THE
PROCESS
OF LEGAL
RESEARCH

THE PROCESS OF LEGAL RESEARCH
Successful Strategies

Third Edition

CHRISTINA L. KUNZ, Professor of Law

DEBORAH A. SCHMEDEMANN, Professor of Law

ANN L. BATESON, Director of the Law Library,
Associate Dean, Associate
Professor of Law

MATTHEW P. DOWNS, Professor of Law

C. PETER ERLINDER, Professor of Law

all of William Mitchell College of Law

CLIFFORD M. GREENE, Popham, Haik, Schnobrich,
& Kaufman, Ltd.,
Minneapolis, Minnesota

Little, Brown and Company
BOSTON   TORONTO   LONDON

Library of Congress Catalog Card No. 92-71001

ISBN: 0-316-50720-2

Third Edition
Fifth Printing
MV-NY

Published simultaneously in Canada by Little, Brown & Company (Canada) Limited

Printed in the United States of America

This book is dedicated to the 3300 students of William Mitchell College of Law who have worked with and helped us to improve these materials during the past eleven years

and

to the faculty, administration, and staff of William Mitchell College of Law, whose unwavering support for skills instruction has made this book possible.

Summary of Contents

Table of Contents

Chapter 8. Administrative Materials: Searching for Primary Authority

List of Illustrations

Chapter 6

Chapter 7

Chapter 8

List of Tables

Preface to the Student

There are many ways to teach legal research. Some law schools offer lectures on legal research sources. Others assign readings in textbooks that describe legal research sources in great detail. Still others provide library tours and allow students to learn by trial and error how to use the sources pointed out to them.

This book teaches legal research by enabling you to explore the sources yourself, at your own pace, as you examine the sample pages and as you use the sources to solve a research problem. You will learn by doing, not merely by listening to a lecture or by reading a book. You will learn in the library, not in a lecture hall. After all, the true measure of whether education is successful is not whether you have been taught something, but whether you have learned it well enough to be able to apply it to a wide range of new settings.

The process of legal research is analytical, not just mechanical. A skilled researcher uses analytical skills in the formulation of legal issues and their answers, as well as in the selection of research sources and the accompanying formulation of a research strategy. This book teaches those analysis skills in a step-by-step fashion, meshing together legal research and legal reasoning.

As we approach the 21st century, our research sources are increasingly appearing in a widening range of media—microfiche, CD-ROM, computers, and print. This proliferation of media choices increases the pressure on a legal researcher to understand the strengths and weaknesses of the various research sources in each of these media. This book takes the view that you first need to understand the nature of the information you are seeking; only then can you make an intelligent decision about which medium will allow you the best access to that information.

Research results and publication formats are ever-changing. The information, illustrations, and research results in this book are current as of the time each chapter was completed (late 1991 to early 1992). However, since this book is in the print medium, it cannot be continually updated. You should assume that the contents of this book are subject to the updating rules set out in this book for other sources.

We hope that this book will help you to approach research situations in the manner in which attorneys approach them.

Christina L. Kunz
Deborah A. Schmedemann
Ann L. Bateson
Matthew P. Downs
C. Peter Erlinder
Clifford M. Greene

April 1992

Acknowledgments

First and foremost, we would like to recognize the work of Tami Dokken Sandberg, Todd Chantry, Diane Gnotta, Jim Reichert, and Rich Korman, our research assistants. They worked hard, long, and diligently on the new problem sets, illustrations, and copyright permissions for this edition. We also would like to salute the work of Scott G. Johnson and Cindy Ley Curtis, our research assistants on the first edition, and Susan Smoot, Mark Wisser, Bill Scullion, Rod Smeltzer, Pat Arsenault, Mark Paige, Pam Strom, and Mary Torkildson, our research assistants on the second edition. The perspectives of all of our research assistants have been invaluable in making this book more accessible to first-year students. We are very appreciative of the quality and energy of their work over the years.

More so than other publications by law school faculty, this book draws on the talents and hard work of the College's professional librarians. Librarians Betty Karweick, Pat Dolan, Phyllis Marion, Paddy Satzer, and Anne Anderson tracked down laser prints, photo-magnetic transfers, missing books, inter-library loans, and new editions. They also answered our questions and offered top-notch suggestions. Anna Cherry provided special assistance on computer-based sources. Betty Karweick provided her expertise on cases, *Shepard's Citations,* and statutes. Pat Dolan assisted on the court rules chapter.

Professors John Jackson (Capitol University) and Michael Steenson (William Mitchell) graciously provided their substantive expertise on jury instructions. Professor Ken Kirwin (William Mitchell) contributed to the polishing of the fact situation on intentional infliction of emotional distress. Professor Kevin Millard, now in practice in Colorado, wrote the first draft of a chapter for the first edition of this book, breaking important new ground for his fellow authors.

We are grateful for the expertise of Cheri Fenstermaker and Cal Bonde, the College's word processing specialists. They endured countless revisions, deletions, "supermoves," and "supercopies" that only Legal Writing faculty would dare produce and edit. We also thank Judy Holmes for the continuity of her administrative support on this edition as well as the previous edition.

The College's faculty and administration have shown considerable interest and support for the project. The financial resources have been constant and unwavering since the day in the spring of 1981 when then-Associate Dean Melvin B. Goldberg gave his blessing to this project with the immortal words: "Of course, none of this is carved in stone. In fact, I take it that this proposal is barely written on paper."

We have been fortunate enough to receive the insights and encouragement of our colleagues around the country as they read various drafts and gave us valuable feedback on the improvements needed in the first edition. We would like to thank Norman Brand, formerly Professor and Legal Writing Director at Albany Law School and now a securities and labor law arbitrator in California; Helene S. Shapo, Professor and Legal Writing Director at Northwestern University School of Law; Kathleen Price, who recently was appointed Law Librarian of Congress; and the anonymous reviewers for our publisher.

This book has been blessed with talented professionals on the publisher's end of the phone. Nick Niemeyer played a key role in bringing our manuscript to the attention of Little, Brown and Company and has always taken an active interest in the book's evolution and progress; we thank him for his keen insights into the market of legal education. Richard Heuser originally acquired the manuscript for this book; we have appreciated his attention, his enthusiasm, his good advice, and his genuine interest in this book. Richard Audet has been our editor on both the first and third editions; we are awed by his talents (and his tenacity) and are grateful for his willingness to tackle this book again. Sandy Doherty, the editor of the second edition, contributed superb editing and a welcome sense of humor to the previous edition. Elizabeth Kenny has skillfully managed the administrative arm of this book for all three editions. We also want to recognize the expert design work of the late Roy Brown and of Maureen Kaplan, who formulated and executed a design that made this book more accessible to its readers. George Nichols has worked on the massive art packet in this and earlier editions. Finally, Carol McGeehan took over as the Law School Books Editor at Little, Brown at the outset of this edition; she has proven to be a fast study and a source of countless good ideas. Her professional talents have enabled this edition to break new ground and to come to fruition a year early.

We especially would like to thank our spouses, companions, families, and friends for their support and their interest in this project. Every three years, they, like us, have been called upon to endure long hours and high stress levels. We thank them from the bottom of our hearts.

We also would like to acknowledge those publishers who permitted us to reprint copyrighted material in this book.

Chapter 2: The Opening Steps of Legal Research

Research Situation: Reprinted with permission of William Mitchell College of Law; copyright © 1990, 1991.

Illustration 2-1: Reprinted by permission from page 627 of *Legal Thesaurus/Dictionary: A Resource for the Writer and the Computer Researcher* by William Statsky; copyright © 1985 by West Publishing Company. All rights reserved.

Illustration 2-2: Copyright © 1980. The Michie Company. Reprinted from *Modern Legal Glossary,* by Kenneth R. Redden and Enid L. Veron, with special permission from The Michie Company, Charlottesville, Virginia. All Rights Reserved.

Illustration 2-3: Reprinted with permission from *Black's Law Dictionary,* Sixth Edition. Copyright © 1990 by West Publishing Company.

Illustration 2-4: From *The Plain Language Law Dictionary* by Robert E. Rothenberg. Copyright © 1981 by Medbook Publications, Inc. Used by permission of Penguin, a division of Penguin Books USA Inc.

Illustration 2-5: Reprinted with permission of Barron's Educational Series, Inc., copyright © 1991, from *Law Dictionary* by Steven H. Gifis.

Illustration 2-6: Reprinted with permission from *Oran's Dictionary of the Law,* Second Edition. Copyright © 1991 by West Publishing Company.

Illustrations 2-7 and 2-8: Reprinted with permission of Anderson Publishing Company, copyright © 1986. All rights reserved.

Illustration 2-9: Reprinted with permission from *Black's Law Dictionary,* Sixth Edition. Copyright © 1990 by West Publishing Company.

Illustration 3-1: Reprinted with permission of Lawyers Cooperative Publishing, a division of Thomson Legal Publishing Inc., copyright © 1968.

Illustration 3-2: Reprinted from C.J.S., copyright © 1954 with permission of the West Publishing Company.

Illustration 3-3: Reprinted from C.J.S., copyright © 1991 with permission of the West Publishing Company.

Illustration 3-4: Reprinted with permission of Lawyers Cooperative Publishing, a division of Thomson Legal Publishing Inc., copyright © 1968.

Illustration 3-5: Reprinted from C.J.S., copyright © 1954 with permission of the West Publishing Company.

Illustration 3-6: Reprinted with permission of Lawyers Cooperative Publishing, a division of Thomson Legal Publishing Inc., copyright © 1991.

Illustration 3-7: Reprinted from C.J.S., copyright © 1991 with permission of the West Publishing Company.

Illustration 3-8: Reprinted with permission of Lawyers Cooperative Publishing, a division of Thomson Legal Publishing Inc., copyright © 1991.

Illustration 3-9: Reprinted from *Prosser and Keeton on the Law of Torts,* W. Page Keeton et al., 5th ed. 1984, copyright © 1984, with permission of the West Publishing Company.

Illustration 3-10: Copyright © 1983 by Shepard's/McGraw-Hill, Inc. Reproduced by permission. Further reproduction is strictly prohibited.

Illustrations 3-13 and 3-14: Reprinted with permission of the Library of Congress, copyright © 1991.

Illustrations 3-16 and 3-17: Reprinted from *Prosser and Keeton on the Law of Torts,* W. Page Keeton et al., 5th ed. 1984, copyright © 1984 with permission of the West Publishing Company.

Illustration 3-18: Reprinted with permission of Daniel S. Kleinberger and Christina L. Kunz, copyright © 1991.

Illustration 3-19: Reprinted by permission. Copyright © 1982 by University of Oregon and Dean M. Richardson.

Illustration 3-20: Reprinted by permission. Copyright © 1982 by University of Oregon.

Illustration 3-21: Copyright © 1991, Information Access Company, CURRENT LAW INDEX™.

Illustration 3-22: *Index to Legal Periodicals,* September 1982 to August 1983, "Subject and Author Index," page 439. Copyright © 1983 by The H.W. Wilson Company. Material reproduced with permission of the publisher.

Illustration 3-23: Copyright © 1991, Information Access Company, *LegalTrac* Database.

Illustration 3-24: Copyright © 1990 by Shepard's/McGraw-Hill, Inc. Reproduced by permission. Further reproduction is strictly prohibited.

Illustration 3-25: Reprinted with permission of Lawyers Cooperative Publishing, a division of Thomson Legal Publishing Inc., copyright © 1985.

Illustration 3-26: Reprinted with permission of Lawyers Cooperative Publishing, a division of Thomson Legal Publishing Inc., copyright © 1986.

Illustration 3-27: Copyright © 1991 by Shepard's/McGraw-Hill, Inc. Reproduced by permission. Further reproduction is strictly prohibited.

Illustration 3-28: Copyright © 1989 by Shepard's/McGraw-Hill, Inc. Reproduced by permission. Further reproduction is strictly prohibited.

Illustrations 3-29 and 3-30: Reprinted with permission of Lawyers Co-

Chapter 5: Case Law

Chapter 6: Introduction to Computer-Assisted Legal Research

hibited. Reprinted with permission from WESTLAW, copyright © 1992 by West Publishing Co.

Illustration 6-5: Reprinted with permission of Thomson Professional Publishing Inc., copyright © 1992.

Illustration 6-6: Reprinted with permission from WESTLAW, copyright © 1992 by West Publishing Co.

Illustration 6-7: Reprinted with permission of Thomson Professional Publishing Inc., copyright © 1992.

Illustration 6-8: Reprinted with permission from WESTLAW, copyright © 1992 by West Publishing Co.

Illustration 6-9: Reprinted with permission from WESTLAW, copyright © 1992 by West Publishing Co.

Illustrations 6-10 and 6-11: Reprinted with the permission of Mead Data Central, Inc., provider of the LEXIS®/NEXIS® services, copyright © 1992.

Illustration 6-13: Reproduced from 563 P.2d 511, copyright © 1992, with permission of the West Publishing Company.

Chapter 7: Statutes and Constitutions

Illustration 7-11: Reprinted from 29 U.S.C.A. § 654, copyright © 1985, with permission of the West Publishing Company.

Illustration 7-12: Reprinted from U.S.C.C.A.N., copyright © 1991, with permission of the West Publishing Company.

Illustration 7-13: Reprinted with permission of Lawyers Cooperative Publishing, a division of Thomson Legal Publishing Inc., copyright © 1990.

Illustration 7-14: Reprinted from Minn. Stat. Ann., copyright © 1992, with permission of the West Publishing Company.

Illustrations 7-15 to 7-17: Copyright © 1986 by Shepard's/McGraw-Hill, Inc. Reproduced by permission. Further reproduction is strictly prohibited.

Illustration 7-18: Certain materials reproduced in this illustration are reprinted with permission of the West Publishing Company. Copyright © 1992.

Illustration 7-19: Certain materials reproduced in this illustration are reprinted with permission of the West Publishing Company. Copyright © 1990.

Illustration 7-20: Certain materials reproduced in this illustration are reprinted with permission of the West Publishing Company. Copyright © 1992.

Illustrations 7-21 and 7-22: Reprinted with the permission of Mead Data Central, Inc., provider of the LEXIS®/NEXIS® services, copyright © 1992.

Illustration 7-23: Reprinted with permission of American Association of Law Libraries, Fred B. Rothman & Co., and Nancy P. Johnson, copyright © 1988.

Illustrations 7-24 to 7-26: Reprinted from U.S.C.C.A.N., copyright © 1970, with permission from West Publishing Co.

Illustrations 7-27 and 7-28: Copyright © 1971 by Congressional Information Service, Inc. (Bethesda MD). All rights reserved. Reprinted with permission.

Illustrations 7-29 and 7-30: Copyright © 1991 by Congressional Information Service, Inc. (Bethesda MD). All rights reserved. Reprinted with permission.

Illustrations 7-36 to 7-38: Reprinted from WESTLAW, copyright © 1992, with permission from West Publishing Co.

Illustrations 7-39 and 7-40: Reprinted with the permission of Mead Data Central, Inc., provider of the LEXIS®/NEXIS® services, copyright © 1992.

Illustration 7-41: Reprinted from 534 F.2d 541, copyright © 1976, with permission of the West Publishing Company.

Illustration 7-42: Reprinted from U.L.A., copyright © 1991, with permission of the West Publishing Company.

Illustration 7-43: The statutes reprinted or quoted verbatim in this illustration are taken from the *Rhode Island General Laws Annotated,* copyright © 1988, by The Michie Company, and are reprinted with the permission of The Michie Company. All rights reserved.

Illustrations 7-44 and 7-45: Reprinted from U.L.A., copyright © 1991, with permission of the West Publishing Company.

Illustrations 7-46 and 7-47: Reprinted from U.L.A., copyright © 1990, with permission of the West Publishing Company.

Illustration 7-48: Reprinted from WESTLAW, copyright © 1992, with permission of the West Publishing Company.

Chapter 8: Administrative Materials

Illustration 8-1: Reprinted with permission of Lawyers Cooperative Publishing, a division of Thomson Legal Publishing Inc., copyright © 1990.

Illustration 8-9: Copyright © 1986 by Shepard's/McGraw-Hill, Inc. Reproduced by permission. Further reproduction is strictly prohibited.

Illustration 8-14: Copyright © 1984 by Shepard's/McGraw-Hill, Inc. Reproduced by permission. Further reproduction is strictly prohibited.

Illustration 8-15: Reprinted from 683 F.2d 361, copyright © 1982, with permission of the West Publishing Company.

Illustration 8-16: Reproduced with permission from *Employment Safety & Health Guide,* published and copyrighted by Commerce Clearing House, Inc., 4025 W. Peterson Ave., Chicago, Illinois, 60646, copyright © 1990, 1991.

Illustration 8-17: Reproduced with permission from *Employment Safety & Health Guide,* published and copyrighted by Commerce Clearing House, Inc., 4025 W. Peterson Ave., Chicago, Illinois, 60646, copyright © 1989.

Illustrations 8-18 to 8-24: Reproduced with permission from *Employment Safety & Health Guide,* published and copyrighted by Commerce Clearing House, Inc., 4025 W. Peterson Ave., Chicago, Illinois, 60646, copyright © 1991.

Illustration 8-25: Reproduced with permission from *Employment Safety & Health Guide,* published and copyrighted by Commerce Clearing House, Inc., 4025 W. Peterson Ave., Chicago, Illinois, 60646, copyright © 1990.

Illustration 8-26: Reproduced with permission from *Occupational Safety & Health Decisions,* published and copyrighted by Commerce Clearing House, Inc., 4025 W. Peterson Ave., Chicago, Illinois, 60646, copyright © 1972.

Illustrations 8-27 to 8-31: Reprinted with permission from WESTLAW, copyright © 1992 by West Publishing Co.

Illustrations 8-32 to 8-35: Reprinted with the permission of Mead Data

Central, Inc., provider of the LEXIS®/NEXIS® services, copyright ©
1991.

Illustration 8-36: Reprinted with permission of Thomson Professional
Publishing Inc., copyright © 1991.

Illustration 8-37: Reprinted with the permission of Mead Data Central,
Inc., provider of the LEXIS®/NEXIS® services, copyright © 1991.

Illustration 8-38: Reprinted with permission of BNA ONLINE, copyright
© 1992. Reprinted with permission from WESTLAW, copyright © 1992
by West Publishing Co.

Illustrations 8-40 and 8-41: Reproduced with permission from *Employment Safety & Health Guide,* published and copyrighted by Commerce
Clearing House, Inc., 4025 W. Peterson Ave., Chicago, Illinois, 60646,
copyright © 1990.

Illustrations 8-42 and 8-43: Reproduced with permission from *Employment Safety & Health Guide,* published and copyrighted by Commerce
Clearing House, Inc., 4025 W. Peterson Ave., Chicago, Illinois, 60646,
copyright © 1991.

Chapter 9: Rules Governing Practice and Procedure

Illustration 9-1: Reprinted from *Federal Civil Judicial Procedure and
Rules,* copyright © 1991, with permission of the West Publishing Company.

Illustration 9-3: Reprinted from U.S.C.A., copyright © 1992, with permission of the West Publishing Company.

Illustration 9-4: Reprinted with permission of Lawyers Cooperative Publishing, a division of Thomson Professional Publishing Inc., copyright
© 1984.

Illustration 9-5: Reprinted from Fed. Prac. Dig. 2d, copyright © 1980,
with permission of the West Publishing Company.

Illustration 9-6: Reprinted from Fed. R. Dig. 3d, copyright © 1987, with
permission of the West Publishing Company.

Illustration 9-7: Copyright © 1992 by Matthew Bender & Co., Inc. Reprinted with permission from *Moore's Federal Practice* by James Wm.
Moore. All rights reserved.

Illustration 9-8: Reprinted from *Federal Practice and Procedure,* copyright © 1987, with permission of the West Publishing Company.

Illustration 9-9: Copyright © 1991 by Shepard's/McGraw-Hill, Inc. Reproduced by permission. Further reproduction is strictly prohibited.

Illustration 9-10: Reprinted from *Federal Civil Judicial Procedure and
Rules,* copyright © 1991, with permission of the West Publishing Company.

Illustrations 9-11 and 9-12: Reprinted from WESTLAW, copyright © 1992,
with permission of the West Publishing Company.

Illustrations 9-13 and 9-14: Reprinted with the permission of Mead Data
Central, Inc., provider of the LEXIS®/NEXIS® services, copyright ©
1992.

Illustration 9-15: Reprinted from *Federal Civil Judicial Procedure and
Rules,* copyright © 1991, with permission of the West Publishing Company.

Illustrations 9-16 and 9-17: Reprinted from WESTLAW, copyright © 1992,
with permission of the West Publishing Company.

Illustrations 9-18 to 9-21: Reprinted with the permission of Mead Data Central, Inc., provider of the LEXIS®/NEXIS® services, copyright © 1992.

Chapter 10: Researching Non-Legal Materials

THE
PROCESS
OF LEGAL
RESEARCH

Analysis

Legal Research Sources

Identify
research
terms

Dictionaries,*
Thesauri,
Glossaries

Read
commentary
sources for
background
& primary
authority
references

Encyclopedias, Treatises,*
Continuing Legal Education Materials,*
Legal Periodicals,* American Law Reports,*
Restatements,* Pattern Jury Instructions

Formulate
issues

Read &
analyze
primary
authority
(the law)

Case
Reporters,*
Digests,*
Citators*

Statutes,*
Constitutions,*
Legislative
History*

Adminis-
trative
Materials:
Rules,* Decisions,*
Looseleafs*

Rules
Governing
Practice &
Procedure*

Model &
Uniform
Laws*

Discern
underlying
premises
to explore

Non-Legal
Materials*

Commentary
Sources
Revisited

*Sources available (in part) through computer-assisted legal research

A. THE PROFESSION OF LAW AND LEGAL RESEARCH

1. Legal Research and the Practice of Law

Law* is one of the learned professions. "Profession" is defined as "a calling requiring specialized knowledge and often long and intensive academic preparation." To be "professional" is to be "characterized by or conforming to the technical and ethical standards of a profession." *Webster's New Collegiate Dictionary* 911 (1981).

Law school is only the beginning of the "long and intensive academic preparation" of a lawyer. Lawyers continue to study law throughout their careers as they research legal principles applicable to their clients' situations and apply pertinent and current principles to those situations. A lawyer's "specialized knowledge" is ever-expanding and ever-changing.

One goal of this book is to provide an introduction to the technical skills lawyers use in researching the law. You will learn, for example, how to use a case digest, interpret statutes, "Shepardize" authorities, and write computer searches. An equally important goal of this book is to impart the technical standards by which the profession, legal system, and clients judge the performance of lawyers in the area of research. For example, you will learn that it is not sufficient to rely on excerpts or descriptions of what the law says; you must read the law yourself. You will learn that lawyers must present the law as it currently stands, not as it stood yesterday.

The goal of this initial discussion is to introduce the ethical component of legal research. The very first rule of the Model Rules of Professional Conduct as drafted by the American Bar Association—Rule 1.1—states in its entirety: "A lawyer shall provide competent representation to a client. Competent representation requires the legal knowledge, skill, thoroughness and preparation reasonably necessary for the representation." Model Rules of Professional Conduct Rule 1.1 (as amended 1984). Complying with the rule includes "inquiry into and analysis of the factual and legal elements of the problem." *Id.* cmt. In other words, the rules of the profession require that a lawyer know what the law is; to know what the law is, you must research it.

---

*Many of the readers of this book are law students (typically, first-year law students); some are lawyers; others are legal assistants or studying to be legal assistants. To make for easy reading, we have written about lawyers and law students for the most part. We trust that readers who are or will be legal assistants will read "legal assistant" rather than "lawyer" as appropriate.

Serious consequences may follow inadequate research. Failure to know the law may lead to disciplinary action. *See, e.g., People v. Yoakum,* 552 P.2d 291 (Colo. 1976); *Nebraska State Bar Ass'n v. Holscher,* 230 N.W.2d 75 (Neb. 1975). Inadequate research may also result in liability for legal malpractice. For example, in *Smith v. Lewis,* 530 P.2d 621 (Cal. Sup. Ct. 1975), the court approved an award of $100,000 against a lawyer who had failed to apply principles of law commonly known to well-informed attorneys and to discover principles readily accessible through standard research techniques. Furthermore, few attorneys wish to tarnish their professional reputations (and economic potential) by becoming known for poor research.

It is not surprising that competent research is emphasized in the rules on lawyer discipline and legal malpractice, for solid research is the foundation of the service lawyers perform for their clients and society. An attorney cannot counsel clients accurately and thoughtfully without knowing the legal rules applicable to their conduct. Moreover, an attorney cannot represent clients' interests zealously and responsibly without knowing the legal rules defining their rights and obligations. Furthermore, attorneys have obligations to the legal system as well as to clients. Lawyers encourage compliance with legal rules as they counsel clients, ensure the proper functioning of our judicial system as they represent clients in various kinds of disputes, and further the rational development of the law as they represent clients' interests before the legislature and administrative bodies. Clearly, to fulfill these obligations well, lawyers must know the applicable legal rules.

2. Criteria for Excellence in Legal Research

What, then, distinguishes the performance of an ethical lawyer in the area of legal research? To a great extent, doing an excellent job in legal research is no different from doing an excellent job in other forms of research. It requires thoroughness, updating, critical reading and thinking, and efficiency. Let's examine some of these qualities.

First, you must cover all of the bases necessary to address fully the legal issues raised by your fact situation, and you must cover them well. As you will soon see, the law does not come wrapped in a tidy, clearly labeled package. Discerning what the law is requires gathering bits and pieces from a variety of sources, sorting them according to their relative weight and relevance to your problem, and combining them into as cohesive an analysis as possible. To do this well, you must look at a wide range of potentially relevant sources, and you must read what you find carefully, looking both for general guidance and specific details pertinent to your problem. Good legal research is noteworthy for its breadth and depth.

Second, thorough research requires being completely current. One Monday morning, one of the authors of this book took a group of first-year law students to hear oral arguments before the Minnesota Court of Appeals, an appellate court one level below the state's highest court, the Minnesota Supreme Court. Before the attorneys in one of the cases could begin, the chief judge asked whether the two attorneys planned to address the decision in a particular case. The case had been decided by the Minnesota Supreme Court the preceding Friday afternoon. The chief judge clearly expected the attorneys to be aware of it and prepared to address it.

Third, good legal research entails critical reading and thinking. It is not enough to simply find the most current sources and principles; you must come to understand them well. This understanding grows out of a respect for legal authority. The law is made by judges, legislators, and administrative agencies through words. You must read the lawmakers' language very closely and critically (even down to the grammar and punctuation). You must honor their word choices, even though you might prefer that they had written something more favorable to your client or more in keeping with your personal views or easier to understand. You must grapple with ambiguity (and there will be ambiguity!) by thinking hard about such things as the purpose and consequences of the law. This obligation to respect the legal authorities explains the emphasis lawyers place on legal citation, a topic discussed in more detail in Part D below.

Fourth, good legal research is accomplished efficiently. Observe that the Model Rule quoted on page 2 calls for work that is "reasonably necessary for the representation." As you will soon discover, it is quite possible to spend hours researching a simple point of law. You—and, more important, your clients—will not be able to afford that luxury in many situations. In essence, you must impose on yourself a rule of reason. Your goal should be to maximize the return you get from each hour spent in research, so that your reasonable expenditure of time and effort yields the best possible results. Of course, the best way to ensure efficiency is to become very technically proficient. The rest of this book should start you on your way toward that goal.

3. Ethical Principles for Learning Research

Law students also are subject to ethical constraints. You owe your fellow students a duty not to impede their professional education. Law students tend to be competitive people. A certain amount of competition is, of course, healthy. Too much, however, can cause one to engage in behavior that is unfair to others—and damaging to oneself because of the lost opportunities to learn from fellow students who are alienated by excessive competitiveness. There are at least two ways in which excessive competitiveness can arise in research.

First, as you will soon find, an inevitable consequence of asking a group of students to research the same issue or set of issues is that several (or many) students will need to or want to use the same book, often at the same time. The problem sets in this text will work effectively only if the sources are in the library and in good condition. Do not hide, mark in, or otherwise alter the sources you use. Use them as quickly as you can without compromising your own learning. Reshelve them promptly (unless your library has a "no reshelving" rule).

Second, some students may think it advantageous to present a commentator's legal analysis as their own—in short, to plagiarize. The tradition of legal citation requires that you provide a citation to your source every time you set forth a legal proposition—and this rule governs ideas coming not only from sources that constitute the law (cases and statutes, for example), but also ideas coming from various forms of commentary and the briefs of other attorneys. You must provide a citation not only when you use direct quotations, but also when you paraphrase material. Keep in mind that a thoroughly cited paper indicates that the author has performed thorough research and knows how to present the views of others. In short, it is the mark of a professional to indicate what your sources are.

In doing legal research, you will be looking for the rule of law that solves the question raised by your client's situation. You no doubt will read many pronouncements of legal principles. How do you discern which of these is "the law" on your topic? The key lies in identifying whether the pronouncement applies directly to your question and whether the pronouncement accurately reflects the law as set forth by the government.

Laws created by the government are "primary authority." Rules of law emanate from the federal, state, and local governments—the legislature, the judiciary, and administrative agencies. Many rules of law are products of the interplay among those branches. For example, the rule of law in a workplace safety dispute may be the decision of a federal judge interpreting a regulation drafted by a federal agency, which in turn implements a federal statute enacted by Congress.

The pronouncements of private parties, standing alone, do not have the force and effect of law and therefore are not primary authority. Such "commentary" on the law is "secondary authority." Secondary authority is very important to the development of the law and to lawyers' understanding of the law. For example, a prominent labor law scholar may write an article on how the federal regulations on workplace safety should be interpreted, and a federal judge may be persuaded by that article.

The following is an overview of the categories of legal research material. You may wish to consult Table 1.1 on page 6, which indicates the relationship among these sources and their finding tools.

1. Primary Authority

"Primary authority" constitutes the law and is issued by a branch of the government or a government body acting in its lawmaking capacity. As has been noted, three branches of government generate primary authority.

First, legislative bodies at the federal, state, and local levels create constitutions, statutes, charters, and ordinances. Legislation generally does not apply to a particular past or present dispute; it is enacted to govern future situations. Pieces of legislation are compiled into codes. In enacting legislation, a legislature also creates background material on why the legislation was enacted and what legislators understood certain legislative language to mean; this background legislative material is compiled into legislative history sources. Ambiguities in legislative language are to be interpreted according to the legislature's intent.

Second, the judiciary at the federal and state levels decides cases based on controversies that already have arisen between people, between legal entities (such as a city or a corporation), or between a person and a legal entity. Some disputes arise under a statute or other legislation; the court's task then is to construe the statutory language and apply it to the facts of the dispute. Other cases grow out of situations to which legislation does not apply; the court's task then is to develop and apply a judge-made rule of law. In either case, the court writes an opinion that sets forth the result in the case and the governing legal principles. In the American legal system, a court's opinion constitutes "precedent" to be followed in subsequent similar cases

TABLE 1.1. Legal Research Materials.

Primary Authority (mandatory and persuasive)

Legislative	Judicial	Administrative
Constitutions	Cases	Regulations
Statutes	Some rules of practice	Decisions
Charters	& procedure	
Ordinances		
Legislative history		
Some rules of practice & procedure		

Secondary Authority (persuasive only)

Commentary	Other Persuasive Materials
Dictionaries	Restatements
Encyclopedias	Uniform and model laws
Treatises	Pattern jury instructions
CLE materials	
Legal periodicals	
A.L.R. annotations	

Finding Tools (used to locate primary and secondary authority)

Citators
Digests
Other primary and secondary authorities

in the same court system. Judges' opinions are compiled into case reporters.

Third, in the United States various administrative agencies at the federal, state, and local levels make a vast amount of administrative law. Agencies are created by "enabling statutes," which direct those agencies to perform specified tasks. An agency may promulgate rules to interpret the enabling statutes and further direct the performance of the agency's duties. In enforcing the law, an agency also may adjudicate disputes arising under the enabling legislation and agency rules. Agency actions may be reviewed by the judiciary for constitutionality, compliance with the enabling statutes, lack of arbitrariness, or adequate factual support.

The judicial and legislative branches also enact rules governing how courts and the parties before them operate. These rules are compiled into codes of procedure.

Primary authority can be categorized not only according to the lawmaking body creating it, but also according to its "weight" in a particular case. For any specific situation, some primary authority is mandatory; it governs the situation. Other authority is persuasive; it may provide guidance but is not dispositive of the outcome.

An authority's weight is determined by its jurisdiction and the jurisdiction of the fact situation. If, for example, you were researching a workplace safety issue in the state of Minnesota, federal law would be mandatory, unless the federal government has ceded its power to the state. Then the law of Minnesota would be binding. On the other hand, law made by Georgia lawmakers would be only persuasive. The concept of jurisdiction is a complicated one, discussed in more detail at several points in this text.

2. Secondary Authority

Secondary authority is anything other than primary authority that a court could use as a basis for decision, should the matter you are researching come before a court. Secondary authority does not have the force and effect of law; in doing research, you should rely on and cite primary authority whenever possible. You should use secondary authority only when primary authority is unclear, unavailable, or unfavorable. Of course, you cannot ignore unfavorable primary authority; secondary authority merely furnishes a basis for an argument as to what the law should be.

Some secondary authority nonetheless borders on being as persuasive as primary authority. For example, a treatise by a leading scholar in a given field may be highly persuasive to lawyers and judges.

Secondary authority includes commentary sources, some of which closely resemble research materials used in other disciplines: treatises, periodicals, dictionaries, and encyclopedias of various sorts. Although the methods of using some of these commentary sources may vary a bit from those you have learned in other research contexts, the basic principles should be familiar.

In addition, continuing legal education (CLE) materials are materials from programs conducted by attorneys for attorneys. American Law Reports (A.L.R.) annotations provide synopses of recent legal developments, with a focus on court decisions.

Secondary authority also includes other materials that can be used persuasively and are unique to legal research: Restatements, uniform and model statutes, and pattern jury instructions. In the Restatements, groups of leading scholars and lawyers have set out what they perceive the law or the law's trend to be. The Restatements are regarded as particularly important secondary authority. Uniform and model statutes are drafted by various organizations whose goal is to promote uniformity or to provide a statute that reflects the viewpoints of the organization's members. Pattern jury instructions are models for judges to use in instructing jurors as to the law.

3. Finding Tools

Several research tools contain no statements of the law but rather function solely as finding tools. They may merely list primary and secondary authorities under various topics, or they may contain brief abstracts of what the authorities say. These finding tools are not authority of any type and are never cited. The finding tools in legal research are fairly unusual in format. They include digests and *Shepard's Citations.*

In addition, as you read primary and secondary authority, you will encounter references to other primary and secondary authority. For example, a legal periodical article will provide numerous references in the footnotes. A judicial opinion may refer to a statute. Thus, primary and secondary authorities also serve as finding tools.

Keep in mind that on occasion you may use a source that combines all three of these categories of materials. The chief example is the looseleaf service. A looseleaf service contains a range of materials relating to a narrow area of law, such as labor law, environmental law, tax law, consumer credit, or consumer protection. These materials may include statutes, regulations, cases, commentary, and finding tools.

C. MEDIA USED IN LEGAL RESEARCH

If all legal materials and research tools appeared only in books or other print media, law libraries would be in much larger buildings than they currently are. As you will soon discover, print is only one of the media in which legal sources appear. The others are microforms (microfilm and microfiche), CD-ROM, and online databases.

You are already very familiar with print materials such as books and journals, and you may be familiar with microforms. Microforms include both microfilm and microfiche. Microfilm is photographic film that contains images that have been reduced in size. The amount of the reduction varies depending on the source, but reduction ratios of 24:1 and 18:1 are common. Microfilm is available in both rolls and cartridges.

A microfiche is a flat sheet of film, which resembles a note card. A typical microfiche is four inches by six inches and contains 98 pages of text in seven rows of 14 columns. These pages typically have been reduced 24 times. A microfiche usually has a print heading that identifies its contents.

CD-ROM stands for "compact disk, read only memory." A CD-ROM disk is a plastic disk that contains information stored in pits molded into the surface of the disk. A laser beam is used to read the information. A CD-ROM disk can hold many types of information, including text, graphics, audio, and video. A typical CD-ROM disk holds the equivalent of about 250,000 typed pages or 1,500 standard floppy computer disks.

Online databases are collections of data and text in computer-readable form. "Online" means the information in a database is stored in a computer at a remote location. You reach the database via a personal computer, a modem, and a telephone line. The information you receive from the remote database is displayed on a terminal at your location.

Each of these media has its advantages and its disadvantages, and you will no doubt develop a preference for some media over others. Nevertheless, you should become adept at locating and using information in all of them for three reasons:

(1) the information you need may be published in only one of the media;
(2) the information you need may be published in multiple media, but the medium you prefer may not be the one most conveniently or economically available to you; and
(3) different media are effective for different purposes.

For example, if you wish to do background reading, a print source is usually your best choice. If you wish to scan index listings for citations to useful articles, a CD-ROM index may be your best choice. If you need the most current available information, an online system is often your best choice. If you need to read an out-of-print document or a document that is hard to store in print such as a newspaper, your library may have the document only in microform.

Table 1.2 on page 9 summarizes the factors to consider in choosing among media.

It is critical to remember that the more important category is the *type of authority* you are researching, not its *medium*. Thus, if you are researching a workplace safety problem governed by federal law, you may begin by researching commentary—for example, legal periodicals. You may use a

TABLE 1.2. Factors to Consider in Choosing among Media.

Factors to Consider	Print	Microfilm/ Microfiche	CD-ROM	Online
How do you locate information within the medium?	Must use the index, table of contents, and other finding aids provided by the publisher—or browse.	Must use the index, table of contents, and other finding aids provided by the publisher—or browse.	May use the finding aids provided by the publisher. You also may be able to search for words you pick.	Usually must create your own "search" by identifying and combining relevant terms.
How easy is it to browse in this medium?	Easy to browse.	You may dislike browsing on a microform reader. Microfilm does not permit you to bypass pages. Quality of filming varies.	Varies with systems; some allow paging through documents.	You may be limited to browsing the documents retrieved by your search. You can view only one screen at a time.
How easy is it to copy information from this medium?	Must make handwritten notes or photocopy relevant information.	If the microform machine does not have a printer, you must take notes. If it does, you may make copies; quality of copies varies.	You may be able to print information, download information to a computer disk, or both. Some systems allow you to add your own notes.	You may be able to print or download information to a computer disk.
How up-to-date is the information in this medium?	Information may be outdated by the time it is published. Some print sources are updated; some are not. Frequency of updating varies.	Currency is not a strength of this format. Microforms are often not updated.	Many disks are updated at regular intervals. The intervals vary, but often are monthly or quarterly. Some systems allow access to online updates.	Some information is updated on a "same day" basis. Other information is no more up-to-date than the information in a print counterpart.
What special expertise is needed to use this medium?	Understanding of indexing is helpful.	Knowledge of how to locate microforms in your library and how to use microform equipment.	Knowledge of a system's hardware and software.	Knowledge of how to find computer databases, write computer searches, and browse results. Searching and browsing techniques vary somewhat among databases.
What is the primary cost of using this medium?	Your time.	Your time.	Your time, unless you use an online update.	Online time, in addition to your time.

print, CD-ROM, or online index, and you may find the article itself in print, in microform, or online. Regardless of the media, your research in periodicals entails use of a finding tool and secondary authority. Similarly, you will look for federal statutes, administrative regulations and decisions, and, ultimately, cases. You may find these in print or you may find them online. Either way, the authority is primary, mandatory authority.

D. WRITING CITATIONS

Once you find a primary or secondary authority to which you plan to refer, you will need to determine its proper citation form.

Legal citation is the rather stylized system lawyers use to provide references to their sources. Proper and complete citation for each statement of law enables fellow lawyers, judges, legislators, and others to assess the weight and reliability of the statement. Although citation is one of the more tedious aspects of legal research, you will come to realize that it is the way you prove to others that your research is sound. Initially, you will feel that citations interrupt the flow of your prose, but eventually you will realize that an experienced legal reader skips over citations until and unless the cites become relevant.

Readily understandable cites thus are important because they communicate the precise location of the authority relied on so the reader in turn can consult that authority. Citation form in legal writing should be uniform to ensure that citations are comprehensible by all readers and in all jurisdictions. *The Bluebook: A Uniform System of Citation* (15th ed. 1991), fondly known as "the Bluebook," sets out the rules most lawyers use in citing legal authority. *The Process of Legal Research* contains Citation Notes that point you to the appropriate rules in *The Bluebook* and provide examples of proper citation form.

Note that most of the examples in *The Bluebook* are in a typeface convention employed in scholarly writing, but not applicable to practice documents such as briefs and memoranda (which are common in most Legal Writing courses). You must use Practitioners' Note P.1 and the back inside cover of *The Bluebook* to convert the typeface in the examples to the typeface for briefs and memos.

E. ORGANIZATION OF THIS BOOK

This book has the following eleven chapters:

1. Introduction
2. The Opening Steps of Legal Research: Analysis and Vocabulary Development
3. Commentary Sources: Searching in Secondary Authority
4. Issue Formulation for Primary Authority Research
5. Case Law: Searching for Primary Authority
6. Introduction to Computer-Assisted Legal Research
7. Statutes and Constitutions: Searching for Primary Authority
8. Administrative Materials: Searching for Primary Authority
9. Rules Governing Practice and Procedure: Searching for Primary Authority

Most chapters cover a set of functionally related sources. The exceptions are this chapter and Chapters 2, 4, 6, and 11.

Each chapter covering a set of related sources contains a description of how the sources are created and their role in legal research; the basics, complete with examples, of how to use the sources; and instructions about how to cite them. Illustrations of sample pages are interspersed throughout the chapters to show you what the research sources actually look like. In addition, a realistic research problem is resolved in the text over the course of Chapters 2 through 6; another research problem is resolved in Chapters 7 and 8. Chapter 9 addresses a third simple problem, and Chapter 10 revisits the problem covered in Chapters 2 through 6. You will see how the steps set out in each chapter lead to pertinent sources and pertinent material in those sources. You also will see how material in one source leads to materials in other sources. The materials eventually combine to resolve the research problem.

Gathered at the end of the book are problem sets, arranged by chapter, for you to complete after you have done the relevant reading. To complete a problem set, you will select one of the ten scenarios ("research situations") and then walk through the research steps you have just read about, answering a series of questions designed to guide your research. The chapters and related problem sets are based on programmed instruction and a hands-on approach to learning.

You may have wondered why the book does not lead off with primary authority and proceed to secondary authority, if primary authority is the more important. The reason is simple: The book's organization tracks the process of legal research most often used, especially for researching an area that is new to the researcher. As the flowchart to this book illustrates (see page 1), that research process generally entails the following steps:

(1) Analyze factual and legal categories; then identify research terms through the use of dictionaries and related sources (Chapter 2).

(2) Read commentary sources for background and to obtain references to primary authority (Chapter 3).

(3) Formulate precise issues (questions of law and fact) to be answered by application of primary authority to the research problem (Chapter 4)

(4) Locate, read, and analyze primary authority, which may take the form of
   (a) cases (Chapter 5),
   (b) statutes and constitutions (Chapter 7),
   (c) administrative materials (Chapter 8), or
   (d) rules governing practice and procedure (Chapter 9).

(5) Discern and research the underlying factual premises of the law in non-legal sources, as needed (Chapter 10).

This list omits Chapter 6, which provides an introduction to computer-assisted legal research (CALR). The information provided online by the two CALR services, WESTLAW and LEXIS, is generally available as well in print form. However, computer technology affords research methods that are not possible in print documents—hence the necessity for a separate chapter devoted to CALR search methods. Moreover, you will understand CALR search methods only after you have learned some of the basics of print research—hence the placement of the CALR chapter midway through the book. Furthermore, CALR is most useful as a means of researching and updating case law—hence the placement of the CALR chapter after the chapter on print research in case law. If you scan the detailed table of contents, you will see that CALR research is covered within the remaining chapters as a parallel track to print research. This concept of parallel tracks will make sense after you have acquired the basics of CALR in Chapter 6.

Finally, Chapter 11 shows you how all of the skills taught in the book combine to produce various research strategies for a fairly complicated research problem. More specifically, this concluding chapter shows you the actual process used by four of the authors of the book, all researching the same problem. It concludes with observations about the similarities and differences in their approaches. Note the reference to "various strategies." As you will see, there is no single way to conduct legal research. There are certain basic rules to follow and many variations.

F. SUCCESSFUL STRATEGIES

The subtitle of this book is "Successful Strategies." Webster's defines "strategy" as "the art of devising or employing plans or stratagems toward a goal." *Webster's New Collegiate Dictionary* 1141 (1981). This text seeks to further your ability to perform legal research strategically in several senses. This chapter has, we hope, helped you to identify the "goal" or purpose of legal research: to locate authority pertinent to your client's situation. Throughout this text, we have sought to provide sequences of research steps—that is, a "plan"—designed to yield useful results and to do so efficiently. Finally, we hope you will see the "art" of successful legal research: that the process is not mechanical and that it entails judgment, skill, and creativity.

Chapter 2 provides an overview of and detailed instruction in the opening steps of legal research.

The Opening Steps of Legal Research: Analysis and Vocabulary Development

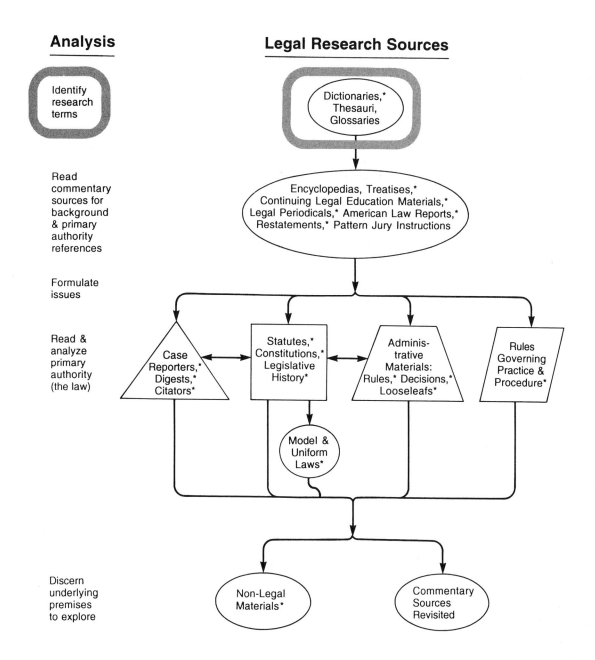

Analysis

Identify research terms

Read commentary sources for background & primary authority references

Formulate issues

Read & analyze primary authority (the law)

Discern underlying premises to explore

Legal Research Sources

Dictionaries,* Thesauri, Glossaries

Encyclopedias, Treatises,* Continuing Legal Education Materials,* Legal Periodicals,* American Law Reports,* Restatements,* Pattern Jury Instructions

Case Reporters,* Digests,* Citators*

Statutes,* Constitutions,* Legislative History*

Administrative Materials: Rules,* Decisions,* Looseleafs*

Rules Governing Practice & Procedure*

Model & Uniform Laws*

Non-Legal Materials*

Commentary Sources Revisited

*Sources available (in part) through computer-assisted legal research

A. RESEARCH AS A STRATEGY

Legal research is a skill that you are learning in order to enhance your ability to solve legal problems. By learning how to skillfully choose and gain access to legal research materials, you will enlarge the pool of resources available to help you resolve legal issues. To become proficient at choosing and gaining access to legal research materials, you must analyze the legal problem being worked on, the strengths and weaknesses of the available sources, and your own areas of knowledge and ignorance. This analysis must continue all the way through the research process.

A good researcher envisions legal research as a set of research "game plans" (or strategies) and knows when to select which strategy. During this course on legal research as well as in your coursework in legal writing, you will learn to formulate research strategies that tell you which source, of several sources, you should consult and in what order you should consult sources. You also will learn when to research a source using computer-assisted legal research (CALR) and when you will gain better results by researching that same source in a print medium. Finally, you will develop strategies for choosing terms to research and selecting arguments to pursue.

Your research strategies should be flexible. Successful researchers continually reevaluate their research methodology and consider alternative research approaches as they find that various sources or research approaches are helpful or fruitless. Thus, even the most diligent researcher, armed with the latest technology, will not be successful if he or she approaches legal research with a mechanical checklist, devoid of flexibility and analysis.

Here are the basic steps of a successful research strategy:

(1) Analyze the facts of the situation to ascertain what topics you need to research.

(2) Use dictionaries, glossaries, and thesauri to clarify the meaning of the terms generated from factual and legal analysis and also to generate additional research vocabulary.

(3) Take accurate and efficient research notes, including citation information (this step continues throughout the rest of the research process).

(4) Begin to formulate an outline or flowchart of the topic.

(5) Locate and read commentary sources to give yourself an overview of the topics involved.

(6) Revise and add to your outline or flowchart to reflect your new knowledge.

(7) Pinpoint areas of intersection between fact and law and phrase them as issues for your research.

(8) Locate and read mandatory primary authority that resolves or yields good points on those issues (if you cannot find any mandatory primary authority or wish to argue for a change in the law in your jurisdiction, you also should locate and read persuasive primary authority and secondary authority).

(9) Revise your outline or flowchart, reevaluate the issues, and do additional research as needed.

(10) Quit researching when you are no longer coming across new relevant information (even though there may be hundreds of cases and articles you have not yet read).

In this chapter, we will discuss the first four steps in detail. The remaining steps will be discussed at various points throughout the remainder of the book.

B. OUR FIRST RESEARCH SITUATION

Before you enter the library to work on a legal research project, you should analyze the facts before you. All of the problem sets in this book contain "research situations" for you to resolve. Likewise, the following research situation will be discussed and eventually resolved in Chapters 2 through 6.

Claudia Perkins, a 35-year-old marketing researcher, had been working for the same firm in Topeka, Kansas, for almost 15 years. Recently the firm was sold, and the management notified the employees that each had the option of withdrawing his or her share of the firm's profit-sharing plan or allowing the funds to remain in escrow until the new owners formed their own profit-sharing plan. If Perkins chose to withdraw her funds, they would be made available to her in six months.

Perkins saw this as a wonderful opportunity to finally purchase her own home in Topeka, using the profit-sharing proceeds for a down payment. She knew that the house of her dreams, located in a suburb only a mile from Perkins' rental unit, had just gone on the market. Perkins contacted Suzanne Swift, the owner, and inquired whether she would agree to a six-month lease with an option to buy at the end of the lease (when the profit-sharing proceeds would be available). Swift agreed to the arrangement, but only if Perkins would pay a premium during the six-month lease period to compensate Swift for taking the house off the market; this premium was to be $200 per month above the normal rental value for this type of unit. Perkins, in turn, would agree to pay the premium rent only if that additional rent would be applied to the purchase price upon Perkins' exercise of the purchase option. Swift and Perkins agreed to those terms.

Perkins moved into the house and immediately began redecorating. She also worked several weekends cleaning up the lawn and gardens.

Perkins made friendly gestures to her neighbors, waving to them from her work in the garden, but no one returned her greetings. Soon thereafter, Perkins learned that several neighbors had contacted Swift to voice their displeasure that she had "rented to a black person." Perkins, who is African-American, had formerly lived in an integrated neighborhood. The neighborhood surrounding Swift's house was exclusively white.

By the end of the fourth month, Perkins was convinced that this was the home for her despite the neighbors' lack of friendliness. She was looking forward to exercising her purchase option.

Two weeks later, however, the neighborhood was shocked by two widely publicized cross-burnings, both within four blocks of Perkins' house. Perkins, concerned about her security, consulted the police. They suggested turning on yard lights at night and coming home before dark.

A few days later, Perkins stepped from her house one morning to find garbage strewn across the publicly owned sidewalk directly in front of her house. Mixed in with the garbage were several dead rats. The word "nigger" was scrawled in chalk on the sidewalk next to the garbage.

Made sick to her stomach by the sight, Perkins called the police. She also took the day off from work to clean up the mess. By the end of the day she was nauseated and dizzy from the shock, anger, and stress of the day's events.

Perkins secured the house and called friends to make arrangements to stay with them for a few days. She still was unable to sleep at night, and her performance at work slipped because she could not concentrate. Perkins considered not going through with her purchase. Yet she had invested considerable time and effort on the decorating and on the yard and gardens. She also had made five rental payments, including $1,000 that she would forfeit if she did not exercise her purchase option.

After several days, she moved back to the house and tried to convince herself that this problem was only temporary and that the purchase option was worth exercising. But by the end of the week, she was still fearful. Her sleepless nights and slipping work performance continued. She occasionally suffered from painful stress headaches. She became short-tempered with friends and afraid equally of leaving the house and of coming home. She had several friends stay overnight. Her friends soon tired of that.

After three weeks, Perkins finally decided that she had to forfeit her option. She planned to tell Swift the next morning, but that evening she received a phone call from a sympathetic neighbor who lived across the street. This neighbor had witnessed the garbage dumping and told Perkins that John Bartow, who lived two doors up the street from Perkins, was the perpetrator. The neighbor explained that Bartow had dumped the garbage because he and other neighbors did not want an African-American person moving onto the block.

Upon hearing this, Perkins decided that she might want to stay and fight. She contacted a senior attorney in your firm the next morning and has requested a speedy evaluation of her rights against Bartow. The purchase option has not yet expired. The senior attorney wishes to know whether Perkins can recover for her emotional distress. If so, and Bartow is made aware of this, Bartow may cease the harassment; furthermore, Perkins may be able to recover damages. Confine yourself to this question and do not discuss the amount of damages.

C. THE STARTING POINT: FACTUAL AND LEGAL ANALYSIS

Law applies to factual circumstances; without a context, the law is difficult to understand. Thus, the facts in a particular situation furnish the connection between a client and the law. As you might surmise, some of these facts are much more important than others.

Since you are unlikely as a beginning researcher to know with certainty which facts and law might be helpful, you should use the following six categories to help you generate and identify key words and concepts:

(1) *Persons or Parties:* This category refers to the group, class, or status of the persons involved in the situation (infant, partnership, etc.) or to relationships (parent/child, landlord/tenant, etc.) that may have legal significance.

(2) *Item or Subject Matter:* This category refers to the item (gun, automobile, train, etc.) or subject matter (joint venture agreement, accounts receivable, etc.) that spawned the problem.

(3) *Timing and Location:* This category refers to the timing (night, after business hours, during work hours, etc.) and the location (school, river, etc.) of the situation or injury.

(4) *Relief Sought:* This category refers to the result (money damages, injunction, criminal penalty, etc.) desired by one or more of those who seek legal advice or who ultimately may bring this situation to the attention of a dispute resolution body.

(5) *Legal Theories:* This category refers to the legal basis that might give rise to liability for harm suffered (breach of contract, negligence, assault, etc.) or provide a defense to liability (consent, privilege, etc.).

(6) *Procedure:* This category refers to procedural concerns (pending motions, statute of limitations, venue, jurisdiction, statute of frauds, timely filing, etc.).

The first three categories are factual, while the last three are legal. As you learn more about the law, you will be able to more easily hone in on the legally relevant facts and do so within a wider range of legal subject areas.

Be flexible in determining which facts matter. Even experienced researchers find that facts that initially seemed unimportant can take on increased significance as research changes their perception of the applicable law. Remember to remain open to researching these new factual topics. In addition, the six categories above (if used diligently) can bring these seemingly unimportant facts to your attention at an earlier research stage. The categories also can jog your memory so that you do not forget to research an entire category.

Here's how the initial factual and legal analysis for the Perkins research situation might look:

(1) *Persons or Parties:* neighbors, African-American vs. Euro-American, female vs. male, adults

(2) *Item or Subject Matter:* garbage, rats, racial epithet, racism, discrimination in home ownership

(3) *Timing and Location:* night, before Perkins exercised her option, sidewalk, in front of house, residential neighborhood

(4) *Relief Sought:* recovery for emotional distress, an end to Bartow's harassment

(5) *Legal Theories:* not yet known

(6) *Procedure:* none so far

Not all of the facts in the first three categories will eventually be relevant to the resolution of this legal dispute. However, this early stage of factual analysis is too soon for you to start eliminating possibilities.

Note that you do not yet know the legal theory of this dispute (fifth category). Do not panic. You seldom will begin your research in command of all of the relevant topics, but your preliminary research on the terms in the factual and legal categories should eventually lead you to one or two legal theories that support Perkins' need for relief. In addition, there is no lawsuit pending, so there is nothing in the procedure (sixth) category.

Be sure to consider the interrelationship of items in these six categories. For instance, you may want to know whether it makes any legal difference that the perpetrator of this incident left rats and garbage (second category) on a public sidewalk (third category). Does it add to Perkins' damages (if any) (fourth category) that the incident took place at night (third category)? Additionally, you might decide to look into how the legal claim (fifth category, yet unknown) is affected by the facts that the victim of the garbage incident was an African-American (first category) while the perpetrator was Euro-American (first category), and that racism (second category) was a motivating factor for the incident.

D. INITIAL RESEARCH GOAL: GENERATING RESEARCH VOCABULARY

In this initial stage of research, you need to generate a research vocabulary by these three means:

(1) constructing the "ladders of abstraction" for each category in your factual and legal analysis,
(2) finding synonyms for those terms, and
(3) establishing precise definitions of the terms in your six-category factual and legal analysis.

1. Constructing Ladders of Abstraction

A "ladder of abstraction" is a list of related terms ordered from general to specific, abstract to concrete, inclusive to exclusive. The most general term forms the top rung of the ladder and the most specific term forms the bottom rung of the ladder. A common tool in cognitive psychology, a ladder of abstraction enables a person who is unfamiliar with a topic to quickly sort out the hierarchical relationships among general and specific terms.

For instance, the factual category "Location" in the Perkins problem is
the top rung of the following ladder:

Location

neighborhood

residence

sidewalk

paved, urban, public sidewalk

Each lower rung is a subset of the rung above it; for instance, neighborhood
is a subset of location, residence is a subset of neighborhood, and so on.

Creating or expanding a ladder of abstraction is also a good means by
which to brainstorm about a factual or legal category in your six-category
analysis. For instance, you can brainstorm about the factual category "Persons
or Parties" in the Perkins problem and thereby greatly expand the initial
analysis shown on page 17. Here is the expanded ladder of abstraction:

Persons or Parties

neighbors, adults, different sexes, different races

female and male, minority and majority races, black
and white, African-American and Euro-American

2. Finding Synonyms

The other way to expand a ladder of abstraction horizontally is by generating synonyms for the terms that make up each rung of the ladder. For
instance, the factual category "Item" in the Perkins problem initially contains
only the terms "garbage" and "rats." The resulting ladder of abstraction would
look like this:

Item

garbage

rats

Employing the brainstorming strategy of the previous section, you then could
expand this ladder vertically by adding more rungs to it. For instance, from
"garbage" to "item" may seem like an abrupt jump. What set does garbage
belong to? One possibility is an even more general category like "smelly
stuff." Additionally, you might ask what other components, besides rats, the
idea of garbage contains. The resulting ladder of abstraction would look like
this:

Item

smelly stuff

garbage

wastepaper, food, leaves, rats, broken items

Now you would generate synonyms for these terms and end up with something like this:

Item

smelly, repulsive, offensive stuff

garbage, refuse, waste, litter, junk, trash, debris

wastepaper, food, leaves, rats, broken items

Similarly, you can generate the following ladder from the factual category "Subject Matter" in the Perkins problem:

Subject Matter

racism

racial epithet, discrimination in home ownership

Brainstorming might yield something like this:

Subject Matter

racism, discrimination, segregation

racial epithet, cross-burning, segregated
neighborhoods, implicit racial threats, discrimination in
home ownership

Finally, you can add synonyms by using dictionaries and thesauri, and end up with something like this:

Subject Matter

racism, discrimination, segregation, injustice, bias,
prejudice, apartheid, bigotry, ostracism, ghettoization

racial epithet, racial slurs, cross-burning, segregated
neighborhoods, implicit racial threats, discrimination in
home ownership

Finding synonyms is a valuable initial research step because you may be unsuccessful in locating research materials discussing your research topics if you do not use the same vocabulary used by the indexes and tables of contents in those materials. This requirement is true of both print and electronic (computer) research.

In other areas of research you have undertaken, you may not have worried much about generating a research vocabulary if the topics you researched did not have much specialized vocabulary. Or perhaps you were not asked to research a particular topic until you had been taught its special vocabulary. If you were not under much time pressure, you may have generated additional synonyms and related terms as you ran into dead ends, but you did not worry about how many extra "billable hours" you spent researching in this manner. Moreover, your sources may have contained many cross-references.

However, in legal research, every legal topic has its share of specialized vocabulary. Furthermore, even seasoned attorneys frequently are asked to research topics they never studied in school. And nearly all legal research is done under time pressure. Moreover, many legal research sources do not contain enough cross-references and synonyms to bail out a novice researcher.

You can adapt to this new set of research pressures by being more savvy and methodical about how you approach each new legal research project. You should take preparatory research steps before you plunge into the mainstream of your research. Using dictionaries, glossaries, and thesauri, you should generate a list of words and phrases that may appear in one or more research sources. The thesauri in various computer word-processing programs also are helpful. You then can use this vocabulary while consulting indexes and tables of contents and in searches in computers, CD-ROM sources, and microforms.

The synonyms that were added to the middle rung of the "Subject Matter" ladder of abstraction on page 20 came from *West's Legal Thesaurus/Dictionary*. The "Racism" entry from that source appears in Illustration 2-1 below; it contained cross-references to segregation, injustice, bias, and prejudice. The entry "Segregation" in turn contained a huge collection of synonyms: classification, isolation, grouping, partition, differentiation, exile, splitting up allocation, detachment, segmentation; racism; apartheid, bigotry, discrimination, ostracism, ghettoization. It also gave cross-references to division, separation, quarantine, bias, and prejudice. The entries for "Bias" and "Prejudice" were not quite as productive. Note that you do not need to add all the synonyms you uncover to your ladder of abstraction, but only those that strike you as potentially helpful to your research.

ILLUSTRATION 2-1. William P. Statsky, *West's Legal Thesaurus/Dictionary: A Resource for the Writer and the Computer Researcher* 627 (1985).

Rabid, *adj.* See extreme, ardent, emotional, wild, hysterical, hot.

Race 1. *n.* A major division of mankind, having in common certain physical peculiarities constituting a comprehensive class appearing to be derived from a distinct primitive source (pride in her race). Stock, breed, tribe, ancestry, stirps, parentage, ethnic stock, strain, clan, generation, people, nation, lineage, kin. See also genealogy, family. **2.** *n.* Contest (presidential race). Campaign, competition, run, chase, trial. **3.** *v.* To move rapidly in a contest of speed (race to the recorder's office). Dash, scramble, run, bolt, dart, compete, hurry, accelerate, hustle, rush, fly, pursue, gallop.

Race-notice recording statute A state law that provides that an unrecorded conveyance is invalid as against a subsequent purchaser for value who records without knowledge of the prior unrecorded instrument. The first to record in the chain of title without notice of a prior unrecorded deed or mortgage has superior rights.

Race recording statute A state law that provides that the party who records an instrument of conveyance has the better claim regardless of notice of prior unrecorded instruments. The first to record regardless of notice of an unrecorded deed or mortgage earlier in time has superior rights.

Racism, *n.* See segregation, injustice, bias, prejudice.

Racist, *adj.* See narrow (2), fanatic.

Rack, *n.* **1.** A frame. Lattice, scaffold, skeleton, trestle, grate. **2.** See pain.

3. Establishing Legal Definitions

You may be wondering whether to use non-legal dictionaries and thesauri in your research. If you are unfamiliar with the area of the law that you are investigating, you should be very cautious about using a layperson's definition until you first have checked whether the term has a different or particular meaning in the legal system. Thus, your initial research approach should be to check law dictionaries and thesauri for a legal definition or synonym. Only if you come up dry should you consult a non-legal dictionary or thesaurus for definitions and synonyms in laypersons' vocabulary.

a. Law Dictionaries, Glossaries, and Thesauri

Your law library may have some or all of the law dictionaries, glossaries, and thesauri listed in Table 2.1 on page 24.

Citation Note: The citations in Tables 2.1 and 2.2 (page 31) are in the form generally required by Rule 15 of *The Bluebook,* except that they are missing page numbers, which would usually follow the title. *See* Rule 3.3. Some frequently cited books, like *Black's* and *Ballentine's* dictionaries, have special citation forms that omit the names of authors and editors. *See* Rule 15.7(a).

Law dictionaries and glossaries contain definitions and may also include pronunciations, word derivations, citations to related sources, and various tables. Their features differ markedly, as shown in Table 2.1. Leaf through Illustrations 2-1 through 2-9 on pages 21 and 26-29 to see for yourself how much these books differ in complexity of language, coverage of terms, length of definitions, and inclusion of supporting cites. Basically, dictionaries and glossaries in Table 2.1 fall into four categories:

(1) The dictionaries by Gilmer, Gifis, Martin, Oran, and Rothenberg define essential terms in plain English and are suitable for a beginning law student. They achieve their brevity partly by using extensive cross-referencing for terms used in the definitions; they also do not define infrequently used terms. These sources are usually paperbacks and are inexpensive.

(2) *Radin* and *Modern Legal Glossary* are hardcover dictionaries that contain an intermediate number of entries.

(3) *Black's* and *Ballentine's* define a huge range of terms in extensive definitions using legal terminology that is geared to a reader with legal training. Both sources are available as hardcover books and are fairly expensive. An abridged, less expensive version of *Black's* is also available in paperback.

(4) *Words and Phrases* compiles definitions from various cases. Its 50 volumes are updated by pocket parts.

Black's Law Dictionary is available on WESTLAW (a computer-assisted research tool). See Chapter 6.

Law thesauri (also listed in Table 2.1) are especially useful for finding alternative search terms to use in indexes and computer-assisted legal research. *West's Legal Thesaurus/Dictionary* contains definitions, synonyms, and antonyms. Burton's *Legal Thesaurus* is more typical of thesauri; it contains extensive synonyms, associated concepts, and sometimes synonymous foreign phrases and words.

In the Perkins research situation, many of the terms in your six-category factual and legal analysis do not appear in the law dictionaries in Table 2.1

because they are non-legal terms. For instance, there are no entries for neighbor, African-American, Euro-American, male, female, garbage, epithet, home ownership, night, sidewalk, residential neighborhood, or pre-option timing. This is because these terms are not defined differently in the law than they are in everyday life. More of the terms are included in the law thesauri in Table 2.1, because the scope of these sources is broader than purely legal terms.

You may have noticed that we have not yet generated ladders of abstraction for any of the law categories in our six-category factual and legal analysis. That is because the terms in these categories nearly always will have specialized legal meanings and therefore should be researched initially in law dictionaries, glossaries, and thesauri.

The same also is true of some terms in the factual-category ladders; for instance, racism, discrimination, and segregation on the "Subject Matter" ladder have specialized legal meanings and therefore should be initially researched in legal sources.

b.   Using Legal Definitions to Build Ladders of Abstraction

How could law dictionaries, glossaries, and thesauri be used in the Perkins research situation? The legal analysis on page 18 tells you that you know almost nothing about the categories of "legal theory," "relief sought," and "procedure," except that Perkins wants Bartow to stop causing her emotional distress and possibly to pay her money for her past emotional distress. You do not know enough in these three categories to construct any ladders of abstraction, so you need to work on the legal definition of "emotional distress."

In Illustration 2-2 on page 26, *Modern Legal Glossary* defines "emotional distress" in part as follows: "[u]sually an intentional tort in which a person acts in an extreme and outrageous manner, causing severe emotional distress or mental anguish in another." This definition mentions a new term, "intentional tort," which is defined in *Black's* (Illustration 2-3 on page 26) as "[a] tort in which the actor . . . possessed intent or purpose to injure." "Tort," in turn, is defined in Rothenberg's dictionary (Illustration 2-4 on page 27) in part as "[a] wrong committed by one person against another," but not a "criminal wrong" or one "arising out of a contract."

You may have noticed that these three definitions have enabled you to construct the top portion of the ladder of abstraction for "Legal Theory." Thus far you know that "emotional distress" is a subset of "intentional tort," which in turn is a subset of "tort," which is a legal theory. At this point the ladder would look as follows:

Legal Theory

tort

intentional tort

emotional distress

Now you need more information about the bottom portion of the ladder.

Return to the first definition from *Modern Legal Glossary;* it mentions "mental anguish" as synonymous with "emotional distress." In Illustration 2-5 on page 27, Gifis' dictionary defines "mental anguish" as "compensable injury embracing all forms of mental pain, . . . including deep grief, distress, anxiety and fright." Oran's dictionary (Illustration 2-6 on page 28) notes that

TABLE 2.1. General-Coverage Law Dictionaries, Glossaries, and Thesauri.

Dictionaries and Glossaries:	Length and Size	Cross-References to Other Definitions	Plain English
Ballentine's Law Dictionary (3d ed. 1969).	1387 pp./ full-size	yes	no
Black's Law Dictionary (6th ed. 1990).	1622 pp./ full-size (also published in abridged edition)	yes	no
A Concise Dictionary of Law (Elizabeth Martin ed., 2d ed. 1990).	448 pp./ pocket-size	yes	yes
Steven H. Gifis, *Law Dictionary* (3d ed. 1991).	537 pp./ pocket-size	yes	yes
The Law Dictionary (Wesley Gilmer, Jr., ed., 6th ed. 1986).	346 pp./ pocket-size	yes	yes
Daniel Oran, *Oran's Dictionary of the Law* (2d ed. 1991).	500 pp./ pocket-size	yes	yes
The Plain-Language Law Dictionary (Robert E. Rothenberg ed., 1981).	378 pp./ pocket-size	yes	yes
Max Radin, *Radin Law Dictionary* (2d ed. 1970).	376 pp./ pocket-size	yes	no
Kenneth R. Redden & Enid L. Veron, *Modern Legal Glossary* (1980).	570 pp./ intermediate size	some	yes
Words and Phrases (perm. ed. 1940-present) (updated by pocket parts).	more than 50 volumes/ full-size	some	no
Thesauri:			
William C. Burton, *Legal Thesaurus* (2d ed. 1991).	518 pp./ full-size	yes	n/a
William P. Statsky, *West's Legal Thesaurus/Dictionary: A Resource for the Writer and the Computer Researcher* (1985).	813 pp./ intermediate size	yes	yes

Pronunciation	Cites to Other Sources	Table of Legal Abbreviations	Other Features
yes (some)	yes	yes	explanations of some federal statutes and all uniform acts
yes (some)	yes	yes	U.S. Constitution, time chart of U.S. Supreme Court, organizational chart of U.S. government, table of British regnal years
no	no	no	
yes (some)	yes	only those used in text	U.S. Constitution, ABA Model Code of Professional Responsibility, ABA Model Rules of Professional Conduct, federal judicial circuits, federal judicial system, U.S. Supreme Court justices
yes (some)	only to statutes, uniform and model acts, Restatements	only those used in text	Latin and French maxims translated and explained; explanation of federal, uniform, and model acts
yes (some)	no	included as entries in text	appendix on how to cut back on legalese, two appendices on legal research and analysis, U.S. government organizational chart, table on sources of law, table on National Reporter System
no	no	only those used in text	Declaration of Independence, U.S. Constitution, legal holidays, basic tax information (outdated), justices of U.S. Supreme Court and federal courts (somewhat outdated), tables on marriage and divorce laws, Social Security information, federal agency addresses, immigration law information
no	yes	yes	manual on citation (inconsistent with *Bluebook*), Declaration of Independence, U.S. Constitution, U.S. Supreme Court justices, British and English regnal years, ABA Model Code of Professional Responsibility, selected legal maxims translated
no	only to famous cases	included as entries in text	entries to famous cases and trials; classic law books; ancient codes; brief biographies of outstanding persons in law; foreign expressions; professional associations; government agencies; international organizations
no	yes (extensive)	yes	digest-style paragraphs from various cases; updated annually with pocket parts
no	no	no	associated concepts, extensive index
only the emphasis syllable	no	no	antonyms, synonyms

ILLUSTRATION 2-2. Kenneth R. Redden & Enid L. Veron, *Modern Legal Glossary* 168 (1980).

EMINENT DOMAIN. The power of a government to take private property for public purposes upon payment of just compensation to the owner.

EMOTIONAL DISTRESS. Usually an intentional tort in which a person acts in an extreme and outrageous manner, causing severe emotional distress or mental anguish in another. Typical examples are bullying tactics used by bill collectors or landlords.

EMPLOYEES TRUST. A trust arrangement established by a corporate employer for the benefit of compensation

The procedure itself is described in Rule 35 of the Federal Rules of Appellate Procedure. It is also used by state courts.

ENCUMBRANCE TO PROPERTY. Binding claim or liability attached to real property. Encumbrances are generally liens which affect the title to the property or restrictions which affect the physical use of property, such as easements or encroachments.

ENDANGERED SPECIES ACT OF 1973. Empowers the Secretary of the Interior to declare a species of plant, animal, bird, or fish to be end

ILLUSTRATION 2-3. *Black's Law Dictionary* 811 (6th ed. 1990).

811

INTERDICTION

Intentional tort. A tort in which the actor is expressly or impliedly judged to have possessed intent or purpose to injure.

Intentione /intènshiyówniy/. In old English law, a writ that lay against him who entered into lands after the death of a tenant in dower, or for life, etc., and held out to him in reversion or remainder.

Intent to kill. An element in certain aggravated assaults and batteries which requires the prosecution to prove the intent to kill in addition to the other elements of the assault and battery. *See* Aggravated assault; Malice aforethought; Premeditation.

Inter /intər. Lat. Among; between.

Interception. Within Federal Communications Act, prohibiting interception of communication by wire or radio, indicates taking or seizure by the way or before arrival at destined place, and does not ordinarily connote obtaining of what is to be sent before, or at the moment, it leaves the possession of the proposed sender, or after, or at the moment, it comes into possession of intended receiver. Communications Act of 1934, § 605, 47 U.S. C.A. § 605; Goldman v. United States, N.Y., 316 U.S. 129, 62 S.Ct. 993, 995, 86 L.Ed. 1322. *See* Eavesdropping; Wiretapping.

Interchangeably. By way of exchange or interchange. This term properly denotes the method of signing deeds, leases, contracts, etc., executed in duplicate, where each party signs the copy which he delivers to the other.

"[m]ental anguish (or mental suffering) . . . may be as limited as the immediate mental feelings during an injury or as broad as prolonged grief, shame, humiliation, despair, etc."

These definitions expand your ladder of abstraction horizontally (with synonyms), as well as vertically by one rung, as shown here:

Legal Theory

tort

intentional tort

emotional distress, mental anguish, mental suffering, mental pain

deep or prolonged grief, anxiety, fright, shame, humiliation, despair

ILLUSTRATION 2-4. *The Plain-Language Law Dictionary* 346 (Robert E. Rothenberg ed., 1981).

27

Title retention. A LIEN or MORTGAGE to secure the purchase price of PROPERTY.

To assume and pay and save harmless. A phrase used in the transfer of PROPERTY, the new OWNER agreeing to assume the MORTGAGE and to secure the former owner against loss should the mortgage not be paid off.

To do time. To serve a term in jail (slang).

To have and to hold. Words used in a transfer (conveyance) of PROPERTY from one person to another, meaning that the property is to pass to that person, to be owned by him, and to pass on to his HEIRS when he dies.

cargo, a tax upon a vessel

Took and carried away. Words used in a SUIT against a person accused of STEALING.

Tort. A wrong committed by one person against another; a CIVIL, not a criminal wrong; a wrong not arising out of a CONTRACT; a violation of a legal DUTY that one person has toward another. (NEGLIGENCE and LIBEL are torts.) Every tort is composed of a legal OBLIGATION, a BREACH of that obligation, and DAMAGE as the result of the breach of the obligation.

Tort, personal. A wrong to a person, such as ASSAULT, or a wrong resulting in damage to a person's

ILLUSTRATION 2-5. Steven H. Gifis, *Law Dictionary* 296 (3d ed. 1991).

MEMORANDUM   296   MERCHANT

argument headings, tables of cases, etc.

OFFICE MEMORANDUM an informal discussion of the merits of a mat

114 So. 529. Compare **pain and suffering.**

MENTAL CRUELTY a ground for **divorce,** consisting of a course of behavior by one spouse toward the

specific mens rea. See, e.g., 343 U.S. 790. These are usually crimes of **strict liability.**

MENTAL ANGUISH compensable **injury** embracing all forms of mental pain, as opposed to mere physical pain, including deep grief, distress, anxiety and fright. See

goods in question, or holding himself out as a person who deals in such goods, was not a "merchant" for purposes of implied **warranty.** 473 F. Supp. 35, 38.

Merchants include car dealers, 397 N.Y.S. 2d 677, 681; producers of remanufactured engines, 551 F.

However, if you consulted Gilmer's dictionary (Illustration 2-7 on page 28), you would find that it contradicts your present understanding of emotional distress. Gilmer says that emotional distress is a form of injury but is not by itself a tort. Gilmer also gives a comparative cross-reference—indicated by the signal *"Cf."*—to "outrage." (*The Bluebook* says that *"Cf."* means that the "[c]ited authority supports a proposition different from the main proposition but sufficiently analogous to lend support." Rule 1.2(a).)

ILLUSTRATION 2-6. Daniel Oran, *Oran's Dictionary of the Law* 269 (2d ed. 1991).

liability for crimes that

Mensa et thoro   (Latin) "Bed and board." Describes a type of limited **divorce** (see that word) or legal separation.

Mental anguish (or mental suffering)   Nonphysical harm that may be compensated for by **damages** in some types of lawsuits. *Mental anguish* may be as limited as the immediate mental feelings during an injury or as broad as prolonged grief, shame, humiliation, despair, etc.

Mental cruelty   See **cruelty.**

Mercantile   Commercial; having to do with buying and selling, etc.

for an institution that may perform

ILLUSTRATION 2-7. *The Law Dictionary* 121 (Wesley Gilmer, Jr., ed., 6th ed. 1986).

m.p.h. 23 U.S.C. § 154; 87 Stat. 1010 (

eminent domain, the right which a government retains over the property of individuals to take it for public use *(q.v.),* in return for a fair compensation. It is often exercised for ordinary governmental purposes, *e.g.,* public highways and public buildings, and for certain private purposes, *e.g.,* pipelines and railroads.

emotional distress, a form of injury *(q.v.)* resulting from tortious *(q.v.)* conduct; it is not in itself a tort *(q.v.).* (2) Variously, mental suffering, mental anguish, nervous shock, and includes all highly unpleasant mental reactions, *e.g.,* fright, horror, grief, shame, embarrassment, anger, chagrin, disappointment, and worry; it is only when emotional distress is extreme that possible liability arises. Cf. *outrage.*

empanel, see *impanel.* See also, *panel.*

facts gathered from observation, experience, or

In Illustrations 2-8 and 2-9 on page 29, Gilmer and *Black's* define the tort of "outrage" and set out many of its elements. *Black's* equates the tort of outrage with "intentional infliction of serious mental distress," but does not define that phrase. Gilmer's definition of "outrage" ends with a cite to the Restatement (Second) of Torts; Restatements are discussed in Chapter 3 at page 104.

The resulting ladder of abstraction for "Legal Theory" is shown below:

Legal Theory

tort

intentional tort

outrage, intentional infliction of serious mental distress

emotional distress, mental anguish, mental suffering, mental distress

deep or prolonged grief, anxiety, fright, shame, humiliation, despair

---

243   **PAC**

ties made out of court. (2) The situation of a plaintiff who has been nonsuited or is otherwise unable to maintain his lawsuit.

out of the state, descriptive of a person who is a nonresident (*q.v.*) of the state or is temporarily outside of the state and beyond the reach of its process.

outer barrister, see *utter barrister.*

outlawry, formerly, an English procedure, by which a person was put out of the protection of the law for wilfully avoiding the execution of the process of the courts.

outrage, a tort, by extreme and outrageous conduct intentionally or recklessly causing severe emotional distress to another. Liability has been found only where the conduct has been so outrageous in character, and so extreme in degree as to go beyond all possible bounds of decency and to be regarded as atrocious and utterly intolerable in a civilized community. Restatement (Second) of Torts § 46, Comment d. Cf. *emotional distress.*

over, above; beyond. In conveyancing, a gift or limitation which is to come into existence upon the termination of preceding estate.

checks upon a bank, for a greater amount

ILLUSTRATION 2-9. *Black's Law Dictionary* 1102 (6th ed. 1990).

...lawry. In old English law, a process by which a defendant or person in contempt on a civil or criminal process was declared an outlaw. If for treason or felony, it amounted to conviction and attainder.

In the United States, the process of outlawry seems to be unknown, at least in civil cases. Hall v. Lanning, 91 U.S. 160, 23 L.Ed. 271.

Outline. The line which marks the outer limits of an object or figure; an exterior line or edge; contour.

Outlot. In early American land law (particularly in Missouri), a lot or parcel of land lying outside the corporate limits of a town or village but subject to its municipal jurisdiction or control. Term now generally refers...

Output contract. *See* Contract; Entire output contract.

Outrage. A grave injury; injurious violence. The tort of "outrage" (intentional infliction of serious mental distress) requires that defendant engage in outrageous and extreme conduct which results in intentionally or recklessly inflicted severe emotional distress. Spencer v. King County, 39 Wash.App. 201, 692 P.2d 874, 880.

Outriders. In old English law, bailiffs-errant employed by sheriffs or their deputies to ride to the extremities of their counties or hundreds to summon men to the county or hundred court.

Outright. Free from reserve or restraint; direct; posi-... down-right; altogether; entirely; openly

---

This is a fairly complete ladder. Often you will not be able to glean this much information from dictionaries and thesauri alone. The top rung of the ladder ("Legal Theory") is one of the six categories, but will not be a useful research term. The next two rungs—"tort" and "intentional tort"—help you to see the big picture within which outrage and emotional distress fit. The next rung down—"outrage"—furnishes synonyms for your research, as do the bottom two steps.

You can link these separate ladders of abstraction to see the relationship between the law and a set of facts, as shown on page 30. Although, for lack of space, not all of the contents of the individual ladders above were included in these linked ladders, you can see how those individual ladders fit together to expand your initial six-category factual and legal analysis of the Perkins research situation. During your future research, you would modify these linked ladders to reflect additional topics and your continual reassessment of the facts.

Ladders of abstraction are a valuable brainstorming tool for generating additional indexing vocabulary from the terms in your six-category factual analysis. The problem sets for Chapter 3 ask you to devise ladders of abstraction for the key legal terms and facts.

c.   Tips on Using Dictionaries

Illustrations 2-2 through 2-9 jumped around among various dictionaries because no single dictionary or thesaurus contained all of these terms. In fact, only a few dictionaries contained more than half of the terms. On this particular research project, the larger dictionaries did not contain more terms than the smaller dictionaries. Although this jumping around among dictionaries is frustrating, it is much less frustrating than using an index in a commentary source without being able to find any useful entries because you did not generate enough research vocabulary.

As an efficient researcher, you should tailor your choices among thesauri, dictionaries, and glossaries to the particular needs of your research problem instead of using the same source in all research situations. No single source will define all of the terms you are researching, and some entries will be more detailed or more concise than others. Keep the following strategy in mind: When you are looking up a more specialized word, you should use a larger or more specialized dictionary to increase your chances of finding the word. On the other hand, when you need a short usable definition of a common legal term, save time by using a compact dictionary.

You may have noticed that law dictionaries sometimes include citations to cases and statutes from which the definitions were derived. Generally, these cites are not particularly useful. They may omit an important piece of information—the year of decision or enactment—so you do not know how

LINKED LADDERS OF ABSTRACTION

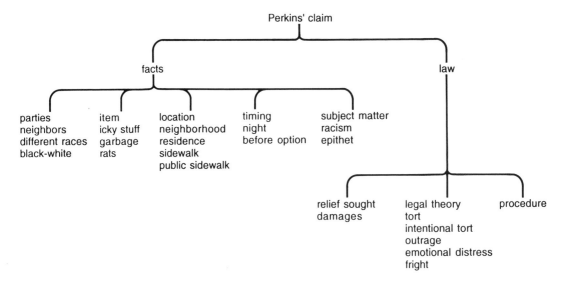

dated or unreliable these cases and statutes are. In addition, the case or statute cited usually originated in a factual setting or jurisdiction that differs from the one you are researching. For instance, if your fact situation arose in Pennsylvania but the dictionary cites only a definition from a California case, you first will need to research whether the Pennsylvania courts will agree with the California definition.

A brief note on alternative alphabetizing techniques: You should be aware that terms can be alphabetized word by word or letter by letter. In word-by-word alphabetizing, "out of the state" appears before "outer barrister" (see Illustration 2-8 on page 29). In letter-by-letter alphabetizing, "Intentional tort" appears before "Intent to kill" (see Illustration 2-3 on page 26). If you forget to watch for this distinction, you might not be able to find the term for which you are searching.

d. Specialized Law Dictionaries

For certain purposes or subjects, you also may be able to consult a wide selection of specialized law dictionaries, a fraction of which are listed in Table 2.2 below. "Special purpose" law dictionaries cover all areas of the law but serve a specialized function such as listing abbreviations. "Special subject" law dictionaries cover only a limited area of the law such as the law of the European Community. (For some comic relief from the study of law, consult *White's Law Dictionary* (D. Robert White ed., 1985) for whimsical and sometimes irreverent definitions and cartoons on legal topics.)

None of these specialized dictionaries is helpful to our current research project. However, one of these sources deserves special mention because of

TABLE 2.2. A Sampling of Specialized Law Dictionaries.

Special Purpose

Doris M. Bieber, *Dictionary of Legal Abbreviations* (Mary M. Prince ed., 3d ed. 1988).

Bryan A. Garner, *A Dictionary of Modern Legal Usage* (1987).

Special Subject

Robert L. Bledsoe & Boleslaw A. Boczek, *The International Law Dictionary* (1987).

John Bouvier, *Bouvier's Law Dictionary and Concise Encyclopedia* (Francis Rawle ed., 3d rev. 1914) (3 volumes; of historical value).

Ralph C. Chandler et al., *The Constitutional Law Dictionary* (1985) (3 volumes).

Elyse H. Fox, *The Legal Research Dictionary: From Advance Sheets to Pocket Parts* (1987).

Rudolph Heimanson, *Dictionary of Political Science and Law* (1967).

Robert Herbst, *Dictionary of Commercial, Financial and Legal Terms* (4th ed. 1985-89) (English, French, and German).

Latin Words & Phrases for Lawyers (R.S. Vasan ed., 1980).

Ernest A. Lindbergh, *International Law Dictionary: English-French-German* (1991).

Jack C. Plano & Roy Olton, *The International Relations Dictionary* (4th ed. 1988).

The Prentice-Hall Dictionary of Business, Finance and Law (1983).

Peter G. Renstrom, *The American Law Dictionary* (1991) (terms in American judicial system).

Jacob E. Schmidt, *Attorney's Dictionary of Medicine and Word Finder* (1962-present) (4-volume looseleaf, frequently updated).

Stroud's Judicial Dictionary of Words and Phrases (5th ed. 1986).

its usefulness to a beginning legal writer and because it is available online on LEXIS. *A Dictionary of Modern Legal Usage* contains definitions of words common to legal writing and notes on frequently misused or confused legal terms. It also contains short essays on points of grammar and style in legal writing. It is the legal equivalent of Fowler's *A Dictionary of Modern English Usage,* a classic text on grammar and usage.

E. TAKING NOTES

A system of note-taking is essential to keep track of where you have been, what you have found, and where you found it. There is no "right" way to keep track of your research. However, you may find it helpful to set up a separate page or notebook section for each issue—that is, to keep your notes segregated by issue. At a minimum, you should record:

(1) the sources you checked and the information needed for their citations;

(2) the topics, words, issues, and index entries that you researched in each source;

(3) the content found in each source, including the significance of certain quotes, facts, and issues (and the page numbers on which you found them);

(4) additional relevant sources of potentially relevant authority referred to in that source; and

(5) your process of updating each source by using supplements and citators.

No doubt you and your classmates have your own systems of note-taking that will merely require some fine-tuning to accommodate the five items listed above. Some sample research notes taken from the definitions and synonyms in Illustrations 2-2 to 2-9 appear on page 33. The arrows show how a term found in one source then led the researcher to another definition. These notes do not contain any updating information because none of these sources are updated. Nor do these notes contain complete citations to the sources consulted because that information is already available in Table 2.1.

Of course, this "step" of note-taking continues throughout your research.

Notes on Content	Source	References
emotional distress	MLG	
intentional tort	p. 168	
mental anguish		
extreme & outrageous actions		
ex.: bullying by bill collectors, landlords		
intentional tort	Black's	
tort in which actor had intent or purpose to injure	p. 811	
tort	Rothenberg	
not a crime, not a contract right	p. 346	
violation of legal duty of one to another		
elements: obligation		
breach of obligation		
damages from breach		
mental anguish	Gifis	114 So. 529
mental pain, as opposed to physical pain	p. 296	
includes deep grief, distress, anxiety, fright		
compensable injury		
same as mental suffering	Oran	
may be compensated by damages	p. 269	
can be as ltd. as immediate feelings or as broad as		
prolonged grief, shame, humiliation, or despair		
emotional distress	Gilmer	
not a tort by itself	p. 121	
injury from tortious conduct		
includes mental suffering, mental anguish, nervous		
shock, and all highly unpleasant mental		
reactions, such as fright, horror, grief, shame,		
embarrassment, anger, chagrin, disappointment,		
worry		
cf. outrage		
outrage	Gilmer	Restmt 2d Torts
tort	p. 243	§ 46 comment d
elements		
intentionally or recklessly		
by extreme & outrageous conduct		
(must go beyond all possible bounds of		
decency; be atrocious & utterly intolerable in		
civilized community)		
causing severe emotional distress to another		
grave injury, injurious violence	Black's	Spencer v. King Cnty,
same as intentional infliction of serious mental	p. 1102	39 Wash. App. 201
distress		692 P.2d 874, 880

F. BEGINNING THE OUTLINE OR FLOWCHART

Using notes like those above, you now can begin an outline of your research on this project:

I. tort = violation of legal duty of one to another
    A. not a crime, not a contract
    B. elements
        1. obligation
        2. breach of obligation
        3. damages from breach

C. intentional tort = tort done with intent or purpose to injure
   1. outrage = intentional infliction of serious mental distress
     a. one kind of intentional tort
     b. elements of outrage
       (1) intentional or reckless conduct by D
       (2) extreme & outrageous conduct by D
         (a) goes beyond all possible bounds of decency
         (b) must be atrocious & utterly intolerable in civilized community
       (3) caused P's severe emotional distress
         (a) emotional distress
           (i) synonyms: mental anguish, mental suffering, mental distress, mental pain
           (ii) includes grief, shame, humiliation, despair, anxiety, fright, horror, embarrassment, anger, chagrin, disappointment, worry
         (b) 2 interpretations: feelings can be immediate (narrow) or prolonged (broad)
     c. examples: bullying by bill collector, landlord
     d. damages, payment, compensation available

If outlining is difficult for you or if you think better visually, consider making a flowchart instead of an outline. A flowchart of the material outlined above appears on page 35.

G. SETTING GOALS AND LIMITS FOR YOUR RESEARCH PROJECT

Very few research projects require the researcher to learn everything about the subject in question. Even fewer require the researcher to read every source on the subject, no matter how redundant or poorly organized.

And yet researchers who are unfamiliar with a research topic too often start their research thinking that they should find and read everything on the subject. These researchers often are attempting to overcome their insecurity by research overkill and by becoming more of an expert than the project demands. These researchers spend 50 hours on a 30-hour project and have little to show for it.

Other researchers begin their research without any specific idea of what they hope to accomplish within their research. Fifty hours later they are still researching and wondering whether they will ever know when to stop.

The answer to both of these situations is to understand why this particular research needs to be done at this particular time. You must understand the needs of your client and, if you are researching for another attorney or judge, the needs of your audience.

For instance, in the Perkins situation, you know that your client desires an end to Bartow's harassment and possibly damages for the harm he already has inflicted. Other possible relief need not be researched at this time. You also know that the dispute is still in a pre-lawsuit setting, so no research on court rules, procedures, and documents is needed yet. You also know that the person needing the research is an experienced attorney, so you need not define each and every legal term, except insofar as you need those definitions

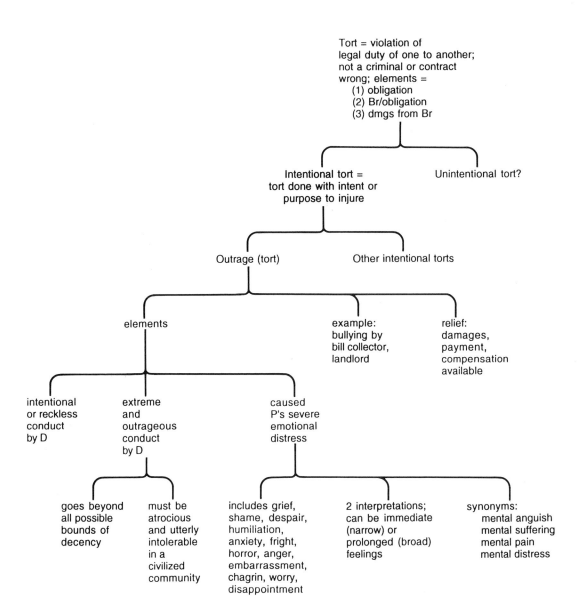

for your own understanding. You do not yet know the availability of research sources on this subject, so you next must proceed to Chapter 3 on commentary sources.

In addition, the scope of research necessary to complete a particular research project is shaped by such factors as the research sources available on that subject, the forum or setting, the role of the person needing the research, the timing of the request with reference to the ongoing process, and your own expertise on the subjects your are researching. All research projects must begin with an analysis of these factors and needs.

Commentary Sources: Searching in Secondary Authority

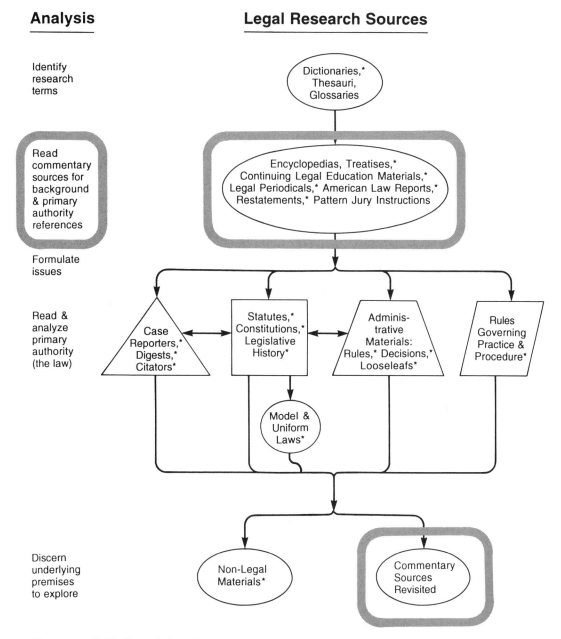

Analysis

Identify research terms

Read commentary sources for background & primary authority references

Formulate issues

Read & analyze primary authority (the law)

Discern underlying premises to explore

Legal Research Sources

Dictionaries,* Thesauri, Glossaries

Encyclopedias, Treatises,* Continuing Legal Education Materials,* Legal Periodicals,* American Law Reports,* Restatements,* Pattern Jury Instructions

Case Reporters,* Digests,* Citators*

Statutes,* Constitutions,* Legislative History*

Administrative Materials: Rules,* Decisions,* Looseleafs*

Rules Governing Practice & Procedure*

Model & Uniform Laws*

Non-Legal Materials*

Commentary Sources Revisited

*Sources available (in part) through computer-assisted legal research

A. INTRODUCTION TO COMMENTARY SOURCES

1. Overview

Secondary authority is not "the law"; primary authority is. You could eventually come to understand a new area of the law by reading primary authority at the start of your research process. However, a savvy researcher more quickly gains an understanding of an area of law by first reading a good survey or an overall analysis of the area. These sources comment on the law; hence the name "commentary sources." They are more accessible and often more coherent than primary authority. They present a "big picture" understanding of the overall structure of relevant primary authority. They also may alert the researcher to legally significant facts or additional legal topics that he or she missed in the initial factual and legal analysis. Thus, secondary authority increases your research efficiency by accelerating your initial understanding of relevant primary authority.

Secondary authority also functions as a finding tool by providing citations to other sources that may be useful in your continuing research. If you locate a cite to a case or statute, that primary authority may lead you to still other primary and secondary authority.

Finally, secondary authority provides skillful analyses, critiques, and projections of trends. These qualities are especially valuable at the end of one's research, when one has read most of the relevant primary authority.

Thus, commentary sources serve three important purposes:

(1) they familiarize the researcher with the subject being researched by providing a valuable overview,
(2) they furnish citations to relevant primary authority, and
(3) they provide expert analysis of the law's trends, policies, and defects.

As you become a seasoned legal researcher, you may be able to skip the step of using commentary sources to familiarize yourself with a particular area, because you no longer need background information or overview. However, you probably will still use commentary sources as finding tools and sources of expert analysis.

Chapter 3 covers seven types of commentary sources in the following order:

encyclopedias
treatises
CLE materials
legal periodicals
A.L.R. annotations
Restatements
pattern jury instructions

The chapter introduces you first to several sources that closely resemble authorities used in other fields and then moves on to sources unique to law. You may find this material easier to assimilate if you note the parallels between sources in other fields and these sources.

As you skim through the illustrations for Chapter 3, you will see just how different these commentary sources are. They differ in such respects as format, organization, coverage, and currency. Encyclopedias and A.L.R. annotations are written by the publisher's staff, who may or may not be experts. Treatises, CLE materials, Restatements, and pattern jury instructions are written by experts in the field (attorneys, judges, and professors). Legal periodicals are written by the same collection of experts as well as selected law students. However, despite the expertise of some of these authors, their work is still merely commentary on the law and is not binding on governmental lawmaking bodies.

Consulting all of the available secondary authority is redundant and inefficient. The final part of Chapter 3 will assist you in formulating a research strategy for choosing among the seven types of secondary authority. On a grid-style chart (see page 127), you will be asked to compare their strengths, weaknesses, and differing functions. Then you will be able to select a combination of secondary authority that best suits the topic, your fact situation, your experience level, and the type of research you are about to undertake.

To learn about research in non-legal sources that may have information pertinent to legal problems, see Chapter 10. Some of these sources have formats parallel to some of the sources discussed in this chapter.

2. Your Research Situation

This chapter demonstrates the use of the above-listed commentary sources to find material pertinent to the Perkins problem described at pages 15-16 in Chapter 2. Recall that in Chapter 2 we developed the following potentially useful research terms:

(1) *Persons or Parties:* neighbors, different races, minority and majority races, black and white, African-American and Euro-American, different sexes, female and male, adults

(2) *Item or Subject Matter:* racism, racial intolerance, bigotry, discrimination, segregation, cross-burnings, racial epithets, segregated neighborhoods, implicit racial threats, discrimination in home ownership; garbage, refuse, waste, litter, junk, trash, debris, wastepaper, food, leaves, rats, broken items; offensive, repulsive, smelly stuff

(3) *Timing and Location:* night, before Perkins exercised her option; residence, neighborhood, in front of house, sidewalk (urban, paved, public), walkway, pedestrian way, passageway

(4) *Relief Sought:* recovery of damages for emotional distress, an end to Bartow's harassment

(5) *Legal Theories:* tort, intentional tort, outrage, intentional infliction of serious mental distress, emotional distress, mental anguish, mental suffering, mental distress, deep or prolonged grief, anxiety, fright, shame, humiliation, despair

(6) *Procedure:* none so far

We will use these terms in the remaining sections of this chapter to locate pertinent commentary on the Perkins research situation.

B. ENCYCLOPEDIAS

1. What Is an Encyclopedia?

Like encyclopedias in areas outside the law, law encyclopedias are sources with broad coverage and alphabetical organization. The scope of law encyclopedias can be a nation, an individual state, or a specialty area.

American Jurisprudence, Second Edition (Am. Jur. 2d) and *Corpus Juris Secundum* (C.J.S.) are both national law encyclopedias that encompass all American jurisdictions, both state and federal. They are descended from two older encyclopedias (now outdated), *American Jurisprudence* and *Corpus Juris.*

Law encyclopedias are organized alphabetically into broad topics that are subdivided into narrower subtopics. (Am. Jur. 2d uses the term "topic," while C.J.S. uses the term "title." This chapter will use the term "topic.") Within each major topic, the subtopics are numbered by section. The sections within each topic are organized as follows: Definitions and general provisions appear first, individual elements and requirements follow, and procedural and evidentiary subtopics conclude the entry. Illustration 3-1 on page 43 is an excerpt from Am. Jur. 2d's discussion of tortious recovery for mental distress. Illustration 3-2 on pages 44-45 shows an excerpt from the C.J.S. discussion of "Other Particular Torts"—a catch-all category; the pocket-part supplement for this section contains discussion and cases on intentional infliction of emotional or mental distress (see Illustration 3-3 on page 46). Note that the wording of an encyclopedia passage is often broadly phrased because the editors seek to encompass and describe many jurisdictions whose laws often differ in some respects. A good technique is to skim the text until you locate a passage that applies directly to your research problem, then use the accompanying footnotes as a finding tool. The footnotes contain case citations (usually in alphabetical order by jurisdiction), commentary citations, and cross-references to other related publications issued by that publisher.

> *Citation Note:* When citing to Am. Jur. 2d or C.J.S., you must cite to the volume, abbreviated name of the encyclopedia, topic, section, and year. For example, Illustration 3-1 is cited as 38 Am. Jur. 2d *Fright, Shock, and Mental Disturbance* § 55 (1968). Illustration 3-2 is cited as 86 C.J.S. *Torts* § 48 (1954). *See* Rule 15.7(a) of *The Bluebook.* Note that, by itself, 86 C.J.S. § 48 (1954) is a useless citation, because the reader cannot locate the correct § 48 without first knowing the topic name.

Both encyclopedias contain several tables that make them easier to use. Each topic volume contains a list of abbreviations of cited sources, such as case reporters and periodicals. The C.J.S. table appears in each bound volume, while the Am. Jur. 2d table is located in the pocket part to each volume.

At the front of each bound volume, Am. Jur. 2d provides a Table of Parallel References that converts the older *American Jurisprudence* (first series) sections to the current Am. Jur. 2d sections. C.J.S. (which, as "Secundum" indicates, is itself a second series) contains no such table converting *Corpus Juris* (first series) sections to second-series sections, but many of the original C.J.S. topics have been revised in replacement volumes. At the beginning of each topic, either in the bound volume or in the pocket part, C.J.S. provides a Table of Corresponding Sections, which converts the original C.J.S. section numbers to the revised section numbers.

2. How to Locate Pertinent Material

There are three research approaches for locating useful encyclopedia passages:

(1) the topic outline approach
(2) the index approach
(3) the Table of Statutes, Rules, and Regulations Cited

a. The Topic Outline Approach

Near the front of each C.J.S. topic (not index) volume is the List of Titles—a list of all of the major topics that appear in that encyclopedia. Am. Jur. 2d has an equivalent list in its *Desk Book* volume and in each index volume; it is called the Table of Abbreviations. It really is a list of all of the topics in the encyclopedia, along with their abbreviations. You can use such lists to locate a relevant topic.

To research the Perkins problem in Chapter 2, you would use either of these topic lists to locate promising topics. This is a mind-numbing task because it involves looking through pages of single-spaced topics, but it is a good way to jog your memory on areas you have not yet thought of researching. In Am. Jur. 2d, some promising topics are Extortion, Blackmail, and Threats; Fright, Shock, and Mental Disturbance; Highways, Streets, and Bridges; Libel and Slander; Torts; and Trespass. In C.J.S., some promising topics are Malicious Mischief; Libel and Slander; Property; Threats and Unlawful Communications; Torts; and Trespass.

ILLUSTRATION 3-1. Sample Encyclopedia Text: 38 Am. Jur. 2d *Fright, Shock, and Mental Disturbance* § 55, at 69 (1968).

43

that should be awarded therefor must, as in other cases, be left to the sound judgment of the jury.[11]

Other courts take the view that mental suffering caused by disfigurement is too remote and indefinite to constitute a proper element of damages.[12] It has been held that there can be no recovery for mental suffering caused by disfigurement of the person where the injury causing the disfigurement was not caused maliciously and the disfigurement is of such a character that it cannot possibly render the plaintiff's presence objectionable to any person or result in making him an object of pity or ridicule.[13]

§ 55. Anxiety, apprehension, and worry.

Among the many types of mental disturbances are anxiety, apprehension, and worry. The rules relating to the special types are those that govern mental disturbances in general.[14] It is accordingly held that where defendant is charged with negligence and he has not produced any direct physical injury or impact, he is not liable for causing anxiety, apprehension, or worry;[15] but that where there is a physical impact or injury, the negligent defendant is liable for the anxiety or worry which naturally results from his conduct.[16] Moreover, where the misconduct is wilful or intentional, and it causes severe anxiety or worry, the defendant is liable for causing such mental distress.[17]

One who has a cause of action for a tort resulting in a personal injury or illness may recover for mental distress caused by a reasonable anxiety, apprehension, or worry concerning the future effect or result of the injury,[18] such as the anxiety or worry of an injured person as to how long he will be disabled, and whether he will have to have an operation,[19] the anxiety

11. Fehely v Senders, 170 **Or** 457, 135 P2d 283, 145 ALR 1092.

12. Southern P. Co. v Hetzer (CA8) 135 **F** 272; Camenzind v Freeland Furniture Co. 89 **Or** 158, 174 P 139; Maynard v Oregon R. & Nav. Co. 46 Or 15, 78 P 983.

13. Diamond Rubber Co. v Harryman, 41 **Colo** 415, 92 P 922.

14. §§ 1–44, supra.

15. Southern Exp. Co. v Byers, 240 **US** 612, 60 L ed 825, 36 S Ct 410; Wilcox v Richmond & D. R. Co. (CA4) 52 **F** 264; Kalen v Terre Haute & I. R. Co. 18 **Ind** App 202, 47 NE 694; Sperier v Ott, 116 **La** 1087, 41 So 323; Wyman v Leavitt, 71 **Me** 227; Spade v Lynn & B. R. Co. 168 **Mass** 285, 47 NE 88, subsequent app 172 **Mass** 488, 52 NE 747; Morton v Western U. Teleg. Co. 53 **Ohio** St 431, 41 NE 689; Kneass v Cremation Soc. 103 **Wash** 521, 175 P 172, 10 ALR 442.

16. Hayes v New York Cent. R. Co. (CA2 NY) 311 **F2d** 198; Merrill v Los Angeles Gas & E. Co. 158 **Cal** 499, 111 P 534; Jansen v Minneapolis & St. L. R. Co. 112 **Minn** 496, 128 NW 826; Elliott v Arrowsmith, 149 **Wash** 631, 272 P 32.

17. Craker v Chicago & N. W. R. Co. 36 **Wis** 657.

18. East Alabama Express Co. v Dupes, 271 **Ala** 504, 124 So 2d 809.
Annotation: 71 ALR2d 341, § 2.

In Smith v Boston & M. R. Co. 87 **NH** 246, 177 A 729, the plaintiff was injured when struck by a train. For a time she had a fear that her legs might be paralyzed; but they did not in fact become paralyzed. It was held that her fear was a proper element of damages.

The circumstances of a particular case have been held to justify a recovery against a wrongdoer for purely mental suffering arising from information received by the injured person from a doctor to whom he went for treatment of the original injury. Ferrara v Galluchio, 5 NY2d 16, 176 NYS2d 996, 152 NE2d 249, 71 ALR2d 331. Annotation: 71 ALR2d 343, § 5.

19. Hayes v New York Cent. R. Co. (CA2 NY) 311 **F2d** 198; East Alabama Express Co. v Dupes, 271 **Ala** 504, 124 So 2d 809.

Damages for a neurosis with respect to cancer have been held recoverable in a malpractice action against three radiologists whose treatment of plaintiff's shoulder resulted in a chronic radiodermatitis, where the plaintiff's claim of a cancerophobia was corroborated by the circumstances consisting, among other matters, of common knowledge that wounds which do not heal over long periods frequently become cancerous, and of a statement made to the plaintiff by a dermatologist suggesting that the shoulder be checked periodically because of the possibility of the development of cancer. Ferrara v Galluchio, 5 NY2d 16, 176 NYS2d 996, 152 NE2d 249, 71 ALR2d 331.

ther malice[56] nor want of probable cause[57] is an essential element of the cause of action. Neither is it essential to the existence of the cause of action that the person sued without authority shall have questioned or challenged the authority of the person in fact conducting the suit at the time it is being prosecuted.[58]

It is not a sufficient ratification to make out a defense that the party named as plaintiff in the prior action has permitted himself to be defaulted in an action, for services incident to the suit, brought against him by the person actually suing,[59] or that such party, on being notified of the suit being conducted in his name, merely repudiates the action and takes no further steps to have it dismissed.[60] While the action is usually brought by those against whom the unauthorized suit was directed,[61] such unauthorized conduct has also been treated as furnishing the foundation for an action against the person assuming to sue by the one whose name was used without authority, for injury resulting to the latter from such action.[62]

§ 47. Unfounded Application for Patent

Application for a patent, although made by one aware that he is not entitled thereto and that another is, does not constitute a tort.

Application for a patent, although made by one aware that he is not entitled thereto and that another is, at the time of application, does not constitute a tort.[63]

§ 48. Other Particular Torts

Various acts or conduct has been held to constitute, or not to constitute, an actionable tort under the facts and circumstances of the particular case.

Various acts or conduct has been held to constitute,[64] or not to constitute,[65] an actionable tort under the facts and circumstances of the particular case. Thus, the violation of a public law has been held actionable, regardless of fraud or deceit,[66]

Ill.—Merriman v. Merriman, **8** N.E. 2d 64, 290 Ill.App. 139.
62 C.J. p 1149 note 14.

56. U.S.—**Corpus Juris quoted in** London & Lancashire Indemnity Co. of America v. Duner, C.C.A.Ill., 135 F.2d 895, 899, 146 A.L.R. 1119.
62 C.J. p 1150 note 15.

57. Ill.—Merriman v. Merriman, 8 N. E.2d 64, 290 Ill.App. 139.
Mass.—Smith v. Hyndman, 10 Cush. 554—Bond v. Chapin, 8 Metc. 31.

58. U.S.—**Corpus Juris quoted in** London & Lancashire Indemnity Co. of America v. Duner, C.C.A.Ill., 135 F.2d 895, 899, 146 A.L.R. 1119.
Me.—Moulton v. Lowe, 32 Me. 466.

Authority prior to suit immaterial
In action for damages occasioned by defendant's wrongful prosecution of suit against plaintiff in name of alleged corporation which admittedly had been legally dissolved more than five years before suit was commenced, fact that defendant was at one time president of corporation and authorized to bring suit in its name was immaterial.—London & Lancashire Indemnity of America v. Duner, C.C.A.Ill., 135 F.2d 895.

59. Me.—Foster v. Dow, 29 Me. 442.

60. Me.—Moulton v. Lowe, 32 Me. 466.

61. U.S.—London & Lancashire Indemnity Co. of America v. Duner, C.C.A.Ill., 135 F.2d 895.
62 C.J. p 1149 notes 12–14, p 1150 notes 15–19.

62. N.C.—Hackett v. McMillan, 17 S.E. 433, 112 N.C. 513, 21 L.R.A. 862—Metcalf v. Alley, 24 N.C. 38.

63. N.Y.—Strelitzer v. Schnaier, 119 N.Y.S. 977, 135 App.Div. 384.

Application for patents generally see Patents §§ 99–148.

64. Wyo.—Miller v. Scoggin, 189 P. 2d 693, 64 Wyo. 248.
Civil liability with respect to threats see Threats and Unlawful Communications § 27.

Communicating venereal disease
Okl.—Mashunkashey v. Brewer, 58 P.2d 564, 177 Okl. 253—Panther v. McKnight, 256 P. 916, 125 Okl. 134.

Vaccination
The vaccination of one person by another without his consent, or of person incapable of understanding consequences by reason of youth, creates liability.—Gulf & S. I. R. Co. v. Sullivan, 119 So. 501, 155 Miss. 1, 62 A.L.R. 191.

Refusal to execute or nondelivery of deed
(1) Where deeds of mineral interest and drafts for the consideration were delivered to bank by escrow agent for transmittal to drawee and collection and one deed contained a typographical inadvertence, action of cashier in prevailing on grantor to withdraw one deed and to deed the interest to the cashier and another was tortious, rendering the bank cashier and the new grantee liable to the drawee for nondelivery of the deed.—Grantham v. McCaleb, 30 So. 2d 312, 202 Miss. 167.

(2) Defendant, who, through mistake, recorded deed which described plaintiff's land, was held liable for damages resulting from refusal to execute quitclaim deed.—Smith v. Hubbard, 1 P.2d 363, 150 Okl. 199.

Personal relations
A merchandise corporation, addressing and mailing to customer at his residence a postal card which contained request to call one signing feminine name thereto at certain telephone number and was received and read by addressee's wife, who concluded therefrom that addressee had clandestine love affair with another woman and thereupon left him, committed a tort entitling addressee to recover damages from corporation.—Freeman v. Busch Jewelry Co., D.C. Ga., 98 F.Supp. 963.

65. Ga.—Clack v. Thomason, 195 S. E. 218, 57 Ga.App. 253.
N.Y.—Schnipper v. Flowood Realty Corp., 122 N.Y.S.2d 178.
Ohio.—Bartow v. Smith, 78 N.E.2d 735, 149 Ohio St. 301, 15 A.L.R.2d 94—Moore v. Travelers Ins. Co., 59 N.E.2d 225, 74 Ohio App. 420.
Or.—Hinish v. Meier & Frank Co., 113 P.2d 438, 166 Or. 482, 138 A.L. R. 1.
S.C.—Holloman v. Life Ins. Co. of Virginia, 7 S.E.2d 169, 192 S.C. 454.

Destruction of gambling paraphernalia
There are no property rights in gambling paraphernalia, as such paraphernalia are a "public nuisance" and damage for destruction thereof cannot be recovered.—Reese v. State, 143 S.W.2d 395, 140 Tex.Cr. 101.

66. Okl.—Panther v. McKnight, 256 P. 916, 125 Okl. 134.

Statutory tort
Neither fraud nor deceit is element of right of statutory tort action against party knowingly issuing check without sufficient funds.—North Adams Beef & Produce Co. v. Cantor, 156 A. 879, 103 Vt. 514.

ILLUSTRATION 3-2. *(continued)* 45

86 C. J. S.   **TORTS § 48**

and a person who by a consciously wrongful act intentionally deprives another of a right to vote in a public election or to hold public office is liable to the other in an action of tort;[67] and one guilty of a nontrespassory invasion of another's interest in the private use and enjoyment of land is liable for damages if such other has property rights and privileges in respect of the use or enjoyment interfered with, the invasion is substantial, the actor's conduct is a legal cause of the invasion, and the invasion is either intentional and unreasonable or unintentional and otherwise actionable under the rules governing liability for negligent, reckless, or ultrahazardous conduct.[68]

Acts of public officers. Since the exercise by one man of a legal right cannot be a legal wrong to another, discussed supra § 14, one who, in a lawful manner, merely sets a public officer in motion to perform a lawful act within the scope of his authority is not liable for damages to another as a result of such officer's unauthorized act in the performance of his duties.[69] However, a person is liable where he authorizes a public officer to do an unlawful act or a lawful act in an unlawful manner, or to abuse, exceed, or disregard his duty or authority, or where he counsels, directs, or participates in the doing of any unlawful act which the process or authority of the officer will not legally justify.[70]

Injurious falsehood. One may be legally responsible for written or oral falsehoods maliciously circulated, which are made with the intention of producing injury, and do result in injury to another,[71]

but it has been held that such liability may be imposed only if the false statements are not actionable as libels or slanders, either because they are not defamatory or for other reasons.[72] The action for injurious falsehood is distinguished from an action of libel or slander which is founded on false defamatory statements;[73] the former action is one on the case for damages willfully and intentionally done without just cause, occasion, or excuse,[74] and, since the false statement injures him only by misleading other persons into action that is detrimental to him, it is governed by more lenient rules of liability,[75] although rules with respect to absolute privilege in libel and slander actions have been applied to actions for injurious falsehood based on nondefamatory statements.[76]

Interference with right of inheritance or destruction of will. Ordinarily the wrongful deprivation of a person of his just bequest under a will or the unlawful and malicious destruction of a will resulting in loss to a beneficiary or legatee is an actionable tort,[77] and a legatee may maintain such an action although the legacy to him cannot be established and admitted to probate as part of the destroyed will because only one witness supports the existence of a gift and a statute relating to the probate of destroyed wills requires the testimony of several witnesses.[78] However, the authorities are divided on the question whether an actionable tort is committed by maliciously interfering with a prospective right of inheritance, or by maliciously interfering with the making of a will.[79] Some authorities hold that no action lies on the theory that no legal or enforceable right has been invaded or

67. N.M.—Valdez v. Gonzales, 176 P. 2d 173, 50 N.M. 281.
Tort liability for malicious removal of officer see Officers § 70.
Civil liability of election officers see Elections § 64.

68. Cal.—Tooke v. Allen, 192 P.2d 804, 85 Cal.App.2d 230.
Nuisance and nonnuisance cases
Principle is most frequently applied in nuisance cases, but has equal application to nonnuisance cases.—Tooke v. Allen, supra.

69. Mo.—McAnarney v. Commonwealth Loan Co., App., 208 S.W.2d 480.

70. Mo.—McAnarney v. Commonwealth Loan Co., supra.

71. Ill.—Pendleton v. Time, Inc., 89 N.E.2d 435, 339 Ill.App. 188.
N.Y.—Raschid v. News Syndicate Co., 191 N.E. 713, 265 N.Y. 1—Gale v. Ryan, 31 N.Y.S.2d 732, 263 App.Div. 76—Advance Music Corp. v. Am. Tobacco Co., 50 N.Y.S.2d 287, 183

Misc. 645—Dubourcq v. Brouwer, 124 N.Y.S.2d 61, affirmed 124 N.Y. S.2d 842, 282 App.Div. 861.
Pa.—Louis Wolfberg, Inc. v. Palace Credit Clothing Co., Com.Pl., 87 Pittsb.Leg.J. 229.
Tex.—Page v. Layne-Texas Co., Civ. App., 258 S.W.2d 366, error granted.
Negligent false statements see Negligence § 20.

72. N.Y.—Dubourcq v. Brouwer, 124 N.Y.S.2d 61, affirmed 124 N.Y.S.2d 842, 282 App.Div. 861.

73. N.Y.—Dubourcq v. Brouwer, supra—Lucci v. Engel, 73 N.Y.S.2d 78.

74. N.Y.—Musso v. Miller, 38 N.Y.S. 2d 51, 265 App.Div. 57—Bradick v. Deetjen, 118 N.Y.S.2d 256.

75. N.Y.—Lucci v. Engel, 73 N.Y.S. 2d 78.

76. **Judicial proceedings**
Allegation in course of an adoption proceeding that plaintiff had shown no desire to fulfil the role

of father and had shown no interest whatever in his minor child was absolutely privileged, and could not form the basis of an action for libel or of an action for injurious falsehood.—Lucci v. Engel, supra.

77. U.S.—McGregor v. McGregor, D. C.Colo., 101 F.Supp. 848.
Ky.—Allen v. Lovell's Adm'x, 197 S. W.2d 424, 303 Ky. 238.
Mich.—Creek v. Laski, 227 N.W. 817, 248 Mich. 425, 65 A.L.R. 1113.
Ohio.—Morton v. Petitt, 177 N.E. 591, 124 Ohio St. 241.

78. Mich.—Creek v. Laski, 227 N.W. 817, 248 Mich. 425, 65 A.L.R. 1113.

79. Kan.—Axe v. Wilson, 96 P.2d 880, 150 Kan. 794.
Question whether such action will lie is not controlling where particular relief sought by plaintiff, in action for damages for malicious interference with plaintiff's alleged right of inheritance, was obtainable in action to contest will.—Axe v. Wilson, supra.

86 CJS 185

TORTS § 48
Page 971

page 971

68. U.S.—Frederick v. Burg, D.C.Pa., 148 F.Supp. 673.

Cal.—Barkett v. Brucato, 264 P.2d 978, 122 C.A.2d 264.

Ga.—Brooks v. Ready Mix Concrete Co., 96 S.E.2d 213, 94 Ga.App. 791.

Pa.—Muehlhausen v. Delaware Valley Holding Co., 9 Bucks 188—Lower Alsace Tp. v. Furillo, 55 Berks 20, 54 Mun. 230.

Wash.—Brillhardt v. Ben Tipp, Inc., 297 P.2d 232, 48 Wash.2d 722.

Freedom from mental distress directly caused by wanton or outrageous conduct is entitled to legal protection independent of any other cause of action,[68.5] and where severe mental pain or anguish is inflicted through a deliberate and malicious campaign of harassment or intimidation, a remedy is available in the form of an action for the intentional infliction of emotional distress.[68.10]

68.5. Ala.—Norris v. Moskin Stores, Inc., 132 So.2d 321, 272 Ala. 174.

Kan.—Dawson v. Associates Financial Services Co. of Kansas, Inc., 529 P.2d 104, 215 Kan. 814—Henderson v. Ripperger, 594 P.2d 251, 3 Kan. App.2d 303.

Recently recognized doctrine

Pa.—Papieves v. Lawrence, 263 A.2d 118, 437 Pa. 373, 48 A.L.R.3d 233.

Conduct must be outrageous in the extreme

Ariz.—Hixon v. State Compensation Fund, App., 565 P.2d 898, 115 Ariz. 392.

Ill.—Public Finance Corp. v. Davis, 343 N.E.2d 226, 36 Ill.App.3d 99, affd. 360 N.E.2d 765, 4 Ill.Dec. 652, 66 Ill.2d 85.

Mich.—Warren v. June's Mobile Home Village & Sales, Inc., 239 N.W.2d 380, 66 Mich.App. 386.

Mo.—Smith v. Standard Oil, Division of Amoco Oil Co., App., 567 S.W.2d 412.

Or.—Rockhill v. Pollard, 485 P.2d 28, 259 Or. 54.

Conduct must exceed all bounds usually tolerated by decent society

U.S.—Sigler v. Mutual Ben. Life Ins. Co., D.C.Iowa, 506 F.Supp. 542, affd., C.A., 663 F.2d 49.

Iowa—Meyer v. Nottger, 241 N.W.2d 911.

Conduct need not satisfy expectations of reasonableness

U.S.—Chuy v. Philadelphia Eagles Football Club, D.C. Pa., 431 F.Supp. 254. Affd., C.A., 595 F.2d 1265.

Conduct calculated to cause severe emotional distress in a person of ordinary sensibilities

U.S.—Garris v. Schwartz, C.A.Ill., 551 F.2d 156.

Tort of outrage

U.S.—Holmes v. Oxford Chemicals, Inc., D.C.Ala., 510 F.Supp. 915, affd. 672 F.2d 854.

Wash.—Grimsby v. Samson, 530 P.2d 291, 85 Wash.2d 52, 77 A.L.R.3d 436—Contreras v. Crown Zellerbach Corp., 565 P.2d 1173, 88 Wash.2d 735—Jackson v. Peoples Federal Credit Union, 604 P.2d 1025, 25 Wash.App. 81.

68.10. U.S.—Kahle v. Glosser Bros., Inc., C.A.Pa., 462 F.2d 815—Galella v. Onassis, D.C.N.Y., 353 F.Supp. 196, affd. in part, revd. in part on oth. grds., C.A., 487 F.2d 986.

Ala.—American Road Service Co. v. Inmon, 394 So.2d 361.

Cal.—Kachig v. Boothe, 99 Cal.Rptr. 393, 22 C.A.3d 626—Cervantes v. J. C. Penney Co., Inc., 156 Cal.Rptr. 198, 595 P.2d 975, 24 C.3d 579.

Colo.—DeCicco v. Trinidad Area Health Ass'n, 573 P.2d 559, 40 Colo.App. 63—First Nat. Bank in Lamar v. Collins, 616 P.2d 154, 44 Colo.App. 228—Vigoda v. Denver Urban Renewal Authority,

App., 624 P.2d 895, affd. in part, revd. in part on oth. grds., Sup., 646 P.2d 900.

Conn.—Hiers v. Cohen, 329 A.2d 609, 31 Conn.Sup. 305.

Mass.—George v. Jordan Marsh Co., 268 N.E.2d 915, 359 Mass. 244, 46 A.L.R.3d 762.

N.Y.—Callarama v. Associates Discount Corp. of Del., 329 N.Y.S.2d 711, 69 Misc.2d 287—Lopez v. City of New York, 357 N.Y.S.2d 659, 78 Misc.2d 575.

Wash.—Contreras v. Crown Zellerbach Corp., 565 P.2d 1173, 88 Wash.2d 735.

Wis.—Muhich v. Family Finance Corp., 241 N.W.2d 619, 72 Wis.2d 625.

Unavailable for violation of matrimonial action confidentiality statute

N.Y.—Freihofer v. Hearst Corp., 480 N.E.2d 349, 65 N.Y.2d 135, 490 N.Y.S.2d 735.

Elements different from those governing invasion of privacy

N.Y.—Nader v. General Motors Corp., 255 N.E.2d 765, 25 N.Y.2d 560, 307 N.Y.S.2d 647, stating District of Columbia law.

Conduct held not actionable on theory of intentional infliction of mental distress

U.S.—Beckham v. Safeco Ins. Co. of America, C.A.Cal., 691 F.2d 898—Kush v. American States Ins. Co., C.A.7(Ill.), 853 F.2d 1380.

Ariz.—Hixon v. State Compensation Fund, App., 565 P.2d 898, 115 Ariz. 392.

Cal.—Scott v. McDonnell Douglas Corp., 112 Cal.Rptr. 609, 37 C.A.3d 277.

Ill.—Public Finance Corp. v. Davis, 343 N.E.2d 226, 36 Ill.App.3d 99, affd. 360 N.E.2d 765, 4 Ill.Dec. 652, 66 Ill.2d 85, 87 A.L.R.3d 187.

Mass.—Casamasina v. Worcester Telegram & Gazette, Inc., 307 N.E.2d 865, 2 Mass.App. 801.

Mich.—Warren v. June's Mobile Home Village & Sales, Inc., 239 N.W.2d 380, 66 Mich.App. 386.

Mo.—Smith v. Standard Oil, Division of Amoco Oil Co., 567 S.W.2d 412.

N.Y.—Costlow v. Cusimano, 311 N.Y.S.2d 92, 34 A.D.2d 196.

Okl.—Breeden v. League Services Corp., 575 P.2d 1374.

Pa.—Salerno v. Philadelphia Newspapers, Inc., 546 A.2d 1168, 377 Pa.Super. 83.

Wash.—McMenamin v. Bishop, 493 P.2d 1016, 6 Wash. App. 455.

Wis.—Muhich v. Family Finance Corp., 241 N.W.2d 619, 72 Wis.2d 625.

Destruction of parent-child relationship

Mich.—Bhama v. Bhama, 425 N.W.2d 733, 169 Mich. App. 73.

Absence of privilege essential to recovery

Cal.—State Rubbish Collectors Ass'n v. Siliznoff, 240 P.2d 282, 38 Cal.2d 330—Agostini v. Strycula, 42 Cal.Rptr. 314, 231 Cal.App.2d 804—Fletcher v. Western Nat. Life Ins. Co., 89 Cal.Rptr. 78, 10 C.A.3d 376, 47 A.L.R.3d 286.

Exercise of legal right must be in permissible way and in good faith

Cal.—Fletcher v. Western Nat. Life Ins. Co., 89 Cal. Rptr. 78, 10 C.A.3d 376, 47 A.L.R.3d 286.

Redress for economic loss only when resulting from emotional distress

Cal.—Fletcher v. Western Nat. Life Ins. Co., 89 Cal. Rptr. 78, 10 C.A.3d 376, 47 A.L.R.3d 286.

Immediate family member covered

Mich.—Warren v. June's Mobile Home Village & Sales, Inc., 239 N.W.2d 380, 66 Mich.App. 386.

Wash.—Grimsby v. Samson, 530 P.2d 291, 85 Wash.2d 52, 77 A.L.R.3d 436.

Factors to be considered

Ill.—Public Finance Corp. v. Davis, 343 N.E.2d 226, 36 Ill.App.3d 99, affd. 360 N.E.2d 765, 4 Ill.Dec. 652, 66 Ill.2d 85, 87 A.L.R.3d 187.

Wash.—Grimsby v. Samson, 530 P.2d 291, 85 Wash.2d 52, 77 A.L.R.3d 436.

Bodily harm not required

Wash.—Grimsby v. Samson, 530 P.2d 291, 83 Wash.2d 52, 77 A.L.R.3d 436.

Scope of liability

U.S.—Conway v. Spitz, D.C.Pa., 407 F.Supp. 536.

Ohio—Yeager v. Local Union 20, Teamsters, Chauffeurs, Warehousemen, & Helpers of America, 453 N.E.2d 666, 6 Ohio St.3d 369, 6 O.B.R. 421, (overruling Bartow v. Smith, 149 Ohio St. 301, 78 N.E.2d 735).

Independent cause of action

Okl.—Bennett v. City Nat. Bank & Trust Co., App., 549 P.2d 393.

Collection of debt

Ala.—Norris v. Moskin Stores, Inc., 132 So.2d 321, 272 Ala. 174.

Ill.—Public Finance Corp. v. Davis, 360 N.E.2d 765, 4 Ill.Dec. 652, 66 Ill.2d 85, 87 A.L.R.3d 187.

Kan.—Dawson v. Associates Financial Serv. Co. of Kan., Inc., 529 P.2d 104, 215 Kan. 814.

Ohio—Housh v. Peth, 135 N.E.2d 440, 99 Ohio App. 485, affd. 133 N.E.2d 340, 165 Ohio St. 35.

Wash.—Jackson v. Peoples Federal Credit Union, 604 P.2d 1025, 25 Wash.App. 81.

Possibility of trivial or fictitious claims irrelevant

Mass.—Boyle v. Wenk, 392 N.E.2d 1053, 378 Mass. 592.

Intentional infliction of mental distress

Cal.—Kinnamon v. Staitman and Snyder, 136 Cal.Rptr. 321, 66 C.A.3d 893.

Ill.—Farnor v. Irmco Corp., 392 N.E.2d 591, 29 Ill.Dec. 894, 73 Ill.App.3d 851.

Mich.—Warren v. June's Mobile Home Village & Sales, Inc., 239 N.W.2d 380, 66 Mich.App. 386.

Pa.—Jones v. Nissenbaum, Rudolph and Seidner, 368 A.2d 770, 244 Pa.Super. 377.

Mental infliction of mental distress

Md.—Jones v. Harris, 371 A.2d 1104, 35 Md.App. 556, affd. 380 A.2d 611, 281 Md. 560, 86 A.L.R.3d 441.

Conduct judged objectively

Ill.—McCaskill v. Barr, 414 N.E.2d 1327, 47 Ill.Dec. 211, 92 Ill.App.3d 157.

Application of doctrine; factors considered

Mo.—United Tel. Co. of Missouri v. Horn, App., 610 S.W.2d 701.

Wis.—Evrard v. Jacobson, App., 342 N.W.2d 788, 117 Wis.2d 69.

"Severe emotional distress" defined

Wis.—Evrard v. Jacobson, App., 342 N.W.2d 788, 117 Wis.2d 69.

The elements of the tort are that the conduct must be intentional or reckless; it must be extreme and outrageous; there must be a causal connection between the wrongful conduct and the emotional distress; and the emotional distress must be severe.[68.11]

68.11 Md.—Harris v. Jones, 380 A.2d 611, 281 Md. 560.

Mo.—LaBrier v. Anheuser Ford, Inc., App., 612 S.W.2d 790.

Nev.—Star v. Rabello, 625 P.2d 90, 97 Nev. 124.

Engage in sexual intercourse with knowledge of transmittable disease

Md.—B.N. v. K.K., 538 A.2d 1175, 312 Md. 135.

The First and Fourteenth Amendments prohibit a public figure from recovering damages for the tort of intentional infliction of emotional distress.[68.12]

68.12 Actual malice required

(1) In general.

Note: 1.   additions to footnote 68 on page 971
        2.   new text, to be inserted after footnote 68 on page 971
        3.   footnote 68.5 in new text
        4.   footnote 68.10 in new text
        5.   new text, to be inserted after previous new text
        6.   footnote 68.11 in new text
        7.   new text, to be inserted after previous new text
        8.   footnote 68.12 in new text

You then would locate the volumes that contain those topics. Carefully read the introductory material at the beginning of the topic. See Illustrations 3-4 and 3-5 on pages 48-50. You always should read the scope note at the beginning of the topic to make sure that topic covers what you think it does. In Am. Jur. 2d, you also should read the "Treated elsewhere" section to see if another topic gives even better coverage or covers a related issue that you have forgotten about.

As Illustrations 3-4 and 3-5 demonstrate, each topic also begins with one or two topic outlines. Most topics contain two outlines: a short summary outline and a longer section-by-section outline of the entire topic. You can save time by using the summary outline to locate the useful portion of the section-by-section outline. You then can use the detailed outline to zero in on the precise sections you wish to read.

b. The Index Approach

As in other research sources, an encyclopedia index is an alphabetical listing of topics, subtopics, and cross-references. In legal encyclopedias, the index appears in separate volumes. Examine an index volume of either encyclopedia. (See Illustrations 3-6 and 3-7 on pages 51-52.) Each index volume contains a table of topic abbreviations used in the index. Always check any supplements to the index volumes to find updated index entries. These supplements may be paperback volumes or pocket parts; a "pocket part" is a thin paper pamphlet inserted in the back of a hardbound volume.

In addition, within each topic volume there is another index covering the topics in that volume, except for the topics that continue in a subsequent volume. A disadvantage of these indexes is that they are not updated by pocket parts.

Note in Illustrations 3-6 and 3-7 that these indexes utilize subtle differences in typeface and indentation to show hierarchical relationships between adjacent items. Some students become quite confused when they forget to check whether they are looking at an index entry within an entry within another entry (a sub-subtopic within a subtopic within a topic). Many other indexes in legal research sources also utilize these same subtle distinctions between typefaces and indentations.

See page 53 for an example of notes taken during a search through the Am. Jur. 2d index to research the Perkins problem in Chapter 2. The end results of this index search pointed mainly to the following topics:

Breach of Peace
Damages
Fright, Shock, and Mental Disturbance
Civil Rights and Discrimination

There also were a few sections in Torts and Insults, but the above four topics were so "loaded" with promising sections that they became the first research priority. These Sample Research Notes do not reflect specific sections under the topic "Civil Rights and Discrimination" because the index entries for this topic span 24 pages of triple-column entries, which made the index approach impractical for this topic. You could save time and obtain better results by using the table of contents approach on this topic.

As already noted, Illustration 3-1 on page 43 shows a portion of the section from "Fright, Shock, and Mental Disturbance." Although the text and footnotes of § 55 were not very helpful to the Perkins problem, the § 55

FRIGHT, SHOCK, AND MENTAL DISTURBANCE

Scope of Topic: This article discusses mental or emotional disturbance or distress, including fright, nervous shock, anxiety, and the like, as the basis of a cause of action, and, in an action where there is another compensable injury, as an element of damages.

Treated elsewhere are many applications of the basic principles and certain exceptions as to the rules as to mental disturbance or anguish as an element of damages in actions for specific types of injuries, or in actions against special types of tortfeasors. Thus, the following are treated in other articles in this work: recovery and damages for mental suffering and anguish in actions for assault and battery (see 6 Am Jur 2d, ASSAULT AND BATTERY § 183), personal injuries (see 22 Am Jur 2d, DAMAGES §§ 195–198), wrongful death (see 22 Am Jur 2d, DEATH §§ 126, 135), the mishandling of a corpse (see 22 Am Jur 2d, DEAD BODIES §§ 43–45), wrongful dishonor of a check (see 10 Am Jur 2d, BANKS § 576), defamation (see LIBEL AND SLANDER), breach of the right of privacy (see PRIVACY), malicious prosecution (see

NUISANCES), seduction

public amusement (see 4 Am Jur 2d,   § 10).
Injury to animals by fright is treated in another article (see 4 Am Jur 2d, ANIMALS § 133).

I. MENTAL OR EMOTIONAL DISTURBANCE WITHOUT PHYSICAL EFFECT (§§ 1–12)

II. MENTAL OR EMOTIONAL DISTURBANCE CAUSING BODILY INJURY OR ILLNESS (§§ 13–24)

[38 Am Jur 2d]—1   **1**

III. PARTICULAR CIRCUMSTANCES (§§ 25–44)

IV. PARTICULAR DISTURBANCES AND INJURIES (§§ 45–57)

I. MENTAL OR EMOTIONAL DISTURBANCE WITHOUT PHYSICAL EFFECT

ILLUSTRATION 3-4. *(continued)*   **49**

update material in the pocket part cited two cases that granted causes of action for "intentional infliction of mental or emotional distress." Examine carefully Illustration 3-8 on page 54.

The index approach was less involved in C.J.S., where the index entry "Emotional Distress" pointed directly to "Torts § 48." See Illustration 3-7 on page 52. Likewise, the index entry "Emotions" listed "Torts § 48" under "Harassment or intimidation, intentional infliction of emotional distress." Even more so than in Am. Jur. 2d, the text and footnotes of the cited section in the main volume were not at all helpful; they merely listed and described "Other particular torts," none of which seemed applicable. See Illustration 3-2 on pages 44-45. However, the § 48 update material in the pocket part added textual material and extensive footnotes on a separate cause of action, intentional infliction of mental or emotional distress. See Illustration 3-3 on page 46.

Remember that less complicated research is not necessarily more successful research. Consider whether a less complicated index might also be an index with fewer cross-references. Alternatively, fewer cross-references might be indicative of better, more centralized organization of the subject.

The index approach is useful when you know enough vocabulary to locate a particular topic. However, some indexes may be frustrating for a beginning researcher because they contain unfamiliar vocabulary. Other indexes may be too general to enable a researcher to locate a narrow topic. In these instances, the researcher has two choices: (1) use the topic outline approach rather than the index approach or (2) consult a dictionary, glossary, or thesaurus for definitions and additional indexing vocabulary (see Chapter 2).

c. Table of Statutes, Rules, and Regulations Cited

If you begin your Am. Jur. 2d research knowing the citation to a federal statute, regulation, court rule, or uniform act, you can locate relevant sections in Am. Jur. 2d by using the separate volume entitled Table of Statutes, Rules,

86   C. J. S.

TORTS

This Title includes injuries from breach of duty **or** obligation not founded on contract, as affecting only the persons injured, not the public; nature and extent of liability of the wrongdoers in general; and civil remedies for such injuries.

Matters not in this Title, treated elsewhere in this work, see Descriptive-Word Index

Analysis

Sub-Analysis

ILLUSTRATION 3-6. [General Index D-I] Am. Jur. 2d 413 (1991). 51

GENERAL INDEX

EMINENT DOMAIN—Cont'd

Wharves (this index)
Widening of highways or streets. Highways and streets, supra
Wife. Husband and wife, supra
Wild lands, cultivation of, Em Dom §§ 34, 44
Wills (this index)
Wires for electric lines, Em Dom §§ 212-214, 331, 332, 344, 345
Withdrawal of deposited money, Em Dom § 263
Witnesses
  generally, Em Dom §§ 420, 423, 425-427, 429, 441
- expert and opinion evidence, supra
- fees of expert witnesses, Em Dom § 477
- instructions to jury, Em Dom § 418
- mandamus to compel hearing of testimony, Em Dom § 490
- venue of condemnation proceedings, Em Dom § 382
Words and phrases, generally, Em Dom §§ 1, 157, 173
Writs
- assistance writ, obtaining possession of condemned land, Assist § 5
- injunctions, supra
- **Mandamus** (this index)
- process, supra
- prohibition, Em Dom § 493
Wrongful death liability, Em Dom § 481
Wrongful entry or damage. Trespass, supra
Zoning and Planning (this index)

EMISSION

Adultery, emission as element of, Adult § 3
Automatic fire extinguisher, coverage of insurance against discharge, Ins § 521
Carbon Monoxide (this index)
Incest, emission as essential, Incest §§ 5, 16
Pollution (this index)
Rape, Rape § 3

"EMIT"

Money, meaning of term "emit" in United States Constitutional provision as to bills of credit, Money § 14

EMOLUMENTS

Compensation (this index)

EMOTIONAL INSANITY

Incompetent or Insane Persons (this index)

EMOTIONAL OUTBURSTS OR DISTURBANCES

Contempt, Contempt § 80
Divorce and separation, Div & S § 157
Exclusion of public from courtroom, Crim L §§ 669, 886
Federal practice and procedure, Fed Prac §§ 64, 92
Rewards, Reward § 6

EMOTION OR FEELINGS

Abatement of action for injuries to feelings, Abat & R § 68
Admissions and declarations, proof of emotion, Evid § 650
Apprehension (this index)
Civil rights, emotional distress as affecting awarding of damages in discriminatory housing case, Civ R § 496
Collection and credit agencies, liability for infliction of emotional distress, Coll & Cr A § 12

EMOTION OR FEELINGS—Cont'd

Continuance or adjournment of proceeding, Contin §§ 57, 58, 114-116
Crying (this index)
Damages, generally, Damg §§ 253, 539
Discharge of jury, spectator's emotional outburst as ground for, Trial § 1105
Distress. **Fright, Shock or Mental Anguish** (this index)
Disturbed persons. **Incompetent or Insane Persons** (this index)
Embarrassment, Humiliation or Disgrace (this index)
Excitement (this index)
Expert and opinion evidence, Expert §§ 359-361
Facial Expressions (this index)
Federal Rules of Evidence (this index)
Fraud and deceit, damages for emotional distress, Fraud § 342
Fright, Shock and Mental Anguish (this index)
Funeral directors and embalmers, Dead B §§ 149, 153-155; Funeral D § 22
Grief (this index)
Homicide (this index)
Husband and Wife (this index)
Hysteria (this index)
Injunctions, injury to feeling as irreparable, Inj § 49
Instructions to jury, Trial § 904
Interference, damages for emotional distress, Interfer §§ 57, 60
Jealousy (this index)
Judges (this index)
Judicial notice, Evid § 114
Jury and Jury Trial (this index)
Libel and Slander (this index)
Love and Affection (this index)
Master and servant, damages for wrongful discharge as including injury to feelings, M & S § 63
Monopolies, injury to feelings, Monop § 635
Name, Name §§ 32, 45
New Trial (this index)
Outbursts. **Emotional Outbursts or Disturbances** (this index)
Passion (this index)
Prejudice or Bias (this index)
Privacy (this index)
Religious societies, emotional depravation resulting from expulsion of member, Relig Soc § 34
Search and seizure, recovery of damages for emotional distress from wrongful search or seizure, Search § 122
Sentimental Considerations (this index)
Social Security (this index)
Support of Persons (this index)
Taxation, payment of illegal tax under apprehension, State Tax §§ 1098, 1099
Temper or Anger (this index)
Trespass, injury to feelings, Tresp § 8
Trial court's powers with respect to emotions of litigants, Trial § 39
Waste, effect of diminution of value resting on emotional grounds, Waste § 1
Wills (this index)
Workers' Compensation (this index)
Zoning, hospital for emotionally disturbed persons, Zoning § 159

EMPANELING JURY

Jury and Jury Trial (this index)

EMPHYSEMA

Social security, Soc Sec § 862
Workers' compensation for, Workm C §§ 289, 303

"EMPLOYED IN MANUFACTURE"

Defined or construed, State Tax § 193

"EMPLOYED WITHIN THE STATE"

Defined or construed, State Tax § 283

EMPLOYEE CASH OR DEFERRED ARRANGEMENTS

Pensions and Retirement (this index)

EMPLOYEE-DISTRIBUTORS

Newspapers, periodicals, and press associations, Newsp § 89

EMPLOYEE RETIREMENT INCOME SECURITY ACT

Pensions and Retirement (this index)

EMPLOYEE SIMPLIFIED PENSION PLANS

Pensions and Retirement (this index)

EMPLOYEE STOCK APPRECIATION RIGHT PLANS

Pensions and retirement funds, Pens § 111

EMPLOYEE STOCK OWNERSHIP PLANS

Generally, Corp §§ 429, 435, 2065, 2524; Pens §§ 25, 75
Assets of plan, Pens §§ 590, 610
Crediting pre-ERISA service, Pens § 187
Federal securities regulation, Pens §§ 103, 105, 110, 111, 114
Loans, Pens §§ 680-686
Payment of benefits, Pens § 406
Percentage coverage tests, Pens § 235
Profit-sharing plans, Pens § 25
Retroactive amendments to satisfy qualification requirements, Pens § 163
Stock bonus plans distinguished, Pens § 25
Tax returns, Pens § 768

EMPLOYEE TAX REDUCTION ACT STOCK OWNERSHIP PLANS

Pensions and retirement funds, Pens § 111

EMPLOYER AND EMPLOYEE

Employment (this index)

EMPLOYER ASSOCIATIONS

Labor and Labor Relations (this index)

EMPLOYER OR EMPLOYEE IDENTIFICATION NUMBERS

Corporations, Corp § 183
Pensions and retirement funds, Pens §§ 767, 768, 785, 917

EMPLOYERS' LIABILITY ACTS

Federal Employers' Liability Act (this index)
Federal Tort Claims Act (this index)
State liability acts. **Master and Servant** (this index)
Workers' Compensation (this index)

EMPLOYERS' LIABILITY INSURANCE

Generally. **Insurance** (this index)
Federal Employers' Liability Act (this index)
Workers' compensation, Ins §§ 721, 722

EMPLOYMENT

Generally. **Master and Servant** (this index)
Job Discrimination (this index)
Labor and Labor Relations (this index)
Plant and Job Safety (this index)

413

EMINENT DOMAIN—Continued
Vendor and purchaser—Continued
    Pendency of action, **Ven&Pur** § 196
    Pending proceedings, encumbrances, **Ven&Pur** § 203
    Preliminary plans or rumors as to taking by, mistake,
        Ven&Pur § 51
    Probability as grounds for rescission, **Ven&Pur** § 159
    Purchase money paid, recovery, **Ven&Pur** § 552
    Purchase price, abatement or deductions, **Ven&Pur** § 263
Venue,
    Generally, see **Title Index to Eminent Domain**
    Change of venue, operation and effect, **Venue** § 201
    Mandamus against state officer, **Venue** § 45
    Restraining, **Venue** § 38
Verdict, this index
Verification,
    Answer, **Em Dom** § 262
    Confirmation or setting aside report of commissioners,
        application, **Em Dom** § 315
    Petition, **Em Dom** § 253
Vested rights,
    Abandonment, compensation, **Em Dom** § 338
    Completion of taking, **Em Dom** § 135
    Interest allowable from date, **Em Dom** § 176
View, see **Title Index to Eminent Domain**
Viewers, see **Title Index to Eminent Domain**
Waiver, see **Title Index to Eminent Domain**
Waiver of tort and action on contract, **Actions** § 110
War and national defense, land by state of municipality, autho-
    rization by eviction suit, **War&ND** § 177
Waters and water rights, see **Title Index to: Eminent Domain;**
    Waters
Wharves, Docks and Piers, this index
Wife. Husband and Wife, this index
Wills,
    Income and profits incident to gift, **Wills** § 1101
    Property charged with legacy, **Wills** § 1306
Withdrawal, this index
Witnesses, see **Title Index to Eminent Domain**
Woods and forests, national forests, right of way, **Woods&F**
    § 11
Zoning and Land Planning, this index

EMISSARY
Defined, **Vol. 30**

EMISSION
Defined, **Vol. 30**
Pollution, generally, this index
Rape,
    Abandonment of effort at intercourse because of emission
        as precluding conviction of assault with intent,
        Rape § 32
    Element, **Rape** § 10
    Emissio seminis, intent to produce without intent to pen-
        etrate insufficient for attempt or assault with intent,
        Rape § 24
    Emissio seminis as rape as dependent on penetration, **Rape**
        § 10

EMIT
Defined, **Vol. 30**

EMMENAGOGUES
Defined, **Vol. 30**

EMOLUMENT
Defined, **Vol. 30**

EMOTIONAL DISTRESS
Damages, this index
Motor vehicles, operation causing, damages, **Motor V** § 560
Torts,
    Elements, **Torts** § 48
    Public figure recovering damage for intentional infliction
        of, **Torts** § 48

EMOTIONAL MATURITY
Defined, **Vol. 30**

EMOTIONS
Attorney and client,
    Disbarment, grounds, **Atty&C** § 69
    Discipline, defenses, **Atty&C** § 64
Evidence,
    Demonstrative or real evidence, **Evid** § 602
    Judicial notice, **Evid** § 79
    Opinion evidence, effect on human body, **Evid** § 546(97)
    Similar acts, **Evid** § 580
Federal civil procedure,
    Emotional stability, evidence, instructions to jury, **Fed Civ**
        Proc § 990
    Final argument, objections, **Fed Civ Proc** § 932
    Misconduct of counsel, cure, **Fed Civ Proc** § 926
Harassment or intimidation, intentional infliction of emotional
    distress, **Torts** § 48
Motor vehicles, collision, bodily injury, **Ins** § 829
Wills, emotional reasons, signing by mark, **Wills** § 172
Witnesses,
    Emotional incapacity, interest or bias, **Witn** § 538
    Emotional instability, credibility, **Witn** § 461
    Outcries by spectator, cross-examination right, **Witn** § 368
Workmen's compensation, emotional disturbances. **Work C**
    § 201
    Aggravation by, **Work C** § 173
    Fights, **Work C** § 226
    Heart attack, **Work C** §§ 184, 627

EMPADRONAMIENTO
Defined, **Vol. 30**

EMPALAMIENTO
Defined, **Vol. 30**

EMPALEMENT
Defined, **Vol. 30**

EMPANNEL
Defined, **Vol. 30**

EMPARA
Defined, **Vol. 30**

EMPARAMENTO
Defined, **Vol. 30**

EMPARNOURS
Defined, **Vol. 30**

EMPATE
Defined, **Vol. 30**

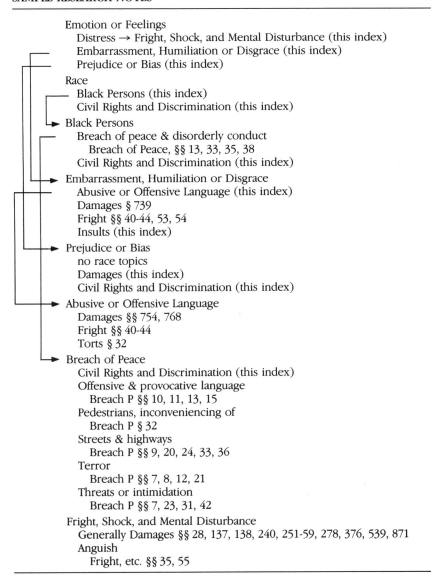

Emotion or Feelings
    Distress → Fright, Shock, and Mental Disturbance (this index)
    Embarrassment, Humiliation or Disgrace (this index)
    Prejudice or Bias (this index)
Race
    Black Persons (this index)
    Civil Rights and Discrimination (this index)
Black Persons
    Breach of peace & disorderly conduct
        Breach of Peace, §§ 13, 33, 35, 38
    Civil Rights and Discrimination (this index)
Embarrassment, Humiliation or Disgrace
    Abusive or Offensive Language (this index)
    Damages § 739
    Fright §§ 40-44, 53, 54
    Insults (this index)
Prejudice or Bias
    no race topics
    Damages (this index)
    Civil Rights and Discrimination (this index)
Abusive or Offensive Language
    Damages §§ 754, 768
    Fright §§ 40-44
    Torts § 32
Breach of Peace
    Civil Rights and Discrimination (this index)
    Offensive & provocative language
        Breach P §§ 10, 11, 13, 15
    Pedestrians, inconveniencing of
        Breach P § 32
    Streets & highways
        Breach P §§ 9, 20, 24, 33, 36
    Terror
        Breach P §§ 7, 8, 12, 21
    Threats or intimidation
        Breach P §§ 7, 23, 31, 42
Fright, Shock, and Mental Disturbance
    Generally Damages §§ 28, 137, 138, 240, 251-59, 278, 376, 539, 871
    Anguish
        Fright, etc. §§ 35, 55

and Regulations Cited. This table lists every section of Am. Jur. 2d that discusses or cites a particular court rule or a particular section of a federal statute, regulation, or uniform act.

3. How Encyclopedias Are Updated

Some topic volumes are not of recent vintage. The volume in Illustration 3-1 was published in 1968 and that in Illustration 3-2 was published in 1954. Clearly, topic volumes must be updated. As already noted, both Am. Jur. 2d and C.J.S. are updated by pocket parts—annual supplements that slip into the inside back cover of each hardbound volume. Always check the supplements for additions to and changes in the text and footnotes.

Am. Jur. 2d also provides a New Topic Service—a looseleaf binder and an occasional bound volume containing topics added after publication of the

FRIGHT, SHOCK, AND MENTAL DISTURBANCE § 56

have to explain credit problems with various lenders, that it was very embarassing for his wife, and that he "felt like scum" whenever he was turned down for a loan, was legally insufficient to support an award for mental anguish; even if the purchaser's feelings could be considered to rise to the level of mental anguish, the purchaser's testimony as to those feelings was all related to his credit hassles, and the purchaser failed to show that his credit problems were in fact caused by the seller, in that there was no proof that the seller ever made a credit report to anyone concerning its lawsuit against the purchaser. Roberts v U.S. Home Corp. (1985, **Tex** App San Antonio) 694 SW2d 129.

A hospital employee's allegation that her supervisor repeatedly insulted her by insisting that she, like all persons older than age 40, was senile and a liar, failed as a matter of law to state a cause of action for intentional infliction of emotional distress. The alleged conduct, although objectively offensive and uncivil, was not so egregious as to be actionable, and the employee provided no details of the specific employment setting so as to show the supervisor abused his position as the employee's superior in the workplace. Yurick v Superior Court (1989, 3rd Dist) 209 **Cal** App 3d 1116, 257 Cal Rptr 665.

§ 55. Anxiety, apprehension, and worry

Practice aids: Bell, The Bell Tolls: Toward Full Tort Recovery For Psychic Injury. 36 U Fla LR 333, Summer, 1984.

Gale and Goyer, Recovery for Cancer Phobia and Increased Risk of Cancer. 15 Cum LR 723, 1984-1985.

Intentional infliction of emotional distress by employer. 45 Am Jur Proof of Facts 2d 249.

Turezyn, When Circumstances Provide a Guarantee of Genuineness: Permitting Recovery for Pre-Impact Emotional Distress. 28 Bos C LR 881, September, 1987.

Additional case authorities for section:

Hospital was liable for emotional harm suffered by daughter of hospital inmate to whom telegram was negligently sent falsely advising daughter of her mother's death where anxiety neurosis condition suffered by plaintiff was supported by objective manifestations thereof. Johnson v State 37 **NY**2d 378, 372 NYS2d 638.

Facts that employee was excluded from certain meetings allegedly necessary to performance of his job, that employee found materials and papers on desk were constantly rearranged so as to annoy him, that employee was advised he was being given new assistant without prior consultation and without plans for such assistant, that employee never received any communication concerning job performance from superior, that employee received rumors that his job was in jeopardy, and that employee's superior continually evaded employee's request for meeting concerning employment status and made intimations that new assistant would replace employee, were insufficient to state cause of action for intentional infliction of mental or emotional distress. Beibler v W.R. Grace, Inc. (1978, ED Pa) 461 **F** Supp 1013.

Plaintiff adequately stated a cause of action against a pet store owner and the owner's insurer for intentional infliction of emotional distress where she alleged that a skunk bit her in the store, that the owner sold the skunk after it bit her, that the skunk was consequently lost prior to the incubation period necessary to see whether it had rabies, that the insurer intentionally exposed her to death by directing the owner to keep this information from her, and that she suffered severe emotional distress when she learned the information had been intentionally withheld and that there was a possibility that she had been exposed to a fatal disease. Kirkpatrick v Zitz (1981, **Fla** App D1) 401 So 2d 850.

In order for workers who had been exposed to asbestos to recover for their fear of cancer, they would have to prove that they were suffering from serious fear or emotional distress or clinically diagnosed phobia of cancer, that fear was proximately caused by exposure by asbestosis, that fear was reasonable, and that defendants were legally responsible for their exposure to asbestos. Devlin v Johns-Manville Corp. (1985) 202 **NJ** Super 556, 495 A2d 495.

§ 56. Loss of enjoyment

Additional case authorities for section:

Mental distress caused by impairment of enjoyment of life was factor in determining award for pain and suffering of worker injured in blast at plant manufacturing military trip flares. Aretz v United States (1978, SD Ga) 456 F Supp 397 (applying **Ga** law).

topic volumes. In time, these new topics and the pre-existing topics are reissued in replacement volumes. Be sure to check this binder before you complete your research. None of the new topics in the binder as of the end of 1991 pertained to the Perkins problem in Chapter 2.

4. State Encyclopedias

In some states, a private publisher issues a law encyclopedia covering the constitution, cases, and statutes of that state. The format and function of these state encyclopedias are very similar to those of the previously discussed encyclopedias. The major difference is that Am. Jur. 2d and C.J.S. include both federal law and the law of all states, while most state encyclopedias concentrate on the law of a single state.

You can locate a state encyclopedia by browsing the shelves containing the collection of research materials for that state or by consulting a legal research guide for that state. You also can consult the library catalog (see page 61) under the subject heading "Law—[name of state]." Some state encyclopedias call themselves "digests" and other misleading names. Be sure to categorize these sources based on their format and function, not their titles.

State law encyclopedias vary considerably as to quality and depth of coverage. You will want to evaluate each state encyclopedia separately and adapt your research steps accordingly. State encyclopedias may be accessible by means of the following research approaches:

(1) the topic outline approach
(2) the index approach
(3) the table of cases approach

The topic outline approach and the index approach have been discussed with reference to C.J.S. and Am. Jur. 2d. As for the table of cases approach, some state encyclopedias contain a table of cases that lists alphabetically the cases discussed or cited in that encyclopedia. There also may be a table of cases listing the defendants first. This table is especially useful in criminal cases and in cases where you know only the name of the defendant. You will use this table when you already know a case name and are seeking a general discussion of the area of law covered in the case.

5. Specialized Encyclopedias

In addition to the general-coverage encyclopedias Am. Jur. 2d and C.J.S., there also are specialized encyclopedias, such as the sampling listed in Table 3.1 below. Check your library for more.

TABLE 3.1. Specialized Encyclopedias.

Encyclopedia of Crime & Justice (Sanford H. Kadish ed., 1983) (4 volumes).
Encyclopedia of Human Rights (Edward Lawson ed., 1991).
Encyclopedia of the American Constitution (Leonard W. Levy et al. eds., 1986) (4 volumes).
Encyclopedia of the American Judicial System: Studies of the Principal Institutions & Processes of Law (Robert J. Janosik ed., 1987) (3 volumes).
Encyclopedia of the European Communities (1991).
The Guide to American Law: Everyone's Legal Encyclopedia (1983) (12 volumes).
Eric H.K. Lee, *Encyclopedia of Arbitration Law* (1984-present).
J.K. Mason & R.A. McCall Smith, *Butterworths Medico-Legal Encyclopaedia* (1987).
William J. Miller, *Encyclopedia of International Commerce* (1985).
Modern Legal Systems Cyclopedia (Kenneth Robert Redden ed., 1984-present).
Edmund J. Osmanczyk, *The Encyclopedia of the United Nations and International Relations* (2d ed. 1990) (previous edition titled *The Encyclopedia of the United Nations and International Agreements*).
A.G. Toth, *The Oxford Encyclopaedia of European Community Law* (1990-present).

C. TREATISES AND CONTINUING LEGAL EDUCATION (CLE) MATERIALS

1. Treatises and CLE Materials Compared

Treatises and continuing legal education (CLE) materials each cover only one area of law in each volume or set of volumes. The area may be a broad area such as contracts, torts, or civil procedure in the federal courts; or it may be a narrower area, such as assault or landlord-tenant law. Thus, these sources are useful to you only when you know which area of law encompasses the problem you are researching. The other commentary sources covered in this chapter (with the exception of Restatements) all cover a wide range of subjects in a single volume or set of volumes.

Both treatises and CLE materials can be located by similar research means (library catalog or shelf browsing), although dissimilar means are available as well.

Because of their similarities, these two kinds of research materials are being covered in the same part of this chapter.

2. What Is a Treatise?

Law treatises are commentary sources written by private authors, usually law professors, legal scholars, and attorneys. The format of a treatise is not unique to legal publications. A treatise contains a scholarly examination of the subject matter, often supplemented by footnotes with supporting citations and tangential remarks. See Illustration 3-9 on page 57. For a less typical treatise format, see Illustration 3-10 on pages 58-59. Some treatises are still in use after many years, especially if the law is relatively stable or the author was prescient. However, treatises in rapidly changing areas of the law usually are replaced frequently with new editions.

Treatises excel in scholarly, integrated analysis of a discrete area of the law. This analysis can be useful to you at two junctures: (1) when you begin researching and are still unfamiliar with the basic vocabulary, issues, sub-issues, arguments, and policies in that area; and (2) when you have done much of your research but still need assistance in tying together some of your primary authority. In both instances, treatises serve you well by giving you the "big picture."

Treatises appear in print, on CD-ROM, and on computer-assisted legal research systems. A print treatise may consist of a single volume or multiple volumes. In an unfamiliar area of law in which there are both single-volume and multi-volume treatises, you might first examine a single-volume treatise to gain familiarity with the basics of the subject, then read the more detailed discussion in a multi-volume treatise. Of course, if you are familiar with the subject matter, you might go directly to a multi-volume treatise.

You may have heard the term "hornbook" since entering law school, and you may wonder if a hornbook is a treatise. "Hornbook" generally refers to a single-volume treatise that explains the basic principles of law in a particular field. Hornbooks are often written by a top scholar in a field and usually are designed with the needs of law students in mind. They explain the basic principles of an area of law in narrative form, rather than casebook form. Thus, they can serve as supplemental reading for law school courses. Perhaps hornbooks can best be thought of as treatises designed especially

ILLUSTRATION 3-9. Sample Treatise Text: W. Page Keeton et al., *Prosser and Keeton on the Law of Torts* § 12, at 61 (5th ed. 1984).

57

quirements of the rule are rigorous, and difficult to satisfy.[55] Yet, such extreme outrage has been found, as in the leading Wilkinson case,[56] in decoying a woman suspected of insanity to a hospital by a concocted tale of an injured husband and child;[57] in spreading the false rumor that the plaintiff's son had hanged himself;[58] in bringing a mob to the plaintiff's door at night with a threat to lynch him unless he left town;[59] and in wrapping up a very gory dead rat instead of a loaf of bread, for a sensitive soul to open.[60] An invitation to illicit intercourse, insufficient in itself,[61] becomes extreme outrage when it is prolonged or repeated to the point of hounding, and accompanied by advertising in the form of indecent pictures or exposure.[62]

The extreme and outrageous nature of the conduct may arise not so much from what is done as from abuse by the defendant of some relation or position which gives the defendant actual or apparent power to damage the plaintiff's interests. The result is something very like extortion. Again the leading case is an English one, Janvier v. Sweeney,[63]

where a private detective, representing himself to be a police officer, threatened to charge plaintiff with espionage unless she surrendered private letters in her possession. Not far removed from this are the cases of bullying a school girl, with threats of prison and public disgrace, unless she signed a confession of immoral misconduct,[64] and the threats of an association of rubbish collectors to beat the plaintiff up, destroy his truck, and put him out of business, unless he paid over proceeds from a territory which they had allocated to one of their members.[65]

It is on this basis that the tort action has been used as a potent counter-weapon against the more outrageous high-pressure methods of collection agencies and other creditors. These are sufficiently well known,[66] ranging from violent cursing, abuse, and accusations of dishonesty,[67] through a series of letters in lurid envelopes bearing a picture of lightning about to strike, which repeatedly threatened arrest, ruination of credit, or a suit which is never brought,[68] or telephone calls around the

---

See also Second Restatement of Torts, § 46, comment *k*.

Ohio held back, in Bartow v. Smith, 1948, 149 Ohio St. 301, 78 N.E.2d 735, where defendant reviled a pregnant woman on the public street. The case is commented on, in 1949, 27 Mich.L.Rev. 436; 1949, 27 Tex. L.Rev. 730 ("distinctly and inexcusably retrogressive").

55. For an illustration, see Harris v. Jones, 1977, 281 Md. 560, 380 A.2d 611.

56. Supra, this section.

57. Savage v. Boies, 1954, 77 Ariz. 355, 272 P.2d 349.

58. Bielitski v. Obadiak, 1921, 61 Dom.L.Rep. 494.

59. Wilson v. Wilkins, 1930, 181 Ark. 137, 25 S.W.2d 428. Cf. Ruiz v. Bertolotti, 1962, 37 Misc.2d 1067, 236 N.Y.S.2d 854 (threat of harm to plaintiffs, Negroes, and their children, if they moved into neighborhood); Flamm v. Van Nierop, 1968, 56 Misc.2d 1059, 291 N.Y.S.2d 189 (hounding plaintiff on the streets).

60. Great Atlantic & Pacific Tea Co. v. Roch, 1930, 160 Md. 189, 153 A. 22.

61. See supra, this section.

62. Samms v. Eccles, 1961, 11 Utah 2d 289, 358 P.2d 344; Mitran v. Williamson, 1960, 21 Misc.2d 106, 197 N.Y.S.2d 689. Cf. Webber v. Gray, 1957, 228 Ark. 289, 307 S.W.2d 80, where defendant, a former mistress of plaintiff, hounded him and his family, with incidents of

aggravation, in an effort to renew the association. Also Halio v. Lurie, 1961, 15 A.D.2d 62, 222 N.Y.S.2d 759, where a man who had jilted a woman wrote her jeering verses and taunting letters; and Tate v. Canonica, 1960, 180 Cal.App.2d 898, 5 Cal.Rptr. 28, where a man was driven to suicide by threats and accusations not set forth.

63. [1919] 2 K.B. 316.

64. Johnson v. Sampson, 1926, 167 Minn. 203, 208 N.W. 814.

65. State Rubbish Collectors Association v. Siliznoff, 1952, 38 Cal.2d 330, 240 P.2d 282.

66. See Birkhead, Collection Tactics of Illegal Lenders, 1941, 8 Law & Contemp.Prob. 78; Borda, One's Right to Enjoy Mental Peace and Tranquility, 1939, 28 Geo.L.J. 55; Berger, The Bill Collector and the Law, 1968, 17 De Paul L.Rev. 327: Notes, 1939, 34 Ill.L.Rev. 505; 1957, 24 U.Chi.L.Rev. 572; 1957, 14 Wash. & Lee L.Rev. 167; 1957, 35 Chicago-Kent L.Rev. 145.

67. Kirby v. Jules Chain Stores Corp., 1936, 210 N.C. 808, 188 S.E. 625; American Security Co. v. Cook, 1934, 49 Ga.App. 723, 176 S.E. 798; American Finance & Loan Corp. v. Coots, 1962, 105 Ga.App. 849, 125 S.E.2d 689 (including pointing revolver).

68. Barnett v. Collection Service Co., 1932, 214 Iowa 1303, 242 N.W. 25; LaSalle Extension University v. Fogarty, 1934, 126 Neb. 457, 253 N.W. 424. Cf. Christensen v. Swedish Hospital, 1962, 59 Wn.2d 545, 368

ILLUSTRATION 3-10. Sample Treatise Text: Carolyn McKinney Garrett, *Cause of Action for Intentional Infliction of Emotional Distress,* in 7 *Shepard's Causes of Action* 663-65, 667 (1983).

CAUSES OF ACTION   7 COA 663

CAUSE OF ACTION FOR INTENTIONAL INFLICTION OF EMOTIONAL DISTRESS

by Carolyn McKinney Garrett, JD

COA ACTION GUIDE

PRIMA FACIE CASE

- A prima facie case in an action for intentional infliction of emotional distress requires proof that:
    1. the conduct of the defendant was outrageous [§§5–7];
    2. the defendant acted intentionally or recklessly [§8];
    3. severe emotional distress was suffered by the plaintiff [§9]; and
    4. the conduct of the defendant was the proximate cause of the emotional distress suffered [§10].

DEFENSES

- A defense to an action for intentional infliction of emotional distress may by established by proof that:
    1. the conduct of the defendant was not outrageous.   §11
    2. the conduct of the defendant was not intentional or reckless. §12
    3. the defendant's conduct did not cause the plaintiff to suffer emotional distress.   §13
    4. the emotional distress suffered by the plaintiff was not severe. §14
    5. the defendant's conduct consisted of the assertion of legal rights in a permissible way.   §15

---

664   EMOTIONAL DISTRESS   7 COA 663

PERSONS ENTITLED TO RECOVER

- Action may be brought by the person toward whom the defendant's conduct was directed and, under certain circumstances, by a person who was not the object of the defendant's conduct, but who witnessed the conduct.   §16

ILLUSTRATION 3-10. *(continued)* 59

RECOVERY

- Compensatory damages are recoverable for the emotional distress suffered, bodily harm which results from the emotional distress, economic losses which result from the emotional distress or its physical consequences, and loss of consortium. §22
- Plaintiff may be entitled to punitive damages. §23

CONTENTS

TABLE OF CASES

INDEX

I. INTRODUCTION

§1. Scope

This article discusses the cause of action for intentional infliction of emotional distress. The elements the plaintiff must prove in establishing a prima facie case are discussed in §§4–10. Defenses that may be raised are consid-
entitled to recover and persons who are

for students or beginners in a field. They are an excellent place to begin your research on an unfamiliar legal topic.

Chapters in treatises often are organized by sections or paragraphs. You should note this mode of organization for two reasons: (1) indexes and supplements usually refer to sections or paragraphs (instead of pages) if the source is organized in this manner; (2) Rule 3.4 of *The Bluebook* requires citations to sections or paragraphs, instead of to page numbers, if the source is organized by sections or paragraphs.

> *Citation Note:* Rule 15 of *The Bluebook* covers all books. Unless the special citation forms in Rule 15.7 apply, the citation includes the volume number (if the treatise has more than one volume), the author's (or authors') full name (or names), and the full main title of the book as they appear on the title page (not the cover); the page, section, or paragraph number; and the edition and year in parentheses. A subtitle is given only if it is particularly relevant. Rule 15.2. Here is a straight-forward example: 3 E. Allan Farnsworth, *Contracts* § 12.16 (2d ed. 1990). Consult Rule 3.2(a) for conventions governing volume numbers and Rule 3.4 for conventions governing paragraphs and sections. If the book is organized by sections or paragraphs, cite to the section or paragraph first; follow with a page number only if it is needed for further specificity.
>
> Illustration 3-9 is from a treatise with multiple authors: W. Page Keeton et al., *Prosser and Keeton on the Law of Torts* § 12 (5th ed. 1984). Rule 15.1.1 states that if there are more than two authors, the name of the first author is followed by "et al."
>
> Illustration 3-10 is from a collection of articles and therefore is cited as Carolyn McKinney Garrett, *Cause of Action for Intentional Infliction of Emotional Distress, in* 7 *Shepard's Causes of Action* 663, 663-65, 667 (1985). Note that the volume number precedes the name of the treatise here, not the name of the article author.
>
> According to Practitioners' Note P.1 on typefaces in *The Bluebook,* you must italicize or underscore book and article titles cited in court documents and legal memoranda. This book uses italics, but your typewriter or word processor may necessitate underlining.

3. How to Find a Treatise

Treatises can be found in many ways, some of them obvious and some of them ingenious:

(1) Look in the library catalog to find out what your library owns. Or, if you want a larger selection, you can seek assistance from librarians who can consult OCLC, RLIN, and other local or national cataloging systems.

(2) Find out the call number range of the subject matter and browse the relevant shelves. In addition, ask at the library reserve desk to see reserve treatises within that call number range. You may be able to browse the reserve stacks.

(3) Look in the front or back of a textbook for a list of treatises published by the same publisher. Or look in a textbook for footnotes and bibliographies that cite treatises in the subject area.

(4) Go to your law school bookstore looking for hornbooks on a particular topic.

Only the first two search methods need more elaboration; the others are self-explanatory.

The catalog of your library's holdings may be in print, on microfiche, or on an online computer database. Print or microfiche catalogs in law libraries most often use the same three entry points used in card catalogs found elsewhere: subject, author, and title. Most computerized card catalogs provide access by subject, author, title, and call number "cards." Some computerized card catalogs also offer "key word" search methods.

If you do not know the author or title of a treatise, you should search the catalog by subject. Searching by subject is not always as easy as you might think, because you must find the relevant standard subject heading used by the cataloger. Catalogs contain cross-references to help you find standard subject headings.

If you are having difficulties finding a useful subject heading in a library catalog but you know of at least one source on point, locate that source in the catalog by means of its author or title. Then use the relevant subject headings listed for that source as subject heading searches to find other related sources. See "Subject" listings in Illustration 3-11 below and Illustration 3-12 on page 62. (Note that Illustration 3-12 lists the subject headings of "Torts," "Actions and defenses," and "Trial practice" for *Shepard's Causes of Action.* However, in some libraries it may be cataloged under a different

ILLUSTRATION 3-11. Computerized Catalog Entry for W. Page Keeton et al., *Prosser and Keeton on the Law of Torts* (5th ed. 1984).

```
CALL #       KF1250 .P73 1984
LOCATIONS    Reserve(5 copies)

TITLE        Prosser and Keeton on the law of torts / W. Page Keeton. general
                editor ; W. Page Keeton ... [et al.]
EDITION      5th ed.
IMPRINT      St. Paul, Minn. : West Pub. Co., 1984.
DESCRIPT     xxxi, 1286 p. ; 26 cm.
SERIES       Hornbook series student edition.
```

```
NOTE         Kept up to date by pocket supplements.
             Rev. ed. of: Handbook of the law of torts / William L. Prosser.
                4th ed. 1971.
             Cover title: Prosser and Keeton on Torts.
             Spine title: Torts.
             Includes index.
             Also known as Prosser on torts.
```

```
SUBJECT      Torts --United States.
ALT AUTHOR   Keeton, Page.
             Prosser, William Lloyd, 1898-1972. Handbook of the law of torts.
             Prosser, William Lloyd, 1898-1972.
ALT TITLE    Prosser and Keeton on torts.
             Torts.
             Prosser on torts.
1 > Reserve(4 copies)
    LIB. HAS: 1984-
    Latest received:  1988
```

```
CALL #         KF1250 .S53 1983
LOCATIONS      Main

TITLE          Shepard's causes of action / prepared by Shepard's editorial
               staff.
IMPRINT        Colorado Springs, CO : Shepard's/McGraw-Hill ; New York : McGraw
               -Hill, [1983]
DESCRIPT       v. ; 27 cm.
NOTE           Includes index.
```

```
CONTENTS       Cause of action for motor vehicle brake defects under strict
               products liability -- Recovery under worker's compensation
               caused by work connected stress without physical cause or
               result -- Cause of action against pharmacist or druggist for
               injury or death from use of drug or medicine -- Cause of action
               in tort for bad faith refusal of insurer to pay claim of
               insured -- Cause of action by "at will" employee for wrongful
               discharge -- Cause of action against retail store or its
               employees for false imprisonment or false arrest of suspected
```

```
               shoplifter -- Cause of action for malpractice involving
               psychiatrist -- Cause of action for discrimination under the
               Federal Equal Credit Opportunity Act [15 USC [double section
               symbol] 1691 et seq.] -- Cause of action for violation of
               odometer disclosure requirements of Motor Vehicle Information
               and Cost Savings Act [15 USC [double section symbol] 1988, 1989
               ] -- Action against United States under 26 USC [section symbol]
               7422 for refund of taxes paid by individual taxpayer.
```

```
SUBJECT        Torts --United States a
               Actions and defenses --United States.
               Torts --United States --Trial practice.
               Trial practice --United States.
ALT AUTHOR     Shepard's/McGraw-Hill.
ALT TITLE      Causes of action.
1 >  Cumulative index
     Latest received:  1991

2 >  Pocket parts
     Latest received:  1991
```

subject heading: Civil Procedure—Actions—General—Treatises. This is more consistent with the treatise's overall focus.)

Another method is to consult the three-volume set entitled *Library of Congress Subject Headings.* These subject headings are the starting point for the creation of many library catalogs. They also offer you a shortcut to efficient use of a library catalog. Read "Introduction" in volume 1 to learn more about the "symbols" used in each volume. See Illustration 3-13 on page 63. No subject headings result from any of the search terms for the Perkins problem in Chapter 2, except for "Torts." See Illustration 3-14 on page 64. The only

ILLUSTRATION 3-13. Symbols Guide, 1 *Library of Congress Subject Headings* lvii (1991).

63

Symbols

UF   Used For
BT   Broader Topic
RT   Related Topic
SA   See also
NT   Narrower Topic

Use of these symbols in the expression of relationships between headings is explained in the Introduction.

For those libraries maintaining manual card catalogs, the following may be used as a guide.

Agriculture – Equipment and supplies
   see
Agricultural machinery

Crops – Machinery
   see
Agricultural machinery

Farm machinery
   see
Agricultural machinery

Machinery
   see also
Agricultural machinery

Farm equipment
   see also
Agricultural machinery

Farm mechanization
   see also
Agricultural machinery

Machine-tractor stations
   see also
Agricultural machinery

Agricultural machinery
   see also subdivision Machinery
   under names of crops, e.g.
   Corn – Machinery

Agricultural machinery
   see also
Agricultural implements

Agricultural machinery
   see also
Agricultural instruments

Agricultural machinery *(May Subd Geog)*
[S671–S760]
UF Agriculture – Equipment and supplies
     Crops – Machinery
     Farm machinery
BT Machinery
RT Farm equipment
     Farm mechanization
     Machine-tractor stations
SA subdivision Machinery under names of
     crops, e.g. Corn – Machinery
NT Agricultural implements
     Agricultural instruments
     . . .

The change in codes for cross references does not require users to alter the style of cross reference cards made for card catalogs.

The USE and UF can be translated into "see" and "see from" respectively.
The BT and RT can be translated into "see also from".
The SA and NT can be translated into "see also".

Tort liability of school districts
  (May Subd Geog)
    UF School districts—Tort liability
    BT Government liability
        School districts—Law and legislation
        Torts
    RT Liability for school accidents
Tort liability of social service agencies
  (May Subd Geog)
    UF Social service—Malpractice
        Social service—Tort liability
    BT Liability (Law)
        Negligence
        Tort liability of charitable
          organizations
        Torts
Tort liability of social workers
    USE Social workers—Malpractice
Tort liability of stockbrokers
    USE Stockbrokers—Malpractice
Tort liability of surveyors
    USE Surveyors—Malpractice
Tort liability of tax consultants
    USE Tax consultants—Malpractice
Tort liability of teachers
    USE Teachers—Malpractice
Tort liability of the government
    USE Government liability
Tort liability of the state
    USE Government liability
Tort liability of trade-unions
  (May Subd Geog)
    UF Trade-unions—Tort liability
    BT Liability (Law)
        Negligence
        Torts
Tort liability of unincorporated societies
  (May Subd Geog)
    UF Unincorporated societies—Tort
          liability
    BT Liability (Law)
        Negligence
        Tort liability of corporations
        Torts
Tort liability of United States Armed Forces
  medical personnel
    USE United States—Armed Forces—
          Medical personnel—Malpractice
Tort liability of universities and colleges
  (May Subd Geog)
    UF Universities and colleges—Tort
          liability
    BT Liability (Law)
        Negligence
        Tort liability of corporations
        Torts
Tort liability of works councils
  (May Subd Geog)
    UF Works councils—Tort liability
    BT Liability (Law)
        Negligence
        Torts
Torticollis
    UF Stiff neck
        Wryneck
    BT Musculoskeletal system—Diseases
        Neck—Diseases
    — Psychosomatic aspects
Tortie and white cats
    USE Calico cats
Torties (Cats)
    USE Tortoiseshell cats
Tortillas
    ₍TX770₎
    BT Bread
        Cookery
        Corn meal
Tortipelvis *(May Subd Geog)*
    UF Twisted pelvis
    BT Dystonia musculorum deformans
        Pelvis—Abnormalities

Tortoise beetles
    ₍QL596.C5₎
    UF Beetles, Tortoise
        Cassididae
        Cassidinae
    BT Chrysomelidae
    NT Cassida
        Eggplant tortoise beetle
Tortoise shell
    USE Tortoiseshell
Tortoises
    USE Turtles
Tortoises (Mining)
    USE Kettlebottoms (Mining)
Tortoiseshell *(May Subd Geog)*
    UF Tortoise shell
    BT Shells
Tortoiseshell and white cats
    USE Calico cats
Tortoiseshell art objects *(May Subd Geog)*
    BT Art objects
Tortoiseshell cats *(May Subd Geog)*
    ₍SF449.T₎
    UF Torties (Cats)
    BT Cat breeds
Tortoiseshell turtle
    USE Hawksbill turtle
Tortola (V.I.) *(Not Subd Geog)*
    BT Islands—British Virgin Islands
        Virgin Islands
Torton family
    USE Tuten family
**Tortosa Disputation, Tortosa, Spain, 1413-
1414**
    UF Tortosa disputation, 1413-1414
    BT Religious disputations
Tortosa disputation, 1413-1414
    USE Tortosa Disputation, Tortosa, Spain,
          1413-1414
Tortricidae *(May Subd Geog)*
    ₍QL561.T8 (Zoology)₎
    ₍SB945.T78 (Plant pests)₎
    UF Archipinae
        Atteriidae
        Ceracidae
        Chlidanotidae
        Epiblemidae
        Eucosmidae
        Grapholithidae
        Olethreutidae
        Schoenotenidae
        Sparganothidae
    BT Lepidoptera
        Moths
    NT Acleris
        Ancylis
        Cacoecia
        Carpocapsa
        Choristoneura
        Endothenia
        Eulia
        Grapholitha
        Laspeyresia
        Paralobesia
        Rhopobota
        Rhyacionia
        Sparganothis
        Tortrix
        Zeiraphera
Tortrix
    ₍QL561.T8₎
    BT Tortricidae
    NT Pea green moth
Tortrix fumiferana
    USE Spruce budworm
Tortrix luteolana
    USE Sparganothis pilleriana
Tortrix murinana
    USE Choristoneura murinana
Tortrix nigridia
    USE Spruce budworm

Tortrix pilleriana
    USE Sparganothis pilleriana
Tortrix viridana
    USE Pea green moth
Torts *(May Subd Geog)*
    UF Civil wrongs
        Injuries (Law)
        Quasi delicts
        Wrongful acts
    BT Actions and defenses
        Liability (Law)
        Obligations (Law)
    RT Accident law
        Negligence
    NT Abuse of rights
        Administrative responsibility
        Alienation of affections
        Assault and battery
        Attractive nuisance
        Chicanery (Law)
        Competition, Unfair
        Conspiracy
        Constitutional torts
        Copyright—Unauthorized reprints
        Damages
        Danger (Law)
        Death by wrongful act
        Dilapidations
        Discovery abuse
        Duress (Law)
        False imprisonment
        Fraud
        Fraudulent conveyances
        Government liability
        Joint tortfeasors
        Liability for animals
        Liability for condition and use of land
        Liability for environmental damages
        Liability for fire damages
        Liability for landslide damages
        Liability for nuclear damages
        Liability for oil pollution damages
        Liability for water pollution damages
        Libel and slander
        Lost earnings damages
        Lost profits damages
        Malicious accusation
        Malicious prosecution
        Malpractice
        Nuisances
        Personal injuries
        Plagiarism
        Proximate cause (Law)
        Res ipsa loquitur doctrine
        Respondeat superior
        Seduction
        Strict liability
        Tort liability of charitable
          organizations
        Tort liability of corporations
        Tort liability of highway departments
        Tort liability of hospitals
        Tort liability of insurance companies
        Tort liability of municipal corporations
        Tort liability of parks
        Tort liability of partnerships
        Tort liability of recreation agencies
        Tort liability of school districts
        Tort liability of social service agencies
        Tort liability of trade-unions
        Tort liability of unincorporated
          societies
        Tort liability of universities and
          colleges
        Tort liability of works councils
        Trespass
        Trover and conversion
        Waste (Law)
    — Conflict of laws
        USE Conflict of laws—Torts

4483

narrower term ("NT") on point is "Personal injuries," which is no more useful than "Torts" for locating treatises in the library catalog. Thus, the Library of Congress headings are not particularly helpful here, but they frequently are.

Subject headings that match titles of law school courses generally are of sufficient breadth to merit a treatise. For example, treatises discussing tort recovery for mental or emotional distress were found under the subject heading "Torts—United States." Searches under narrower subjects were uniformly unsuccessful, as shown in Illustration 3-15 on page 66. If you do not find a treatise on a narrow legal topic (or perhaps even if you do), you should consider trying to find one on a broader topic, depending on whether you need detailed or "big picture" information.

If you search a computerized catalog, pay close attention to the example screens and help screens. Be careful to correctly spell the title, the author's name, or the subject heading. For instance, the subject heading "tort" yields a much shorter list of sources than does the subject heading "torts." The same is true of "contract" instead of "contracts." Worse yet, a misspelled author's name or a misworded title will cause your search to be unsuccessful. So will searching for an author's name in the title or subject file, and so on. Moreover, if your computerized catalog does not allow you to browse beyond the "cards" retrieved by your search, you thereby lose some opportunities to catch or correct a misspelled or misworded title, subject search, or author's name, as well as opportunities for some lucky finds.

Illustrations 3-11 and 3-12 on pages 61 and 62 show the kind of bibliographic information found on a catalog "card" (be it paper, fiche, or computerized). "Location" tells you the name of the collection in which that source is located (for instance, the reserve collection). "Call number" tells you the order in which the sources in that collection are arranged.

Your library may have some treatises online or on CD-ROM but they may not appear in your library's catalog. Alternatively, the catalog may list each CD-ROM holding by the title on the disk, but may not list separately each source on the disk, some of which may be treatises. For instance, the *West CD-ROM Federal Civil Practice Library* contains portions of a well-known multi-volume civil procedure treatise, Charles A. Wright et al., *Federal Practice and Procedure* (1969-present). However, your library's catalog may not contain any listing for the CD-ROM version of the treatise.

If you need a larger selection of treatises than those found in the catalog of your law library, consult the reference librarians in your law library. They may have online access to regional and national cataloging systems and may have access to online catalogs from other local libraries as well. They also may be able to show you how to dial in to some of those sources.

You also may find treatises by consulting bibliographies such as *Law Books in Print*. Most bibliographic reference tools are accessible by subject, author, and title. Some cover in-print titles; others cover out-of-print titles.

b. Browsing the Shelves or the Computerized Catalog

Most libraries use one of two call number systems—Library of Congress or Dewey Decimal; other specialized classification systems also exist. Under the Library of Congress system, most American law-related publications appear under the "KF" listing. In the Dewey Decimal system, American law-related publications appear in Classes 340-349.

A good research strategy for finding a treatise in a new area of the law is to use the card catalog or a list posted in your library (see Table 3.2 on page 67) to ascertain the call numbers of the broad topic you are researching.

ILLUSTRATION 3-15. Sample Subject Searches: Innovative Interfaces, Inc., Public Access Catalog System.

```
You searched for the SUBJECT: emotional distress
 Your SUBJECT not found, Nearby SUBJECTS are:

 1   Eminent Domain United States Trial Practice  ........ 1 entry
 2   Emission Control Devices Automobiles --> See AUTO .... 1 entry
 3   Emission Control Devices Motor Vehicles --> See MOTOR  1 entry
 4   Emmigration And Immigration Trial Practice  .......... 1 entry
         Your entry  Emotional Distress   would be here
 5   Emotional Health --> See MENTAL HEALTH  .............. 1 entry
 6   Emotional Stress --> See STRESS (PSYCHOLOGY)  ........ 1 entry
 7   Emotionally Disturbed Children --> See MENTALLY ILL .. 1 entry
 8   Emotions --> See Related Subjects  ................. 7 entries


You searched for the SUBJECT: mental distress
 Your SUBJECT not found, Nearby SUBJECTS are:

 1   Mental Deficiency --> See MENTAL RETARDATION  ........ 1 entry
 2   Mental Discipline --> See Related Subjects  ........ 3 entries
 3   Mental Diseases --> See Related Subjects  .......... 3 entries
 4   Mental Disorders --> See Related Subjects  ......... 3 entries
         Your entry  Mental Distress   would be here
 5   Mental Health --> See Related Subjects  ............ 9 entries
 6   Mental Health Aged United States  ................... 1 entry
 7   Mental Health Clinics --> See COMMUNITY MENTAL HEALTH  1 entry
 8   Mental Health Counseling --> See Also PSYCHOTHERAPY .. 1 entry


You searched for the SUBJECT: intentional infliction of emotional
           distress
  Your SUBJECT not found, Nearby SUBJECTS are:

 1   Intensive Care Units --> See Also CRITICAL CARE MEDIC  1 entry
 2   Intensive Medicine --> See CRITICAL CARE MEDICINE  ... 1 entry
 3   Intent Criminal --> See CRIMINAL INTENT  ............. 1 entry
 4   Intent Letters Of --> See LETTERS OF INTENT  ......... 1 entry
         Your entry  Intentional Infliction Of Emotional Distress
           would be here
 5   Inter American Cooperation --> See PAN-AMERICANISM .. 1 entry
 6   Inter American Relations --> See PAN-AMERICANISM .... 1 entry
 7   Inter Library Loans --> See Related Subjects .......2 entries
 8   Inter Library Loans  ................................ 1 entry


You searched for the SUBJECT: outrage
 Your SUBJECT not found, Nearby SUBJECTS are:

 1   Outdoor Recreation United States  ................... 1 entry
 2   Outer Space Exploration  ............................ 1 entry
 3   Outlaw Strikes --> See WILDCAT STRIKES  ............. 1 entry
 4   Outlaws --> See Also PIRATES  ...................... 1 entry
         Your entry  Outrage   would be here
 5   Over The Counter Drugs --> See DRUGS, NONPRESCRIPTION  1 entry
 6   Overcrowding Of Prisons --> See PRISONS --OVERCROWDIN  1 entry
 7   Overcrowding Prisons  ............................... 1 entry
 8   Overcrowding Prisons United States  ................. 1 entry
```

TABLE 3.2. Library of Congress Call Numbers in the KF Classification (Law of the United States).

Administrative Law   KF 5401-5425
Antitrust   KF 1631-1657
Banking   KF 966-1032
Bankruptcy   KF 1501-1548
Business Associations, generally   KF 1355-1480
Children and Law   KF 479, 540-550
Civil and Political Rights   KF 4741-4788
Civil Procedure   KF 8810-9075
Commercial Transactions   KF 871-962
Conflict of Laws   KF 410-418
Constitutional Law   KF 4501-5130
Contracts, quasi-contracts   KF 801-1244
Copyright   KF 2986-3080
Corporations   KF 1384-1480
Criminal Law   KF 9201-9479
Criminal Procedure   KF 9601-9797
Education Policy and Law   KF 4101-4257
Employment Discrimination   KF 3464-3469
Environmental Law   KF 277.E5, JX 1291+
Equity   KF 398-400
Evidence
   In civil cases   KF 8931-8969
   In criminal cases   KF 9660-9677
Federal Courts   KF 8700-8807
Immigration Law   KF 4801-4848
Insurance Law   KF 1146-1238
International Law   JX 1-6731
Jurisprudence   KF 379-382
Juvenile Criminal Law   KF 9771-9827
Labor Law   KF 3300-3580
Land-Use Planning   KF 5691-5710
Legal History   KF 350-374
The Legal Profession   KF 297-334
Legal Research and Writing   KF 240-251
Legislative Process   KF 4945-4952
Local Government/Municipal Law   KF 5300-5332
Marital Relations and Dissolution   KF 501-553
Medical Legislation   KF 3821-3829
Mental Health Law   KF 3828-3829
Oil and Gas   KF 1841-1870
Patents   KF 3091-3192
Public Safety   KF 3941-3977
Real Property   KF 560-698
Regulation of Industry, Trade, and Commerce   KF 1600-2940
Secured Transactions   KF 1046-1062
Securities Regulations   KF 1428-1457, KF 1066-1083
Social Legislation   KF 3300-3771
Taxation   KF 6271-6645
Torts   KF 1246-1327
Trial Advocacy Principles/Tactics   KF 8911-8925
Uniform State Laws   KF 165
Water Resources   KF 5551-5590
Wills and Trusts   KF 726-780

You then can browse the shelves of books with those call numbers, looking for useful treatises. You also should browse the reserve stacks, if allowable, so that you don't overlook sought-after treatises placed on reserve. Experienced researchers regularly use this research method.

Some computerized catalogs have a useful feature that allows you to "shelf" browse online. Note that this allows you to find even those books that are checked out.

c. Recognizing a Treatise

As a researcher new to legal research, you may find it difficult to determine what is and what is not a treatise. Regardless of whether you are browsing shelves of books, looking at lists of sources, or flipping through a stack of cards, the following tips will come in handy:

- Do not expect the word "treatise" to appear in the title or the subject heading. If it does, you got lucky.
- Sources with "cases and problems," "cases and materials," or "casebook" in the title or subject heading are textbooks for class, not treatises. They contain very little commentary and are not efficient sources for legal research.
- Sources with titles or a publisher's name containing "Institute," "Seminar," "Advanced Education," "Continuing Education," or "Legal Education" are probably not treatises; they may be continuing legal education (CLE) materials.
- "Restatements" of the law are not treatises.
- A treatise will have an index.
- Most treatises are written by individual authors, not institutional authors or members of a publisher's editorial staff. The source from which Illustration 3-10 is drawn is an exception because it is written by members of the publisher's editorial staff.
- None of the commentary sources illustrated and discussed in the other parts of this chapter are treatises.

4. How to Select the Best Treatise

Selecting the best treatise for your needs requires that you consider the following:

(1) *Author:* Research the author to make sure that he or she is considered an expert in the field. Read his or her affiliations on the title page. If you are still in doubt, consult faculty or library staff, or look up the author in a biographical dictionary such as *Who's Who in American Law* or *The A.A.L.S. Directory of Law Teachers*. You also could consult a legal periodicals index to find reviews of the author's past work. (See Part D at pages 81-89.)

(2) *Publisher:* As you become a more experienced researcher, you will develop your own opinions about various publishers' reputations for quality, reliability, and accuracy. For the time being, you may want to ask reference librarians and other experienced legal researchers for their opinions.

(3) *Currency:* Make sure that the treatise is up-to-date. There may be a delay between completion of the treatise and its publication, so always compare the preface date with the publication date. Check for pocket-part or pamphlet supplements. If you are using a looseleaf treatise, check for dates on the pages or some indication of the date of the last updating.

(4) *Clarity:* Make sure that the treatise is clearly worded and articulate. Also look for sensible organization in the table of contents.

(5) *Index:* If you will be using the index, you should select a treatise with a good cross-referencing system in the index to help circumvent the limitations of your own vocabulary. Also look for an index with an adequate but not excessive level of detail.

(6) *Coverage:* Make sure that the treatise covers your topic adequately. Every treatise lacks detail in certain areas and does not cover some topics at all. On the other hand, some treatises may include more detail than you need, wasting valuable research time. For instance, you may choose a single-volume treatise over a multi-volume treatise for efficiency's sake.

(7) *Accuracy:* Make sure that the treatise is accurate and unbiased. Treatises can differ greatly in style and tone. While some merely interpret the law as it is, others endeavor to state what it should be, and some do both. Apparent inconsistencies among treatises may be due to philosophical differences among the authors. Thus, you may need to compare your treatise to other sources.

In the Perkins problem, the selection of torts treatises was very extensive. As an example, we have chosen a well-known single-volume torts treatise, colloquially known as "Prosser on Torts," the fifth edition of which is written by four well-reputed co-authors. See Illustration 3-9 on page 57. West Publishing Company publishes reliable hornbooks, and this hornbook scores high on clarity, coverage, and accuracy. The weak points are the thin index with poor cross-referencing and the out-of-date 1988 supplement.

We also have chosen a multi-volume treatise covering a wide range of causes of action. *Shepard's Causes of Action* was written by the publisher's staff and uses a format that is atypical for a treatise. See Illustration 3-10 on pages 58-59. Shepard's/McGraw-Hill is a high-quality legal publisher, the text is exceptionally clear and well organized, and coverage is very thorough. The index is nicely accessible, and the supplements are up-to-date. The table of contents is poor because the articles are not arranged in any logical manner, aside from their order of publication.

If you were researching this topic for the first time, you might want to consult the single-volume treatise first, followed by the more extensive coverage of the multi-volume treatise.

5. How to Use a Treatise

a. Summary Table of Contents/Detailed Table of Contents

In many books and for many research problems, it is less time-consuming and more fruitful to find the relevant sections of a treatise by consulting its table of contents rather than its index. There are several reasons for this. You can scan the entire treatise's contents in several minutes and thereby jog your memory for additional issues and vocabulary. See Illustration 3-16 on page 71. You also can see whether the author organizes the topic differently than you do. Thus, using a table of contents keeps you from being tripped up by your own insular view of the topic and indexing vocabulary.

Many treatises include both a summary table of contents and a detailed table of contents. The summary table of contents may enable you to locate the pertinent section in the detailed table of contents without perusing the entire detailed table of contents. Use it!

b.   Index

The index to a treatise allows you to find the major discussion of a topic as well as the scattered minor discussions of the same topic. Indexing vocabulary is not "standardized" among treatises; you may overlook a relevant index entry simply because you do not recognize a synonym or subdivision of the term for which you are searching. Therefore, you always should use law dictionaries, glossaries, and thesauri to cultivate alternative vocabulary for searching indexes.

Some single-volume treatises are abridged versions of multi-volume treatises by the same author. The indexes in these related single-volume and multi-volume works may be similar in organization and may use similar terminology. Being able to use similar indexes increases your research efficiency.

If you have done your best to find an entry in a particular index but have failed, do not assume that you are at fault—the treatise may not contain the information you seek or its index entry may be inaccessible. Move on to another treatise to ease your frustration.

The easiest way to locate a tort dealing with emotional distress in Prosser was to skim the table of contents to find "Infliction of Mental Distress"— § 12. See Illustration 3-16 on page 71. The index was not nearly as easy; the only search term from Chapter 2 that worked in the index was "Mental Distress." See Illustration 3-17 on page 72. No other related terms were cross-referenced in the index.

Section 12 in Prosser first discusses the history of tort recovery for intentional infliction of mental distress, then examines the tort's various elements, policies, and factual settings. See Illustration 3-9 on page 57, which gives an excerpt from that discussion.

In *Shepard's Causes of Action* (1983), the table of contents to the set was bulky and not very accessible. The index was much more helpful in locating a good article and contained many of the search terms from Chapter 2. The most on-point entry was the chapter entitled "Cause of Action for Intentional Infliction of Emotional Distress," which appears at pages 663 to 713 in volume 7. (See Illustration 3-10 on pages 58-59.) It begins with summary information (prima facie case, defenses, persons entitled to recover, etc.), a mini-table of contents to the article, and a mini-index to the article. The text is supplemented with frequent lists of cites from all relevant jurisdictions, Am. Jur. 2d, C.J.S., and A.L.R. annotations (see page 91).

c.   Table of Cases

A table of cases enables you to locate text or footnotes about a particular case. These tables are common in treatises. The table of cases approach is useful only if you know the name of a case on point and if the case is cited in the treatise.

d.   Update Services: Pocket Parts and Supplements

When you use any legal research source (not just treatises), you always should check the year of publication on the front or back of the title page. If your source is not up-to-date, you should look to see if the source has an update service containing the text of or discussion about recent cases, statutes, and administrative materials that might have changed the law since the publication date.

Fortunately, most multi-volume treatises have update services, as do some

Table of Contents

CHAPTER 1. INTRODUCTION

CHAPTER 2. INTENTIONAL INTERFERENCE WITH THE PERSON

CHAPTER 3. INTENTIONAL INTERFERENCE WITH PROPERTY

CHAPTER 4. DEFENSES TO INTENTIONAL INTERFERENCE WITH PERSON OR PROPERTY

single-volume treatises. Update services are organized by page, paragraph, or section to correspond to the page, paragraph, or section of the original volume. Update services assume several forms:

Pocket parts: These updates are pamphlets that slip into a pocket on the inside back or front cover of each volume. Pocket parts usually are replaced annually and are cumulative for the period since publication of the original volume. Be sure to check the date of publication of the pocket part in order to guard against relying on an out-of-date pocket part.

Supplemental volumes: Some sources issue separate volumes or paperback pamphlets updating the original volumes. In addition, if a pocket part becomes too large, it may be replaced with a paperbound volume. Always check the publication date of any supplemental material to find out if still more updating is necessary.

Looseleaf supplements: Sources bound in looseleaf binders may be updated with looseleaf supplements that are inserted periodically into the looseleaf volumes. These supplements often are printed on colored paper to distinguish them from the original material. Be sure to check the date of any supplement you are using.

Looseleaf page replacements: Sources bound in looseleaf binders may be updated with replacement pages that arrive at regular intervals or on an "as needed" basis. These pages are inserted into the binders by the library staff members, who also remove outdated pages. For this reason, looseleaf pages frequently are dated. Looseleaf services with weekly or monthly replacement pages are especially valuable because of their current information.

Update services often contain supplementary indexes, which add index entries for new areas of law and sometimes change index entries for difficult portions of the original indexing system. In these instances, you must use both the original index and the supplementary index in order to locate all pertinent passages.

A lawyer has a professional duty to update his or her research. To skip updating is to risk being embarrassed by a judge, opposing counsel, or client who notes your reliance on out-of-date authority. In addition, an attorney's failure to update his or her research can be grounds for malpractice. Always update your research.

Citation Note: Rule 3.2(c) in *The Bluebook* governs citations to supplements. To cite a separately paginated supplement, use the correct citation form for the source and identify the supplement and its date in parentheses. For example: W. Page Keeton et al., *Prosser and Keeton on the Law of Torts* § 12 (Supp. 1988). If you are citing material that is split between the main volume and the supplement, use the correct citation form for the source and include the year of publication of the main volume as well as that of the supplement. For example: W. Page Keeton et al., *Prosser and Keeton on the Law of Torts* § 12 (5th ed. 1984 & Supp. 1988).

Your research on the Perkins research situation could be updated as follows: The 1988 pocket part to Prosser supplied additional text and footnotes, but as of this writing a more recent pocket part was not available. On the other hand, the 1991 pocket part to volume 7 of *Shepard's Causes of Action* contained 16 pages of updating material.

6. What Are CLE Materials?

Many states require attorneys licensed in their state to continue to take courses on the law. And even in states without mandatory continuing legal education (CLE), attorneys need courses on new areas of law and on subjects they did not take in law school. Around this need has grown a small industry of CLE-sponsoring organizations at both the state and national levels.

Most CLE programs are taught by more than one presenter, and most of the presenters are attorneys. Many presenters prepare materials that may include an outline or text of the presentation and photocopies of important cases, statutes, rules, or regulations, especially recent ones. These materials typically are photocopied directly from typewritten text and documents and are bound in a looseleaf binder. See Illustration 3-18 on page 75. These binders then are given to the program attendees and are sold to law libraries.

Because of this informal publishing method and budget constraints, many CLE materials lack indexes and comprehensive, detailed tables of contents. That means that you may have to leaf through the entire binder to find out if a particular topic is covered.

CLE programs often are designed for one of two purposes—to impart new knowledge and skills or to maintain and improve existing skills. A program created to meet the first purpose may be at an orientation, basic, or advanced level. A program created for the second purpose may be a new developments course or a refresher course. Pay attention to these purposes and levels, if noted, because they will tell you how useful the materials will be to you. If you are new to a subject, you likely will be lost in a refresher or advanced course.

7. When to Look for CLE Materials

CLE materials are helpful to your research when you need the comprehensive analysis of a treatise but cannot find one that is suitable because your topic is too recent, too practice-oriented, or too state-focused. The analysis in CLE materials frequently is less scholarly than in treatises but often has more detailed case and statutory analysis. Many CLE materials focus on the law of a single jurisdiction.

CLE materials are especially valuable when you need cutting-edge analysis of fast-breaking law. No other commentary source covers new law so rapidly. CLE materials may be available as quickly as a month after a new statute, case, or regulation is issued.

You may not want to use CLE materials if you need a source with an index or a comprehensive, detailed table of contents, because these research aids frequently are missing in CLE materials.

8. How to Find Pertinent CLE Materials

You can locate CLE materials by using the library catalog or by browsing the shelves. In addition, some national CLE materials such as those from the American Law Institute/American Bar Association (ALI-ABA) and the Practicing Law Institute (PLI) are available online on WESTLAW.

a. Using the Library Catalog

CLE materials usually will have a title or a publisher's name containing one or more of the following words: "Institute," "Seminar," "Advanced Education," "Continuing Education," or "Legal Education." Thus, key word searching for these terms on a computerized catalog will be the most efficient strategy. A title search using these terms usually will be unsuccessful because these words may not appear at the beginning of a title. An author search will

ILLUSTRATION 3-18. Sample Page of CLE Material: Daniel S. Kleinberger & Christina L. Kunz, *Legal Writing for Effect* 10 (1991) (sponsored by Minnesota Institute of Legal Education).

75

Such information must be accurate, clear, and conspicuous.

v. Section 1667c requires clear and conspicuous disclosure of certain information in the advertising of "consumer leases."

c. Fair Credit Reporting Act, 15 U.S.C. §§ 1681-1681t

i. Section 1681d requires clear, prompt, accurate, and written disclosure of the intended procurement of an investigative consumer report, as well as the consumer's rights to further information.

ii. Section 1681g requires a consumer reporting agency to clearly and accurately disclose certain information to a consumer in certain instances.

3. Combatting the law's substantive disfavor

a. Construing the document against the drafter

b. Where the law is suspicious of a power being exercised and accordingly requires some sort of disclosure, incoherence can be especially costly.

i. McCarthy Well Co. v. St. Peter Creamery, Inc., 389 N.W.2d 514, 518 (Minn. Ct.

Legal Writing
Plain English Writing
10

work if CLE-sponsoring organizations are listed as authors; however, individual CLE presenters often are not listed as authors. Subject heading searches will locate CLE materials as well as other sources on that topic.

You can find the titles of relevant CLE materials by obtaining the catalogs of CLE-sponsoring organizations in the jurisdiction you are researching. You then can perform a title search for those CLE materials.

In addition, PLI annually publishes *Index to Course Handbooks,* a compilation of PLI's CLE materials. ALI-ABA publishes *The CLE Journal and Register,* a bimonthly collection of articles and reports on CLE training, followed by

- a one-year calendar of future CLE programs
- detailed course listings by state for the next six months
- detailed course listings by subject for the next six months
- index to courses for the next six months (including courses for which no detailed information is available)
- CLE publications
- sponsor abbreviations
- membership list of the Association of Continuing Legal Education Administrators

b. Browsing the Shelves

You can find out the call number of your research topic and then physically browse the shelves. In addition to looking for the CLE words listed above, you also should look for looseleaf notebooks and binders, which frequently (but not always) contain CLE materials. Remember that CLE materials from the same publisher will not be shelved together if they are not on the same topic, unless your library places CLE materials in a separate collection.

There were no CLE materials on the Perkins research situation in the jurisdiction we consulted.

D. LEGAL PERIODICALS

1. What Is a Legal Periodical?

a. Functions of Legal Periodicals

Like treatises, encyclopedias, and other sources covered in this chapter, legal periodicals are secondary authority. Articles in legal periodicals are written by private authors, not by courts, legislatures, or administrative agencies. Articles in legal periodicals do not constitute the law; instead, they analyze, describe, and comment on the law.

You will use legal periodicals primarily for two distinct purposes. First, you will find useful background information for your research in primary authority. Second, some articles propose legal reforms, which you may use to support an argument on your client's behalf before a court, legislature, or administrative agency.

In terms of background, all articles in legal periodicals describe and analyze the law. Thus, an article may be helpful as you synthesize a set of cases or work through a difficult statute or agency regulation. Furthermore, articles generally provide a wealth of references to primary authority, such as cases and statutes, and to other secondary authority, such as treatises and other articles. These references, found in the footnotes, make legal periodicals useful as finding tools for further research. Some articles provide basic factual information and references to non-legal sources as well.

Please note: The citation form used in legal periodical footnotes differs somewhat from that used in other legal writing, such as in the memos and briefs that lawyers write. Compare the quick reference tables inside the front and back covers of *The Bluebook*. *See also* Rule 2.

A few articles provide more than background and reference notes; they are a moving force in the law. These articles generally are written by well-known scholars or practitioners in a field and reflect serious research and thought. Lawyers and even judges may cite these seminal articles as substantial, although not primary, authority. For example, many scholars attribute the constitutional and tort doctrines recognizing a right to privacy to an 1890 article in the *Harvard Law Review. See* Samuel D. Warren & Louis O. Brandeis, *The Right to Privacy,* 4 Harv. L. Rev. 193 (1890). Few of the many articles written each year attain this status.

Periodicals have several particular advantages and drawbacks compared to treatises, encyclopedias, and other commentary sources. Periodicals generally are the best source for discussion of very new legal questions, since it takes less time to write and publish an article than it does to publish other materials. Furthermore, an article generally covers its subject in more depth than do the other commentary sources; indeed, you may find a 50-page article on a very narrow topic. Since the function of legal periodicals is to present interesting legal thought, you may find the most original thought on a subject in a periodical article. Indeed, in some cases, you will find a series of articles on the same subject, each presenting a different viewpoint and responding to the others.

It is important, however, to keep in mind as you read periodical articles that you are not necessarily reading the conventional view on your subject. Note also that the footnote references are current only to the date of the article's publication, whereas other commentary sources have update services.

In your ongoing investigation of the Perkins problem, your research in periodicals might lead you to an article by Professor Dean Richardson, published in the 1982 *Oregon Law Review.* This article would be helpful for several reasons. As you can see from the synopsis on the first page (Illustration 3-19 on page 78), Richardson's article presents the elements of the tort of intentional infliction of emotional distress, argues that the tort is applicable to racist conduct, and describes pertinent cases. As the footnotes show, the article also provides citations to primary authority (the Washington Supreme Court case of *Contreras*) and other commentary (Derrick Bell, Jr.'s book titled *Race, Racism, and American Law*).

b. Types of Legal Periodicals and Articles

The term "legal periodicals" usually calls to mind law reviews of general scope published by groups of selected students at law schools around the country. These law reviews carry the names of their schools, for example, *Chicago-Kent Law Review, Harvard Law Review,* and *Indiana Law Review.* They are considered general in scope because they publish articles on a wide range of legal topics. Articles in these law reviews tend to be scholarly or theoretical; they generally explore the policies underlying the law, may expose the weaknesses of current legal rules, and advocate new approaches.

DEAN M. RICHARDSON*

Racism: A Tort of Outrage

RACISM is a disease that defies easy remedy. It is an affliction that affects the way people think, feel, and act. When American law has addressed racism, it has concentrated on widely accepted patterns of action or "institutional structures."[1] Consequently, much ugly individual behavior has gone unchallenged. Individual racist acts, even when they clearly violate standards of human decency, usually fall outside the scope of criminal and civil rights laws. Partly out of respect for freedom of thought and speech and partly because racism is so firmly embedded in American culture, the law has had little impact on racist attitudes. This Article argues that the tort of outrage,[2] also called intentional infliction of emotional distress or outrageous conduct, has great potential as a means of recovery for persons injured by racist conduct and as a method for changing racist beliefs and attitudes. The elements of the tort of outrage are explained in Part I; the application of the tort to episodes of racial misconduct is discussed in Part II; cases employing the tort of outrage in a racial context are examined in Part III; special problems are addressed in Part IV.

I

THE TORT OF OUTRAGE

The *Restatement (Second) of Torts* defines the tort of outrage simply: "One who by extreme and outrageous conduct intentionally or

---

* Professor of Law, Willamette University College of Law. B.A. (1966) University of Rochester; J.D. (1969), Syracuse.

[1] An "institutional structure" is any well-established, habitual, or widely accepted pattern of action or organizational arrangement, whether formal or informal. For example, the residential segregation of almost all Negroes in large cities is an "institutional structure." So is the widely used practice of denying employment to applicants with any nontraffic police record because this tends to discriminate unfairly against residents of low-income areas where police normally arrest young men for minor incidents that are routinely overlooked in wealthy suburbs. A. DOWNS, RACISM IN AMERICA AND HOW TO COMBAT IT 5–6 (1970), *quoted in* D. BELL, RACE, RACISM, AND AMERICAN LAW 88 (1972). "Institutional structures" include behavior that is intentional and unintentional. *Id.*

[2] The Washington Supreme Court employed this label in Contreras v. Crown Zellerbach Corp., 88 Wash. 2d 735, 565 P.2d 1173 (1977) (*passim*), and in Grimsby v. Samson, 85 Wash. 2d 52, 530 P.2d 291, 292 (1975).

The *Oregon Law Review,* which published the Richardson article (Illustration 3-19 on page 78), is a general-scope law review.

Most scholarly journals outside of law are edited by prominent scholars. Most law reviews, by contrast, are edited by students; students select each article, evaluate the ideas, verify the support given for the ideas, and edit the author's work. In addition, students write some short pieces and edit each other's work. This experience is widely viewed as very beneficial to the students because it builds research and writing skills. However, some critics have argued that the law's chief vehicle for scholarly discussion should be edited by law faculty or other proven lawyers or scholars. They argue that the complex legal problems discussed in law reviews require experience in the law or interdisciplinary insights most law students do not yet have.

In any event, law reviews publish several types of articles. Long articles with extensive citations written by practitioners, professors, or judges are called "articles"; shorter, less extensively cited pieces by outside authors may be called "essays." On occasion, a law review will publish a feature article by a prominent author followed by short discussions of the feature article, labeled "commentaries." A "symposium" is a collection of articles, with or without student pieces, on the same topic. The Richardson piece on racism is an article in a symposium issue devoted to the topic of race relations.

In general, student pieces are called "notes" or "comments" if they cover a fairly broad topic. Student pieces are called "case notes" or "case comments" or "recent developments" if they cover a narrow topic, such as a new court decision. The label "recent development" is also used for a lengthy survey of an area of law co-written by a group of students. Some issues also contain "book reviews" written by lawyers.

A law review's table of contents generally classifies its contents by these categories. Illustration 3-20 on page 80 shows a table of contents for a special issue or symposium in which all of the pieces are articles. It is important to determine which type of article you are reading in order to evaluate its authoritative weight and to cite it properly. (For convenience, the word "article" is used in the rest of this chapter to refer to any piece in a legal periodical.)

> *Citation Note:* Rule 16 in *The Bluebook* governs citation to articles in legal periodicals. The standard citation consists of the author's name, the article title, the volume number of the law review, the name of the law review, the page number on which the article begins, the page number on which the cited material is located, and a parenthetical containing the date of publication. The name of the law review should be abbreviated according to Table T.13 (in the blue pages). If the law review does not use volume numbers, use the publication date as the volume number and delete the parenthetical date. The proper citation to the second page of the Richardson article from Illustration 3-19 on page 78 is: Dean M. Richardson, *Racism: A Tort of Outrage,* 61 Or. L. Rev. 267, 268 (1982).
>
> Citations to signed pieces written by students include a label, such as "Note" or "Comment," after the author's name. Short signed student articles may be cited by providing the author's name, label (such as "Recent Case"), the volume number, law review abbreviation, page number, and date.
>
> You should consult Rule 16 for special rules for citing book reviews, symposia, and other types of articles and for guidance on matters such as multiple authors and unsigned student work.

1982

OREGON LAW REVIEW

VOLUME 61
NUMBER 2

UNIVERSITY
OF OREGON

AN ISSUE ON
RACE RELATIONS

Contents

Second-class postage paid at Eugene, Oregon 97403
Copyright © 1982 by University of Oregon.

A second category of legal periodicals is the special interest legal periodical. These periodicals generally focus on a well-defined area of law; for example, the *Industrial Relations Law Journal* focuses on labor and employment law. Some special interest periodicals are interdisciplinary, such as the *Journal of Psychiatry and Law*. Special interest periodicals are edited and published by various organizations. Some special interest periodicals are published by law schools and edited by student staffs or faculty; they thus resemble general-scope law reviews in some respects. Other special interest periodicals are published by commercial publishers or bar association sections and are generally called "journals." Their articles typically are less theoretical and more practical than those found in reviews published by law schools.

The third major category of legal periodicals is bar association journals, such as the *ABA Journal*. Many national, state, and local bar associations and sections as well as similar professional organizations publish journals that contain articles on the law as well as news of interest to members. As a general rule, the articles in these journals are more practical than theoretical; they usually focus on how to accomplish a particular legal task. The news in these journals can be of great value. For example, a bar journal may cover changes in court rules or opinions by the state professional responsibility board for lawyers.

Fourth, commercial legal newspapers are exactly what the name suggests: newspapers that report current legal news, important court decisions, changes in court rules, and other legal developments. Some are national in coverage (such as the *National Law Journal*); others cover one city or state.

Finally, commercial publishers publish newsletters on specific legal topics. These newsletters generally are short; are issued monthly, weekly, or even daily; and cover very recent developments. They provide information on new cases, statutes, and regulations, as well as on non-legal developments. Most are not indexed in the finding tools described below in section 2, although many are self-indexed. In very new areas of the law, newsletters can be indispensable.

It is worth noting that non-legal periodicals often are of great interest to lawyers. Many legal problems touch on fields such as medicine and economics. Articles from journals in those fields can provide valuable insight. Chapter 10 covers research in non-legal materials.

c. Publication Media of Legal Periodicals

The traditional and still classic medium in which periodicals are published is print; most periodicals are initially published that way. Some periodicals also appear in other media, including microforms and online databases. Some periodicals appear on CD-ROM. To determine whether your library has a periodical in one of these media, ask your librarian.

2. How to Find Pertinent Articles in Legal Periodicals

Sometimes in the course of your research in other sources, you will find a reference to a legal periodical article. At other times, when you are just beginning your research by looking for an article, you will use a system no different from that used for finding a periodical article of any other sort—an index. There are several major indexes to law reviews, legal journals, and legal newspapers. They are published in various media as well. This chapter covers print, microform, and CD-ROM services. (See Chapter 6 for general coverage of computer-assisted legal research.)

In searching for a legal periodical article, you should keep several strategies in mind. First, determine the years in which the most pertinent and helpful articles probably were published. You generally will want to obtain the most current information available. Recent articles are more useful than older articles, especially if you are looking for an article to provide background on the current state of the law. On the other hand, you may wish to focus on a particular year or two when you know that an important legal development occurred, since periodical articles on a topic generally appear within a year or two of a major development in an area.

Second, to make your research comprehensive, you may well want to locate a good share (if not all) of the articles on point. To do so often requires the use of several research terms. In general, it is wise to look under several subject headings and subheadings. The task of finding related subject headings is facilitated by the cross-reference systems many index services use. You also may wish to search in more than one index, for example, a case index as well as a subject index. (These indexes are described below.)

Third, try to judge which type of article will be most useful to you. For example, an article by a recognized expert in the area is generally preferable to a student-written comment, especially if you are seeking support for a novel legal argument. An article in a bar association journal may be your best choice if you are seeking practical information on how to handle a particular type of case. A symposium is likely to afford a broad range of views and cover several facets of a topic, making it a good starting point as a general rule. For example, the special issue on race relations in the *Oregon Law Review* would be a useful starting point for research of the Perkins problem.

Similarly, be sure to select index services carefully. Index services for legal periodicals are commercial products, and each has features aimed at securing a niche in the legal research market. You should learn those features and choose the service that best suits your research style and the issue you are researching. Among the factors to consider are coverage (number and type of periodicals indexed, as well as years covered), indexing vocabulary and cross-references, types of indexes (subject, author, title, etc.), cumulation schedule, search strategies, and publication media. These features change from time to time as the services modify their products to remain competitive.

Finally, read the instructions for the index service you use, and do so regularly. These instructions may appear in the first few pages of a printed volume, on the front of a microfilm reader, on the first screen or two of a computer program or CD-ROM reader, or in a user's manual.

a. Print Indexes

The traditional medium for periodical indexes is print. Two major print indexes cover most legal periodicals written in English: *Current Law Index* and *Index to Legal Periodicals.* You also may consult several more specialized print indexes from time to time. Table 3.3 on page 83 summarizes the important characteristics of the major print indexes.

(1) Current Law Index

Current Law Index (C.L.I.) is a print service published since 1980 by Information Access Corporation. It indexes over 700 legal periodicals, including law reviews, bar journals, and interdisciplinary journals, from the

TABLE 3.3. Major Print Indexes.   83

Current Law Index since 1980	over 700 general-scope law reviews, special interest periodicals, bar association journals, and journals from law-related fields from the United States, Canada, the United Kingdom, Ireland, Australia, and New Zealand
Index to Legal Periodicals since 1908	over 500 legal periodicals, yearbooks, annual institutes, and annual reviews from the countries covered by *Current Law Index*
Index to Periodical Articles Related to Law since 1958	periodicals not generally covered in the indexes listed above insofar as articles pertain to law and are of research value
Index to Foreign Legal Periodicals since 1960	over 400 primarily non-Anglo-American legal periodicals and periodicals dealing with international and comparative law

United States, Canada, the United Kingdom, Ireland, Australia, and New Zealand. All articles, case notes, and book reviews in covered journals are indexed.

C.L.I. is published twelve times per year, with three issues serving as quarterly cumulations and the final volume as the bound annual cumulation. As with all legal sources published in such a fashion, it is important to consult all of the volumes needed to cover the time frame you are researching. Thus, if you wish to search current law, you should start with the most recent pamphlets and work your way back in time through the bound volumes until you find enough references. If it is likely that articles on your topic appeared in a specific year or two, begin with the volumes for that period.

Each C.L.I. volume contains four separate indexes. The most generally useful index is the subject index (Illustration 3-21 on page 84), which employs the indexing headings developed by the Library of Congress. These headings also are used in most card and online catalogs (see Part C at page 62). Many topics are divided by subheadings; it is useful to scan these before reading the entries so that your research is well focused. It also is wise to review the cross-references found at the beginning or end of a topic for additional headings. The articles are listed by date of publication, with the most recent articles appearing at the beginning of the list of entries under each heading or subheading.

Review the list of potential research terms for the Perkins problem developed in Chapter 2 and restated in Part A of this chapter at page 41. "Mental distress (law)" is a subject heading in C.L.I., and the Richardson article appears under the subheading "analysis" (see Illustration 3-21). Note that C.L.I. provides two cross-references under "mental distress": "negligence" and "torts." Although articles about negligence are not likely to be pertinent to the Perkins problem (because Bartow's conduct was intentional, not negligent), you might consider looking for additional references under "torts."

C.L.I. also contains a table of cases and a table of statutes. These tables index articles that contain substantial analysis and pertain in large part to a single case (or several cases) or statute. These indexes would be useful if you already knew the name of a case or statute for your problem and wished to locate commentary on that authority.

Finally, C.L.I. has an author/title index. You would be most likely to use

ILLUSTRATION 3-21. Subject Index, 4 *Current Law Index* 556 (1983).

MELICETE INDIANS — **SUBJECT INDEX**

MELICETE Indians *see*
Malecite Indians

MELVILLE, Max
Max Melville. (Six of the greatest: a tribute to outstanding lawyers in Colorado history) by Edward E. Pringle *12 Colo. Law. 1073-1074 July '83*

MEMBERSHIP corporations *see*
Corporations, Nonprofit

MEMORIA technica *see*
Mnemonics

MEMORY
Amnesia, confabulation and lying. (National Symposium on Lying - Australian Academy of Forensic Sciences and the World Psychiatric Association - April 23, 1983) (transcript) by A.K. Lethlean *16 Austl. J. For. Sci. 39-45 Sept '83*
Law cover. (practice of law and memory) (New South wales) by Ian S. Bowden *20 Law Soc'y J. 683(2) Nov '82*
Prototype formation of faces: a case of pseudo-memory. (from 72 British Journal of Psychology 499-503, 1981) by Robert L. Solso and Judith E. McCarthy *8 Soc. Act. & L. 83-87 July-Aug '82*
see also
Amnesia
Mnemonics

MEMORY, Disorders of
see also
Amnesia

MEMORY training *see*
Mnemonics

MEMPHIS and Shelby County Bar Association
Memphis bar fires executive director. by Vicki Quade *9 B. Leader 5 Nov-Dec '83*

MEN
The exclusion of women from influential men's clubs: the inner sanctum and the myth of full equality. by Michael M. Burns *18 Harv. C.R.-C.L.L. Rev. 321-407 Summ '83*
Comparing annual and weekly earnings from the Current Population Survey. by Nancy Rytina *v106 Monthly Labor Review p32(5) April '83*
Real Men cry: fighting stereotypes. *11 Human Rights 4 Wntr '83*

MEN, Discrimination against *see*
Sex discrimination against men

MENCAP
A home of one's own. (homes for mentally handicapped people - Great Britain) (editorial) *J. Soc. Welfare L. 129 May '83*

MENDEL'S law
see also
Genetics

MENDENALL Ministries. Community Law Office
The Mendenhall ministry. (Mississippi) by Suzanne Griggins *4 CLS Q. 13-15 Wntr '83*

MENDICANCY *see*
Begging

MENNONITES
see also
Amish

MENOCAL, Armando M., III
How Public Advocates made poverty law (almost) profitable. by Susan Milstein *5 Am. Law. 77-80 Dec '83*
Performance testing: a valuable new dimension or a waste of time and money? by Douglas D. Roche, Armando M. Menocal III, Jane Peterson Smith and Albert M. Sacks *52 B. Exam. 12-29 Nov '83*

MEN'S etiquette *see*
Etiquette for men

MENS rea *see*
Criminal intent

MENSURATION
see also
Measuring instruments

MENTAL depression *see*
Depression, Mental

MENTAL discipline
see also
Memory
Mnemonics

MENTAL distress (law)
see also
negligence
torts

-analysis

Psychological effects at NEPA's threshold. by George J. Skelly *83 Colum. L. Rev. 336-377 March '83*
Dillon revisited: toward a better paradigm for bystander cases. by John David Burley *43 Ohio St. L.J. 931-949 Fall '82*
Liability to bystanders for negligently inflicted emotional harm - a comment on the nature of arbitrary rules. by Richard N. Pearson *34 U. Fla. L. Rev. 477-516 Summ '82*
Racism: a tort of outrage. by Dean M. Richardson *61 Or. L. Rev. 267-283 Spr '82*

-cases

Torts - wrongful death - parent allowed to recover damages for loss of companionship and society as well as damages for mental anguish for death of minor child under Texas Wrongful Death Act. (case note) Sanchez v. Schindler 651 S.W.2d 249 (Tex. 1983) by Vicky Hallick Robbins *15 St. Mary's L.J. 185-205 Wint '83*
Damages - per diem damages in North Carolina. (case note) Weeks v. Holsclaw 295 S.E.2d 596 (N.C. 1982) by Robert S. Thompson *19 Wake Forest L. Rev. 645-674 Aug '83*
The cognizability of psychological impacts under NEPA. (Recent administrative law decisions from the District of Columbia Circuit) (case note) People Against Nuclear Energy v. Nuclear Regulatory Commission 678 F.2d 222 (D.C. Cir. 1982) *42 Md. L. Rev. 619-638 Summ '83*
Tort law - wrongful birth and wrongful life actions - damages - the Pennsylvania Supreme Court has held that an infant cannot bring an action for wrongful life, but parents of the infant can maintain a cause of action for wrongful birth and recover damages for mental distress and physical inconvenience incident to the birth. (case note) Speck v. Finegold 439 A.2d 110 (Pa. 1981) by Margaret M. Boldt *21 Duq. L. Rev. 1113-1136 Summ '83*
Worker's compensation: psychological injury resulting from protracted stress is not compensable through workers' compensation. (Annual Survey of Rhode Island Law for the 1981-1982 Term) (case note) Seitz v. L. & R. Industries 437 A.2d 1345 (R.I. 1981) by Catherine E. Welker *17 Suffolk U.L. Rev. 493-499 Summ '83*
Product manufacturers' strict liability for emotional injuries in Iowa. (case note) Walker v. Clark Equipment Co. 320 N.W.2d 561 (Iowa 1982) by Martha J. Van Vooren *68 Iowa L. Rev. 853-870 May '83*
Torts - mother can recover for mental anguish caused by birth of defective child due to physician's negligence. (case note) Haught v. Maceluch 681 F.2d 291 (5th Cir. 1982) by Leo Camp *21 J. Fam. L. 567-570 May '83*
Nuclear power regulation - NEPA: the D.C. Circuit holds the psychological health effects in the restart of a nuclear reactor are recognized by NEPA and requires the Nuclear Regulatory Commission to evaluate these factors when assessing the safety of restarting the undamaged reactor at Three Mile Island, PA. (case note) by Susan B. Rush *23 Nat. Resources J. 459-466 April '83*
Redefining environmental policy in the stressful aftermath of a nuclear accident. (case note) People against Nuclear Energy v. Nuclear Regulatory Commission 678 F.2d 222 (D.C. Cir. 1982) by Louis J. Caccavaro Jr. *18 New Eng. L. Rev. 449-486 Spr '83*
Tort law - negligence - negligent infliction of emotional distress - bystander recovery - the Supreme Judicial Court of Maine has held that a mother who became emotionally distressed as a result of seeing her infant son gag and choke on foreign material contained in baby food asserted a valid cause of action for negligent infliction of emotional distress. (case note) Culbert v. Sampson's Supermarkets 444 A.2d 433 (Me. 1982) by Samuel F. Reynolds Jr. *21 Duq. L. Rev. 797-814 Spr '83*
Tort law - negligent infliction of emotional distress - should the Florida Supreme Court replace the impact rule with a foreseeability analysis? (case note) Champion v. Gray 420 So. 2d 348 (Fla. Ct. App. 1982) by David Richard Lenox *11 Fla. St. U.L. Rev. 231-254 Spr '83*
Tort law: damages for emotional distress - bystander may recover for mental distress caused by witnessing a negligent act. (case note) by Stacy E. West *61 Wash. U.L.Q. 317-329 Spr '83*
Intentional infliction of emotional distress: cognizable under the federal Tort Claims Act. (case note) Gross v. United States 676 F.2d 295 (8th Cir. 1982) by Bruce M. Ford *28 S.D.L. Rev. 376-387 Spr '83*
Potential psychological harm under NEPA. (case note) People Against Nuclear Energy v. Nuclear Regulatory Commission 678 F.2d 222 (D.C. Cir. 1982) by Jill E. Horner *32 Cath. U.L. Rev. 495-520 Wntr '83*
Torts - mother's claim of child enticement and intentional infliction of emotional distress against her ex-husband as a result of alleged removal of children from her custody is not excluded from federal diversity jurisdiction by the domestic relations exception. (case note) Wasserman v. Wasserman 671 F.2d 832 (4th Cir. 1982) by Kenneth Dunn *21 J. Fam. L. 370-371 Jan '83*
Trial practice - government immunity and liability - while court may raise issue of governmental liability for pain and suffering, sua sponte raising of issue after summation caused defendant unfair surprise and prejudice. (case note)(Survey of recent developments in New Jersey law) Rivera v. Gerner 446 A.2d 508 (N.J. 1982) by Nathalie Berger *13 Seton Hall L. Rev. 435-437 Wntr '83*
Searching for a bright line test. (atomic power-plants) (case note) People Against Nuclear Energy v. Nuclear Regulatory Commission 678 F.2d 222 (D.C. Cir. 1982) by Karen Goodwin *15 Conn. L. Rev. 303-325 Wntr '83*
Allowing a bystander to recover emotional distress damages caused by witnessing peril to a victim. (case note) Walker v. Clark Equipment Co. 320 N.W.2d 561 (Iowa 1982) by Sharon Ficquette *6 Am. J. Trial Advocacy 356-358 Fall '82*
Environmental - Three Mile Island in your neighborhood. (case note) People Against Nuclear Energy v. Nuclear Regulatory Commission 51 U.S.L.W. 3339 (1982) by Lynn Thomas Ziolko *1982 Ariz. St. L.J. 1009-1029 Fall '82*
Infliction of mental distress absent physical injury. (case note) Kennedy v. McKeeson Co. 451 N.Y.S.2d 530 (1982) by Bob Moletteire *6 Am. J. Trial Advocacy 355-356 Fall '82*
Landlord-tenant - Massachusetts Supreme Judicial Court awards damages to tenant for emotional distress caused by landlord's substandard maintenance of apartment. (case note) Simon v. Solomon 431 N.E.2d 556 (Mass. 1982) by Joseph A. Lambert *16 Suffolk U.L. Rev. 865-881 Fall '82*
Insurance law - emotional distress damages in commercial contract action - emotional distress damages are not recoverable by insured for breach of disability insurance contract absent proof that damages for emotional distress were contemplated by the parties at the time of contract formation. (case note) Kewin v. Massachusetts Mutual Life Insurance Co. 295 N.W.2d 50 (Mich. 1980) by Randall J. Bramer *60 U. Det. J. Urb. L. 120-136 Fall '82*
Intentional infliction of emotional distress - escaping the impact rule in Arkansas. (case note) M.B.M. Co. v. Counce 596 S.W.2d 681 (Ark. 1980) by Ronald E. Goins *35 Ark. L. Rev. 53-548 Summ '82*
Torts: parent who hears about injury to child after accident occurs and subsequently witnesses child's death in hospital cannot recover for resulting emotional distress. (Pennsylvania Supreme Court Review, 1981) (case note) Yandrich v. Radic 433 A.2d 459 (Pa. 1981) by Andrea L. Parry *55 Temp. L.Q. 781-801 Summ '82*
Torts: Pennsylvania recognizes action for wrongful birth and full damage recovery but denies child's wrongful-life action. (Pennsylvania Supreme Court Review, 1981) (case note) Speck v. Finegold 439 A.2d 110 (Pa. 1981) by William Hildenbrand *55 Temp. L.Q. 810-842 Summ '82*
Torts - loss of consortium - right of a child to a cause of action for loss of society and companionship when the parent is tortiously injured. (case note) Berger v. Weber 303 N.W.2d 424 (Mich. 1981) by Veleta P. Brooks-Burkett *28 Wayne L. Rev. 1877-1899 Summ '82*
Expanding loss of parental society and negligent infliction of emotional distress - allowing recovery despite worker's compensation exclusive remedy provisions. (case note) Ferriter v. Daniel O'Connell's Sons, Inc. 413 N.E.2d 690 (Mass. 1980) by Janet M. Boes *13 U. Tol. L. Rev. 1401-1436 Summ '82*
Insurer's liability for bad faith damages. (case note) Timmons v. Royal Globe Insurance Co. 53 Okla. B.J. 1898 (1982) by Stephanie L. Jones *18 Tulsa L.J. 348-358 Wntr '82*
Negligent infliction of emotional distress absent physical impact or subsequent physical injury. (case note) Molien v. Kaiser Foundation Hospitals 616 P.2d 813 (Cal. 1980) by Carl J. Spector *47 Mo. L. Rev. 124-133 Wntr '82*
Remedy for an odious diagnostic error. (case note) Molien v. Kaiser Foundation Hospitals 27 Cal. 3d 916 (1980) by Rosalyn Flitcraft *14 U.W.L.A.L. Rev. 61-88 Ann '82*
The need for workers' compensation reform in Ohio's definition of injury. (case note) Szymanski v. Halle's Department Store 407 N.E.2d 502 (Ohio 1980) by Ellen L. Knight *31 Clev. St. L. Rev. 145-173 Wntr '82*
Arguing per diem damages in summation. (case note) Cox v. Valley Fair Corp. 83 N.J. 381 (1980) by Aimee L. Manocchio *11 Seton Hall L. Rev. 461-498 Spr '81*

-evaluation

In death cases, do husbands suffer greater mental anguish than wives over the loss of the opposite spouse? Grief over a wife's death as a subsequent cause of death to the husband. *30 Current Med. 1-2 May '83*

-history

Payment for pain and suffering through history. by Jeffrey O'Connell and Keith Carpenter *50 Ins. Counsel J. 411-417 July '83*

-law and legislation

Emotional distress damages for cancerphobia: a case for the DES daughter. by Corey Scott Cramin *14 Pac. L.J. 1215-1239 July '83*
Malicious, intentional and negligent mental distress in Florida. by Patricia V. Russo *11 Fla. St. U.L. Rev. 339-367 Summ '83*
Debt collection practices: Iowa remedies for abuse of debtors' rights. by William A. Reilly II *68 Iowa L. Rev. 753-785 May '83*
Administering the tort of negligent infliction of mental distress: a synthesis. by Terri Krivosha Herring *4 Cardozo L. Rev. 487-518 Spr '83*
The employment-at-will doctrine: recent judicial developments. by Eric A. Taussig *19 Law Notes 43-52 Spr '83*
Negligent injury to family relationships: a reevaluation of the logic of liability. by Laurie J. Barsella *77 Nw. U.L. Rev. 794-817 Feb '83*
Making up for lost time: recovering for shortened life expectancy. by Nicole Schultheisw and Paul D. Rheingold *19 Trial 44-47 Feb '83*
Negligence and financial loss. (Great Britain) by Alec Samuels *127 Solicitor's J. 60-61 Jan 28 '83*
Loss of consortium and engaged couples: the frustrating fate of faithful fiancees. by Kris Treu *44 Ohio St. L.J. 219-237 Wntr '83*
New package, old toy: The Alabama Supreme Court recognizes the tort of outrageous conduct. by Kimberly W. West *34 Ala. L. Rev. 181-196 Wntr '83*
Liability for negligently inflicted nervous shock. (Great Britain) by Harvey Teff *99 Law Q. Rev. 100-112 Jan '83*
Damages for injured feelings in Australia. by Peter R. Handford *5 U. New S. Wales L.J. 291-308 Dec '82*

556

this index if you wished to locate articles by a particular author or reviews of a particular book. As with the tables of cases and statutes, you are most likely to use this index at a late stage in your research.

(2) Index to Legal Periodicals

The *Index to Legal Periodicals* (I.L.P.) dates to 1908 and is the most established index to legal periodicals. I.L.P. indexes articles in over 500 legal periodicals from the same countries covered by C.L.I. Very short articles are not indexed. Thus, I.L.P. is more inclusive than C.L.I. because it is an older service; I.L.P. is also less inclusive because it covers fewer articles per year.

In format, I.L.P. both resembles and diverges from C.L.I. It follows much the same publication and cumulation schedule as C.L.I. I.L.P. contains a subject index that is merged with the author index (Illustration 3-22 on page 86). While I.L.P. uses a system of headings, subheadings, and cross-references as does C.L.I., the headings are not necessarily the same as in C.L.I. Some researchers perceive that the I.L.P. headings are more "legal," while C.L.I. uses headings that are closer to ordinary English. I.L.P. lists articles alphabetically by title, rather than by date of publication. A nice feature of I.L.P. is the list of subject headings found at the beginning of recent bound volumes.

I.L.P. also publishes a thesaurus that provides terms that are narrower ("NT") or broader ("BT") than the term you have looked up or are related to it ("RT") (much like the listing of Library of Congress headings). The thesaurus also signifies those terms that are most useful with the designation "USE." (See Illustration 3-13 on page 63.)

Again, recall the list of research terms developed for the Perkins problem. A search for articles in I.L.P. in the 1982-1983 volume under "mental distress" (the term that worked well in C.L.I.) would not yield the Richardson article for two reasons. First, I.L.P. uses the term "emotional distress" in lieu of "mental distress." (Note the importance of generating synonyms for your research terms!) Second, I.L.P. does not list the Richardson article under "emotional distress" (perhaps because the title refers to the tort of "outrage") but rather under the broader heading of "torts." (Note the importance of extending the ladder of abstraction developed in Chapter 2!) See Illustration 3-22.

Finally, I.L.P. contains a table of cases and a table of statutes, as does C.L.I. I.L.P. also contains a book review index.

(3) Other Print Indexes

There are many other print indexes to legal periodicals. In certain fields, such as tax, there are specialty index services. The *Index to Periodical Articles Related to Law* (I.P.A.R.L.) indexes periodicals not covered in other major indexes—including social science, business, and technical journals as well as popular magazines—insofar as their articles pertain to law.

If your research pertains to the law of a particular foreign jurisdiction, you may wish to consult an index covering journals from that country, such as the *Index to Canadian Legal Periodical Literature* and *Legal Journals Index* (for British law). The *Index to Foreign Legal Periodicals* (I.F.L.P.) indexes over 400 legal periodicals and other sources covering international and comparative law and the law of countries other than the United States, United Kingdom, Canada, and Australia.

Some law reviews periodically publish indexes to their own recent volumes. These indexes, which generally are bound along with the law review's issues, usually are organized by subject, title, and author. An index of this

TORTS—*Continued*

Property—landlord and tenant—exculpatory clause in residential lease absolving lessor of tort liability for common areas is void as against public policy. 52 Miss L J 913-25 D '82

Proving loss of consortium: the view from another perspective. G. D. Gage. 19 Trial 56-7 F '83

Psychiatric malpractice: identifying areas of liability. A. F. Wilkinson. 18 Trial 73-7 O '82

Public policy exception to the employment-at-will rule: Illinois creates an amorphous tort: Palmateer v. International Harvester Co. 421 N E 2d 876 (Ill) 59 Chi-Kent L Rev 247-85 '82

Punitive damages in constitutional tort actions 57 Notre Dame Law 530-46 F '82

Question of seduction: the case of Macmillan v. Brownlee [[1940] 2 W W R 455] T. Thorner, G. N. Reddekopp. 20 Alta L Rev 447-74 '82

Racism: a tort of outrage. D. M. Richardson. 61 Or L Rev 267-83 '82

Recent trends in school tort immunity. J. Siegel. 71 Ill B J 240-6 D '82

Recognition and recovery for bad faith torts. R. Bourhis. 18 Trial 46-9+ D '82

Recognizing and meeting medical malpractice defenses. C. D. Burt. 18 Trial 46-8 O '82

Renteria v. County of Orange et al [147 Cal Rptr 447]: civil action against employer and fellow employees for intentional tort not barred by exclusive remedy provision of workmen's compensation act. 12 U W L A L Rev 125-36 Spr '80

Requiem for a heavyweight: a farewell to Warren and Brandeis's privacy tort. D. L. Zimmerman. 68 Cornell L Rev 291-367 Mr '83

Rocking the torts. 46 Mod L Rev 224-31 Mr '83

Silkwood v. Kerr-McGee Corp (667 F 2d 908): preemption of state law for nuclear torts? 12 Envtl L 1059-81 Summ '82

Slipping and falling accidents. C. Bennett. 126 S J 600-2 S 17 '82

Smith v. Atlas Off-Shore Boat Services (653 F 2d 1057): retaliatory discharge, a new maritime tort. 22 S Tex L J 605-12 '82

Some thoughts on the constitutionality of Good Samaritan statutes. B. Sullivan. 8 Am J L & Med 27-43 Spr '82

Sovereign immunity—discretionary function exemption to the Tort Claims Act: Larson v. Independent School District No. 314. 289 N W 2d 112 (Minn) 5 Hamline L Rev 103-21 Ja '82

Statutory and common law considerations in defining the tort liability of public employee unions to private citizens for damages inflicted by illegal strikes. 80 Mich L Rev 1271-302 My '82

Statutory reform of "toxic torts": relieving legal, scientific, and economic burdens on the chemical victim. J. Trauberman. 7 Harv Envtl L Rev 177-296 '83

Statutory vicarious parental liability: review and reform. 32 Case W Res L Rev 559-93 '82

Step backward for the infant plaintiff in preconception tort actions: Albala v. City of New York [429 N E 2d 786 (NY)] 15 Conn L Rev 161-81 Fall '82

Successor landowner liability for environmental torts: robbing Peter to pay Paul? 13 Rutgers L J 329-59 Wint '82

Superfunds and tort law reforms—are they insurable? R. A. Schmalz. 38 Bus Law 175-92 N '82

Surgeons and anesthesiologists, vicarious liability and the continued trend toward specialization and decentralization in the operating room. 9 Ohio North L Rev 437-64 Jl '82

Survey of bad faith claims in first party and industrial proceedings. L. D. Bess, J. A. Doherty. 49 Ins Counsel J 368-75 Jl '82

Taming of a duty—the tort liability of landlords. O. L. Browder. 81 Mich L Rev 99-156 N '82

Terrorism as a tort in violation of the law of nations. 6 Fordham Int'l L J 236-60 82/'83

Thomas v. Inmon [594 S W 2d 853 (Ark)]: parental immunity in Arkansas statement of the case. 35 Ark L Rev 509-18 '81

To certify or not to certify: the use of the class action device in mass tort litigation. L. L. Rivkin, J. Silberfeld. 33 Fed'n Ins Counsel Q 105-29 Wint '83

Tort & workmen's compensation law—recognizing a child's action for loss of parental consortium: reconciling cognate actions with workmen's compensation provisions: Ferriter v. Daniel O'Connell's Sons, Inc., 413 N E 2d 690 (Mass) 15 Suffolk U L Rev 1082-103 Jl '81

Tort law—merchant's duty to protect its customers from third-party criminal acts—Foster v. Winston-Salem Joint Venture [281 S E 2d 36 (NC)] 18 Wake Forest L Rev 114-33 F '82

Tort law—negligence—requirement of specificity of victim as a prerequisite to imposition of a duty to warn in third party situations. Thompson v. County of Alameda [614 P 2d 728 (Cal)] N. Rubin. 4 Glendale L Rev 166-88 '79/'80

Tort liability for cult deprogramming: Peterson v. Sorlien [299 N W 2d 123 (Minn)] 43 Ohio St L J 465-89 '82

Tort of custodial interference—toward a more complete remedy to parental kidnappings. 1983 U Ill L Rev 229-60 '83

Tort—worker compensation—employer immunity—an employee is not precluded by the Ohio workers' compensation laws from enforcing a common law remedy for intentional torts committed by his employer. Blankenship v. Cincinnati Milacron Chemicals, Inc. 433 N E 2d 572 (Ohio) 51 U Cin L Rev 682-96 '82

Torts—abrogation of parental immunity—Anderson v. Stream, 295 N W 2d 595 (Minn) 8 Wm Mitchell L Rev 273-83 '82

Torts—an unemancipated minor can maintain an action against his parent for negligence torts committed outside the area of parental authority and discretion—Turner v. Turner [304 N W 2d 786 (Iowa)] 31 Drake L Rev 948-54 '81/'82

Torts and trials: fifty years of evolution. M. M. Belli, sr. 19 Trial 36-8 Jl '83

Torts: comparative negligence: intrafamily immunity: parental liability for juvenile vandalism; bystander liability; wrongful birth; the constitutionality of medical malpractice statutes; and the Federal Torts Claims Act. 1982 Ann Surv Am L 373-429 F '83

Torts: civil liability in the use of deadly force in North Carolina. 4 Campbell L Rev 391-409 Spr '82

Torts—damages—procedure of discounting damage awards to present value abandoned under federal law in order to account for the effect of future inflation: Pfeifer v. Jones & Laughlin Steel Corp., 678 F 2d 453 28 Vill L Rev 253-70 N '82

Torts—husband's gunpoint rape of wife constituted "intentional," "outrageous" conduct not subject to doctrine of interspousal immunity. Lusby v. Lusby, 390 A.2d 77 (Md) 6 Tex S U L Rev 463-80 '81

Torts—immunity—sovereign immunity is unavailable as a defense in tort actions against the state or its political subdivisions. 53 Miss L J 227-36 Mr '83

Torts in sports—"I'll see you in court!" 16 Akron L Rev 537-53 Wint '83

Torts—interspousal immunity in Kansas: a vestige of a bygone era—Guffy v. Guffy [631 P 2d 646 (Kan)] 30 Kan L Rev 611-24 Summ '82

Torts—loss of consortium—child who suffers loss of society and companionship may bring an action for loss of parental consortium when parent is negligently injured. Berger v. Weber, 303 N W 2d 424 (Mich) 60 U Det J Urb L 137-51 Fall '82

Torts—loss of consortium—right of a child to a cause of action for loss of society and companionship when the parent is tortiously injured. 28 Wayne L Rev 1877-99 Summ '82

Torts—medical malpractice—locality rule requires that physicians be held to standard of reasonably competent practitioner in Mississippi or adjacent area. 53 Miss L J 353-68 Je '83

Torts—Ohio parental immunity role—an unemancipated child is barred by the Ohio rule of parental immunity from recovery in a negligence suit instituted against its parent—Karam v. Allstate Insurance Co. 436 N E 2d 1014 (Ohio) 12 Cap U L Rev 173-7 Fall '82

Torts opinions of Judge Domenick L. Gabrielli. R. J. Tymann. 47 Alb L Rev 323-32 Wint '83

Torts—parent-child—negligent supervision and instruction protected by parent-child immunity—Foldi v. Jeffries, 440 A 2d 58 (NJ) 13 Seton Hall L Rev 398-413 '83

Torts—parental immunity: a time for change. Ard v. Ard, 414 So 2d 1066 (Fla) 35 U Fla L Rev 181-8 Wint '83

Torts—sovereign immunity trilogy:—Commercial Carrier [Commercial Carrier Corp. v. Indian River County, 371 So 2d 1010 (Fla)] revisited but not refined—Department of Transportation v. Neilson, 419 So 2d 1071 (Fla); Ingham v. Department of Transp. 419 So 2d 1081 (Fla); City of St. Petersburg v. Collom, 419 So 2d 1082 (Fla) 10 Fla St U L Rev 702-22 Wint '83

Toxic tort litigation: the management challenge. A. M. Keller. 19 Trial 50-4 Ap '83

Trade disputes, economic torts and the constitution: the legacy of Talbot [Talbot (Ireland) Ltd. v. Merrigan. Judgment of April 30, 1981 Supreme Court, Ireland] T. Kerr. 16 Ir Jur 214-61 Wint '81

Uncommon law rule of liability for slip and fall accidents: Stewart v. 104 Wallace Street, Inc. [432 A 2d 881 (NJ)] & Mirza v. Filmore Corporation [456 A 2d 518 (NJ)] 35 Rutgers L Rev 425-52 Wint '83

What behavior constitutes sexual harassment? P. Linenberger. 34 Lab L J 238-47 Ap '83 sort can be helpful if there is a specialty journal in the subject area you are researching.

b. Alternatives to Print Indexes

Some of the print indexes described above, including C.L.I. and I.L.P., are available in non-print formats as well. These formats afford the benefits of total cumulation and additional search methods. This section focuses on the CD-ROM version of C.L.I., because (as of the writing of this book) it is the most widely available service. Table 3.4 below summarizes the information in this section.

(1) LegalTrac

LegalTrac is a CD-ROM service that encompasses the material found in C.L.I. and more. *LegalTrac* covers over 800 major English-language legal periodicals as well as selected articles from other periodicals. It dates back to 1980 and is updated monthly.

LegalTrac is a totally cumulative service: All listings on a topic appear in a single listing under a subject heading. Thus, you need not collect and page through multiple volumes as with C.L.I. The feature of total cumulation is one of the major advantages of *LegalTrac*. Of course, CD-ROM disks have limited capacity. At some point, the capacity will be exceeded; it may then be necessary to consult multiple disks.

To search *LegalTrac*, you simply start the *LegalTrac* reader and enter your research term when prompted to do so. When there is an exact match between your term and a *LegalTrac* heading, *LegalTrac* will present a screen with your term highlighted. If there is no exact match, you will receive a message to that effect as well as the heading that best matches your subject alphabetically. Once you have found an appropriate heading, you may wish to browse the subheadings and related headings listed on the screen by paging up and down several screens.

When you have identified the best heading and subheading, press the "ENTER" key to obtain a listing of pertinent articles (see Illustration 3-23 on page 88). Press the "PRINT" key to obtain a print-out of pertinent citations.

If you were to use *LegalTrac* to find articles for the Perkins problem and entered the term "mental distress," you would come to the heading of "Mental Distress (Law)" with 27 subtopics. As of fall 1991, there were 38 articles listed under the subheading "Analysis"; the Richardson article was number 29. The Richardson article also could be found by searching "racism," where it is the first entry under the subheading "Remedies."

The cumulative nature and wide coverage of *LegalTrac* are apparent when you compare Illustrations 3-21 and 3-23. There are only 4 articles listed in the C.L.I. 1983 volume under "Mental distress (law)—analysis," while there

TABLE 3.4. Media of Periodical Indexes.

Current Law Index	print
	CD-ROM (*LegalTrac*)
	microform (*Legal Resource Index*)
	also online
Index to Legal Periodicals	print
	CD-ROM (*WILSONDISC*)
	also online

```
                                              LegalTrac database
MENTAL DISTRESS (LAW)
 -Analysis


    1.      Stress claims 'crisis' blamed on settlements:
            judges cites insurers' laxity. (California) by Hallye
            Jordan 37 col in. v104 The Los Angeles Daily Journal
            July 11 '91 p1 col 2



    2.      Sources of judicial reluctance to use psychic harm
            as a basis for suppressing racist, sexist and
            ethnically offensive speech. by David Goldberger v56
            Brooklyn Law Review Wntr '91 p1165-1212




    29.     Racism: a tort of outrage. by Dean M. Richardson
            v61 Oregon Law Review Spr '82 p267-283



    30.     Real estate broker liable for emotional distress.
            by Joseph Posner 24 col in. v95 The Los Angeles Daily
            Journal March 26 '82 p4 col 4
```

are 38 under the same heading and subheading in *LegalTrac.* Some of the *LegalTrac* entries would not appear in C.L.I., for example, the *Los Angeles Daily Journal* article (entry number 30).

As you become more advanced in your knowledge of a subject and in your use of *LegalTrac,* you may wish to try additional search strategies. For example, you can search for articles by a specific author by using the method described above. You can focus your subject search by use of the "expanded search" method, which allows you to enter not only a subject heading but also an important term that you believe will appear somewhere in the entries for pertinent articles. Press the "HELP" key to obtain information on how to do this.

(2) Other Services

The information available through *LegalTrac* is also available in a less popular and useful medium, microfilm, under the name *Legal Resource Index* (L.R.I.). L.R.I. is a cross between C.L.I. and *LegalTrac.* It cumulates years of entries, as does *LegalTrac.* But it is used by scrolling through the pages on the microfilm reader, much as C.L.I. is used by flipping through print pages.

WILSONDISC is a service that parallels *LegalTrac* in many respects. It comes in CD-ROM format. Its basic search method parallels that of *LegalTrac:*

entry of a research term or name, review of a screen of alphabetically similar headings, selection of the preferred heading, and then review of the citations listed under that heading. A second search method permits you to enter words you expect to find in pertinent entries; the researcher fills these words into a set of blanks (such as author/name or subject).

WILSONDISC differs from *LegalTrac* in that its base is the I.L.P. index, not C.L.I. Coverage of I.L.P. begins in 1981. WILSONDISC also encompasses over 20 other indexes, such as the *Social Sciences Index.*

c. Methods of Finding Very Recent Articles: Current Awareness Services

Although the time lag between the issuance of a legal periodical and its appearance in the indexes described above is relatively short, you may wish to consult a "current awareness service," which provides virtually immediate listings of newly issued legal periodical articles. *Current Index to Legal Periodicals* (C.I.L.P.), for example, lists newly issued articles by subject matter and sets out the tables of contents of new issues. C.I.L.P. covers over 300 legal periodicals, is issued weekly, and is produced in print and online. Check with your library's reference staff for any other such services carried by your library.

d. Summary

As you develop research skills, you probably also will develop preferences for certain research tools. In choosing among periodical indexes, consider such factors as these:

(1) The dates of articles you wish to find: Only I.L.P. covers articles published before the 1980s. More recent articles are covered in I.L.P., C.L.I., and their microform and CD-ROM equivalents.

(2) The periodicals you wish to search: Although the major indexes (I.L.P., C.L.I., and their related services) cover many journals, they do not cover all periodical articles. For example, you will need to consult I.P.A.R.L. for articles from other fields that are related to law. If your research is in a specialized field such as tax law, a specialty index may be most appropriate.

(3) How focused your search is: The CD-ROM services permit searches that are narrower than the subject headings and subheadings of the print indexes.

(4) Your preferences as to medium: If you work well browsing in a book, consider the print indexes. If you prefer to hone in closely on a list of potential articles, consider the CD-ROM services. Note that there are slight differences between print indexes, such as the order in which articles are listed under the subject headings.

It is important to be reasonably proficient in more than one index because few libraries will contain a full selection. You should take some time to experiment with various index services.

3. *Shepard's Law Review Citations*

On occasion, you will find an article that addresses your issue directly and sets forth an important new idea. You may want to know whether the idea has been received favorably by courts or other legal scholars. *Shepard's*

Law Review Citations enables you to locate references to law review articles found in court decisions and other law reviews (Illustration 3-24 below). You will encounter *Shepard's Citations* again in Chapter 5; the following is a brief introduction.

The first step in using *Shepard's Citations* is to identify your "cited source." If you are interested in finding out whether the Richardson article (Illustration 3-19 on page 78) has been referred to by courts or other law review writers, the Richardson article would be your "cited source." It is found in volume 61 of the *Oregon Law Review,* starting at page 267. Thus, you would look up *Oregon Law Review,* volume 61, page 267 in *Shepard's.* Under that heading you would find a list of "citing sources," that is, published court decisions and law review articles that refer to the Richardson article. The first number in each entry is a volume number, the second a page number where the reference to the cited source may be found. To decipher what the abbreviation in the middle means, you would use the table of abbreviations at the front of the *Shepard's* volume. For example, the citing source reference

ILLUSTRATION 3-24. *Shepard's* Entries for the Richardson Article, in *Shepard's Law Review Citations* 501 (Supp. 1986-1990).

OREGON LAW REVIEW

Vol. 61

Vol. 54	Vol. 55	Vol. 56	Vol. 57	Vol. 58	Vol. 59	Vol. 60	Vol. 61
—293—	—3—	—3—	—3—	—3—	—3—	—59—	—3—
49LLR608	W Va	67OLR49	19UCD411	14FSU26	30Buf112	20LWR387	67OLR112
52MoL18	164WV272	67OLR69		60NDL949	40FLR714	22LWR1	
	66OLR224	67OLR110	—31—		36SCR415	64OLR66	—157—
—337—		67OLR586	Haw	—61—		11WmM989	34Buf96
Ore	—85—		762P2d175	74CaL70	—43—		1988BYU368
305Ore284	65OLR554	—31—			Ore	—157—	1987DCL810
751P2d774		71ILR679	—51—	—151—	300Ore209	19EnL303	38LR5
	—197—	41StnL1550	66TxL812	7ALJ642	709P2d232	22LWR17	44MdL740
—539—	67OLR110			15Cap2	39HLJ974	64OLR66	81NwL595
100HLR1044		—191—	—203—	88CR276			41RLR1170
	—227—	65OLR572	34Buf742	22Goz513	—159—		39StnL335
	Ore		53ChL750	85McL433	1986IILR409		57UCR1206
	76OrA601	—235—	72Cor65	16VLP217	56JBK(9)33		13WmM706
	711P2d139	Ore	1986IILR600				
		303Ore14	55KCR190	—311—	—243—		—201—
	—479—	734P2d1334	61NDL380	28AzL535	30VR1184		1989BYU95
	22HUL968	66OLR225	62NYL495	20UCD221			38Cth842
	50LCP(2)30		67TxL711		—363—		17RLJ487
		—287—	21VLP79	—411—	Ore		25SDL1044
	—493—	26Wsb420	21VLP98	N J	300Ore28		41StnL50
	Ore		30VR729	109NJ73	303Ore286		20Suf863
	83OrA129	—331—	92WVL60	533A2d393	706P2d932		30W&M47
	730P2d615	Okla		1985DuL410	735P2d616		13WmM714
	70MnL772	775P2d868	—377—	72VaL318	66OLR284		
		Ore	39HLJ846	64WsL784			—245—
		97OrA82	101HLR666				40AkL800
				—483—			27AzL397
		—539—	—399—	N C			30AzL419
		65OLR530	39HLJ844	323NC274			56ChL695
		72VaL1064		372SE719			
			—505—				—267—
			Del				35Buf152
			550A2d1119				103HLR654
			66WQ674				41StnL12
							—317—
							35Buf89
							17RLJ484
							25SDL1066
							13WmM720

to "35Bufl52" indicates that the Richardson article is referred to at page 52 of volume 35 of the *Buffalo Law Review.*

Shepard's Law Review Citations began publication in 1957 and now covers articles published in over 200 law reviews. *Shepard's* consists of bound volumes updated by one or more softcover or paper pamphlets. In using any set of *Shepard's,* you should always be sure that you have checked all pertinent volumes. Look on the cover of the most recent pamphlet for the list of volumes to collect.

E. A.L.R. ANNOTATIONS

1. What Is an A.L.R. Annotation?

Lawyers Cooperative Publishing writes and publishes a substantial research source entitled "American Law Reports." Called "A.L.R." for short, this source probably occupies one or two aisles in your law library. These A.L.R. volumes contain two kinds of resources: cases and "annotations." Each annotation and its related case cover the same legal topic. However, you hardly ever will use A.L.R. as a source of cases because Rule 10.3.1 of *The Bluebook* prefers two other types of case reporters over A.L.R. (See Chapter 5 on cases.) Thus, your main reason for consulting A.L.R. is to find an annotation that addresses your research topic.

An annotation is an article covering a topic that is considerably narrower than a topic heading in an encyclopedia and about the same breadth as the subject of many legal periodical articles. Most annotations tend to focus on issues of current controversy (especially when the courts are split or inconsistent) and on issues that are factually sensitive (when a case with similar facts would be helpful). These topics are frequently in areas such as torts, property, contracts, evidence, and criminal law. Annotations also address constitutional, administrative, and statutory issues. Each annotation is written by an attorney on the publisher's staff.

A.L.R. has been published in series over the following years:

A.L.R.1st (1919-1948)
A.L.R.2d (1948-1965)
A.L.R.3d (1965-1980)
A.L.R.4th (1980-1991)
A.L.R.5th (1992 to date)
A.L.R. Fed. (1969 to date)

Until 1969, A.L.R.1st, A.L.R.2d, and A.L.R.3d covered both state and federal topics. Since 1969, A.L.R. Fed. has covered federal topics, while A.L.R.3d and A.L.R.4th have covered state topics. A.L.R.5th, introduced in 1992, follows the same convention. Each year, a handful of new volumes is added to the A.L.R.5th and A.L.R. Fed. series. Contrary to what you might think, the annotations in each new series of A.L.R. do not necessarily replace or update the annotations in the previous series, nor does the new series contain the same topics as the previous series. However, some early A.L.R. annotations have been superseded by more up-to-date annotations in later series. Because many of the annotations in the first and second series have been superseded or have become outdated, this chapter focuses on the third, fourth, fifth, and federal series.

ANNOTATION

MODERN STATUS OF INTENTIONAL INFLICTION OF MENTAL DISTRESS AS INDEPENDENT TORT; "OUTRAGE"

TOTAL CLIENT-SERVICE LIBRARY® REFERENCES

38 Am Jur 2d, Fright, Shock, and Mental Disturbance §§ 1, 2, 4–12

Annotations: See the related matters listed in the annotation, infra.

8 Am Jur Pl. & Pr Forms (Rev), Damages, Forms 201 et seq.; 12 Am Jur Pl & Pr Forms (Rev), Fright, Shock, and Mental Disturbance, Forms 21–26

3 Am Jur Proof of Facts 722, Damages, Proof 32, Mental Anguish

5 Am Jur Trials 921, Showing Pain and Suffering; 23 Am Jur Trials 479, Determining the Medical and Emotional Bases for Damages

US L Ed Digest, Damages §§ 153–157; Torts §§ 1, 3

L Ed Index to Annos, Damages; Intent; Torts

ALR Quick Index, Damages; Emotional Disturbance; Intentional Tort; Mental Anguish; Shock; Torts

Federal Quick Index, Damages; Emotional Distress; Intentional Torts; Mental Anguish; Torts

Auto-Cite®: Any case citation herein can be checked for form, parallel references, later history, and annotation references through the Auto-Cite computer research system.

In addition, most A.L.R. annotations are updated in minor respects in their own pocket-part supplements.

The format of annotations in A.L.R.3d and A.L.R.4th generally follows the format of the annotation in Illustration 3-25 on pages 92-95. Note the following features of this annotation:

(1) title

(2) Total Client-Service Library References (these are citations to related materials published by this publisher, Lawyers Cooperative Publishing)

(3) table of contents for this annotation

(4) index to this annotation

(5) Table of Jurisdictions Represented (including sections in which cases in that jurisdiction appear)

(6) text of the annotation, organized by section, as shown in the table of contents:

    (a) Scope (of this annotation)

    (b) Related matters (cites to related A.L.R. annotations)

ILLUSTRATION 3-25. *(continued)* 93

38 ALR4th   Torts—Intentional Mental Distress
38 ALR4th 998

Modern status of intentional infliction of mental distress as independent tort; "outrage"

INDEX

TABLE OF JURISDICTIONS REPRESENTED
Consult POCKET PART in this volume for later cases

(c) Background and summary

(d) cases recognizing intentional infliction of emotional distress as an independent tort (including cases from Kansas, the jurisdiction of the Perkins situation)

(e) cases declining to recognize intentional infliction of emotional distress as an independent tort

(f) a split among the Florida cases

The organization of the items in (6)(d), (e), and (f) is typical of an A.L.R. annotation. A.L.R. annotations frequently catalog the splits among and in jurisdictions.

ILLUSTRATION 3-25. *(continued)* 95

Ind: §§ 4	**SD:** §§ 3
Iowa: §§ 3	**Tenn:** §§ 3
Kan: §§ 3	**Tex:** §§ 4
Ky: §§ 4	**Utah:** §§ 3
Me: §§ 3	**Vt:** §§ 3
Md: §§ 3	**Va:** §§ 3
Mass: §§ 3	**Wash:** §§ 3
Mich: §§ 3	**W Va:** §§ 3
Minn: §§ 3	**Wis:** §§ 3

§ 1. Introduction

[a] Scope

This annotation collects and analyzes the state and federal cases decided since 1970[1] in which the courts have explicitly recognized or refused to recognize the existence of the independent tort more or less interchangably referred to as "the inten-

---

§ 1[a] TORTS—INTENTIONAL MENTAL DISTRESS 38 ALR4th
38 ALR4th 998

tional infliction of emotional distress," or "outrage."

Outside the scope of this annotation are cases which, in discussing or disposing of claims for the intentional infliction of emotional distress, only implicitly recognize or refuse to recognize the existence of such a cause of action and which contain no discussion of the elements of the tort.

The purpose of the present annotation is thus not to reveal the factual circumstances under which claims for the intentional infliction of emotional distress have succeeded and failed, but rather to collect cases reflecting the recognition or nonrecognition of the tort, in general, in the various jurisdictions.

[b] Related matters

Civil liability for insulting or abusive language—modern status. 20 ALR4th 773.

lessly causing employee emotional distress. 86 ALR3d 454.

Liability of hospital or similar institution for giving erroneous notification of patient's death. 77 ALR3d 501.

Recovery for mental or emotional distress resulting from injury to, or death of, member of plaintiff's family arising from physician's or hospital's wrongful conduct. 77 ALR3d 447.

Recovery of damages for emotional distress resulting from discrimination because of sex or marital status. 61 ALR3d 944.

Recovery for mental anguish or emotional distress, absent independent physical injury, consequent upon breach of contract in connection with sale of real property. 61 ALR3d 922.

Civil liability of undertaker in connection with embalming or preparation of body for burial. 48 ALR3d 261.

Annotations in the A.L.R.5th series follow a slightly different format than their predecessors and contain some additional research features:

(1) title

(2) prefatory statement (an abstract of the annotation, brief of the related case, cross-reference to page of related case in that volume)

(3) table of contents for this annotation
(4) research references
    (a) Total Client-Service Library References (related material published by Lawyers Cooperative Publishing)
        (i) encyclopedias and texts (including Am. Jur. 2d)
        (ii) practice aids
        (iii) federal statutes
        (iv) A.L.R. digests and indexes (related entries)
    (b) Research Sources (found to be helpful by author of annotation; includes sources published by other companies)
        (i) texts
        (ii) encyclopedias
        (iii) law reviews
        (iv) computer word searches for other sources
        (v) West Digest Key Numbers (see Chapter 5)
(5) index to this annotation
(6) Jurisdictional Table of Cited Statutes and Cases (alphabetized by jurisdiction; constitutional and statutory provisions included only if cited by a case in that annotation)
(7) text of annotation (no change in format from previous series)

The features in item (4)(b) will be added to A.L.R.4th, starting with the September 1992 pocket parts.

In reading an A.L.R. annotation in any series, you first should read the scope note to check the annotation's coverage. If the annotation misses the mark, use the list of related matters to find other applicable annotations. If the annotation is on point, read its summary as well as its internal table of contents to get a sense of the annotation's scheme of presentation. Then use the annotation's index or its table of contents to locate the points that interest you.

The annotation in Illustration 3-25 on page 92 addresses the "Modern Status of Intentional Infliction of Mental Distress as Independent Tort; 'Outrage.'" A reading of the scope section revealed the annotation to be on a useful topic. The related matters section yielded citations to several other useful annotations. The table of contents to the annotation revealed that §§ 2, 3, and 4 (but not 5) would be worth reading. The index to the annotation contained entries like "Coercion," "Defamation," "Racial insults," and "Rubbish collectors' association." The Table of Jurisdictions Represented pointed to § 3 as containing Kansas cases. And §§ 2, 3, and 4 contained considerable information about cases favoring and disfavoring this kind of tort claim. The case preceding this annotation, *Hubbard v. United Press International, Inc.,* is one of the leading cases on this topic. (In A.L.R.5th, the related cases appear together at the end of each volume, rather than preceding the annotations.)

Citation Note: The annotation in Illustration 3-25 would be cited as Annotation, *Modern Status of Intentional Infliction of Mental Distress as Independent Tort; "Outrage,"* 38 A.L.R.4th 998 (1985). Rule 16.5.5 in *The Bluebook* also requires the author's full name at the beginning of the cite, but no author was listed on this annotation, either at the beginning or at the end of the annotation. In early A.L.R. volumes, the author's name never appeared. Later, initials appeared at the end of the annotation or, still later, at the beginning of the annotation. In recent volumes, the author's name appears at the beginning of the annotation if the author still is in a position at the company to be a good "contact person" on the subject. Again, Rule 10.3.1 implies that A.L.R. almost never will be cited as the reporter of a case.

2. How to Locate Pertinent Annotations

A.L.R. annotations are accessible by four approaches:

(1) the index approach
(2) the digest approach
(3) the table approach
(4) the computer and citator approaches

A summary and flowchart of A.L.R. research methods appear on the inside front cover of all volumes of A.L.R.5th and some volumes of A.L.R.4th (volume 31 and later) and A.L.R. Fed. (volume 73 and later).

a. The Index Approach

Locate the A.L.R. volumes entitled *Index to Annotations*. This index encompasses the second, third, fourth, fifth, and federal series of A.L.R. The first series of A.L.R. is indexed in its own *Word Index* and *Quick Index.*

For the Perkins problem, you might look in this index under terms such as "emotional distress," "intentional tort," and "outrage." Unfortunately, none of these terms appears in the index. However, "outrageous conduct" appears where "outrage" might have been and refers you to another topic, "emotional injury." The same is true of related terms—"mental anguish," "mental distress," and "mental suffering"; they all contain cross-references to "emotional injury."

Under the index topic "Emotional Injury," the following entries look promising:

Abusive language: civil liability for insulting or abusive language—modern status, 20 ALR4th 773, §§ 3, 5

Libel and slander—discrimination, recovery of damages for emotional distress resulting from racial, ethnic, or religious abuse or discrimination, 40 ALR3d 1290, § 10

Outrageous conduct—intent, modern status of intentional infliction of mental distress as independent tort, "outrage", 38 ALR4th 998

Illustration 3-26 on page 98 shows the portion of the index containing the latter entry.

The following cross-references to other major topics (noted in bold type in the index) also look worth pursuing:

Anxiety
Embarrassment, Humiliation, and Disgrace
Intentional, Wilful, and Wanton Acts
Psychic Trauma

Note that this 1986 volume has a pocket part at the front of the volume that brings its entries up-to-date. As of the date of this writing, nothing else promising appeared in the pocket part under "Emotional Injury," but you should always check. Anything you find will speed up your research, because it will update the material in the main (1986) index volume.

INDEX TO ANNOTATIONS

EMOTIONAL INJURY—Cont'd

Medical care or treatment—Cont'd

- plastic surgery, cost of future cosmetic plastic surgery as element of damages, 88 ALR3d 117, § 10

Names, rights and remedies of parents inter se with respect to the names of their children, 92 ALR3d 1091, § 9

New Trial (this index)

No-fault insurance, what constitutes sufficiently serious personal injury, disability, impairment, or the like to justify recovery of damages outside of no-fault automobile insurance coverage, 33 ALR4th 767, § 4[a]

Obscene telephone calls, forum state's jurisdiction over nonresident defendant in action based on obscene or threatening telephone call from out-of-state, 37 ALR4th 852

Outrageous conduct

- intent, modern status of intentional infliction of mental distress as independent tort, "outrage", 38 ALR4th 998
- medical practitioner, recovery for emotional distress resulting from statement of medical practitioner or official allegedly constituting outrageous conduct, 34 ALR4th 688

EMOTIONAL INJURY—Cont'd

Privacy

- "single publication," what constitutes "single publication" within meaning of single publication rule affecting action for lible and slander, violation of privacy, or similar torts, 41 ALR4th 541, § 5
- uninvited entry into another's living quarters as invasion of privacy, 56 ALR3d 434, §§ 3[a], 6
- unsolicited mailing, distribution, house call, or telephone call as invasion of privacy, 56 ALR3d 457, § 14[b]

Products liability, bystander recovery for emotional distress at witnessing another's injury under strict products liability or breach of warranty, 31 ALR4th 162

Psychic Trauma (this index)

Punitive damages

- actual damages, sufficiency of showing of actual damages to support award, 40 ALR4th 11, §§ 8, 9, 11[a], 13-16[a-d]
- building and construction contracts, recovery for breach of building and construction contracts, 40 ALR4th 110, § 6

Rape, what constitutes penetration in prosecution for rape or statutory rape, 76 ALR3d 163, 76 ALR3d 163

Your first reading priority should be the entry that contains the largest number of terms you were looking for. The "Outrageous conduct" entry (38 A.L.R.4th 998) meets this test. It also looks the most promising for another reason: The entire annotation is listed as being on point, while only part of the annotations on "Abusive language" and "Libel and slander" are listed as being on point.

As an additional feature, *Index to Annotations* also gives cross-references to specific topic names in *A.L.R. Digests.*

b.   The Digest Approach

Another way that A.L.R. annotations can be located is by using the volumes entitled *A.L.R. Digests.* A "digest" is a research source that synopsizes or abstracts a set of articles, cases, or other lengthy works. These digest paragraphs are grouped by topic to facilitate their use in locating the relevant article, case, or other work. The major topics then are ordered alphabetically. Thus, a digest is neither primary nor secondary authority but, rather, a finding tool. For that reason, a digest is never cited or quoted.

There is one *A.L.R. Digest* apiece for the first and second series as well as a unified digest for the third, fourth, fifth, and federal series. A how-to-use guide appears at the front of the first volume. These digests also help you to find other A.L.R. topics and citations to other related sources published by Lawyers Cooperative Publishing, such as *American Jurisprudence* (an encyclopedia) and *United States Code Service* (a statutes publication).

Unfortunately, the digest approach is not very efficient in A.L.R. You have to peruse a five-page list in order to select one or more of 400 digest topics.

In the Perkins problem, the most likely topics are "Torts," "Civil Rights," and "Highways and Streets." Of these topics, "Torts" looks the most promising because Perkins is not pursuing a civil rights claim nor is she seeking any remedy peculiar to highways and streets. After you turn to the "Torts" topic in the digest, you would skim the table of contents to the topic and select "Mental or Emotional Tranquility"—§ 21 (generally) and § 22 (fright, threats). Within each of those sections, you would read a five- or six-page list of titles to annotations and other sources, very few of which are as useful as the sources found more quickly using the index approach. Although you might find the annotations located through the index approach, the more likely result is that you would be led on a few wild-goose chases trying to eliminate the wide range of entries in this digest.

In short, you should use the index approach for your research in A.L.R. rather than the digest approach.

c. The Table Approach

The Table of Laws, Rules, and Regulations appears near the end of the last volume of the *Index to Annotations*. This table tells you which annotations cite particular provisions of federal statutes, federal administrative regulations, federal court rules, uniform laws, model acts, Restatements, and codes of ethics. If you already know the citation to one of these kinds of sources, this table is your fastest access method to an on-point A.L.R. annotation.

d. The Computer and Citator Approaches

You may use an online word search to locate pertinent annotations in a computer database. In addition, computer searches to locate related sources are listed in A.L.R.5th and in pocket parts to A.L.R.4th after 1991.

If you have an annotation citation, you can find out which cases have cited it by using *Shepard's Citations for Annotations*. You may recall a similar *Shepard's* set for sources citing various legal periodical pieces; see Part D of this chapter at page 89. Illustration 3-27 on page 100 shows that the annotation at 38 A.L.R.4th 998 has been cited by courts in California, Florida, North Dakota, New York, and Virginia.

If you are looking for an A.L.R. annotation that cites a particular case, you could look up the case's citation in *Shepard's Citations for Annotations* or *Shepard's* for any of the case reporters in the citation (see Chapter 5). Illustration 3-28 at page 101 shows the *Shepard's* entries for 330 N.W.2d 428, the reporter citation for the *Hubbard* case. Look under volume 330, page 428. Each of these entries is an A.L.R. annotation that cites *Hubbard*. The first entry (in parentheses) is the cite to the *Hubbard* opinion, which precedes the annotation at 38 A.L.R.4th 998.

3. Using the Annotation History Table

After you find a reference to a useful annotation, consult the pocket part to that volume to see if the annotation has been supplemented or superseded. The Annotation History Table in the tables volume of the *Index to Annotations* gives you the same information. For instance, the Annotation History Table

Vol. 36 — AMERICAN LAW REPORTS, 4th SERIES (Annotations)

Vol. 36
-144-
Tex
783SW584
81A4425n
-212-
69A4784n
69A41129n
85A4288n
-395-
DC
560A2d511
80A411n
-419-
87A4808n
-502-
62A4184n
-684-
84A4273n
-807-
68A41017n
85A4816n
-907-
82A4241n
-941-
84A4423n
-978-
81A41010n
82A4897n
-997-
Miss
569So2d1185
-1046-
Calif
267CaR416
-1126-
Del
571A2d740
93ARF137n
93ARF418n
-1139-
Ariz
772P2d40
-1159-
71A417n
-1169-
85A41051n
-1175-
Va
405SE441
-1182-
Cir. 1
708FS461

Vol. 37
-10-
Ill
552NE1285
ND
456NW119
87A4989n
87A41112n
102ARF891n
104LE1048n
-110-
Cir. 9
874F2d659

-167-
Del
575A2d1184
Miss
573So2d767
Mo
795SW550
Ohio
550NE979
66A4590n
70A41036n
83A4299n
84A4317n
84A4659n
87A4575n
87A4576n
-286-
Ala
83A4248n
-304-
Ala
570So2d759
Colo
794P2d212
NJ
590A2d1154
Cir. 7
736FS205
Calif
270CaR684
DC
574A2d1350
Iowa
452NW388
ND
450NW780
85A4958n
87A4451n
-480-
63A41022n
-510-
83A4632n
84A4317n
-565-
Md
550A2d375
-635-
86A4414n
100ARF38n
-646-
63A4660n
66A4317n
66A4347n
68A4699n
69A4418n
70A4789n
70A4797n
-724-
71A4308n
78A4222n
83A4299n
-751-
Del
564A2d677
-773-
81A4382n
-787-
Cir. 9
105BRW592
Idaho
788P2d849
ND
434NW718

-842-
71A4945n
-852-
83A41009n
-948-
Calif
272CaR823
795P2d1280
NJ
563A2d459
-972-
Cir. 4
747FS1198
-987-
Iowa
440NW899
62A4329n
85A4816n
-1004-
82A4897n
-1168-
NM
793P2d283
66A41248n
-1179-
66A41248n
68A4516n
81A4752n
86A4936n
-1196-
68A4299n
-1206-
70A4903n

Vol. 38
-25-
Kan
774P2d361
-117-
83A4790n
-170-
Cir. 3
103BRW640
-200-
NC
382SE859
68A4230n
68A4828n
-267-
66A4513n
-339-
81A4208n
-355-
83A4115n
84A41059n
94LE844n
-378-
Wyo
811P2d996
85A4480n
-496-
84A4624n
84A4640n
86A4952n
-515-
Calif
258CaR504
Pa
574A2d633
84A4624n
84A4640n
86A4997n

-538-
86A4833n
-583-
84A41125n
-628-
70A4903n
-648-
83A41063n
-756-
78A41033n
81A41103n
-768-
71A4308n
78A4222n
-900-
67A4514n
69A4879n
81A4490n
-930-
Calif
275CaR361
83A41063n
104LE1079n
-998-
Calif
770P2d284
Fla
561So2d409
ND
435NW920
NY
536NYS2d
[1016
Va
400SE162
-1022-
Cir. 1
924F2d13
-1064-
85A4958n
-1114-
62A4329n
93ARF758n
-1170-
Ariz
770P2d358
-1194-
W Va
380SE38
68A4269n
69A4743n
98ARF548n
-1237-
Mich
445NW156

Vol. 39
-6-
ND
436NW225
72A415n
80A4974n
-114-
80A4952n
-129-
80A4951n

-229-
Mo
770SW261
-399-
70A427n
85A4958n
-450-
66A4513n
-465-
87A4734n
93ARF137n
-517-
86A4936n
-556-
66A4261n
78A4731n
-691-
W Va
380SE38
-705-
81A41035n
-742-
Mo
765SW199
66A4217n
-824-
Nebr
441NW160
-859-
NY
541NYS2d
[821
-879-
84A4190n
-899-
W Va
390SE14
71A4557n
98ARF663n
-967-
Ga
392SE896
66A41248n
86A4936n
-983-
66A41248n
-1011-
Va
382SE308
100ARF671n
-1047-
Cir. 8
707FS1147
Colo
812P2d699
Wis
456NW576
72A4634n
85A4957n
87A4451n
-1203-
W Va
400SE299

Vol. 40
-11-
Cir. 1
753FS412
85A41081n

-147-
W Va
382SE540
-304-
80A411n
-333-
86A4789n
17ARF522s
-381-
Ark
763SW648
Kan
771P2d942
Md
589A2d1338
Utah
791P2d889
-535-
78A4731n
-553-
Ill
558NE248
-575-
71A41149n
72A4877n
83A4663n
83A4667n
84A4317n
-594-
66A4590n
69A4907n
70A4985n
70A41093n
102LE1042n
-627-
Pa
561A2d1255
-662-
Mich
463NW250
85A41051n
-684-
NC
398SE662
-741-
95LE928n
95LE945n
-812-
Ala
537So2d948
86A4213n
-846-
78A4222n
-867-
Tenn
774SW633
78A415n
86A4890n
-908-
Wyo
811P2d261
-968-
84A4423n
-998-
98ARF782n
-1062-
Mass
571NE350
93ARF757n
-1089-
86A4213n
-1114-
80A41128n
103LE953n

-1218-
66A423n
72A465n

Vol. 41
-10-
Cir. 6
740FS478
-47-
67A4966n
72A415n
78A4156n
-60-
93ARF534n
-99-
W Va
380SE38
-111-
W Va
380SE38
-112-
La
556So2d8
-131-
Mo
792SW422
Pa
582A2d26
12CoLR209
-292-
Cir. 10
97BRW617
-351-
78A4731n
-353-
Mont
781P2d278
-361-
Cir. 11
97BRW1020
66A4317n
66A4347n
68A4699n
69A4418n
70A4789n
-416-
70A4176n
78A41108n
-481-
89McL125
70A4176n
78A41108n
-541-
83A41009n
85A4816n
-573-
72A4136n
-588-
68A4516n
72A4840n
81A41752n
-597-
Del
562A2d597
-612-
Utah
786P2d1344
-730-
80A4951n

-773-
Tex
777SW825
-774-
Mo
776SW888
-812-
NY
546NYS2d27
82A4986n
85A4480n
93ARF534n
-877-
82A41040n
85A4480n
-973-
78A4819n
-1095-
Calif
258CaR641
85A4957n
11CoLR110
-1129-
75MnL435
62A4264n
84A4658n
86A4213n
-1189-
95LE895n
-1216-
99A3967s

Vol. 42
-12-
Ariz
755P2d1190
-188-
86A4890n
-253-
87A4807n
87A4808n
-272-
83A41009n
-293-
85A41081n
-392-
Calif
266CaR621
266CaR622
Mo
776SW487
72A4423n
-516-
70A4136n
-543-
69A4879n
-586-
78A4760n
-676-
80A4951n
-795-
Fla
565So2d792
-839-
80A473n
-879-
Ind
535NE1193
NY
536NYS2d
[831

ILLUSTRATION 3-28. *Shepard's* Entries for 330 N.W.2d 428, in *Shepard's Citations for Annotations* [Part 2] 390 (1989).

101

Vol. 327 — NORTHWESTERN REPORTER, 2d SERIES

– 603 –	**– 59 –**	**– 343 –**	63A4.814n	**– 878 –**	**– 250 –**	**– 555 –**	**– 923 –**
(212Neb915)	(120McA465)	21A3.845s	66A4.96n	(110Wis2d	(110Wis2d	84A3.242s	(110Wis2d
78A3.1255s	63.3RF856s	57A4.896n	**– 585 –**	309)	393)	9A4.20s	733)
– 606 –	**– 65 –**	**– 348 –**	(121McA98)	31A3.565s	34A3.652s	**– 605 –**	37A4.657n
(212Neb901)	(120McA485)	36A3.900s	50A4.1116n	**– 894 –**	**– 263 –**	78A3.910s	37A4.675n
89.3.399s	13A4.1226s	**– 377 –**	50A4.1144n	(110Wis2d	(110Wis2d	**– 624 –**	
– 611 –	**– 70 –**	(121McA306)	**– 598 –**	381)	414)	51A3.1087s	
(213Neb98)	(120McA506)	62A3.110s	(121McA137)	60A3.333s	80A3.369s	**– 630 –**	**Vol. 330**
63A4.1178n	39A4.697n	**– 380 –**	85A3.351s	41A4.853n	**– 275 –**	51A3.727s	
– 622 –	**– 82 –**	(120McA765)	87A3.93s	**– 898 –**	(110Wis2d	**– 648 –**	**– 16 –**
(213Neb123)	(120McA552)	9A4.972s	**– 602 –**	(110Wis2d	447)	4A3.361s	(415Mch443)
99A3.288s	57A4.626n	**– 389 –**	(121McA153)	431)	36A3.1403s	30A3.9s	18A3.259s
– 624 –	**– 92 –**	(121McA36)	37A3.127s	92A3.1164s	**– 295 –**	3A4.998s	**– 22 –**
(213Neb126)	(120McA606)	98.3.160s	**– 619 –**	**– 913 –**	94A3.975s	**– 660 –**	(415Mch483)
43A3.699s	14.3.1227s	**– 402 –**	(121McA203)	33A3.17s	**– 306 –**	80A3.219s	33A4.767s
– 628 –	**– 95 –**	(121McA192)	81A3.1192s		8A4.464s	43A4.637n	33A4.779n
(120McA708)	(120McA708)	42A4.162n	**– 622 –**		45A4.293n	**– 666 –**	**– 33 –**
62A3.314s	33A3.703s	**– 406 –**	(121McA212)	**Vol. 329**	**– 346 –**	96A3.968s	(415Mch512)
63A3.88s	34A4.243n	(121McA208)	78A3.339s		(213Neb364)	**– 673 –**	79A3.417s
– 674 –	35A4.295n	**– 419 –**	60A3.651s	**– 17 –**	25A3.7s	19A4.1082s	**– 52 –**
(110Wis2d	**– 108 –**	(121McA374)	**– 653 –**	34A3.16s	**– 378 –**	**– 697 –**	(415Mch628)
188)	(120McA806)		(121McA424)	**– 22 –**	64A4.348n	(415Mch328)	84A3.242s
61A3...				Case 1	64A4.536n	93A3.7s	**– 64 –**

– 832 –	**– 279 –**	16A4.1127s	30A3.9s		**– 506 –**	13A3.1364s	**– 263 –**
(415Mch31)	(110Wis2d	50A4.861n	**– 792 –**	(110Wis2d	(121McA827)	56A4.57n	20A3.320s
84A3.375s	146)	**– 551 –**	(213Neb335)	522)	96A3.804s	56A4.277n	**– 291 –**
	66A3.1018s	(121McA266)	51A3.556s	6A4.555s	**– 513 –**	**– 890 –**	43A3.566s
Vol. 328	**– 293 –**	71A3.753s	**– 795 –**	**– 178 –**	(122McA1)	(110Wis2d	**– 306 –**
	14A3RF447s	**– 554 –**	(213Neb349)	(110Wis2d	35A4.652n	581)	31A3.565s
– 5 –	**– 308 –**	(121McA281)	31A3.565s	530)	**– 522 –**	51A3.8s	**– 314 –**
(120McA23)	61A3.906s	38A3.10s	**– 844 –**	27A4.778n	(122McA35)	54A3.352s	(415Mch558)
27A4.123n	**– 314 –**	95A3.15s	56A4.965n	**– 210 –**	23A3.1416s	74A3.1001s	34A3.16s
– 29 –	43A3.221s	**– 556 –**	**– 847 –**	(110Wis2d	**– 528 –**	78A3.339s	**– 389 –**
(120McA283)	**– 323 –**	(121McA324)	13A3.1057s	725)	(122McA51)	96A3.22s	(416Mch217)
96A3.22s	21A3.206s	22A3.717s	46A3.240s	66A4.327n	48A3.1096s	4A4.13s	(36A4.911)
19A4.326s	94A3.141s	68A4.539n	74A3.1001s	68A4.762n	**– 533 –**	**– 921 –**	**– 428 –**
– 51 –	**– 328 –**	68A4.655n	11A4.1118s	**– 240 –**	(122McA63)	(110Wis2d	(38A4.971)
(120McA388)	78A3.421s	**– 566 –**	12A4.96s	(110Wis2d	10A3.359s	736)	86A3.454s
18A4.961s	**– 333 –**	(121McA47)	39A4.751n	369)	**– 541 –**	37A4.660n	90A3.393s
40A4.748n	7A3.8s	(37A4.279)	**– 862 –**	34A4.191s	(122McA80)	37A4.665n	52A4.934n
	27A4.160n	**– 576 –**	18A3.1376s	**– 243 –**	32A4.774s	66A4.370n	
		(121McA73)		(110Wis2d		68A4.740n	
		94A3.748s		356)			
		45A4.819n		65A3.1128s			

390

in Illustration 3-29 on page 102 indicates that the annotation cited in Illustration 3-25 (38 A.L.R.4th 998) has not been supplemented or superseded. The pocket part to the annotation volume agrees.

Note that the entries in this table mean that the older annotation (or section) has been superseded *by* the newer annotation. The shorthand for the entry seems at first glance to say the reverse.

4. How A.L.R. Annotations Are Updated

Instead of consulting the Annotation History Table, you could consult the pocket part to the annotation volume to see if the annotation has been supplemented or superseded. The annotations in A.L.R.3d, A.L.R.4th, A.L.R.5th, and A.L.R. Fed. are updated by annual pocket parts. As shown in Illustration

ANNOTATION HISTORY TABLE

ALR4th

35 ALR4th 441
§ 17 Superseded 50 ALR4th 843

57 ALR4th 911
§§ 3, 7[a] Superseded 98 ALR Fed 124

ALR Fed

4 ALR Fed 343 Superseded 92 ALR Fed 333	**24 ALR Fed 808** § 11 Superseded 99 ALR Fed 30	**36 ALR Fed 9** § 23 Superseded 91 ALR Fed 178
5 ALR Fed 674 §§ 13-15 Superseded 92 ALR Fed 733	**27 ALR Fed 537** § 3[c] Superseded 91 ALR Fed 178	**37 ALR Fed 320** § 6 Superseded 85 ALR Fed 118
8 ALR Fed 675 §§ 2.5, 3 Superseded 97 ALR Fed 369	**27 ALR Fed 702** § 16 Superseded 95 ALR Fed 262	**38 ALR Fed 578** §§ 15, 16 Superseded 85 ALR Fed 118
12 ALR Fed 163 Superseded 91 ALR Fed 16	**28 ALR Fed 26** § 35 Superseded 85 ALR Fed 864	**44 ALR Fed 148** § 6 Superseded 97 ALR Fed 40
12 ALR Fed 233 § 8 Superseded 100 ALR Fed 880	**29 ALR Fed 482** § 6 Superseded 101 ALR Fed 27	**53 ALR Fed 348** §§ 7-9 Superseded 101 ALR Fed 813, § 4[a] Superseded 103 ALR Fed 698
12 ALR Fed 910 Superseded 81 ALR Fed 36	**30 ALR Fed 19** §§ 19-28 Superseded 92 ALR Fed 436	
15 ALR Fed 288 Superseded 99 ALR Fed 278	**31 ALR Fed 900** Superseded 95 ALR Fed 262	**58 ALR Fed 616** §§ 5, 6 Superseded 90 ALR Fed 825
17 ALR Fed 675 § 7 Superseded 101 ALR Fed 751	**33 ALR Fed 393** § 2 Superseded 85 ALR Fed 880	**65 ALR Fed 574** Superseded 87 ALR Fed 500

3-30 on page 103, the pocket part in 38 A.L.R.4th updates the annotation you have been researching by citing additional cases from Kansas, the jurisdiction of the Perkins problem.

> *Citation Note:* To cite material in both the main volume and the 1991 pocket part, you would cite to the annotation but change the final parenthetical containing the year to read as follows: (1985 & Supp. 1991). *See* Rule 3.2(c) of *The Bluebook.*

The A.L.R.2d annotations are updated by a separate set of volumes entitled *A.L.R.2d Later Case Service.* The volumes of *A.L.R.2d Later Case Service* also are updated by pocket parts. The annotations in A.L.R. (first series) are supplemented by the *A.L.R. Blue Book of Supplemental Decisions,* a collection of permanent volumes and a paperbound volume that is updated annually until it is replaced by the next bound volume.

A.L.R. subscribers (law libraries and firms) can bring their research up-to-the-minute by calling the Latest Case Service "hot line" for cases decided since the last supplement. The telephone number is listed on the front cover of the pocket parts for A.L.R.3d, A.L.R.4th, A.L.R.5th, and A.L.R. Fed. (annotation volumes only, not digest volumes).

ILLUSTRATION 3-30. Supplement to Annotation, *Modern Status of Intentional Infliction of Mental Distress as Independent Tort; "Outrage,"* 38 A.L.R.4th 59 (Supp. 1991).

103

SUPPLEMENT **38 ALR4th 998–1035**

For latest cases, call the toll free number appearing on the cover of this supplement.

BNA IER Cas 1142 (requirements of proof for tort of intentional infliction of emotional distress more severe than for emotional distress as incidental damage caused by tort of wrongful discharge); Oswald v LeGrand (1990, Iowa) 453 NW2d 634; Mills v Guthrie County Rural Electric Coop. Assn. (1990, Iowa) 454 NW2d 846 (customers brought action against electric cooperative arising from electrical fire in customers' hog farrowing facility caused by imbalance in electrical voltage; conduct not sufficiently outrageous to permit claim); Vaughn v AG Processing, Inc. (1990, Iowa) 459 NW2d 627, 55 CCH EPD P 40555; Engstrom v State (1990, Iowa) 461 NW2d 309.

Morgan v Olds (1987, Iowa App) 417 NW2d 232 (doctor did not act outrageously or disregard probability of causing emotional distress by failing to take heroic measures after patient was weaned from respirator); Strauss v Cilek (1987, Iowa App) 418 NW2d 378; Coontz v Gordon Jewelry Corp. (1989, Iowa App) 439 NW2d 223 (to recover damages for intentional infliction of emotional distress plaintiff must show defendant's conduct was outrageous, defendant acted intentionally or recklessly, and plaintiff suffered severe and extreme emotional distress as result of defendant's actions); Benishek v Cody (1989, Iowa App) 441 NW2d 399, 113 CCH LC P 56123 (employer's accusation to two employees that he believed someone embezzled money and termination of both employees after giving them two weeks to tell employer who took money was not conduct amounting to outrageous behavior).

Kan—Bowman v Doherty (1984) 235 Kan 870, 686 P2d 112 (allegations of attorney's wanton conduct in failing to obtain continuance so that plaintiff missed hearing on criminal matter were sufficient to state cause of action); Neufeldt v L.R. Foy Constr. Co. (1985) 236 Kan 664, 693 P2d 1194; Burgess v Perdue (1986) 239 Kan 473, 721 P2d 239 (conduct of physician in telling decedent's mother that state neurological institute had her son's brain in a jar was untactful but not outrageous); Moore v State Bank of Burden (1986) 240 Kan 382, 729 P2d 1205, cert den (US) 96 L Ed 2d 376, 107 S Ct 2484 (conduct by bank in making erroneous setoff of depositor's social security funds against legitimate indebtedness owed to bank, after consultation with counsel and without any showing of intent to injure plaintiff, not sufficiently outrageous).

Fletcher v Wesley Medical Center (1984, DC Kan) 585 F Supp 1260, 119 BNA CRRM 2217 (applying Kan law); Earth Scientists (Petro Services), Ltd. v United States Fidelity & Guaranty Co. (1985, DC Kan) 619 F Supp 1465 (applying Kan law; plaintiff corporation was incapable of suffering emotional distress; tort of outrage inapplicable); Polson v Davis (1986, DC Kan) 635 F Supp 1130 (applying Kan law; circumstances of termination of employment failed to meet two threshhold requirements necessary to arrive at elemantry analysis of alleged conduct, i.e., (1) extremeness and outrage and (2) severity of plaintiff's distress thereby caused); Crow v United States (1987, DC Kan) 659 F Supp 556 (applying Kan law; no actionable case by plaintiff acquitted of mail fraud charges); Maxedon v Texaco Producing, Inc. (1989, DC Kan) 710 F Supp 1306, summary judgment den (DC Kan) 1989 US Dist LEXIS 4618 (applying Kan law; damages for pollution of land; cause of action not established); EEOC v General Motors Corp. (1989, DC Kan) 713 F Supp 1394, 51 CCH EPD P 39305 (applying Kan law; employer's transfer of employee back to shift with co-worker who had sexually harassed employee not sufficiently outrageous).

Ky—Pearce v Courier-Journal (1985, Ky App) 683 SW2d 633, 11 Media L R 1498; Whittington v Whittington (1989, Ky App) 766 SW2d 73 (fraud and adultery by estranged husband not sufficiently outrageous).

Stewart v Pantry, Inc. (1988, WD Ky) 715 F Supp 1361, 4 BNA IER Cas 526 (dismissal of at-will employee based on polygraph test did not amount to extreme or outrageous conduct; applying Ky law).

La—Smith v Mahfouz (1986, La App 3d Cir) 489 So 2d 409, cert den (La) 494 So 2d 1181 (intentional, reprehensible violation of property rights, without pecuniary damage, outrageous enough to sustain award of damages for intentional infliction of emotional distress); Muslow v A.G. Edwards & Sons, Inc. (1987, La App 2d Cir) 509 So 2d 1012, cert den (La) 512 So 2d 1183; Engrum v Boise Southern Co. (1988, La App 3d Cir) 527 So 2d 362 (allegations in employee's complaint that employer fired him without conducting adequate investigation, issued payroll check that appeared to be altered, caused employee's arrest when employer knew he was innocent, and engaged in continuous pattern of conduct intended to cause him mental harm, stated claim for intentional infliction of emotional distress).

Duhe v Delta Air Lines, Inc. (1986, ED La) 635 F Supp 1414 (applying La law).

Me—Staples v Bangor Hydro-Electric Co. (1989, Me) 561 A2d 499, 4 BNA IER Cas 918 (former employer's conduct in humiliating employee at staff meetings and demoting him without cause did not warrant submitting case to jury on issue of intentional infliction of emotional distress).

59

5. Specialized Sets of A.L.R. Annotations

As of the date of this writing, multi-volume collections of specialized A.L.R. annotations were available in two subject areas: environmental law and federal criminal law and procedure. In addition, single-volume collections of A.L.R. annotations (entitled *Critical Issues*) were available on wrongful death, trademarks, the Freedom of Information Act, drunk driving prosecutions, and the Federal Rules of Evidence. More are planned by the publisher. If your research lies in one of these specialized areas, you can streamline your A.L.R. research by using the applicable collection. They are updated annually.

F. RESTATEMENTS AND PATTERN JURY INSTRUCTIONS

1. Restatements and Pattern Jury Instructions Compared

The research materials in this part of the chapter constitute a different kind of secondary source. Thus far, most of the secondary sources you have studied have been commentary sources in which the authors synthesized, summarized, and criticized the primary authority in a given area. This is true of encyclopedias, treatises, CLE materials, legal periodicals, and A.L.R. annotations.

However, Restatements and pattern jury instructions diverge from those characteristics because they are

(1) written in rule form, with explanations following;
(2) written and revised through a deliberative process by more than one expert; and
(3) often considered for adoption by courts, which incorporate the rule into the law of that court's jurisdiction.

Like the commentary sources above, these sources are not written or published by the government, so they are not primary authority even though they look like it and have fooled many a first-year law student. They frequently are accompanied by extensive comments that serve as both commentary and quasi-legislative history ("quasi" because they are not the comments of the enacting government body). When part of this kind of secondary source is adopted by a court, the adopted language then becomes primary authority in that jurisdiction because it is part of a case. However, the drafters' comments are infrequently adopted, even though they frequently are reprinted or quoted along with the adopted language.

Restatements seek to unify the common law (case law) on a national basis, while pattern jury instructions seek to unify jury instructions in a particular jurisdiction. These differences in purpose also lead to differences in research materials and in the uses to which you put these materials.

2. What Are the Restatements?

a. Historical and Philosophical Roots

To use the Restatements most effectively, you must understand some of the history of the "Restatement movement." The Restatements are products of the primary theoretical conflicts that shaped twentieth-century American jurisprudence.

The immense geographic and industrial growth of the United States in the mid-nineteenth century generated an increasing amount of litigation and case law. Legal scholars known as "the rationalists" were concerned about apparent inconsistencies in the flood of decisions, which left courts, attorneys, and citizens without a secure understanding of the law. The rationalists believed that the law consisted of immutable principles that could be reduced to a consistent, organized, and scientific system. They sought to impose this vision of consistency and order on the common law.

Legal "realists," on the other hand, concluded that the laws governing people were not derived from immutable laws of nature. Rather, legal realists maintained that the common law often reflected the needs of particular litigants, the biases of judges, and the prevailing social ethic of the day.

This philosophical challenge by the realists, coupled with a continuing onslaught of seemingly contradictory case law, caused the rationalists to mobilize in the hope of enhancing predictability and organization in American common law. In 1923, leading American legal thinkers organized the American Law Institute (ALI). The objective of this organization was to reduce the uncertainty and complexity of American common law by reformulating common law principles into one authoritative, rule-like source. The tangible results of this effort are the Restatements of the Law.

The authors of the first series of Restatements (1932-1944) set a lofty goal: to "restate" precisely the principles of the existing common law. By so doing, the drafters hoped to produce "an authority greater than that now accorded to any legal treatise, an authority more nearly on a par with that accorded the decisions of the courts." Report of the Committee on the Establishment of a Permanent Organization for the Improvement of the Law Proposing the Establishment of an American Law Institute, Feb. 23, 1923, The American Law Institute 50th Anniversary 34 (1973). In the first Restatement series the drafters did not take into account "what the law ought to be . . . [if that] result had no judicial support or was a minority position." A. James Casner, *Restatement (Second) of Property as an Instrument of Law Reform,* 67 Iowa L. Rev. 87, 88 (1981). This meant that the early Restatements' declaration of a majority rule had the potential of retarding the growth of a minority rule and inhibiting the natural (albeit infrequent) occurrence of judicial overthrow of existing doctrines. *See id.* at 91.

However, in 1966 the ALI changed its policies to allow prediction as well as restatement of the law. Subsequently, the Reporter of the Restatement (Second) of Property opined that "in determining what the law is that is to be restated, due consideration is to be given to the position that a court might be expected to take if it made a fresh examination of all relevant aspects of the problem in light of current circumstances." *Id.* at 90.

b. The Drafting Process

In a continuing effort to keep the Restatements reasonably current, the ALI has published a second series for many of the Restatement topics and a third series for a single topic. (See Table 3.5 on pages 106-109.) The second and third series usually reflect a more current analysis of the state of the law and may also reflect emerging trends. Caution: In the next decade, new Restatement subjects may be covered for the first time in the second or third series, without being covered in the previous series.

TABLE 3.5. Restatement Features.

| Subject | Series & Date(s) of Adoption* | Table of Contents | | Scope & Location of Index | | |
		location	coverage	Restatement series	Restatement subject	volume
Agency	1st (1933)	front of each volume	Agency 1st series	General Index	end of last volume	no
	2d (1957)	front of each volume	Agency 2d series	no	end of last topical volume	no
Conflict of Laws	1st (1934)	front of volume	Conflicts 1st series	General Index	end of volume	no
	2d (1969, 1988)	front of each volume	Conflicts 2d series	no	end of last topical volume	no
Contracts	1st (1932)	front of each volume	Contracts 1st series	General Index	end of last volume	no
	2d (1979)	front of each volume**	Contracts 2d series	no	end of last topical volume	no
Foreign Relations	2d (1962)	front of volume	Foreign Relations 2d series	no	end of volume	no
	3d (1986)	front of each topical volume	Foreign Relations 3d series	no	end of last topical volume	no
Judgments	1st (1942)	front of volume	Judgments 1st series	General Index	end of volume	no
	2d (1980)	front of each volume**	Judgments 2d series	no	end of last topical volume	no
Property	1st (1936, 1940, 1944)	front of each volume	only that volume, except that volumes I & II are merged	General Index	no	end of volume; volumes I & II are merged
(Landlord & Tenant)	2d (1976)	front of each volume	Prop. (L.&T.) 2d series	no	no	end of volume
(Donative Transfers)	2d (1981, 1984, 1987)	front of each volume	Prop. (D.T.) 2d series	no	no	end of volume
Restitution	1st (1936)	front of each volume	Restitution 1st series	General Index	end of topical volume	no

Parallel Tables of Section Numbers	Case Digests Separated by Series?	Statutory Notes	Reporter's Notes	Tables of		References to	
				Cases	Statutes	A.L.R. Annotations	West Topic & Key Numbers
tent. drafts → 1st series	n/a	no	no	no	no	no	no
none	1st appendix volume: w/in each section; other appendix volumes: w/in each volume	no	first appendix volume	no	no	first appendix volume	first appendix volume
tent. drafts → 1st series	n/a	no	no	no	no	no	no
1st ↔ 2d series tent. drafts ↔ 2d series	1st appendix volume: w/in each section; other appendix volumes: w/in each volume	no	after each section in topical volume	first appendix volume	no	first appendix volume	first appendix volume
tent. drafts → 1st series	n/a	no	no	no	no	no	no
tent. drafts ↔ 2d series UCC → 2d series	1st appendix volume: w/in each section; other appendix volumes: as marked on binding	no	after each section in topical volume	end of last topical volume	end of last topical volume	first appendix volume	first appendix volume
2d series → proposed official draft	w/in the supplement	no	after each section	end of volume	end of volume	no	no
3d → 2d series tent. drafts ↔ 3d series	w/in each volume or supplement	no	after each section in topical volume	end of last topical volume[†]	end of last topical volume[†]	end of last topical volume	end of last topical volume
tent. drafts → 1st series	n/a	no	no	no	no	no	no
1st → 2d series tent. drafts ↔ 2d series	w/in each volume or supplement	no	after each section in topical volume	end of last topical volume	end of last topical volume[††]	first appendix volume	first appendix volume
tent. draft → 1st series	n/a	no	no	no	no	no	no
none	n/a because 1st series did not cover landlord-tenant law	after each section in topical volume	after each section in topical volume	end of last topical volume[†††]	end of last topical volume[†††]	end of last topical volume	end of last topical volume
1st ↔ 2d series (each volume has own tables)	w/in each supplement	after each section in topical volume	after each section in topical volume	each volume has own table[†††]	each volume has own table[†††]	each volume has own table	each volume has own table
tent. draft → 1st series	w/in each section	no	no	no	no	no	no

TABLE 3.5. *(continued)*

Subject	Series & Date(s) of Adoption*	Table of Contents location	Table of Contents coverage	Scope & Location of Index: Restatement series	Scope & Location of Index: Restatement subject	Scope & Location of Index: volume
Security	1st (1941)	front of volume	Security 1st series	General Index	end of volume	no
Torts	1st (1934, 1938, 1939)	front of volume	only that volume	General Index	no	end of volume
	2d (1963, -64, -76, -77)	front of each volume**	only that volume	no	no	end of volume
Trusts	1st (1935)	front of each volume	Trusts 1st series	General Index	end of last volume	no
	2d (1957)	front of each volume	Trusts 2d series	no	end of last topical volume	no
(Prudent Investor Rule)	3d (1990)	front of volume	Trusts (P.I.R.) 3d series	no	end of volume	no

*The Bluebook requires the date of adoption, not publication.
**Appendix volumes may contain tables of contents for both series.
†Also has Table of Authorities and Table of International Agreements.
††Has separate table for Federal Rules of Civil Procedure.
†††Also has Table of Secondary Authorities.

When the ALI decides to prepare a new Restatement on a particular topic, it appoints a "Reporter," who is an eminent scholar in the field. With the help of assistants, that Reporter prepares an initial draft of the new series for the topic. A committee of advisers who are experts in that field review and revise the draft. The revised draft then is reviewed by the ALI's Council—a group of 50 or so judges, attorneys, and professors—who may refer the draft back to the Reporter or approve it as a "tentative draft" and submit it to the annual meeting of the ALI members. After the ALI membership has debated and discussed the tentative draft, it is released to the public and to the legal profession, where it engenders further debate. Most Restatements appear in a great number of tentative drafts until treatment of the subject has been completed. Some tentative drafts are even cited by courts to reflect the current thought of the ALI. Then a "proposed official draft" is submitted to the ALI Council and membership. If the proposed official draft is approved by the Council and then the ALI membership, it becomes an "official draft" and is published in final form.

There are a number of tentative drafts currently in progress on new topics such as The Law Governing Lawyers, Property (Servitudes), and Unfair Competition. These tentative drafts are not listed in Table 3.5 because they are not yet official drafts. Current information can be obtained from the latest *Annual Report* of the American Law Institute.

The prestige of the Reporters and reviewers of the Restatements has made the Restatements unusually authoritative compared to other secondary sources. As of April 1, 1990, the Restatements had been cited by the courts 110,887 times. American Law Institute, *Publications* at R1 (1991). The Re-

Parallel Tables of Section Numbers	Case Digests Separated by Series?	Statutory Notes	Reporter's Notes	Tables of		References to	
				Cases	Statutes	A.L.R. Annotations	West Topic & Key Numbers
tent. drafts → 1st series	n/a	no	no	no	no	no	no
tent. drafts → 1st series	n/a	no	no	no	no	no	no
none	consult Table 3.6, page 119	no	first appendix volume	no	no	first appendix volume	first appendix volume
tent. drafts → 1st series	n/a	no	no	no	no	no	no
none	1st appendix volume: w/in each section; other appendix volumes: w/in each volume	no	first appendix volume	first appendix volume	no	first appendix volume	first appendix volume
none	none yet	no	after each section in topical volume	end of volume	end of volume	end of volume	end of volume

statements are particularly useful as persuasive support for legal arguments that have not been addressed by the courts in a particular jurisdiction. When no primary authority supports an argument, a Restatement section may be used persuasively to suggest what the law should be.

c.   Format

Each Restatement subject is organized according to numbered chapters. Each chapter covers a major portion of that Restatement subject. The chapters, in turn, are divided into topics, which are in turn divided into sections. The legal rule is printed in boldface, followed by two kinds of explanation: comments and illustrations. The comments offer insight into the reasons why the ALI adopted this rule of law; they also clarify the scope and meaning of the proposition. The illustrations use examples to further define the legal proposition, its scope, and the comments. Some of the examples are based on the facts of real cases.

Illustration 3-31 on pages 110-111 shows § 46 of the second series of the Restatement of Torts. Subsection (1) addresses the Perkins research situation and sets out the conditions to her recovery, if this subsection has been adopted by the Kansas courts.

Citation Note: According to Practitioners' Note P.1(h) in *The Bluebook,* Restatement cites are in roman type in court documents and legal memoranda. Titles are abbreviated according to Table T.6, and comments and illustrations are abbreviated according to Table T.17. *See* Rules 3.5 and 12.8.5. Here are some sample cites:

TOPIC 5. THE INTEREST IN FREEDOM FROM EMOTIONAL DISTRESS

§ **46.** Outrageous Conduct Causing Severe Emotional Distress

(1) One who by extreme and outrageous conduct intentionally or recklessly causes severe emotional distress to another is subject to liability for such emotional distress, and if bodily harm to the other results from it, for such bodily harm.

See Appendix for **Reporter's Notes, Court Citations, and Cross References**

71

---

§ **46**   TORTS, SECOND   Ch. 2

(2) Where such conduct is directed at a third person, the actor is subject to liability if he intentionally or recklessly causes severe emotional distress

> **(a) to a member of such person's immediate family who is present at the time, whether or not such distress results in bodily harm, or**
>
> **(b) to any other person who is present at the time, if such distress results in bodily harm.**

See Reporter's Notes.

Caveat:

The Institute expresses no opinion as to whether there may not be other circumstances under which the actor may be subject to liability for the intentional or reckless infliction of emotional distress.

Comment:

a. This Section is concerned only with emotional distress which is inflicted intentionally or recklessly. As to the negligent infliction of emotional distress, see §§ 312, 313, 436, and 436 A.

b. As indicated in Chapter 47, emotional distress may be

~~cases where other interests have~~

~~the rules stated in §§~~

c. The law is still in a stage of development, and the ultimate limits of this tort are not yet determined. This Section states the extent of the liability thus far accepted generally by the courts. The Caveat is intended to leave fully open the possibility of further development of the law, and the recognition of other situations in which liability may be imposed.

d. Extreme and outrageous conduct. The cases thus far decided have found liability only where the defendant's conduct

See Appendix for **Reporter's Notes, Court Citations, and Cross References**

72

ILLUSTRATION 3-31. *(continued)* 111

Ch. 2 **EMOTIONAL DISTRESS** **§ 46**

has been extreme and outrageous. It has not been enough that the defendant has acted with an intent which is tortious or even criminal, or that he has intended to inflict emotional distress, or even that his conduct has been characterized by "malice," or a degree of aggravation which would entitle the plaintiff to punitive damages for another tort. Liability has been found only where the conduct has been so outrageous in character, and so extreme in degree, as to go beyond all possible bounds of decency, and to be regarded as atrocious, and utterly intolerable in a civilized community. Generally, the case is one in which the recitation of the facts to an average member of the community would arouse his resentment against the actor, and lead him to exclaim, "Outrageous!"

The liability clearly does not extend to mere insults, indignities, threats, annoyances, petty oppressions, or other trivialities. The rough edges of our society are still in need of a good deal of filing down, and in the meantime plaintiffs must necessarily be expected and required to be hardened to a certain amount of rough language, and to occasional acts that are definitely inconsiderate and unkind. There is no occasion for the law to intervene in every case where some one's feelings are hurt. There must still be freedom to express an unflattering opinion, and some safety valve must be left through which irascible tempers may blow off relatively harmless steam. See Magruder, Mental and Emotional Disturbance in the Law of Torts, 47 Harvard Law Review 1033, 1053 (1936). It is only where there is a special relation between the parties, as stated in § 48, that there may be recovery for insults not amounting to extreme outrage.

Illustrations:

1. As a practical joke, A falsely tells B that her husband has been badly injured in an accident, and is in the hospital with both legs broken. B suffers severe emotional distress. A is subject to liability to B for her emotional distress. If it causes nervous shock and resulting illness, A is subject to liability to B for her illness.

2. A, the president of an association of rubbish collectors, summons B to a meeting of the association, and in the presence of an intimidating group of associates tells B that B has been collecting rubbish in territory which the association regards as exclusively allocated to one of its members. A demands that B pay over the proceeds of his

See Appendix for Reporter's Notes, Court Citations, and Cross References

Restatement (Second) of Torts § 46 (1964).
Restatement (Second) of Torts § 46 cmt. a (1964).
Restatement (Second) of Torts § 46 cmt. a, illus. 1 (1964).
Restatement (Second) of Torts § 847A (Tent. Draft No. 17, 1974).

Note that each Restatement illustration must be cited to a particular comment. The year cited is the year of adoption, not publication, unless the version cited contains subsequent amendments, in which case you should give the year of the last amendment, even if the cited section was not affected by those amendments. Rule 12.8.5.

The Restatements also are available online, as discussed in Chapter 6.

d. Clearing Up Misconceptions about the Restatements

First, you should be aware that differences among jurisdictions are not reflected in the Restatement rules. The Restatements purport to set forth a unitary common law, not the common law of any particular jurisdiction. Indeed, your jurisdiction may not follow the Restatement view. Thus, uncritical acceptance of a Restatement is not warranted and is possibly dangerous, because the Restatements are not primary authority. The Minnesota Supreme Court reminded the bar that the Restatements are not "law" until adopted by the court. In *Conover v. Northern States Power Co.,* 313 N.W.2d 397, 404 n.4 (Minn. 1981), Justice Simonett noted: "The issue here, of course, is more than the narrow one of construing Restatement language. Even if the Restatement expressly said employees of independent contractors are included in 'others,' it would be for us to decide if we wished to adopt such a rule."

Second, a court may adopt only portions of a Restatement section or may adopt the section but not the comments or the illustrations.

Third, the issuance of a second or third series of the Restatement does not repeal or otherwise affect an earlier version of the Restatement that has been adopted by a court or a legislature. The primary authority of the adopting state cannot be affected by the ALI's subsequent issuance of a new series of the Restatement. Furthermore, a state may have adopted an assortment of Restatement sections from different series.

Fourth, the Restatements' rule-based format may make the law appear to be more stable than it is if the researcher does not take the time to find out whether the rule is the subject of increasing criticism or whether it reflects an emerging rule not yet adopted by a majority of the states. The Reporter of the Restatement (Second) of Property noted that a reader could be misled if the Restatement adopted a rule not supported by current law but did not alert the reader to this lack of support. To avoid this result, the second and third series of the Restatement contain Reporter's Notes on each section, which

> disclos[e] the extent of . . . judicial decisions that have considered the issue. An examination of these Notes will reveal whether the restatement [rule] represents a choice between conflicting views and if a choice, whether [the chosen rule] is a minority position. These Notes also reveal whether the Restatement's position is a development of an area that has not received statutory or judicial consideration.

A. James Casner, *Restatement (Second) of Property as an Instrument of Law Reform,* 67 Iowa L. Rev. 87, 100 (1981). These Notes are not present in the first series of the Restatement.

Fifth, some commentators believe the Restatements do not embody dispassionate and accurate recording of existing common law. Rather, they argue that the Restatements actually reflect compromises between the divergent views of the participants in the ALI drafting and approval process; these compromises may have been adopted to achieve consensus among the ALI members rather than to achieve the goals of the Restatement process. Consequently, as the legal realists would have predicted, the Restatements are at times inconsistent, vague, or ambiguous.

3. How to Find Pertinent Material in the Restatements

Any thorough research project that involves use of the Restatements should address three questions:

(1) Are there Restatement sections relevant to my research problem?
(2) How did the authors of the Restatement construe the relevant sections?
(3) How have courts or secondary authorities interpreted the relevant Restatement sections (discussed in section 4 below)?

a. Finding a Relevant Section

In order to find the proper Restatement section, you must determine which Restatement subject, if any, encompasses your research issue. Consult the list of subjects in the first column of Table 3.5 beginning on page 106. You may wish to use other secondary sources to decide which subject or subjects apply to your fact situation.

Next you must determine which series on that subject will be useful in your research. The various Restatement series and their dates of adoption (as required by *The Bluebook*) are reflected in Table 3.5. If you are using the Restatements because you have a citation from another source to a particular section in a particular series, you may need to use only that series. On the other hand, you should consider consulting the earlier series if you have questions about the derivation of the current series' rule; the predecessor rule may demonstrate the countervailing rationales to the rule in the later series. By the same token, if you have a cite to an earlier series, you should consider consulting a later series to learn of emerging rules or rules that have attained majority status since the earlier series.

In the Perkins research problem, we know that the subject is torts and that recovery for emotional distress is an emerging tort theory, so the second series likely will be more fertile research ground than the first series.

Once you know which subject and series you need to use, you can locate an applicable Restatement section using either

(1) the table of contents approach or
(2) the index approach.

A table of contents is located in the front of each Restatement volume. It usually encompasses the entire subject in that series. However, in a few subjects (indicated in Table 3.5), the table of contents covers only topics found in that particular volume. Thus, for multi-volume Restatement subjects, you occasionally will have to examine the table of contents in more than one volume to find the appropriate topic.

A one-volume comprehensive index covers all of the Restatement subjects in the first series. The second and third series have no comprehensive index. In addition, each Restatement subject generally has its own index, which is located in the last topical (non-appendix) volume of each set. Exceptions to this index structure are noted in Table 3.5; these subjects have an index in the back of each volume indexing only sections located in that volume. Thus, for multi-volume Restatement subjects, you occasionally will have to consult indexes in more than one volume.

In the Perkins research project, both the table of contents and the index were helpful. The table of contents first led to Chapter 2 on intentional invasions of interests in personalty, which included Topic 5 on interest in freedom from emotional distress. Within Topic 5, § 46 covered outrageous conduct causing severe emotional distress. See Illustration 3-31 at pages 110-111. Similarly, the index listed § 46 under "emotional distress" but not under "mental distress."

b. Using Restatement Material to Interpret a Restatement Section

Once you have located a section number, be sure to look for it first in a main volume, not in an appendix volume or a supplement. They may look very similar. Read the boldface rule carefully: Remember that nearly every word was deliberated over by the ALI and that some subtle meanings may escape you on the first reading or two. Also read related Restatement rules so that you understand the full context of the section you are researching; these related rules include cross-referenced sections, sections in the vicinity of the section you are researching, and other sections that look promising in the Restatement index or table of contents.

Once you have read all of the pertinent rules, skim the comments and illustrations under each rule to locate the ones dealing with language or concepts that you need clarified. (See Illustration 3-31 on pages 110-111.) Read those comments and illustrations just as carefully as you read the rule.

In the Perkins research project, § 46 is a valuable "find" with a wealth of information. The rule stated in § 46(1) allows Perkins recovery for her emotional distress if

(1) Bartow's conduct was
    (a) extreme and outrageous and
    (b) intentional or reckless; and
(2) Bartow's conduct caused Perkins severe emotional distress.

Although Illustration 3-31 ends at comment d, § 46 really ends after comment *l* and illustration 22. Comment d discusses what constitutes extreme and outrageous conduct and gives four illustrations of what kind of conduct does and does not qualify. None of the illustrations are particularly analogous to Perkins' situation. Comment f details how "[t]he extreme and outrageous character of the conduct may arise from the actor's knowledge that the other is peculiarly susceptible to emotional distress, by reason of some physical or mental condition or peculiarity." Although none of the five illustrations is on point, comment f might cause you to wonder if Bartow tried to capitalize on Perkins' susceptibility to emotional distress because of her race, the racial difference between Perkins and her neighbors, and possibly the recent cross-burning. Comment i discusses the requirement of intention or recklessness. Comment j discusses how severe the emotional distress has to be in order to merit recovery. Comment k notes that bodily harm is not required but, if it is not present, "the courts may perhaps tend to look for more in the way of outrage as a guarantee that the claim is genuine . . . ."

Next locate the Reporter's Notes on that particular section; they are published in the main or appendix volumes to second- and third-series Restatements. Consult Table 3.5 (beginning on page 106) for the location of the Reporter's Notes. They explain the drafting history of the Restatement sections and provide commentary and analysis from the Reporter. (There are no Reporter's Notes to the first-series Restatements.) Illustration 3-32 on page 116 shows the Reporter's Notes on § 46. The Notes cite the books and articles that influenced the development of this section, as well as the cases that served as a basis for the illustrations.

If you decide to use more than one series, there are several ways you can find the equivalent section in another series on the same topic. Some subjects include tables that convert first-series sections to second-series sections and vice versa; these subjects are noted in Table 3.5. (Some tables even convert tentative-draft sections to final sections.) In addition, the Reporter's Notes for second- and third-series sections usually indicate at the outset which initial-series section was the predecessor for the subsequent-series section.

4. How to Find Sources Citing the Restatements

You can locate sources that cite particular Restatement sections by using

(1) finding tools within the Restatements,
(2) *Shepard's Restatement of the Law Citations,* or
(3) a table in A.L.R.

a. Finding Tools within the Restatements

The Restatements have collected a list of cases that have cited a particular Restatement section. This "digest" of cases contains the holding and citation of the case as well as a code that tells which portion of the Restatement was involved and how it was treated by the court.

The 1944 Permanent Edition of Restatement in the Courts (which may be shelved separately from the series) lists and summarizes all cases citing all Restatements from 1932 to 1944. Within each second- and third-series Restatement subject, the appendix volumes and their supplements list and summarize cases from 1945 to fairly recently that have cited a particular Restatement rule, comment, or illustration. See Illustration 3-33 on page 117. In the first appendix volume for some subjects, each section contains separate headings for first-series case digests and second-series case digests (if any). Consult Table 3.5 (beginning on page 106) for organizational differences among the various subjects' appendix volumes. In the subsequent appendix volume, the first-series case digests appear at the front of the volume, followed by the second-series case digests, then the third-series case digests (if any).

More recent cases can be found in *Interim Case Citations to the Restatement of the Law,* which updates all of the appendix volumes but contains only case citations and treatments, not summaries of those cases. See Illustration 3-34 on page 118.

Research in the appendix volumes of the Restatement (2d) of Torts presents special challenges, because of inaccurate tables of contents, inaccurate headers, differing organization, and one volume in which the sections are not arranged logically. Table 3.6 on page 119 shows how the sections are divided among the appendix volumes. The first appendix volume for each set of sections contains the Reporter's Notes and references to A.L.R. annotations and Key Numbers for each Restatement section. In those volumes, each section also contains separate headings for first-series case digests and second-series case digests (if any). However, in the first appendix volume

§ 45 A   TORTS, SECOND   Ch. 2

Charge of larceny and circumstances accompanying same as detention that will support action for false imprisonment. 31 A.L.R. 314.

Action for false imprisonment predicated upon institution of, or conduct in connection with, lunacy proceedings. 145 A.L.R. 711.

TOPIC 5. THE INTEREST IN FREEDOM FROM EMOTIONAL DISTRESS

§ 46. Outrageous Conduct Causing Emotional Distress.

REPORTER'S NOTES

This Section was revised, and the Comments rewritten, in the 1948 Supplement to the Restatements. It has again been revised, and the Comments rewritten, to keep pace with the continued development of the law. As to this development, see Magruder, Mental and Emotional Disturbance in the Law of Torts, 49 Harv. L. Rev. 1033 (1936); Prosser, Intentional Infliction of Mental Suffering: A New Tort, 37 Mich. L. Rev. 874 (1939); Eldredge, Modern Tort Problems, 71–102 (1941); Smith, Relation of Emotions to Injury and Disease: Legal Liability for Psychic Stimuli, 30 Va. L. Rev. 194 (1944); Wade, Tort Liability for Abusive and Insulting Language, 4 Vand. L. Rev. 63 (1950); Prosser, Insult and Outrage, 44 Cal. L. Rev. 40 (1956).

Extreme and outrageous conduct: Illustration 1 is based on Wilkinson v. Downton, 2 Q.B.D. 57 [1897]. See also Bielitski v. Obadisk, 15 Sask. L.R. 155, 61 Dom. L. Rep. 494, 23 A.L.R. 351 (1921); Savage v. Boies, 77 Ariz. 355, 272 P.2d 349 (1954). Cf. Great Atlantic & Pacific Tea

Co. v. Roch, 160 Md. 189, 153 A. 22 (1931).

Illustration 2 is taken from State Rubbish Collectors Association v. Siliznoff, 38 Cal. 2d 330, 240 P.2d 282 (1952).

Illustration 3: Compare Samms v. Eccles, 11 Utah 2d 289, 358 P. 2d 344 (1961); Mitran v. Williamson, 21 Misc. 2d 106, 197 N.Y.S. 2d 689 (1960); Halio v. Lurie, 15 App. Div. 2d 62, 222 N.Y.S.2d 759 (1961).

Illustration 4 is taken from Brooker v. Silverthorne, 111 S.C. 553, 99 S.E. 350, 5 A.L.R. 1283 (1919). Cf. Martin v. Lincoln Park West Corp., 219 F.2d 622 (7 Cir. 1955); Ex parte Hammett, 259 Ala. 240, 66 So. 2d 600 (1953); Halliday v. Cienkowski, 333 Pa. 123, 3 A.2d 372 (1939); Flowers v. Price, 190 S.C. 392, 3 S.E.2d 38 (1939); Atkinson v. Bibb Mfg. Co., 50 Ga. App. 434, 178 S.E. 537 (1935); Kramer v. Ricksmeier, 159 Iowa 48, 139 N.W. 1091, 45 L.R.A. N.S. 928 (1913); Galvin v. Starin, 132 App. Div. 577, 116 N.Y.Supp. 919 (1909); Stavnezer v. Sage-Allen & Co., 146 Conn. 460, 152 A.2d 312 (1959); Slocum v. Food Fair

See also cases under division, chapter, topic, title, and subtitle that includes section under examination.

Ch. 2   **APPENDIX**   **§ 46**

cause of action. Cucinotti v. Ortmann, 399 Pa. 26, 159 A.2d 216, 218.

Pa. 1963. 1948 Supp. cit. but dist. In action for injunctive relief against surveillances by defendant and money damages for invasion of privacy and intentional infliction of emotional distress, plaintiff could not maintain such action against defendant, who was enagaged by party against whom plaintiff had a claim for personal injuries sustained by her. Forster v. Manchester, 410 Pa. 192, 189 A.2d 147, 151, 152.

Tex. 1953. Illus. 4 cit. and dist. Damages were not recoverable for mental suffering caused by manner in which defendant attempted to collect usurious interest in absence of proof of physical injury. Harned v. E-Z Finance Co., 151 Tex. 641, 254 S.W.2d 81, 84.

Utah, 1961. 1948 Supp. cit. in ftn. in sup. Action by married woman for injury caused by emotional distress she claimed to have suffered because defendant persistently annoyed her with proposals that she have illicit sexual relations with him could not be based upon mere negligence, but, though harm not accompanied by bodily impact or physical injury, an action may be based upon severe emotional distress where defendant intentionally engaged in some conduct toward plaintiff and defendant's purpose was to inflict emotional distress or any reasonable person would have known that such would result, and actions are of such nature as to be considered outrageous and intolerable in that they offend against the generally accepted standards of decency and morality. Samms v. Eccles, 11 Utah 2d 289, 358 P.2d 344, 347.

Cross References to

1. **Digest System Key Numbers**
   Damages ☞48 et seq.
   Threats ☞10
   Torts ☞6, 8

2. **A.L.R. Annotation**
   Right to recover for mental pain and anguish alone, apart from other damages. 23 A.L.R. 361, s. 44 A. L. R. 428, 56 A.L.R. 657.
   Recovery for physical consequences of fright resulting in a physical injury. 11 A.L.R. 1119, s. 40 A.L.R. 983, 76 A.L.R. 681, 98 A.L.R. 402.
   Recovery for mental shock or distress in connection with injury to or interference with tangible property. 28 A.L.R.2d 1070.
   Recovery for emotional disturbance or its physical consequences, in the absence of impact or other actionable wrong. 64 A.L.R.2d 100, 108 et seq.
   Right of debtor to recover for mental pain and anguish caused by methods pursued by creditor in attempt to collect claim. 91 A.L.R. 1495.
   Recovery by tenant for mental anguish occasioned by wrongful eviction. 17 A.L.R.2d 936.
   Anxiety as to future disease, condition, or death therefrom, as element of damages in personal injury action. 71 A.L.R.2d 338, 342.
   Humiliation and mental suffering as element of damages recoverable by one wrongfully induced to enter into illegal, void, or nonexistent marriage. 72 A.L.R.2d 994.
   Mental distress as element of damages for wrongful suspension or expulsion of member. 74 A.L.R.2d 783, 811.

Cit.—cited; fol.—followed; quot.—quoted; sup.—support.
A complete list of abbreviations faces page 1.

TORTS 2d

Section 46

C.A.3, 1990. Kraus v. Consolidated Rail Corp., 899 F.2d 1360, 1361. Subsec. (1) cit. in disc.

C.A.9, 1990. Cook v. Lindsay Olive Growers, 911 F.2d 233, 239. Com. (d) quot. in case quot. in disc.

C.A.10, 1990. Merrick v. Northern Natural Gas Co., 911 F.2d 426, 432. Com. (d) quot. in case quot. in disc.

C.A.11, 1990. Hart v. U.S., 894 F.2d 1539, 1548. Cit. in case cit. in disc., com. (d) quot. in case quot. in disc.

C.A.11, 1990. Von Stein v. Brescher, 904 F.2d 572, 584. Subsecs. (d) and (e) quot. in cases quot. in disc.

C.A.D.C. 1990. Abourezk v. New York Airlines, Inc., 895 F.2d 1456, 1459. Quot. in case cit. in disc.

D.Md. 1990. Poyer v. Sears Roebuck Co., Inc., 741 F. Supp. 98, 101. Cit. in disc.

D.Minn. 1990. Meleen v. Hazelden Foundation, 740 F. Supp. 687, 693. Quot. in case quot. but dist.

D.N.H. 1990. Bourque v. Town of Bow, 736 F. Supp. 398, 404. Quot. in disc., subsec. (1), com. (d) quot. in disc.

D.N.J. 1990. Lacy v. Cooper Hospital/University Medical Center, 745 F. Supp. 1029, 1034-1035. Com. (d) quot. in case quot. in disc., com. (h) quot. in

E.D.Pa. 1990. Quitmeyer v. S.E. Pa. Transp. Authority, 740 F. Supp. 363, 368. Subsec. (1) quot. in disc., com. (d) quot. in sup. and cit. generally in ftn.

W.D.Pa. 1990. McWilliams v. AT & T Information Systems, Inc., 728 F. Supp. 1186, 1194. Cit. in disc.

W.D.Va. 1990. Simmons v. Norfolk & Western Ry. Co., 734 F. Supp. 230, 232. Com. (d) quot. in sup.

N.D.W.Va. 1989. White v. National Steel Corp., 742 F. Supp. 312, 342. Quot. in case quot. in sup., com. (d) quot. in case quot. in sup.

Ala. 1990. Continental Cas. Ins. Co. v. McDonald, 567 So.2d 1208, 1211, 1217, 1219-1220. Com. (d) quot. gen. in case quot. in disc., coms. (e) and (f) quot. in disc., coms. (e), (g) and (j) cit. in case quot. in disc.

Cal.App. 1990. Christensen v. Superior Court, 271 Cal. Rptr. 360, 373. Cit. in sup.

Del. 1990. Cummings v. Pinder, 574 A.2d 843, 845. Subsec. (1) cit. in sup.

D.C.App. 1990. Saunders v. Nemati, 580 A.2d 660, 661, 664. Cit. and quot. in disc.

Fla.App. 1990. Baker v. Florida Nat. Bank, 559 So.2d 284, 288. Cit. in disc., coms. (d) and (g) quot. in disc.

Fla.App. 1990. Lashley v. Bowman, 561 So.2d 406, 408-410. Subsec. (1) quot. in sup., com. (d) quot. and cit. in sup., com. (e) and illus. 5 cit. in sup.

covering §§ 708 to 840E, the sections and their case digests are arranged in the order indicated in Table 3.6. The table of contents does not show this contorted organizational scheme. The major clues are "headers" (the lines at the top of each page) that refer you to notes, which indicate that certain pages contain only first-series case digests.

In the subsequent appendix volumes and supplements, the first-series case digests are located in the initial part of the volume or supplement, followed by the second-series case digests. However, in the earlier volumes indicated in Table 3.6, the words in the headers do not reflect this organization; they all read "Torts 2d" or a similar term. Thus, you must flip through the book looking for the point where the section numbers start to repeat themselves. In the later volumes indicated in Table 3.6, the headers accurately reflect whether the case digests contain first- or second-series cases. Ignore the table of contents, because it frequently only lists the second-series sections contained in that volume, but does not reflect the actual organization of the volume.

One last peculiarity: Sections 402A and 402B did not appear in the first series but have been frequently litigated since their second-series adoption.

TABLE 3.6. Organization of Case Digests in the Restatement (2d) of Torts: First-Series Cases and Second-Series Cases.

Individual Volume Contents	Organization in First Appendix Volume			Organization in Subsequent Appendix Volumes and Supplements
§§ 1-309	separate headings within each section			1st-series digests at front of volume or supplement; 2d-series digests follow; headers inaccurate in 1964-75 and 1976-84 volumes; headers accurate from 1984 on
§§ 310-402	separate headings within each section			same as §§ 1-309
§§ 402A-503	separate headings within each section			same as §§ 1-309; §§ 402A & 402B have no 1st-series cases and are in separate volume
§§ 504-587	separate headings within each section			1st-series digests at front of volume or supplement; 2d-series digests follow; all headers accurate
§§ 588-707A	separate headings within each section			same as §§ 504-587
§§ 708-840E	*pages*	*series*	*sections*	same as §§ 504-587
	1-131	1st	708-816	
	342-392	2d	712-774B	
	393-412	1st & 2d	817-821	
	413-476	1st	822-840	
	477-552	2d	821A-840E	
§§ 841-951	separate headings within each section			same as §§ 504-587

After the first appendix volume, these sections have their own appendix volumes, and there are no first-series cases in them.

Table 3.5 (beginning on page 106) catalogs which Restatements contain the following features:

(1) tables of cases and statutes cited in that Restatement subject or at least in the Reporter's Notes, from which tables you may be able to find a pertinent Restatement section by the name of a leading case or by the citation to a statute;

(2) citations to A.L.R. annotations that pertain to the topic of a particular Restatement section; and

(3) West Topics and Key Numbers that pertain to the topic of a particular Restatement section (see Chapter 5).

See Illustration 3-33 on page 117 for the latter two features.

b.   Finding Tools outside the Restatements

Shepard's Restatement of the Law Citations began publication in 1976, covers all series of the Restatements, and usually is within a month of being current. It lists published cases, A.L.R. annotations, and selected legal periodical articles that have cited each Restatement section, comment, and illustration. You may recall a similar *Shepard's* set for sources citing various legal periodical pieces; see Part D of this chapter. Be sure to locate the heading for the correct Restatement section in the correct series.

Illustration 3-35 on page 120 shows the hardbound *Shepard's* entry for § 46 of the second-series Torts Restatement. As of November 1991, there were six pages of citations for § 46. Note the separate sub-listings of sources that

§ 41   **TORTS, SECOND**

Comments	DC	612F2d273	606FS879	1FlS2d156	67NYM253	480So2d1247	606P2d953
a to h	399A2d218	616F2d89	607FS1175	112GaA684	118NYM562	Alk	659P2d88
548FS332	448A2d862	646F2d1291	609FS673	154GaA159	122NYM303	705P2d456	695P2d1277
	Ind	667F2d23	609FS996	176GaA229	16▢A435	Ariz	106NE746
§ 42	439NE199	692F2d914	609FS1197	64H468	253Or122	540P2d196	174NE163
548FS306	Mich	697F2d1124	613FS220	244Ia687	258Or612	551P2d575	343NE230
41NY557	327NW894	703F2d1158	613FS497	100Ida849	259Or55	578P2d155	360NE767
8OhM195	NJ	724F2d18	615FS308	104Ida334	282Or243	603P2d931	371NE375
NY	250A2d770	750F2d814	617FS1042	107Ida1138	282Or737	605P2d40	388NE268
362NE963	Ohio	759F2d275	617FS1365	347IIA302	287Or455	610P2d463	392NE159
394NYS2d	474NE367	762F2d220	617FS1549	361IIA103	291Or725	619P2d1035	427NE311
[163	Wash	303FS119	618FS928	56IIA113	292Or152	624P2d875	433NE1367
Ohio	544P2d58	315FS753	63FRD33	66IIA85	39OrA320	629P2d1005	Ind
221NE218	Wis	369FS150	94FRD740	70IIA237	51OrA602	650P2d499	426NE1307
Comment a	184NW172	372FS1075	12BRW469	74IIA27	57OrA211	653P2d18	Iowa
638F2d861	Comment b	390FS998	18BRW244	100IIA855	6▢S374	685P2d734	57NW918
	556F2d1193	422FS394	289Ala631	105IIA240	399Pa26	688P2d617	179NW582
§ 43	415Mch218	431FS262	268Ark279	26IID644	410Pa192	Ark	203NW255
547F2d692	93NJS229	432FS690	274Ark225	22Il2d83	437Pa378	596SW687	252NW423
103CA3d944	96NJS13	435FS356	266Ark1069	1KA2d216	494Pa511	597SW94	328NW498
186Ct268	50Wis2d295	446FS395	118Az476	3KA2d514	231PaS449	623SW519	334NW129
36TnA9	Mich	454FS1212	124Az304	7KA2d608	244PaS382	Calif	334NW756
Calif	327NW894	455FS152	124Az461	215Kan819	257PaS60	5CaR33	346NW801
163CaR338	NJ	458FS1384	125Az461	216Kan201	262PaS335	42CaR317	360NW776
Colo	225A2d592	461FS1016	127Az258	219Kan582	279PaS504	54CaR84	372NW197
663P2d1056	232A2d427	462FS1342	127Az499	225Kan478	293PaS126	73CaR111	Kan
Conn	Wis	468FS479	128Az197	227Kan920	294PaS269	79CaR204	529P2d109
440A2d974	184NW172	469FS488	129Az169	232Kan536	304PaS432	86CaR90	531P2d2
Tenn	Comment c	472FS948	133Az197	233Kan279	324PaS152	89CaR88	549P2d881
251SW142	Comment c	473FS990	133Az561	2MaA802	332PaS59	97CaR581	563P2d514
	556F2d1193	476FS649	141Az97	359Mas252	333PaS616	103CaR891	592P2d861
§ 44	587F2d1058	487FS1301	141Az609	371Mas142	334PaS45	108CaR489	597P2d687
407F2d792	549FS341	491FS1042	24AzA577	380Mas835	342PaS381	131CaR552	611P2d153
530F2d1213	174GaA347	495FS346	27AzA126	381Mas519	251SoC98	136CaR278	645P2d920
693F2d487	415Mch219	501FS69	134CA2d633	385Mas95	273SoC770	136CaR820	657P2d566
358FS949	100Nev634	504FS163	171CA2d109	386Mas549	276SoC160	162CaR202	662P2d1223
112DPR813	16▢A23	510FS260	180CA2d904	3McA692	283SoC166	192CaR496	Ky
348Mo702	253Or335	512FS139	231CA2d808	66McA390	146NJS518	193CaR674	584SW407
Colo	Fla	514FS557	245CA2d529	101McA732	153NJS83	206CaR7	666SW733
663P2d1056	382So2d682	514FS1033	10CA3d394	114McA17	178NJS315	206CaR484	671SW250
Mo	Ga	521FS4	20CA3d302	117McA706	180NJS428	210CaR822	La
155SW77	330SE110	530FS768	60CA3d296	119McA714	193NJS260	286P2d478	155So2d913
Comment a	Mich	530FS779	66CA3d170	129McA76	198NJS431	339P2d911	217So2d444
519F2d45	327NW895	531FS72	67CA3d763	129McA460	217Ten478	468P2d218	335So2d488
1982IILR852	Nev	534FS691	101CA3d921	133McA590	151Tex647	510P2d1041	362So2d1145
Comment c	691P2d445	536FS602	144CA3d229	134McA350	215Va341	Colo	Mass
556F2d1193	Ohio	537FS1390	145CA3d790	137McA245	136Vt474	476P2d756	268NE320
Comment d	474NE367	538FS334	158CA3d922	138McA134	4WAp150	536P2d841	307NE866
24OrA765	Ore	544FS653	160CA3d122	141McA113	15WAp684	580P2d400	355NE317
Ore	454P2d640	546FS225	164CA3d640	141McA684	22WAp617	645P2d294	406NE676
547P2d1401	Comment d	548FS336	2C3d498	422Mch602	25WAp84	655P2d425	413NE697
	24OrA765	553FS238	9C3d579	281Md564	29WAp387	658P2d1376	431NE561
§ 45	Ore	553FS938	35CC726	35MdA559	31WAp425	Conn	437NE177
412F2d536	547P2d1401	560FS227	35CoA403	302NC447	32WAp154	93A2d295	Md
Comment b	Comment e	561FS203	40CoA456	193Neb370	40WAp863	480A2d614	371A2d1106
12C3d719	591F2d1271	565FS498	173Col177	210Neb69	21Wis2d357	484A2d946	380A2d613
Calif		565FS914	31CS308	214Neb156	114Wis2d307	DC	502A2d1115
117CaR246	**§ 46**	570FS200	40CS62	219Neb358	54W2d447	412A2d957	Me
527P2d870	et seq.	572FS906	40CS167	96Nev946	85W2d58	415A2d1076	401A2d154
	Okla	572FS919	139C1308	97Nev126	88W2d736	443A2d37	Mich
	549P2d397	573FS372	50DC2d44	122NH652	91W2d320	Fla	143NW614
§ 45A		574FS1488	53DC2d466	124NH217	94W2d95	319So2d112	239NW382
556F2d1193	**§ 46**	576FS433	70DC2d756	84NM480	96W2d675	373So2d818	300NW691
591F2d1271	404F2d165	585FS69	71DC2d59	97NM214	100W2d741	382So2d153	318NW561
250Ark456	455F2d860	585FS762	6DC3d766	43NY557	103W2d146	426So2d973	326NW618
415Mch218	470F2d4	585FS1261	10DC3d142	58NY127	162WV127	429So2d1290	341NW528
16▢A23	533F2d399	586FS902	11DC3d259	65NY143	Ala	438So2d59	341NW817
104NJS576	540F2d1230	587FS225	14DC3d187	35NYAD113	270So2d87	467So2d278	349NW532
14WAp567	586F2d885	588FS1155	18DC3d493	49NYAD1026	392So2d537	471So2d166	351NW567
50Wis2d295	595F2d1273	594FS831	23DC3d762	66NYAD507	394So2d362	Ga	357NW673
Ark	599F2d381	595FS298	24DC3d222	78NYAD944	400So2d373	145SE780	358NW909
465SW331		595FS739	24DC3d712	83NYAD20	415So2d1100	267SE785	366NW12
		601FS1154	25DC3d601	84NYAD514	428So2d640	335SE447	
		605FS513	28DC3d411	84NYAD815	431So2d1261	Haw	
		605FS1521	31DC3d344	109NYAD966	461So2d1311	643P2d535	*Continued*
				56NYM1060	466So2d122	Idaho	

334

have cited specific comments for the sections preceding § 46. Also note that a handful of Kansas cases have cited § 46.

As with all *Shepard's* citators, the only information provided is the citation itself and sometimes a one-letter or two-letter notation, not an explanation of how the Restatement segment is used in the case. The major disadvantage of *Shepard's* is the absence of summaries explaining the facts or holdings of the cases cited. Thus, using the Restatement appendix volumes may be more efficient for finding pertinent cases than using *Shepard's* because the appendix case summaries reduce the need to read every case cited. However, the appendix volumes are not nearly as current as *Shepard's* and do not cover the range of secondary sources included in *Shepard's.*

In addition, the last volume of the A.L.R. *Index to Annotations* has a table listing annotations that refer to various Restatement sections.

c. Application to the Perkins Research Situation

In the Perkins problem, the Restatement appendix volumes, their supplements, and the *Interim Case Citations* provided a wealth of case citations, some of which seemed pertinent. Your next step would be to read those cases. Likewise, *Shepard's* yielded a large collection of case citations but sorting them was difficult. You definitely would skim the cases from Kansas, the jurisdiction of the Perkins problem. You also could select the cases cited under the Restatement comments of most interest to you. For instance, comment d on extreme and outrageous conduct focuses on a key element of the tort that is in question in the Perkins problem.

5. What Are Pattern Jury Instructions?

At the end of a jury trial, be it civil or criminal, the jury must be instructed on the law of the case before it retires to the jury room for deliberations. These jury instructions may be created by the judge or by the attorneys litigating the case. They may be created from scratch, from published cases, or from a pattern jury instruction guide. Procedures vary quite a bit from court to court.

Pattern jury instructions are a published collection of tried-and-true jury instructions drawn from statutes or published cases, revised jury instructions based on past instructions courts have criticized, or new jury instructions reflecting new law or a unique fact situation. The authors or Reporters of these compilations may be private authors, a group of judges, a bar association, a supreme court committee, or any combination of these groups. However, even if judges are involved in compiling the collection, pattern jury instructions are still commentary sources because they are not issued by a court as the law.

Most of these sources are updated annually with pocket parts or other supplements.

Illustration 3-36 on page 122 shows a page from a leading compilation of pattern jury instructions used in federal courts, Edward J. Devitt, Charles B. Blackmar & Michael A. Wolff, *Federal Jury Practice and Instructions* (4th ed. 1987). These instructions were compiled by a federal judge, a state court judge, and a law professor. Each section contains a jury instruction, followed by notes stating the source of the instruction and briefly discussing related law in several federal appellate jurisdictions.

Illustration 3-37 on page 123 shows a page from a state jury instruction guide. ("JIG" stands for jury instruction guide.) These pattern jury instructions

Ch. 81   **INJURY CLAIM—INTENTIONAL TORTS**   § 81.05

the accused. Singleton v. New York, 632 F.2d 185 (2d Cir.1980), cert. denied 450 U.S. 920, 101 S.Ct. 1368, 67 L.Ed.2d 347 (1981 N.Y.).

Under Michigan law a person giving incorrect information to prosecutor may be held liable for malicious prosecution. Cann v. Ford Motor Co., 658 F.2d 54 (2d Cir.1981), cert. denied 456 U.S. 960, 102 S.Ct. 2036, 72 L.Ed.2d 484 (1982).

Ninth Circuit

In Rannels v. S.E. Nichols, Inc., 591 F.2d 242 (3d Cir.1979), the court expounded on the essential elements of malicious prosecution under Pennsylvania law, and reversed an order dismissing the complaint.

§ 81.05   Intentional Infliction of Emotional Distress

In order to find for the plaintiff on his claim of intentional infliction of emotional distress, the plaintiff must show by a preponderance of the evidence the following:

First, the conduct of the defendant was extreme and outrageous;

Second, the conduct was intentional or reckless;

Third, the plaintiff suffered emotional distress as a result of the defendant's conduct; and,

Fourth, the emotional distress was severe.

NOTES

In General

Restatement Second of Torts § 46, Comments d and j (1965).

Third Circuit

For an action claiming intentional infliction of emotional distress by a false reporting of a disease, see Chuy v. Philadelphia Eagles Football Club, 431 F.Supp. 254 (E.D.Pa.1977), affirmed 595 F.2d 1265 (3d Cir.1979).

Plaintiff failed to state a cause of action for intentional infliction of emotional distress where he alleged employer did not adequately deal with employee's alcoholism and refused to rehire employee even after successful rehabilitation. Bradshaw v. General Motors Corp., Fisher Body Div., 805 F.2d 110, 113, 4 (3d Cir.1986).

Ninth Circuit

For case discussing intentional infliction of emotional distress, see Miller v. Fairchild Industries, Inc., 797 F.2d 727 (9th Cir.1986).

ILLUSTRATION 3-37. Sample State Jury Instructions, 4 Minn. Dist. Judges Ass'n
Comm. on Jury Instruction Guides, *Minnesota Practice:
Minnesota Jury Instruction Guides—Civil* 349 (Michael K.
Steenson, Reporter, 3d ed. 1986).

123

INTENTIONAL TORTS   **JIG 505**

JIG 505

INTENTIONAL INFLICTION OF EMOTIONAL DISTRESS

The intentional infliction of emotional distress requires proof of four elements:

First, the conduct of ＿＿＿＿＿＿＿ must be so ex-
name of defendant
treme and outrageous that it passes the boundaries of decency and is utterly intolerable to the civilized community.

Second, the conduct must be intentional or reckless.

Third, that intentional conduct must cause emotional distress to ＿＿＿＿＿＿＿ .
name of plaintiff

Fourth, the distress must be so severe that no reasonable person could be expected to endure it.

AUTHORITIES

Restatement, Second, Torts § 46 (1965), reads as follows:

(1) One who by extreme and outrageous conduct intentionally or recklessly causes severe emotional distress to another is subject to liability for such emotional distress, and if bodily harm to the other results from it, for such bodily harm.

(2) Where such conduct is directed at a third person, the actor is subject to liability if he intentionally or recklessly causes severe emotional distress

(a) to a member of such person's immediate family who is present at the time, whether or not such distress results in bodily harm, or

(b) to any other person who is present at the time, if such distress results in bodily harm.

The Minnesota Supreme Court adopted the first paragraph of section 46 in *Hubbard v. United Press Int'l*, 330 N.W.2d 428 (Minn. 1983). The court discussed the elements of an emotional distress claim as follows:

The commentary to the Restatement emphasizes the high threshold standard of proof required of a complainant before his case may be submitted to a jury. We have previously noted that the type of actionable conduct referred to in the were compiled by a law professor who served as a "Reporter" (see the previous discussion of the Restatement Reporters) working in conjunction with an association of state court trial judges.

In addition, there are some excellent specialized collections of pattern jury instructions on subjects such as medical issues, tort actions, employment law, antitrust cases, and business tort litigation.

6. When to Look For Pattern Jury Instructions

Of course, you should consult pattern jury instructions when you are looking for jury instructions for a trial.

Pattern jury instructions also provide limited commentary and cites to leading cases in a specific jurisdiction, so they are useful even in an advisory or non-litigative setting. However, their limited coverage restricts their use in doing background research on the law of that particular jurisdiction.

In addition, a good jury instruction should be in layperson's language and thus may be helpful to an attorney who needs to explain the law to a layperson client.

7. How to Find Pertinent Pattern Jury Instructions

Pattern jury instruction volumes can be located by means of a library catalog or by shelf browsing. The easiest way to locate federal pattern jury instructions is to locate the source in Illustration 3-36 on page 122, then use its call number (1) to do a call number search on a computerized catalog to locate other federal pattern jury instructions or (2) to browse the shelves. Another possibility is to locate the *West CD-ROM Federal Civil Practice Library,* which contains the source in Illustration 3-36, as well as pattern jury instruction collections from the Fifth and Ninth Circuits.

Locating state pattern jury instructions is tougher. You can locate them in a library catalog by doing a subject search under the requisite jurisdiction for the following terms: jury trial, jury practice, jury instructions, pattern jury instructions, model jury instructions, and sample jury instructions. If this search is unsuccessful, try a key word search for the same terms on a computerized catalog but be prepared for a large number of entries. In addition, some pattern jury instructions are part of treatises on state practice and procedure; these collections may not show up in a search of the library catalog.

Most pattern jury instructions are accessible through their tables of contents and indexes. Some pattern jury instructions also have tables of cases, statutes, and court rules, so that you can locate a pertinent jury instruction if you have a cite to a leading case, a pertinent statute, or a pertinent court rule.

The pattern jury instructions shown in Illustrations 3-36 and 3-37 pertain to the Perkins research problem and were easily accessible by both table of contents and index approaches. Both sets of notes after the instructions cite first and foremost to § 46 of the second-series Restatement of Torts, leading one to think that the Restatement section is a "find" of major consequence. The *Hubbard* case cited in Illustration 3-37 is the same case that appears before the A.L.R. annotation illustrated earlier in Part E (Illustration 3-25).

1. Setting Goals for Your Use of Commentary Sources

In Chapter 2, your starting point was the six categories of factual and legal analysis. After that, your initial research goal was to generate a research vocabulary by forming ladders of abstraction and finding synonyms and legal definitions. Then you moved into commentary sources to obtain

(1) an overview of the subject;
(2) citations to other commentary sources and key primary sources; and
(3) expert analysis of the law's trends, policies, and defects.

However, the question left open at the outset of Chapter 3 was how you decide which type(s) of commentary source to consult. This final part of Chapter 3 assesses some of the strengths, weaknesses, and differences of the various kinds of commentary sources.

2. Choosing Commentary Sources Suited to Your Research Project

All of the secondary sources covered in this chapter serve dual functions as both commentary sources and finding tools; they provide commentary as well as citations to other commentary and primary sources. Because much of the information in these sources is fairly redundant, you do not need to research in each of these sources on every research project. But how do you know when to use which source?

There are few hard-and-fast rules about when to use one source instead of another. Rather, there are various factors to consider. Each source is strong on some factors and weak on others. Once you have decided which factors are most important for your specific task, you can rank the sources. Indeed, you can create descending levels of preference, so that you drop down to the next source when the more preferred source does not satisfy your research needs. The grid-style chart on page 127 is designed to help you identify the factors.

The strategy of commentary research lies in recognizing and weighing these factors. Scan the factors listed across the top of the chart. Which of them seem more important than the others? Do your rankings change according to the type of situation you are researching? How so? What additional factors would you add to this chart?

You may notice some patterns evolving. Here are but a few:

The generality of an encyclopedia can be extremely helpful at the outset of a research project but is frustrating later on when you need more specificity. Conversely, the narrowness of an A.L.R. annotation or a legal periodical article may not be helpful at the outset of a research project, when you need "big picture" information; however, they may be of great assistance if your research has advanced to the stage where you are seeking the answer to a narrow, well-defined question. Thus, a wider scope of coverage usually comes at the expense of detailed coverage. Encyclopedias try to cover the full range of legal topics in general terms, while A.L.R. annotations and legal periodical articles attempt detailed coverage of the "hot spots" in law practice and legal scholarship. Treatises and Restatements usually fall somewhere in between these extremes.

The less cohesive the organizational scheme of the source, the more dependent you are on the research aids by which you locate pertinent material in the source. Treatises, Restatements, and pattern jury instructions have a comprehensive topical organizational scheme, so their indexes are an adequate back-up to their tables of contents. Encyclopedias are organized alphabetically by subject matter, so a good index is essential to back up the table of contents; tables of cases and statutes are helpful too. A.L.R. annotations have no overall organization and must be located through indexes, tables, and other sources. Likewise, legal periodicals have no overall organization and must be located through several commercial indexes and other sources.

On the other hand, both A.L.R.s and legal periodicals are published serially rather than as a set, so they are better able to respond to the changing profile of the law than are encyclopedias, treatises, and other sources published as a complete set. Thus, A.L.R.s and legal periodicals trade off comprehensive organization in favor of attention to current controversies.

Updating is another factor to consider. Many commentary sources are updated annually but some are never updated. This latter group includes some treatises, all CLE materials, and legal periodicals. Some finding tools in the Restatements are updated more often than once a year. The *Shepard's Citators* associated with legal periodicals, A.L.R.s, and Restatements are regularly updated.

In a brief to a court or in a memorandum to a partner, the "citability" of various commentary sources depends largely on the reputation and credibility of the author. In the case of staff writers for encyclopedias and A.L.R. annotations, one doesn't know the author's credentials, so an assessment of "citability" is more difficult than it is with treatises, which generally have well-known authors. In legal periodicals, articles usually are ordered according to the prestige and credibility of the authors, permitting a fairly easy assessment of citability.

By now, you and your classmates have worked on a wide range of research situations in the problem sets. What kind of fact situations are well served or poorly served by each type of commentary source? Do some of these sources favor or avoid certain subjects? Which sources do well on questions of law (with fixed facts) and which sources do well on mixed questions of law and fact? What other patterns and trade-offs do you see? What impact do they have on your developing commentary preferences?

By the time you have completed this book, you should begin to develop some preferences as to the more important factors differentiating commentary sources. The polishing of a research strategy, however, requires experience and encounters with a wide range of fact situations and research settings.

3. Prioritizing and Selecting Leads within a Single Commentary Source

When you use an index or table of contents to find pertinent material on an unfamiliar subject, you often generate so many leads that you cannot or should not track down all of them. How should you prioritize and select among those leads?

	encyclopedias	treatises	CLE materials	legal periodicals	A.L.R. annotations	Restatements	pattern jury instructions
Breadth of Coverage							
Depth of Coverage							
Organizational Scheme (alphabetical, topic, serial)							
Table of Contents							
Index							
Other Means by Which to Find Pertinent Material							
Attention to Current Controversies							
Updating Frequency & Content							
Citability & Credibility							
Clarity, Lack of Bias, Accuracy							
Subjects Covered Well							
Subjects Not Covered Well or Not Covered at All							
Citing Sources Information (internal or *Shepard's*)							
Attention to Factual Analysis							
Attention to Policy							
Other Strengths							
Other Weaknesses							

Rather than skimming all of these leads to determine their value, you first should prioritize these leads in order of how much promise they show. Otherwise, you will be reading overlapping commentary as well as some not-so-useful commentary. This is a waste of valuable time. One way to prioritize is to determine which concepts and terms in your factual and legal analysis in Chapter 2 (with subsequent additions as discovered; see pages 19, 20, and 28) have greater importance than others to this particular research project. You also should give high priority to commentary leads with a larger number of key terms in their titles. Yet another way to prioritize is to think about the strengths and weaknesses of particular commentary sources and to select the leads that capitalize on the strengths of the sources, not their weaknesses.

Remember to look for clues like this before you plow through a list of possible leads in no particular order. You want to increase your chances of a "lucky hit" and thereby decrease the number of pages you have to read to get the same amount of information.

4. When to Cite Commentary Sources

Recall that primary sources have the force and effect of law. All other research sources are secondary sources, which in turn can be divided into commentary and finding tools. If your memory needs refreshing on this point, reread Chapter 1.

You should cite primary sources—cases, statutes, rules of court, regulations—whenever possible. Never rely on commentary alone without investigating and reading the primary sources yourself. Reading the full texts of primary sources gives you the full flavor of the law. It also allows you to detect ambiguities, misinterpretations, and perhaps even mistakes made by the commentator. Keep in mind that none of these commentary sources is written under governmental authority. A commentary source should not be cited if primary authority—for example, a case or a statute—also supports the proposition.

However, commentary sources can be cited for some propositions that do not require primary authority citation. For instance, a commentary source could be cited to support a statement as to the number of jurisdictions adopting a certain rule of law. Commentary also may be cited for its criticism or policy analysis of an established rule of law.

Finding tools are never cited.

Issue Formulation for Primary Authority Research

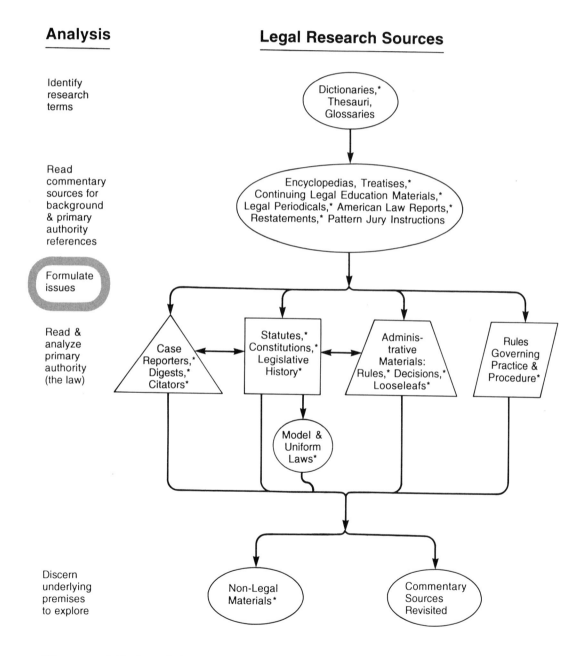

Analysis

Legal Research Sources

Identify
research
terms

Dictionaries,*
Thesauri,
Glossaries

Read
commentary
sources for
background
& primary
authority
references

Encyclopedias, Treatises,*
Continuing Legal Education Materials,*
Legal Periodicals,* American Law Reports,*
Restatements,* Pattern Jury Instructions

Formulate
issues

Read &
analyze
primary
authority
(the law)

Case
Reporters,*
Digests,*
Citators*

Statutes,*
Constitutions,*
Legislative
History*

Adminis-
trative
Materials:
Rules,* Decisions,*
Looseleafs*

Rules
Governing
Practice &
Procedure*

Model &
Uniform
Laws*

Discern
underlying
premises
to explore

Non-Legal
Materials*

Commentary
Sources
Revisited

*Sources available (in part) through computer-assisted legal research

A. HOW TO FORMULATE AND ORDER ISSUES

While performing the steps set out in Chapters 2 and 3, you will have begun to tentatively identify and frame the issues raised by the application of legal principles to your specific facts. By the end of your commentary research, you need to put these issues on paper and refine them. This process is the core of the analytical process inherent in legal research. If you ask the right questions, your research will be focused and efficient, and your solution is likely to be the correct one.

Legal issues involve questions about how the *law* relates to the *facts* of the case. The following question contains only law: "What is the definition of severe emotional distress?" The following question contains only facts: "Did the defendant place the garbage in front of plaintiff's house?" (An issue about disputed facts can be resolved only by the jury or trier of fact, not by your legal research.) However, the following issue shows the desired relationship between law and fact: "Did the plaintiff suffer severe emotional distress from the garbage placed in front of her house?" Your issues should show how the law relates to the facts of the case, because your legal research and writing are directed toward informing your reader how the law relates to this particular fact situation.

There may be more than one issue, or there may be a single issue with multiple sub-issues. In dealing with multiple issues or sub-issues, the issue-framing process is the same but the difficulties are compounded because you must cope with the problem of ordering related and unrelated issues.

Sub-issues often evolve out of a list of "elements" (requirements), criteria, guidelines, or factors used to determine a single legal concept such as a cause of action (breach of contract, battery); a defense (qualified privilege, frustration of purpose); a legal status (a protected class, an incompetent person); or a remedy (eviction, specific performance). For instance, in the example problem, the main issue and its sub-issues on the cause of action might be as follows:

(1) Can Perkins establish a cause of action for intentional infliction of emotional distress (IIED) against Bartow?

   (a) Did Bartow engage in extreme and outrageous conduct when he placed the garbage in front of Perkins' house in order to keep her out of the neighborhood?

   (b) Was Bartow's conduct reckless or intentional when he placed the garbage in front of Perkins' house in order to keep her out of the neighborhood?

   (c) Did Perkins suffer severe emotional distress when she experienced dizziness, nausea, sleeplessness, shock, anger, fear, headaches, and an inability to function at work?

   (d) Was Perkins' severe emotional distress caused by Bartow when she had an extreme reaction immediately after he dumped garbage in front of her house?

These sub-issues are based on the elements of the cause of action, IIED, as stated in some jurisdictions and as related to the facts of this case.

Other sub-issues may examine the possibility of alternative remedies:

(2) Is Perkins entitled to any relief for IIED?
    (a) May Perkins obtain damages from Bartow?
    (b) If not, may Perkins obtain an injunction prohibiting more harassing conduct by Bartow?

If you continued to revise and expand the outline or flowchart in Chapter 2 (see pages 33-35) as you did your research in commentary sources, these issues and sub-issues would be apparent from that outline or flowchart. It also would be apparent that you could formulate sub-subissues as well. For example, issue (1)(a) could have the following sub-subissue:

> Did Bartow's garbage dumping in front of Perkins' house constitute extreme and outrageous conduct because he knew that Perkins, as an African-American, was peculiarly susceptible to emotional distress in the setting of a segregated neighborhood and a recent cross-burning?

This is a viable research issue, but when you write up your research results, you might decide not to list all of your sub-subissues for fear of losing the reader.

Issues and sub-issues need to be ordered logically according to certain rules or organizing principles. You may place issues in the order that the facts occurred (chronologically) or in the order they would be presented in court (claim, defense, rebuttal). Issues such as jurisdiction and statute of limitations logically precede other issues, because if their legal requirements are not met, the entire lawsuit will be dismissed. Issues dealing with the legal claim or cause of action should precede issues dealing with the relief or remedy sought, because only a limited range of remedies is available for each cause of action. There are additional logical ways to order issues, but all of them are premised on the theory that you should address issues in a logical order that allows the reader to understand the research subject matter in the easiest possible fashion.

Sometimes a point will arise more than once in your issues. For example, plaintiff's peculiar susceptibility crops up in the issue of extreme and outrageous conduct, as well as in the issue of the severity of plaintiff's emotional distress. You should research both legal aspects, but when you write up your research results, you may use a cross-reference in the later discussion to incorporate portions of the previous discussion.

When you research in an unfamiliar subject matter, you formulate issues slowly. They evolve as your research progresses, necessitating frequent revisions, additions, and deletions in your initial set of issues. However, if you are researching in a subject matter that you know well, you can spot the issues easily at the outset of your research, and you will revise them less often and less drastically.

B. HOW TO USE PRIMARY AUTHORITY

Once you have analyzed the facts, gained some background information from commentary sources, and tentatively framed the issues, you are ready to look for authority that resolves the legal issues in your fact situation. Your research approach in this step depends in large part on the type of authority that addresses the legal issues raised by the facts.

As a beginning researcher, you probably will not know the type of primary authority that is likely to govern the outcome of the legal issues you have identified. Therefore, cases, statutes, constitutions, ordinances, administrative regulations and rulings, and court rules should all be considered as possible sources for primary authority as you begin your research. However, you should have received some leads on primary authority from your research in the commentary sources.

Most frequently, the objective of legal research is to discern which authority (if any) the courts in your jurisdiction must follow. This is called "mandatory primary authority." It includes that jurisdiction's cases, statutes, constitution, ordinances, administrative regulations and rulings, and court rules. A "jurisdiction" is the territory within which mandatory primary authority operates or controls. (Of course, the courts actually resolve very few disputes, but you can ascertain the law in your jurisdiction by determining what the court would do if the case came before the court.)

If no mandatory primary authority addresses your issue, or if a change in the law is possible, you should look elsewhere for a solution. In such instances, the courts often will choose to base their decisions on "persuasive primary authority." Persuasive primary authority is primary authority that is not binding on the deciding court; it furnishes guidance to the deciding court and may be used to persuade the deciding court to overrule its existing mandatory primary authority. Persuasive primary authority includes primary authority from other jurisdictions (which would be mandatory if it were from the deciding court's jurisdiction).

Another alternative to the lack of mandatory primary authority is secondary authority, in the form of commentary sources. By its very nature, secondary authority lacks the force and effect of law, but it may provide persuasive reasoning. Although you initially consulted commentary sources to obtain an overview of the subject being researched, keep in mind that commentary sources can serve three research functions:

(1) providing an overview of the subject,
(2) furnishing leads on relevant primary and other secondary authority, and
(3) providing in-depth analysis on the law and its underlying policy.

The third function is the reason for consulting commentary sources at the end of your research as well as at the outset.

Thus, the objective of your legal research should be to locate mandatory primary authority, persuasive primary authority, and secondary authority, in that order of preference. The most effective analysis will be based primarily on mandatory primary authority. The other alternatives should be explored only if mandatory primary authority does not exist, you want the mandatory primary authority to be overruled, you want other authority to bolster the result of the primary authority, or you want other authority to explain the policies behind the primary authority.

C. RESEARCH AS A NON-LINEAR PROCESS

The research process described thus far is much tidier and more linear than your actual legal research is likely to be. Your first impression of the issues, and hence your key facts and vocabulary, may be off-target. Reaching a dead end early in your research may tell you that you need to reformulate your research terms. Or you may need to consult several commentary sources before you fully understand the issues, because the various commentary sources differ in content, function, and accessibility. Or you may need to read about several related areas of primary authority before you are sure you have located the most pertinent area.

Furthermore, every legal researcher must continually reevaluate which facts are legally significant, which legal rules apply, and whether the issues need to be revised or expanded as the research progresses. This process continues until the research project is complete. Very often the final statement of the legal issues will be quite different from the initial statement formulated early in the research process. This development of the issues is a natural result of learning more and more about the legal rules governing the problem in question.

Legal analysis and its accompanying research and writing are components in a spiraling process. You begin with an analysis of the facts, preliminary research, and an analysis of the law thus far uncovered, then proceed to continued research and more analysis, followed by composition. However, research and analysis do not cease when you begin to compose. Often you will find midstream in the composing process that you missed an important aspect of the problem or that you misanalyzed an issue. You must then return to the research and analysis steps until all of the pieces fit.

D. WHEN TO CALL IT QUITS

Unfortunately, there is not a clearly defined point at which you can be certain that your research is complete. Generations of beginning researchers have asked "When do I stop?" without receiving a clear-cut answer. As you gain experience you will develop your own sense of when to stop. But, even then, the point at which you decide to stop will vary with different issues and research goals. However, there are a few guidelines that will help you decide whether your research is sufficient.

First, once you've completed your background research and exhausted the research possibilities in the jurisdiction in which the controversy arises, think carefully before exploring persuasive primary authority or secondary authority. Only read persuasive primary authority that is directly on point or closely analogous.

Second, don't search forever for the case, statute, or other source that is squarely on point and answers all of your issues. Legislatures and agencies do not address all problems. Moreover, it is rare that two cases will be precisely the same, and only very commonplace issues are likely to be replicated in several cases. Remember that legal issues requiring research are almost always those that do not have obvious or clear answers.

Third, apply the law of diminishing returns and stop looking for new sources when the same issues and authorities keep turning up. When you stop uncovering new rules of law, you probably have a grasp on the available authority, even though you have yet to read some sources.

Fourth, do not stop until you have updated every authority you find. Once you have found relevant authority, you must make certain that you have found the most recent expression of the law. By using citators and other updating methods, such as supplements to hardbound sources, you can determine whether the authority you have found is current. You have not finished your research until you have updated every authority and determined that there have been no changes in the law.

Fifth, at the end of your research consult recent commentary sources to make certain you have remembered all the issues. As you conclude your research, the commentary sources you used earlier will have far more meaning for you and will help to identify issues you may have missed.

Sixth, once you have satisfied the five guidelines above, begin writing, even though you are not fully comfortable with your analysis. You will find that your understanding of the law, the facts, and possible shortcomings in your research will emerge as you begin writing down the results of your research and analysis. Don't be afraid to take a second look at your authorities or your research strategies during the writing process. Many times, the importance of certain factors or the shortcomings of a certain authority will become clear to you only after you have put pen to paper (or hands to keyboard).

Case Law: Searching for Primary Authority

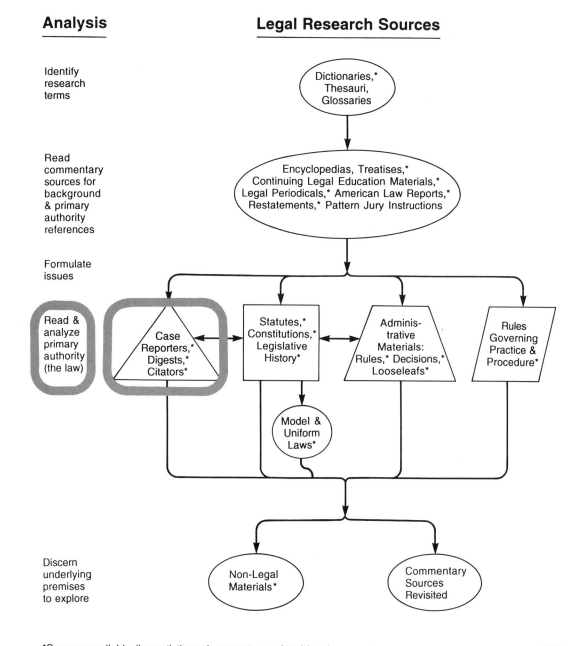

Analysis

Identify research terms

Read commentary sources for background & primary authority references

Formulate issues

Read & analyze primary authority (the law)

Discern underlying premises to explore

Legal Research Sources

Dictionaries,* Thesauri, Glossaries

Encyclopedias, Treatises,* Continuing Legal Education Materials,* Legal Periodicals,* American Law Reports,* Restatements,* Pattern Jury Instructions

Case Reporters,* Digests,* Citators*

Statutes,* Constitutions,* Legislative History*

Administrative Materials: Rules,* Decisions,* Looseleafs*

Rules Governing Practice & Procedure*

Model & Uniform Laws*

Non-Legal Materials*

Commentary Sources Revisited

*Sources available (in part) through computer-assisted legal research

A.   Introduction

B.   Goals of Case Law Research
    1.   Jurisdiction of the Court
        a.   The Court System: Federalism
        b.   State Courts
        c.   Federal Courts
    2.   Level of the Court
    3.   History and Treatment of a Case

C.   Case Reporters: Where Court Decisions Are Published
    1.   What Is a Reporter?
    2.   Parts of a Court Decision
        a.   Case Name and Citation Information
        b.   Docket Number
        c.   Syllabus
        d.   Headnotes
        e.   Names of Counsel and Presiding Judges/Justices
        f.   Opinion of the Court
        g.   Disposition by the Court
    3.   Organizational Scheme: Official and Unofficial Reporters
    4.   Parallel Citations
    5.   First, Second, or Third Series
    6.   Researching Recent Court Decisions
        a.   Slip Opinions
        b.   Advance Sheets
        c.   *The United States Law Week* and *United States Supreme Court Bulletin*
        d.   Newspapers

D.   Digests
    1.   What Is a Digest?
    2.   The West Digest System and Key Number System
        a.   The Digests
        b.   The West Key Number System
        c.   How to Use the West System
        d.   Updating Case Law Research
    3.   Non-West Digests

E.   Case Citators
    1.   Introduction: What They Are and Why You Need Them
    2.   *Shepard's* Case Citators
        a.   State Case Law Citators: The State Citators
        b.   State Case Law Citators: The Regional Citators
        c.   Federal Case Law Citators
    3.   Steps in Using *Shepard's Citations*
    4.   Reading the Citation Lists
        a.   The Citing Sources
        b.   Components of the Citation Lists
            (1)   Parallel Citations
            (2)   History Citations
            (3)   Case Treatment Citations
            (4)   Other Citations
        c.   The Order of the Citations
    5.   Using *Shepard's* Effectively
    6.   Updating

A. INTRODUCTION

The law serves many functions. It facilitates and regulates relations between people by means of rules created by institutions having the authority to govern society. These rules govern people's personal and business dealings by defining acceptable behavior. The law governs simple matters such as traffic ordinances and fishing regulations. The law also regularizes more sophisticated matters such as contracts between a buyer and a seller. The law establishes standards that assist parties in avoiding disputes and provides procedures for amicably resolving the disputes that do occur.

"The law" is difficult to define comprehensively because it emanates from many different sources. The law encompasses rulings by courts, as well as constitutions, statutes, regulations enacted pursuant to legislative authorization, and administrative decisions interpreting those regulations. Legislative acts, including statutes and ordinances, typically address the general concerns of society and regulate future conduct. Case law adjudicates past conduct and generally addresses only the facts of a single dispute and issues raised by the parties involved in a specific lawsuit. As you will learn, however, specific lawsuits may apply indirectly to more than the specific parties to the lawsuit because of the doctrine of *stare decisis*.

The law has evolved from tradition or custom and reflects societal practice or norms; historically, customs adopted by the community were the only laws. In feudal Europe, for example, the customs observed in each of the many feudal manors dictated tenants' rights, the ownership and transfer of property rights, inheritance, marital relations, criminal procedure, and business relations. The feudal manors' most prevalent customs became the "common law" only after the first court system was established. Some of the practiced traditions varied significantly between manors. The variances in customs were reconciled and tempered by the newly established courts. Widely followed customs were adopted in their entirety. The judges based their decisions on their own reasoning as they sought ultimately to achieve desirable societal goals and to treat the populace uniformly.

These early court decisions were not formally recorded; nevertheless, they became the common law and formed the law of the land. The binding authority of the early courts' case law gave rise to one of the fundamental doctrines of judicial decision-making—*stare decisis et non quieta movere,* which means "to adhere to precedent and not to unsettle things which are settled." Even today, the doctrine of *stare decisis* remains central to American jurisprudence.

Stare decisis requires a court to adhere strictly to precedent, that is, to follow its own decisions and the decisions rendered by higher appellate courts in its jurisdiction, unless they have been overturned by statute. Because of precedent, judges and other decision-makers are bound to apply existing, well-reasoned principles and are not free to react with personal biases or predilections to controversies presented to them. Because these precedents are binding, situations involving the same or similar circumstances receive equal treatment under the law. This equal treatment promotes uniformity and impartiality, which fosters confidence in the law and in our legal system. On a societal level, adherence to precedent provides standards to which people may look for guidance in conducting their personal or business affairs.

A basic paradox arises from the doctrine of *stare decisis*. Strict adherence to *stare decisis* dictates that judicially established common law precedents should not shift with the passage of time. That is, a new case brought before the court should be decided just as a similar case with similar issues was decided a century before. Clearly, *stare decisis* is not interpreted in such a manner. The law is not a static entity; it is flexible and adapts to changing conditions, needs, and norms of society. Sometimes, legislative enactments compel courts to rule differently. In the absence of statutes, judges overrule previous decisions when they are convinced that the old law is no longer applicable or when society or justice is best served by doing so.

For instance, in *Plessy v. Ferguson,* 163 U.S. 537 (1896), the United States Supreme Court held that "separate but equal" treatment of persons of color was not a violation of the equal protection clause of the United States Constitution. If, 60 years later, the Court felt totally constrained to follow precedent strictly, the landmark decision of *Brown v. Board of Education,* 347 U.S. 483 (1954), would never have been decided as it was. Fortunately, the Supreme Court recognized the historical ills of segregation, noting that "separate" could not be and is not "equal." It should be noted that the Court was not swayed by the wishes of the majority of the public, but clearly had considered the benefits that would inure to all of society by its overruling of precedent. Hence, it is not the ruling of the original decision that is paramount; the reasoning behind judicial decision-making is also important. When the reasoning of the original decision is faulty or ceases to merit societal support, then precedent should be overruled.

The concepts of *stare decisis* and legal precedent are highly regarded in modern judicial decision-making. Indeed, rather than overrule precedent directly, judges generally strive to indicate differences in the facts of cases so as to distinguish precedent they consider outmoded. The law changes slowly. Courts are persuaded to abandon or change an established rule of law only when they are convinced by a persuasive argument that a better rule is possible; or that continued adherence to a precedent would bring about unintended, erroneous results; or that societal norms have been altered such that different public goals should be promoted.

An attorney who seeks changes in the rule of previous case law should show factual differences that distinguish cases, faulty reasoning in the earlier cases, or major changes in public policy that would persuade the court that a particular rule of law is outmoded. It is an attorney's role to analyze existing rules creatively and intelligently, and then to suggest appropriate changes. When a court embraces these changes, new common law is articulated and the prior law is overruled or distinguished.

B. GOALS OF CASE LAW RESEARCH

This chapter is designed to help you gain the skills necessary to research case law quickly and efficiently. The fundamental goal of case law research is to find binding precedent, or if binding precedent does not exist or you wish to alter it, to find the most persuasive authority available. To determine binding or persuasive authority, you must consider several factors. These include the jurisdiction of the court, the level of the court, the history of the case, and the treatment of the case by subsequent courts.

a.   The Court System: Federalism

The United States is a federation of states. Each state has a separate governmental structure as provided by that state's constitution. Similarly, the federal government is governed by the United States Constitution. State and federal constitutions and statutes define the jurisdiction and structure of the various courts. There may be occasional changes in the geographic boundaries covered by a court, the subject matter that it has under its jurisdiction, and its structure. For example, in 1980 and 1982 Congress substantially restructured the federal courts. It reorganized the Fifth Circuit and created the Eleventh Circuit Court of Appeals and altered the jurisdiction of the Federal Circuit. In state court systems, such reorganizations may require a constitutional amendment. In 1982, for example, an amendment to the Minnesota Constitution created the Minnesota Court of Appeals, which heard its first case in 1983.

b.   State Courts

The court systems in all 50 states are similar in that they have trial-level courts and at least one appellate court. Beyond this, however, the court structure and nomenclature vary from state to state. Kansas has a typical court structure:

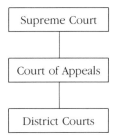

Some states, such as New York, have slightly different court structures and nomenclatures: New York's highest court or "court of last resort" is called the Court of Appeals, and its intermediate court is called the Supreme Court, Appellate Division. Some states, such as Maine and Montana, do not have an intermediate court between the trial court and the court of last resort. You need not memorize the jurisdiction or function of each court; that information appears in the individual state code or rules of court. The state and federal court system is summarized in *The Bluebook,* Table T.1.

c.   Federal Courts

Trial courts at the federal level are called United States District Courts. There are 89 district courts for the 50 states, plus one each for the District of Columbia and Puerto Rico, and one each for the territories of Guam, the Northern Mariana Islands, and the Virgin Islands. The number of federal districts in a state varies; each state has at least one district court and some have as many as four. For example, Washington has two federal district courts— the Western District and the Eastern District. Oregon has only one district court, and California has four—Northern, Eastern, Central, and Southern.

The jurisdiction of the federal courts is enumerated in Article III, Section 2 of the United States Constitution; all other matters are reserved for state courts. Generally, federal district courts have original jurisdiction for civil actions arising under the United States Constitution and federal laws of the United States, such as issues relating to admiralty, civil actions against a foreign state, and civil actions between parties of different states, or between a citizen of the United States and a citizen of a foreign country, where the amount in controversy exceeds $50,000. For some matters, such as patents and copyrights, the federal courts have exclusive jurisdiction. Although the jurisdictional boundaries of federal district courts are within state lines, federal district court jurisdiction is completely separate from state court jurisdiction.

The intermediate appellate courts in the federal system are called the United States Courts of Appeals. Appeal from a federal district court is typically to a United States Court of Appeals and ultimately to the Supreme Court of the United States, the country's highest federal court. Of the 13 federal appellate circuits in the United States Courts of Appeals system, 12 have regional jurisdiction. Eleven numbered courts of appeals encompass several states apiece; the District of Columbia Circuit encompasses the District of Columbia. The Federal Circuit Court of Appeals has jurisdiction to hear subject matter disputes involving patent, copyright, and trademark appeals from any of the federal district courts, as well as controversies originating in the United States Claims Court and in the United States Court of International Trade. (See Illustration 5-1 at page 141.)

The federal system also includes specialized trial courts or appellate courts, such as the United States Tax Court, the United States Claims Court, Bankruptcy Courts, the United States Court of Military Appeals, the United States Court of Veterans Appeals, and the United States Court of International Trade. The Bankruptcy Court has jurisdiction, for example, over bankruptcy controversies referred to it by a district court. The Claims Court hears non-tort claims against the federal government for money damages. The Court of International Trade typically deals with controversies involving international trade and customs.

The Supreme Court must consider some cases; in others, its review is discretionary. For example, if a case involves state legislation that the state supreme court has ruled does not violate the federal constitution, review is mandatory; review of an action brought in federal courts that raises federal questions is discretionary.

The jurisdiction of a court is determined by federal or state constitutions or statutes. Under our federal system of government, state courts have jurisdiction over issues and disputes separate and distinct from the federal courts, except in a few special circumstances, and the case law of one state is not binding on the court of another state.

One of the most common exceptions occurs when a party seeks to bring a claim in federal court under "diversity jurisdiction." Residents of the United States may claim diversity jurisdiction if the controversy involves citizens of different states and the amount of damages alleged exceeds $50,000. Because the parties come from different states, the federal court serves as a neutral forum to hear the dispute. In this situation, the federal court will apply appropriate state law, which is determined by a choice of law based on the state that has the most significant contact with regard to the litigation or, if one of the parties is a corporation, based on the situs of its principal place of business.

You will have ascertained that most decisions of a federal court are not

ILLUSTRATION 5-1. The Federal Judicial Circuits, as Shown in *1992 Judicial Staff Directory* 469 (Ann L. Brownson ed., 6th ed. 1991).

141

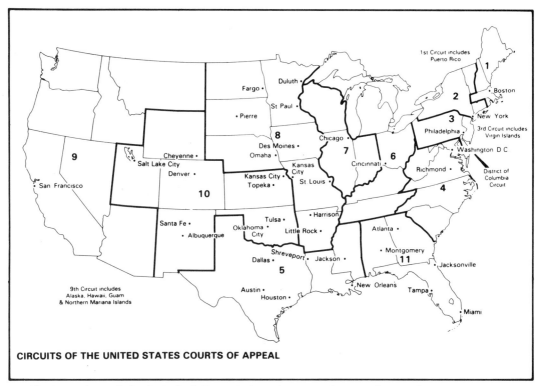

CIRCUITS OF THE UNITED STATES COURTS OF APPEAL

The Court of Appeals for the Federal Circuit sits in Washington, D.C. Its jurisdiction is by subject matter, not geography.

binding on state courts, and most decisions of a state court are not binding on a federal court. State and federal courts respect each other's decisions, however, and a decision from another jurisdiction may provide persuasive authority, although not mandatory authority.

In order to better understand the concept of jurisdiction, consider the facts of the Perkins problem raised in previous chapters and the issue of whether it is possible to bring a cause of action in tort under the common law doctrine of intentional infliction of emotional distress (also called "outrage") when a party addresses another party using racial epithets. For illustrative purposes, read the excerpts from the case of *Bradshaw v. Swagerty,* 1 Kan. App. 2d 213, 563 P.2d 511 (1977), reproduced in Illustration 5-2 on pages 142-145.

In *Bradshaw,* the Kansas Court of Appeals ruled that racial epithets were mere insults and that the plaintiff could not, therefore, support a cause of action for the tort of outrage (intentional infliction of emotional distress). By ruling this way, the Kansas Court of Appeals affirmed the Kansas trial court's earlier ruling.

When you research case law on the issue of intentional infliction of emotional distress (or outrage) regarding conduct that took place in the state of Kansas, Kansas law is binding. The decision of a court in another state, such as Washington, is not mandatory authority and is not binding on the Kansas court. Although the facts and issues in the Kansas case may be very similar to those raised in the Washington case, the Washington court does not have jurisdiction. The Washington decision may, however, be used as

BRADSHAW v. SWAGERTY

Cite as, Kan.App., 563 P.2d 511

Kan. **511**

ghue v. Gaffy, 54 Conn. 257, 266, 7 A. 552. The trial court erred in refusing to direct a verdict for the defendant Lippe on the slander count." (p. 385, 294 A.2d p. 333.)

[9] We find certain similarities between *Moriarty* and the present case. The statements were made in public, the utterances did not charge a crime or improper conduct or lack of skill or integrity in one's profession or business, and there were no allegations of special damages.

The two cases are distinguishable in that the statements in the present case were made in a judicial proceeding where the speaker was clothed with absolute immunity.

Although we do not condone the use of such words, we agree with the *Moriarty* decision that the allegedly slanderous words are not actionable *per se* and the matter becomes one of law for the court. Furthermore, it would appear from common knowledge and experience that such words do not have the same meaning in today's society as they did in the past. Hence, even if the expression were not privileged, the words were not actionable.

We now turn our attention to plaintiff's argument that Count IV states a cause of action against the defendant Sanborn for invasion of privacy. Basically, plaintiff contends that defendant Sanborn had for several years conducted continuing investigations of his private and business affairs, ostensibly in Sanborn's capacity as district attorney, but in fact such conduct was outside the scope of his authority.

Defendant Sanborn responds that his actions were within the scope of his authority as district attorney for Sedgwick County, Kansas.

[10–13] It has long been recognized that the county or district attorney is the chief law enforcement official in his jurisdiction and that a criminal proceeding is a matter of state concern and the control of it is in the county attorney. (*State v. Pruett,* 213 Kan. 41, 515 P.2d 1051; *State v. Kilpatrick,* 201 Kan. 6, 439 P.2d 99.) It is his duty to inquire into the facts of violations. If the

inquiry disclose the fact that an offense has been committed, he must institute proceedings for its punishment. (*State v. Trinkle,* 70 Kan. 396, 78 P. 854.) By statute he is given the authority to conduct inquisitions and to grant immunity to witnesses. (K.S.A. 22–3101 and 22–3102.) The same policy considerations requiring absolute immunity for communications made during the course of a prosecution require immunity for conduct in investigations which may lead to a prosecution. We hold that the power of the district attorney to investigate alleged violations within his jurisdiction is unquestionable and his motive in so doing may not be the subject of a lawsuit against him.

Finally, plaintiff raises as one of his points of appeal that the trial court erred in denying his motion for leave to amend his petition. On oral argument, plaintiff conceded that he could not improve upon his previously amended petition. Such admission disposes of this point.

For the reasons set forth in this opinion, the judgment is affirmed as to both defendants.

○══[KEY NUMBER SYSTEM]

1 Kan.App.2d 213

Rodney BRADSHAW, Appellant,

v.

Daniel L. SWAGERTY, Appellee.

No. 48321.

Court of Appeals of Kansas.

April 15, 1977.

Action for slander and outrage was brought against attorney for statements allegedly made by attorney. The Hodgeman District Court, C. Phillip Aldrich, J., rendered summary judgment for the attorney, and plaintiff appealed. The Court of Ap-

512 Kan. 563 PACIFIC REPORTER, 2d SERIES

5 peals, Foth, J., held that: (1) in the absence of allegations of special damages, complaint alleging that plaintiff had been called a "nigger," and "bastard," and a "knot-headed boy" failed to allege actionable slander per se, and (2) epithets complained of were mere insults, and thus facts could not be construed to make out tort of "outrage."

Affirmed.

1. Libel and Slander ⚷100(7)

Unless defamatory words are slanderous per se they are not actionable unless the plaintiff pleads and proves special damages.

2. Libel and Slander ⚷6(1)

Slander per se is limited to statements falling into four categories: imputation of a crime; imputation of a loathsome disease; words reflecting on plaintiff's fitness for his office, profession or trade; and the imputation of unchastity in a woman.

3. Libel and Slander ⚷6(1)

Words of general abuse, regardless of how rude, uncouth or vexatious, are not slanderous per se and cannot support recovery in a slander action in the absence of a showing of special damages.

4. Libel and Slander ⚷6(1)

An imputation of bastardy or illegitimacy is not slander per se.

5. Libel and Slander ⚷6(1)

The term "nigger" is one of insult, abuse and belittlement, but it is not slander per se.

6. Libel and Slander ⚷80, 89(1)

Complaint alleging that, during the course of a heated argument, defendant had called plaintiff a "nigger," a "bastard," and a "knot-headed boy" failed to allege terms that were slanderous per se, so that, in the absence of allegation of special damages, plaintiff was precluded from recovering for slander.

7. Torts ⚷3

One who by extreme and outrageous conduct intentionally or recklessly causes severe emotional distress to another is subject to liability for such emotional distress, and if bodily harm to the other results from it, for such bodily harm.

8. Torts ⚷3

Liability for "outrage" does not extend to mere insults, indignities, threats, annoyances, petty oppressions, or other trivialities.

9. Torts ⚷3 6

It is for the court in the first instance to determine whether the defendant's conduct was so outrageous as to permit recovery in cause of action for tort of "outrage."

10. Torts ⚷26(1)

Allegation that, during course of a heated argument, defendant had called plaintiff a "nigger," a "bastard," and a "knot-headed boy" failed to make out tort of "outrage."

Syllabus by the Court

1. Unless defamatory words are slanderous *per se* they are not actionable unless the plaintiff pleads and proves special damages.

2. Slander *per se* is limited to statements falling into four categories: imputation of a crime; imputation of a loathsome disease; words reflecting on plaintiff's fitness for his office, profession or trade; and the imputation of unchastity in a woman.

3. Words of general abuse, regardless of how rude, uncouth or vexatious, are not slanderous *per se* and cannot support recovery in a slander action in the absence of a showing of special damages. 7

4. An imputation of bastardy or illegitimacy is not slanderous *per se.*

5. The term "nigger" is one of insult, abuse and belittlement, but is not slanderous *per se.*

6. The tort of "outrage" requires extreme and outrageous conduct on the part of the defendant. It is for the court in the first instance to determine whether the defendant's conduct was so outrageous as to permit recovery.

7. Liability for "outrage" clearly does not extend to mere insults, indignities,

Note: 5. Syllabus by a reporter editor
6. Headnotes and Key Numbers
7. Syllabus by the court

BRADSHAW v. SWAGERTY   Kan. **513**
Cite as, Kan.App., 563 P.2d 511

threats, annoyances, petty oppressions, or other trivialities.

8. In an action for slander and outrage based upon insults hurled in the course of a heated argument it is *held,* the trial court properly entered summary judgment for the defendant on both counts.

B. A. Lightfoot, Jetmore, for appellant.

B. G. (Skip) Larson and Max Eugene Estes, Williams, Larson, Voss, Strobel & Estes, Dodge City, for appellee.

Before REES, P. J., and FOTH and SWINEHART, JJ.

FOTH, Judge:

Plaintiff Rodney Bradshaw brought this action for slander and outrage, with both counts arising out of a single verbal encounter with the defendant, Daniel L. Swagerty. On the basis of depositions and answers to interrogatories the trial court rendered summary judgment for the defendant, and plaintiff has appealed. There is no claim that discovery was not complete. The question, therefore, is whether, taking plaintiff's evidence in the light most favorable to him, he had a submissible case under either of his theories.

The defendant is a lawyer who, in March, 1975, was retained by the Southwest Grain company to collect accounts allegedly owed by plaintiff and his brother Paul. Defendant was also Hodgeman county attorney. On March 19 plaintiff appeared at defendant's office in response to a collection letter inviting a discussion of the accounts. Plaintiff asserted the defense of infancy, and threatened countersuit if sued. He also helped himself to candy from a dish in defendant's office, much to defendant's irritation. The discussion grew heated, and descended to the name-calling which forms the basis of plaintiff's suit.

At some point during the discussion plaintiff's brother Paul appeared. Although Paul apparently took no active part in the encounter, it was to him that the allegedly slanderous words were first published. According to plaintiff's deposition,

in the course of the argument defendant at one time or another called him a "nigger" and a "bastard." Plaintiff is a young black man, of concededly legitimate birth. (The term "knot-headed boy" was also pleaded, but its use does not appear in the depositions.)

Defendant admitted using the term "bastard," but denied that he "directly" called plaintiff a "nigger." In any event, when the two brothers refused to leave defendant summoned a deputy sheriff, who escorted them out. The deputy returned to defendant's office and asked what had happened. Defendant's recounting of the events resulted in the second publication of the alleged slander.

[1] Do the terms used (assuming all of them were) constitute actionable slander? We note first that plaintiff pleaded only that he had suffered "humiliation, embarrassment and loss of reputation." He testified that "the incident in the defendant's office had not affected his employment, but had affected his relations with others in the community." Thus he neither pleaded nor offered to prove special damages. Barring special damages plaintiff has no cause of action for slander unless the words spoken are slanderous *per se. Bennett v. Seimiller,* 175 Kan. 764, 267 P.2d 926.

[2] At common law slander *per se* was limited to four categories: imputation of a crime; imputation of a loathsome disease; words reflecting on plaintiff's fitness for his office, profession or trade; and the imputation of unchastity in a woman. Prosser, Law of Torts (4th ed.), pp. 754–760; 50 Am.Jur.2d, Libel and Slander, sec. 10; 53 C.J.S. Libel and Slander § 14. And *cf.,* Restatement (Second), Torts, sec. 569 (Tent. Draft No. 11).

No single Kansas case has adopted the common law categories *in toto,* but each of the four has been recognized: *Sweaney v. United Loan & Finance Co.,* 205 Kan. 66, 468 P.2d 124 (imputation of a felony); *Bennett v. Seimiller,* supra (criminal offense, loathsome disease, prejudice to trade or business); *Munsell v. Ideal Food Stores,* 208 Kan. 909, 494 P.2d 1063 (unfitness for em-

ILLUSTRATION 5-2. *(continued)* 145

514 Kan. **563 PACIFIC REPORTER, 2d SERIES**

ployment); *Cooper v. Seaverns*, 81 Kan. 267, 105 P. 509 (unchastity).

[3, 4] Plaintiff offers no authority from this jurisdiction or any other holding the epithets in question here to be slanderous *per se.* The annotation appearing at 53 A.L.R. 548 indicates that an imputation of bastardy or illegitimacy is generally held not slanderous *per se,* although it might be actionable where it affected property rights acquired through inheritance. As to the closely allied epithet "son of a bitch," Connecticut's highest court, after finding that a charge of police brutality was not actionable, went on to say:

> "Other words uttered in the presence of those assembled, 'clown,' 'big fat ape,' 'smart aleck,' 'big fat oaf,' and 'stupid son of a bitch,' were here merely gross and vulgar expressions of abuse. The general rule has long been that such words of general abuse, regardless of how rude, uncouth or vexatious are not slanderous per se and cannot support recovery in a slander action in the absence of a showing of special damages. Notes, 13 A.L.R.3d 1286, 1290, 37 A.L.R. 883, 885."

(*Moriarty v. Lippe,* 162 Conn. 371, 385, 294 A.2d 326 [1972].)

See, also, *Sampson v. Rumsey,* 1 Kan.App. 2d 191, 563 P.2d 506 (decided April 15, 1977).

[5] The term "nigger" is one of insult, abuse and belittlement harking back to slavery days. Its use is resented, and rightly so. It nevertheless is not within any category recognized as slanderous *per se.* "Knot-headed boy," if that expression was used, can only be construed to be the same type of general verbal abuse.

[6] We hold that none of the alleged terms was slanderous *per se.* Since there was no plea or evidence of special damages, the trial court correctly entered its summary judgment for defendant on this count.

[7] The remaining issue is whether the facts may be construed to make out the tort of "outrage." Kansas has adopted the Restatement rule:

> "(1) One who by extreme and outrageous conduct intentionally or recklessly causes

severe emotional distress to another is subject to liability for such emotional distress, and if bodily harm to the other results from it, for such bodily harm." (Restatement [Second], Torts, sec. 46, p. 71.)

See, *Vespa v. Safety Fed. Savings & Loan Ass'n.,* 219 Kan. 578, 549 P.2d 878; *Dotson v. McLaughlin,* 216 Kan. 201, 531 P.2d 1; *Dawson v. Associates Financial Services Co.,* 215 Kan. 814, 529 P.2d 104.

[8] In *Dotson* the court noted that liability attaches only to extreme and outrageous conduct, and quoted with approval from the Restatement notes:

> "The liability clearly does not extend to mere insults, indignities, threats, annoyances, petty oppressions, or other trivialities. The rough edges of our society are still in need of a good deal of filing down, and in the meantime plaintiffs must necessarily be expected and required to be hardened to a certain amount of rough language, and to occasional acts that are definitely inconsiderate and unkind. There is no occasion for the law to intervene in every case where some one's feelings are hurt. There must still be freedom to express an unflattering opinion, and some safety valve must be left through which irascible tempers may blow off relatively harmless steam." (216 Kan. at 210, 531 P.2d at 8.)

[9, 10] It is for the court in the first instance to determine whether the defendant's conduct was so outrageous as to permit recovery. *Dotson v. McLaughlin,* supra. It appears to us that the trial court was fully justified in regarding the epithets complained of here as "mere insults" of the kind which must be tolerated in our rough-edged society. Summary judgment for the defendant was therefore proper on the "outrage" count as well as the slander count.

Affirmed. ————

persuasive authority, particularly if you are advocating a change in the law or if the Kansas courts have never ruled on the issue.

In fact, review *Gomez v. Hug,* 7 Kan. App. 603, 645 P.2d 916 (1982), which is a later discussion by the Kansas Court of Appeals. In *Gomez,* the Kansas Court of Appeals again considered whether racial epithets could give rise to recovery under the tort theory of intentional infliction of emotional distress. Read the edited excerpt of the case that has been reproduced in Illustration 5-3 (see pages 147-151).

2. Level of the Court

The level of a court is an important consideration in your search for an authoritative statement of case law. Lower courts are bound by the decisions of higher courts within the same jurisdiction; logically, higher courts are not bound by the decisions of lower courts. Consequently, a trial court considers the decisions of an appellate court in the same jurisdiction to be mandatory primary authority.

Judges frequently cite earlier, analogous cases to support their reasoning. This suggests that a court has examined similar issues, policy considerations, and rules on previous occasions, and later cases have been decided with the same result. Whenever possible, trial courts and appellate courts will cite to the supreme (or highest court) within that jurisdiction.

Reexamine the text in *Gomez* reproduced in Illustration 5-3, noting those passages where the Kansas Court of Appeals cites to several Kansas Supreme Court decisions: *Whitsel v. Watts,* 98 Kan. 508, 159 P. 401 (1916); *Dawson v. Associates Financial Services Co.,* 215 Kan. 814, 529 P.2d 104 (1974); and *Dotson v. McLaughlin,* 216 Kan. 201, 531 P.2d 1 (1975). The Kansas Court of Appeals cited these three Kansas Supreme Court decisions to trace the development of the tort of intentional infliction of emotional distress and to review the elements necessary to seek recovery under that tort. Hence, the Kansas Court of Appeals kept its decision in *Gomez* within the confines of previous Kansas Supreme Court doctrine, and at the same time expanded the doctrine to cover racial epithets.

Note how the Kansas Court of Appeals cited to and relied to some extent on a Washington Supreme Court decision, *Contreras v. Crown Zellerbach,* 88 Wash. 2d 735, 565 P.2d 1173 (1977). Although this decision is not binding on the Kansas court, it provided persuasive authority. The court's reliance on *Contreras* shows that the Kansas court was persuaded to some extent by the fact that the Washington court had previously considered a case with similar facts and similar issues, and had held that racial epithets could support a claim for intentional infliction of emotional distress.

The *Gomez* case, decided in 1982, would now carry greater authority than the *Bradshaw* case, decided in 1977. Remember that both of these cases, however, were decided at the court of appeals level and not by the Kansas Supreme Court. Although these cases serve as binding authority on later Kansas District Court and Kansas Court of Appeals decisions, they are not binding on later Kansas Supreme Court decisions.

3. History and Treatment of a Case

The history of a case, another important consideration in case law research, includes every court action and decision made with regard to the specific case under consideration. To understand this concept fully, recall the *Bradshaw* case. Assume that *Bradshaw* had been appealed to the Kansas

147

[Note: This excerpt has been edited by the authors and reset by the publisher of this book.]

Silvino GOMEZ, Appellant,

v.

Roland HUG and Board of County Commissioners of Shawnee County, Kansas, Appellees.

No. 53111.

Court of Appeals of Kansas.

June 3, 1982.

. . .

Syllabus by the Court

1. In an appeal from summary judgment granted to the individual defendant, the record is examined and it is *held*: (1) The trial court erred in sustaining the motion for summary judgment on the issues of assault and outrage. (2) The trial court did not err in sustaining the motion for summary judgment on the issues of defamation and deprivation of civil rights pursuant to 42 U.S.C. § 1983, all as set forth with more particularity in the opinion.

2. County commissioners are elected officials whose powers are conferred upon them by statute. They act independently as public officers, not as agents of the commission; therefore, the county cannot be held liable under the doctrine of respondeat superior for acts of neglect or misconduct attributed to individual commissioners.

Pedro Luis Irigonegaray and Pantaleon Florez, Jr., of Hawver & Irigonegaray, P. A., Topeka, for appellant.

Terry E. Beck, of Tilton, Dillon, Beck & Crockett, Topeka, for appellee Roland Hug.

Donna Voth, Asst. County Counselor, Topeka, for appellee Bd. of County Com'rs.

Before REES, P. J., MEYER, J., and RICHARD W. WAHL, District Judge, Assigned.

RICHARD W. WAHL, District Judge, Assigned: . . .

On April 21, 1978, Silvino Gomez was employed as a supervisor at the Shawnee County fairgrounds. His immediate supervisor was the fairgrounds administrator, Robert Kanatzer. During the evening hours of April 21, 1978, Gomez and Kanatzer were engaged in preparing an area of the fairgrounds for a horse show. They learned of a waterline break and, after determining the problem, proceeded to the administrator's office to phone a piping contractor.

Appellee Roland Hug, a member of the Board of County Commissioners of Shawnee County, and a companion, Robert Corbett, were in Kanatzer's office when Gomez and Kanatzer arrived. As they entered the office, Hug asked Kanatzer, "What is that fucking spic doing in the office?" Hug then repeated the question, again referring to Gomez as a "fucking spic." Hug then ordered Gomez over to where he was, again referring to Gomez as a "fucking spic." Gomez complied with Hug's order to approach him and inquired of Hug as to what he meant by that name. Gomez testified in his deposition that the following exchange took place between him and Hug:

"A. . . . 'Commissioner, you have repeatedly stated that remark throughout the day and in the past day or two. Can you give me your interpretation of a fucking spic?' He said, 'You are a fucking spic.' I said, 'What does it mean?' He said, 'A fucking Mexican greaser like you, that is all you are. You are nothing but a fucking Mexican greaser, nothing but a pile of shit.' And he repeated it over and over and he raised his fist and he said, 'Now what are you going to do about it?' He got that close to me (indicating) and said, 'What are you going to do about it?' He kept hollering it out and hollering it out. He said, 'Go ahead and do something about it, you fucking Mexican greaser. I have told you what you are. You are nothing but a fucking spic.' And he repeated it over and he kept shaking his fists in front of my eyes and pounding on the desk and he would come up to me and say, 'Are you going to do something, you coward, you greaser, you fucking spic? What are you going to do? Don't stand there like a damn fool because that is all you are is a pile of shit.'

"Q. [by Mr. Beck] These are the exact words that you are using? Are these all exact quotes of Mr. Hug that you are giving us here right now?

"A. Yes. He repeated it over and over.

"Q. You stated he was pounding the desk with his fist?

"A. Pardon?

"Q. Did you say he was pounding the desk with his fist?

"A. He caught me offguard when he said that to me because I didn't expect that to come from a Commissioner. In fact, I didn't expect it to come from anyone. But we are speaking about Roland Hug. He kept threatening me. What was I going to do about it? He kept putting his fist in front of my face and pounding on that table, 'What are you going to do about it?' and repeating it over and over that I was nothing but a fucking spic. 'Now, you said you know what the definition of a spic is. You are nothing but a fucking spic and a Mexican greaser,' and he kept repeating it over and over, and he kept shaking his fist in front of me. I was froze because I was afraid of the man. For the first time in my life, I was terrified of one man calling me that. I was afraid for my job. I was afraid for my family."

It is variously estimated that this tirade lasted from five to fifteen minutes. After the exchange between Gomez and Hug, Kanatzer escorted Gomez out of the office and took him home. Gomez appeared to be upset.

Gomez began having serious medical problems. He sought medical advice and treatment from Dr. D. J. Weber, his family physician, Dr. Vinod Patel, a neurologist, and Dr. James N. Nelson, a psychiatrist. Both Dr. Nelson and Dr. Patel stated in their reports that Gomez' medical problems were related to the complained-of incident. Gomez was hospitalized from July 5, 1978, through July 18, 1978. He was unable to work due to his health-related problems and finally resigned his job with the county in November, 1979.

Appellees moved for summary judgment and the motion was sustained and judgment entered for the appellees. Gomez appealed.

K.S.A. 60–256(*c*) provides that a motion for summary judgment may be sustained only if the record before the court shows "that there is no genuine issue as to any material fact and that the moving party is entitled to a judgment as a matter of law." . . .

[4] Viewing the record in a light most favorable to Gomez, and giving him the benefit of all inferences that may be drawn from the record, this Court cannot say that reasonable persons could reach but one conclusion from this evidence. When the other acts and circumstances are considered—that Gomez and Hug had previously had problems which resulted in litigation; that Hug was Gomez' employer; that Hug was obviously very angry; that the fist-shaking, pounding of the table and the shouting of invectives lasted from five to fifteen minutes—this Court cannot say, as a matter of law, that Gomez could not have been in immediate apprehension of bodily harm.

In viewing the totality of the situation, this Court believes that the trial court erred in granting summary judgment on the issue of whether Hug assaulted Gomez. It is a question to be determined by a jury.

Did the district court err in determining, as a matter of law, that Gomez had

ILLUSTRATION 5-3. (*continued*) 149

no cause of action for intentional inflic-tion of emotional distress by Hug?

[5] The Kansas Supreme Court con-sidered a comparable wrong in *Whitsel v. Watts,* 98 Kan. 508, 159 P. 401 (1916). There, the plaintiff suffered a miscar-riage after being frightened when the defendant jumped from his buggy, ran towards the plaintiff in an angry, threatening manner, swearing, shak-ing his fist and saying, "You are fooling with the wrong person this time." The Court, speaking through Chief Justice Johnston, held:

"Defendant insists that he inflicted no bodily injury upon her, that no physical injury was in fact threat-ened, that there was no assault upon her and that proof of a mere fright furnishes no basis for a recovery. It has long been the rule here that there can be no recovery for fright or men-tal anguish unless it results in or is accompanied by physical injury to the person. (*Shelton v. Bornt,* 77 Kan. 1, 93 Pac. 341.) The plaintiff, however, is not asking a recovery for fright alone, but for the personal injuries directly resulting from fright caused by the willful tort of the defendant. It is argued that as the acts of the defendant did not amount to an as-sault she has no right to recover; but the defendant's liability does not de-pend upon whether his wrongful on-set constituted an assault. The plaintiff is seeking to enforce a civil liability for the consequences of the wrong and the general rule is that a wrongdoer is liable in damages for injuries which are the natural and reasonable consequences of his wrongful act, whatever name may be fittingly applied to the wrong." 98 Kan. at 509, 159 P. 401.

In *Dawson v. Associates Financial Services Co.,* 215 Kan. 814, 529 P.2d 104 (1974), the plaintiff, a former em-ployee of Associates, was delinquent on a car loan from Associates due to hav-ing lost her job when she developed multiple sclerosis. She received four phone calls from Associates about the account similar in content to calls she had had to make to delinquent debtors when she worked there. She referred them to her insurance carrier on the first call. On the second call Associates threatened to repossess the car, sell it and hold her responsible for any defi-ciency. On the third call plaintiff was told when the car would be repossessed, that it would ruin her credit rating, and would somehow involve her parents' business. On the fourth call, plaintiff got emotional and told Associates to call her attorney. After receiving these calls, plaintiff suffered physical distress and had to go under a doctor's care.

In *Dawson,* the Court adopted the rule from Restatement (Second) of Torts § 46(1) (1965), which provides:

"One who by extreme and out-rageous conduct intentionally or recklessly causes severe emotional distress to another is subject to lia-bility for such emotional distress, and if bodily harm to the other results from it, for such bodily harm."

The Court further held:

"[T]hat it is for the court to deter-mine, in the first instance, whether the defendant's conduct may reason-ably be regarded as so extreme and outrageous as to permit recovery, or whether it is necessarily so, and where reasonable men may differ, the ques-tion is for the jury to determine." 215 Kan. at 824, 529 P.2d 104.

. . . The Supreme Court, speaking through now Chief Justice Schroeder, concluded:

"Certainly creditors must be per-mitted to pursue reasonable methods of collecting debts, and debtors are protected only from extreme and out-rageous conduct. Nonetheless, meth-ods of collecting debts which might be reasonable in some circumstances, might also be regarded as outrageous in others where it is known that the debtor is particularly susceptible to emotional distress due to a disease such as multiple sclerosis. Here the appellant made claim for payments on an insurance policy which Associates had sold her. . . ." 215 Kan. at 825, 529 P.2d 104.

Dotson v. McLaughlin, 216 Kan. 201, 531 P.2d 1 (1975), was an action for invasion of privacy, but the Court also considered the matter of outrageous conduct. The Court, at page 210, 531 P.2d 1, quoted comment *d* from § 46 of Restatement (Second) of Torts:

> " 'The cases thus far decided have found liability only where the defendant's conduct has been extreme and outrageous. . . . Liability has been found only where the conduct has been so outrageous in character, and so extreme in degree, as to go beyond all possible bounds of decency, and to be regarded as atrocious, and utterly intolerable in a civilized community. Generally, the case is one in which the recitation of the facts to an average member of the community would arouse his resentment against the actor, and lead him to exclaim "outrageous!"
>
> " 'The liability clearly does not extend to mere insults, indignities, threats, annoyances, petty oppressions, or other trivialities. The rough edges of our society are still in need of a good deal of filing down, and in the meantime plaintiffs must necessarily be expected and required to be hardened to a certain amount of rough language, and to occasional acts that are definitely inconsiderate and unkind. There is no occasion for the law to intervene in every case where some one's feelings are hurt. There must still be freedom to express an unflattering opinion, and some safety valve must be left through which irascible tempers may blow off relatively harmless steam. . . .' (p. 73.)"

. . . *Bradshaw v. Swagerty,* 1 Kan.App.2d 213, 563 P.2d 511 (1977), was an action for slander and outrage. The epithets in question were "nigger," "bastard" and possibly "knot-headed boy." Plaintiffs legitimacy was conceded. The trial court granted summary judgment to the defendant on both counts. The appellate court agreed that these words were " 'mere insults' of the kind which must be tolerated in our rough-edged society." 1 Kan.App.2d at 216, 563 P.2d 511. . . .

In the instant case the appellees rely heavily on *Bradshaw v. Swagerty,* 1 Kan.App.2d 213, 563 P.2d 511, and *Dotson v. McLaughlin,* 216 Kan. 201, 531 P.2d 1. The reliance is misplaced. The cases are distinguishable. In *Bradshaw,* the plaintiff was in an attorney's office concerning a collection letter. During the interview he was called a "nigger," a "bastard" and possibly a "knot-headed boy." However tasteless such outbursts are, they do not sink to the abysmal degradation of the words used by Hug. They did not wield a similar emotional impact upon their target.

In *Dotson,* the facts are so dissimilar that it is of no help. McLaughlin was simply complaining of the frequency of Dotson's calls while trying to collect a note.

The relative positions of Gomez and Hug are important here. Hug was the employer. Gomez was the employee. Hug spoke from the position of a county commissioner. These remarks had been made to Gomez by Hug over a period of several days. The tirade unleashed upon Gomez on April 21, 1978, was terrifying to him. He was afraid of Hug, afraid for his job, afraid for his family. Each party argues a different meaning from these statements of Gomez' fear. It is an issue for the trier of fact.

ILLUSTRATION 5-3. *(continued)* 151

Contreras v. Crown Zellerbach, 88 Wash.2d 735, 565 P.2d 1173 (1977), concerned the allegations of a Mexican-American that he had been the object of racial insults, humiliation and embarrassment during the course of his employment. The Washington Court found that liability for infliction of mental distress could attach under the facts alleged. The Court held at p. 741, 565 P.2d 1173:

"When one in a position of authority, actual or apparent, over another has allegedly made racial slurs and jokes and comments, this abusive conduct gives added impetus to the claim of outrageous behavior. Restatement (Second) of Torts § 46 comment *e*. The relationship between the parties is a significant factor in determining whether liability should be imposed."

We can agree with the comment from Restatement of Torts quoted above. We cannot agree that it was for the trial court to rule that what was said to Gomez was a mere insult, a petty oppression or other triviality. This was a matter for the jury. Certainly there is no occasion for the law to intervene in every case where someone's feelings are hurt. Certainly the rough edges of our society still need smoothing down and there must still be freedom to blow off harmless steam. But this vituperation was well beyond the bounds of freedom to blow off harmless steam. It is not a burden of American citizenship in the State of Kansas that such vitriolic bullying as was turned by Hug against Gomez, and its emotional and physical consequences, must be accepted without possibility of redress and accepted as often as it amuses the speaker to utter it. Kansas courts are not so impotent. At the very least the victim of such an attack has the right to have his grievance heard by a jury of average members of the community to know whether they would exclaim, "Outrageous!"

It cannot be said that reasonable persons could reach but one conclusion from the evidence in this case. The trial court erred in sustaining the motion for summary judgment as to the allegation of intentional infliction of emotional distress by the defendant Hug. . . .

Supreme Court and it had ruled that racial epithets could be considered so outrageous as to sustain a cause of action for intentional infliction of emotional distress even if unaccompanied by any other injury. If the appeal had been filed and the Kansas Supreme Court had ruled in this manner (it did not; this is merely a hypothetical), the Kansas Supreme Court would have reversed the Kansas Court of Appeals decision. As a result, the appellate court decision would no longer have precedential value for the issue on which *Bradshaw* was reversed.

Your research would be inaccurate and incomplete (and perhaps grounds for a malpractice action) if you relied exclusively on the Kansas Court of Appeals decision and ignored the subsequent history. To be thorough and complete, you must trace the entire history of every case relied on. You always must look for later court action that may have affected the final disposition of any case.

"Status" refers to the disposition of a case and its currentness. For instance, the *Bradshaw* case, decided in 1977, has been finally disposed of. That is, there are no appeals pending and its disposition is final. If *Bradshaw* had been appealed to the Kansas Supreme Court and the Kansas Supreme Court had not yet handed down its decision, the case's status would be questionable at best. Although currentness is an important consideration, the age of the case is not determinative. For instance, although *Bradshaw* was decided 15 years ago, the case law contained in its decision will still be "current" if no comparable or higher court of the same jurisdiction has rendered a contrary decision. Hence, "currentness" is directly related to the status of the case and refers more to whether contrary mandatory case law has been rendered than to the age of the decision.

"Treatment" describes how a case has been analyzed by later court decisions. If a decision has been relied on by other cases as mandatory or persuasive authority, its value as precedent may be enhanced. On the other hand, if a case has been treated skeptically by later court decisions, the authority of the earlier case is greatly weakened. Courts sometimes reflect this skepticism by limiting the holding of the earlier decision narrowly to the facts. Of most significance are those rare occasions when the court directly overrules an earlier decision, which is a straightforward indication that the reasoning articulated in an earlier case was faulty. To justify different holdings in cases that raise similar issues, courts often distinguish an earlier case from the case at hand based on differing facts or circumstances.

For example, you may have noted that the Kansas Court of Appeals distinguished *Gomez* from its earlier decision in *Bradshaw* on the basis that the plaintiff, Gomez, and the defendant, Hug, had an employee/employer relationship. The Kansas Court of Appeals considered the employer/employee relationship special enough to give rise potentially to outrageous conduct on the part of the employer, Commissioner Hug, when he shouted racial epithets at his employee, Gomez.

That *Bradshaw* was distinguished exemplifies what we mean by treatment. The authority of *Bradshaw* has thereby been somewhat weakened, and the common law tort of intentional infliction of emotional distress involving racial epithets has been expanded slightly to include consideration of the relationship of the parties.

Other treatment that cases may receive includes "explained," "followed," "overruled," or "criticized." These terms are largely self-explanatory; you will encounter them again later in this chapter when you learn about citators. Since the treatment given an earlier decision by subsequent court decisions indicates the relative authority carried by the earlier decision, your research is not complete if you have not analyzed fully any treatment your case has received in later decisions.

So far, common law doctrine as articulated by court decisions has been discussed. Your research would be incomplete if you failed to also consider the effect that the legislature may have on the authority of court decisions. Specifically, the status of a decision may be affected by legislation passed after a court decision was rendered. For example, assume that the Kansas legislature enacted a "hate crime statute" or "civil rights act" or "human rights legislation" providing that racial epithets directed toward individuals with the intent to cause egregious emotional distress would give rise to recovery in tort. If that had occurred, plaintiffs such as Gomez or Bradshaw could rely on these statutes, and the court would be bound to follow them, assuming such statutes sustain constitutional challenge. Recently, in many states, the courts have relied on state civil rights acts or employment discrimination statutes to extend the common law tort theory of intentional infliction of emotional distress to include racial epithets such as those uttered in *Bradshaw* and *Gomez*. The interrelationship of statutes to the common law and the authority of legislative enactments will be studied in Chapter 7.

1. What Is a Reporter?

A "reporter" is a series of books containing a collection of court decisions designated for publication by a court or courts and arranged in roughly chronological order. Reporters do not include the transcripts of court proceedings nor the texts of briefs submitted by the parties.

Most court reporters are organized by geography or by the court rendering the decision. A few, such as state reporters, use both means of organization.

Decisions of the federal courts are published according to the court rendering the decision. The *United States Reports,* for example, publishes only the decisions of the United States Supreme Court; *West's Federal Reporter* publishes the decisions of the United States Courts of Appeals; and *West's Federal Supplement* reports the decisions of the federal trial courts.

The most comprehensive case reporting system is West Publishing Company's National Reporter System. This system of reporters includes both state court decisions and decisions of the federal courts, published in separate reporter volumes.

West's "regional" reporters include appellate state court decisions for each of the 50 states. In the late nineteenth century, West divided the United States into seven regions from which its regional reporters derive their names— Atlantic, North Eastern, North Western, Pacific, South Eastern, South Western, and Southern. A state's appellate court cases are published according to that state's location within these regional assignments. See Table 5.1 below.

Do not confuse, however, these geographical designations with jurisdiction. For example, *West's Pacific Reporter* includes decisions of many states, such as Kansas and Washington. (At the time the regions were designated,

TABLE 5.1. The West National Reporter System: Regional Reporters.

The West National Reporter System divides the 50 states into seven geographic regions:

National Reporter	States Covered
West's Atlantic Reporter (A. or A.2d)	Connecticut, Delaware, Maine, Maryland, New Hampshire, New Jersey, Pennsylvania, Rhode Island, Vermont, and the District of Columbia
West's North Eastern Reporter (N.E. or N.E.2d)	Illinois, Indiana, Massachusetts, New York, and Ohio
West's North Western Reporter (N.W. or N.W.2d)	Iowa, Michigan, Minnesota, Nebraska, North Dakota, South Dakota, and Wisconsin
West's Pacific Reporter (P. or P.2d)	Alaska, Arizona, California, Colorado, Hawaii, Idaho, Kansas, Montana, Nevada, New Mexico, Oklahoma, Oregon, Utah, Washington, and Wyoming
West's South Eastern Reporter (S.E. or S.E.2d)	Georgia, North Carolina, South Carolina, Virginia, and West Virginia
West's South Western Reporter (S.W. or S.W.2d)	Arkansas, Kentucky, Missouri, Tennessee, Texas, and Indian Territories
West's Southern Reporter (So. or So. 2d)	Alabama, Florida, Louisiana, and Mississippi

the Pacific states were not so populated, which explains why *West's Pacific Reporter* covers so many states, including Kansas.) As discussed previously, the Washington court has absolutely no jurisdiction over Kansas matters. Likewise, the regional groupings have nothing to do with authority. Remember that cases decided in one state are merely persuasive authority (not mandatory authority) for other state courts.

The second part of West's National Reporter System includes reporters covering the federal courts, including the federal specialty courts. Table 5.2, set out on page 155, enumerates the many federal courts included in the National Reporter System and names the appropriate reporter.

Some state court decisions are published in state reporters as well as in the West reporters. These state reporters contain only the decisions of the specified court(s) of that state. *Kansas Reports,* for example, contains only Kansas Supreme Court decisions, and *Kansas Court of Appeals Reports* contains only decisions of the Kansas intermediate appellate court.

Not all court decisions are published. Most states publish their highest courts' opinions; however, most publish only selected intermediate court decisions. Some states also publish selected trial court decisions or decisions of specialty courts, such as tax, family, or criminal matters; the authority of these trial courts may be limited and should be carefully checked before relying on their decisions.

The United States Supreme Court submits all of its opinions for publication. The federal courts of appeals and the federal district courts do not make available all of their decisions for publication—only those cases that the judges believe raise new issues or principles of law. Hence, you may hear of decisions in the news media that were never officially published. However, the written decisions or orders and the trial materials are public record and can be obtained from the clerk of the court.

Many unpublished opinions are included in the LEXIS or WESTLAW databases. You need to be aware, however, that in some jurisdictions the court is unwilling to accept as authority those opinions that have been marked as unpublished. If you wish to cite an unpublished opinion, check the court rules of the relevant jurisdiction to see if the court will accept the opinion as authority.

2. Parts of a Court Decision

Refer to Illustration 5-2 (pages 142-145) to see the various parts of the court's decision: the case name and citation; the docket number; the syllabus and headnotes; the names of counsel and judges; the opinion of the court; and the disposition by the court.

a. Case Name and Citation Information

The report of a case decision contains a great deal of information. The first item of information to note is the case name. The name of the Kansas case in Illustration 5-2 is *Bradshaw v. Swagerty.* The case name or title indicates the parties to the suit. Although correct citation form requires the listing of only the first-named plaintiff and the first-named defendant, there may in fact be several plaintiffs, defendants, or cross-complainants involved in the litigation.

The plaintiff's name usually precedes the defendant's name in the case title. In some jurisdictions, the order of the names is reversed on appeal when the defendant appeals. In those jurisdictions, the petitioner's or appellant's name is listed first, the respondent's or appellee's second. Refer to

TABLE 5.2. The West National Reporter System: Federal and Specialized Reporters.

The West National Reporter System also covers the federal courts.

National Reporter	Federal Court
West's Supreme Court Reporter (S. Ct.)	Supreme Court of the United States, 1882-present
West's Federal Reporter (F. or F.2d)	U.S. Circuit Courts, 1880-1912 Commerce Court of the U.S., 1911-1913 District Courts of the U.S., 1880-1932 U.S. Court of Claims, 1929-1932; 1960-1982 U.S. Courts of Appeals, 1891-present U.S. Court of Customs and Patent Appeals, 1929-1982 U.S. Emergency Court of Appeals, 1943-1961 Temporary Emergency Court of Appeals, 1972-present
West's Federal Supplement (F. Supp.)	U.S. Court of Claims, 1932-1960 U.S. District Courts, 1932-present U.S. Customs Court, 1956-1980 U.S. Court of International Trade, 1980-present Judicial Panel on Multi-District Litigation, 1968-present

There are also specialized reporters covering various other federal matters.

West's Bankruptcy Reporter (B.R.)	U.S. Bankruptcy Courts and the U.S. District Courts (publishes bankruptcy decisions not published in F. Supp.) Supreme Court of the United States and the U.S. Courts of Appeals (contains reprints of bankruptcy decisions) 1979-present (all of the above courts)
West's Federal Rules Decisions (F.R.D.)	U.S. District Courts (contains decisions involving Federal Rules of Civil Procedure or Federal Rules of Criminal Procedure, which are not published in F. Supp.), 1939-present (civil), 1946-present (criminal)
West's Military Justice Reporter (M.J.)	U.S. Court of Military Appeals and Courts of Military Review, 1975-present
United States Claims Court Reporter (Cl. Ct.)	U.S. Claims Court U.S. Courts of Appeals U.S. Supreme Court (contains reprints of claims decisions) 1982-present (all of the above courts)
West's Veterans Appeals Reporter (Vet. App.)	U.S. Court of Veterans Appeals, 1991-present

Rule 10.2 in *The Bluebook* for proper case title citation. (See the Citation Note on page 156 for further information regarding proper case citation form.)

The second piece of information you should notice, which also is reproduced in Illustration 5-2, is the citation to the volume and the title of the *official* reporter series in which the case has been published, and the page at which the court's opinion begins in that reporter. This citation reads as follows: 1 Kan. App. 2d 213.

Looking at this citation, the number 1 indicates the volume of the state reporter that includes the decision; "Kan. App. 2d" indicates the reporter title and the series of the reporter, *Kansas Court of Appeals Reports,* second series; and the number 213 indicates the page on which the case begins. From this citation you can tell that *Bradshaw* was decided by the Kansas Court of Appeals because Table T.1 of *The Bluebook* tells you that "Kan. App. 2d" indicates that the case is published in *Kansas Court of Appeals Reports* (Kan. App. 2d), which includes only Kansas Court of Appeals decisions. If the decision had been decided by the Kansas Supreme Court, it would have been reported in *Kansas Reports,* which is cited merely as "Kan." The case itself, as Illustration 5-2 shows, also names the court that decided the case and the date—April 15, 1977—on which the decision was rendered.

The *Bradshaw* case is published in two reporters; hence, 563 P.2d 511 is a parallel citation to the regional reporter, specifically, volume 563 of *West's Pacific Reporter,* second series, and the case begins on page 511 of that volume. See the Citation Note on page 160 for additional information on parallel citations.

The cases found in reporters are published in rough chronological order according to the date the decision was rendered. Since decisions are not published in alphabetical order by title or by subject, an accurate citation provides the only realistic means for locating reported cases.

> *Citation Note:* Rule 10 of *The Bluebook* governs case citation. A proper case citation includes the case name, the published sources in which the case may be found, the year of the decision, and any appropriate historical information. The level and jurisdiction of the court must also be reflected in your citation. Tables T.1, T.6, T.7, and T.9 provide correct abbreviations for various parts of a citation. Case names should be modified according to Rule 10.2 and Table T.6.

b.   Docket Number

The docket number for *Bradshaw* is 48321. The docket number is assigned by the clerk of court and is used to identify all papers submitted to that particular court regarding this case. Although this information is not included in a case citation if the case is published, it is useful when you wish to obtain background documents about the case. You would also use this docket number when requesting information from the clerk of court.

c.   Syllabus

Case reports usually begin with a brief synopsis or summary of the facts, the issues considered, and the resolution of the case. This synopsis is often referred to as a "syllabus" of the case, particularly if it is written by the court rather than by the editor of the reporter, which is more typical. Note that in the *Bradshaw* case, there is a synopsis written by an editor and there is also a brief syllabus written by the court, or actually by a designee of the court such as the Reporter of Decisions.

Although a syllabus may assist your research by providing a brief overview of a case, it should not be relied on as authority in place of the court's full decision. Sometimes, the syllabus does not reflect accurately the court's opinion. Consequently, an attorney who relies on a syllabus may be surprised to find that his or her case is based on an incorrect interpretation of the law. For example, in *United States v. Detroit Timber & Lumber Co.*, 200 U.S. 321, 337 (1906), an attorney relying on a United States Supreme Court syllabus claimed a point of law was settled. The syllabus had misinterpreted the point of law, however, and the Supreme Court explained that a syllabus is simply a reporter's interpretation of the case and is published for an attorney's convenience. To this day, the United States Supreme Court cites *Detroit Lumber* as authority in the warning it prints at the top of its opinions that contain a syllabus: "The syllabus constitutes no part of the opinion of the court but has been prepared by the Reporter of Decisions for the convenience of the reader."

d. Headnotes

A unique feature of West reporters is the short paragraphs that follow the syllabus. These paragraphs are called headnotes. They summarize specific rules of law discussed in the court's opinion and are assigned specific West Topics and Key Numbers. (The West Key Number System is explained at page 164.) Like syllabi, headnotes offer a quick preview of a case but are not a substitute for the decision itself. They are not written by the court and carry no authoritative value. Thus, they should be used merely as a research tool; they are never in support of any legal proposition.

e. Names of Counsel and Presiding Judges/Justices

The published report of a case usually includes the names of each party's counsel. An attorney who demonstrated particular expertise in handling a case may be a valuable person for you to contact if your research involves a similar issue. In *Bradshaw,* B.A. Lightfoot represented the appellant; the appellee was represented by B.G. (Skip) Larson and Max Eugene Estes.

The *Bradshaw* case was heard before a three-judge panel comprised of Judges Rees, Foth, and Swinehart. The separate designation just prior to the body of the opinion indicates the author of the majority opinion; in this instance, Judge Foth wrote the majority opinion.

You should become conscious of judicial nomenclature. Persons presiding on trial and intermediate courts are typically called "Judges" but members of the highest courts, including the United States Supreme Court, are called "Justices." The "Chief Judge" or the "Chief Justice" is typically specially appointed, convenes the court, and carries out administrative duties related to managing the workings of the court, such as assigning persons to author certain opinions. The presiding justice of the United States Supreme Court is called the "Chief Justice of the United States."

f. Opinion of the Court

An opinion is the reasoning and the decision of the judge or judges who heard the case. In an opinion, the court explains why it decided the case as it did. The court's opinion is neither a transcript of the proceedings nor a record of the evidence. The court does, however, usually set forth the pertinent facts of the case. In addition, the court summarizes the issues raised by those facts, relates the relief sought by the parties, and, in the case of appellate opinions, sets forth any errors made by the lower court and their bearing on the outcome of the case.

The major portion of an opinion is the court's application of the law to the facts. Each opinion includes a statement of the relevant controlling authority, be it statutes, administrative rules or decisions, or other cases. The court also may explain the underlying principles and reasoning governing its decision—the *ratio decidendi* for its decision.

Not every word in a decision carries precedential value. On occasion, a court may make broad policy statements in its opinion about a rule of law on an issue not directly before the court nor essential to its resolution. Or a court may use a case with a narrow issue to discuss a broader area of the law. These discussions are called *obiter dicta*. Such statements carry very little precedential authority because they are not the basis of the court's holding. Thus, you should rely on dicta with great caution.

Decisions of a court may be unanimous, in which case the opinion expresses the views of the entire panel of judges hearing the case. When a decision is not unanimous, the majority opinion may be accompanied by concurring or dissenting opinions written by other judges. A concurring opinion supports the majority holding and may offer an additional rationale, or may even view the case from a different perspective, but with the same holding. A dissenting opinion differs with the majority holding; the dissent may or may not include a written rationale for so holding. A case reporter contains all opinions. You should pay particular attention to dissenting or concurring opinions, for these opinions may reflect well-reasoned analysis that the court may embrace if later confronted with a similar issue.

The number of judges who hear a case varies from jurisdiction to jurisdiction. The United States Supreme Court has nine justices, and the federal courts of appeals have six to twenty-eight judges who normally sit in three-judge panels. In special circumstances, all of the judges within the federal courts of appeals may sit *en banc,* which means all the judges sit together to hear the case. Many judges have been appointed at the federal district court level, but typically only one judge hears a trial or the related motions.

g. Disposition by the Court

The disposition by the court is the court's order—for example, "affirmed," "reversed," or "remanded." "Affirmed" means that the lower court's decision stands. "Reversed" means that the lower court's decision has been overturned by an opposite ruling by the appellate court. Cases are "remanded" for further factual findings by the trial court, and for resolution consistent with the appellate court's ruling. On occasion, an appellate court may rule "in part." "In part" means that one or more of the issues presented to the appellate court receives a ruling that is different from the other issues; consequently, a decision rendered by a trial court may be both "reversed in part" and "affirmed in part" by an appellate court.

Often, an appellate court's entire decision is nothing more than the order stating that "the opinion of the lower court is affirmed." Such an order is often only one paragraph long and is called a "memorandum decision." Because the memorandum decision does not clearly describe the issues and facts of the case, the prior history of the case should be given as part of the case citation. *See* Rule 10.7 of *The Bluebook*.

3. Organizational Scheme: Official and Unofficial Reporters

Some states compile, print, and bind the decisions of their courts. Similarly, the Supreme Court of the United States relies on the United States Government Printing Office, a federal government agency, to publish its opinions in a series of volumes known as *United States Reports*. These governmentally authorized reporters are called "official" reporters.

Often there is a significant time lag between the issuance of a court's opinion and the publication of official reporters. This lag makes it difficult for attorneys to obtain recent court decisions necessary for credible research. The resulting demand by attorneys for recent decisions created a market for unofficial reporters of state and federal courts.

Because of the popularity of the West National Reporter System, many states have reassessed the need for state-subsidized case reporters. In states that have discontinued their official reporters, the courts rely on commercial publishing companies to print their decisions. Until 1948, for example, Florida published its own reporter called *Florida Reports,* using an officially authorized state printer. Since that date, attorneys in Florida have looked to *West's Southern Reporter* for the decisions of the Florida Supreme Court.

On the federal level, West publishes the *Supreme Court Reporter,* which carries United States Supreme Court decisions. The United States Government Printing Office continues to publish *United States Reports,* which is the official reporter and is the proper reporter to cite. However, the time lag is so great between the announcement of the Supreme Court's decision and publication by the Government Printing Office that other sources, such as *West's Supreme Court Reporter,* are typically relied on for research.

There is no official reporter for the lower federal courts; decisions of the United States Courts of Appeals are published in *West's Federal Reporter.* Decisions of the United States District Courts are found in *West's Federal Supplement.* See Table 5.2 at page 155.

Other companies, such as Lawyers Cooperative, publish case reporters. One set of unofficial reporters frequently used is Lawyers Cooperative's *United States Supreme Court Reports, Lawyers' Edition.* This set includes all United States Supreme Court decisions as well as selected research aids. Among the research aids of special interest are the summaries of counsels' briefs that are included as appendices to the decisions. Additionally, the publisher has included annotations that direct the researcher to related secondary sources published by Lawyers Cooperative such as *American Law Reports, American Jurisprudence, American Jurisprudence Proof of Facts,* and *American Jurisprudence Trials.*

The terms "reporter" and "reports" often are used interchangeably. Technically, "reporter" is usually used in connection with unofficial court publications, and "reports" usually refers to the official publication.

Citation Note: Note that the case of *Gideon v. Wainwright,* a 1963 United States Supreme Court case, may be found in *United States Reports, West's Supreme Court Reporter,* and Lawyers Cooperative's *United States Supreme Court Reports, Lawyers' Edition.* According to *The Bluebook,* you should cite only the official reporter despite the existence of parallel citations. Hence, the correct citation for *Gideon v. Wainwright* is 372 U.S. 335 (1963).

If *United States Reports* is not yet published, *West's Supreme Court Reporter* is the next preferred source to cite. If the opinion is not yet cited there, you may use *United States Supreme Court Reports, Lawyers' Edition.* If the opinion has not been published in any of the previous three reporters, cite to *The United States Law Week.* The Citation Note on pages 162-163 provides information on citing *The United States Law Week. See* Table T.1 of *The Bluebook.*

4. Parallel Citations

Many decisions are published in both official and unofficial reporters. You may rely on both versions of the published cases for authority, although the official version governs if there is a discrepancy in text between the official and unofficial versions. Because readers may have either the official or the unofficial reporter in their libraries, a parallel citation may be useful to researchers. However, you only include the parallel citation, if available, in documents presented to a state court for those decisions decided by a court within that state.

You are most likely to find parallel citations in the following sources:

(1) within the case report
(2) *National Reporter Blue Book*
(3) the Tables of Cases volumes in the various digests
(4) *Shepard's Citations* (see below at page 172)
(5) computer-assisted legal research tools such as LEXIS and WESTLAW

Citation Note: Consider the Kansas case of *Bradshaw v. Swagerty.* If you are citing *Bradshaw* in a document to be submitted to a Kansas court, you must include a parallel citation: *Bradshaw v. Swagerty,* 1 Kan. App. 2d 213, 563 P.2d 511 (1977). As noted earlier, this complete citation includes the official reporter, *Kansas Court of Appeals Reports,* second series (Kan. App. 2d), as well as the parallel citation to the unofficial reporter, *West's Pacific Reporter,* second series (P.2d). Rule 10.3.1 and Table T.1 of *The Bluebook* indicate the reporters for each court and their abbreviations.

Obviously, if a state has ceased publication of an official reporter, there is no parallel citation. However, the state and court must then be designated in the parenthetical: *Hubbard v. United Press International,* 330 N.W.2d 428 (Minn. 1983). If the court had been the Minnesota Court of Appeals, the parenthetical would contain the abbreviation "Minn. Ct. App." rather than "Minn." Rule 10.4 and Tables T.1 and T.7 of *The Bluebook* indicate the abbreviations for each court.

If you cite a case decision rendered by a court in another state, you need only cite to the regional reporter. For example: *Contreras v. Crown Zellerbach Corp.,* 565 P.2d 1173 (Wash. 1977). Give the abbreviated name of the state in parentheses—as in the *Contreras* example—and add the abbreviated name of the court of decision if the court is not the highest court in the state.

See Rule 10.3.1 and Practitioners' Note P.3 of *The Bluebook* for additional information on parallel citations.

Because of the sheer bulk of cases decided by courts in California, Illinois, and New York, West's National Reporter System contains separate reporter series for the decisions of those states: *West's California Reporter, West's Illinois Decisions,* and *West's New York Supplement.* The California and New York reporters cover many California and New York intermediate and lower court decisions, in addition to the decisions of the highest courts.

Proper citation requires parallel citations to these specialized reporters in documents submitted to the New York or California courts respectively, in addition to the regional reporters and the official state reports. Therefore, if the document is submitted to the New York or California courts respectively, there may be three parallel citations for New York or California cases. For example, the case of *People v. Romero,* decided by the Supreme Court of California, is found in *California Reports,* third series; *West's Pacific Reporter,* second series; and *West's California Reporter.* The correct citation would be: *People v. Romero,* 31 Cal. 3d 685, 646 P.2d 824, 183 Cal. Rptr. 663 (1982). *See* Rule 10.3.1, the tables in Part T, and Practitioners' Note P.3 in *The Bluebook.*

The *National Reporter Blue Book* is a companion to West's National Reporter System. It contains tables with cross-references between unofficial and official citations. By looking up the reporter, volume, and page of your case, you can find the parallel citation.

Illustration 5-4 below is taken from the *National Reporter Blue Book*. Note that if you have only the official citation to *Bradshaw v. Swagerty*—1 Kan. App. 2d 213—you can use these tables to find the parallel citation—563 P.2d 511—as indicated.

5. First, Second, or Third Series

You have probably noticed that many state reports and most of the West Reporters have been divided into first, second, or third series. When you see the citation 646 P.2d 824, "P.2d" means that the case is in the *Pacific Reporter, second series*. The publishing company numbered the volumes of the first series to a certain number, stopped that sequence, and then numbered the next volume as volume 1, second series. This second series is not a second edition or a second printing of the cases from the first series; rather, a later series is merely a compilation of more recent cases. To avoid confusion, you must always carefully cite to the correct series.

6. Researching Recent Court Decisions

a. Slip Opinions

Recent decisions of a court are first published in print as "slip opinions." A slip opinion is a mimeographed or typeset version of a single decision. Some courts make slip opinions commercially available; others do not.

Federal and state court slip opinions are frequently available on LEXIS and WESTLAW. In most circumstances, slip opinions are available on these databases much sooner than they are available in a printed source.

ILLUSTRATION 5-4. *National Reporter Blue Book* 331 (Supp. 1980).

I KANSAS COURT OF APPEALS REPORTS, SECOND SERIES

Kan. App.2d Pg.	Vol.	P.2d Pg.	Kan. App.2d Pg.	Vol.	P.2d Pg.	Kan. App.2d Pg.	Vol.	P.2d Pg.	Kan. App.2d Pg.	Vol.	P.2d Pg.	Kan. App.2d Pg.	Vol.	P.2d Pg.	Kan. App.2d Pg.	Vol.	P.2d Pg.
1	561	892	142	562	142	276	563	531	404	573	614	544	571	56	667	573	625
7	562	94	150	562	138	285	564	153	416	566	29	546	571	350	671	573	1096
12	561	880	155	563	485	291	563	1112	421	566	33	557	571	58	675	574	224
18	561	885	164	563	492	301	564	552	429	566	38	564	571	62	682	573	1099
22	561	880	171	563	1073	309	564	558	437	566	389	568	571	65	683	573	1100
29	561	877	180	563	497	310	564	559	445	571	1	574	570	1374	688	574	229
32	562	445	186	563	502	315	564	563	452	571	6	581	571	70	695	573	628
44	562	453	191	563	506	323	564	568	460	570	1100	592	570	1380	699	573	1103
57	562	102	198	563	515	331	564	574	464	571	11	607	571	78	704	573	632
64	562	98	203	563	1070	338	564	579	472	571	338	610	571	358	709	574	960
70	561	904	213	563	511	349	564	588	481	571	17	622	571	80	722	573	1106
75	561	897				356	564	593	494	571	26	630	573	622	727	573	1110
84	562	464	222	563	1069	362	566	18	503	571	32	634	573	1081	730	573	635
94	562	117	228	563	1086	366	566	21	509	571	36	642	573	1087	732	573	1112
103	562	108	243	563	1096	374	566	384	517	571	42	649	573	1092	736	573	234
114	562	127	251	563	1103	382	567	22	525	571	48	652	573	1095	744	573	637
131	561	907	254	563	522	394	566	26	532	571	345	654	573	214	748	573	1115
137	562	123	267	563	1106	397	566	775	540	571	53	659	574	217			

b. Advance Sheets

Because it takes a fair amount of time for recent case decisions to be edited and cumulated into hardbound volumes, publishing companies publish paper pamphlets called "advance sheets." These advance sheets provide the text of new decisions. The decisions contained in the advance sheets are paginated just as they will be when compiled in the hardbound volume; hence, the citation will remain the same when the bound volume is published. After the bound volume is received, the advance sheets are discarded.

c. *The United States Law Week* and *United States Supreme Court Bulletin*

Two excellent sources for recent United States Supreme Court decisions are *The United States Law Week* (Bureau of National Affairs, Inc.) and the *United States Supreme Court Bulletin* (Commerce Clearing House, Inc.). Both of these looseleaf services publish decisions weekly.

In addition to reporting recent Supreme Court decisions, these services include summaries of arguments recently heard by the Court and index cases that have been docketed by the Supreme Court. You will find the most recent information regarding the status of cases for which review has been petitioned in the tables of *The United States Law Week* and *United States Supreme Court Bulletin.* By status, we mean the disposition of the case such as "certiorari granted or denied" or "rehearing granted or denied." "Certiorari" refers to the discretionary petition filed to the Supreme Court seeking review of a lower court decision. "Rehearing" refers to the petition filed to the Supreme Court for reconsideration after a decision has been rendered by the Court; rehearing is rarely granted.

The United States Law Week provides summaries of selected federal and state decisions of particular interest as well. The indexes in both publications are strong, but the *United States Supreme Court Bulletin* is particularly helpful in finding Supreme Court decisions by subject of the issues presented in recent court cases.

d. Newspapers

Most states publish legal newspapers that often contain the texts of state appellate court decisions. These newspapers also may report cases docketed and changes in court rules, provide legal notices to parties involved in legal disputes, report on decisions regarding professional ethics, and give some court calendars for the week. You should become familiar with the legal newspaper for your state and rely on it for recent court decisions as well as professional notices and news.

You should not undervalue major public newspapers as sources of information. Immediately following the announcement of important Supreme Court decisions, the *Washington Post* and the *New York Times* often publish portions of the decisions, often with commentary by the editorial staff or by noted legal scholars.

> *Citation Note:* According to Rule 10.3.1 of *The Bluebook,* if you rely on a case decision that is not published in a reporter, you must cite a looseleaf service, a widely used computer database, a slip opinion, or a newspaper, in that order of preference. Citations to any of these sources must include the exact date of the case as specified by Rule 10.5.

As the Citation Note on page 159 explained, *The United States Law Week* may be cited if a recent United States Supreme Court decision has not yet been published in a reporter. For example: *Jacobson v. United States,* 60 U.S.L.W. 4307 (U.S. Apr. 7, 1992). Citation Notes in Chapter 6 (see page 215) and Chapter 8 (see page 373) provide further information on computer citation and looseleaf citation. *See* Rule 16.4 of *The Bluebook* for newspaper citation.

A proper slip opinion citation includes the title, the docket number, the court, and the complete date of the case's most recent action. For example: *Brooks v. Cook,* No. 89-56077 (9th Cir. July 22, 1991). To cite to a specific page in the slip opinion, include the page number in the following manner: *Brooks v. Cook,* No. 89-56077, slip op. at 4 (9th Cir. July 22, 1991).

D. DIGESTS

1. What Is a Digest?

The law is better indexed, digested, compiled, and annotated than any other subject field of knowledge. Because cases are published roughly by date of decision, it is nearly impossible to research a case law topic effectively without using secondary sources as finding tools. Digests assist you in finding relevant case law by topic.

A digest is both a subject index and a topical outline of case law. It consists of a series of brief summaries or abstracts gleaned from the points of law in a court's decision. These brief abstracts (or "digests") are organized by topic, such as "torts" or "damages"; often the topics are further broken down into narrower subtopics, such as "intentional, reckless or outrageous conduct" or "injuries to others."

Each digest series is compiled by court, by jurisdiction, or by geography—just as reporters are. There are state digests, regional digests, federal digests, court-specific digests, and a national digest, the American Digest System. *West's Kansas Digest,* for example, contains abstracts of state court appellate decisions for the state of Kansas as well as federal court decisions for cases originating in the federal courts located in Kansas. *West's Pacific Digest* contains summaries of state court decisions for the states covered by the regional *West's Pacific Reporter. West's Federal Practice Digest* contains summaries of reported federal appellate and federal trial court decisions, and the *United States Supreme Court Digest* contains summaries of United States Supreme Court opinions.

Computer-assisted research tools such as WESTLAW and LEXIS have broadened the availability of court decisions by allowing researchers to search the full texts of decisions. Nonetheless, it is crucial that you learn how digests work because, in some circumstances, digest searching is more efficient than full-text searching on LEXIS or WESTLAW. Furthermore, the computer databases do not yet contain older case decisions for many jurisdictions, and some lawyers do not have access to WESTLAW or LEXIS.

Remember that digests are finding tools and carry no authority. The digest entries are very brief and are written by editors employed by the digest publishing companies. Therefore, you might gather information that is incorrect or misleading if you rely solely on the case digests, and you must read and analyze each decision yourself.

2. The West Digest System and Key Number System

a. The Digests

The West Digest System is the most comprehensive and most commonly used digest system. Historically, there was a close relationship between the West National Reporter System and the West Digest System; there were corresponding digests for the regional and federal case reporters.

In recent years, however, some of the regional digests have been discontinued; examine Table 5.3 on page 165 and notice that, currently, only four of the seven regional reporters have a corresponding digest. West discontinued *South Western Digest* in 1958, *North Eastern Digest* in 1970, and *Southern Digest* in 1988. To conduct a digest search for the decisions contained in the corresponding three regional reporters, you must refer to the appropriate state digest or to the American Digest System, discussed below. As noted earlier, there is also a Supreme Court digest for United States Supreme Court decisions, and there is a federal digest system that covers the many trial and intermediate appellate federal courts.

The West Digest System also contains a digest for each state except Utah, Nevada, and Delaware. The Dakotas and Virginias are each combined in one digest. In general, state digests are preferable to regional digests because the state digests are not as bulky as regional digests. State digests are more focused; you need not read through case abstracts from other jurisdictions. The state digests also are more comprehensive than regional digests; unlike a regional digest, a state digest contains the cases arising in or appealed from the federal courts for that state.

West also publishes a massive series entitled the American Digest System, which is a comprehensive set of digests containing all the digest entries contained in West's federal, state, and regional digests. This system is bulky because it contains so many cases. Since the precedent set by cases in your jurisdiction is mandatory authority, you may not need to research the law of other jurisdictions. However, it is sometimes valuable to know how other jurisdictions have resolved the issue in question; for instance, your jurisdiction may not have considered your issue yet. In such situations, the American Digest System may be helpful.

The American Digest System consists of three sequential sets of digests: the *Century Edition,* the *Decennial Digests,* and *West's General Digests.* The *Century Edition* covers all cases published from 1658 to 1896. The *Decennial Digests* follow from that point, cumulating cases published during each five-year or ten-year span. Cases published most recently are digested annually in *West's General Digests,* which consist of multiple volumes published periodically throughout the year.

b. The West Key Number System

West Publishing Company developed a "Key Number System" to organize the digest summaries. Under this system, West has organized the entire body of law into general topics and subtopics according to specific issues and sub-issues. Key Numbers have been assigned to the issues and sub-issues for purposes of organization and ease of retrieval.

The term "Key Number" is somewhat misleading. A Key Number actually contains two parts: (1) the topic and (2) the Key Number. Since the second part (the Key Number) repeats for each topic, a complete Key Number must

Digests	Coverage
Supreme Court:	
United States Supreme Court Digest	Supreme Court of the U.S., 1754-date
Federal:	
Federal Digest	Federal Courts, 1754-1938
Modern Federal Practice Digest	Federal Courts, 1939-1961
West's Federal Practice Digest, 2d	Federal Courts, 1961-1975
West's Federal Practice Digest, 3d	Federal Courts, 1975-date
West's Federal Practice Digest, 4th	Federal Courts (supplements *West's Federal Practice Digest, 3d*)
West's Bankruptcy Digest	*West's Bankruptcy Reporter* and other units of the National Reporter System
West's Military Justice Digest	*West's Military Justice Reporter*
United States Claims Court Digest	*United States Claims Court Reporter*

West also has separate digests for the Fifth and Eleventh Circuits.

Regional:

Currently, West publishes regional digests for four of its seven regional reporters. Although state digests include references to federal decisions issued by the federal courts located within the state, regional digests do not include federal court decisions.

West's Atlantic Digest	*West's Atlantic Reporter*
West's North Western Digest	*West's North Western Reporter*
West's Pacific Digest	*West's Pacific Reporter*
West's South Eastern Digest	*West's South Eastern Reporter*

State:

Digests are published for all states except Utah, Nevada, and Delaware. District of Columbia Court of Appeals decisions are also digested in the *Maryland Digest*. North Dakota and South Dakota are both contained in the *West's Dakota Digest*, and the Virginias share the *West's Virginia and West Virginia Digest*.

Federal and State Coverage:

American Digest System:	All reported state and all federal court decisions
Century Edition of the American Digest (1658-1896)	
Decennial Digests (1897-1986; ten decennials)	
West's General Digests (1986-date; now in 8th series)	

state both the topic and the Key Number. You will waste valuable research time if you do not keep notes on both the topic and the Key Number.

There is a close relationship between the reporters published by West and the West digests. The West Key Number System ties case headnotes from the West reporters to the case abstracts in the West digests. For example, the same text appears in case headnote number 7 for *Bradshaw* as published in *West's Pacific Reporter* (see Illustration 5-2 on page 143) and under Key

Number "Torts 3" found in *West's Kansas Digest*. (See Illustration 5-5 on page 167.)

You may be able to ascertain from the case headnotes that several Key Numbers may be relevant, but not all of them. For example, in *Bradshaw*, "Torts 3" and "Torts 26(1)" are relevant. A quick glance at the headnotes that refer to Key Numbers on libel and slander suggests that those Key Numbers refer to issues that are tangential to our focus on the issue of intentional infliction of emotional distress.

One of the major benefits of the Key Number System is that you can use that same Key Number to find cases on the same topic and subtopic in any of the digests published by West. This is significant because once you find a Key Number, by using that same Key Number in other state or federal West digests you are easily directed to case decisions raising the same topic but in other jurisdictions. Hence, Key Number "Torts 3" involves the same topic throughout the West system, and you can find decisions unique to each jurisdiction merely by using a different digest series.

Lawyers Cooperative also publishes a digest of United States Supreme Court decisions. Although the topics are consistent with other publications published by Lawyers Cooperative, such as its A.L.R. annotations and encyclopedias, the topics or subtopics used in its system are not directly correlated to topics and Key Numbers in West's digests, and vice versa.

c. How to Use the West System

Consider the Perkins fact situation involving the intentional infliction of emotional distress, which has been discussed previously. To find case law applicable to situations where a person seeks recovery for emotional distress because of outrageous racial epithets, you first must select a digest that covers the appropriate jurisdiction. *West's Kansas Digest* (the state digest) and *West's Pacific Digest* (the regional digest) both include Kansas cases. The American Digest System does as well, but the set is so bulky that it is not advisable to begin your research there if you have other options. Once you have selected a digest, you can gain access to it by using any of the following research approaches:

(1) the "Descriptive Word Index" approach
(2) the topic outline approach
(3) the Key Number approach
(4) the table of cases approach

The Descriptive Word Index approach employs the general index volumes that are a part of each digest series. The index is usually located in the first or last volumes of the set. This index functions like any other index, except that it refers you to a topic and a Key Number instead of a volume and page.

When using a Descriptive Word Index, employ the same skills learned in using dictionaries, thesauri, periodicals, or encyclopedias. Remember to use legal descriptive words or terms; for example, look under "torts" or "personal injury" but not "harm" or "anger." Be precise in your language and topic selection. It is often best to start out with broad topics and then to seek for more specialized terms.

The topic outline approach is helpful if you already are familiar with the topic involved. As noted above, the digest is organized and arranged alphabetically by topics. Thus, if you know a digest topic that applies to your research, you may save time by selecting the volume containing the desired

TORTS ☞3

so time began on April 11 and concluded on May 10, which was Sunday, so notice of appeal filed on May 11, a Monday, was timely, pursuant to statute providing that last day of time period cannot fall on Saturday or Sunday. K.S.A. 74–2426(b), 77–613(b, d); Rules Civ.Proc., K.S.A. 60–206(a).—Matter of Newton Country Club Co., 753 P.2d 304, 12 Kan.App.2d 638, review denied.

Kan.App. 1977. Rule that notice of appeal must have been filed with the clerk of the district court within 30 days of entry of judgment has two exceptions: the district court judge may accept pleadings and other papers, note the filing date on them, and then promptly transmit them to the clerk, and secondly, when the final day of a time period falls on a Saturday, Sunday or legal holiday, the period is automatically extended to the next working day; however, in the instant case, appellants were not within either exception, since, first, their notice of appeal was placed in the mail on February 4, the final day for filing, and neither the judge nor clerk was in receipt of the notice on that day, and since, secondly, February 4 was a Friday and was not a legal holiday. Rules of Civil Procedure, rules 5(e), 6, 6(a, e), K.S.A. 60–205(e), 60–206, 60–206(a, e).—Kittle v. Owen, 573 P.2d 1115, 1 Kan.App.2d 748.

TORTS

Cases involving mental or emotional injury from intentional, reckless, or outrageous conduct, formerly classified to this topic, are now classified to Damages ☞50.10 et seq.

Library references
C.J.S. Torts §§ 1 et seq., 13, 17, 18.

☞1. Nature and elements in general.

D.Kan. 1990. Kansas did not recognize tort for breach of implied covenant of good faith and fair dealing; that duty was imposed in contract, and conduct departing from that duty was breach of contractual obligation.—Pizza Management, Inc. v. Pizza Hut, Inc., 737 F.Supp. 1154.

Kan. 1984. Tort of bad faith is not recognized. —State Farm Fire and Cas. Co. v. Liggett, 689 P.2d 1187, 236 Kan. 120.

Kan. 1982. Tort of bad faith is not recognized in Kansas and cannot be utilized as independent tort giving rise to punitive damages in action for breach of insurance contract.—Guarantee Abstract & Title Co., Inc. v. Interstate Fire and Cas. Co., Inc., 652 P.2d 665, 232 Kan. 76.

Kan. 1980. Kansas law does not recognize tort of bad faith; legislative provisions authorizing certain penalties against an insurer for lack of good faith are sufficient remedies for an aggrieved insured. K.S.A. 40–2404(9)(f), 40–2406(a, b), 40–2407.—Spencer v. Aetna Life & Cas. Ins. Co., 611 P.2d 149, 227 Kan. 914.

Kan. 1974. In a debtor-creditor relationship, actions of the creditor are compensable when they would be highly offensive to a reasonable man.—Dawson v. Associates Financial Services Co. of Kansas, Inc., 529 P.2d 104, 215 Kan. 814.

Kan.App. 1988. Claim arises in tort when a party violates some duty imposed on him by law.—L.R. Foy Const. Co., Inc. v. Professional Mechanical Contractors, 766 P.2d 196, 13 Kan.App.2d 188.

Kan.App. 1988. "Tort" is violation of duty imposed by law, a wrong independent of contract.—Pittman v. McDowell, Rice & Smith, Chartered, 752 P.2d 711, 12 Kan.App.2d 603, review denied.

Kan.App. 1981. Where tort liability is predicated on conduct less culpable than "intentional" the general rule is to compare fault and causation.—Sandifer Motors, Inc. v. City of Roeland Park, 628 P.2d 239, 6 Kan.App.2d 308.

☞2. What law governs.

C.A.Kan. 1980. Under Kansas law, lex loci delicti is the prevailing rule for determining where a cause of action arose.—Hawley v. Beech Aircraft Corp., 625 F.2d 991.

D.Kan. 1990. Under Kansas choice of law rules, Massachusetts law governed contract claims raised by Kansas purchaser of computer from Massachusetts seller, in that choice of law provision in purchase contract provided for same; however, Kansas law would govern plaintiff's related tort claims in that that state was where injury was suffered. K.S.A. 84–1–105(1).—Ritchie Enterprises v. Honeywell Bull, Inc., 730 F.Supp. 1041.

Kan. 1986. Kansas tort law governs the nature of the cause of action available to injured party where injury occurs in Kansas.—Brown v. Kleen Kut Mfg. Co., 714 P.2d 942, 238 Kan. 642.

Kan. 1985. In conflict of law situations, the law of the state where the tort occurred should apply.—Ling v. Jan's Liquors, 703 P.2d 731, 237 Kan. 629.

☞3. Right, duty, or obligation violated. ①

C.A.Kan. 1979. Malpractice suit, still pending, against physician, was not such an action as would establish basis for tort of outrageous conduct under Kansas law.—Tappen v. Ager, 599 F.2d 376.

Kan. 1987. Before there can be any recovery in tort there must a violation of a duty owed by one party to the person seeking recovery.—Koplin v. Rosel Well Perforators, Inc., 734 P.2d 1177, 241 Kan. 206.

Kan. 1976. Conduct of vice-president of assignee of mortgage which had foreclosed on plaintiff's property, in making an unannounced visit to plaintiff's home and in releasing information to realtor concerning judgment and redemption period fixed in foreclosure action, was not sufficiently extreme or outrageous to justify liability to plaintiff on theory of "outrage."—Vespa v. Safety Federal Sav. and Loan Ass'n, 549 P.2d 878, 219 Kan. 578.

Kan. 1974. Business community must be given some latitude to pursue reasonable methods of collecting debts even though such methods might often result in some inconvenience or embarrassment to the debtor.—Dawson v. Associates Financial Services Co. of Kansas, Inc., 529 P.2d 104, 215 Kan. 814.

Methods of collecting debts which might be reasonable in some circumstances might also be regarded as outrageous in others where it is known that the debtor is particularly susceptible to emotional distress due to a disease such as multiple sclerosis.—Id.

Kan.App. 1977. Breach of contract may be a material failure of performance of a duty arising under or imposed by agreement, while a tort is a violation of a duty imposed by law.—Chavez v. Saums, 571 P.2d 62, 1 Kan.App.2d 564.

Where a contractual relationship exists between attorney and client, and, at same time, a duty is imposed by or arises out of circumstances surrounding or attending the transaction, the breach of the duty is a "tort."—Id.

Kan.App. 1977. One who by extreme and outrageous conduct intentionally or recklessly causes severe emotional distress to another is subject to liability for such emotional distress, and if bodily harm to the other results from it, for such bodily harm.—Bradshaw v. Swagerty, 563 P.2d 511, 1 Kan.App.2d 213. ②

Liability for "outrage" does not extend to mere insults, indignities, threats, annoyances, petty oppressions, or other trivialities.—Id.

It is for the court in the first instance to determine whether the defendant's conduct was so topic and glancing through the topic outline. For instance, you may be aware that intentional infliction of emotional distress is a tort; hence, the topic outline for "Torts" may provide an appropriate entry into the digest. Locate the appropriate volume in the digest series covering "Torts" and look directly at the topic outline. For example, examine Illustration 5-6 on pages 170-171, which shows the topic outline for "Torts."

Obviously, you can avoid both the Descriptive Word Index approach and the topic outline approach if you already know the topic and Key Number. As you become familiar with a specialized area of the law, you may find that you remember certain Key Numbers. Or you may already have before you a case decision that you know is on point; the headnotes in the reporter will reference Key Numbers.

Each set of digests contains a table of cases, which usually is located in the last volume of the set. This table allows you to find the citation to a case by using only the names of parties to the suit. For example, you can find the citation to *Bradshaw v. Swagerty* by searching *West's Kansas Digest* table of cases volume. Usually, this search would occur using an alphabetical approach by name of the plaintiff or first-named party—"Bradshaw." West also includes a Defendant-Plaintiff Table of Cases in addition to the traditional table of cases, making it possible to use the table of cases approach even if you can identify only one of the named parties—"Swagerty." Obviously, this approach is used to locate cases only in situations where you have a case name but not its citation.

Using any of the approaches described above would lead you to the Key Number "Torts 3." You first find the volume that covers the topic "Torts" and then look for the Key Number "3" in *West's Kansas Digest* to find cases that discuss the tort of outrage or intentional infliction of emotional distress. Examine Illustration 5-5 on page 167. Notice that listed under the topic and Key Number "Torts 3" there is a digest entry for the case *Bradshaw v. Swagerty,* as well as other cases that may lend additional authority to your case law research.

Based on your previous examination of the headnotes for the *Bradshaw* case, you already know that Key Number "Torts 3" is relevant; it is prudent to also examine other related Key Numbers. This can be accomplished simply by scanning Key Numbers just before and just after "Torts 3" or by reexamining the topic outline in Illustration 5-6. This is important because the subtopics assigned by the digest editorial staff may be more narrowly drawn than your research project warrants. For our research situation, Key Numbers "Torts 3" and "Torts 7" are both relevant.

As you have already learned, encyclopedias and A.L.R. annotations do a good job of providing an overview of legal topics. These publications also contain case law references in their texts and in their extensive footnotes. Likewise, digests often include references to secondary sources. For instance, in Illustration 5-5, you may have noticed that there is a "Library references" heading, under which is a cross-reference to a legal encyclopedia, C.J.S. (*Corpus Juris Secundum*), which is also a West publication. Digests sometimes also include cross-references to practice books. Similarly, digests published by companies other than West may cross-reference companion encyclopedias or practice books published by those companies.

d. Updating Case Law Research

The law is not static, and recent court decisions are very important. Hardbound digest volumes are updated annually by pocket parts. Pocket parts, which are inserted either in the front or back cover of each hardbound digest volume, are pamphlets containing supplemental, updated information.

It is critical that you always check the pocket part. At the time this book was written, the entry in the pocket part for Key Number "Torts 3" of *West's Kansas Digest* indicates that another topical Key Number has been added to the digest series since *Bradshaw v. Swagerty* was decided. In Illustration 5-5 on page 167, note that a new topic and number have been added to the digest: "Damages 50.10 et seq." Hence, to perform thorough, current research, it is necessary then to also check Key Number "Damages 50.10 et seq."

More recent update services for digests are published in softcover "advance pamphlets" that are a part of the digest series. Advance pamphlets are supplemental softcover volumes that are issued periodically after the pocket parts are printed; annually, these advance pamphlets are cumulated into new pocket parts. These pamphlets provide references to cases published two or three months earlier.

Finally, you should check the advance sheet of a recent related reporter. For instance, to update digests for Kansas, it is prudent to check the recent advance sheets accompanying *West's Pacific Reporter,* second series. The advance sheets of the West reporters include a section of new case digests.

Hence, to update the digests thoroughly, you must (1) always check the bound volume, (2) any pocket parts and advance pamphlets to the digest, and (3) the advance sheets of the related reporter. This process ensures current and accurate research.

To update case law using the *Decennial Digests* and *West's General Digests* you would employ a similar process. *West's General Digests* can be updated by examining the digest section in the advance sheets of any recent West reporter. To conduct a complete historical search using the American Digest System, you must consult all the available advance sheets, the *West's General Digests* volumes, then each *Decennial,* and finally the *Century Edition.*

On occasion, an entire digest series is no longer updated, and a new series is started. The *Federal Digest* series was not updated after 1938, and a later series that digested cases after that date was introduced, entitled *Modern Federal Practice Digest.* In turn, the *Modern Federal Practice Digest* was no longer updated after 1961, and *West's Federal Practice Digest, 2d, West's Federal Practice Digest, 3d,* and *West's Federal Practice Digest, 4th* were introduced. For complete coverage, it is necessary to use all series of a digest. If only recent cases are desired, it is necessary to use only the most recent series. In the introductory pages of each digest is a listing of the dates indicating the scope or coverage for that digest series.

It is important to distinguish between *edition* and *series.* On occasion, an entire new edition is published that supersedes previous editions. For example, the second edition of *West's Minnesota Digest* totally replaced the first edition. However, a second, third, or fourth series updates by adding digests of more recent decisions, but does not replace previous series.

3. Non-West Digests

Several of the digests not published by West also compile and digest case law by topic. These digests also direct the user to other texts by the publisher. A frequently used digest is the *United States Supreme Court Digest, Lawyers' Edition.* This digest refers you not only to case law, but also to A.L.R. annotations and other practice books published by Lawyers Cooperative Publishing.

TORTS

SUBJECTS INCLUDED

Injuries from breach of duty or obligation not founded on contract, as affecting only the persons injured, not the public

Nature and extent of liability of the wrongdoers in general and with respect to particular torts not covered by specific topics

Civil remedies for such injuries

SUBJECTS EXCLUDED AND COVERED BY OTHER TOPICS

Damages for torts, see DAMAGES and specific topics relating to particular injuries

Distinction between tort and contract actions, see ACTION, ELECTION OF REMEDIES

Particular remedies for torts, see TRESPASS, ACTION ON THE CASE, TROVER AND CONVERSION, and other specific topics

Public injuries, wrongful acts as, see CRIMINAL LAW and specific topics relating to particular offenses

Specific torts, relating to particular—

> Classes of persons committing them, see INFANTS, MENTAL HEALTH, PARTNERSHIP, CORPORATIONS, and other specific topics

> Forms of injury to person or property, see ASSAULT AND BATTERY, DEATH, FRAUD, NEGLIGENCE, and other specific topics

> Kinds of property or estates or interests in property affected, see MINES AND MINERALS, ANIMALS, LANDLORD AND TENANT, and other specific topics

> Occupations or transactions in which injuries are inflicted, see CARRIERS, PHYSICIANS AND SURGEONS, and other specific topics

> Personal relations, liabilities incurred in, see HUSBAND AND WIFE, PARENT AND CHILD, MASTER AND SERVANT, and other specific topics

For detailed references to other topics, see Descriptive-Word Index

ILLUSTRATION 5-6. *(continued)* 171

9A Kan D—81

TORTS

Analysis.

For detailed references to other topics, see Descriptive-Word Index

Because West's headnotes, topics, and Key Number System have copyright protection, other digests cannot use them. However, other publishers use comparable systems of cross-references.

E. CASE CITATORS

1. Introduction: What They Are and Why You Need Them

Once you have found a case that is relevant to your research, you must verify that it is still good law—that is, that (1) it has not been reversed on appeal by a higher-level court, or (2) it has not been overruled in a different case decided by the same court or a higher court, or (3) its authority has not been altered by subsequent legislation. You also must determine its current weight of authority, as well as its applicability to the facts of your research situation, by examining how other, later cases have treated the case. To determine whether legislation has altered the authority of a case, you would do statutory research as described in Part A of Chapter 7. To determine the judicial history and treatment of a case, you use a citator.

A citator is a document listing references in later sources that have cited earlier sources. A later source is called a "citing source." The earlier source is the "cited source." *Shepard's Citations,* published by Shepard's/McGraw-Hill, Inc., are the most commonly used citators. Although other publishers produce citators (primarily for specialized subjects such as tax law), *Shepard's Citations* have played such an important role in legal research that they have given rise to the term "Shepardize," which means to look for references to a citation in a citator.

2. *Shepard's* Case Citators

Shepard's publishes case citators that correspond to the state, regional, and federal reporters. These case citators serve four functions:

(1) They provide parallel citations to your cited case.
(2) They trace the history of your cited case.
(3) They help you determine the treatment of your cited case by leading you to other cases that have cited your case.
(4) They provide some references to commentary sources.

a. State Case Law Citators: The State Citators

If your research involves a state court decision, such as the *Bradshaw* case, you may use a state or regional *Shepard's,* or both, to Shepardize the decision.

Shepard's publishes a state citator for each of the 50 states. As you would expect, these state citators allow you to Shepardize a case by its official reports citation, if it has one. As you might not expect, however, state citators also allow you to Shepardize a state court decision by its regional reporter citation. You use one part of a state *Shepard's* to Shepardize a decision by its official citation; you use a different part of a state *Shepard's* to Shepardize a decision by its regional reporter citation. *Shepard's* refers to these separate parts for each reporter title and reporter series for which it prints citations as "divisions." Because our example case, *Bradshaw v. Swagerty,* 1 Kan. App. 2d 213, 563 P.2d 511 (1977), has both an official reports citation and a regional reporter citation, you may Shepardize it in *Shepard's Kansas Citations* using either the state reports division (*Kansas Court of Appeals Reports,* second series) or the regional reporter division (*West's Pacific Reporter,* second series).

Both divisions of a state citator list citing cases from the state courts within the jurisdiction and from federal courts. However, the official state reports division lists subsequent citations using the official state reports citations, while the regional reporter division of the state *Shepard's* lists citations to later cases from the state using regional reporter citations. This means that if you Shepardize the *Bradshaw* case in *Shepard's Kansas Citations* using its "Kan. App. 2d" citation, the citing references from Kansas cases will be from the *Kansas Court of Appeals Reports,* second series (or later, if the publisher adds series); however, if you Shepardize the *Bradshaw* case in *Shepard's Kansas Citations* using its "P.2d" citation, the citing references from Kansas cases will be from the *West's Pacific Reporter,* second series (or later, if the publisher adds series).

Another difference between the official state reports division and regional reporter division of a state citator is that the official reports division lists citations to your case that have appeared in additional sources, such as opinions of the state's attorney general, state bar publications, selected legal periodicals, and annotations in American Law Reports and *United States Supreme Court Reports, Lawyers' Edition.* Compare Illustrations 5-7 and 5-8 on pages 174-175 to understand this difference. (Citations from such sources appear in the regional reporter division of the state citator only when there is no corresponding official state reports.)

Because the citing sources listed in each division of the state citator are different and because the frequency of publication of the citing sources in the two divisions may differ, you may wish to Shepardize the citation to your case in both the state reports and regional reporter divisions of a state citator.

b. State Case Law Citators: The Regional Citators

In addition to publishing state citators, Shepard's also publishes a citator for each of the regional reporters in the National Reporter System. Thus, you may Shepardize the *Bradshaw* case in *Shepard's Pacific Reporter Citations* as well as in *Shepard's Kansas Citations.* The primary differences between regional citators and state citators are that (1) regional citators include citations to your cited case from the courts of every state, not just from federal courts and the courts of the state in which the case arose, and (2) while regional citators include citations to your case in the *ABA Journal,* they do not pick up the references in state legal periodicals and attorney general opinions, which are found in the state citators. Review Illustrations 5-8 and 5-9 on pages 175-176 for a comparison of the listings for the *Bradshaw* case from *Shepard's Pacific Reporter Citations* and *Shepard's Kansas Citations* (*Pacific Reporter,* second series, division).

A good strategy for Shepardizing cases from your state is to start with *Shepard's* state citator, checking, if applicable, both the state reports division and the regional reporter division. By doing so you will retrieve all mandatory case law authority from your state and possibly some commentary. Then expand your research to the *Shepard's* regional reporter edition and search for persuasive authority.

You also may wish to use a regional citator if your research in commentary or other sources has led you to a persuasive case from another jurisdiction because the regional reporter citator will tell you if the case has been cited by the courts of your state.

ILLUSTRATION 5-7. List of Citing Sources for the *Kansas Court of Appeals Reports*, Second Series, in *Shepard's Kansas Citations* [Case Ed., Part 2] 21 (1986).

KANSAS COURT OF APPEALS REPORTS, SECOND SERIES, Vols. 1-9

Cited in

Kansas Reports, Vols. 221-236
Kansas Court of Appeals Reports, Second Series, Vols. 1-9
United States Supreme Court Reports, Vols. 429-463
Lawyers' Edition, United States Supreme Court Reports, Second Series, Vols. 50-84
Supreme Court Reporter, Vols. 97-104
Federal Reporter, Second Series, Vols. 546-762
Federal Supplement, Vols. 425-607
Federal Rules Decisions, Vols. 72-105
Bankruptcy Reporter, Vols. 1-48
The Journal of the Bar Association of the State of Kansas, Vols. 45-53
Kansas Judicial Council Bulletin, 1977-1983
University of Kansas Law Review, Vols. 25-32
Washburn Law Journal, Vols. 16-24
California Law Review, Vols. 65-72
Columbia Law Review, Vols. 77-84
Cornell Law Review, Vols. 62-69
Georgetown Law Journal, Vols. 65-72
Harvard Law Review, Vols. 90-97
Law and Contemporary Problems, Vols. 41-46
Michigan Law Review, Vols. 75-82
Minnesota Law Review, Vols. 61-68
New York University Law Review, Vols. 52-58
Northwestern University Law Review, Vols. 72-78
Stanford Law Review, Vols. 29-36
Texas Law Review, Vols. 55-62
University of California at Los Angeles Law Review, Vols. 24-31
University of Chicago Law Review, Vols. 44-51
University of Illinois Law Forum, 1977-1980
University of Illinois Law Review, 1981-1984
University of Pennsylvania Law Review, Vols. 125-132
Virginia Law Review, Vols. 63-70
Wisconsin Law Review, 1977-1984
Yale Law Journal, Vols. 86-93
American Bar Association Journal, Vols. 63-70

and in annotations of

Lawyers' Edition, United States Supreme Court Reports, Second Series, Vols. 50-75
American Law Reports, Vols. 79 *A*3 - 34 *A*4
American Law Reports, Federal, Vols. 34-69

NOTE-Citations to Kansas Court of Appeals cases reported in the Pacific Reporter as cited in Kansas cases in the Pacific Reporter and in federal cases may be obtained by referring to the Pacific Reporter divisions of Shepard's Kansas Citations, Case Edition.

Citations to Kansas Court of Appeals cases reported in the Pacific Reporter as cited in all units of the National Reporter System may be obtained by referring to Shepard's Pacific Reporter Citations.

PACIFIC REPORTER, SECOND SERIES, Vols. 1–699

(Kansas Cases)

Cited in

Pacific Reporter, Second Series (Kansas Cases), Vols. 1–699
United States Supreme Court Reports, Vols. 282–463
Lawyers' Edition, United States Supreme Court Reports, Vols. 75 LE–84 LE
Supreme Court Reporter, Vols. 51–104
Federal Reporter, Second Series, Vols. 50–762
Federal Supplement, Vols. 1–607
Federal Rules Decisions, Vols. 1–105
Bankruptcy Reporter, Vols. 1–48

NOTE—With respect to Kansas cases which are reported only in the Pacific Reporter, citations to such cases in the Kansas Reports, in articles in legal periodicals, and in annotations of the American Law Reports are also shown in this division. With respect to Kansas cases which are also reported in the Kansas Reports, reference should be made to the Kansas Reports division of Shepard's Kansas Citations, Case Edition for such citations.

　　Citations to Kansas cases reported in the Kansas reports prior to the Pacific Reporter as cited in all units of the National Reporter System or in Vols. 1–283 Illinois Appellate Court Reports, Vols. 1–19 Ohio Appellate Reports or Vols. 1–101 Pennsylvania Superior Court Reports which were published prior to the time that cases reported in those three series of state reports began also to be reported in the National Reporter System may be obtained by referring to the Kansas reports divisions of Shepard's Kansas Citations, Case Edition.

　　Citations to Kansas cases reported in the Pacific Reporter as cited in all units of the National Reporter System or in Vols. 1–283 Illinois Appellate Court Reports, Vols. 1–19 Ohio Appellate Reports or Vols. 1–101 Pennsylvania Superior Court Reports which were published prior to the time that cases reported in those three series of state reports began also to be reported in the National Reporter System may be obtained by referring to Shepard's Pacific Reporter Citations.

c.　Federal Case Law Citators

　　If your research involves a United States Supreme Court case, use *Shepard's United States Citations,* Case Edition, to determine the history and treatment of your case by subsequent cases. This *Shepard's* title lists citations to your cited case in later federal and state court opinions, plus a few other sources.

　　Similarly, if you are researching a case reported in *West's Federal Reporter* or *West's Federal Supplement,* use the appropriate unit of *Shepard's Federal Citations* to find citations to later cases that have cited your case. As you may recall, *West's Federal Reporter* reports federal appellate court cases, and *West's Federal Supplement* reports federal district court cases. *Shepard's Federal Citations* is divided into separate sets of bound volumes for each of these two reporters. To locate the correct volumes for a citation, look for the identifier *Federal Reporter* or *Federal Supplement* on the spines of the bound volumes and on the covers of paperbound supplements.

PACIFIC REPORTER, SECOND SERIES, Vols. 1–725

Cited in

Pacific Reporter, Second Series, Vols. 1–725
United States Supreme Court Reports, Vols. 282–469
Lawyers' Edition, United States Supreme Court Reports, Vols. 75 LE–91 LE
Supreme Court Reporter, Vols. 51–106
Federal Reporter, Second Series, Vols. 50–799
Federal Supplement, Vols. 1–640
Federal Rules Decisions, Vols. 1–110
Bankruptcy Reporter, Vols. 1–63
Claims Court Reporter, Vols. 1–9
Military Justice Reporter, Vols. 1–22
Atlantic Reporter, Vols. 155 At–515 A2d
California Reporter, Vols. 1–229
New York Supplement, Vols. 251 NYS–505 NYS2d
Northeastern Reporter, Vols. 177 NE–497 NE
Northwestern Reporter, Vols. 237 NW–392 NW
Southeastern Reporter, Vols. 159 SE–348 SE
Southern Reporter, Vols. 135 So–494 So2d
Southwestern Reporter, Second Series, Vols. 40–716
American Bar Association Journal, Vols. 41–71

and in annotations of

Lawyers' Edition, United States Supreme Court Reports, Vols. 93 LE–75 LE
American Law Reports, Vols. 75 AR–39 A4
American Law Reports, Federal, Vols. 1–72

To find law review articles that have cited a federal case, use *Shepard's Federal Law in Selected Law Reviews.* It lists citations to reported federal cases that have appeared in articles published in approximately 20 major law reviews.

3. Steps in Using *Shepard's Citations*

To use *Shepard's* effectively, you must understand both how to Shepardize and how to read the citation lists in a citator. This section of the chapter outlines the steps in Shepardizing; the next section discusses how to read the citation lists.

To use *Shepard's* effectively, follow these steps:

(1) Read your case in a reporter and note its citation in the reporter you are using.

(2) Note the numbers of the headnotes in the case that are relevant to the issue or issues you are researching. The lists of citing cases in *Shepard's Citations* include references to headnotes from the cited

cases, so you will want to know the relevant headnote numbers from a cited case when you look at the citation lists.

(3) Pick the appropriate *Shepard's Citations* title or titles. If you do not know if there is a *Shepard's* title for your citation, consult your librarian or check your library's catalog. You may find the *Shepard's* titles owned by your library by doing a title search in your library's catalog under the word *"Shepard's"* or by doing a subject search using the subject heading "Annotations and citations (law)." If you have more than one *Shepard's* title, or more than one division within a title, to choose from, turn to the list of citing sources for the relevant divisions and compare them to decide which *Shepard's* titles or divisions you will use.

(4) Find the most recent paper supplement to the bound volumes of your *Shepard's Citations* title. The gold, red, or white supplement should generally be no more than three months old. If it is older than that, ask your librarian if a newer supplement is available.

(5) Look at the part of the cover of the most recent paper supplement that is headed, "What Your Library Should Contain." (See Illustration 5-10 on page 178.) Use that part to determine what constitutes a complete set of *Shepard's* volumes for the title you have chosen. Set these volumes in order on a convenient shelf or work table.

(6) Select from the complete set of volumes for your *Shepard's* title those volumes that include the citation you are checking. Choose only those volumes that include citations to the reporter volume and series in which your case is printed. For example, in October 1991 a complete set of *Shepard's Pacific Reporter Citations* included: (a) 1987 Bound Volume 1 (Parts 1-4), with each part containing citations to different volumes of *West's Pacific Reporter,* first series; (b) Bound Volume 2 (Parts 1-5), with each part listing citations to different volumes of *West's Pacific Reporter,* second series; and (c) a 1987-1990 Bound Supplement and two paperback supplements, all of which listed citations to volumes in both the first and second series of *West's Pacific Reporter.* To Shepardize the *Bradshaw* case by its regional reporter citation, 563 P.2d 511, you need to use only Bound Volume 2, Part 5, plus the 1987-1990 Bound Supplement and any later paper supplements.

(7) Scan the Preface and Illustrative Case at the front of any bound volume of your *Shepard's* title for instructions on how to use and interpret *Shepard's.* See Illustration 5-11 on page 179 for an example of an Illustrative Case.

(8) Turn to the appropriate division in each of your *Shepard's* volumes. Use the table of contents or the page headings printed at the top of each page to find the appropriate division. To Shepardize *Bradshaw* in *Shepard's Pacific Reporter Citations,* for example, you would turn to the *Pacific Reporter,* second series, division. A common mistake is to turn to the wrong division within a citator—to turn, for example, to a first series division when your citation is to a second series case (or vice versa). Whenever you cannot find an entry for your citation or the entry you have found seems incorrect, consider the possibility that you may be in the wrong division of the citator.

(9) Find citations to your cited case by locating the volume and page number that correspond to your citation. Volume numbers are pref-

VOL. 62   JUNE, 1991   NO. 10

Shepard's

Kansas

Citations

ANNUAL CUMULATIVE SUPPLEMENT

(USPS 656430)

IMPORTANT NOTICE

Do not destroy the June, 1991 gold paper-covered
Annual Cumulative Supplement until it is removed
from the "What Your Library Should Contain" list on
the front cover of any future supplement.

WHAT YOUR LIBRARY SHOULD CONTAIN:

1986 Bound Volume, Cases (Parts 1 and 2)*
1986 Bound Volume, Statutes*
*Supplemented with June, 1991 Annual Cumulative Supplement
   Vol. 62 No. 10*

DESTROY ALL OTHER ISSUES

SEE TABLE OF CONTENTS ON PAGE III

SEE "THIS ISSUE INCLUDES" ON PAGE IV

**RECYCLE YOUR
OUTDATED
SUPPLEMENTS**

When you receive new supplements
and are instructed to destroy the
outdated versions, please consider
taking these paper products to a local
recycling center to help conserve our
nation's natural resources. Thank you

SHEPARD'S
M C G R A W · H I L L

ILLUSTRATION 5-11. Example of a *Shepard's* Illustrative Case, in *Shepard's Citations,* Case Editions, Bound Volumes.

179

ILLUSTRATIVE CASE

Pacific Reporter, Second Series

Vol. 553

-423-
(87Wsh2d298)

D430US952
D51L℥801
D97SC1594
s510P2d233   — 1
cc553P2d442
cc554F2d369

559P2d⁴²602
564P2d838
566P2d²¹1264
578P2d⁴¹878
583P2d²¹625
589P2d¹⁹262
d589P2d²¹287
j589P2d288
f599P2d1274
605P2d²⁶1277
627P2d²⁶577
628P2d¹513
628P2d²¹817
638P2d1216
639P2d²¹773
639P2d²789
639P2d²⁶840
639P2d²¹841   — 2
j639P2d843
e649P2d832
652P2d²⁶967
655P2d³⁷1181
655P2d³⁸1181
658P2d¹1261
668P2d²⁹576
675P2d²¹202
675P2d²²202
j675P2d207
676P2d⁶499
j676P2d973
680P2d²¹420
683P2d³⁸209
704P2d³⁷692
719P2d²⁶535

Idaho
615P2d⁶123   — 4
Nev
582P2d²⁵792

La
354So2d775   — 5
Md
501A2d73

58.℀²1024s
89.℀³467n
89.℀³487n
9.℀⁴1152n   — 7
9.℀⁴1165n
23.℀⁴298n
35.℀⁴29n
35.℀⁴44n

Citations to the case of *State of Washington v. Ralph Williams' North West Chrysler Plymouth, Inc.* as reported in Volume 553 Pacific Reporter, Second Series at page 423 are shown in the left margin of this page in the same form in which they appear in the Pacific Reporter, Second Series division of this edition.

Cross references to a cited case as also reported in a series of state reports and the American Law Reports are shown enclosed in parentheses immediately following the page number of that case when first available and are not repeated in subsequent volumes. Thus the reference "(87 Wsh2d 298)" immediately following the -423- page number of the *Ralph Williams'* case indicates that that case is also reported in Volume 87 Washington Reports, Second Series at page 298 and the absence of an American Law Reports reference enclosed in parentheses indicates that the *Ralph Williams'* case is not also reported in the American Law Reports.

Citations to each cited case are grouped as follows:

1. citations by state and federal courts analyzed as to the history of the cited case;
2. other citations by courts of the state in which the cited case was decided analyzed as to the treatment accorded the cited case;
3. other citations by federal courts analyzed as to the treatment accorded the cited case;
4. citations, arranged alphabetically by states, by courts of states covered by the Pacific Reporter other than the state in which the cited case was decided analyzed as to the treatment accorded the cited case;
5. citations, arranged alphabetically by states, by courts of states covered by any units of the National Reporter System other than Pacific Reporter;
6. citations in articles in the American Bar Association Journal;
7. citations in annotations of Lawyers' Edition, United States Supreme Court Reports and the American Law Reports; and
8. citations in selected legal texts.

For the purpose of illustration only, this grouping has been indicated by bracketing the citations accordingly. It will be noted that as yet there are no citations in groups three and six.

In indicating the history and treatment of a cited case, the letter-form abbreviations shown on page xvi are used.

An examination of the citations relating to the history of the cited case indicates that an appeal was dismissed "D" by the United States Supreme Court in a case reported in 430 United States Supreme Court Reports "US" 952 as well as in 51 Lawyers' Edition, United States Supreme Court Reports, Second Series "L℥" 801 and in 97 Supreme Court Reports "SC" 1594. Another phase of the same case "s" is shown in a case reported in 510 Pacific Reporter, Second Series "P2d" 233. Connected cases "cc" are reported in 553 P2d 442 and 554 Federal Reporter, Second Series "F2d" 369.

An examination of the treatment accorded the cited case in subsequent Washington cases reported in the Pacific Reporter, Second Series indicates that it has been distinguished "d" in a case reported in 589 P2d 287, followed "f" in a case reported in 599 P2d 1274 and explained "e" in a case reported in 649 P2d 832. The *Ralph Williams'* case was also cited in aced by the word "Vol." and are set off in large bold type. The volume number in the heading on the top left-hand side of a page is the volume number of the first cited source on that page. The volume number on the right-hand side of the facing page is the number of the last volume cited on that page. Page numbers, also printed in boldface type, are centered in the columns and set off by dashes on both sides. (See Illustration 5-12 on page 181.)

(10) Skim the list of citing cases and select those cases you wish to read in full.

(11) Locate the correct reporter volumes and read those cases.

(12) Shepardize the relevant citing cases. Begin again at step (1).

4. Reading the Citation Lists

a. The Citing Sources

When you use a citator, it is important that you understand the scope of the information included. Citators are lists of citations compiled from specific sources during a specific period of time. A combined list of all the sources the editors checked to compile a particular *Shepard's* title appears at the beginning of each volume. A list of the sources the editors reviewed to compile the citations for a particular division within the title appears at the beginning of that division. Do not confuse these separate lists. As you may recall from the discussion of state citators, the citing sources differ from division to division within the same volume. Furthermore, the citing sources may change over time. You may wish to review again Illustrations 5-7, 5-8, and 5-9 on pages 174-176 for a comparison of the citing sources for the *Bradshaw* case as found in two divisions of *Shepard's Kansas Citations* and in *Shepard's Pacific Reporter Citations*.

b. Components of the Citation Lists

Case citation lists may include four types of information for a case: (1) parallel citations; (2) case history information; (3) information about the treatment of the case in later, different cases; and (4) secondary sources that have cited the case.

Refer to the citation list for the *Bradshaw* case from *Shepard's Pacific Reporter Citations* as you read the following discussion. The list is part of Illustration 5-12 on page 181. Recall that the *West's Pacific Reporter* citation for *Bradshaw* is 563 P.2d 511.

(1) Parallel Citations

Shepard's case citators list parallel references to a cited case. The parallel references may be to the case as reported in the official reports for the state, an unofficial reporter, or to a report of the case in American Law Reports, whichever are appropriate. These parallel references appear in parentheses immediately after the page number of the cited case. Parallel references are printed when they first become available and are not reprinted in subsequent volumes of *Shepard's*. In Illustration 5-12, "(1KA2d213)" is the parallel citation for the cited case, 563 P.2d 511.

(2) History Citations

Shepard's indicates the history of a cited case, if any, immediately after the parallel citation(s) for the case or immediately after the page number if

Vol. 563			PACIFIC REPORTER, 2d SERIES				
Okla	US reh den	**– 408 –**	**– 418 –**	**– 440 –**	US reh den	Haw	597P2d⁹687
f613P2d²462	in441US917	(222Kan1)	(222Kan50)	(222Kan140)	in434US1002	706P2d¹130	637P2d1178
Ill	607P2d¹410	563P2d⁵1067	d564P2d³539	574P2d⁸149	579P2d³151	89A2540s	637P2d⁶1179
436NE32	620P2d⁷770	575P2d¹35	e565P2d³294	574P2d¹²151	579P2d⁵156	39A21003n	645P2d⁵921
Md	635P2d¹251	575P2d²903	e565P2d⁶294	574P2d⁶562	587P2d⁵865		d645P2d⁶922
394A2d823		575P2d³903	d565P2d295	582P2d287	o587P2d866	**– 483 –**	645P2d926
Mo	**– 395 –**	575P2d⁴903	574P2d³164	598P2d⁹556	f597P2d³1106	Case 1	657P2d¹⁰566
591SW147	(98Ida337)	576P2d³656	574P2d⁴176	620P2d⁶825	606P2d²1039	s561P2d889	662P2d
17A31010s	US cert den	576P2d⁴656	j574P2d³179	625P2d⁸1141	606P2d³1039		[¹⁰122⁹
22A21387s	in434US891	577P2d⁴46	574P2d³195	629P2d⁶181	609P2d³232	**– 483 –**	673P2d⁸1122
4A2935n	j595P2d1089	578P2d⁵1111	e574P2d⁴196	654P2d¹⁰423	609P2d⁴232	Case 2	693P2d⁷1197
	j660P2d53	578P2d¹1149	574P2d³209	667P2d⁷390	438US⁵179	s562P2d453	Cir. 8
– 371 –	690P2d⁵899	f579P2d¹714	574P2d³212	j667P2d392	57L½⁵687		578F2d¹697
(39CoA14)	Kan	580P2d¹892	d575P2d³541	675P2d²75	98SC⁵2688	**– 483 –**	578F2d²698
623P2d⁴55	d602P2d²1274	582P2d⁵255	576P2d³1095	675P2d⁸75	Cir. 10	Case 3	Cir. 10
f638P2d²277	Wyo	587P2d¹328	d576P2d⁴1097	681P2d¹⁰617	611F2d¹806	s562P2d94	635FS²1147
638P2d²779	612P2d¹832	587P2d²328	580P2d⁵1299	681P2d⁶683	611F2d⁵806		Pa
678P2d³572	612P2d⁷833	587P2d⁸910	f594P2d⁵271	Utah	5A2394s	**– 485 –**	499A2d650
	f612P2d⁹839	590P2d⁵1031	614P2d¹1003	627P2d⁶536	10A23359s	Case 3	15A2108s
– 373 –		592P2d¹895	642P2d³140	NJ	24A21275n	(1KA2d155	87A3216n
(39CoA28)	DC	592P2d⁵895	d642P2d⁴140	390A2d1191		a575P2d504	38A21010n
568P2d¹1164	408A2d47	592P2d³896	669P2d³667	61A2677s	**– 467 –**	626P2d³226	
653P2d¹401	Fla	592P2d⁴896	j669P2d680	5A21136n	(222Kan197)	626P2d⁴226	**– 515 –**
	423So2d386	594P2d¹233	703P2d¹769		588P2d⁵956	Ind	(1KA2d198)
– 377 –	Me	594P2d²233	Iowa	**– 446 –**	597P2d⁵1111	397NE319	578P2d268
(39CoA54)	464A2d166	d594P2d⁸234	291NW343	(222Kan155)	620P2d²843		578P2d⁹269
r572P2d837	NY	595P2d¹1112	31A21078s	s532P2d1064	667P2d³884	**– 492 –**	Mo
	366NE1308	595P2d³1113		574P2d⁶185	676P2d88	(1KA2d164)	628SW651
– 379 –	397NYS2d	[952	**– 422 –**	586P2d²65	681P2d³636	(97A33981)	
(39CoA194)	419NYS2d	f597P2d¹674	(222Kan73)	f609P2d¹177	681P2d²1074	576P2d2624	**– 518 –**
710P2d¹1175	[991	e598P2d¹1059	582P2d¹260	f609P2d²1177	684P2d³422	581P2d³825	(1KA2d217)
724P2d²93	Pa	602P2d¹102	DC	f609P2d³1177	718P2d³638	608P2d⁴1391	592P2d¹870
	395A2d1348	f605P2d¹597	402A2d1220	56A21170s		623P2d¹916	697P2d83
– 382 –	395A2d1358	f605P2d²597		11A3737s	**– 470 –**	654P2d484	q697P2d¹84
(39CoA197)	422A2d632	f605P2d³597	**– 425 –**		(222Kan201)	Ark	
703P2d²652	422A2d634	d612P2d¹636	(222Kan118)	**– 451 –**	cc563P2d474	698SW517	**– 522 –**
	Tex	614P2d³434	576P2d⁶245	(222Kan162)	574P2d³936	4A27s	Case 3
– 384 –	613SW26	618P2d⁸833	d643P2d⁶1114	573P2d⁴975	f591P2d³168		(1KA2d254)
(39CoA189)	Va	631P2d¹241	Cir. 6	576P2d⁶605	596P2d³188	**– 497 –**	624P2d476
571P2d²309	325SE726	631P2d²241	e510FS¹834	576P2d⁶1074	598P2d³555	(1KA2d180)	
616P2d²179	20A23988s	642P2d¹1000	Alk	579P2d⁶168	603P2d²1036	574P2d⁵977	**– 531 –**
622P2d⁶76	75A23616s	642P2d²1000	646P2d⁵250	582P2d⁴310	631P2d³666	623P2d⁵531	(1KA2d276)
622P2d⁷76	RLPB§1.62	646P2d¹1098	Ariz	617P2d⁸104	631P2d⁴666	f636P2d²181	cc625P2d624
626P2d²699		646P2d²1098	d664P2d⁶668	639P2d⁴464	646P2d³1067	Ariz	630P2d1200
647P2d⁴691	**– 400 –**	647P2d⁵1312	Pa	660P2d⁶564	647P2d³1296	579P2d²570	d666P2d
663P2d⁹261	(98Ida342)	f653P2d²427	498A2d877	680P2d260	Okla	1A2454n	[¹²1188
d676P2d²1236	f673P2d¹435	673P2d¹1166	SD	680P2d924	640P2d³1384		686P2d⁷874
677P2d³1390		673P2d²1166	378NW252	Idaho	33A23798s	**– 502 –**	686P2d⁸874
677P2d⁵1390	**– 402 –**	677P2d¹1014		648P2d³207		Case 2	
683P2d⁴378	(98Ida344)	687P2d¹654	**– 431 –**	Wash	**– 474 –**	(1KA2d186)	**– 538 –**
701P2d⁴1248	632P2d¹677	687P2d²654	(222Kan127)	671P2d⁴275	(222Kan175)	Ind	(172Mt280)
Ill	637P2d²1166	711P2d¹154	580P2d³1368	Md	cc563P2d470	397NE319	cc537P2d325
395NE765	q653P2d¹814	711P2d²154	580P2d⁴1368	439A2d549	563P2d471		567P2d¹450
399NE1021	Iowa	721P2d¹275	q590P2d596	32A2434s	574P2d¹1365	**– 506 –**	571P2d
438NE470	288NW347	721P2d²275	597P2d⁷1091	34A31256s	582P2d⁵287	(1KA2d191)	[¹²1165
Mo			f599P2d³1034		590P2d²1072	563P2d²8514	572P2d²512
670SW869	**– 404 –**	**– 414 –**	f599P2d⁴1034	**– 456 –**	e602P2d²1343	579P2d²164	f573P2d¹195
Pa	(98Ida346)	Case 1	f599P2d⁸1034	(222Kan169)	606P2d²119	620P2d⁷843	575P2d¹877
514A2d105	580P2d³78	s561P2d880	f599P2d¹1035	565P2d²258	607P2d⁵1347	724P2d²688	f575P2d¹79
24A2460n	581P2d³338	630P2d1090	f599P2d⁵1035	565P2d⁶258	100A21433s	Nev	578P2d¹292
EDP§5.37	589P2d⁷92	25A2598s	j608P2d1357	567P2d⁴890		657P2d⁵104	578P2d¹1152
	594P2d³629		610P2d¹⁰664	567P2d⁶892	**– 476 –**	Wyo	f587P2d¹413
– 387 –	602P2d³49	**– 414 –**	612P2d⁷1217	704P2d¹⁰395	(222Kan206)	651P2d⁵1102	592P2d¹8161
(39CoA218)	j619P2d1114	Case 2	659P2d⁴240	Wyo		714P2d1234	595P2d⁷362
602P2d²6	691P2d²1174	(222Kan26)	724P2d146	566P2d³222	**– 478 –**	Iowa	605P2d¹1065
635P2d²889	j718P2d1205	597P2d620	Colo	566P2d⁴222	(222Kan209)	258NW310	611P2d¹611
	Me	647P2d¹826	644P2d49	649P2d³221	648P2d258	13A31286s	613P2d⁴1384
– 390 –	388A2d519	673P2d¹1203	Mont	649P2d⁴221			615P2d¹905
(58Haw1)		717P2d1067	e606P2d³1513	j654P2d146	**– 480 –**	**– 511 –**	632P2d¹1135
	– 405 –	718P2d¹609	Utah		(222Kan212)	(1KA2d213)	664P2d¹943
– 391 –	(98Ida347)	Cir. 10	672P2d¹⁰738	**– 461 –**	f573P2d³103	592P2d²479	668P2d1032
(58Haw4)	587P2d¹308	731F2d¹471	Minn	(222Kan189)	f573P2d²103	592P2d²7862	704P2d¹67
US cert den	663P2d²1088	489FS¹1301	369NW507	US cert den	f573P2d⁵103	594P2d⁹254	710P2d¹713
in440US911	685P2d¹834	619FS¹1475		in434US833	661P2d²796	594P2d²255	
		30A39s			661P2d⁹796	597P2d⁷687	
					694P2d¹1330	597P2d⁸687	

244

there are no parallel citations. *Shepard's* includes both the prior and subsequent history of your cited case. You always can recognize a history citation because it includes one of the *Shepard's* history abbreviations that are listed at the beginning of any *Shepard's* volume. Be especially alert for the "r" and "m" abbreviations; "r" means that a case has been reversed on appeal, and "m" means that it has been modified. See Illustration 5-13 on page 183 for a list of the *Shepard's* history abbreviations. Our example case, *Bradshaw,* has no reported prior or subsequent history.

> ***Citation Note:*** Rule 10.7 of *The Bluebook* requires that the subsequent history of a case be given whenever the case is cited in full. However, the history of a case on remand or denial of a rehearing may be omitted "unless relevant to the point for which the case is cited." The prior history of a case must be given only if the cited case "does not intelligibly describe the issues in the case," perhaps because the decision is a memorandum decision, or if the prior history "is significant to the point for which the case is cited."

(3) Case Treatment Citations

Next, *Shepard's* lists citations to your cited case in later court decisions. The basic format for each citation includes (1) the volume number of the citing source; (2) the title of the citing source, in abbreviated format; and (3) the page number of the citing source on which you will find the reference to the cited source.

You may clarify the title of any *Shepard's* cited or citing source by using the list, "Abbreviations—Reports," which appears at the beginning of any *Shepard's* volume. See Illustration 5-14 on page 184.

Shepard's alerts you to how some later decisions have treated your case through the use of treatment codes, which appear at the beginning of some of the citations. (See Illustration 5-13 on page 183 for a list of the treatment codes.) *Shepard's* treatment codes tell you if a later case has explicitly overruled your case (noted by an "o"). However, since the overruling may or may not relate to the issue in the case that you are researching, you must read the later opinion to understand its impact on your case. Treatment codes also tell you if a later decision criticizes your case (noted by a "c"), explains it (noted by an "e"), follows it (noted by an "f"), or distinguishes it (noted by a "d"). You always should consider treatment information when weighing the precedential value of your cited case. For example, a decision that has been followed consistently may be more authoritative than one that has been criticized consistently.

In assigning treatment codes, the *Shepard's* editors rely on the specific language in a case. Therefore, if one case overrules another implicitly rather than explicitly, you may not learn that through a *Shepard's* treatment code. Furthermore, you may not assume that the absence of a treatment code means anything more than that the editors did not find it appropriate to assign one of the codes to a citing case. If a citation does not have a treatment code, you must check it to learn its significance! Treatment codes are merely aids to assist you in selecting or ruling out some cases to read.

The case you are Shepardizing may involve more than one issue, and you may not need to research all of them. For example, the *Bradshaw* case involves issues of libel and slander as well as issues related to the tort of intentional infliction of emotional distress. (See Illustration 5-2 on page 143, which reproduces the headnotes from the *Bradshaw* case as reported in

ILLUSTRATION 5-13. *Shepard's* Abbreviations—Analysis, in *Shepard's Citations,* Case Editions, Bound Volumes and Cumulative Supplements.

183

ABBREVIATIONS—ANALYSIS

History of Case

a	(affirmed)	Same case affirmed on appeal.
cc	(connected case)	Different case from case cited but arising out of same subject matter or intimately connected therewith.
D	(dismissed)	Appeal from same case dismissed.
De	(denied)	Review or rehearing denied.
Gr	(granted)	Review or rehearing granted.
m	(modified)	Same case modified on appeal.
Np	(not published)	Reporter of Decisions directed not to publish this opinion.
Op	(original opinion)	Citation of original opinion.
r	(reversed)	Same case reversed on appeal.
Re	(republished)	Reporter of Decisions directed to publish opinion previously ordered not published.
s	(same case)	Same case as case cited.
S	(superseded)	Substitution for former opinion.
v	(vacated)	Same case vacated.
US cert den		Certiorari denied by U. S. Supreme Court.
US cert dis		Certiorari dismissed by U. S. Supreme Court.
US reh den		Rehearing denied by U. S. Supreme Court.
US reh dis		Rehearing dismissed by U. S. Supreme Court.

Treatment of Case

c	(criticised)	Soundness of decision or reasoning in cited case criticised for reasons given.
d	(distinguished)	Case at bar different either in law or fact from case cited for reasons given.
e	(explained)	Statement of import of decision in cited case. Not merely a restatement of the facts.
f	(followed)	Cited as controlling.
h	(harmonized)	Apparent inconsistency explained and shown not to exist.
j	(dissenting opinion)	Citation in dissenting opinion.
L	(limited)	Refusal to extend decision of cited case beyond precise issues involved.
o	(overruled)	Ruling in cited case expressly overruled.
p	(parallel)	Citing case substantially alike or on all fours with cited case in its law or facts.
q	(questioned)	Soundness of decision or reasoning in cited case questioned.

ABBREVIATIONS—COURTS

Cir. DC–U.S. Court of Appeals, District of Columbia Circuit
Cir (number)–U.S. Court of Appeals Circuit (number)
Cir. Fed.–U.S. Court of Appeals, Federal Circuit
CCPA–Court of Customs and Patent Appeals
CIT–United States Court of International Trade
ClCt–Claims Court (U.S.)
CtCl–Court of Claims (U.S.)
CuCt–Customs Court
ECA–Temporary Emergency Court of Appeals
ML–Judicial Panel on Multidistrict Litigation
RRR–Special Court Regional Rail Reorganization Act of 1973

ILLUSTRATION 5-14. Example of *Shepard's* Abbreviations—Reports, in *Shepard's Citations,* Case Editions, Bound Volumes and Cumulative Supplements.

ABBREVIATIONS—REPORTS

AA–Antitrust Adviser, Third Edition (Shepard's, 1987)

AABA–Atwood & Brewster, Antitrust and American Business Abroad (Shepard's, 1981)

A2d–Atlantic Reporter, Second Series

AB–American Bankruptcy Reports

ABA–American Bar Association Journal

ABA(2)–American Bar Association Journal, Part 2

ABn–American Bankruptcy Reports, New Series

AC–American Annotated Cases

AD–American Decisions

ADC–Appeal Cases, District of Columbia Reports

Advo–Givens, Advocacy (Shepard's, 1985)

AE–Acret, Architects and Engineers (Shepard's, 1984)

AEn–Buck, Alternative Energy (Shepard's, 1982)

AFW–Newberg, Attorney Fee Awards (Shepard's, 1987)

AgD–Eglit, Age Discrimination (Shepard's, 1982)

AgL–Davidson, Agricultural Law (Shepard's, 1981)

AGSS–Laritz, Attorney Guide to Social Security Disability Claims (Shepard's, 1986)

AL–Turley, Aviation Litigation (Shepard's, 1986)

A2–American Law Reports, Second Series

A3–American Law Reports, Third Series

A4–American Law Reports, Fourth Series

Ala–Alabama Supreme Court Reports

AlA–Alabama Appellate Court Reports

Alk–Alaska Reports

AR–American Law Reports

ARF–American Law Reports, Federal

AMP–Bauernfeind, Income Taxation: Accounting Methods and Periods (Shepard's, 1983)

AN–Abbott's New Cases (N.Y.)

AnC–New York Annotated Cases

AR–American Reports

ARAP–Analytical Review: A Guide to Analytical Procedures (Shepard's, 1988)

ARD–Application for Review Decisions

Ark–Arkansas Reports

ARm–O'Reilly, Administrative Rule-making (Shepard's, 1983)

AS–American State Reports

At–Atlantic Reporter

AtSN–Attorney Sanctions Newsletter (Shepard's)

Az–Arizona Reports

AzA–Arizona Court of Appeals Reports

Boy–Boyce's Reports (Del.)

BP–Drake & Mullins, Bankruptcy Practice (Shepard's, 1980)

BRW–Bankruptcy Reporter (West)

BTA–United States Board of Tax Appeals Reports

BTCL–Givens, Business Torts and Competitor Litigation (Shepard's, 1989)

C2d–California Supreme Court Reports, Second Series

C3d–California Supreme Court Reports, Third Series

C3dS–California Supreme Court Reports, Third Series (Special Tribunal Supplement)

CCA–Court of Customs Appeals Reports; Court of Customs and Patent Appeals Reports (Customs)

CA2d–California Appellate Reports, Second Series

CA3d–California Appellate Reports, Third Series

CA3S–California Appellate Reports, Third Series Supplement

CaA–California Appellate Reports

CAH–Acret, Construction Arbitration Handbook (Shepard's, 1985)

Cal–California Supreme Court Reports

CaR–California Reporter

CaU–California Unreported Cases

CCL–Court of Claims Reports (U.S.)

CCLM–Acret, California Construction Law Manual (Shepard's, 1982)

CCPA–Court of Customs and Patent Appeals Reports (Patents)

CCRL–Davis/Strobel Capital Cost, Recovery and Leasing (Shepard's, 1987)

CD–Decisions of the Commissioner of Patents

CER–Anderson, Chapter 11 Reorganizations (Shepard's, 1983)

West's Pacific Reporter, second series.) To help you select the citing cases that
185

Case Law:
Searching for
Primary Authority

discuss those points of law you are interested in researching, *Shepard's* links
its citing references to the headnotes of the cited case. In any citing reference,
a raised number to the left of a page number corresponds to the headnote
number from the cited case that is discussed on that page of the citing case.
For example, notice the entry "597P2d^{8}687" in Illustration 5-12 on page 181.
The raised "8" refers to headnote 8 in *Bradshaw v. Swagerty,* as reported in
West's Pacific Reporter, second series. The principle of law summarized in
that headnote is discussed on page 687 of volume 597 of *West's Pacific Reporter,* second series.

The only trick to using the headnote numbers effectively is to remember
that the headnote numbers written in the citing sources correspond to headnotes in the cited reporter. In other words, if your cited source is a case
reported in *West's Pacific Reporter,* second series, it is the headnote numbers
from the case as printed in that source that are referred to in the citing
sources. If your cited source is the case as reported in *Kansas Court of Appeals
Reports,* second series, it is the headnote numbers from the case as printed
in that source that are referred to in the citing sources. The headnotes in the
two sources are compiled and numbered by different editors. They are not
identical.

Headnote numbers, like history and treatment codes, help you to focus
and speed your *Shepard's* research.

(4) Other Citations

The remaining citations consist primarily of citations from secondary
sources, such as legal periodicals, annotations in *United States Supreme Court
Reports, Lawyers' Edition* and American Law Reports, and selected legal texts.
In state citators, these may be preceded by citations from state attorney
general's opinions.

c. The Order of the Citations

The citing sources in a *Shepard's* case citator are grouped in a specified
order. An understanding of that order will help you use a citator more
effectively. For example, you will use the regional reporter citators more
effectively if you understand that in a regional citator the first citations to a
case after the history citations are citations to the case from the courts of the
state that decided the original case. You may determine the order of the
citations for a particular *Shepard's* title by studying the Illustrative Case that
appears at the beginning of the *Shepard's* bound volumes for the title. (Again,
see Illustration 5-11 on page 179 for an example of a *Shepard's* Illustrative
Case.)

5. Using *Shepard's* Effectively

A *Shepard's* citation list is often very long and can appear overwhelming.
It will seem less so if you keep the following hints in mind:

(1) Use *Shepard's* early in your research. Doing so may help you avoid
spending too much time on a mandatory primary authority that has
been reversed or overruled. It may lead you to a better authority
than the one with which you began your research. It may also alert
you to the number of citing sources available to you and thus help
you plan your time.

(2) Use the headnote numbers and treatment codes to help you focus your research.

(3) Work from the newest supplement backward and work from the bottom of a citation list to the top. That way you will be finding the newest citing sources first. Often the analysis in those sources will include a discussion of the important earlier sources, so if you fail to get to the earlier sources, you may have covered them anyway.

(4) Adapt your *Shepard's* research to your research needs. If your earlier research in encyclopedias, treatises, periodicals, A.L.R.s, Restatements, or cases has shown that the point of law you are researching is well settled, you may need only check a few recent citations. On the other hand, if you are researching a developing or changing area of law or an area in which the law differs among jurisdictions, you may need to explore the reasoning of a larger number of cases.

6. Updating

There is a time lag between when a case is decided and when the citations in the case are reflected in *Shepard's Citations*. You have not completed your Shepardizing until you have updated every citation that is important to your research. You may update the citations in some state citators by using *Shepard's Express Citations,* a new monthly or bimonthly update service that now exists for some state citators. In addition, Shepard's maintains a computerized updating service, and subscribers may call Shepard's directly for updates. Finally, you may update your *Shepard's* research online on LEXIS or WESTLAW by creating your own citator from the computer databases. You will be shown how to do this in the next chapter.

Introduction to Computer-Assisted Legal Research

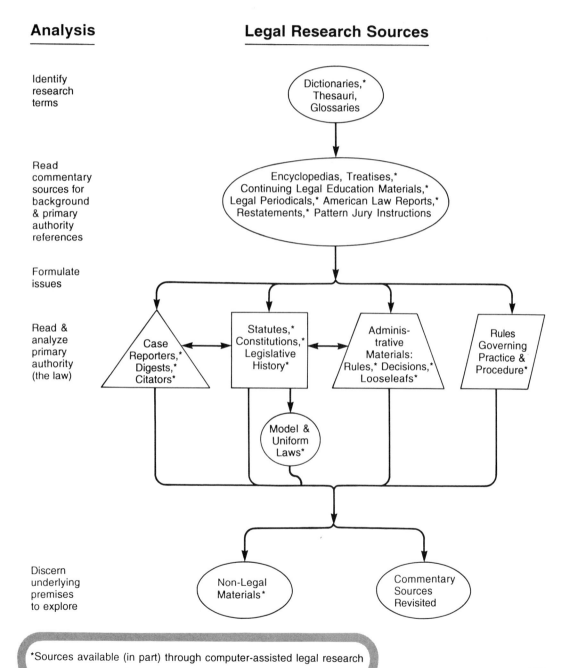

Analysis

Identify research terms

Read commentary sources for background & primary authority references

Formulate issues

Read & analyze primary authority (the law)

Discern underlying premises to explore

Legal Research Sources

Dictionaries,* Thesauri, Glossaries

Encyclopedias, Treatises,* Continuing Legal Education Materials,* Legal Periodicals,* American Law Reports,* Restatements,* Pattern Jury Instructions

Case Reporters,* Digests,* Citators*

Statutes,* Constitutions,* Legislative History*

Administrative Materials: Rules,* Decisions,* Looseleafs*

Rules Governing Practice & Procedure*

Model & Uniform Laws*

Non-Legal Materials*

Commentary Sources Revisited

*Sources available (in part) through computer-assisted legal research

A. INTRODUCTION

Until now, the research sources you have used have been primarily print sources. Many sources that are available to you in print are also available to you online, and some sources are available to you only online. This chapter introduces you to online searching on the two major computer-assisted legal research systems, LEXIS and WESTLAW.

Because citators are among the easiest and most appropriate sources to use online, the chapter begins with online citators. Then it introduces you to full-text searching. Full-text searching is the process by which the computer attempts to match words (and the relative positions of those words) that you specify against (almost) all the words in all the documents you select to search.

The discussion of full-text searching in this chapter focuses on case law research, but the principles you will learn are also applicable to full-text searching in the commentary sources you have already learned about. The remaining chapters of the book discuss both print and online research and build on the concepts developed in this chapter.

B. ONLINE CITATORS

LEXIS and WESTLAW contain some citators with which you are already familiar and some that will be new to you. This discussion begins with the familiar citator, *Shepard's*.

1. *Shepard's Citations* Online

a. Description

Many *Shepard's Citations* titles are available on LEXIS and WESTLAW. The computer (online) versions of *Shepard's* generally contain the same information as the corresponding print versions, but the information appears in slightly different formats.

Look first on pages 190-191 at Illustrations 6-1 and 6-2, the LEXIS *Shepard's* screens for *Bradshaw v. Swagerty*. At the top of a screen, LEXIS tells you how many documents you retrieved with the citation you "entered"—that is, typed into the computer—and which of those documents you are viewing. For *Bradshaw,* you retrieved two documents. That is because citations to *Bradshaw v. Swagerty* by its 563 P.2d 511 citation appear in two different *Shepard's* titles, *Shepard's Pacific Reporter Citations* and *Shepard's Kansas Citations.* LEXIS searched both *Shepard's* titles for you automatically. It displays the citations from each title in separate LEXIS documents.

In the next four lines of the *Shepard's* display, LEXIS describes the document you are viewing. First, under the heading "CITATIONS TO," LEXIS verifies the citation you entered as your search—in our example, 563 P.2d 511. Then, under the heading "SERIES," LEXIS tells you the name of the corresponding print *Shepard's* title in which you would find the same citations. For document one (Illustration 6-1), that would be *Shepard's Pacific Reporter Citations;* for document two (Illustration 6-2), *Shepard's Kansas Citations.* (Remember that in a state *Shepard's* citator you can Shepardize a case by its regional reporter citation, as well as by its official state reports citation if it has one.)

```
               (c) 1992 McGraw-Hill, Inc. - DOCUMENT 1 (OF 2)

CITATIONS TO: 563 P.2d 511
SERIES: SHEPARD'S PACIFIC REPORTER CITATIONS
DIVISION: PACIFIC REPORTER, 2d SERIES
COVERAGE: Shepard's 1987 Volume & Supplements Through 12/91 Supplement.

NUMBER  ANALYSIS            CITING REFERENCE              PARA   NOTES
------  ----------------    ------------------------      ----   ----------
   1    parallel citation      (1 Kan.App.2d 213)
   2                         592 P.2d 479                    2
   3                         592 P.2d 862                    7
   4                         594 P.2d 254                    9
   5                         594 P.2d 255                    2
   6                         597 P.2d 687                    7
   7                         597 P.2d 687                    8
   8                         597 P.2d 687                    9
   9                         637 P.2d 1178
  10                         637 P.2d 1179                   6
  11                         645 P.2d 921                    5
  12    distinguished        645 P.2d 922                    6
  13                         645 P.2d 926
  14                         657 P.2d 566                   10
  15                         662 P.2d 1225                  10
  16                         673 P.2d 1122                   6
  17                         693 P.2d 1197                   7
                               Cir. 4
  18                         831 F.2d 53                     3
  19                         831 F.2d 53                     6
                               Cir. 8
  20                         578 F.2d 697                    1
  21                         578 F.2d 698                    2
                               Cir. 10
  22                         635 F.Supp. 1147                2
  23                         730 F.Supp. 361                 2
                               Pa
  24                         499 A.2d 650
  25                          15 A.L.R.2d 108                      annot supp
  26                          87 A.L.R.3d 216                      annot.
  27                          38 A.L.R.4th 1010                     annot.
```

Then LEXIS tells you the "DIVISION" within the *Shepard's* volume in which you would find citations to your cited case. For document one, the division is *West's Pacific Reporter,* second series; for document two, the division is *West's Pacific Reporter,* second series (Kansas Cases).

Finally, LEXIS tells you exactly which print volumes correspond to your online search. By comparing the volumes listed online in the "COVERAGE" line with the volumes of the print *Shepard's* in the same series, you will be able to tell if the online version of *Shepard's* is complete or if you must use the print version to complete your Shepardizing. For example, document one for the *Bradshaw* case includes citations beginning with the 1987 bound volumes of *Shepard's Pacific Reporter Citations.* Since the 1987 bound volumes are the oldest *Shepard's Pacific Reporter Citations* volumes, coverage of this *Shepard's* title online includes the earliest *Shepard's* citations. Document two includes citations beginning with the 1986 bound volumes of *Shepard's Kansas Citations.* Again, because the 1986 bound volumes are the oldest *Shepard's Kansas Citations* volumes, coverage of this *Shepard's* title online includes the earliest *Shepard's* citations. Although it may seem that *Shepard's* coverage beginning with 1986 or 1987 bound volumes would not be complete, remember that the 1986 and 1987 dates on the citators refer to the

ILLUSTRATION 6-2. The Second LEXIS *Shepard's* Document for *Bradshaw v. Swagerty*, 563 P.2d 511.

191

```
              (c) 1992 McGraw-Hill, Inc. - DOCUMENT 2 (OF 2)

CITATIONS TO: 563 P.2d 511
SERIES: SHEPARD'S KANSAS CITATIONS
DIVISION: PACIFIC REPORTER, 2d SERIES (Kansas Cases)
COVERAGE: Shepard's 1986 Volumes Through 12/91 Supplement.

NUMBER  ANALYSIS              CITING REFERENCE              PARA   NOTES
------  ---------------       -----------------------       ----   ----------
   1    parallel citation         (1 Kan.App.2d 213)
   2                          592 P.2d 479                    2
   3                          592 P.2d 862                    7
   4                          594 P.2d 254                    9
   5                          594 P.2d 255                    2
   6                          597 P.2d 687                    7
   7                          597 P.2d 687                    8
   8                          597 P.2d 687                    9
   9                          637 P.2d 1178
  10                          637 P.2d 1179                   6
  11                          645 P.2d 921                    5
  12    distinguished         645 P.2d 922                    6
  13                          645 P.2d 926
  14                          657 P.2d 566                   10
  15                          662 P.2d 1225                  10
  16                          673 P.2d 1122                   6
  17                          693 P.2d 1197                   7
  18                          578 F.2d 697                    1
  19                          578 F.2d 698                    2
  20                          831 F.2d 53                     3
  21                          831 F.2d 53                     6
  22                          635 F.Supp. 1147                2
  23                          730 F.Supp. 361                 2
```

dates those *Shepard's* volumes were reprinted, not to the dates of the earliest citations listed in those volumes.

It is also important to look at the currency of *Shepard's* online coverage. For the *Bradshaw* case, both *Shepard's* documents were current through their December 1991 paper supplements when this text was written. Although you might assume that *Shepard's* online would be more up-to-date than its print counterpart, that is generally not so. Shepard's updates its print and online versions at the same time. Sometimes the most current *Shepard's* supplement appears online before it arrives in the library; sometimes it appears in the library first.

Most of the LEXIS screen is filled with information about the citing documents. This information is presented in five columns. The names of the columns and their functions are as follows:

NUMBER: You may enter this number into LEXIS to retrieve the full text of the corresponding document.

ANALYSIS: The analysis words correspond to the history and treatment codes used in the print *Shepard's* to explain the relationship between the citing document and the cited case.

CITING REFERENCE: The citations are the same as those in the print *Shepard's*, and they appear in the same order, except that citations from the supplements are integrated into their appropriate places. The page number is the page on which the citation to the cited case appears.

PARA: The "para" number is the number of the headnote in the cited case that reflects the issue being discussed by the citing case.

NOTES: Notes may provide additional information.

Now look on pages 193 and 194 at Illustrations 6-3 and 6-4, the WESTLAW *Shepard's* screens for *Bradshaw*. The WESTLAW version of *Shepard's* first tells you that you have reached the *Shepard's* service in WESTLAW. Then WESTLAW tells you how many documents your citation has retrieved and which of those documents you are viewing. "Rank 1 of 2" means you retrieved two documents, and you are viewing the first document. The first line also tells you the total number of "pages" (computer screens) in the *Shepard's* display for the document you are viewing and the number of the page you are viewing. For *Bradshaw,* the first document has three pages; the second document has two.

Next, the WESTLAW *Shepard's* verifies the citation you entered on the "CITATIONS TO" line. On the "CITATOR" line, WESTLAW tells you the name of the corresponding print *Shepard's* title in which you would find the same citations, and on the "DIVISION" line WESTLAW tells you the part within that *Shepard's* title in which you would find the citations. On the "COVERAGE" line, WESTLAW tells you which print volumes of the *Shepard's* title are included in the display.

Then the WESTLAW *Shepard's* presents information about the citing documents in four columns. The names of those columns and their functions are as follows:

Retrieval No.:   You may enter this number into WESTLAW to retrieve the full text of the corresponding citing document.

Analysis: Analysis includes the history or treatment code used by *Shepard's* to explain the relationship between the citing document and the cited case. It also includes the meaning of the codes. The column indicates a parallel citation by the phrase "Same Text" and an annotation by "N Anno," or "S Anno Sup" when the annotation appears in a supplement.

Citation: The citations are the same as those in the print *Shepard's,* and they appear in the same order, except that citations from the supplements are integrated into their appropriate places. WESTLAW sometimes adds the first page of the citing document before the number of the page on which the citation to the cited case appears.

Headnote No.:   This number is the number of the headnote in the cited case that reflects the issue being discussed by the citing case.

If you compare the *Shepard's* displays on LEXIS and WESTLAW, you will notice only minor differences between them. WESTLAW prints the *Shepard's* codes (as well as the explanations of the codes), while LEXIS has dispensed with the codes and prints only their explanations. WESTLAW often adds the first page of a citing document, while LEXIS follows the *Shepard's* format of

ILLUSTRATION 6-3. The First WESTLAW *Shepard's* Document for *Bradshaw v. Swagerty*, 563 P.2d 511.

193

```
                              SHEPARD'S   (Rank 1 of 2)          Page 1 of 3
CITATIONS TO: 563 P.2d 511
CITATOR: PACIFIC REPORTER CITATIONS
DIVISION: Pacific Reporter 2nd
COVERAGE: First Shepard's volume through Dec. 1991 Supplement
Retrieval                                          Headnote
   No.     ----Analysis---- ------Citation------     No.
           Same Text        (  1 Kan.App.2d 213)
    1                       592 P.2d 477, 479          2
    2                       592 P.2d 860, 862          7
    3                       594 P.2d 251, 254          9
    4                       594 P.2d 251, 255          2
    5                       597 P.2d 682, 687          7
    6                       597 P.2d 682, 687          8
    7                       597 P.2d 682, 687          9
    8                       637 P.2d 1175, 1178
    9                       637 P.2d 1175, 1179        6
   10                       645 P.2d 916, 921          5
   11     D  Distinguished 645 P.2d 916, 922          6
   12                       645 P.2d 916, 926

NOTE:   Check Shepard's PreView (SP), Insta-Cite (IC), and QuickCite (QC).
Copyright (C) 1992 McGraw-Hill, Inc.; Copyright (C) 1992 West Publishing Co.
```

```
                              SHEPARD'S   (Rank 1 of 2)          Page 2 of 3
CITATIONS TO: 563 P.2d 511
CITATOR: PACIFIC REPORTER CITATIONS
DIVISION: Pacific Reporter 2nd
Retrieval                                  Headnote
   No.     Analysis -------Citation-------   No.
    1            657 P.2d 561, 566           10
    2            662 P.2d 1214, 1225         10
    3            673 P.2d 1112, 1122          6
    4            693 P.2d 1194, 1197          7

                      Cir. 4
    5            831 F.2d 51, 53              3
    6            831 F.2d 51, 53              6

                      Cir. 8
    7            578 F.2d 691, 697            1
    8            578 F.2d 691, 698            2

                      Cir. 10
    9            635 F.Supp. 1130, 1147       2

Copyright (C) 1992 McGraw-Hill, Inc.; Copyright (C) 1992 West Publishing Co.
```

```
                              SHEPARD'S   (Rank 1 of 2)          Page 3 of 3
CITATIONS TO: 563 P.2d 511
CITATOR: PACIFIC REPORTER CITATIONS
DIVISION: Pacific Reporter 2nd
Retrieval                                  Headnote
   No.    -Analysis-- ------Citation-------   No.
                      Cir. 10
    1            730 F.Supp. 357, 361         2

                       Pa
    2            499 A.2d 648, 650
          S  Anno Sup  15 A.L.R.2d at 108
          N  Anno      87 A.L.R.3d at 216
          N  Anno      38 A.L.R.4th at 1010

Copyright (C) 1992 McGraw-Hill, Inc.; Copyright (C) 1992 West Publishing Co.
```

```
                          SHEPARD'S   (Rank 2 of 2)        Page 1 of 2
CITATIONS TO: 563 P.2d 511
CITATOR: KANSAS CITATIONS
DIVISION: Pacific Reporter 2nd
COVERAGE: First Shepard's volume through Dec. 1991 Supplement
Retrieval                                         Headnote
   No.       ----Analysis---- ------Citation------    No.
              Same Text       (  1 Kan.App.2d 213)
    1                         592 P.2d 477, 479        2
    2                         592 P.2d 860, 862        7
    3                         594 P.2d 251, 254        9
    4                         594 P.2d 251, 255        2
    5                         597 P.2d 682, 687        7
    6                         597 P.2d 682, 687        8
    7                         597 P.2d 682, 687        9
    8                         637 P.2d 1175, 1178
    9                         637 P.2d 1175, 1179      6
   10                         645 P.2d 916, 921        5
   11       D  Distinguished 645 P.2d 916, 922        6
   12                         645 P.2d 916, 926

NOTE:  Check Shepard's PreView (SP), Insta-Cite (IC), and QuickCite (QC).
Copyright (C) 1992 McGraw-Hill, Inc.; Copyright (C) 1992 West Publishing Co.




                          SHEPARD'S   (Rank 2 of 2)        Page 2 of 2
CITATIONS TO: 563 P.2d 511
CITATOR: KANSAS CITATIONS
DIVISION: Pacific Reporter 2nd
Retrieval                              Headnote
   No.       Analysis -------Citation-------    No.
    1                657 P.2d 561, 566            10
    2                662 P.2d 1214, 1225          10
    3                673 P.2d 1112, 1122           6
    4                693 P.2d 1194, 1197           7
    5                578 F.2d 691, 697             1
    6                578 F.2d 691, 698             2
    7                831 F.2d 51, 53               3
    8                831 F.2d 51, 53               6
    9                635 F.Supp. 1130, 1147        2
   10                730 F.Supp. 357, 361          2

Copyright (C) 1992 McGraw-Hill, Inc.; Copyright (C) 1992 West Publishing Co.
```

printing only the page on which the reference to the cited case appears. WESTLAW numbers the pages in its *Shepard's* displays, but LEXIS does not.

WESTLAW has two unique updating services for its online *Shepard's*. The first, called *Shepard's Preview,* lists the newest citing cases as reported in West's National Reporter System advance sheets. *Shepard's Preview* looks like a stripped-down version of *Shepard's*. The second, called QuickCite, allows you to automatically search case law databases for citations to your case name and citation. Using the computer's searching ability to update *Shepard's* is important because a citing case reference may be available in a full-text case database four to six weeks before the same citing reference is available even in *Shepard's Preview*. You will be shown how to use *Shepard's Preview* and QuickCite in one of the problem sets for this chapter.

Both LEXIS and WESTLAW allow you to update *Shepard's* through full-text searching, which you will learn about later in this chapter.

Although the illustrations only show the *Shepard's* displays for *Bradshaw* by its *Pacific Reporter* citation, recall that a state case often may be Shepardized by an official state citation as well as by a regional reporter citation. When a case has both citations, you may wish to Shepardize it by both, since there are differences in the citing references you will retrieve. (If you do not remember these differences, review Chapter 5.)

b. Comparison of *Shepard's* Online and the Print *Shepard's*

Both online versions of *Shepard's* have advantages over the print version. First, they allow you to search multiple citators at the same time. As you may recall, our online search for citations to *Bradshaw v. Swagerty* retrieved citing references from two different *Shepard's* titles—*Shepard's Pacific Reporter Citations* and *Shepard's Kansas Citations*.

Second, the online *Shepard's* displays integrate information from the main volumes and supplements into a single list of citations. You do not have to look in as many locations as in the print versions for the information you need.

Third, the online versions are easier to read. They display citing references only for the citation you entered. Assuming you entered the correct citation, you do not have to worry about being in the wrong division or column of the citator. In addition, the online versions present information in a clearer format. The print is bigger, the headnote or paragraph numbers are clearly displayed rather than embedded within the citation of the citing document, and the *Shepard's* treatment and analysis codes are explained on the screen.

Fourth, the online versions sometimes give you more information than the print version. This information may include, for example, a comment about a citing document or the number of the first page of the citing document.

Fifth, with *Shepard's* online you can ask the computer to show you only citing documents that meet the criteria you specify. You can, in effect, create customized *Shepard's* lists. For example, you can ask the computer to display only those citing cases that discuss the issue represented by a particular headnote in your cited case or that contain a particular history or treatment code. (You will learn how to do this in one of the problem sets for this chapter.)

Finally, the two online *Shepard's* provide links between the citations of the citing documents and the full texts of those citing documents, making it fast and easy for you to scan the citing documents for relevance. You will be shown how these links work in the problem set.

Shepard's online has two disadvantages. First, not all *Shepard's* titles or divisions are available online. Second, coverage of some *Shepard's* titles online does not include the early print *Shepard's* volumes; therefore, you must always check the scope of coverage.

2. Auto-Cite and Insta-Cite

a. Purposes

In addition to putting *Shepard's* online, LEXIS and WESTLAW have their own online citators. The LEXIS citator, a service of Lawyers Cooperative Publishing, is called Auto-Cite; the WESTLAW citator is called Insta-Cite. These online citators can be used to verify the accuracy of a case citation, to obtain parallel citations, to determine the direct history of a case, and to determine the negative indirect (or precedential) history of a case.

"Direct" history traces the movement of the same case through the appellate process. It would include, for example, a citation to the case as decided at the federal district court level, the court of appeals level, and the United States Supreme Court level, if the case has in fact been decided on all three levels. (If your case has been reversed or vacated on appeal, you will want to know.)

"Indirect" history notes how decisions outside the direct history of a case affect the precedential value of that case. Negative indirect history includes cases that diminish the authority of the cited case or that question or criticize it. (If your case has been overruled by a decision in another case, you will want to know that too.) Both direct and indirect history help you determine the current weight of authority of the case you are researching.

The online citators also help you to expand your research. Auto-Cite provides references to A.L.R. and *United States Supreme Court Reports, Lawyers' Edition* annotations that have cited your case, and it also cites cases to which your case makes negative reference. Insta-Cite refers to topics in C.J.S. that have cited your case.

b. Comparison with *Shepard's*

There are a number of differences between Auto-Cite and Insta-Cite on the one hand and *Shepard's* (either online or in print) on the other. First, Auto-Cite and Insta-Cite are much more up-to-date because they are totally electronic citators rather than citators based on a print publication. In fact, Auto-Cite and Insta-Cite both typically include direct case history information within five days after a history case is received by their publishers. Because of their currency, it is wise to check your case citations on Auto-Cite or Insta-Cite as a last step before submitting your research to a court, administrative agency, client, or colleague.

Second, Auto-Cite and Insta-Cite do not cite every case that refers to a case you are researching, as *Shepard's* does; they cite only cases that are part of the direct history of your case or cases that are in disharmony with your case—cases that may adversely affect its precedential value. Because they are more limited and focused in the cases they cite, you may wish to begin your research with an Auto-Cite or Insta-Cite search. If you learn that a case has been reversed or overruled or that its precedential value has been substantially weakened, then you may avoid some unnecessary research. Remember, however, that Auto-Cite and Insta-Cite are not intended to replace *Shepard's* with its complete citation coverage.

Table 6.1 on page 197 lists the differences between *Shepard's* (either online or in print) on the one hand and Auto-Cite and Insta-Cite on the other. For a visual impression of the differences, compare Illustrations 6-5 and 6-6 on page 198 with Illustration 5-12 on page 181.

c. Description

The Auto-Cite and Insta-Cite displays for *Bradshaw* do not fully convey the capacities or complexities of the systems. Therefore, to see more fully how the electronic citators work, look at the information they display for a second case, *Farmer v. United Brotherhood of Carpenters & Joiners*, 430 U.S. 290 (1977). Illustration 6-7 on page 199 is a partial Auto-Cite display for *Farmer.*

Auto-Cite presents information in one or more of six parts:

(1) "CITATION YOU ENTERED" identifies the case you are researching.

Function	*Shepard's*	Auto-Cite/Insta-Cite
Citation verification information—case name, jurisdiction, citation, date		x
Parallel citations	x	x
History of a case	x	x
References to related cases—those dealing with same parties and facts but different issues	x	x
Citations that affect the precedential value of the cited case	x	x
Citations from all cases citing the cited case	x	
Analysis of citing case, indicating its effect on cited case	x	x
Indication of whether citing case relates to a particular headnote or paragraph of cited case	x	
Citations from selected law reviews	x	
Provides a single source of information from all jurisdictions, federal or state		x

It includes the name and citation of the case, parallel citations, and the year of the decision. In addition, if a case listed in this or any other section of the display has been discussed in an A.L.R. or *United States Supreme Court Reports, Lawyers' Edition* annotation, a number preceded by an asterisk refers you to the annotation, which appears in a later part of the Auto-Cite display. Note the *1 in our example.

(2) "SUBSEQUENT APPELLATE HISTORY" identifies later decisions in the direct appellate history of the case. Note that *Farmer* was remanded. The decision on remand appears in volume 96 of BNA's *Labor Relations Reference Manual* beginning on page 3314.

(3) "SUBSEQUENT TREATMENT HISTORY" identifies later decisions outside of the direct history of the case that are in disharmony with the case and may adversely affect its precedential value. In our example, *Hyles v. Mensing* refused to follow *Farmer.* That refusal is noted in *Jackson v. Southern California Gas Co.* Both the *Hyles* and *Jackson* decisions were amended ("amd") by later decisions. The indented entries under those cases indicate that the indented citations refer to those cases rather than *Farmer.*

(4) "PRIOR HISTORY" identifies earlier decisions in the history of the case you entered. Note that *Farmer* was first published under the name *Hill v. United Brotherhood of Carpenters & Joiners* and that *Hill* was vacated by *Farmer.*

(5) "MAKES NEGATIVE REFERENCE TO" identifies those cases with which the case you entered disagrees. Our example case does not make negative reference to other cases.

(6) "ANNOTATIONS CITING THE CASE(S) INDICATED ABOVE WITH ASTERISK(S)" provides citations to annotations that discuss cases listed in the Auto-Cite display. If an annotation has been superseded or supplemented, this information appears in parentheses after the citation to the annotation.

Now look at Illustration 6-8 on page 200, the Insta-Cite screen for *Farmer.* Insta-Cite presents case information in three parts: (1) direct history, (2) negative indirect history, and (3) secondary sources.

```
Auto-Cite (R) Citation Service, (c) 1992 Lawyers Cooperative Publishing

563 P2D 511:


CITATION YOU ENTERED:

Bradshaw v Swagerty*1, 1 Kan App 2d 213, 563 P2d 511 (1977)

ANNOTATIONS CITING THE CASE(S) INDICATED ABOVE WITH ASTERISK(S):

*1   Modern status of intentional infliction of mental distress as independent
     tort; "outrage", 38 ALR4th 998, sec. 3.

     Recovery by debtor, under tort of intentional or reckless infliction of
     emotional distress, for damages resulting from debt collection methods, 87
     ALR3d 201, sec. 5.

     Civil liability for insulting or abusive language not amounting to
     defamation, 15 ALR2d 108, supp sec. 4.

To search for collateral annotations referring to the annotation(s) above, type
the citation and press the TRANSMIT key.
```

ILLUSTRATION 6-6. The WESTLAW Insta-Cite Display for *Bradshaw v. Swagerty*, 563 P.2d 511.

```
     Insta-Cite


     CITATION: 563 P.2d 511
     =>   1  BRADSHAW V. SWAGERTY, 1 Kan.App.2d 213, 563 P.2d 511
             (Kan.App., Apr 15, 1977) (NO. 48321)


                          SECONDARY SOURCES

     CORPUS JURIS SECUNDUM (C.J.S.) REFERENCES
             53 C.J.S. Libel and Slander Sec.18 Note 4
             53 C.J.S. Libel and Slander Sec.27 Note 33
             53 C.J.S. Libel and Slander Sec.162 Note 55
             86 C.J.S. Torts Sec.15 Note 11 (Pocket Part)
             86 C.J.S. Torts Sec.19 Note 50 (Pocket Part)
             86 C.J.S. Torts Sec.20 Note 59 (Pocket Part)
     (C) Copyright West Publishing Company 1992
```

Direct history appears first. Cases are listed in chronological order, beginning with the earliest case. Each entry includes the case name and citation, parallel citations, the name of the court deciding the case, the full date of the decision, and the docket number of the case. "MEM" or "TABLE" appears before the docket number if the decision was a memorandum decision or appeared in a table. On a separate line following each case and preceding the next is the history explanation that relates the following case to a preceding case. A citation is connected to the one immediately above it unless the word "AND" precedes the citation, in which case it is connected to an earlier case in the list. The case you are Insta-Citing is highlighted on

ILLUSTRATION 6-7. The LEXIS Auto-Cite Display for *Farmer v. United Brotherhood of Carpenters & Joiners,* 430 U.S. 290.

199

Auto-Cite (R) Citation Service, (c) 1992 Lawyers Cooperative Publishing

430 US 290:

CITATION YOU ENTERED:

Farmer v United Brotherhood of Carpenters & Joiners*1, 430 US 290, 51 L Ed 2d 338, 97 S Ct 1056, 94 BNA LRRM 2759, 81 CCH LC P 13056 (1977),

SUBSEQUENT APPELLATE HISTORY:

    on remand Hill v United Brotherhood of Carpenters and Joiners, Local 25*2, 96 BNA LRRM 3314 (Cal App 1977)

SUBSEQUENT TREATMENT HISTORY:

    and (not followed by Hyles v Mensing*3, 849 F2d 1213, 1988 US App LEXIS 8302, 3 BNA IER Cas 840, 128 BNA LRRM 2746, 109 CCH LC P 10568 (CA9 Cal 1988),

        amd Hyles v Mensing, 3 BNA IER Cas 1248, 129 BNA LRRM 2336 (CA9 Cal 1988))

    as stated in Jackson v Southern California Gas Co.*4, 881 F2d 638, 1989 US App LEXIS 11014, 4 BNA IER Cas 1092, 131 BNA LRRM 3238, 50 CCH EPD P 39204, 112 CCH LC P 11390 (CA9 Cal 1989),

        amd, reh den Jackson v Southern California Gas Co.*5, 52 CCH EPD P 39470, 113 CCH LC P 11689 (CA9 Cal 1989)

PRIOR HISTORY:

Hill v United Brotherhood of Carpenters & Joiners*6, 49 Cal App 3d 614, 122 Cal Rptr 722, 90 BNA LRRM 2467, 77 CCH LC P 11057 (2nd Dist 1975),

    vacated (BY CITATION YOU ENTERED)

ANNOTATIONS CITING THE CASE(S) INDICATED ABOVE WITH ASTERISK(S):

*1 Modern status of intentional infliction of mental distress as independent tort; "outrage", 38 ALR4th 998, sec. 3.

    Legality of hiring-hall arrangement under Labor Management Relations Act, 38 ALR2d 413, supp sec. 3 (sec. 3(b) superseded by Union's discriminatory operation of exclusive hiring hall as unfair labor practice under sec. 8(b) of the National Labor Relations Act (29 USCS sec. 158(b)), 73 ALR Fed 171).

    Construction of provision of Labor Management Relations Act (Taft-Hartley Act) conferring jurisdiction on Federal district courts in actions for violation of contract between employer and labor organization, 17 ALR2d 614, supp sec. 9.

---

the screen. It is also identified by a symbol that looks like an arrow. The direct history section also includes related references, that is, references to other cases arising from the same facts but involving different issues.

Direct history is followed by negative indirect history. Insta-Cite, unlike Auto-Cite, only displays indirect history for the citation you entered. It does not display the indirect history of the other cases in the Insta-Cite display for the citation you entered.

Finally, *Corpus Juris Secundum* references to the case are listed under the heading "Secondary Sources."

```
Insta-Cite


CITATION: 430 U.S. 290
                         DIRECT HISTORY

     1  Hill v. United Broth. of Carpenters and Joiners of America, Local 25
           49 Cal.App.3d 614, 122 Cal.Rptr. 722, 90 L.R.R.M. (BNA) 2467,
           96 L.R.R.M. (BNA) 3314, 77 Lab.Cas.  P 11,057
           (Cal.App. 2 Dist., Jun 30, 1975) (NO. CIV. 43751)
        Certiorari Granted by
     2  Hill v. United Brotherhood of Carpenters and Joiners of America,
           Local 25, 423 U.S. 1086, 96 S.Ct. 876, 47 L.Ed.2d 96
           (U.S.Cal., Jan 26, 1976) (NO. 75 804)
        AND Motion Denied by
     3  Hill v. United Broth. of Carpenters and Joiners of America, Local 25
           425 U.S. 969, 96 S.Ct. 2163, 48 L.Ed.2d 792
           (U.S.Cal., May 19, 1976) (NO. 75 804)
        AND Judgment Vacated by
=>   4  FARMER V. UNITED BROTH. OF CARPENTERS AND JOINERS OF AMERICA, LOCAL
           25, 430 U.S. 290, 97 S.Ct. 1056, 51 L.Ed.2d 338,
           94 L.R.R.M. (BNA) 2759, 81 Lab.Cas.  P 13,056
           (U.S.Cal., Mar 07, 1977) (NO. 75-804)

                    NEGATIVE INDIRECT HISTORY

   Abrogation Recognized by
     5  Aragon v. Pappy, Kaplon, Vogel & Phillips, 214 Cal.App.3d 451,
           262 Cal.Rptr. 646, 114 Lab.Cas.  P 11,878
           (Cal.App. 2 Dist., Sep 28, 1989) (NO. B034347), opinion modified
           (Oct 23, 1989)
   Holding Limited by
     6  Brown v. Southwestern Bell Telephone Co., 901 F.2d 1250,
           134 L.R.R.M. (BNA) 2363, 115 Lab.Cas.  P 10,081,
           5 Indiv.Empl.Rts.Cas. (BNA) 655 (5th Cir.(Tex.), May 24, 1990)
           (NO. 89-1768), rehearing denied (Jun 22, 1990)
   Limitation of Holding Recognized by
     7  Jackson v. Southern California Gas Co., 881 F.2d 638,
           131 L.R.R.M. (BNA) 3238, 50 Empl. Prac. Dec. P 39,204,
           52 Empl. Prac. Dec. P 39,470, 112 Lab.Cas.  P 11,390,
           113 Lab.Cas.  P 11,689, 4 Indiv.Empl.Rts.Cas. (BNA) 1092
           (9th Cir.(Cal.), Jul 28, 1989) (NO. 87-6506)


                        SECONDARY SOURCES

CORPUS JURIS SECUNDUM (C.J.S.) REFERENCES
          51A C.J.S. Labor Relations Sec.523 Note 5 (Pocket Part)
          51A C.J.S. Labor Relations Sec.525 Note 6 (Pocket Part)
          51A C.J.S. Labor Relations Sec.525 Note 16 (Pocket Part)
          51A C.J.S. Labor Relations Sec.525 Note 21 (Pocket Part)
          51A C.J.S. Labor Relations Sec.525 Note 23 (Pocket Part)
          51A C.J.S. Labor Relations Sec.525 Note 24 (Pocket Part)
          51A C.J.S. Labor Relations Sec.525 Note 30 (Pocket Part)
  (C) Copyright West Publishing Company 1992
```

The cases listed in an Insta-Cite display are numbered. You may retrieve a listed case by entering its number.

d. Comparison of Auto-Cite and Insta-Cite

Auto-Cite and Insta-Cite differ from each other in a number of ways. Table 6.2 on page 201 shows some of the differences at the time this text was written.

Auto-Cite	Insta-Cite
Case coverage	
About 330 reporters, plus slip opinions and unpublished opinions found on LEXIS	About 400 reporters, plus slip opinions and unpublished opinions found on WESTLAW
Citation verification coverage (case names and citations)	
From 1658	State cases from 1879 Federal cases from 1754
Case history information	
Direct history from 1658	Direct history Federal cases from 1754 State cases from 1879
Precedential history from 1658	Precedential history from 1972
Related references (cases involving same parties and facts but different issues)	
From 1658	From September 1983
Format	
List or paragraph style	List style
Unique features	
"Citation you requested makes negative reference to" entries	References to C.J.S.
References to A.L.R. and *United States Supreme Court Reports, Lawyers' Edition* annotations	

C. FULL-TEXT SEARCHING

1. Introduction

The online citators on LEXIS and WESTLAW are relatively easy to understand and use. Full-text searching on those systems is more complex. Recall that full-text searching is the process by which the computer attempts to match words (and the relative positions of those words) that you specify against (almost) all the words in the documents you select to search. This part of the chapter introduces you to the concepts you need to understand to do full-text searching on both systems effectively. These include (1) how information is organized and located in a computer system; (2) how to write effective online searches; (3) how searching for information in a computer-assisted research system compares with and contrasts to searching for information in print indexes; and (4) when to use a computer-assisted system for legal research.

2. Databases

a. Introduction to Databases

Information in a computer-assisted legal research (CALR) system is organized into units called databases on WESTLAW and called libraries, which contain files, on LEXIS. When you search for information on a CALR system, you search in a database or file. This chapter uses the term "database" to mean both database or file.

A database is a collection of documents that may be searched as a unit on a computer. The nature of the documents varies from database to database. There are two major categories of databases: bibliographic databases and full-text databases. Bibliographic databases refer you to more complete sources of information; that is, they function primarily as finding tools. *Index to Legal Periodicals* and *Legal Resource Index* online are examples of bibliographic databases. Full-text databases, on the other hand, contain the full text of the information you seek. Databases containing the full texts of legal periodical articles and cases are examples of full-text databases. Although LEXIS and WESTLAW contain some bibliographic databases, they are important research systems mainly because they contain the full texts of a wide variety of primary and secondary sources.

b. Identifying Online Databases

As you would expect, it is crucial to know whether there is a database containing the material you wish to research. There are two simple methods for identifying databases and obtaining the code you must enter into the computer to reach a database. The first is to use a print database directory for a system. Both LEXIS and WESTLAW publish print directories of their databases. These are free to use.

The other method is to consult a system's online directory. Both LEXIS and WESTLAW have online directories that the systems automatically present after you sign on. An online directory typically will be more up-to-date than its print counterpart. You pay connect costs when you use an online directory.

See Illustrations 6-9 to 6-11 on pages 203-205 to get an idea of the range of databases available on LEXIS and WESTLAW.

c. Choosing a Database

The appropriate database for your search will, of course, depend on the jurisdiction whose law governs your research situation, on whether you can find mandatory primary authority, and on whether you also wish to find persuasive primary authority and commentary.

As you may have suspected from looking at Illustrations 6-9 to 6-11, the same information may be available in more than one database on the same system. To search either LEXIS or WESTLAW efficiently, you should, as a general rule, begin your search with the smallest appropriate database because a smaller database may cost less to search than a larger one. For example, you may be able to retrieve Kansas case law for the Perkins problem by searching a database that includes only Kansas cases or by searching a database that contains cases from the courts of all the states. If you want to retrieve only Kansas cases, it is more efficient and cost-effective to search the database that contains only Kansas cases.

Your choice of a database may affect your choice of search terms. If you choose a subject database, do not search for words that will be found in all the documents in the database. For example, if you are searching in a tax database, you should not enter the word "tax" as a search term.

ILLUSTRATION 6-9. The First Two WESTLAW Directory Screens.   203

```
_____ WELCOME to the WESTLAW DIRECTORY _____P1_____

GENERAL MATERIAL    TEXT & PERIODICAL      CITATORS      SPECIALIZED MAT'L
Federal        P2   Law Reviews,  P320  Insta-Cite,  P357  ABA          P359
State          P6     Texts & CLEs       Shepard's,         BNA          P361
DIALOG       P145   Restatements         Shepard's PreView  C. Boardman  P365
News & Info. P183   & Unif. Laws P356    & QuickCite        Dictionary   P367
------------------- TOPICAL MATERIAL --------------------  Directories  P368
Antitrust    P191   Family Law    P232  Legal Ser.   P279  Gateways (D&B, P372
Bankruptcy   P194   Financial Ser P235  Maritime Law P283   Dow Jones, etc.)
Business     P197   First Amend.  P240  Military Law P285  Historical   P373
Civil Rights P203   Gov't Benefit P242  Product Liab P287  Other Pub's  P390
Commun. Law  P206   Gov't Cont.   P245  Real Prop.   P290  TaxSource    P401
Corporations P208   Health Ser.   P251  Sci. & Tech. P293  WESTLAW      P402
Crim. Just.  P213   Immigration   P257  Securities   P296   Highlights
Education    P217   Insurance     P259  Soc. Science P304  Other Serv.  P404
Energy       P220   Intell. Prop. P263  Taxation     P307   (NEW, FIND, etc.)
Environment  P225   International P267  Transport.   P315  EZ ACCESS    P405
                    Labor         P272  Worker Comp. P317  Customer Info P406
If you wish to:
  View another Directory page, type P followed by its number and press ENTER
  Select a known database, type its identifier and press ENTER
  Obtain further information, type HELP and press ENTER




____WESTLAW DIRECTORY WELCOME SCREEN_____P1_____
____GENERAL FEDERAL DATABASES                                   P2_____
------------------------
FEDERAL DATABASES INDEX        CASE LAW                CASE LAW
Admin. Law .... Enter P5   ALLFEDS Federal Cases   CTA10  10th Circuit
Case Law ...... This Page  SCT     Supreme Court   CTA11  11th Circuit
Historical --              CTA     Courts of Appeals CTADC D.C. Circuit
  Case Law ..... Enter P386 CTA1   1st Circuit     CTAF   Fed. Circuit
  Stats. & Regs. Enter P375  CTA2   2nd Circuit     DCT    District Cts.
Specialized ... Next Page  CTA3    3rd Circuit     DCTR   Reported Cases
  DIALOG ....... Next Page  CTA4   4th Circuit     DCTU   Unrepor. Cases
Statutes and               CTA5    5th Circuit     CLCT   Claims Court
  Regulations .. Enter P4   CTA6    6th Circuit
Territory                  CTA7    7th Circuit     TERRITORIAL CASE LAW
  Case Law ..... This Page  CTA8   8th Circuit     MP-CS  N. Mariana Is.
-------------------------  CTA9    9th Circuit


If you wish to:
  Select a database, type its identifier, e.g., ALLFEDS and press ENTER
  View information about a database, type SCOPE followed by its identifier
    and press ENTER
```

d. Determining Scope of Coverage

Once you have identified a potentially useful database, you should determine its scope of coverage. Scope refers to both the content of the material available online and the time span covered by the database. Do not assume that an online version of a source is the same as its print version. For example, in fall 1991, LEXIS and WESTLAW coverage of Kansas Supreme Court decisions began with cases decided in 1945.

You may determine the scope of a database by using a print source such as the *LEXIS/NEXIS Library Contents and Alphabetical List,* the *LEXIS Libraries Guide,* the *WESTLAW Database List,* or the *WESTLAW Reference Manual.* You may also obtain scope information online by using the GUIDE library on

```
                       LIBRARIES -- PAGE 1 of 2
Please TRANSMIT the NAME (only one) of the library you want to search.
- For more information about a library, TRANSMIT its page (PG) number.
- To see a list of additional libraries, press the NEXT PAGE key.
NAME    PG NAME    PG NAME    PG NAME    PG NAME    PG NAME    PG NAME    PG

- - - - - L E X I S - U S - - - - - - - - - - PUBLIC      FINANCIAL --NEXIS--
GENFED  1 CODES    1 LEGIS    1 STATES   1 CITES    6 RECORDS   COMPNY 15 NEXIS  13
                                                     ASSETS   6 MERGER 15 BACKGR 13
ADMRTY  2 FEDCOM   3 MILTRY   4 CORP     2 LAWREV   6 DOCKET   6 NAARS  15 BANKS  14
BANKNG  2 FEDSEC   3 PATENT   4 EMPLOY   2 MARHUB   6 INCORP   6            CMPCOM 13
BKRTCY  2 FEDTAX   3 PENBEN   4 HEALTH   3 LEXREF   6 LIENS    6 --INT'L-- CONSUM 13
COPYRT  2 IMMIG    3 PUBCON   4 INSRLW   3 ABA      6            WORLD  16 ENRGY  14
ENERGY  2 INTLAW   3 PUBHW    4 MEDMAL   3 BNA      6 --MEDIS-- ASIAPC 16 ENTERT 13
ENVIRN  2 ITRADE   3 REALTY   4 PRLIAB   4 TAXRIA   6 GENMED  12 EUROPE 16 INSURE 13
ESTATE  2 LABOR    3 TRADE    5 STENV    4 ALR      6 MEDEX   12 MDEAFR 16 LEGNEW 14
ETHICS  2 LEXPAT   3 TRDMRK   5 STSEC    4            MEDLNE  12 NSAMER 16 MARKET 14
FAMILY  2 M&A      4 TRANS    5 STTAX    4 -ASSISTS-             PEOPLE 14
FEDSEN  3 MSTORT   5          UCC        5 PRACT    12 POLITICAL           SPORTS 13
                             UTILTY     5 GUIDE    12 CMPGN   14           TRAN   14
                                                      EXEC    14
        AC for AUTO-CITE      LXE (LEXSEE) to retrieve a case/document by cite
        SHEP for SHEPARD'S    LXT (LEXSTAT) to retrieve a statute by cite
     Press ALT-H for Research Software Help; Press ESC for the Utilities Menu




                       LIBRARIES -- PAGE 2 of 2
Please TRANSMIT the NAME (only one) of the library you want to search.
- For more information about a library, TRANSMIT its page (PG) number.
- To see a list of additional libraries, press the PREV PAGE key.
NAME    PG NAME    PG NAME    PG NAME    PG NAME    PG NAME    PG NAME    PG

- - - - - - - L E X I S - U S - - - - - - - - LEXIS-UK  LEXIS-CW  LEXIS-FR
ALA     7 GA       7 MD       7 NJ       8 SD       8 ENGGEN 10 COMCAS 10 INTNAT 11
ALAS    7 HAW      7 MASS     7 NM       8 TENN     8 UKTAX  10 AUST   10 LOIREG 11
ARIZ    7 IDA      7 MICH     7 NY       8 TEX      8 SCOT   10 NZ     10 PRIVE  11
ARK     7 ILL      7 MINN     7 NC       8 UTAH     8 UKJNL  10            PUBLIC 11
CAL     7 IND      7 MISS     8 ND       8 VT       9 NILAW  10            REVUES 11
COLO    7 IOWA     7 MO       8 OHIO     8 VA       9            EC-LAW
CONN    7 KAN      7 MONT     8 OKLA     8 VI       9            EURCOM 10
DEL     7 KY       7 NEB      8 ORE      8 WASH     9
DC      7 LA       7 NEV      8 PA       8 WVA      9            LEXIS-IR
FLA     7 MAINE    7 NH       8 PR       8 WISC     9            IRELND 10
                             RI        8 WYO      9
                             SC        8
     Press ALT-H for Research Software Help; Press ESC for the Utilities Menu
```

LEXIS or by entering a "scope" command on WESTLAW. You will be shown how to use the GUIDE library and the scope command in one of the problem sets for this chapter.

e. A Comparison of CALR and Print Sources

In terms of the documents available, a CALR system has some advantages and some disadvantages compared with traditional print sources. The first advantage is currentness of the available information. Computer databases may include information before it appears in other sources because information can be "published" and "sent" to you more quickly on a computer than it can be printed and mailed to you.

ILLUSTRATION 6-11. A LEXIS File Screen.   **205**

```
Please TRANSMIT, separated by commas, the NAMES of the files you want to search.
You may select as many files as you want, including files that do not appear
below, but you must transmit them all at one time.  To see a description of a
file, TRANSMIT its page (PG) number.
                    FILES - PAGE 1 of 6 (NEXT PAGE for additional files)

 NAME   PG  NAME   PG  NAME   PG  NAME   PG  NAME   PG  NAME    PG  NAME   PG

 - - - - - - - - - - - - C A S E S - - - - - - -  - - - - - - - C O D E S - - - - -
 ALA     1  HAW    13  MICH   25  NC     37  UTAH   47  ALLAG  63  STTRCK 55  DCCODE 10
 ALAS    2  IDA    14  MINN   27  ND     37  VT     48  ALLENV 63  ALLCDE 64  FLCODE 11
 ARIZ    3  ILL    15  MISS   28  OHIO   38  VA     49  ALLPUC 63  STRGTR 64  GACODE 12
 ARK     4  IND    16  MO     29  OKLA   39  VI     50  ALLSEC 63  ALCODE  1  HICODE 13
 CAL     5  IOWA   17  MONT   30  ORE    40  WASH   51  ALLSOS 63  AKCODE  2  IDCODE 14
 COLO    7  KAN    18  NEB    31  PA     41  WVA    52  ALLTAX 63  AZCODE  3  ILCODE 15
 CONN    8  KY     20  NEV    32  RI     43  WISC   53             ARCODE  4  INCODE 16
 DEL     9  LA     21  NH     33  SC     44  WYO    54             CACODE  5  IACODE 17
 DC     10  ME     22  NJ     34  SD     44                        COCODE  7  KSCODE 18
 FLA    11  MD     23  NM     35  TENN   45  MEGA   64  OMNI2  64  CTCODE  8  KYCODE 20
 GA     12  MASS   24  NY     36  TEX    46  OMNI   64  HIGHCT 64  DECODE  9  KYSTAT 20
NOTE:  The CODE files cannot be combined using Custom File Selection.
SEE NEXT PAGE FOR ADDITIONAL CODE FILES.
Press ALT-H for Research Software Help; Press ESC for the Utilities Menu
```

A second advantage is that computer databases may contain information that is not available in your library in another form because (1) the information is not sold in another form, or (2) your library did not buy another form, or (3) the information has been checked out of your library. Furthermore, the information in a computer is always available unless the computer is "down" or all available terminals are in use; it cannot be "checked out" to someone else.

A third advantage of CALR is convenience. You can do computer-assisted legal research almost anywhere you have a personal computer, a modem, a telephone, and the appropriate software; you are not confined to a library.

On the other hand, a CALR system may not carry a source you need. Or it may not cover the time period in which you are interested, most likely because it does not extend back far enough in time. In addition, there are some forms of information that computer systems generally do not handle well; graphics are the most notable example.

Both LEXIS and WESTLAW are constantly adding new databases and expanding the coverage of existing databases. Do not assume that today's coverage is the same as yesterday's. Always check to see if material you need has become available online.

How you use a computer system is also different from how you use a book. As you will see later, these differences also give the computer some advantages and disadvantages.

3. Search Formulation

Because LEXIS and WESTLAW cannot understand questions phrased in natural language, you must translate a research situation into language the systems can understand. In technical jargon, you must draft what LEXIS calls a "search request" and WESTLAW calls a "query."

Searches can be designed and evaluated in terms of two characteristics: recall and precision. Recall is the ratio of relevant records retrieved to all the relevant records in the database. It answers the question: Did you retrieve all or almost all of the relevant documents in your database?

Precision is the ratio of relevant records retrieved to all records retrieved. It answers the question: Are most or all of the documents you retrieved relevant? Although high precision is important, do not be fooled into thinking precision alone is an accurate measure of search effectiveness. If precision is high but your search is poorly drafted, you may have missed some of the most relevant documents.

Recall and precision tend to vary inversely. Therefore, know which is more important to you. Do you need to retrieve a few highly relevant documents, or do you want to find all or almost all relevant documents? If you need high recall, you may be willing to tolerate (and pay for) low precision. That is, you may accept retrieving some irrelevant documents in order to get all relevant ones. On the other hand, if you do not need high recall, you probably do not want to pay to wade through many irrelevant documents. You should design your search according to these needs.

There are four kinds of searches: (1) a search for a single unique word, (2) a search for a word or concept that has single-word alternatives, (3) a search for a multiple-word concept, and (4) a search for multiple concepts. Since the Perkins problem involves a multiple-word concept, intentional infliction of emotional distress, it obviously requires a type (3) or (4) search. However, since these searches build on the other, simpler searches, the discussion that follows begins with the simplest search and ends with the most complex. Throughout the discussion that follows, brackets designate a computer search.

a. The Search for a Single Unique Word

The simplest search you can do on a computer—and the only search that does not require use of computer searching conventions—is a search for a single word that can be expressed in only one way. Even this search, however, is not as simple as you might expect, because you must know what the computer recognizes as a word.

To a computer, any unbroken string of alphabetical, numerical, or alphanumerical characters is a word. However, embedded punctuation, such as periods, hyphens, and parentheses, can create multiple words or single words, depending on the surrounding characters, the type of punctuation, and the system you are using. Therefore, you must be sure to look up how to write your search if it includes a word with punctuation—for example, a statute or rule number such as 12(b)(6).

Also, some words, such as "and," "or," and "of," are too common to search on a computer. These terms, called "noise words" by LEXIS and "stop words" by WESTLAW, vary somewhat between the two systems. A list of LEXIS noise words appears in the *Reference Manual for the LEXIS/NEXIS Services*. A list of WESTLAW stop words appears in the *WESTLAW Reference Manual*.

Computer searches that involve single unique words are very efficient searches and yield very complete results.

b. The Search for a Word That Has Single-Word Alternatives

Most searches involve words that may be expressed in more than one way. The search for a word that may be expressed by a variety of single-word alternatives or by various forms of the same word is somewhat more difficult than a search for a single unique word, although it still is a fairly easy search.

Your success in searching for the word depends largely on how successful you are at recognizing the alternatives that may be used to express
it; how adept you are at using root expanders and universal characters; and
how adept you are at recognizing and applying a system's rules for plurals,
possessives, and equivalent terms.

(1) Alternative Terms

Because LEXIS and WESTLAW perform searches by matching words rather
than by searching for concepts, you must consider all possible alternative
terms for any concept you wish to search or you may not retrieve all the
relevant documents. Alternative terms may include synonyms, antonyms,
broader terms, narrower terms, and related terms. You may wish to use a
legal or general-purpose thesaurus to help you generate alternative terms.

For example, if you want to search for all cases that discuss intentional
infliction of emotional distress in the context of racism, you may need to use
"racism" and "discrimination" as search terms, and you will have to tell the
computer that you wish to search for the terms as alternatives.

The computer technique for joining terms that are intended as alternative
terms is to use an "or" connector. The search [racism or discrimination] tells
LEXIS or WESTLAW to retrieve a document if it contains either or both of
those terms.

(2) Variant Forms of the Same Word

After you have identified alternative search terms, you also must consider
the variant forms for each of those terms.

(a) Variant Noun and Verb Forms; Root Expanders and Universal Characters

Variant forms for a noun include its related verb forms. For example,
"discrimination" may be expressed as "discriminated," "discriminates," or
"discriminating." Variant forms for a verb include its different tenses and its
related noun form. For example, "inflict" may be expressed as "inflicts,"
"inflicted," and "inflicting," as well as by the related noun form "infliction."
Variant forms for "racism" include "race" and "racial."

Root expansion is a technique whereby you search for different words
that share the same root, without having to type each of those words. Root
expansion both minimizes typing, which uses chargeable time, and helps you
retrieve all possible forms of a term as it might appear in a document.

LEXIS and WESTLAW share two root expansion symbols: the exclamation
point (!) and the asterisk (*). The exclamation point is an unlimited root
expander. Typing an exclamation point after the root of a word instructs the
computer to search for all terms that begin with that root, whatever the lengths
of the terms. For example, [discriminat!] retrieves "discrimination," "discriminated," "discriminates," and "discriminating."

The asterisk is a limited root expander. One asterisk at the end of a root
term instructs the computer to retrieve the root term and any term that is
one letter longer than the root. Placing two asterisks after the root retrieves
the root term and any term that is one or two letters longer, and so on.
Carefully consider which expander to use. If you need more than three
asterisks, it may be more efficient to use an exclamation point as an unlimited
root expander. Use the limited root expander (or write out in full the desired
alternative search terms) whenever use of the unlimited root expander might
retrieve too many irrelevant terms. For example, do not use [rac!] to retrieve

documents discussing race, racism, or racial incidents because that root with the unlimited expander will also generate documents that contain "racketeering," "racetrack," "racquetball," and many other unrelated concepts. Generally, you should be cautious about using very short root terms with the unlimited root expander.

The asterisk may also be used within a word to substitute for a character. For example, [mari*uana] retrieves both "marijuana" and "marihuana." When typed within a word, each asterisk holds a place for one character. Therefore, the search [judg*ment] will not retrieve the word "judgment."

Neither the asterisk nor the exclamation point may be used at the beginning of a word.

(b) Plurals and Possessives

Variant forms for a noun include plurals and possessives. Both LEXIS and WESTLAW automatically retrieve a "regular plural" when you enter the singular form of a word. A regular plural is a plural that ends in "s," "es," or "ies." WESTLAW automatically retrieves many "irregular" plurals, such as children and women, too. On LEXIS, by contrast, if you want to retrieve the singular and plural of a term that has an irregular plural, you must enter both the singular and plural forms. LEXIS automatically retrieves the singular form of a regular plural when you enter the plural; WESTLAW does not.

LEXIS also automatically retrieves the singular and plural possessive forms when you enter either the singular or plural form of a word that has a regular plural. If you search for a word that does not have a regular plural, entering the singular automatically retrieves only the singular possessive, and entering the plural automatically retrieves only the plural possessive. On WESTLAW, entering the singular form of a word automatically retrieves the singular and plural possessives. Entering the plural retrieves only the plural possessive. The point to remember is that for both systems if you use the singular form of a word, you generally retrieve the singular, plural, and singular and plural possessive forms. Thus, your best strategy is usually to search for the singular form of a word.

(c) Equivalent Terms

LEXIS and WESTLAW both automatically generate equivalents of certain terms. That is, when you enter one form of these terms, it is not necessary to enter a form LEXIS or WESTLAW lists as an equivalent. For example, if you enter [kan], LEXIS and WESTLAW also retrieve Kansas and vice versa.

Both systems generate equivalents for names of states; months and days of the week; some numbers; and terms related to the history of a case. For example, "affirmed" equals "affd" and "aff'd."

A list of terms that have automatically generated equivalents on LEXIS appears in the *Reference Manual for the LEXIS/NEXIS Services*. A list of terms that have automatically generated equivalents on WESTLAW appears in the *WESTLAW Reference Manual*.

c. The Search for a Multiple-Word Concept

Some searches include multiple-word concepts, such as intentional infliction of emotional distress. The search for a multiple-word concept often involves initialisms, compound terms, or phrases. Therefore, you must know how the systems treat these forms.

Initialisms are strings of letters that are usually pronounced as letters. A.C.L.U., a substitute for American Civil Liberties Union, is an example of an initialism.

On WESTLAW, if you enter an initialism that contains periods but no spaces, WESTLAW retrieves the other forms of the initialism automatically. For example, if you enter [a.c.l.u.], WESTLAW retrieves documents containing "A.C.L.U.," "A. C. L. U.," "ACLU," or "A C L U." If you enter one of the other forms of an initialism, however, WESTLAW retrieves only the form you enter. Furthermore, if you enter the initialism, WESTLAW does not retrieve documents containing only the form "American Civil Liberties Union." To retrieve those documents, you would have to enter ["American Civil Liberties Union"] as an alternative search term.

LEXIS does not have a preferred form that retrieves all equivalent initialisms automatically, but some initialisms have automatic equivalents on LEXIS. These are listed in the *Reference Manual for the LEXIS/NEXIS Services.* You will have to enter as alternatives the forms that are not listed as equivalents.

(2) Compound Words

Some terms may be written as one word, multiple words, or a hyphenated word. "Townhouse" is an example. On WESTLAW, if you enter the hyphenated form of a word, you retrieve all three forms. If you do not enter the hyphenated form, the computer retrieves only the form you enter.

LEXIS treats hyphens as spaces. Thus, to LEXIS [town-house] is the same as [town house]. To retrieve all three forms of the term on LEXIS, you would have to enter [townhouse or town house].

(3) Phrases

Sometimes a single concept is expressed as a phrase. "Intentional infliction of emotional distress" is an example. The systems diverge in their treatment of phrases.

On LEXIS, you may search for a phrase exactly as you would search for a single word. For example, to search for the phrase "intentional infliction of emotional distress," just enter [intentional infliction of emotional distress]. Alternatively, you may enter [intentional infliction emotional distress]. LEXIS does not count stop words such as "of," so to LEXIS the two searches are equivalent.

On WESTLAW, you must enclose a phrase in quotation marks to command WESTLAW to look for the words as a phrase. In the absence of quotation marks, WESTLAW is programmed to read a space between words as an "or" instruction. Thus, without quotation marks, WESTLAW would interpret the search [intentional infliction of emotional distress] as [intentional or infliction or emotional or distress]. Furthermore, you must include stop words, such as "of," in a phrase search because WESTLAW, unlike LEXIS, counts them when it searches.

Be very cautious about searching for a concept as a phrase. This approach succeeds only if the concept is always written exactly the same way. "Intentional infliction of emotional distress" is a good search phrase. However, if you search for "assumption of risk" as a phrase, you will not retrieve cases that do not use that exact phrase but that do use such expressions as "assumed the risk" or "the risk was assumed." Often an expression that could be written as a phrase should be written with a numerical connector. You will be shown how to do this later (see page 212).

d. The Search for Multiple Concepts

The most complex search combines two or more concepts. You may be able to research the Perkins problem in a Kansas case law database by using the single concept of intentional infliction of emotional distress; however, if you wish to research the case law of intentional infliction of emotional distress in all jurisdictions, to be cost-effective you should narrow your search to retrieve only those cases most similar to Perkins. To do so, review the sub-issues raised by the Perkins problem.

Then formulate the sub-issues you wish to research, one at a time. A good technique is to write a sub-issue in sentence form as you would do for manual research, and then to underline the terms that might be useful search terms or concepts. Assume that you wish to research the relationship between race or racial incidents and intentional infliction of emotional distress. You might phrase your sub-issue this way: Can racism constitute intentional infliction of emotional distress? This sub-issue contains two concepts: racism and intentional infliction of emotional distress.

Next, list alternative terms for each of the concepts. The following lists show the search concepts and their alternatives:

intentional infliction of emotional distress	racism
tort of outrage	race
	racial
	discrimination
	discriminate
	discriminates
	discriminated
	discriminating

Column 1 uses "tort of outrage" because "outrage" by itself would retrieve many irrelevant documents. Although emotional distress can be expressed in many ways in addition to the two terms listed ("mental distress," "mental anguish," and "emotional suffering" are but a few), you need not list all these alternatives since "intentional infliction of emotional distress" and "tort of outrage" are legal terms of art, at least one of which should appear in any case on point.

Now apply the principles relating to root expansion. (At this stage, you also would apply the principles relating to plurals and possessives, if there were any.) You will be left with the following lists:

intentional infliction of emotional distress	racism
tort of outrage	race
	racial
	discriminat!

Your next task is to join these concepts in a logical way. Computer systems, including LEXIS and WESTLAW, generally share three major connectors: "or," "and," and "not." These connectors are referred to as Boolean connectors because they are derived from Boolean logic, a system that represents the relationships between concepts symbolically.

In addition, some systems, including LEXIS and WESTLAW, have numerical connectors that allow you to require that your search terms appear within a specified number of words of each other; and some systems, including WESTLAW, have grammatical connectors that allow you to require that your search terms appear within the same sentence or paragraph.

You need to understand both the connectors available on the system you are using and the sequence in which the system processes those connectors.

(1) The Boolean Connectors

(a) "Or" Connector

The "or" connector tells the computer to retrieve a document if it contains *one or more* of the terms joined by the connector. Use the "or" connector if your terms are alternatives. Clearly, the terms in column 1 of the example issue are alternatives that should be joined by the "or" connector. The same is true of the terms in column 2. In each instance, the columns include synonymous or related terms. For a document to be relevant, it does not have to include all of the terms in a column of alternative terms. In fact, it is likely that a relevant document will include only one of the synonymous terms. You just don't know which one!

On WESTLAW, you may use a space between words as an alternative to writing out the word "or."

(b) "And" Connector

The "and" connector tells the computer to retrieve a document only if it contains *both* of the terms joined by the "and." Since the "and" connector tells the computer to look for the terms anywhere within the document, it is a very broad connector. The words could be paragraphs or even pages apart. When you use an "and" connector, you may often retrieve documents in which your search terms are not related in the manner you intended. The "and" connector is too broad to use between the columns of search terms in our example issue.

On WESTLAW, you may use an ampersand (&) as an alternative to writing out the word "and."

(c) "Not" Connector

The "not" connector tells the computer to *exclude* a document if it contains a specified term. For example, the search ["intentional infliction of emotional distress" and race or racial or racism but not employ!] seeks to find all documents in the database relating to race and intentional infliction of emotional distress, except those relating to the tort in an employment context.

On LEXIS, type "and not" for the "not" connector. On WESTLAW, type "but not" or the percent symbol (%).

The "not" connector is risky to use because it excludes every document that contains both the terms you want and the terms you think you do not want. The example search would exclude a document if it contained the term "employed" or any term beginning with the root "employ" even if the document was relevant to the issue you were researching. Therefore, use this connector sparingly.

ILLUSTRATION 6-12. The Boolean Connectors.

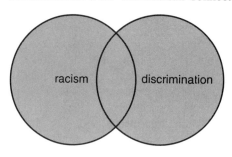

The "Or" Connector

The search [racism *or* discrimination] retrieves documents containing *either* term or *both* terms.

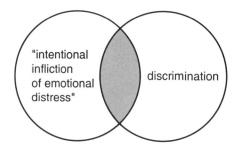

The "And" Connector

The search ["intentional infliction of emotional distress" *and* discrimination] retrieves only those documents containing *both* terms.

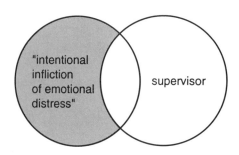

The "Not" Connector

The search ["intentional infliction of emotional distress" *but not* supervisor] retrieves only documents containing "intentional infliction of emotional distress" *but not* supervisor.

See Illustration 6-12 above for a visual representation of the Boolean connectors.

(2) Numerical Connectors

On both LEXIS and WESTLAW, you may require that search terms appear *within a specified number of words* of each other by using "w/n." The "n" represents any number of words from 1 to 255. For example, the search [tort w/3 outrage] tells the computer to retrieve documents in which the word "tort" appears within three words of "outrage." On WESTLAW you may use "/n" as an alternative to "w/n."

LEXIS includes only searchable words when counting words; it omits noise words. WESTLAW counts all words. Thus, the same numerical connector may produce different results in the two systems, even if their databases are identical.

On both LEXIS and WESTLAW, use "w/n" if you do not care which search term appears first in a document. On the other hand, use the "pre/n" connector (or "+n" on WESTLAW) if you want the term on the left to precede the term on the right. For example, if you are searching for all cases that refer to the tort of outrage, you may use the search [tort pre/3 outrage].

There are at least two drawbacks to numerical connectors. First, there is no formula for determining what number to use as the connector. Sometimes terms will appear closer together or further apart in a document than you anticipated. Second, the numerical connectors do not recognize sentences and paragraphs. Therefore, the use of "w/n" or "pre/n" may retrieve a document in which the search terms are in unrelated sentences or paragraphs and have no logical relationship to each other.

(3) Grammatical Connectors

On WESTLAW (but not LEXIS), you may require that your search terms appear in the same paragraph by using the "/p" connector or in the same sentence by using the "/s" connector. In the search ["intentional infliction of emotional distress" /p race or racism or racial], WESTLAW retrieves only documents that contain the phrase "intentional infliction of emotional distress" in the same paragraph as "race" or "racism" or "racial."

Sometimes you will want to require that words or numbers appear in a certain order within a sentence. Use the "+s" connector to require that the term to the left of the connector precede the term to the right within the same sentence. The "+s" connector is especially useful to require that a first name precede a last name or that the volume number of a publication precede the page number.

Grammatical connectors are useful because they allow you to specify that the computer search for your terms in units that occur naturally in the English language. Thus, using grammatical connectors rather than numerical connectors may improve your search results.

(4) Summary of the Major Connectors on LEXIS and WESTLAW

As you have seen, LEXIS and WESTLAW have many of the same connectors, although they may offer different options for writing them. Table 6.3 on page 214 summarizes the major connectors available on LEXIS and WESTLAW.

(5) Sequence of Connectors

Each system processes connectors in a predetermined priority order. You must know this order of operation, or the system may perform a search entirely different from the search you intend. The order of processing on each of the systems is:

LEXIS	WESTLAW
phrases	phrases
or	or
w/n, pre/n, not w/n	pre/n
and	w/n
and not	+s
	/s
	/p
	and
	but not

TABLE 6.3 Major Connectors on LEXIS and WESTLAW.

Description	LEXIS	WESTLAW
Search terms as alternatives	or	or, a space
Within the same document	and	and, &
Within the same paragraph	—	/p
Within the same sentence	—	/s
Within the same sentence, term on left must precede term on right	—	+s
Terms must appear within specified number of words of each other	w/n	w/n, /n
Terms must appear within specified number of words of each other; term on left must precede term on right	pre/n	pre/n, +n
Exclude documents with the terms or relationships following the connector	and not	but not, %
Phrase search	intentional infliction emotional distress	"intentional infliction of emotional distress"

In other words, both systems process a phrase first, the "or" before the numerical connectors, and the numerical connectors before the "and." Both systems process a lower-numbered numerical connector before a higher-numbered connector, except that WESTLAW processes all "pre/n" connectors before any "w/n" connectors.

You can override the normal order of processing (or protect yourself if you do not know it) by using parentheses. LEXIS and WESTLAW process connectors inside parentheses before connectors outside the parentheses. Consider the following WESTLAW search, which is designed to find references to either intentional infliction of emotional distress or the tort of outrage:

"intentional infliction of emotional distress" (tort /3 outrage)

Without the parentheses, the computer would search for "intentional infliction of emotional distress" or "tort" (remember, a space between words means "or") and then for one of those terms within three words of "outrage."

If you do not use parentheses when you should, you will still get a result (albeit not the best one), and you may never know you made a mistake.

(6) A Sample Search for the Perkins Problem

Applying the principles you have learned about connectors and the sequence of connectors, you may now write a complete search for the Perkins sub-issue we have been discussing. These searches will work:

LEXIS: intentional infliction emotional distress or (tort w/3 outrage) w/30 race or racism or racial or discriminat!

WESTLAW: "intentional infliction of emotional distress" (tort /3 outrage) /p race or racism or racial or discriminat!

In these searches, LEXIS and WESTLAW will both process the connectors in the following order:

(1) First, the systems will search for "intentional infliction of emotional distress" or "tort w/3 outrage."

(2) Next, the systems will search for "race," "racism," "racial," or some form of "discriminat!"

(3) Then the systems will search for one of the terms it found at step (1) within 30 words (on LEXIS) or within the same paragraph (on WESTLAW) of "race," "racism," "racial," or some form of "discriminat!"

Citation Note: Rule 10.8.1 permits you to cite an unreported case to any widely used database. A correct citation begins with the name of the case and the docket number. Then give enough information to identify the database; if the database uses a unique citation to identify the case, place that citation next. If you cite a database page number, use an asterisk before the page. Finally, give the court, the full date of the most recent disposition of the case, and the meaning of that date in parentheses if the date is not the date of the decision. An example is: *Opitz v. Davis,* No. C8-90-2158, 1991 WESTLAW 216299, at *3 (Minn. Ct. App. Oct. 29, 1991).

Rule 17.3.1 of *The Bluebook* provides for a document (other than a case) that is available in a computer database and is also separately published and available. It is not necessary to cite the database form unless the separately published document is difficult to obtain. Materials that are unavailable or difficult to obtain in printed form may be cited as *"available in"* a database. When citing materials other than cases as *"available in"* a database, give a complete citation to the document and to the database. If the database uses a unique identifier for a document, include that identifier. An example is: *What Is Not in the Tax Simplification Bills?* Tax Notes Today, Oct. 18, 1991, *available in* LEXIS, Fedtax Library, TNT File, 91 TNT 215-3.

(7) Alternative Methods of Writing Multiple-Concept Searches

You have just learned one method for writing a multiple-concept search. There are alternative methods.

You may search for all the concepts in a multiple-concept search at the same time, but you should not always do so. The simplest search is sometimes best. Some writers suggest that you search for the most specific (that is, concrete, well-defined) concept first. If the number of documents you retrieve is small enough, you may never have to add the other concepts to the search. If you retrieve too many documents, you can then add other concepts, one at a time. For example, for the Perkins problem you could search first for the "intentional infliction of emotional distress" concept and not add the second concept unless you find it necessary to narrow your search results.

A second approach is to search first for the concept that will probably retrieve the fewest number of documents. If you retrieve a small enough group of documents, you may not need to add the other concepts. The first and second approaches (which sometimes coincide—they do for the Perkins problem) may be useful if you need to retrieve all or most of the relevant documents in the system, and you are willing to sort out some irrelevant documents to achieve your objective.

A third strategy, which is useful if you think that combining all your concepts at once will retrieve too few documents, is to begin with the broadest concept or concepts and then to add on narrower concepts to limit your search. The publishers of LEXIS recommend this approach and provide level searching capacity to support it. Simple searches containing only a few concepts do not necessarily need to be divided into levels. For more complex searches, however, there are advantages to using levels. When you start with the most general concept (or concepts) on level 1 and make the search more specific with each additional level, you can analyze your results at each level. If there are very few or no documents at your narrowest search level, you may go back one or more levels to find the more general search that retrieves relevant documents. For our intentional infliction of emotional distress example, you may wish to divide the search into the following levels on LEXIS:

Level 1: intentional infliction emotional distress or (tort w/3 outrage)
Level 2: w/30 race or racism or racial or discriminat!

This search allows you to compare the results of a general search for intentional infliction of emotional distress (level 1) with the results of a search for cases that are factually similar (level 2) to the Perkins problem without running a second search.

On LEXIS, level searching is more economical than running separate searches because there is a charge for each separate search, but there is no charge for adding a level to a search or reviewing results at any level. WESTLAW does not use level searching.

Another strategy that is particularly useful if your search contains a number of vague concepts so that searching for them all at once might retrieve few, if any, documents is to try searching the concepts two at a time and comparing results.

Finally, if your search involves only vague concepts, you may wish to search for the most concrete term for each of the concepts, retrieve some highly relevant documents, and then use terms you find in those documents to help you refine your search. Searching for a few highly relevant documents and using them to help you refine your search is always a good strategy.

(8) Browsing Your Search Results; Modifying Your Search

In each database the documents retrieved by your search will be displayed in a particular order. You should learn that order because it may affect your browsing through the retrieved documents. For example, if you search the case law of all states at the same time, you need to know if the cases are displayed by date of decision, by state, by level of court, or by some combination of those methods. Information about how documents are displayed is available in the *LEXIS Libraries Guide* and in the *WESTLAW Reference Manual.*

As you browse your search results, you may find that your search retrieved too few documents or that it retrieved too many irrelevant documents.

If your search retrieved too few documents and you want to increase recall:

(1) add alternative terms;
(2) use broader search terms;
(3) delete a required term;
(4) use broader connectors; or
(5) search a broader or different database.

If your search retrieved too many irrelevant documents and you need to increase precision:

(1) delete a broad or ambiguous term;

(2) use narrower search terms;

(3) add a required term;

(4) use fewer root expanders or increase the lengths of the roots you are searching for;

(5) use more restrictive connectors;

(6) search a more limited database; or

(7) find a few highly relevant documents and use them to find language to help you rewrite your search.

e. The Segment or Field Search

Just as most books have a common format so that you expect to find certain information in certain locations, so too the documents in each database have a common structure with easily identifiable parts. These parts are called "segments" on LEXIS and "fields" on WESTLAW. The segments or fields vary from database to database. Illustration 6-13 on page 218 shows the WESTLAW fields for a case, using *Bradshaw v. Swagerty* as the example.

The concept of segments or fields is important because it enables you to instruct the computer to look for specified search terms only in particular parts of a document. By doing so, you may limit the number of documents retrieved or retrieve some documents more efficiently.

For example, assume that you know about the intentional infliction of emotional distress case, *Bradshaw v. Swagerty,* but you do not have its citation. You may retrieve this case, and only this case, by doing a name segment search on LEXIS or a title field search on WESTLAW. If you do not limit your search to the name segment or title field, you will also retrieve all the cases in the database that cite *Bradshaw.*

To do a segment or field search, type the name of the segment or field, followed by the terms to be searched, enclosed in parentheses.

For the *Bradshaw* case, the following are good name or title field searches:

LEXIS: name (Bradshaw and Swagerty)
WESTLAW: title(Bradshaw and Swagerty)

You may obtain the names of the segments for a LEXIS document by using the *LEXIS Libraries Guide* or by pressing the SEGMTS key after you have selected a library and file. You may obtain the names of the fields for WESTLAW documents by using the *WESTLAW Reference Manual,* by using the scope command, or by pressing the F or FIELDS key after you have selected a database.

On both LEXIS and WESTLAW, spacing between the name of the field and the left parenthesis is optional. Also, WESTLAW allows you to shorten the name of a field to its first two letters, which is more efficient than typing the full name. For example, you may use "ti" instead of "title" for a title field search.

You may combine fields on WESTLAW, and you may join a field search to a non-field search on both LEXIS and WESTLAW by using the "and" connector.

f. The Date Restriction

Occasionally, you may wish to limit your search to a particular time period. For example, if you did most of your research on the Perkins problem

Synopsis Field

```
                          COPR. (C) WEST 1992 NO CLAIM TO ORIG. U.S. GOVT. WORKS
Citation                                    Page(P)          Database    Mode
563 P.2d 511                    FOUND DOCUMENT P 1 OF 3        KS-CS        P
1 Kan.App.2d 213
(CITE AS: 563 P.2D 511)
                            Rodney BRADSHAW, Appellant,
                                          v.
                            Daniel L. SWAGERTY, Appellee.
    Action for slander and outrage was brought against attorney for statements
 allegedly made by attorney.  The Hodgeman District Court, C. Phillip Aldrich,
 J., rendered summary judgment for the attorney, and plaintiff appealed.  The
 court of Appeals, Foth, J., held that: (1) in the absence of allegations of
 special damages, complaint alleging that plaintiff had been called a 'nigger,'
 and 'bastard,' and a 'knot-headed boy' failed to allege actionable slander per
 se, and (2) epithets complained of were mere insults, and thus facts could not
 be construed to make out tort of 'outrage.'
    Affirmed.
```

1

Note: 1. Synopsis (partial)

Attorney and Judge Fields

```
                          COPR. (C) WEST 1992 NO CLAIM TO ORIG. U.S. GOVT. WORKS
563 P.2d 511                    FOUND DOCUMENT P 2 OF 2        KS-CS        P
(CITE AS: 563 P.2D 511)
   B. A. Lighfoot, Jetmore, for appellants.
   B. G. (Skip) Larson and Max Eugene Estes, Williams, Larson, Voss, Strobel &
Estes, Dodge City, for appellee.

----FOTH, Judge:
END OF DOCUMENT
```

2

3

2. Attorneys
3. Judge

Digest (Topic + Headnote) Field; Title, Citation, and Court Fields

```
                          COPR. (C) WEST 1992 NO CLAIM TO ORIG. U.S. GOVT. WORKS
Citation                                    Page(P)          Database    Mode
563 P.2d 511                    FOUND DOCUMENT P 1 OF 11       KS-CS        P
1 Kan.App.2d 213
(CITE AS: 563 P.2D 511)
237k6(1)
LIBEL AND SLANDER
k. In general.
Kan.App. 1977.
Slander per se is limited to statements falling into four categories:
imputation of a crime;  imputation of a loathsome disease;  words reflecting on
plaintiff's fitness for his office, profession or trade;  and the imputation of
unchastity in a woman.
Bradshaw v. Swagerty,
563 P.2d 511, 1 Kan.App.2d 213
```

4   **8**   **5**   **6**   **7**

4. Topic
5. Headnote (n.b.: Topic + Headnote = Digest)
6. Title
7. Citation
8. Court

some time before your oral argument on the problem, you would want to update your research before the oral argument. You may use a date restriction to restrict your search to a specific day, month, or year, or to a period before, after, or between certain dates. To add a date restriction to a word search, always begin with the "and" connector.

You may enter a date in many formats. The following formats work on both LEXIS and WESTLAW: July 18, 1985; Jul 18, 1985; 7-18-85; and 7/18/85.

To enter a date search on LEXIS, use the word "date" followed by one of these arithmetic indicators: is, =, bef, <, aft, >. Then add the date. Do not use parentheses. The following examples work in LEXIS:

and date is July 18, 1985
and date bef 1985
and date aft 1985
and date aft 7/18/85 and date bef 1/5/89

To enter a date restriction on WESTLAW, use the word "date" or its first two letters, followed by your date enclosed in parentheses. The following examples work in WESTLAW:

& da(July 18, 1985)
& da(bef 1985)
& da(aft 1985)
& da(aft 7/18/85 & bef 1/5/89)

Although these details may seem overwhelming at first, with practice the mechanics of writing a computer search will seem quite simple, and remember that you may always look them up! Becoming an efficient, cost-effective computer researcher is far more difficult.

4. CALR Full-Text Searching versus Searching in Print Indexes

To use CALR effectively, you must understand the difference between CALR full-text searching and searching in print indexes. It is useful to think first about how indexers prepare indexes.

a. How Indexing for Print Sources Works

To prepare an index, the indexer first reads the text to be indexed from the perspective of the index user. Thus, the indexer will probably index the same article on intentional infliction of emotional distress differently for a legal index than for a medical index.

While reading the text, the indexer notes the facts or concepts to be indexed. The indexer may select all or almost all of the facts or concepts, or the indexer may select a more limited number. If the indexer decides not to index a fact or concept, you will not be able to locate it through the index.

The indexer must select a word or phrase to represent each fact or concept to be indexed. Many facts and concepts can be expressed by more than one word or phrase and frequently are, even within the same text. For example, "mental distress" may also be expressed as "mental anguish" or "emotional distress." Nonetheless, the indexer chooses one word or phrase to represent a concept so that all entries relating to that fact or concept, as it is discussed in various sources, will appear together in the index. The indexer may choose a term that is used in the text of the document, or the indexer may select a term that does not appear in the document. An indexer often selects indexing terms from a pre-existing list of terms designed to help the indexer avoid variations in expressing a single concept. The list tells the indexer which of the synonyms, antonyms, or variant forms of a term the indexer should choose and which cross-references to create.

When you use an index, you benefit from—and are at the same time constrained by—the indexer's attempt to control and standardize vocabulary.

b. How CALR Full-Text Searching Works

As you have seen, when you use a computer to do full-text searching you determine the search words you wish to use, and you may use an unlimited number of them. Every word in the database you are searching (except certain very common words such as "and" and "the") is an "index" term. Thus, you may search online for terms that do not appear in the print index for a publication. You also may search for facts or concepts that were not indexed, such as all cases decided by a particular judge or cases in which a particular individual appeared as counsel. You also may specify combinations of terms. For example, you may ask the computer to retrieve documents containing the phrase "intentional infliction of emotional distress" but only if the documents also contain the phrase "hate speech." In addition, you can instruct the computer to retrieve documents containing a specified term or concept, but only if the term or concept appears in a particular part of a document, such as in a case synopsis. You also can instruct the computer to exclude documents that contain a specified term.

c. A Comparison of CALR and Traditional Print Research

Obviously, these differences in search methods constitute one of the major differences between CALR and print research. CALR has the advantage of permitting you to tailor a search to your research needs very precisely. On the other hand, if your search does not include the words in the relevant documents, your CALR search will fail. Print indexes interpose a third person—the indexer—between you and the information you seek. This is an advantage if you and the indexer share an approach to reading the materials and a vocabulary for describing them or if the indexer has more insight than you do; this is a disadvantage if you and the indexer differ in your approach or the indexing is weak.

An advantage of CALR is that a computer database cumulates information that is spread over multiple volumes of a title in print form. Recall, for example, that when you Shepardized a case, the computer checked the main volumes and paperbound supplements simultaneously. Furthermore, on a CALR system you often may search a number of sources at once. For example, on LEXIS and WESTLAW you may search the decisions of many different courts at the same time.

Another advantage of CALR is the speed with which a computer can search for information. A computer search may be a cost-effective alternative to a traditional print search.

On the other hand, there are some obstacles to overcome when using a computer for research. The first stems from the literalness of the computer. People think in concepts; the machine does not—it only recognizes words. For example, "mental distress" and "emotional distress" may mean the same thing to you, but they do not to the computer. Recall that when you search a full-text database, you do not search synonyms automatically as you do in a good print index. You must specifically ask the computer to search for the synonyms. Furthermore, if your database covers a long period of time, you must remember that the popular term for a concept may have changed, and you may need to search for both an older term and a newer one. Similarly, a computer may not be programmed to recognize various forms of the same word. Therefore, if you want to search for some form of the word "inflict," you may need to instruct the computer to find such variant forms as "inflicts," "inflicting," "inflicted," and "infliction." Also, some words have more than one meaning, and the computer will not distinguish among documents containing a word according to the various meanings. Finally, if you misspell a word, the computer will literally search for the misspelling and ignore the word you intended. And it may not tell you that you made a mistake!

A second obstacle is that a computer full-text database does not give you the same search guidance that traditional sources do. For example, it generally does not include cross-references to guide you from general to specific terms or to remind you of synonyms and antonyms for the search terms you have chosen. As you can see, computer research clearly puts the burden of vocabulary control on you, the researcher.

A third obstacle is that search words that are useful in a print index may not be useful for a full-text search. For example, "tort law" may be an appropriate subject heading in a print index, but it is not likely to be a useful search term in a CALR system. When using a CALR system, you must ask yourself which terms are most likely to be used in the documents you are seeking, not just what the documents are about.

Fourth, print research allows you to browse through the index or text of a source and stumble upon an answer. Browsing with a computer is both more difficult and more expensive.

A final and significant obstacle to overcome when doing CALR is the false sense of security that can arise if your computer research gives you some usable results. Just because you have found some relevant documents, do not assume that you have found them all. It is much easier to know what you have found on the computer than what you have missed. You should remember, however, that a computer-assisted search is only part of the process of legal research. Often your search is not going to retrieve every relevant document, but by reading and tracking the history of the documents you do retrieve, you may be able to find any important documents you missed.

5. When to Use a Computer-Assisted System for Legal Research

All legal research costs money because a lawyer charges clients for time. You may not always be aware of the cost of your time when doing print legal research, but such research can be expensive if it is time-consuming. The costs of computer-assisted research are very visible. You (or your firm) will see at the end of each month exactly how much your computer research costs. If the cost of your time plus the computer charges are less than the cost your time alone would have been if you had done print research, then you have done cost-effective research and made the most efficient use of your time. If the cost of your time plus the computer charges are higher than the cost your time alone would have been if you had done print research, then you should have done print research. Knowing when the computer will save you time (and money) instead of adding unnecessary costs is an important skill to develop.

The computer is better suited to some research applications than to others. It is particularly useful for finding

(1) names,
(2) unique terms,
(3) combined terms or concepts (unless all of the terms or concepts are too common or one or more of them has too many alternatives),
(4) specific fact patterns,
(5) narrow legal topics,
(6) words that are not used in a print index,
(7) concepts that are not well-indexed in print,
(8) new topics that are not yet indexed, and
(9) full and accurate bibliographic information, such as the correct citation to a law review article for which you have an incorrect citation.

Of course, the computer is the only source for information that is only available online.

On the other hand, the computer is not as well-suited to researching broad legal concepts or concepts that can be expressed only with common words, vague words, words that have multiple meanings, or words that can be expressed by many alternatives.

As you might have guessed, it is sometimes impossible to write a search that will not retrieve irrelevant documents. For example, if you wish to retrieve all cases involving violence *against* police, it may be impossible to avoid retrieving cases involving violence *by* police.

As you gain experience in using a computer for legal research, you will develop some intuition about when a computer search is likely to be effective.

Although you need not be overly concerned about search costs while you are in law school because law schools pay a flat rate for LEXIS and WESTLAW, it is essential that you develop efficient search habits so you will be able to minimize your search costs when you are searching at a commercial billing rate.

LEXIS and WESTLAW bill somewhat differently, so it is difficult to compare their costs. The components of LEXIS pricing and the approximate costs of those components in November 1991 were as follows:

connect time	$30 an hour
network time	$13 an hour
search charges	Charge varies from file to file. (Range is $6 to $68 and the average charge is $18.) You may determine the charge for a file by pressing the SEGMTS key after selecting the file.
Shepard's and Auto-Cite	$2.50 a search
LEXSEE and LEXSTAT (document retrieval commands)	$4 a citation
offline printing	$.02 per line ($.025 for NEXIS, a related service described in Chapter 10)

The components of WESTLAW pricing and some approximate costs of those components in November 1991 were as follows:

connect time	$22 an hour
network time	$20 an hour
subscription charge	$125 a month
database charge	$125-$240 an hour (depending on amount of use and subscription plan) and 1.65 times that for the combined files, such as "allstates" and "allfeds." The scope screen for a database will tell you if the database is billed at the higher rate.
offline printing	$.02 per line

The biggest difference in pricing between the systems is that LEXIS charges for each search or citation you enter, and WESTLAW charges by the amount of time you use. Thus, if you plan to browse or read a lot online, LEXIS may be less expensive; but if you plan to enter a large number of searches or citations, WESTLAW may be less expensive.

As you work through the problem sets for the rest of this book, try to develop your understanding of when it is more cost-effective to do manual research and when it is more cost-effective to do computer-assisted research.

Statutes and Constitutions: Searching for Primary Authority

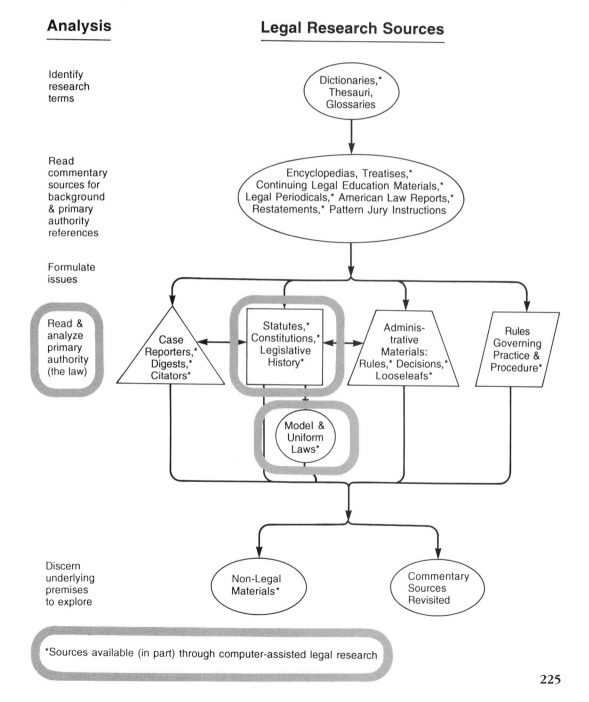

Analysis

Legal Research Sources

Identify research terms

Dictionaries,*
Thesauri,
Glossaries

Read commentary sources for background & primary authority references

Encyclopedias, Treatises,*
Continuing Legal Education Materials,*
Legal Periodicals,* American Law Reports,*
Restatements,* Pattern Jury Instructions

Formulate issues

Read & analyze primary authority (the law)

Case Reporters,*
Digests,*
Citators*

Statutes,*
Constitutions,*
Legislative
History*

Administrative Materials:
Rules,* Decisions,*
Looseleafs*

Rules Governing Practice & Procedure*

Model & Uniform Laws*

Discern underlying premises to explore

Non-Legal Materials*

Commentary Sources Revisited

*Sources available (in part) through computer-assisted legal research

A. Statutes
  1. Introduction
  2. Reading and Analyzing Statutes
  3. An Overview of the Legislative Process
  4. An Overview of Statutory Sources
     a. Slip Laws
     b. Session Laws
     c. Codes
        (1) When to Use a Code
        (2) Your Research Situation
        (3) Federal Codes
           (a) *United States Code* (U.S.C.)
               (i) Index Approach
               (ii) Title Outline Approach
               (iii) Popular Name Approach
               (iv) Conversion Table Approach
           (b) *United States Code Annotated* (U.S.C.A.)
               (i) Annotations
               (ii) Supplements
               (iii) Indexes and Tables
           (c) *United States Code Service* (U.S.C.S.)
               (i) Annotations
               (ii) Supplements
               (iii) Indexes and Tables
           (d) Choosing between U.S.C.A. and U.S.C.S.
        (4) State Codes
  5. *Shepard's* Statutory Citators
  6. Statutes on LEXIS and WESTLAW
     a. WESTLAW
     b. LEXIS
B. Constitutions
  1. The Text
  2. Annotations
  3. Research Techniques
  4. Constitutions on LEXIS and WESTLAW
C. Legislative History
  1. Introduction
     a. What Is Legislative History?
     b. Uses of Legislative History
     c. The Federal Legislative Process
  2. Your Research Situation Restated
  3. Researching Federal Legislative History without CALR
     a. Overview
     b. The Statutory Codes
     c. *United States Code Congressional and Administrative News* (U.S.C.C.A.N.)
     d. Congressional Information Service
     e. The *Congressional Record* and Other Government Publications
        (1) *Congressional Record*
        (2) The *Serial Set* and Related Materials
        (3) Bills
     f. Other Legislative History Sources and Media
  4. CALR in Legislative History

A. STATUTES

1. Introduction

Thus far, you have learned how to use secondary authority to help you locate and understand primary authority, and you have learned how to research one form of primary authority—case law. In this chapter, you will learn to research an additional body of primary authority—federal and state statutes and related materials.

Although both cases and statutes are primary authority, each is analyzed in a different manner. Common law analysis focuses on judicial interpretations of ever-evolving common law principles. Common law typically develops in a case-by-case fashion that directly affects only the parties to a particular case and is concerned primarily with situations that occurred before the case was brought. Decisions that evolve from this process serve as binding or persuasive precedent for future disputes of a similar nature.

In contrast, statutory analysis focuses on the meaning of legal rules enacted by legislatures, not by judges. Legislatures create these legal rules, usually in the form of statutes, to apply to situations that will arise after the legislation goes into effect. While cases apply initially only to the particular parties or situations that are the subject of the case, statutes are usually drafted to apply generally to broad categories of parties and situations. These situations may have been covered by the common law, or they may be situations that the common law does not address.

Some statutes codify, clarify, or supplement the common law. (For example, in some areas of criminal law, the close relationship between common law crimes and criminal statutes makes the common law helpful in interpreting the meanings of statutes.) Some statutes, such as workers' compensation statutes, overturn the common law. Still other statutes create whole new areas of law not covered in the common law, such as labor law. Because constitutions grant legislatures broad powers to create legal rules to govern society, statutes usually take precedence over common law principles that are at odds with statutory provisions.

2. Reading and Analyzing Statutes

There are some similarities and some differences between reading cases and reading statutes. One similarity is that just as cases have common parts, so too do many (but far from all) statutes. The common parts of many statutes include a title, an enacting clause, a popular name, a statement of legislative findings, a statement of legislative purpose, definitions, an applicability provision, operative provisions, enforcement or remedy provisions, and an effective date. These parts may appear in one statutory section or in multiple, sequentially numbered sections. See Illustration 7-1 on pages 229-233 for an example of the parts of a statute.

Separating the components of a statute may help you structure your analysis of the statute's meaning. First, read the title, findings, statement of purpose, or other introductory sections the legislature may have included so you can obtain an overview of the intended effects of the statute. Then read any definitions included by the legislature to help you understand any particularized meanings of the statutory language. Statutory definitions are especially important because the technical nature of legislative drafting often necessitates the use of words whose meanings are not immediately clear to the unsuspecting reader. Then read any applicability provision to determine the people, places, or situations regulated by the statute.

Next read all of the operative sections of the statute to be certain that you understand the relationships among them and any inferences that can be drawn from the context in which the words are used. The operative sections tell you what conduct the statute requires or prohibits. Then read any enforcement or remedy provisions to shed light on the procedures for obtaining compliance with the statute and to determine the consequences of violating it. Finally, especially if the statute you are reading is a newly enacted statute, be sure to check its effective date to determine if it has taken effect or when it will take effect. If the statute does not include an effective date provision, check the code for the relevant jurisdiction to determine the "default" effective date in the jurisdiction.

Pay close attention to every word in a statute. Unlike cases, statutes do not contain dicta. You should assume that each word has a purpose and is potentially significant.

Rules of statutory construction may aid your reading of a statute. Some jurisdictions have statutory provisions that set forth rules for analyzing statutory language. *See, e.g.,* Minn. Stat. ch. 645 (1990 & Supp. 1991). You should determine whether such rules have been enacted in your jurisdiction. In addition, courts have developed rules of statutory construction. Many jurisdictions use the following rules of statutory construction:

(1) Specific provisions prevail over conflicting general provisions.
(2) Later-added provisions prevail over conflicting earlier provisions.
(3) Masculine pronouns include the feminine.
(4) The singular includes the plural; the plural includes the singular.

Other rules and methods of statutory construction can be found in sources such as Norman J. Singer, *Statutes and Statutory Construction* (Sands 4th ed., 1985 rev.).

As you might expect, the rules of statutory construction cannot be applied automatically, and in some cases there are conflicting rules that might apply to the same situation. For instance, a later-added provision might also be

ILLUSTRATION 7-1. Common Parts of a Statute: Occupational Safety and Health Act of 1970, Pub. L. No. 91-596, 84 Stat. 1590-93, 1601, 1602, 1606, 1620.

229

1590   PUBLIC LAW 91-596—DEC. 29, 1970   [84 STAT.

Public Law 91-596

December 29, 1970
[S. 2193]

AN ACT

To assure safe and healthful working conditions for working men and women; by authorizing enforcement of the standards developed under the Act; by assisting and encouraging the States in their efforts to assure safe and healthful working conditions; by providing for research, information, education, and training in the field of occupational safety and health; and for other purposes.

Occupational
Safety and Health
Act of 1970.

Be it enacted by the Senate and House of Representatives of the United States of America in Congress assembled, That this Act may be cited as the "Occupational Safety and Health Act of 1970".

CONGRESSIONAL FINDINGS AND PURPOSE

SEC. (2) The Congress finds that personal injuries and illnesses arising out of work situations impose a substantial burden upon, and are a hindrance to, interstate commerce in terms of lost production, wage loss, medical expenses, and disability compensation payments.

(b) The Congress declares it to be its purpose and policy, through the exercise of its powers to regulate commerce among the several States and with foreign nations and to provide for the general welfare, to assure so far as possible every working man and woman in the Nation safe and healthful working conditions and to preserve our human resources—

(1) by encouraging employers and employees in their efforts to reduce the number of occupational safety and health hazards at their places of employment, and to stimulate employers and employees to institute new and to perfect existing programs for providing safe and healthful working conditions;

(2) by providing that employers and employees have separate but dependent responsibilities and rights with respect to achieving safe and healthful working conditions;

(3) by authorizing the Secretary of Labor to set mandatory occupational safety and health standards applicable to businesses affecting interstate commerce, and by creating an Occupational Safety and Health Review Commission for carrying out adjudicatory functions under the Act;

(4) by building upon advances already made through employer and employee initiative for providing safe and healthful working conditions;

(5) by providing for research in the field of occupational safety and health, including the psychological factors involved, and by developing innovative methods, techniques, and approaches for dealing with occupational safety and health problems;

(6) by exploring ways to discover latent diseases, establishing causal connections between diseases and work in environmental conditions, and conducting other research relating to health problems, in recognition of the fact that occupational health standards present problems often different from those involved in occupational safety;

(7) by providing medical criteria which will assure insofar as practicable that no employee will suffer diminished health, functional capacity, or life expectancy as a result of his work experience;

(8) by providing for training programs to increase the number and competence of personnel engaged in the field of occupational safety and health;

Note: 1. Title
2. Enacting clause and popular name
3. Findings
4. Legislative purpose

(9) by providing for the development and promulgation of occupational safety and health standards;

(10) by providing an effective enforcement program which shall include a prohibition against giving advance notice of any inspection and sanctions for any individual violating this prohibition;

(11) by encouraging the States to assume the fullest responsibility for the administration and enforcement of their occupational safety and health laws by providing grants to the States to assist in identifying their needs and responsibilities in the area of occupational safety and health, to develop plans in accordance with the provisions of this Act, to improve the administration and enforcement of State occupational safety and health laws, and to conduct experimental and demonstration projects in connection therewith;

(12) by providing for appropriate reporting procedures with respect to occupational safety and health which procedures will help achieve the objectives of this Act and accurately describe the nature of the occupational safety and health problem;

(13) by encouraging joint labor-management efforts to reduce injuries and disease arising out of employment.

DEFINITIONS

SEC. 3. For the purposes of this Act—

(1) The term "Secretary" mean the Secretary of Labor.

(2) The term "Commission" means the Occupational Safety and Health Review Commission established under this Act.

(3) The term "commerce" means trade, traffic, commerce, transportation, or communication among the several States, or between a State and any place outside thereof, or within the District of Columbia, or a possession of the United States (other than the Trust Territory of the Pacific Islands), or between points in the same State but through a point outside thereof.

(4) The term "person" means one or more individuals, partnerships, associations, corporations, business trusts, legal representatives, or any organized group of persons.

(5) The term "employer" means a person engaged in a business affecting commerce who has employees, but does not include the United States or any State or political subdivision of a State.

(6) The term "employee" means an employee of an employer who is employed in a business of his employer which affects commerce.

(7) The term "State" includes a State of the United States, the District of Columbia, Puerto Rico, the Virgin Islands, American Samoa, Guam, and the Trust Territory of the Pacific Islands.

(8) The term "occupational safety and health standard" means a standard which requires conditions, or the adoption or use of one or more practices, means, methods, operations, or processes, reasonably necessary or appropriate to provide safe or healthful employment and places of employment.

(9) The term "national consensus standard" means any occupational safety and health standard or modification thereof which (1), has been adopted and promulgated by a nationally recognized standards-producing organization under procedures whereby it can be determined by the Secretary that persons interested

4. Legislative purpose
5. Definitions

ILLUSTRATION 7-1. *(continued)* 231

1592   PUBLIC LAW 91-596–DEC. 29, 1970   [84 STAT.

and affected by the scope or provisions of the standard have reached substantial agreement on its adoption, (2) was formulated in a manner which afforded an opportunity for diverse views to be considered and (3) has been designated as such a standard by the Secretary, after consultation with other appropriate Federal agencies.

(10) The term "established Federal standard" means any operative occupational safety and health standard established by any agency of the United States and presently in effect, or contained in any Act of Congress in force on the date of enactment of this Act.

(11) The term "Committee" means the National Advisory Committee on Occupational Safety and Health established under this Act.

(12) The term "Director" means the Director of the National Institute for Occupational Safety and Health.

(13) The term "Institute" means the National Institute for Occupational Safety and Health established under this Act.

(14) The term "Workmen's Compensation Commission" means the National Commission on State Workmen's Compensation Laws established under this Act.

APPLICABILITY OF THIS ACT

SEC. 4. (a) This Act shall apply with respect to employment performed in a workplace in a State, the District of Columbia, the Commonwealth of Puerto Rico, the Virgin Islands, American Samoa, Guam, the Trust Territory of the Pacific Islands, Wake Island, Outer Continental Shelf lands defined in the Outer Continental Shelf Lands Act, Johnston Island, and the Canal Zone. The Secretary of the Interior shall, by regulation, provide for judicial enforcement of this Act by the courts established for areas in which there are no United States district courts having jurisdiction.

67 Stat. 462.
43 USC 1331
note.

(b)(1) Nothing in this Act shall apply to working conditions of employees with respect to which other Federal agencies, and State agencies acting under section 274 of the Atomic Energy Act of 1954, as amended (42 U.S.C. 2021), exercise statutory authority to prescribe or enforce standards or regulations affecting occupational safety or health.

73 Stat. 688.

(2) The safety and health standards promulgated under the Act of June 30, 1936, commonly known as the Walsh-Healey Act (41 U.S.C. 35 et seq.), the Service Contract Act of 1965 (41 U.S.C. 351 et seq.), Public Law 91–54, Act of August 9, 1969 (40 U.S.C. 333), Public Law 85–742, Act of August 23, 1958 (33 U.S.C. 941), and the National Foundation on Arts and Humanities Act (20 U.S.C. 951 et seq.) are superseded on the effective date of corresponding standards, promulgated under this Act, which are determined by the Secretary to be more effective. Standards issued under the laws listed in this paragraph and in effect on or after the effective date of this Act shall be deemed to be occupational safety and health standards issued under this Act, as well as under such other Acts.

49 Stat. 2036.
79 Stat. 1034.
83 Stat. 96.
72 Stat. 835.

Ante, p. 443.

Report to
Congress.

(3) The Secretary shall, within three years after the effective date of this Act, report to the Congress his recommendations for legislation to avoid unnecessary duplication and to achieve coordination between this Act and other Federal laws.

5. Definitions
6. Applicability section

(4) Nothing in this Act shall be construed to supersede or in any manner affect any workmen's compensation law or to enlarge or diminish or affect in any other manner the common law or statutory rights, duties, or liabilities of employers and employees under any law with respect to injuries, diseases, or death of employees arising out of, or in the course of, employment.

DUTIES

Sec. 5. (a) Each employer—
   (1) shall furnish to each of his employees employment and a place of employment which are free from recognized hazards that are causing or are likely to cause death or serious physical harm to his employees;
   (2) shall comply with occupational safety and health standards promulgated under this Act.
(b) Each employee shall comply with occupational safety and health standards and all rules, regulations, and orders issued pursuant to this Act which are applicable to his own actions and conduct.

PROCEDURE FOR ENFORCEMENT

Sec. 10. (a) If, after an inspection or investigation, the Secretary issues a citation under section 9(a), he shall, within a reasonable time after the termination of such inspection or investigation, notify the employer by certified mail of the penalty, if any, proposed to be assessed under section 17 and that the employer has fifteen working days within which to notify the Secretary that he wishes to contest the citation or proposed assessment of penalty. If, within fifteen working days from the receipt of the notice issued by the Secretary the employer fails to notify the Secretary that he intends to contest the citation or proposed assessment of penalty, and no notice is filed by any employee or representative of employees under subsection (c) within such time, the citation and the assessment, as proposed, shall be deemed a final order of the Commission and not subject to review by any court or agency.
   (b) If the Secretary has reason to believe that an employer has failed to correct a violation for which a citation has been issued within the period permitted for its correction (which period shall not begin to run until the entry of a final order by the Commission in the case of any review proceedings under this section initiated by the employer in good faith and not solely for delay or avoidance of penalties), the Secretary shall notify the employer by certified mail of such failure and of the penalty proposed to be assessed under section 17 by reason of such failure, and that the employer has fifteen working days within which to notify the Secretary that he wishes to contest the Secretary's notification or the proposed assessment of penalty. If, within fifteen working days from the receipt of notification issued by the Secretary, the employer fails to notify the Secretary that he intends to contest the notification or proposed assessment of penalty, the notification and assessment, as proposed, shall be deemed a final order of the Commission and not subject to review by any court or agency.
   (c) If an employer notifies the Secretary that he intends to contest a citation issued under section 9(a) or notification issued under subsection (a) or (b) of this section, or if, within fifteen working days

6. Applicability section
7. Operative provision
8. Enforcement provision

ILLUSTRATION 7-1. *(continued)* 233

1602   PUBLIC LAW 91-596–DEC. 29, 1970   [84 Stat.

80 Stat. 384.

of the issuance of a citation under section 9(a), any employee or representative of employees files a notice with the Secretary alleging that the period of time fixed in the citation for the abatement of the violation is unreasonable, the Secretary shall immediately advise the Commission of such notification, and the Commission shall afford an opportunity for a hearing (in accordance with section 554 of title 5, United States Code, but without regard to subsection (a)(3) of such section). The Commission shall thereafter issue an order, based on findings of fact, affirming, modifying, or vacating the Secretary's citation or proposed penalty, or directing other appropriate relief, and such order shall become final thirty days after its issuance. Upon a showing by an employer of a good faith effort to comply with the abatement requirements of a citation, and that abatement has not been completed because of factors beyond his reasonable control, the Secretary, after an opportunity for a hearing as provided in this subsection, shall issue an order affirming or modifying the abatement requirements in such citation. The rules of procedure prescribed by the Commission shall provide affected employees or representatives of affected employees an opportunity to participate as parties to hearings under this subsection.

⑧

PENALTIES

Sec. 17. (a) Any employer who willfully or repeatedly violates the requirements of section 5 of this Act, any standard, rule, or order promulgated pursuant to section 6 of this Act, or regulations prescribed pursuant to this Act, may be assessed a civil penalty of not more than $10,000 for each violation.

(b) Any employer who has received a citation for a serious violation of the requirements of section 5 of this Act, of any standard, rule, or order promulgated pursuant to section 6 of this Act, or of any regulations prescribed pursuant to this Act, shall be assessed a civil penalty of up to $1,000 for each such violation.

(c) Any employer who has received a citation for a violation of the requirements of section 5 of this Act, of any standard, rule, or order promulgated pursuant to section 6 of this Act, or of regulations prescribed pursuant to this Act, and such violation is specifically determined not to be of a serious nature, may be assessed a civil penalty of up to $1,000 for each such violation.

⑨

(d) Any employer who fails to correct a violation for which a citation has been issued under section 9(a) within the period permitted for its correction (which period shall not begin to run until the date of the final order of the Commission in the case of any review proceeding under section 10 initiated by the employer in good faith and not solely for delay or avoidance of penalties), may be assessed a civil penalty of not more than $1,000 for each day during which such failure or violation continues.

EFFECTIVE DATE

Sec. 34. This Act shall take effect one hundred and twenty days after the date of its enactment.

Approved December 29, 1970.

⑩

8. Enforcement provision
9. Penalty provision
10. Effective date

more general than an earlier specific provision that still seems to apply. Nevertheless, the rules provide some guidance about how courts may analyze an issue of statutory interpretation.

The meaning or constitutionality of a statute may be interpreted by the courts if a statute is challenged in a legal proceeding. Statutory analysis hinges on determining the intent of the legislature in enacting the statute and usually involves answering two major questions. First, did the legislature intend the statute to cover the parties or the situation at issue? Second, if the statute does apply, what effect did the legislature intend the statute to have? Courts are limited to determining what the legislature intended the words of the statute to mean and whether the legislature was within its constitutional authority in enacting that legislation; a court may not create a new statute.

Although determining legislative intent may sound simple, the intent of the legislature is often difficult to ascertain. For example, controversies arise in situations that were not contemplated by those who drafted the legislation, or in historical circumstances that call for new interpretations of the law to respond to unanticipated societal needs.

The rules of statutory construction emphasize the primacy of statutory language and the secondary role that other sources play in the process of interpreting a statute. They forbid the use of other sources, such as legislative history, unless a close reading of a statute reveals an ambiguity or inconsistency in the statute. Therefore, judicial analysis of the legislature's intent begins with a close reading of the language of the statute.

This part of the chapter will give you an overview of how statutes are enacted; it will then teach you how to locate the texts of statutes and how to use statutory annotations to find cases and other sources that may assist you in interpreting statutory language. Part B covers constitutions. Legislative history research is covered in Part C, and research using uniform and model laws is covered in Part D.

3. An Overview of the Legislative Process

To understand statutory texts, you must have a basic understanding of the legislative process. (This process will be explained in more detail in Part C at pages 281-283.) The process of enacting a statute is similar at both the federal and state levels. For purposes of this example, you will follow a bill through Congress.

Proposed legislation, usually called a bill, is introduced into a body of Congress. Each bill is given its own number, which reflects both the body in which it is introduced (i.e., the House or Senate) and the order in which it is introduced. A Senate bill will be identified by a number that begins with "S." for Senate; a House of Representatives bill will be identified by a number that begins with "H.R." For example, S. 673, a 1991 federal bill that would amend the Occupational Safety and Health Act of 1970, was the 673rd bill introduced into the Senate in the 1991 session. The same bill may be introduced in both the House and Senate. In that case it will have two bill numbers, one in the House and the other in the Senate.

A bill becomes a statute after passing through several stages: consideration by House or Senate committees, or both; debate by both houses of Congress and affirmative votes; and signing by the President (or congressional override of a presidential veto).

If the bill becomes law, it is given a new number. On the federal level, this number is called a public law number. A public law number consists of the number of the Congress in which the bill passed, followed by a number that represents the order in which it passed. For example, "Public Law 91-596" (in Illustration 7-1 on pages 229-233) refers to the 596th law passed by the 91st Congress.

235

Statutes and
Constitutions:
Searching for
Primary Authority

4. An Overview of Statutory Sources

a. Slip Laws

Laws are published and compiled in a similar fashion at both the federal and state levels. When a new law is enacted, the law (which may also be called an act) may be separately published as an unindexed "slip law." A slip law may be a single page, or it may run almost to book length. A federal slip law is identified by its public law number.

On the federal level, slip laws are published officially by the United States Government Printing Office. They are also commercially available in *United States Code Congressional and Administrative News* (U.S.C.C.A.N.) pamphlets and in the *United States Code Service* (U.S.C.S.) *Advance* pamphlets. (You will learn more about both of these publications later at pages 256-264.)

Some states publish official copies, in slip law form, of each piece of legislation that has been enacted, but many do not. As a result, commercial publishers of annotated codes at the state level, such as West Publishing Company and The Michie Company, publish unofficial copies of recent enactments in the form of advance session law (legislative) services. Your librarian will be able to tell you whether official slip laws are available for your jurisdiction and to show you your state's advance session law service.

b. Session Laws

At the end of a legislative session, the slip laws for that session are compiled into one or more bound volumes, which are called "session laws" because they contain all the laws enacted during a particular legislative session. Session laws are typically arranged in chronological order by the dates the laws were passed.

The official compilation of federal session laws is called *United States Statutes at Large* [hereinafter *Statutes at Large*]. *Statutes at Large* is a government publication that is available about a year after the close of the congressional session to which it refers. The federal session laws published in *Statutes at Large* are ordered by either chapter numbers or public law numbers. Chapter numbers were once the official federal designation of session laws, although unofficial public law numbers began to appear in the early 1900s. In 1957, the 85th Congress began using public law numbers instead of chapter numbers for the official designation.

> ***Citation Note:*** According to Rule 12.2 of *The Bluebook,* a session law citation is used (1) when the statutory provision does not appear in a code (a collection of statutory provisions organized by subject matter); (2) when a statute appears in so many scattered locations that no useful citation to the code is possible; (3) when the citation supports the historical fact of enactment, amendment, or repeal; or (4) when the language in the current code differs materially from the language in the session law and the title has not been enacted into "positive law" (see list of titles enacted into positive law in Rule 12.2.2(c) of *The Bluebook*).

Rule 12.4 governs session law citation and requires the following form: Occupational Safety and Health Act of 1970, Pub. L. No. 91-596, 84 Stat. 1590. This citation includes the name of the act (Occupational Safety and Health Act of 1970); the chapter or public law number (Pub. L. No. 91-596); and the citation to the session law publication by volume (84), title (Stat. for *United States Statutes at Large*), the first page of the act (1590), and the year of the session law publication (unless that same year appears in the name of the act, as it does in the example). Abbreviations for session law publications appear in Table T.1. If you are citing a specific page, the relevant page number follows the number of the first page of the act. If you are citing to a particular section or subsection, include it after the public law number. For example, Occupational Safety and Health Act of 1970, Pub. L. No. 91-596, § 5, 84 Stat. 1590, 1593. If you know the location of a session law in the *United States Code* (U.S.C. is a codification of session laws that is discussed later at pages 238-247), the U.S.C. citation may be included in a parenthetical at the end of the session law citation. For example, Occupational Safety and Health Act of 1970, Pub. L. No. 91-596, § 5, 84 Stat. 1590, 1593 (codified at 29 U.S.C. § 654 (1988)).

Locate volume 84 of *Statutes at Large* and turn to page 1590, the page on which the Occupational Safety and Health Act of 1970 begins. (See Illustration 7-1 on pages 229-233.) Across the top of each page of text in *Statutes at Large* is a "running heading" that includes the public law number (or chapter number) of the law and the date the session law was enacted. The date of enactment is important because a federal law takes effect upon enactment unless a different time is specified in the law itself. The outside margins of the text of a federal session law typically contain notes that further identify the contents of the law. These notes may include, for example, the popular name of the law, words or phrases that highlight the contents of a particular section, references to the *United States Code* sections where the law will be codified, and cross-references to help you locate other laws that are referred to by the law you are reading. Near the beginning of a law, you will find the original bill number of the law. In Illustration 7-1 (see page 229), S. 2193 is the Senate bill number that was assigned to the act during the legislative process. This number is essential to your research if you want to locate the act's legislative history. You will find additional legislative history references at the end of session laws enacted in 1975 or thereafter.

Session law compilations are important research sources because they

(1) contain the exact text of the laws as enacted;
(2) contain all the laws enacted during a particular legislative session, including private and special laws (legislation directed at individuals or specific matters rather than general policies), budgetary provisions, effective date provisions, and other temporary provisions that are not codified;
(3) make it possible to track changes in a statute from year to year; and
(4) form a permanent historical record of the law, enabling you to find even those laws that have been repealed.

Session laws are difficult to use, however, because they are arranged chronologically rather than by subject, and they do not incorporate in one place the changes that occur over time as laws are amended or repealed.

c. Codes

237

Statutes and
Constitutions:
Searching for
Primary Authority

(1) When to Use a Code

Because the chronologically arranged compilations of session laws are difficult to use for many purposes, laws are also published in subject arrangements called "codes." Codes contain the current text of the general, public, permanent laws of a jurisdiction. They usually omit special laws, private laws, and temporary laws, such as appropriations laws and effective date provisions. Between printings of new sets, codes are typically kept current by supplementary volumes or by pocket parts and supplementary pamphlets containing new or amended statutes.

Unless you are looking for a statute that was never codified, or for an earlier version of a statute, or for a very new law, you generally will begin your statutory research in a code.

You may have more than one code from which to choose. Codes, like cases, are often published in both "official" and "unofficial" forms. A code is "official" if it is published by the government or by a private party authorized to publish in lieu of the government; otherwise, it is "unofficial."

A code may be annotated or unannotated. An annotated code contains digests of cases that interpret the statutory sections, as well as references to useful research sources related to those sections. An unannotated code does not include case digests, and it has few references to related research sources. Generally, official codes are unannotated and unofficial codes are annotated, but there is no necessary relationship between the two concepts. When you are interested in reading only the text of a statute, an unannotated code may be the better research choice, but an annotated code will usually be more useful for statutory research.

(2) Your Research Situation

Assume the following research situation:

The firm that you work for has just been contacted by Carlotta Selleck, the president of a small construction firm, CSB Construction, Inc. She has expressed concern as a result of a safety inspection at the firm's major project.

The firm has been working on the "Mega-Mall," a huge shopping and entertainment complex under construction in a nearby suburb. Your client's workers install heating and air conditioning ductwork. They come in after the structure has been framed and before the drywall is put up. Their work entails both heavy-duty and precision work. Because of the height of the mall, they frequently work 20 or more feet above the nearest floor.

During an unannounced safety inspection, the inspector apparently observed several workers who were not "tied off" (working with safety belts and lines), even though they were 30 feet or more above the floor. The inspector observed that safety lines were available, but some workers were not using them. Although he found no other unsafe conditions, he told the supervisor on the location to "expect a citation."

Selleck has inquired into why the workers were not wearing the safety lines. According to the supervisor, the workers find them constricting, and the safety lines make certain tasks considerably more awkward than they would otherwise be. Thus the workers choose not to wear them, despite what the supervisor asserts is a concerted effort to promote safety. The firm provides all new workers with top-of-the-line safety lines, instructs workers how to use them, and tells workers to wear them at all times. The topic is reviewed at the weekly meetings of the work crew. Workers are told that they may be disciplined for not wearing them, and indeed three workers have received written warnings for failing to wear safety lines during the last month. No worker has been suspended or fired for this behavior, however. The supervisor has been reluctant to fire anyone because the current crew is experienced and works well together. Replacing workers now would be difficult because this job is the firm's biggest project ever, and the mall is being constructed on a fast schedule.

CSB Construction has never had any difficulty passing safety inspections before, and Selleck is concerned. She has asked two basic questions:

(1) Is the firm subject to sanctions? She believes that the firm has done what the law requires in providing safety equipment and requiring its use.

(2) Since the real problem appears to be the refusal of the workers to comply with safety requirements, shouldn't the sanctions be against the workers?

Often it may be unclear to you if a federal or state statute, or both, may apply. Since federal laws sometimes set parameters for state laws, a good strategy is to begin with the federal code and then move to the state code.

(3) Federal Codes

There are three widely used versions of the federal code. The official version is *United States Code* (U.S.C.). The two unofficial versions are *United States Code Annotated* (U.S.C.A.), published by West Publishing Company, and *United States Code Service* (U.S.C.S.), published by Lawyers Cooperative Publishing. These three versions all contain the same statutory sections, and they all use the same organizational scheme of titles and section numbers. You may use similar research approaches in all three.

There are two major differences among these codes. First, the official code, U.S.C., reports only the text of the code, while both U.S.C.A. and U.S.C.S. supplement the text of the code with (1) annotations to decisions that have applied or interpreted particular sections of the code, (2) historical notes, and (3) references to other sources that interpret and analyze the code. Second, the unofficial codes are updated far more frequently than the official code.

To get an overview of the statutory scheme that governs your research situation, we will begin our research in the *United States Code*.

(a) United States Code (U.S.C.)

You can find a statute in U.S.C. if you have a citation to the statute from another source. You also may find a statute by using any of these four different research approaches:

(1) the index approach
(2) the title outline approach
(3) the popular name approach
(4) the conversion table approach

(i) Index Approach

239

Statutes and
Constitutions:
Searching for
Primary Authority

You will usually begin your code research in an index. The U.S.C. index lists federal statutes alphabetically according to their subject matter and the names of the acts. It can give you the exact location of virtually every federal statute found in U.S.C. However, because the main volumes of U.S.C. are reprinted at six-year intervals, you must refer to the index in the most recent cumulative annual bound supplement to locate statutes enacted since the publication of the main index.

Your task is to formulate a description of the subject matter of your research that matches the vocabulary used in the index. As you have already learned, finding the correct vocabulary to use in an index can be frustrating. For example, most students would probably look for statutes governing your research situation under a main heading such as "Safety Lines," "Safety Equipment," or something similar. Although those headings do not appear in the U.S.C. index, a cross-reference under "Safety" tells you to look under "Occupational Safety and Health." If you began your research with the main heading "Employers," you would find a similar cross-reference under the subheading "Safety." If you do not find an index entry using the terms you select, refer back to Chapter 2 for ideas on how to generate alternative research vocabulary.

Under the main heading "Occupational Safety and Health," you will find entries for "Citations for violations, 29 § 658," "Duties of employers and employees, 29 § 654," and "State, Jurisdiction, 29 § 667." See Illustration 7-2 at pages 240-241. The numbers at the end of the second entry, "29 § 654," indicate that a federal statute covering duties of employers and employees under the Occupational Safety and Health Act (OSHA) appears in title 29 of U.S.C. at section 654. (The statute referred to by the "State, Jurisdiction" entry might help you understand if federal or state law applies to your research situation.)

Locate section 654 in the main volume of title 29 of U.S.C. as found in Illustration 7-3 on page 241. Section 654(a), which is sometimes referred to as the "general duty" clause of OSHA, imposes on employers both the general duty to provide a safe workplace and the specific duty to comply with regulations promulgated under the act. (You will learn about regulations in Chapter 8.)

The text of section 654 and of every statute in U.S.C. is followed by a statutory history note. The note gives the public law number, section number, date of enactment, and *Statutes at Large* citation for the original law that created that section of the code and for every law that has amended it. Although these citations are not in proper *Bluebook* citation form, they enable you to turn directly to previous versions of the statute in *Statutes at Large* when researching a statute's history. The statutory history note applies to the entire statutory section. If the note cites more than one act, it will not indicate the year in which any particular provisions were enacted or modified. You would have to read each *Statutes at Large* reference to determine which provisions of the statute were affected and when.

To update your research in U.S.C., look for the same title and section number in the most recent cumulative annual supplement. (You will need to update your research even further, but you will have to use some of the sources described later in this part to do so.)

Citation Note: Rule 12 of *The Bluebook* explains how to cite statutes. Whenever possible, cite the current official code or its supplement. For federal statutes, the current official code is *United States Code*. As of late 1991, the correct citation form for the section reproduced in Illustration 7-3 on page 241 is 29 U.S.C. § 654 (1988). *See* Rule 12.3 of *The Bluebook*. Add the name and original section number of the act if they help identify the statute. If the statute or part of the statute that you are citing has been amended since publication of the main U.S.C. volume, the citation must include both the year of the main volume and the year of the most recent supplement. For example, if part of § 654 were amended and the amendment appeared in the 1989 U.S.C. supplement (which is "Supple-

ILLUSTRATION 7-2. Index Pages from U.S.C.: [General Index N-Q] U.S.C. 362-64 (1988).

GENERAL INDEX   Page 362

to ob-
3h
10
Armed
bstruc-

iterna-

nd dec-
irisdic-

oncern-

ations,
ication

7212

vigable

or of-
to or
penal-

70

nstruc-
tc., by

3 § 502

ion of

for, 33

bstruc-

9

454
606

3 § 409

415

ructing

ion, 16

Billies Bay Wilderness, designation, 16 § 1132 note
Juniper Prairie Wilderness, designation, 16 § 1132 note
Little Lake George Wilderness, designation, 16 § 1132 note
Refuge,
  Creation, etc., 16 § 692 et seq.
  Designation, 16 § 692 note

OCCUPANT RESTRAINT SYSTEM
Defined, safety standards, National Traffic and Motor Vehicle Safety Act, 15 § 1410b

OCCUPATION TRAINING
Vocational Education, generally, this index

OCCUPATIONAL DISEASES
Coal Mines, this index
Mine Safety and Health, this index

OCCUPATIONAL SAFETY AND HEALTH
  Text of Act of 1970. See Popular Name Table
Administration, Asbestos Hazards School Safety Task Force, representative, 20 § 3602
Administrative law judge, Review Commission, 29 § 661
Agency, defined, program for Federal employees, 5 § 7902 note, Ex. Ord. No. 12196
Agricultural credit, loans to farmers for purposes of, 7 § 1942
Alternative Motor Fuels, Interagency Commission on, membership by Administrator, 42 § 6374c
Analysis of statistics, 29 § 673
Applicability of Act, 29 § 653
Appropriations, 29 § 678
Attorney General, civil litigation subject to direction and control of, 29 § 663
Audits, 29 § 674
Citations for violations, 29 § 658
  Enforcement, 29 § 659
  Penalties, 29 § 666
Civil defense workers, protection and incentives, emergency preparedness functions of Secretary of Labor, 50 App. § 2251 note, Ex. Ord. No. 11490
Civil litigation, representation of Secretary in, 29 § 663
Commerce, defined, 29 § 652
Committees, programs for Federal employees, establishment by agency head, membership, powers and duties, 5 § 7902 note, Ex. Ord. No. 12196
Compensation, chairman and members of Review Commission, 5 §§ 5314, 5315
Confidentiality of trade secrets, 29 § 664
Congressional findings, 29 § 651
Contracts,
  National Institute, 29 § 671
  Studies, 29 § 669
Counteracting imminent dangers, procedures, 29 § 662
Declaration of purpose, 29 § 651
Definitions, 29 § 652
Demonstrations, 29 § 669
Department of HHS, programs for Federal employees, liaison with Secretary of Labor, 5 § 7902 note, Ex. Ord. No. 12196
Director, defined, 29 § 652

Page 363   GENERAL INDEX

OCCUPATIONAL SAFETY AND HEALTH—Continued
Discrimination against employee filing complaint, etc., prohibited, 29 § 660
Duties of employers and employees, 29 § 654
Education of employees, 29 § 670
Employee, defined, 29 § 652
Employer, defined, 29 § 652
Enforcement, citations for violations, 29 § 659
Established Federal standard. Standards, post, this heading
Evaluation, carrying out of State plan, 29 § 667
Exemptions from provisions of Act, 29 § 665
Experiments, 29 § 669
  National Institute, 29 § 671
False statements, representations, etc., penalties, 29 § 666
Farmers, loans to, 7 § 1942
Federal Advisory Council on,
  Continuation of, termination date, 5 App. § 14 note, Ex. Ord. No. 12610
  Establishment, membership, powers and duties, 5 § 7902 note, Ex. Ord. No. 12196
Federal agency safety programs and responsibilities, 29 § 668
  Postal Service, applicability to, 39 § 410
Federal register, standards, publication, 29 § 655
General Services Administration,
  Administrator, resolution of conflicting standards for space leased by, etc., programs for Federal employees, 5 § 7902 note, Ex. Ord. No. 12196
  Programs for Federal employees,
    Cooperation to abate unsafe or unhealthy working conditions, 5 § 7902 note, Ex. Ord. No. 12196
    Liaison with Secretary of Labor, 5 § 7902 note, Ex. Ord. No. 12196
Grants,
  Audit, 29 § 674
  To States, 29 § 672
  Statistics, 29 § 673
Hazardous waste operations, standards, promulgation, 29 § 655 note
Hearing, rejection of State plan, 29 § 667
Hearing examiner, Review Commission, 29 § 661
Imminent dangers, procedures to counteract, 29 § 662
Inspection, 29 §§ 657, 669
  Annual report, 29 § 675
Investigations, 29 § 657
Judicial review, orders of Review Commission, 29 § 660
Jurisdiction,
  Restraining conditions or practices of imminent danger, 29 § 662
  Review of orders of Review Commission, 29 § 660
  State, 29 § 667
Labels, standards, 29 § 665
Labor standards. Standards, generally, post, this heading
Limitation, citation for violation of standards, rule, etc., 29 § 658
Loans to small businesses, 42 § 3142-1
Medical examinations, 29 § 669
  Standards, 29 § 655

Natio
by
ad
F
§
Natio
Sa
"Co
Esta
Natio
th
Natio
H
Coa

Dire
A
D

E

M

St

T

Esta
Fed

"Ins
Mili

Min

Tax

Nativ
th
Notic
§
Office
Mar

Per

Order
Rev
Var
Penal
Perso
Petiti
Res

Rev
O

ILLUSTRATION 7-2. *(continued)*   241

ILLUSTRATION 7-3. 29 U.S.C. § 654 (1988).

§ 654. Duties of employers and employees

(a) Each employer—

(1) shall furnish to each of his employees employment and a place of employment which are free from recognized hazards that are causing or are likely to cause death or serious physical harm to his employees;

(2) shall comply with occupational safety and health standards promulgated under this chapter.

(b) Each employee shall comply with occupational safety and health standards and all rules, regulations, and orders issued pursuant to this chapter which are applicable to his own actions and conduct.

(Pub. L. 91-596, § 5, Dec. 29, 1970, 84 Stat. 1593.)

SECTION REFERRED TO IN OTHER SECTIONS

This section is referred to in sections 658, 666 of this title.

§ 655. Standards

(a) Promulgation by Secretary of national consensus standards and established Federal standards; time for promulgation; conflicting standards

Without regard to chapter 5 of title 5 or to the other subsections of this section, the Secretary shall, as soon as practicable during the period beginning with the effective date of this chapter and ending two years after such date, by rule pr̶o̶m̶u̶l̶g̶a̶t̶i̶n̶g̶ ̶a̶n̶ ̶o̶c̶c̶u̶p̶a̶t̶i̶o̶n̶a̶l̶ ̶s̶a̶f̶e̶t̶y̶ ̶o̶r̶

ing the results of research, demonstrations, and experiments. An advisory committee shall submit to the Secretary its recommendations regarding the rule to be promulgated within ninety days from the date of its appointment or within such longer or shorter period as may be prescribed by the Secretary, but in no event for a period which is longer than two hundred and seventy days.

(2) The Secretary shall publish a proposed rule promulgating, modifying, or revoking an occupational safety or health standard in the Federal Register and shall afford interested persons a period of thirty days after publication to submit written data or comments. Where an advisory committee is appointed and the Secretary determines that a rule should be issued, he shall publish the proposed rule within sixty days after the submission of the advisory committee's recommendations or the expiration of the period prescribed by the Secretary for such submission.

(3) On on before the last day of the period provided for the submission of written data or comments under paragraph (2), any interested person may file with the Secretary written objections to the proposed rule, stating the grounds therefor and requesting a public hearing on such objections. Within thirty days after the last day for filing such objections, the Secretary shall publish in the Federal Register a notice specifying the occupational safety or health standard to which objections have been filed and a hearing requested, and specif̶y̶i̶n̶g̶

ment I" to the 1988 version of the U.S.C.), then the correct citation to § 654 as amended would be 29 U.S.C. § 654 (1988 & Supp. I 1989). For the year of the code, choose the year on the spine of the volume, the year on the title page, or the latest copyright year—in that order of preference. *See* Rules 3.2(c) and 12.3.2 of *The Bluebook*.

(ii) Title Outline Approach

As an alternative to the index approach, you may use the title outline approach to locate relevant sections of the code. The *United States Code* is divided into 50 "titles." These titles are listed in the front of each volume of U.S.C. (See Illustration 7-4 on page 243.) Each title is further divided into chapters and subchapters. Once you have found the title that appears to be pertinent to the topic you are researching, turn to the "Table of Titles and Chapters" at the beginning of the volume. See Illustration 7-5 on page 244. To find a relevant chapter number, scan the chapter listings under the title you chose. Then, using the relevant title and chapter number, locate the chapter in the appropriate U.S.C. volume. (Be sure to choose the main volumes, not a supplementary volume. Supplementary volumes will always have "Supplement" on the spine.) Finally, examine the section outline at the beginning of that chapter to find the specific statutory provisions you need. See Illustration 7-6 on pages 245-246.

For example, Illustration 7-4 tells you that title 29 of U.S.C. contains legislation concerning labor. Illustration 7-5 shows that chapter 15 of title 29 contains statutes governing occupational safety and health, and Illustration 7-6 indicates (in part) the sections governing occupational health and safety. Sections 654 (Duties of employers and employees), 658 (Citations), and 667 (State jurisdiction and plans) appear especially relevant to your research situation.

The research approach we have just used—the title outline approach— works well only if you can figure out which title and chapter are likely to encompass statutes pertinent to the topic you are researching. Because a novice legal researcher seldom has enough knowledge of the law to be able to find the correct title or chapter using the title outline approach, this research strategy may initially be less valuable than other research approaches.

(iii) Popular Name Approach

If you know the name of the statute you are seeking, you may use a third research approach, the popular name approach. Locate the U.S.C. volume with the words "Popular Names" printed on the spine. Turn to the section entitled "Acts Cited by Popular Name." You will see that the Occupational Safety and Health Act of 1970 appears in the table. See Illustration 7-7 on page 247. Note that the first entry for OSHA specifies that it has been codified in Title 29 at § 651 and those following. To find statutes enacted since the publication of the main "Popular Names" volume, check the "Popular Names" table in the most recent U.S.C. cumulative supplement.

(iv) Conversion Table Approach

If you begin your research knowing the *Statutes at Large* citation or the public law number for the act you are seeking, or if you have a previous section number for a statute that has been renumbered, you may locate the current version of that statute in the code by using a table. You would consult the "Tables" volumes of U.S.C. and look at Tables I and III.

TITLES OF UNITED STATES CODE

*1. General Provisions.

2. The Congress.

*3. The President.

*4. Flag and Seal, Seat of Government, and the States.

*5. Government Organization and Employees; and Appendix.

†6. [Surety Bonds.]

7. Agriculture.

8. Aliens and Nationality.

*9. Arbitration.

*10. Armed Forces; and Appendix.

*11. Bankruptcy; and Appendix.

12. Banks and Banking.

*13. Census.

*14. Coast Guard.

15. Commerce and Trade.

16. Conservation.

*17. Copyrights.

*18. Crimes and Criminal Procedure; and Appendix.

19. Customs Duties.

20. Education.

21. Food and Drugs.

22. Foreign Relations and Intercourse.

*23. Highways.

24. Hospitals and Asylums.

25. Indians.

26. Internal Revenue Code.

27. Intoxicating Liquors.

*28. Judiciary and Judicial Procedure; and Appendix.

29. Labor.

30. Mineral Lands and Mining.

*31. Money and Finance.

*32. National Guard.

33. Navigation and Navigable Waters.

‡34. [Navy.]

*35. Patents.

36. Patriotic Societies and Observances.

*37. Pay and Allowances of the Uniformed Services.

*38. Veterans' Benefits.

*39. Postal Service.

40. Public Buildings, Property, and Works.

41. Public Contracts.

42. The Public Health and Welfare.

43. Public Lands.

*44. Public Printing and Documents.

45. Railroads.

*46. Shipping; and Appendix.

47. Telegraphs, Telephones, and Radiotelegraphs.

48. Territories and Insular Possessions.

*49. Transportation; and Appendix.

50. War and National Defense; and Appendix.

---

*This title has been enacted as law. However, any Appendix to this title has not been enacted as law.
†This title was enacted as law and has been repealed by the enactment of Title 31.
‡This title has been eliminated by the enactment of Title 10.

Page III

"Table I—Revised Titles" shows where statutes that have been revised or renumbered appear in the current edition of U.S.C. See Illustration 7-8 on page 248.

"Table III—Statutes at Large" lists the acts of Congress in chronological order and indicates where they appear in U.S.C. See Illustration 7-9 on pages 249-250. Abbreviations explain what happened to an act if it does not appear

ILLUSTRATION 7-6. Chapter Outline for Title 29, Chapter 15: 29 U.S.C §§ 651-68 (1988).

245

EFFECTIVE DATE

Section effective May 1, 1974, see section 29(a) of Pub. L. 93-259, set out as an Effective Date of 1974 Amendment note under section 202 of this title.

TRANSFER OF FUNCTIONS

"Equal Employment Opportunity Commission" was substituted for "Civil Service Commission" in subsecs. (b) and (g) pursuant to Reorg. Plan No. 1 of 1978, § 2, 43 F.R. 19807, 92 Stat. 3781, set out in the Appendix to Title 5, Government Organization and Employees, which transferred all functions vested by this section in the Civil Service Commission to the Equal Employment Opportunity Commission, effective Jan. 1, 1979, as provided by section 1-101 of Ex. Ord. No. 12106, Dec. 28, 1978, 44 F.R. 1053.

CROSS REFERENCES

Equal employment opportunities for Federal employees without discrimination because of race, color, religion, sex, or national origin, see section 7201 of Title 5, Government Organization and Employees.

SECTION REFERRED TO IN OTHER SECTIONS

This section is referred to in section 631 of this title; title 5 sections 2302, 7702, 7703; title 22 section 3905.

§ 634. Authorization of appropriations

There are hereby authorized to be appropriated such sums as may be necessary to carry out this chapter.

(Pub. L. 90-202, § 17, formerly § 16, Dec. 15, 1967, 81 Stat. 608, renumbered and amended Pub. L. 93-259, § 28(a)(5), (b)(1), Apr. 8, 1974, 88 Stat. 74; Pub. L. 95-256, § 7, Apr. 6, 1978, 92 Stat. 193.)

AMENDMENTS

1978—Pub. L. 95-256 struck out ", not in excess of $5,000,000 for any fiscal year," after "sums".

1974—Pub. L. 93-259, § 28(a)(5), increased appropriations authorization to $5,000,000 from $3,000,000.

EFFECTIVE DATE OF 1974 AMENDMENT

Amendment by Pub. L. 93-259 effective May 1, 1974, see section 29(a) of Pub. L. 93-259, set out as a note under section 202 of this title.

TRANSFER OF FUNCTIONS

All functions relating to age discrimination administration and enforcement vested by this section in the Secretary of Labor or the Civil Service Commission were transferred to the Equal Employment Opportunity Commission by Reorg. Plan No. 1 of 1978, § 2, 43 F.R. 19807, 92 Stat. 3781, set out in the Appendix to Title 5, Government Organization and Employees, effective Jan. 1, 1979, as provided by section 1-101 of Ex. Ord. No. 12106, Dec. 28, 1978, 44 F.R. 1053.

CHAPTER 15—OCCUPATIONAL SAFETY AND HEALTH

Page 1105   **TITLE 29—LABOR**

Sec.

659. Enforcement procedures.
- (a) Notification of employer of proposed assessment of penalty subsequent to issuance of citation; time for no-~~tification of Secretary by employer~~

Sec.

- (b) Appropriate injunctive relief or temporary restraining order pending outcome of enforcement proceeding; applicability of Rule 65 of Federal Rules of Civil Procedure.
- (c) ~~Notification of affect-~~

of procedure.

660. Judicial review.
- (a) Filing of petition by persons adversely affected or aggrieved; orders subject to review; jurisdiction; venue; procedure; conclusiveness of record and findings of Commission; appropriate relief; finality of judgment.
- (b) Filing of petition by Secretary; orders subject to review; jurisdiction; venue; procedure; conclusiveness of record and findings of Commission; enforcement of orders; contempt proceedings.
- (c) Discharge or discrimination against employee for exercise of rights under this chapter; prohibition; procedure for relief.

661. Occupational Safety and Health Review Commission.
- (a) Establishment; membership; appointment; Chairman.
- (b) Terms of office; removal by President.
- (c) Omitted.
- (d) Principal office; hearings or other proceedings at other places.
- (e) Functions and duties of Chairman; appointment and compensation of administrative law judges and other employees.
- (f) Quorum; official action.
- (g) Hearings and records open to public; promulgation of rules; applicability of Federal Rules of Civil Procedure.
- (h) Depositions and production of documentary evidence; fees.
- (i) Investigatory powers.
- (j) Administrative law judges; determinations; report as final order of Commission.
- (k) Appointment and compensation of administrative law judges.

662. Injunction proceedings.
- (a) Petition by Secretary to restrain imminent dangers; scope of order.

- (i) Violation of posting requirements.
- (j) Authority of Commission to assess civil penalties.
- (k) Determination of serious violation.
- (l) Procedure for payment of civil penalties.

667. State jurisdiction and plans.
- (a) Assertion of State standards in absence of applicable Federal standards.
- (b) Submission of State plan for development and enforcement of State standards to preempt applicable Federal standards.
- (c) Conditions for approval of plan.
- (d) Rejection of plan; notice and opportunity for hearing.
- (e) Discretion of Secretary to exercise authority over comparable standards subsequent to approval of State plan; duration; retention of jurisdiction by Secretary upon determination of enforcement of plan by State.
- (f) Continuing evaluation by Secretary of State enforcement of approved plan; withdrawal of approval of plan by Secretary; grounds; procedure; conditions for retention of jurisdiction by State.
- (g) Judicial review of Secretary's withdrawal of approval or rejection of plan; jurisdiction; venue; procedure; appropriate relief; finality of judgment.
- (h) Temporary enforcement of State standards.

668. Programs of Federal agencies.
- (a) Establishment, development and maintenance by head of each Federal agency.
- (b) Report by Secretary to President.
- (c) Omitted.
- (d) Access by Secretary to records and reports required of agencies.

---

in U.S.C. You would use the "Statutes at Large" conversion table if you had a citation to a public law number or to *Statutes at Large* and wanted to find the current version of the statute in the code. For instance, Illustration 7-9 shows on page 250 the conversion between Public Law 91-596 and 29 U.S.C. § 651 et seq. Also, if you knew the date of enactment of the statute you were researching but did not know its location in U.S.C., the conversion table would give you the corresponding U.S.C. title and section number.

In addition to these conversion tables, U.S.C. also contains a useful table of internal references. See Illustration 7-10 on page 251. You would use this

---

ACTS CITED BY POPULAR NAME   Page 1092

Occupational Safety and Health Act of 1970
Pub. L. 91-596, Dec. 29, 1970, 84 Stat. 1590 (Title 29, § 651 et seq.)
Pub. L. 93-237, § 2(c), Jan. 2, 1974, 87 Stat. 1024
Pub. L. 95-251, § 2(a)(7), Mar. 27, 1978, 92 Stat. 183
Pub. L. 97-375, title I, § 110(c), Dec. 21, 1982, 96 Stat. 1821
Pub. L. 98-620, title IV, § 402(32), Nov. 8, 1984, 98 Stat. 3360

Ocean Dumping Act
See Marine Protection, Research, and Sanctuaries Act of 1972

Ocean Dumping Ban Act of 1988
Pub. L. 100-688, title I, Nov. 18, 1988, 102 Stat. 4139

Pub. L. 99-661, div. A, title IV [IX], § 922(b), (d)(2), Nov. 14, 1986, 100 Stat. 3931, 3932
Pub. L. 100-679, §§ 2-5(a), 6(a), 9, 12, Nov. 17, 1988, 102 Stat. 4055-4058, 4063, 4069

Office of Federal Procurement Policy Act Amendments of 1979
Pub. L. 96-83, Oct. 10, 1979, 93 Stat. 648

Office of Federal Procurement Policy Act Amendments of 1983
Pub. L. 98-191, Dec. 1, 1983, 97 Stat. 1325

Office of Federal Procurement Policy Act Amendments of 1988
Pub. L. 100-679, Nov. 17, 1988, 102 Stat. 4055

Office of Government Reports Act
June 9, 1941, ch. 189, 55 Stat. 247

---

table if you wanted to determine whether the section you are researching is referred to in any other sections of U.S.C. Illustration 7-10 indicates that 29 U.S.C. § 654 is referred to in §§ 658 and 666 of Title 29.

(b)   United States Code Annotated (U.S.C.A.)

U.S.C.A. is the unofficial code published by West Publishing Company and is a part of the West research system. It contains the full text of the United States Code and the United States Constitution; it also contains the Federal Rules of Civil and Criminal Procedure, the Federal Rules of Evidence, court rules for the federal trial and appellate courts, and administrative rules for selected agencies.

(i)   Annotations

In the preceding discussion of U.S.C., you located the OSHA "general duty" clause, title 29, § 654. Turn to Illustration 7-11 at pages 252-255, which shows the same title and section in U.S.C.A.

You will note that U.S.C.A., like U.S.C., publishes statutory history citations immediately after the text of a section. But U.S.C.A. does more. After the statutory history citations, U.S.C.A. may include a "Historical Note." See Illustration 7-11 at page 253. For example, the Historical Note following the text of the OSHA "general duty" clause has three sections:

(1) References in Text (explaining the meaning of general terms such as "this chapter");
(2) Effective Date (specifying the effective date of the section); and
(3) Legislative History (containing citations to *United States Code Congressional and Administrative News,* a West publication that includes some legislative committee reports).

If a statute was preceded by a different statute or has been amended, the prior statute will be cited in a historical note, and the effect of the amendment will be explained.

TABLES

TABLE I—REVISED TITLES

The following tables represent those titles of the United States Code that have been revised and renumbered since adoption of the Code in 1926. These tables show where former sections of the revised titles have been incorporated in this edition of the Code.

Abbreviations

Rep.—Repealed. Where "Rep." appears in the new sections column, the former section was repealed prior to, or at the time of, the enactment of the revised Title, and was not restated in the revised Title.

Elim.—Eliminated. Where "Elim." appears in the new sections column, the former section was not restated in the revised Title and was not repealed.

TITLE 5—GOVERNMENT ORGANIZATION AND EMPLOYEES

[*This title was enacted into law by Pub. L. 89-554, § 1, Sept. 6, 1966, 80 Stat. 378. This table shows where sections of former Title 5 were incorporated in revised Title 5.*]

Title 5 Former Sections	Title 5 New Sections	Title 5 Former Sections	Title 5 New Sections
1, 2	101	69	5535, 5536
3	Rep.	70	5536
4	3345	70a, 70b	5945
5	3346	70c	5942
6	3347	71	5536
7	3348	72	5535
8	3349	73, 73a	Rep.
9	5535	73b	5731
10	2901	73b-1(a), (b)	5724
11, 12	2902	73b-1(c)	5730
13-14a, 15	Rep.	73b-1(d)	5725
16	3331	73b-1(e)	5726
16a	2903, 2904	73b-1(f)	5727
17, 17a	Rep.	73b-2	5703
17b, 17c	2905	73b-3(a) (less 3d-6th provisos)	5722
18	2903		
19	Rep.	73b-3(a) (3d, 4th provisos)	5728
20	2904	73b-3(a) (5th, 6th provisos)	5729
21	2906	73b-3 (less (a))	5723
21a	3332	73b-4	T. 41 § 5a
21b	5507	73b-4a, 73b-4b	5724a
22	301	73b-4c	5726
22-1 (less 3d-5th provisos)	7532	73b-4d	5724
22-1 (3d proviso)	3571, 5594	73b-4e	5724a
22-1 (4th and 5th provisos)	7312	73b-4f	5724
22-2	7533	73b-5	5732
22-3	7531	73c	5727
22a	302	73c-1, 73c-2, 73d	Rep.
23-26c	Rep.	73e	5731
27	6106	73f, 74-75a	Rep.
28	6105	75a-1	Elim.
29, 29a, 30 to 30b-1, 30c to 30e-1, 30f-30m.	Rep.	75b-75d, 76	Rep.
		76a	T. 20 § 244a
30n	6322	77, 77a	Rep.
30n-1	T. 28 § 1823	78, 78a, 78a-1, 79, 80	T. 31 §§ 638a-638e (See Rev. T. 31 Table)
30o	5537		
30p	5515	81, 81a	Rep.
30q	6321	82	5512
30r(a)	6323	83	5946
30r(b)	3551	84	5505
30r(c)	502, 5534	84a	T. 4 § 111
30r(d)	2105	84b, 84c	5517
31-31b, 32	Rep.	84d	5518
33	7154	85	5502
34-35a, 36-37a	Rep.	86	Rep.
38	3341	86a	6104
39, 40	3342	87-87c	6103
41	T. 14 § 632	88	T. 31 § 554 (See Rev. T. 31 Table)
42, 42a	Rep.		
43	3101	89	Rep.
43a	3102	90	T. 28 § 414
		91	T. 28 § 520
			Rep.

Under the heading "Cross References," the editors alert you to related statutes that may be of interest to you.

The Cross References section typically is followed by references to the same topic in other West publications, in this example, *West's Federal Practice Manual.*

The U.S.C.A. section entitled "Library References" gives you the applicable West Topics and Key Numbers and citations to C.J.S., West's legal encyclopedia.

You will sometimes find additional references, such as references to law review articles and other commentary sources, as well as references to the *Code of Federal Regulations,* which is covered in Chapter 8.

The section entitled "Notes of Decisions" provides an important bridge between statutes and cases. It contains digests of cases dealing with the particular statutory section you are reading. See Illustration 7-11 at pages 253-255. These case digests appear under numbered topic headings. The topic headings and their corresponding numbers are listed alphabetically in an index at the beginning of the Notes of Decisions section. When there are many Notes of Decisions, as there are for § 654, the decisions are grouped into broad categories that are listed before the topic headings at the beginning

ILLUSTRATION 7-9. Statutes-at-Large Table for Acts of Congress, [Tables] U.S.C. 95, 949 (1988).

TABLE III—STATUTES AT LARGE

(1789-1978 contained in this volume)

Showing where the Acts of Congress will be found in the United States Code

---

Abbreviations

Rep.—Repealed. Where "Rep." appears in the status column following a U.S.C. reference, an explanation of the repeal can be found under such U.S.C. title and section.

Rev. T.—Revised Title. Where "Rev. T." appears in the status column, the U.S.C. reference is to title and section where the section of the Act of Congress was originally allocated in the U.S.C. To locate the section of the Act in the U.S.C. revised title, see Table I.

Elim.—Eliminated. Where "Elim." appears in the status column following a U.S.C. reference, the reason for the elimination of the text can be found under such U.S.C. title and section. Where "Elim." appears in the status column and the U.S.C. column is blank, the text had at one time appeared as a note to a prior section of the Code.

I.R.C. '39.—Internal Revenue Code of 1939. Where I.R.C. '39 appears in the status column, it is an indication that the provision was repealed or otherwise superseded by the Internal Revenue Code of 1939.

R.S.—Revised Statutes of 1878. Where "R.S." followed by a § number appears in the status column, the provision was restated in the cited section of the Revised Statutes of 1878. See Table II showing where sections of the Revised Statutes of 1878 will be found in the United States Code.

1st Cong.					U.S.C.		
1 Stat.	Chapter	Section	Page	Title	Section	Status
1789—June	1 1	2	23			R.S. § 28
		2	23			R.S. § 29
		2	23			R.S. § 30
		3	23			R.S. § 1836
		3	23			R.S. § 1837
July	27 4	1	28			R.S. § 161
		1	28			R.S. § 199
		1	28			R.S. § 202
		2	29			R.S. § 203
		4	29			R.S. § 203
			49			R.S.

Page 949   **TABLE III—STATUTES AT LARGE**

91st Cong. 84 Stat.	Pub. L.	Section	Page	U.S.C. Title	Section	Status
1970—Dec. 24	91-581	16	1571	30	1015	
		17	1571	30	1016	
		18	1571	30	1017	
		19	1572	30	1018	
			1572	30	1019	
		9(g)				
		9(h)	1585	38	prec. 501	
		10	1585	38	521 nt	
	91-589	1	1586	2	168	
		2	1586	2	168a	
		3	1586	2	168b	
		4	1587	2	168c	
		5	1587	2	168d	
25	91-696	101	2080-1	42	295-295e	Rep.
		201	2080-5	42	295 nt	Elim.
28	91-590	1-3	1587	49	903, 903 nt	Rev. T.
	91-591	2	1588	7	2264	
		3	1588	7	2265	
29	91-596	1	1590	29	651 nt	
		2	1590	29	651	
		3	1591	29	652	
		4	1592	29	653	
		5	1593	29	654	
		6	1593	29	655	
		7	1597	29	656	
		8	1598	29	657	
		9	1601	29	658	
		10	1601	29	659	
		11	1602	29	660	
		12	1603	29	661	
		12(c)(1)	1604	5	5314	
		12(c)(2)	1604	5	5315	
		13	1605	29	662	
		14	1606	29	663	
		15	1606	29	664	
		16	1606	29	665	
		17	1606	29	666	
		17(h)(1)	1607	18	1114	
		17(h)(2)	1607	18	1114 nt	
		18	1608	29	667	

of the Notes of Decisions section. Each of these categories has a separate index. If you choose, you may use the index that appears at the beginning of a category, rather than the full index to the Notes of Decisions.

To find relevant cases, you would skim through the Index to the Notes of Decisions (Illustration 7-11 at pages 253-254) and pick out the headings that might be useful to your research situation. Then you would skim the case digests under your chosen headings to see if you could find any references to decisions on point. A single case may appear under several headings because of its applicability to several topics. After you skimmed the case digests under the most likely headings, you also might wish to skim the other digests, since information often is not indexed where you expect it to be. As you skim the case digests, you might note that subsequent case histories and parallel reporter citations often are included in the annotations.

The case digest paragraphs are not "official." They are subject to the usual limitations of finding tools. Nor are they "citable"; but you may cite a case after you have read it to determine its relevance. You must, of course, Shepardize each applicable case to make certain that it has not been overruled or altered in some other way.

Although West's goal is to be comprehensive rather than selective in its coverage of relevant cases, do not assume that U.S.C.A. cites every case that discusses a statutory section. Nevertheless, the case digests included in the

TABLE IX—INTERNAL REFERENCES

This Table lists those sections of the United States Code that are referred to in other sections of the Code together with citations to the referring sections.

TITLE 1—GENERAL PROVISIONS

Section	Referred to in
1	Title 10 section 101; title 30 sections 1511, 1531; title 31 section 5312; title 32 section 101; title 37 section 101; title 39 section 5215; title 49 section 10102.
2	Title 10 section 101; title 12 section 3702; title 32 section 101; title 37 section 101.
3	Title 10 section 101; title 32 sec-

TITLE 2—THE CONGRESS—Cont.

Section	Referred to in
37	Section 25b of this title.
38a	Section 25b of this title.
39	Section 25b of this title.
40	Section 25b of this title.
40a	Section 25b of this title.
41	Section 25b of this title.
42c	Section 25b of this title.
43b	Section 43b-1 of this title.
43b-2	Section 43b-3 of this title.
46b	Section 25b of this title.
46b-1	Sections 25b, 46b-2 of this title.

Page 759   TABLE IX—INTERNAL REFERENCES

TITLE 29—LABOR—Cont.

Section	Referred to in
441	Sections 435, 437, 1031 of this title.
461	Section 464 of this title.
462	Section 464 of this title.
481	Section 482 of this title.
501	Title 18 sections 1961, 2516.
504	Section 481 of this title.
557a	Section 952 of this title.
623	Sections 626, 631 of this title.
626	Section 633 of this title.
631	Sections 622, 623, 624, 633a of this title; title 5 sections 2302, 7702; title 22 section 3905.
633	Section 626 of this title.
633a	Section 631 of this title; title 5 sections 2302, 7702, 7703; title 22 section 3905.
651	Section 671 of this title.
653	Section 673 of this title; title 15 section 2608.
654	Sections 658, 666 of this title.
655	Sections 656, 657, 658, 666, 667, 668, 669 of this title; title 7 section 1942.
656	Section 655 of this title.
657	Sections 667, 669, 673 of this title.
658	Sections 659, 666, 667 of this title.
659	Sections 660, 666, 667 of this title.
660	Title 15 section 2651.
666	Sections 659, 660, 667 of this title.
667	Section 672 of this title; title 7 section 1942.
668	Title 39 section 410.
669	Section 671 of this title.

TITLE 29—LABOR—Cont.

Section	Referred to in
761a	Section 761 of this title.
761b	Section 761a of this title.
762	Sections 761, 761a of this title; title 38 sections 1904, 4101.
771	Section 706 of this title.
772	Section 776 of this title.
775	Section 776 of this title.
776	Sections 721, 762, 771, 773, 775, 777a, 777b, 777f of this title.
777	Section 762 of this title.
777a	Sections 762, 777 of this title; title 20 section 1425.
777b	Section 777 of this title.
777f	Section 777 of this title.
781	Section 2231 of this title.
784	Section 2231 of this title.
791	Section 794a of this title; title 5 sections 2302, 3102, 7702; title 22 section 3905; title 38 section 2014; title 42 section 5057.
792	Sections 776, 794b of this title; title 42 section 4157; title 49 App. section 1304.
793	Sections 706, 721 of this title.
794	Sections 706, 774, 775, 794a, 1577 of this title; title 5 section 3102; title 12 section 1715z-1a; title 20 sections 1132a, 1232e; title 25 section 2005; title 42 sections 290cc-34, 300w-7, 300x-7, 708, 1437l, 2000d-7, 3608, 5057, 5309, 6727, 8625, 9849, 9906, 10406; title 49 App. section 1612.
794a	Title 22 section 3905; title 42 section 10406.
794c	Title 42 section 5057.

annotations will further your research by providing you with relevant cases that have interpreted or relied on the statute.

If a statute has not yet been the subject of litigation, that section of the code may not have any case digest annotations. In such an instance, legislative history research would be the best method of resolving an ambiguity or inconsistency.

(ii) Supplements

In addition to the annotations, another advantage of U.S.C.A. over U.S.C. is up-to-date information. While U.S.C. supplements may be issued as much as one or two years after the laws in them were enacted, U.S.C.A. main volumes are updated annually by pocket parts (or supplementary pamphlets, if the amount of the updating for a volume has become too much for a pocket part).

West updates the pocket parts or supplementary pamphlets with non-cumulative supplementary pamphlets, which it issues about four times a year. These pamphlets, which are arranged in code section order, include both statutory changes to the code and the newest case annotations and other research aids. Finally, at the end of the year, West issues, as part of this noncumulative supplementary pamphlet series, statutory supplements that print in public law number order those laws passed too late in the session to include in the earlier pamphlets.

ILLUSTRATION 7-11. 29 U.S.C.A. § 654 (West 1985).

Ch. 15   SAFETY AND HEALTH   **29 § 654**

Hatcher v. Bullard Co., 1984, 477 A.2d 1035, 39 Conn.Sup. 250.

v. Fieldcrest Mills, Inc., C.A.N.C.1974, 496 F.2d 1323.

This chapter did not create any duties on part of city employees that would have benefited admin—

Ohio safety requirement, violation of which was basis for additional award of workers' compensation benefits, was not preempted by

—a private remedy, and plaintiff was entitled to recover from employer for alleged negligence in violation of this chapter.   Byrd

Specialties, Inc., D.C.Miss.1974, 386 F.Supp. 1240.

§ 654.   Duties of employers and employees

(a) Each employer—

(1) shall furnish to each of his employees employment and a place of employment which are free from recognized hazards that are causing or are likely to cause death or serious physical harm to his employees;

(2) shall comply with occupational safety and health standards promulgated under this chapter.

(b) Each employee shall comply with occupational safety and health standards and all rules, regulations, and orders issued pursuant to this chapter which are applicable to his own actions and conduct.

(Pub.L. 91–596, § 5, Dec. 29, 1970, 84 Stat. 1593.)

231

ILLUSTRATION 7-11. *(continued)* 253

29 § 654 LABOR Ch. 15

Historical Note

References in Text. This chapter, referred to in subsecs. (a) and (b), was in the original "this Act", meaning Pub.L. 91–596, Dec. 29, 1970, 84 Stat. 1590, as amended. For complete classification of this Act to the Code, see Short Title note set out under section 651 of this title and Tables volume.

Effective Date. Section effective 120 days after Dec. 29, 1970, see section 34 of Pub.L. 91–596, set out as an Effective Date note under section 651 of this title.

Legislative History. For legislative history and purpose of Pub.L. 91–596, see 1970 U.S. Code Cong. and Adm.News, p. 5177.

Cross References

Civil penalty for willful or repeated violations of duties of employer, see section 666 of this title. Grounds to issue citation to employer, see section 658 of this title.

West's Federal Practice Manual

Employee considerations, statutory duties, see § 10410.
Employers, see § 10408.
Standards, generally, see § 10421.

Library References

Labor Relations ⟊10.
C.J.S. Labor Relations § 12.

Notes of Decisions

I. GENERALLY

Subdivision Index

ILLUSTRATION 7-11. *(continued)* 255

29 § 654
Note 47

danger of condition or activity is either actually known to particular employer or generally known in industry. St. Joe Minerals Corp. v. Occupational Safety and Health Review Commission, C.A.8, 1981, 647 F.2d 840.

In a case brought under "general duty clause" of this section, the Secretary must show, among other things, existence of the hazard, recognition of the hazard by employer or industry in general, and worker exposure to the hazard. Bunge Corp. v. Secretary of Labor, C.A.5, 1981, 638 F.2d 831.

Under requirements of this chapter, knowledge of existence of hazardous situation must be determined in light of common experience of an industry, but extent of precautions to take against known hazard is that which a conscientious safety expert would take. General Dynamics Corp., Quincy Shipbuilding Division v. Occupational Safety and Health Review Commission, C.A.1, 1979, 599 F.2d 453.

Determination whether reasonably prudent man familiar with practices of industry would protect against alleged hazard may often be made by reference to custom of relevant industry. Brennan v. Smoke–Craft, Inc., C.A.9, 1976, 530 F.2d 843.

A "recognized hazard" is a condition that is known to be hazardous, and is known not necessarily by each and every individual employer, but is known by taking into account the standard of knowledge in the industry. Brennan v. Occupational Safety and Health Review Commission, C.A.7, 1974, 501 F.2d 1196. See, also, U.S. v. B & L Supply Co., D.C.Tex.1980, 486 F.Supp. 26.

48.   Preventable hazards—Generally

This section does not impose on employers an absolute duty to make safe the working environment of its employees, but it does require employer to abate recognized hazards as to which the Secretary of Labor has met his burden to show that a feasible method exists by which the cited employer could have abated the hazard. Baroid Division of NL Industries, Inc. v. Occupational Safety and Health Review Commission, C.A.10, 1981, 660 F.2d 439.

To prove that employer failed to render its workplace "free" of hazard, as required by "general duty" clause of this section, Secretary may be required to specify particular steps cited employer should have taken to avoid citation, and to demonstrate feasibility and likely utility of such measures. St. Joe Minerals Corp. v. Occupational Safety and Health Review Commission, C.A.8, 1981, 647 F.2d 840.

Duty imposed by this section is intended to be achievable; only preventable hazards are required to be eliminated, and therefore, a hazard is recognized only when Secretary demonstrates that feasible measures can be taken to reduce materially the likelihood of death or serious physical harm resulting to employees. Babcock & Wilcox Co. v. Occupational Safety and Health Review Commis-

Hazardous conduct is not preventable by employer within meaning of this section, if it is so idiosyncratic and implausible in motive or means that conscientious experts, familiar with the industry, would not take it into account in prescribing a safety program, nor is misconduct preventable if its elimination would require methods of hiring, training, monitoring, or sanctioning workers which are either so untested or so expensive that safety experts would substantially concur in thinking the methods infeasible. National Realty & Const. Co., Inc. v. Occupational Safety and Health Review Commission, 1973, 489 F.2d 1257, 160 U.S.App.D.C. 133.

duty to eliminate all foreseeable and preventable hazards. Shimp v. New Jersey Bell Tel. Co., 1976, 368 A.2d 408, 145 N.J.Super. 516.

49.   —— Employee misconduct

Lineman/supervisor's conduct was not reasonably foreseeable to, or preventable by, power company, where power company had demonstrated good faith in its efforts to comply with regulations enumerated by this chapter governing work near power lines, had developed excellent overall safety program, had sponsored linemen training sessions and distributed technical information dealing specifically with subject of grounding, and supervisor, who was electrocuted after failing to follow proper safety procedure, was extremely safety-conscious with unblemished safety record; thus, power company was not liable for violation of this chapter based on lineman/supervisor's failure to comply with regulation. Pennsylvania Power & Light Co. v. Occupational Safety and Health Review Com'n, C.A.3, 1984, 737 F.2d 350.

When corporate employer entrusts to a supervisory employee its duty to assure employee compliance with safety standards, it is reasonable to charge the employer with the supervisor's knowledge, actual or constructive, of noncomplying conduct by a subordinate and, upon a showing of the supervisor's knowledge, it is not unreasonable to require the employer to defend a charge of a serious violation by showing that the failure to prevent violations by subordinates was un-

In addition to using U.S.C.A. pamphlets to update your U.S.C.A. research, you also may use the paperbound *United States Code Congressional and Administrative News* (U.S.C.C.A.N.) pamphlets published by West. These pamphlets are issued monthly, so they may sometimes bring you more up-to-date than U.S.C.A. itself. U.S.C.C.A.N. contains the texts of new laws and amendments to laws in public law number order. You may determine if a particular law has been amended by checking Table 3 in the most recent issue of U.S.C.C.A.N. See Illustration 7-12 on page 257. (The tables in each of the issues of U.S.C.C.A.N. are cumulative, even though the text is not.) Table 3 lists, in code section order, United States Code titles and sections that have been changed by recently enacted legislation, and gives a citation to the corresponding public law that makes the change. This Table does not show any amendments to or repeals of 29 U.S.C.A. § 654.

To summarize: To complete your research using U.S.C.A., you must check the following:

(1) the appropriate bound volume,
(2) the pocket part or supplementary pamphlet to the bound volume, and
(3) the noncumulative U.S.C.A. pamphlets that supplement the pocket parts, or *United States Code Congressional and Administrative News,* or both.

Citation Note: Recall that you must cite to the official code, rather than an unofficial code, if the material appears in the official code. Citations to U.S.C.A. are similar to those to U.S.C. If you are citing a section or sections that appear in the main volume, as well as an amendment that appears in a supplement, you must cite both the main volume and the supplement. *See* Rule 3.2(c) in *The Bluebook.* For example, section 666 of OSHA would be cited as 29 U.S.C.A. § 666 (West 1985 & Supp. 1991) because the text of the statute appearing in the 1985 bound volume was altered by a public law reported in the 1991 supplement. If the cited material is found only in the supplement, delete the publication date for the bound volume. Citations to unofficial codes include the name of the publisher in the parenthetical. *See* Rule 12.3(d).

(iii) Indexes and Tables

In U.S.C.A., you can use all of the research approaches you used in U.S.C.:

(1) the index approach
(2) the title outline approach
(3) the popular name approach
(4) the conversion table approach

Again, the index approach is especially useful. U.S.C.A. has a multi-volume General Index that is issued annually, so it is very up-to-date. In addition, each U.S.C.A. title has an individual title index, which is usually located in the last volume of the title. The title index refers only to material in the main volumes of the title. It may be less up-to-date than the General Index, which includes material in the pocket parts.

The last volume of the General Index contains the "Popular Name Acts" table for all titles. In addition, at the beginning of each volume containing the text of statutes, you will find a table of the "Popular Name Acts" included in that title. The "Popular Name Acts" table in the General Index may be more useful than the "Popular Name Acts" tables in the statute volumes because the table in the General Index is updated more frequently.

ILLUSTRATION 7-12. Table of Code Sections Amended, Repealed, and New, [No. 10] U.S.C.C.A.N. [38], [58] (Dec. 1991).

257

Table 3

U.S. CODE
AND
U.S. CODE ANNOTATED SECTIONS AMENDED, REPEALED, NEW, ETC.
102nd CONGRESS—1st SESSION

The pagination of the Public Laws of this Session contained in the 1991 U.S. Code Congressional and Administrative News is identical with Volume 105 U.S. Statutes at Large. In this table a page reference to "8", for example, will be paged as "105 STAT. 8" in this service and in Volume 105 U.S. Statutes at Large.

U.S. Code and U.S.C.A.		1991–102nd Cong.		105 Stat. at Large and 1991 Cong. News
Title	Sec.	P.L. 102–	Sec.	Page
2	31 nt	90	6(c)	451
	31-1	90	6(c)	451
	31-2(a)(1)	90	314(c)(1) to (3)	470
	31-2(a)(2)	90	314(c)(2)	470
	31-2(a)(2)(B)	90	314(c)(4)	470
	31-2(a)(3)	90	314(c)(1), (2)	470
	31-2(a)(3)(A)	90	314(c)(5)	470
	31-2(a)(3)(B)	90	314(c)(5)	470
	31-2(a)(3)(C)	90	314(c)(5)	470
	31-2(a)(4)	90	314(c)(1), (2)	470
	31-2(a)(5)	90	314(c)(2)	470
	31-2(a)(6)	90	314(c)(2)	470
	31-2(a)(7)	90	314(c)(2)	470
	524(c)(9)(C)	140	112(7)	796
	524(c)(9)(E)	27	101	135
		140	112(8)	796
	527 nts	140	—	784
	533 nts	140	102(b)(4), (5)	793
	589a(b)(2)	140	111(b)(1)	795
	589a(b)(5)	140	111(b)(2)	795
	589a(f)	140	111(c)	795
	589a nt	140	111	795
	994 nt	141	632	876
	1821 nt	27	102	136
	1913 nt	140	303	810
	1930(a)(3)	140	111(a)(1)	795
	1930(a)(6)	140	111(a)(2)	795
	7463	40	402(b)(1)	238
29	701 nt	52	1	260
	720(b)(1)(A)	52	2(a)(1)(A)	260
	720(b)(1)(B)	52	2(a)(1)(B)	260
	720(b)(1)(C)	52	2(a)(1)(C)	260
	720(b)(2)	52	2(b)(1)	260
	720(d)(1)(B)	52	2(a)(2)	260
	721(a)(11)	54	13(k)(1)(A)	276
		119	26(e)	607

U.S.C.A. has both of the conversion tables you consulted in U.S.C. It does not have an Internal Cross Reference Table. You will find the conversion tables in bound volumes marked "Tables." These tables are updated by both bound supplement volumes and pamphlets. They are used like the U.S.C. tables discussed earlier.

(c) United States Code Service (U.S.C.S.)

U.S.C.S. is published by Lawyers Cooperative Publishing. Like U.S.C.A., U.S.C.S. supplements the text of each section of the code with annotations. To locate statutes in U.S.C.S., you can use the same research approaches used in the other codes (the index approach, the title outline approach, the conversion table approach, and the popular name table approach). As you will learn, your choice between the two sets of annotated statutes should be based on the nature of the information you want to gain from your research.

(i) Annotations

Illustration 7-13 on pages 259-262 shows United States Code title 29, § 654 in U.S.C.S. Although § 654 does not, some statutory sections in U.S.C.S. have portions of the text placed in brackets. Keep in mind that such portions are not part of the statute and have been added by the publisher, usually to show the location of various session law sections in the code. Thus, you should not include the bracketed portions when quoting the statute.

Look at the editorial material for § 654 in U.S.C.S. Note that U.S.C.S. provides basic legislative history information, such as the statute's date of enactment and public law number, as do U.S.C. and U.S.C.A. Focus on the "Research Guide." You will notice that U.S.C.S. includes research sources not mentioned in U.S.C.A. That is because U.S.C.S. focuses on sources published by Lawyers Cooperative Publishing, just as U.S.C.A. focuses on research sources published by West Publishing Company.

Another difference between U.S.C.S. and U.S.C.A. is in the organization and indexing of the case annotations. As you may recall from Illustration 7-11 at pages 253-254, U.S.C.A. uses alphabetical topic indexes. U.S.C.S. uses detailed topic outlines. See Illustration 7-13 at pages 260-261.

There also are differences between U.S.C.S. and U.S.C.A. in the content and coverage of the annotations. While West tries to be comprehensive in its coverage of court case annotations, U.S.C.S. aims to be selective, excluding annotations to cases its editors judge obsolete, insignificant, or repetitive. However, U.S.C.S. includes more annotations of administrative agency decisions than does U.S.C.A.

(ii) Supplements

U.S.C.S. is updated by replacement volumes and pocket parts or paper supplements. These, in turn, are further updated by the quarterly *Cumulative Later Case and Statutory Service* (C.L.C.S.S.). C.L.C.S.S. contains the same type of material found in the main volumes and pocket parts, and the material is arranged the same way—by title and section numbers.

C.L.C.S.S. is, in turn, updated by *U.S.C.S. Advance*. This service is a monthly compilation of the texts of slip laws and other legislative and executive branch issuances. The slip laws are arranged in public law number order. Unlike C.L.C.S.S., *U.S.C.S. Advance* does not contain new annotations, but it does contain the statutory changes that occurred after the publication of the last C.L.C.S.S. You will most likely use *U.S.C.S. Advance* in one or more of the following ways: (1) by turning directly to a new public law for which you

ILLUSTRATION 7-13. 29 U.S.C.S. § 654 (Law. Coop. 1990). 259

OCCUPATIONAL SAFETY AND HEALTH   **29 USCS § 654**

§ 654. Duties of employers and employees

(a) Each employer—

(1) shall furnish to each of his employees employment and a place of employment which are free from recognized hazards that are causing or are likely to cause death or serious physical harm to his employees;

(2) shall comply with occupational safety and health standards promulgated under this Act.

(b) Each employee shall comply with occupational safety and health standards and all rules, regulations, and orders issued pursuant to this Act which are applicable to his own actions and conduct.

(Dec. 29, 1970, P. L. 91-596, § 5, 84 Stat. 1593.)

HISTORY; ANCILLARY LAWS AND DIRECTIVES

References in text:

"This Act", referred to in this section, is Act Dec. 29, 1970, P. L. 91-596, 84 Stat. 1590, popularly known as the Occupational Safety and Health Act of 1970, which appears generally as 29 USCS §§ 651 et seq. For full classification of this Act, consult USCS Tables volumes.

Effective date of section:

For the effective date of this section, see the Other provisions note to 29 USCS § 651.

CROSS REFERENCES

USCS Administrative Rules, OSHRC, 29 CFR Part 2200.
This section is referred to in 29 USCS §§ 658, 666.

RESEARCH GUIDE

Federal Procedure L Ed:

17 Fed Proc L Ed, Health, Education, and Welfare §§ 42:1085, 1260.

Am Jur:

2 Am Jur 2d, Administrative Law § 650.

61 Am Jur 2d, Plant and Job Safety—OSHA and State Laws §§ 1–3, 9, 21, 25, 26, 31, 34–38, 40, 43, 57, 58, 67, 78, 82, 88, 101, 102, 106, 112, 124.

Forms:

10A Fed Procedural Forms L Ed, Health, Education, and Welfare § 37:112.

16 Am Jur Pl & Pr Forms (Rev), Labor and Labor Relations, Forms 381, 382, 402–404.

American Law of Products Liability 3d:

4 Am Law Prod Liab 3d, Consumer Product Safety Laws § 62:7.

RIA Coordinators:

15 RIA Employment Coord, Employer Requirements ¶¶ WS-11,072; 13,802; 13,803.

29 USCS § 654 LABOR

15 RIA Employment Coord, Agency and Court Proceedings ¶ WS-15,212.

Annotations:

Economic feasibility as factor affecting validity of, or obligation of compliance with, standards established under Occupational Safety and Health Act (29 USCS § 651 et seq.). 68 ALR Fed 732.

Prohibition of discrimination against, or discharge of, employee because of exercise of right afforded by Occupational Safety and Health Act, under § 11(c)(1) of the Act (29 USCS § 660(c)(1)). 66 ALR Fed 650.

Participation by Occupational Safety and Health Review Commission as party in proceedings for judicial review of its decision. 65 ALR Fed 599.

OSHA violation by employer or third party as providing cause of action for employee. 35 ALR Fed 461.

Who is "Employer" for purposes of Occupational Safety and Health Act (29 USCS §§ 651 et seq.). 27 ALR Fed 943.

Right of employee to injunction preventing employer from exposing employee to tobacco smoke in workplace. 37 ALR4th 480.

Law Review Articles:

VanderWaerdt, Resolving the Conflict Between Hazardous Substances in the Workplace and Equal Employment Opportunity. 21 Am Bus L J 157, Summer, 1983.

Rader, Smotherman, and Ehlke, How to Handle an OSHA Case: An Employer's Rights and Options. 33 Baylor L Rev 493, Summer, 1981.

Gombar, OSHA's General Duty Clause. 9 Barrister 25, Winter, 1982.

38

grams: Implications and ~~...~~ 779, Summer, 1981.

Swinton, Regulating Reproductive Hazards in the Workplace: Balancing Equality and Health. 33 University of Toronto L J 45, Winter, 1983.

Employee Medical Records and the Constitutional Right to Privacy. 38 Washington and Lee L Rev 1267, Fall 1981.

INTERPRETIVE NOTES AND DECISIONS

I. IN GENERAL

1. Promulgation of standards
2. Reservation of place for additional regulations
3. Construction of standards
4. Application of standards
5. —Maritime employment
6. Constitutionality of standards
7. Inspection methods
8. Persons responsible
9. —Dissolved corporation
10. —Joint enterprise
11. —Lessor of equipment
12. —Principal contractor
13. —Subcontractor
14. — —Bringing hazard to prime contractor's attention
15. —Responsibility for employee noncompliance
16. Imputation of knowledge
17. Number of citations
18. Occurrence of accident as establishing violation
19. Necessity of accident to establish violation
20. Necessity of employee exposure to establish violation
21. Record keeping requirements
22. Amendment of citation

39

ILLUSTRATION 7-13. *(continued)* 261

29 USCS § 654

29 USCS § 654, n 128

128. — —Pits

Regulation (29 CFR § 1910.22(c)) was applicable to bus company's maintenance pits since pits were situated in walking and working surface at permanent place of employment and were open as opposed to covered except when there was bus over them. Greyhound Lines-West v Marshall (1978, CA9) 575 F2d 759.

Standard [29 CFR 1926.500(b)(8)] requiring that floor holes into which persons can accidentally walk shall be guarded by railing or cover, is limited in application to holes of such size that employees could accidentally walk into such holes, and consequently employer charged with violation of this standard need not deny existence of unguarded floor holes per se, but it is enough that he denies existence of unguarded floor holes which are of type that require guarding under standard. W. C. Sivers Co. (1972) OSHRC Docket No. 239, 1973–1974 CCH OSHD ¶ 17792.

Interstate motor carrier violated standard [29 CFR 1910.22(c)] requiring covers and/or guardrails to protect personnel from hazards of open pits, tanks, vats, ditches, etc., where it failed to provide guardrails or covers for its four service pits (100 feet long, 31 inches wide, 4 feet deep), even though there was evidence of low level of gravity type hazards at pits, because standard assumes existence of hazard with regard to open pits and does not require that hazard be proven before noncompliance with its terms is established. Lee Way Motor Freight, Inc. (1974) OSHRC Docket No. 1105, 1973–1974 CCH OSHD ¶ 17693.

Standard [29 CFR § 1910.22(c)] requiring covers and/or guardrails to protect personnel from hazards of open pits did not require that hazard be shown to establish violation, rather it was sufficient to show that pit was not covered as required to establish violation; however since hazard presented by failure to provide cover for pit in cold steel mill in which electric coil buggy operated was trifling in view of precautions of providing non-skid shoes and all-grip floor plates and three foot fall distance involved, charge would be modified to de minimis and no penalty would be assessed. National Rolling Mill Co. (1976) OSHRC Docket No. 7987.

Standard (29 CFR § 1910.22(c)) requiring guarding of open pits is not unenforceably vague; standard specifically apprises employer of hazard addressed and what is required to achieve compliance—greater specificity is not required; standard need not specify particular methods of compliance nor require single uniform method of abatement. Greyhound Lines, Inc. (1977) OSHRC Docket No. 76-2334.

Requirement that floor holes "into which persons can accidently walk" be guarded (29 CFR §§ 1910.23(a)(8), 1926.500(b)(8)) does not apply only to holes through which persons can fall. Bechtel Power Corp. (1979) OSHRC Docket No. 13832.

Employer was properly cited for willful violation of 29 CFR § 1910.22(c) in failing to provide guardrails around vats of molten zinc where employer had been previously cited under same standard for failure to have guardrails around galvanizing kettles and acid tanks and was thus aware of requirements of standard and employer's belief that guardrails would make certain operations impossible or create greater hazard, however "sincere," could not be considered "good-faith" belief since employer failed to exercise reasonable diligence to find alternative protection for employees. Acme Fence & Iron Co. (1980) OSHRC Docket No. 78-0982.

129. —Safety lines and belts

Terms "lifeline" and "lanyard" have distinct meanings under OSHA regulations; construction company violated standard requiring use of lifeline (29 CFR § 1926.451(1)(4)) even though employee used lanyard. Fluor Constructors, Inc. v Occupational Safety & Health Review Com. (1988, CA6) 861 F2d 936, 13 BNA OSHC 1956, 1988 CCH OSHD ¶ 28350.

Construction industry personal protective equipment standard (29 CFR § 1926.28(a)) properly can be read to require use of tied-off safety belts where employee is exposed to falling hazard. PPG Industries, Inc. (1977) OSHRC Docket No. 15426.

Prima facie violation of 29 CFR § 1926.105(a) is established if employees are subject to falls of more than 25 feet and none of devices listed in standard are used; complete failure to use safety belts is not excused simply because they cannot be tied off in ideal manner. Sierra Constr. Corp. (1978) OSHRC Docket No. 13638.

Requirement of standard (29 CFR § 1926.556(b)(2)(v)) that tied off body belt be worn when "working" from aerial lift includes act of being transported in aerial lift to or from work level. Salah & Pecci Constr. Co. (1978) OSHRC Docket No. 15769.

Employer can be found in violation of 29 CFR § 1926.28(a) for failing to require wearing of tied-off safety belts even if belts cannot be tied off in ideal manner; employer is not excused from compliance with § 1926.28(a) merely because it is not possible to secure lifelines as required by 29 CFR § 1926.104(b) or to limit length of lanyards as required by 29 CFR § 1926.104(d). Valley Roofing Corp. (1978) OSHRC Docket No. 15800.

Standard at 29 CFR § 1926.451(u)(3) is directed at separate fall hazard associated with have a citation, (2) by using the subject index, or (3) by checking the table called "Code Sections Added, Amended, Repealed, or Otherwise Affected" to see if the statutory section you are researching has been changed recently. Although the textual material in *U.S.C.S. Advance* is not cumulative, the tables and index are cumulative. Therefore, consult the tables and index only in the most recent issue of *U.S.C.S. Advance.*

Thus, to complete your research using U.S.C.S., you must check the following:

(1) the appropriate bound volume,
(2) the pocket part or paper supplement to the bound volume,
(3) the *Cumulative Later Case and Statutory Service,* and
(4) *U.S.C.S. Advance.*

(iii) Indexes and Tables

U.S.C.S. has a multi-volume hardbound General Index, which is updated by a looseleaf *General Index Update Service.* It is important that you check the looseleaf update. In addition, an individual index to each title appears at the end of that title.

Like U.S.C. and U.S.C.A., U.S.C.S. includes conversion tables for Revised Titles and Statutes at Large. In addition, the U.S.C.S. "Tables" volumes also include Tables of Popular Names.

(d) Choosing between U.S.C.A. and U.S.C.S.

U.S.C.A. and U.S.C.S. differ in several respects that may be important for your research. For example, the text of statutes in U.S.C.S. is drawn from *Statutes at Large* while that in U.S.C.A. is drawn from U.S.C. This means that the U.S.C.S. text is precisely that enacted by Congress. On rare occasions U.S.C. may reprint a statute incorrectly and this difference may become important. Also, U.S.C.S. includes annotations for uncodified federal enactments, such as treaties, presidential proclamations, and uncodified laws and resolutions, while U.S.C.A. does not.

Your choice between U.S.C.A. and U.S.C.S. may also be based partly on personal preference. For example, if you want to locate a reference to West's Topics and Key Numbers or to West's legal encyclopedia, C.J.S., you should choose U.S.C.A. However, if you would rather locate A.L.R. annotations, Am. Jur. references, or other sources in the Lawyers Cooperative Publishing system, U.S.C.S. is the better choice. Because each publisher's system includes information not provided by the other, you will probably want to use both U.S.C.A. and U.S.C.S. for most federal statutory research.

Citation Note: When does one cite U.S.C., U.S.C.A., U.S.C.S., or *Statutes at Large?* Rule 12.2.1 in *The Bluebook* dictates the following order of preference (subject to the exceptions in Rule 12.2.2): (1) U.S.C. (current official code); (2) U.S.C.A. or U.S.C.S. (a current unofficial code); and (3) Stat. (official session laws). Thus, you would cite to the current code for statutes currently in force and even those statutes already repealed, if they still appear in the current code. You would not cite an unofficial code unless the section you are citing has been amended so recently that its current text is available only in a more recent unofficial code or its supplement. Session laws are usually cited for historical reasons— for example, you wish to cite the original version of the act or the fact of legislative enactment—because the original act does not appear verbatim in the current code. (This order of citation preference also applies at the state level.)

(4) State Codes

Section 667 of title 29 of the United States Code allows a state to assume responsibility for the development and enforcement of occupational safety and health standards otherwise regulated by federal law if the state submits a plan that is approved by the secretary of labor. Therefore, you must research state law to determine if it applies to Selleck's research situation.

All states have subject compilations of state laws that are updated periodically. These statutory compilations are variously called "Statutes," "Revisions," "Codes," "Compilations," and other terms. While all state codes use an organizational structure based on subject matter, the numbering schemes associated with this structure vary considerably from state to state. Some states, such as Connecticut, use a title and section format similar to U.S.C. Others, such as Indiana, use a title-article-chapter-section format. Still others, such as Minnesota, use a system of whole numbers and decimals to identify chapters and sections.

Many jurisdictions have both official and unofficial codes. Consult Table T.1 in *The Bluebook* for a list of the available codes for each state. Unofficial codes follow the same numbering schemes as the official code. Some state codes are annotated; some are unannotated. Like U.S.C.A. and U.S.C.S., annotated state codes supplement the text of a state statute with references to cases and other sources that have referred to or interpreted that particular statute. They also provide information relating to the statute's legislative history and references to related research sources. You should become familiar with any annotated codes used in your jurisdiction. Pay particular attention to the type of information, in addition to case digests, provided by the annotations and references. Also note the frequency of updates through either pocket parts, paper pamphlets, or other supplements, such as an interim annotation service that updates pocket parts.

> ***Citation Note:*** Rule 12 in *The Bluebook* applies to citations of state as well as federal statutes. Table T.1 in *The Bluebook* provides guidance about how to cite compilations of state statutes.

All state codes contain a subject matter index, a topic outline, or both to assist you in locating topics. Most state codes also have conversion tables similar to those in U.S.C. These tables are essential for tracking statutes that may have appeared in older editions of the code or for converting a session law citation to a code citation.

If Selleck's research situation had arisen in Minnesota, you could find Minnesota's Occupational Safety and Health Act of 1973 by consulting the subject index to either *Minnesota Statutes* or *Minnesota Statutes Annotated.* Reading that statute, you would find (1) that the Minnesota law has an employers' duty clause similar to the federal clause; (2) that the Minnesota law, like the federal law, requires that employees comply with occupational safety and health standards; and (3) that the Minnesota law, like the federal law, provides for the issuance of citations only to employers. *See* Minn. Stat. §§ 182.653, 182.654, 182.666 (1990). Illustration 7-14 on pages 265-267 shows § 182.654. By using the annotated statutes and checking all the related sections, you would find cross-references to the related state administrative rules, which you would check. Unfortunately, the "Notes of Decisions" to these statutory sections show no case on point. You would, therefore, use the federal annotations for assistance, since the Minnesota statute is patterned after federal law and must provide at least as much protection as federal law.

The authority of state codes varies from jurisdiction to jurisdiction. In some states the original session laws are the final official authority for statutory language if there is a conflict between the language of the code and the language of the session law. You should determine whether your state recognizes the state code or its session laws as the primary source for statutory language. You will most likely find a statute that governs the matter.

Sources resembling statutes exist at levels of government lower than the federal and state governments. For instance, a municipality may be established under a "charter" and its governing body (a city council, for example) may promulgate ordinances. These sources are primary authority. Some jurisdictions publish these sources; some do not. Each jurisdiction has its own system (or lack of one). Check with the city clerk or a similar official about how to research the law for a particular local government unit.

5. *Shepard's* Statutory Citators

Shepard's United States Citations and *Shepard's* state citators include statute editions. These statute editions treat statutes in much the same manner as the case editions treat cases. Cited sources in *Shepard's Citations,* Statute

ILLUSTRATION 7-14. Minn. Stat. Ann. § 182.654 (West Supp. 1992).

182.654. Rights and duties of employees

Subdivision 1. Rights and duties of employees include but are not limited to those specified in this section.

Subd. 2. Each employee shall comply with occupational safety and health standards and all rules and orders issued pursuant to this chapter which are applicable to the employee's own actions and conduct.

Subd. 3. Any employee or association of employees is entitled to participate in the development, revision and revocation of standards by submission of comments on proposed standards, participation in hearings on proposed standards, or by requesting the development of standards on a given issue, under section 182.655.

Subd. 4. Each employee or an authorized representative shall be notified by an employer of any application for a temporary order granting the employer a variance from any provision of this chapter or standard or rule promulgated pursuant to this chapter.

Subd. 5. The employee representative shall be given the opportunity to participate in any hearing which concerns an application by an employer for a variance from a standard promulgated under this chapter.

Subd. 6. Any employee who may be adversely affected by a standard or variance issued pursuant to section 182.655 may file a petition stating a position with regard to proposed standard or variance with the commissioner.

Subd. 7. An employee who has been exposed or is being exposed to hazardous substances or harmful physical agents in concentrations or at levels in excess of that provided for by an applicable standard shall be provided by the employer with the opportunities provided in section 182.655, subdivision 10a.

Subd. 8. Subject to rules issued pursuant to this chapter any employee or authorized representative of employees has the right to request an inspection and to consult with the commissioner at the time of the physical inspection of any workplace as provided in section 182.659.

198

OCCUPATIONAL SAFETY AND HEALTH   § 182.654

Subd. 9. No employee shall be discharged or in any way discriminated against because such employee has filed any complaint or instituted or caused to be instituted any proceeding or inspection under or related to this chapter or has testified or is about to testify in any such proceeding or because of the exercise by such employee on behalf of the employee or others of any right afforded by this chapter. Discriminatory acts are subject to the sanctions contained in section 182.669.

Subd. 10. An employee, except an employee employed in a farming operation with ten or fewer employees and no temporary labor camp, or the designated representative of the employee has the right to request and receive from the employer, within a reasonable period of time, access to information the employer is required to provide the employee under section 182.653, subdivisions 4b, 4c, 4d, or 4e. For the purposes of this subdivision and section 182.668, subdivision 5, "designated representative" means a labor organization, as defined in section 179.01, subdivision 6, that represents employees under a valid collective bargaining agreement, or another employee whom an employee or former employee has authorized, in writing, to exercise the employee's rights under this chapter.

Every employee employed in a farming operation with ten or fewer employees and no temporary labor camp, and any agricultural employee association or union representing that employee, shall have the right, upon request, to receive from their employer, within a reasonable period of time, any information on a label that is required by any federal or state health and safety law to be on the container of any substance or chemical to which the employee is routinely exposed.

Subd. 11. An employee acting in good faith has the right to refuse to work under conditions which the employee reasonably believes present an imminent danger of death or serious physical harm to the employee.

A reasonable belief of imminent danger of death or serious physical harm includes but is not limited to a reasonable belief of the employee that the employee has been assigned to work in an unsafe or unhealthful manner with a hazardous substance, harmful physical agent or infectious agent.

An employer may not discriminate against an employee for a good faith refusal to perform assigned tasks if the employee has requested that the employer correct the hazardous conditions but the conditions remain uncorrected.

An employee who has refused in good faith to perform assigned tasks and who has not been reassigned to other tasks by the employer shall, in addition to retaining a right to continued employment, receive pay for the tasks which would have been performed if (1) the employee requests the commissioner to inspect and determine the nature of the hazardous condition, and (2) the commissioner determines that the employee, by performing the assigned tasks, would have been placed in imminent danger of death or serious physical harm.

Laws 1973, c. 732, § 5. Amended by Laws 1983, c. 216, art. 1, § 88; Laws 1983, c. 316, §§ 15, 16, eff. Jan. 1, 1984; Laws 1983, c. 316, § 17, eff. July 1, 1984; Laws 1983, c. 316, § 29, eff. June 15, 1983; Laws 1984, c. 431, § 4, eff. Aug. 1, 1984; Laws 1985, c. 130, § 7; Laws 1985, c. 248, § 70; Laws 1986, c. 444.

Historical and Statutory Notes

1983 Amendment. Laws 1983, c. 316, §§ 15 to 17, substituted "An employee" for "Any employee", substituted "hazardous substances" for "toxic materials", substituted "an applicable standard" for "any applicable standard", substituted "the employer" for "his employer", and "subdivision 10a" for "subdivision 10" in subd. 7, effective January 1, 1984. Added subd. 10, effective January 1, 1984, and subd. 11, effective July 1, 1984.

1984 Amendment. Added the fifth paragraph in subd. 11.

1985 Amendment. Rewrote subd. 11, which prior thereto read:

"An employee acting in good faith has the right to refuse to work under conditions which the employee reasonably believes present an imminent danger of death or serious physical harm to the employee.

"A reasonable belief of imminent danger of death or serious physical harm includes but is not limited to a reasonable belief of the employee that the employee has been assigned to work with a hazardous substance, harmful physical agent or infectious agent under conditions which are inconsistent with the training or information provided by the employer pursuant to section 182.653, subdivision 4b, clauses (g) or (h), section 182.653, subdivision 4c, clause (f), section 182.-

ILLUSTRATION 7-14. *(continued)*   267

653, subdivision 4d, section 182.653, subdivision 4e, section 182.653, subdivision 4f, or section 182.654, subdivision 10.

"An employer may not discriminate against an employee for a good faith refusal to perform assigned tasks if the employee has requested that the employer correct the hazardous conditions but the conditions remain uncorrected.

"An employee who has refused in good faith to perform assigned tasks and who has not been reassigned to other tasks by the employer shall, in addition to retaining a right to continued employment, receive pay for the tasks which would have been performed if (1) the employee requests the commissioner to inspect and determine the nature of the hazardous condition, and (2) the commissioner determines that the employee, by performing the assigned tasks, would have been placed in imminent danger of death or serious physical harm; or (3) the employee requests the commissioner to inspect and determine if a hazardous condition exists, and (4) the commissioner determines that the employer has failed to provide the training required under section 182.653, subdivision 4b, 4c, 4d, 4e, or 4f prior to the employee's initial assignment to a workplace where the employee may be routinely exposed to a hazardous substance or harmful physical agent and the employer has failed to provide the information required under section 182.653, subdivision 4b, 4c, 4d, 4e, or 4f after a request pursuant to section 182.654, subdivision 10 within a reasonable period of time, but not to exceed 24 hours, of the request.

"Nothing in this subdivision shall give a technically qualified individual who elects to participate in the training required under section 182.-

653, subdivisions 4b, 4c, or 4f, the right to refuse to work as provided under this subdivision because his or her employer has failed to provide a training program required under those subdivisions."

1986 Amendment. Laws 1986, c. 444, § 1, removed gender specific references applicable to human beings throughout Minn.Stats. by adopting by reference proposed amendments for such revision prepared by the revisor of statutes pursuant to Laws 1984, c. 480, § 21, and certified and filed with the secretary of state on Jan. 24, 1986. Section 3 of Laws 1986, c. 444, provides that the amendments "do not change the substance of the statutes amended."

Notes of Decisions
Compliance with safety and health standards
    1

---

1. Compliance with safety and health standards

Evidence supported administrative determination that employee's remelting barrel of contaminated scraps during state safety inspection was motivated by desire to call attention to safety concerns, rather than merely act of disgruntled employee, and that employee was discharged for demonstrating safety concern to inspector, and not for violating employer's safety rule, in determining whether employer unlawfully discriminated against employee by discharging him for engaging in protected activity. Bohn v. Cedarbrook Engineering Co., App.1988, 422 N.W.2d 534.

Editions, include annotated and unannotated codes, session law sections that are not included in codes, and local ordinances. (Shepard's also publishes *Ordinance Law Annotations.*)

Each statutory citator contains an illustration, such as that found in Illustration 7-15 on page 268, which shows how to read the statutory citations. Cited statutory sections are listed by number in bold print according to the jurisdiction's numbering scheme. Following each cited source are citing sources that may include (1) subsequent legislative enactments; (2) cases; (3) attorney general opinions (for state statutes); (4) legal periodicals; (5) annotations in A.L.R.s and *United States Supreme Court Reports, Lawyers' Edition;* and (6) legal texts published by Shepard's/McGraw-Hill, Inc. Citations to specific subdivisions of the statute follow citations to the statute as a whole. Illustration 7-16 on page 269 shows the *Shepard's* entries for 29 U.S.C. § 654.

Shepard's statutory citators, like the case citators, provide one- or two-letter abbreviations to indicate the effect of some of the citing sources on the cited source. These abbreviations are explained in the beginning of each *Shepard's* volume. See Illustration 7-17 on page 270. The analysis abbreviations used in *Shepard's Citations,* Statute Editions, differ from those used in the case editions.

UNITED STATES CODE
(Illustrative Statute)

**United
States
Code, 1982
Edition**

TITLE 18

§ 700
Ad82St291   **1**

394US604
459US949
22 LE592
74 LE207
89SC1372
103SC267
Cir. DC
445F2d226
511F2d1312
Cir. 1
343FS165   **2**
397FS263
Cir. 2
324FS1278
Cir. 4
313FS49
317FS138
322FS593
Cir. 5
479F2d1177
Cir. 9
462F2d96
C302FS1112
Cir. 11
758F2d1481
560FS546

41 A3 504n   **4**

Subsec. a
415US582
39 LE617
94SC1251
Cir. DC
445F2d226
C454F2d972
Cir. 2
324FS1278
385FS167
Cir. 5
479F2d1179
407FS497
Cir. 9
C462F2d96
Cir. 11
571FS1025   **6**

Subsec. b
Cir. DC
445F2d226
Cir. 9
C462F2d96

Subsec. c
394US598
22 LE588
89SC1369
Cir. 4
322FS585
Cir. 11
739F2d571
571FS1026

Citations to section "§" 700 of Title 18 of the United States Code, 1982 Edition, are shown in the left margin of this page in the same form in which they appear in the United States Code division of this citator. In Shepard's United States Citations, Statute Edition any citation to a section of the United States Code presently in effect is shown as illustrated here and any citation to a section of the United States Code no longer in effect is shown as referring to the section number of the United States Code of the year when that section number last appeared.

Citations to each cited statutory provision are grouped as follows:

1. amendments, repeals, etc. by acts of Congress subsequent to 1974;
2. citations by the United States Supreme Court and the lower federal courts analyzed as to constitutionality or validity;
3. citations in articles in the American Bar Association Journal;
4. citations in annotations of the Lawyers' Edition, United States Supreme Court Reports and of the American Law Reports;
5. citations in legal texts; and
6. citations to specific subdivisions.

For the purpose of illustration only, this grouping has been indicated by bracketing the citations accordingly. It will be noted that as yet there are no citations in groups three and five.

In indicating the legislative and judicial operation of a cited statute, the letter-form abbreviations shown on page xvi are used.

The first citation shown indicates that section 700 of Title 18 was added "Ad" by an act of Congress printed in 82 United States Statutes at Large "St" at page 291.

As shown in group two, the section has been cited by the United States Supreme Court in two cases. The first case is reported in 394 United States Supreme Court Reports "US" 604 as well as in 22 Lawyers' Edition, United States Supreme Court Reports, Second Series "LE" 592 and 89 Supreme Court Reporter "SC" 1372. These references are followed by several citations in lower federal court opinions reported in either the Federal Reporter, Second Series "F2d" or Federal Supplement "FS". One of these cases, as reported in 302 FS 1112, held the section to be constitutional "C". The section was also cited in an annotation "n" of the American Law Reports, Third Series " A3".

Citing references to specific subdivisions of the section are then shown. Subsection "Subsec." a was held constitutional in two lower federal court cases reported in 454 F2d 972 and 462 F2d 96. Subsections b and c are then shown with the specific references made to each.

Citations by the various federal courts other than the United States Supreme Court appear under headings indicating the federal courts or the judicial circuits from which the citations originated. Thus federal court cases decided in the First Circuit appear under the heading "Cir. 1".

ILLUSTRATION 7-16. *Shepard's* Entries for 29 U.S.C. § 654, in 3 *Shepard's United States Citations* [Statute Ed.] 818-19 (1986).

269

UNITED STATES CODE '82 Ed.

Left panel:

591F2d321	522FS783
747F2d300	Cir. 5
423FS802	489F2d120
Cir. 7	512F2d675
516F2d1084	C518F2d997
Cir. 10	528F2d568
511F2d864	659F2d710
40ARF181n	727F2d417
Subd. 3	744F2d1155
Cir. DC	754F2d582
523F2d1161	374FS1350
40ARF183n	386FS1242
Subd. 4	450FS529
Cir. DC	Cir. 6
489F2d1260	593F2d716
523F2d1161	756F2d29
647F2d1234	416FS32
446FS182	524FS1187
Cir. 1	524FS1198
512F2d1148	Cir. 7
Cir. 3	516F2d1084
447FS1196	561F2d83
498FS412	588F2d1187
593FS1154	752F2d274
Cir. 4	Cir. 8
496F2d1323	487F2d439
522FS783	507F2d1041
Cir. 5	558F2d410
507F2d977	566F2d600
583F2d1365	Cir. 9
591F2d319	511F2d1144
659F2d709	540F2d1015
672F2d1238	692F2d647
762F2d447	402FS171
356FS671	Cir. 10
359FS214	531F2d455
386FS1242	660F2d441
387FS627	43ARF163
423FS802	FRCI§ 9.04
429FS905	27ARF943s
433FS914	31ARF554n
Cir. 6	45ARF785s
494F2d334	47ARF814n
593F2d725	50ARF741s
756F2d29	**Subsec. a**
770F2d608	C430US445
408FS599	C51LE469
Cir. 9	C97SC1262
402FS173	Cir. DC
435FS507	593F2d1329
Cir. 10	685F2d667
521F2d629	Cir. 1
79A3968n	505F2d701
27ARF959n	572FS498
35...	Cir. 2
§ 654	581F2d1056
445...	683F2d674
631LE162	Cir. 3
100SC889	502F2d946
Cir. DC	C519F2d1203
520F2d1163	540F2d160
685F2d667	447FS1196
Cir. 1	Cir. 4
576F2d949	504F2d1255
638F2d275	522F2d777
Cir. 2	539F2d337
487F2d343	606F2d451
492F2d1029	442FS197
Cir. 3	Cir. 5
502F2d946	555F2d440
C519F2d1201	563F2d709
540F2d160	576F2d620
600FS612	581F2d509
Cir. 4	591F2d319
504F2d1255	
522F2d778	*Continued*

Right panel:

595F2d311	C503F2d10	698F2d424	576F2d72	708F2d573	503
638F2d814	538F2d562	769F2d652	576F2d625	27ARF943s	C519
486FS28	601F2d718	418FS628	581F2d509	27ARF948n	584
Cir. 6	685F2d880	Cir. 11	583F2d1366	31ARF551s	592
594F2d569	750F2d28	683F2d363	587F2d232	35ARF51n	622
635F2d549	480FS379	689F2d955	588F2d981	38ARF507s	763
728F2d803	728F2d803	748F2d1471	591F2d320	38ARF518n	489
424FS754	C519F2d85	58ABA255	638F2d815	43ARF159s	600
524FS1188	520F2d1036	AgD§ 5.13	638F2d835	43ARF163n	
524FS1199	530F2d1143	27ARF948n	649F2d1162	43ARF175n	522
Cir. 7	27ARF948n	31ARF551s	658F2d1077	45ARF799n	545
588F2d1184	555F2d440	34ARF94n	659F2d710	47ARF814n	714
Cir. 8	581F2d509	35ARF51n	670F2d14	48ARF471n	750
647F2d842	593F2d1366	43ARF175n	671F2d846	**Subsec. b**	542
Cir. 9	593F2d638	45ARF789n	723F2d412	Cir. DC	
511F2d1141	595F2d310	45ARF795n	747F2d295	647F2d1228	487
546F2d282	620F2d98	45ARF799n	486FS620	Cir. 2	512
577F2d536	621F2d758	47ARF816n	Cir. 6	491F2d1340	528
586F2d686	638F2d834	48ARF475n	540F2d1292	581F2d1058	563
Cir. 10	649F2d1164	50ARF741s	585F2d1328	715F2d59	574
511F2d864	658F2d1078	50ARF742n	594F2d569	Cir. 3	581
521F2d629	659F2d710	**Subd. 2**	**Subd. 2**	502F2d947	583
586F2d1343	659F2d1277	C430US447	625F2d728	534F2d543	588
AgL§ 6.42	718F2d1343	C51LE229	629F2d437	Cir. 5	599
FRCI§ 9.05	729F2d319	C97SC1265	649F2d458	528F2d570	657
27ARF946n	356FS670	Cir. DC	709F2d1095	563F2d709	659
41ARF158n	374FS1350	489F2d1261	712F2d1009	390FS999	744
Subd. 1	423FS802	587F2d1304	728F2d804	Cir. 6	374
445US6	424FS959	617F2d647	728F2d816	593F2d716	386
448US691	496FS1183	746F2d896	775F2d144	728F2d803	423
63LE160	Cir. 6	Cir. 1	Cir. 7	Cir. 7	494
65LE1065	579F2d378	512F2d1148	516F2d1081	516F2d1092	550
100SC884	584F2d132	540F2d544	520F2d1011	Cir. 9	
100SC2889	593F2d719	576F2d948	542F2d28	511F2d1145	585
Cir. DC	594F2d569	589F2d81	557F2d608	546F2d282	649
489F2d1257	597F2d79	643F2d894	657F2d120	Cir. 10	500
499F2d470	625F2d731	692F2d819	658F2d546	577F2d129	
617F2d647	630F2d447	764F2d34	674F2d593	577F2d1114	516
645F2d1097	649F2d457	532FS842	683F2d1107	FRCI§ 9.04	520
671F2d645	728F2d803	Cir. 2	Cir. 8	35ARF51n	557
698F2d512	748F2d341	491F2d1340	507F2d1041	**§ 655**	561
C717F2d1420	Cir. 7	513F2d1033	529F2d650	et seq.	589
741F2d445	501F2d1196	526F2d53	548F2d248	Cir. DC	679
Cir. 1	516F2d1081	568F2d902	566F2d596	561F2d915	
493F2d1064	520F2d1011	581F2d1056	570F2d806	Cir. 7	487
512F2d1148	567F2d735	583F2d61	586F2d1243	430FS302	507
540F2d544	589F2d270	683F2d674	590F2d274	13ARF145s	524
599F2d454	589F2d1339	715F2d59	618F2d31	**§§ 655 to 657**	529
643F2d894	632F2d26	Cir. 3	627F2d150	529F2d650	554
653F2d39	674F2d1187	534F2d541	630F2d628	456FS506	570
742F2d14	760F2d784	539F2d961	666F2d318	**§ 655**	583
532FS842	550FS768	576F2d559	722F2d1416	Cir. DC	593
Cir. 2	Cir. 8	607F2d872	Cir. 9	489F2d1261	666
491F2d1340	494F2d461	613F2d1230	511F2d1141	520F2d1163	
495F2d823	501F2d504	625F2d1077	517F2d988	570F2d1035	435
513F2d1033	507F2d1041	737F2d352	518F2d49	581F2d961	545
540F2d69	551F2d1117	447FS1165	530F2d843	617F2d644	
568F2d902	630F2d628	543FS58	575F2d759	627F2d1161	505
581F2d1056	647F2d842	Cir. 4	577F2d535	647F2d1202	510
583F2d63	650F2d935	C503F2d8	596F2d373	673F2d472	531
649F2d97	674F2d690	504F2d1255	607F2d311	756F2d163	577
683F2d674	Cir. 9	522F2d780	616F2d1113	766F2d582	
713F2d920	511F2d1141	538F2d562	641F2d802	768F2d1486	708
715F2d60	517F2d988	545F2d1384	666F2d1269	377FS1302	AgL
Cir. 3	540F2d1014	594F2d397	703F2d1089	485FS847	ARn
502F2d946	556F2d432	601F2d719	437FS875	Cir. 10	FRC
534F2d541	577F2d537	685F2d880	Cir. 10	505F2d701	22AE
573F2d826	579F2d537	727F2d1359	505F2d870	512F2d1148	25AE
C607F2d872	608F2d374	480FS379	511F2d865	Cir. 2	31AE
622F2d1162	437FS874	Cir. 5	577F2d1114	487F2d348	**Su**
622F2d1178	Cir. 10	497F2d230	594F2d1360	492F2d1029	448U
625F2d1078	576F2d810	502F2d31	623F2d156	513F2d1032	452U
713F2d46	577F2d127	528F2d565	734F2d509	583F2d63	65LI
766F2d811	594F2d1360	539F2d387	738F2d399	610F2d80	69LI
447FS1163	597F2d234	555F2d439	769F2d652	Cir. 3	100S
Cir. 4	660F2d441	576F2d42	418FS628	502F2d950	101S
			Cir. 11		

ABBREVIATIONS—ANALYSIS

Form of Statute

Amend.	Amendment		Proc.	Proclamation
App.	Appendix		Pt.	Part
Art.	Article		Res.	Resolution
Ch.	Chapter		§	Section
Cl.	Clause		St.	Statutes at Large
Ex. Ord.	Executive Order		Subch.	Subchapter
H.C.R.	House Concurrent		Subcl.	Subclause
	Resolution		Subd.	Subdivision
No.	Number		Sub ¶	Subparagraph
¶	Paragraph		Subsec.	Subsection
P.L.	Public Law		Vet. Reg.	Veterans' Regulations
Pr.L.	Private Law			

Operation of Statute

Legislative

A	(amended)	Statute amended.
Ad	(added)	New section added.
E	(extended)	Provisions of an existing statute extended in their application to a later statute, or allowance of additional time for performance of duties required by a statute within a limited time.
L	(limited)	Provisions of an existing statute declared not to be extended in their application to a later statute.
R	(repealed)	Abrogation of an existing statute.
Re-en	(re-enacted)	Statute re-enacted.
Rn	(renumbered)	Renumbering of existing sections.
Rp	(repealed in part)	Abrogation of part of an existing statute.
Rs	(repealed and superseded)	Abrogation of an existing statute and substitution of new legislation therefor.
Rv	(revised)	Statute revised.
S	(superseded)	Substitution of new legislation for an existing statute not expressly abrogated.
Sd	(suspended)	Statute suspended.
Sdp	(suspended in part)	Statute suspended in part.
Sg	(supplementing)	New matter added to an existing statute.
Sp	(superseded in part)	Substitution of new legislation for part of an existing statute not expressly abrogated.
Va	(validated)	

Judicial

C	Constitutional.		V	Void or invalid.
U	Unconstitutional.		Va	Valid.
Up	Unconstitutional in part.		Vp	Void or invalid in part.

ABBREVIATIONS—COURTS

Cir. DC–U.S. Court of Appeals, District of Columbia Circuit
Cir. (number)–U.S. Court of Appeals Circuit (number)
Cir. Fed.–U.S. Court of Appeals, Federal Circuit
CCPA–Court of Customs and Patent Appeals

Shepard's aids you in performing the following research functions in statutory research:

(1) locating citations to other sources that have discussed the statute you are researching;

(2) quickly determining, by means of *Shepard's* abbreviations, the impact of some of the citing sources on the cited statute; and

(3) tracking the history of a statute.

As you learned earlier in this chapter, all of these functions are also fulfilled by the annotated codes. *Shepard's* may provide more citations than an annotated code, but its treatment abbreviations do not give you as much information as do the case digest paragraphs in the annotated codes. *Shepard's* may provide new citations more quickly than an annotated code. Thus, you may sometimes wish to use both sources.

6. Statutes on LEXIS and WESTLAW

Just as you can research case law online, so you can research federal and state statutes online through LEXIS and WESTLAW. This section points out the available databases, describes some of the differences between statutory and other databases, suggests some possible searches, and comments on their usefulness as compared to print research.

a. WESTLAW

WESTLAW has four databases for federal statutes: (1) United States Code (USC), (2) United States Code Annotated (USCA), (3) United States Code Annotated Index (USCA-IDX), and (4) United States Public Laws (US-PL). Unless you were looking for a very new law, you would begin federal code research in one of the first three databases. First, you would decide which database you were going to start with, since your search might be different if you were searching an index than if you were doing a full-text search.

Assume that you will try your search first in the USCA-IDX database. Your search may look something like this: [safety /5 belt line harness equipment]. In January 1992, this search retrieved 39 documents (that is, entries) in the USCA-IDX database. If you list the documents retrieved by this search, you will see the main subject heading under which each document (entry) appears in the index. For example, document number 25 in Illustration 7-18 on page 272 directs you to an entry in the main index under the heading "Occupational Safety and Health." If you browse through all of the subheadings under "Occupational Safety and Health," not just the one retrieved by your search, you will find all the relevant statutes for your research situation. See Illustration 7-19 on page 273. (The actual entry retrieved by your search under the subject heading was not relevant. That entry was "National Institute for Occupational Safety and Health"—"Director"—"Study of diving equipment in connection with safety regulation, leasing program on Outer Continental Shelf.")

The same search retrieved 105 documents in WESTLAW'S USC database. See Illustration 7-20 on page 274. Again, by looking at the list of documents retrieved, you may determine those most likely to be useful.

The same search retrieved even more documents in the USCA database because a search in an annotated code database includes a search of the annotations as well as a search of the code text. If you are likely to find your search terms in both a relevant statutory section and in annotations to different sections, it may be more cost-effective to search an unannotated code. On

```
CITATIONS LIST (Page 1)                    Total Documents:  39
Database: USCA-IDX

    1.   US INDEX: AIRPORTS AND LANDING AREAS

    2.   US INDEX: BOARD AND CARE HOMES

    3.   US INDEX: BUREAU OF JUSTICE ASSISTANCE

    4.   US INDEX: CERTIFIED COAL MINE SAFETY EQUIPMENT

    5.   US INDEX: COAL MINES

    6.   US INDEX: COMMISSIONS AND COMMISSIONERS

    7.   US INDEX: CONGRESS

    8.   US INDEX: CONSUMER PRODUCT SAFETY

    9.   US INDEX: DEFINITIONS

   10.   US INDEX: ESTATES AND TRUSTS
```

```
CITATIONS LIST (Page 3)                    Total Documents:  39
Database: USCA-IDX

   21.   US INDEX: MUNICIPAL AGENCIES

   22.   US INDEX: NATIONAL HOUSING

   23.   US INDEX: NATURAL GAS

   24.   US INDEX: NURSING HOMES

   25.   US INDEX: OCCUPATIONAL SAFETY AND HEALTH

   26.   US INDEX: OCEAN THERMAL ENERGY CONVERSION

   27.   US INDEX: OFFICERS AND EMPLOYEES OF GOVERNMENT

   28.   US INDEX: PORTS AND WATERWAYS SAFETY PROGRAM

   29.   US INDEX: RADIO

   30.   US INDEX: RAILROADS
```

ILLUSTRATION 7-19. WESTLAW Document 25 Retrieved by the Search [safety /5 belt line harness equipment] in the USCA-IDX Database.

273

```
  Citation                     Rank(R)          Page(P)         Database   Mode
                               R 25 OF 39       P 1 OF 14       USCA-IDX   T
    US INDEX: OCCUPATIONAL SAFETY AND HEALTH


                             UNITED STATES CODE ANNOTATED
                                   GENERAL INDEX

                   COPR. (c) WEST 1990  No Claim to Orig. Govt. Works

  OCCUPATIONAL SAFETY AND HEALTH

     Text of Act of 1970.  See Popular Name Table
  Administration,
       Administrator, air pollution prevention and control, hazardous air
           pollutants, Chemical Safety and Hazard Investigation Board, report, 42
           USCA § 7412
       Asbestos Hazards School Safety Task Force, representative, 20 USCA § 3602
       Working group membership, safety study.  Firefighters and Firefighting, this
           index
  Administrative law judge, Review Commission, 29 USCA § 661
  Agency, defined, program for Federal employees, 5 USCA § 7902 nt, EON 12196
  Agricultural credit, loans to farmers for purposes of, 7 USCA § 1942
```

```
                              R 25 OF 39      P 3 OF 14       USCA-IDX   P
       US INDEX:  OCCUPATIONAL SAFETY AND HEALTH/ Contracts, -cont'd

     Contracts,
        National Institute, 29 USCA § 671
        Studies, 29 USCA § 669
     Counteracting imminent dangers, procedures, 29 USCA § 662
     Declaration of purpose, 29 USCA § 651
     Definitions, 29 USCA § 652
     Demonstrations, 29 USCA § 669
     Department of HHS, programs for Federal employees, liaison with Secretary of
        Labor, 5 USCA § 7902 nt, EON 12196
     Director, defined, 29 USCA § 652
     Discrimination against employee filing complaint, etc., prohibited, 29 USCA §
        660
     Duties of employers and employees, 29 USCA § 654
     Education of employees, 29 USCA § 670
     Employee, defined, 29 USCA § 652
     Employer, defined, 29 USCA § 652
     Enforcement, citations for violations, 29 USCA § 659
     Established Federal standard.  Standards, post, this heading
     Evaluation, carrying out of State plan, 29 USCA § 667
     Exemptions from provisions of Act, 29 USCA § 665
```

the other hand, sometimes the annotations for a relevant statutory section will contain your search terms, and the section itself will not. A search of USCA, for example, retrieves 29 U.S.C.A. § 654, while a search of USC does not. Thus, the capacity to search the case annotations is very important.

For your research situation, although you will eventually find the relevant statutes through both a book and an online search, a book search is faster and more cost-effective than an online search.

There are some similarities and some differences between searching cases and searching statutes online. One difference is that there are additional

```
CITATIONS LIST (Page 6)                       Total Documents:  105
Database: USC

   21.   29 U.S.C.A. § 668   UNITED STATES CODE ANNOTATED   TITLE 29.   LABOR
CHAPTER 15--OCCUPATIONAL SAFETY AND HEALTH
§ 668. Programs of Federal agencies

   22.   29 U.S.C.A. § 670   UNITED STATES CODE ANNOTATED   TITLE 29.   LABOR
CHAPTER 15--OCCUPATIONAL SAFETY AND HEALTH
§ 670. Training and employee education

   23.   30 U.S.C.A. § 874   UNITED STATES CODE ANNOTATED
TITLE 30.   MINERAL LANDS AND MINING   CHAPTER 22--MINE SAFETY AND HEALTH
SUBCHAPTER III--INTERIM MANDATORY SAFETY STANDARDS FOR UNDERGROUND COAL MINES
§ 874. Hoisting and mantrips

   24.   30 U.S.C.A. § 951   UNITED STATES CODE ANNOTATED
TITLE 30.   MINERAL LANDS AND MINING   CHAPTER 22--MINE SAFETY AND HEALTH
SUBCHAPTER V--ADMINISTRATIVE PROVISIONS   § 951. Studies and research

   25.   33 U.S.C.A. § 1225   UNITED STATES CODE ANNOTATED
TITLE 33.   NAVIGATION AND NAVIGABLE WATERS
CHAPTER 25--PORTS AND WATERWAYS SAFETY PROGRAM   § 1225. Waterfront safety
```

commands available in the statutory databases. The most important commands and their functions are listed below:

Command	Function
RM:	Presents a directory of Related Materials for the statute; Related Materials include, for example, references to related sources and case annotations
UPDATE:	Displays documents that amend or repeal the statutory section you are viewing
ANNOS:	Displays annotations for an unannotated statute you are viewing
REFS:	Displays references to secondary sources related to the unannotated statute you are viewing
GM:	Displays General Materials (major headings) related to the title, subtitle, chapter, or subchapter containing the statute you are viewing

In addition, a "d" (documents in sequence) command allows you to move backward and forward from a statutory section you have retrieved, even if the neighboring sections were not retrieved by your search. This capacity is very important since statutes often exist in related groups. Enter "d" to move forward one document. Use d+ or d−, followed by a number, to move forward or backward by the number you entered.

Statutes, like cases, have fields, but the fields are different. You may identify the fields, as well as obtain search tips and other useful information, by entering the scope command for the statutory database in which you are interested. (If you do not recall the significance of fields, review Chapter 6 at page 217.)

As of January 1992, WESTLAW has annotated code databases for every state except Montana and Nebraska, and for the District of Columbia, Puerto Rico, and the Virgin Islands. It has unannotated code databases for all 50 states, plus the District of Columbia, Puerto Rico, and the Virgin Islands. It has code index databases for 39 states and the District of Columbia. It has legislative service (session law) databases for all 50 states, the District of Columbia, Puerto Rico, and the Virgin Islands. In addition, WESTLAW has all-state databases for its annotated statutes, unannotated statutes, and legislative services. You may generally search state statutes online the same way you search the federal code online.

b.   LEXIS

You may find the statutes available on LEXIS by selecting its CODES library. (Statutes are also available on LEXIS in other libraries, including GENFED, STATES, and the subject libraries.) Illustration 7-21 (below) shows some of the files available in the CODES library. Note especially the ALLCDE (all codes) and ALLALS (all advanced legislative services) files, which allow you to search at once all documents of the specified type that are available on LEXIS. Note, too, the USCODE and PUBLAW files. The USCODE is a combined file that includes the federal code, the Constitution, and public laws. The code is the U.S.C.S. version. LEXIS currently includes the U.S.C.S. annotations for all titles except title 26. LEXIS does not yet have the U.S.C.S. index online but plans to add it.

LEXIS includes the codes of each of the 50 states and an Advance Legislative Service for many states. You may find the description of a file by entering the number to the right of the file. See Illustration 7-22 on page 276 for some of the descriptions.

The best way to learn how to use a statutory database on LEXIS is to obtain a description of that database by using the GUIDE file.

ILLUSTRATION 7-21. LEXIS Screen of Some of the Files in the CODES Library.

```
Please TRANSMIT, separated by commas, the NAMES of the files you want to search.
You may select as many files as you want, including files that do not appear
below, but you must transmit them all at one time.  To see a description of a
file, TRANSMIT its page (PG) number.
              FILES - PAGE 1 of 12 (NEXT PAGE for additional files)

NAME   PG NAME    PG NAME    PG NAME    PG NAME    PG NAME    PG NAME    PG

   -GROUP-- ----------------------STATE CODES-------------------------- -FEDERAL
ALLCDE  1 ALCODE   3 FLCODE 15 KYSTAT 27 MTCODE 39 OHCODE 50 TXCODE 61 USCODE 71
ALLALS  1 AKCODE   4 GACODE 17 LACODE 28 NECODE 40 OKCODE 52 UTCODE 63 PUBLAW 71
STRGTR  1 AZCODE   5 HICODE 18 MECODE 29 NVCODE 42 ORCODE 53 VTCODE 64 CFR    72
STTRCK  2 ARCODE   6 IDCODE 19 MDCODE 30 NHCODE 43 PACODE 54 VACODE 65 FEDREG 72
TRCK90  2 CACODE   7 ILCODE 20 MACODE 31 NJCODE 44 PRCODE 56 VICODE 66 RECORD 72
TRCK91  2 COCODE   9 INCODE 22 MICODE 33 NMCODE 46 RICODE 57 WACODE 67
          CTCODE 11 IACODE 23 MNCODE 35 NYCODE 47 SCCODE 58 WVCODE 68
          DECODE 12 KSCODE 24 MSCODE 37 NCCODE 48 SDCODE 59 WICODE 69
GUIDE   1 DCCODE 14 KYCODE 26 MOCODE 38 NDCODE 49 TNCODE 60 WYCODE 70
========TABLE OF CONTENTS (TRANSMIT .np commands as indicated below)=========
Federal Materials.. .np     State Bill Text......... .np4   International.. .np7
Adv. Legis. Service .np2     Combined Tracking & Text .np5   Specialty files .np8
State Bill Tracking .np3     Administrative Law...... .np6   How To......... .np9
Press Alt-H for Help or Alt-Q to Quit.
```

```
Please TRANSMIT, separated by commas, the NAMES of the files you want to search.
You may select as many files as you want, including files that do not appear
below, but you must transmit them all at one time.  To see the menu page
containing the first file described below, press the TRANSMIT key.
          DESCRIPTIONS - PAGE 1 of 83 (NEXT PAGE for additional files)

NAME    FILE                          NAME    FILE

ALLCDE  All state code files
        contained in this library.    GUIDE   Descriptions of files in the
                                              CODES library.
ALLALS  All Advance Legislative
        Service files contained in
        this library.

STRGTR  -Combined Regulation Tracking
         files for all 50 states, from
         1990 to present.
Press Alt-H for Help or Alt-Q to Quit.
```

```
Please TRANSMIT, separated by commas, the NAMES of the files you want to search.
You may select as many files as you want, including files that do not appear
below, but you must transmit them all at one time.  To see the menu page
containing the first file described below, press the TRANSMIT key.
        DESCRIPTIONS - PAGE 35 of 83 (NEXT PAGE or PREV PAGE for additional files)

NAME    FILE                          NAME    FILE

MNCODE  -Minnesota Statutes *         MNADMN  -Minnesota Rules *
         (Statutes & Constitution incl.         Administrative Code thru 2/4/91
         laws in force through 1991
         Regular Session)             MNTRCK  -MN tracking from 1/1/92
                                               to present. Pending bills
MNALS   -Advance Legislative Service           tracked from introduction to
         1991, 1990 & 1989 Laws complete       enactment or veto. Bill track-
                                               ing files are updated daily.
*Copyright (c) 1990, 1991 Office of the Revisor of Statutes, State of Minne-
 sota (claimed on those portions of the statutes subject to copyright). The
 text appearing in these databases is produced from material provided by the
 Minnesota Revisor of Statutes. Use of this material is subject to the terms
 of federal copyright and other applicable laws.
Press Alt-H for Help or Alt-Q to Quit.
```

```
Please TRANSMIT, separated by commas, the NAMES of the files you want to search.
You may select as many files as you want, including files that do not appear
below, but you must transmit them all at one time.  To see the menu page
containing the first file described below, press the TRANSMIT key.
        DESCRIPTIONS - PAGE 71 of 83 (NEXT PAGE or PREV PAGE for additional files)

NAME    FILE                          NAME    FILE

USCODE  -United States Code Service   BLTRCK  -Bill status of legislation
         (Federal statutes and                Introduced in the 102nd
          constitution)                        Congress.
         -COVERAGE:                   BLTEXT  -Full text of legislation
         TITLES 1-50 current through           in the 102nd Congress.
         P.L. 102-137, apprv. 10/28/91 CMTRPT  -Congressional  Committee
         *TITLE 26 current through             Reports.
         P.L. 102-2, apprv. 1/30/91   BILLS   -Comb. BLTRCK & BLTEXT files.
         -U.S. Public Laws            PUBLAW  -United States Public Laws
         All laws from the 102nd Cong.         Coverage of 102 Cong, 2nd Sess
                                               through P.L. 102-247, 2/24/92
USNAME  -USCS Popular Name Table               Complete 102 Cong. 1st Sess.,
         Current through P.L. 102-243          101 Cong. & 100 Cong. 2nd Sess.
Press Alt-H for Help or Alt-Q to Quit.
```

Shepard's Citations, Statute Editions, are not available online on either LEXIS or WESTLAW as of January 1992.

277

Statutes and
Constitutions:
Searching for
Primary Authority

B. CONSTITUTIONS

Constitutions are documents that describe government powers and limit government authority. For example, they create legislatures and empower them to enact statutes, and they generally describe both the methods by which statutes may be enacted and the limits placed on legislative power over a particular subject matter. Thus, the first amendment to the United States Constitution limits the power of Congress to pass statutes that infringe on the freedom of speech and religion.

The federal government and each of the 50 states have their own constitutions, and local units of government may have similar governing documents, such as municipal charters. Amendments to these documents alter or supplement the original provisions. Several states have had more than one constitution during their history. Thus, thorough constitutional research may require locating not only the present version of a constitution, but also any former versions or amendments that may exist. It may also require looking into the history of the provision. Researching the historical background of constitutions is beyond the scope of this book. If you need to research the historical background of the federal constitution, consult Morris L. Cohen et al., *How to Find the Law* 208-11 (9th ed. 1989).

1. The Text

At both the federal and state levels, statutory code volumes contain the complete text of the applicable constitution, even though the constitution is not technically a part of the code. Thus, the text of the United States Constitution and its amendments can be found in U.S.C., U.S.C.A., and U.S.C.S. Since the United States Constitution is not frequently amended, the current version is not difficult to identify in the most recent editions of the official and unofficial codes.

State constitutions and amendments are published in the state code volumes. (The United States Constitution is often published in the state codes as well.) State constitutions are amended more frequently than the federal Constitution. These amendments require you to take great care in bringing your research up-to-date. You must check pocket parts, supplements, and other updating sources whenever you do state constitutional research. *Shepard's* statute citators may be particularly helpful in this regard. You also may wish to check state session laws for constitutional amendments the legislature has voted to submit to the electorate.

Citation Note: Constitutional citations are governed by Rule 11 of *The Bluebook.* For provisions currently in force, use the abbreviated name of the jurisdiction, "Const.," and identify the provision. An example: U.S. Const. art. I, § 8.

2. Annotations

In both U.S.C.A. and U.S.C.S., the text of the United States Constitution and its amendments is followed by citations to cases and other sources that refer to the Constitution. Annotated state codes contain similar information for their own constitutions and are used like U.S.C.A. and U.S.C.S. to locate cases and other sources that discuss the state constitution in question.

You may wish to examine the constitutional annotations in both U.S.C.A. and U.S.C.S., as well as in your own state's annotated code. Note the differences between the constitutional annotations in the volumes of the two federal annotated codes. Be certain to note the frequency with which the annotations to both the federal and state constitutions are updated by pocket parts or supplements. The pocket parts or supplements will give you the most recent cases interpreting the constitutional provision you are researching.

Another source for annotations to the United States Constitution is a Library of Congress publication, published under the authorization of the United States Senate, entitled *The Constitution of the United States of America.* It is published at approximately ten-year intervals with annual supplements. It includes the text of the Constitution and amendments, together with annotations of the United States Supreme Court decisions that interpret the United States Constitution. You can use this source much like U.S.C.A. or U.S.C.S. to find cases that interpret sections of the Constitution. Because it is a single volume, it can be more convenient to use than the annotated codes. However, because it refers only to United States Supreme Court decisions, it is far more limited in scope than the annotated codes.

3. Research Techniques

Constitutional research involves many of the research tools you have used so far. Where you start depends on your knowledge of constitutional principles. If you are fortunate enough to know the citation to the constitutional provision relevant to your issue, you can go to an annotated code that contains that provision and locate both the text and annotations. However, you most likely will begin your research without knowing which constitutional provision, if any, has a bearing on your problem.

For an introduction to basic constitutional principles, you may wish to seek out encyclopedias or treatises on constitutional law such as the following:

> *Encyclopedia of the American Constitution* (Leonard W. Levy ed., 1986 & Supp. 1991).
> John E. Nowak & Ronald D. Rotunda, *Constitutional Law* (4th ed. 1991).
> Laurence Tribe, *American Constitutional Law* (2d ed. 1988).

In addition to giving you an overview of a topic, treatises can furnish you with citations to other sources. You could find commentary material in any of the following sources in addition to treatises:

(1) law reviews and journals (often an outstanding source of constitutional commentary),
(2) encyclopedias, and
(3) A.L.R. annotations.

Once you know the constitutional citation, you can refer to the initial volumes of both U.S.C.A. and U.S.C.S. that contain the complete unannotated text of the United States Constitution, followed by an annotated version of the Constitution. A similar method may be used in researching state constitutional provisions.

Having the citation to an applicable case greatly expands the research options available to locate other cases and sources:

(1) The text of the case will contain citations to the sources on which the court relied. These sources may include other case precedent, analogous cases, law review commentary, or treatises.
(2) The version of the case in the appropriate West reporter will include the case's Topic and Key Numbers, which allow you access to the West Digest System.
(3) You can Shepardize the case to locate later cases, A.L.R. annotations, and law review articles that have cited the case.

4. Constitutions on LEXIS and WESTLAW

LEXIS and WESTLAW both have the United States Constitution in their databases. LEXIS includes the U.S.C.S. version, except for the annotations of decisions, in its GENFED library, USCNST file. WESTLAW includes the U.S.C.A. annotated version in its USCA database. Both systems also include state constitutions. You search constitutions online just as you search statutes online.

C. LEGISLATIVE HISTORY

1. Introduction

a. What Is Legislative History?

The legislative history of a statute defies easy categorization. Legislative history is not really primary authority; primary authority exists in the statute itself, the cases interpreting it, and agency law created pursuant to it. Nor is legislative history commentary, in the sense that treatises, encyclopedias, and legal periodical articles are commentary. Legislative history is created before and as the statute is created and thus cannot be said to comment on it; furthermore, legislative history is "written" by legislators, not scholars. Nor is legislative history primarily a finding tool. Although one legislative history source may point you to another legislative history source, any guidance for other research that you might receive while researching legislative history is incidental.

Perhaps the best way to look at legislative history is to view it as a unique form of authority—a collection of documents created by the legislative process. A statute's history consists of the views of legislators and other persons interested in the statute, sundry facts about the circumstances giving rise to the enactment of the statute, and steps of legislative procedure. In many ways, legislative history may strike you as a combination of background information and good intentions.

This part focuses on federal legislative history. In most states, researching state legislative history is fairly difficult. Before beginning legislative history research in your state, you would be wise to seek advice and information from your state's legislative reference librarian or consult one of the texts that provide an overview of state legislative history sources, such as Lynn Hellebust, *State Legislative Sourcebook 1991* (1990).

b. Uses of Legislative History

You are most likely to research legislative history for one of two purposes: (1) to monitor the progress of pending legislation that might affect your client's interests or your practice or (2) to determine the legislative intent behind an enacted statute so as to resolve ambiguities created by the words of the statute. This part focuses on the second purpose. However, as you work through this part, you also may wish to consider how the sources you encounter could be used to monitor the status of pending legislation.

Legislative intent is one of the key factors courts and lawyers look to in interpreting ambiguities in statutes. The general rule is that one should resort to legislative history as an aid only when the statute is ambiguous or unclear, but this rule is not always followed. For general principles of statutory construction and the use of legislative history, see 2A Norman J. Singer, *Statutes and Statutory Construction* §§ 48.01-.20 (5th ed. 1992 rev.).

You may find that some courts view arguments based on legislative history with a skeptical eye. This skepticism is due in part to the difficulty of discerning from the mass of statements, reports, and procedural maneuvers that constitute a legislative history just what the legislature really intended in enacting a statute. Legislative history research rests in part on the premise—or fiction—that some of the statements of individual legislators and witnesses shed light on the intent of the legislature as a whole. It also rests on the premise (perhaps more believable) that one can tell something about legislative intent by studying the versions the bill went through on its way to being enacted.

In deciding how to use a statute's legislative history, you should be careful to account for the vagaries of the legislative process. For example, relying on the "extended remarks" of a member of Congress would be imprudent. Extended remarks are not actually made during a congressional debate, but rather are added later to the published transcript of a debate and are rarely read by other members of Congress. (This procedure was challenged in *Gregg v. Barrett,* 771 F.2d 539 (D.C. Cir. 1985), on the grounds it produces a "corrupt" record of congressional actions. The court declined to consider the claim out of deference to Congress.)

You should acquaint yourself thoroughly with the full legislative history of a statute before using selected parts of it. For example, before relying on the testimony of a witness at a legislative hearing, you should determine whether that witness' views were given credence in later debates, and you should consider the testimony of opposing witnesses and the weight given to them.

You also should research whether the legislature considered any related bills prior to enacting the statute you are researching. It may be highly instructive to know what the legislature rejected before it passed the statute you are investigating.

It is equally important that you always examine the legislative history of both the original statute and its amendments. A legislature generally amends a statute to correct a flaw not seen at the time of original enactment, to respond to new and unforeseen problems, or to accommodate changes in public policy. Thus, the legislative history of the original statute may provide indirect guidance as to what the amendment means. And the legislative history of an amendment usually provides invaluable insight into how the legislature came to interpret the original statute, as well as guidance on what the amendment is intended to accomplish.

You soon will discover that some legislative history is itself no less ambiguous than the statute and that the same history may be used to support both sides of a debate. The majority and dissenting opinions in *North Haven*

Board of Education v. Bell, 456 U.S. 512 (1982), exemplify such a debate. The issue in the case was whether a federal statute barred gender-based discrimination in employment by educational institutions. Justice Blackmun, writing for the Court, answered "yes," relying heavily on the statute's legislative history, especially the remarks of Senator Birch Bayh, who introduced the legislation. Justice Powell, writing for the three dissenters, answered "no"—also relying heavily on the statute's history, including Senator Bayh's remarks. You may wish to read the decision, for the two opinions together constitute a primer on the use of legislative history, covering everything from hearings prior to the bill's introduction to post-enactment events (a rather unusual type of legislative "history").

A final caveat: There may be no instructive legislative history when you want or need it most. For example, in *Brown v. Board of Education,* 347 U.S. 483 (1954), the landmark case establishing that the fourteenth amendment to the United States Constitution does not allow segregated public schools, the Supreme Court sought guidance in the Constitution's legislative history. (Congress drafts and passes amendments to the Constitution, which are then ratified by the states.) The Court discovered that the pertinent section was viewed differently by its opponents and proponents. Furthermore, at the time the amendment was drafted, no one had reason to think about the problem of segregated schools, since African-Americans then usually were uneducated and public schools were rare.

c. The Federal Legislative Process

To research legislative history successfully, you need a basic understanding of the legislative process so that you will understand the roles of the documents you discover. The following provides an overview of the federal legislative process. The processes of bicameral state legislatures in large part parallel the federal process.

The legislative history of a statute almost always predates its introduction in Congress. Proposals for legislation are drafted not only by members of Congress, but also by federal agencies, the President, citizens, and organizations such as unions and industry groups. The original draft of the legislation and explanations by its authors generally constitute the first documents in a statute's legislative history. On occasion, congressional hearings on a problem are conducted prior to the drafting of any legislation; records of such hearings also constitute legislative history. Some of these earlier sources of legislative history are created before the session in which the statute is enacted and thus will appear in sources published before the statute's year of enactment.

Members of Congress introduce proposals for legislation in one of four forms. For the most part, you will be concerned with bills (designated "H.R." or "S.") and joint resolutions (designated "H.J. Res." or "S.J. Res."). Bills are used for most statutes; joint resolutions now are used for minor or unusual statutes. Concurrent resolutions, designated "H. Con. Res." or "S. Con. Res.," and simple resolutions, designated "H. Res." or "S. Res.," merely express facts or principles affecting the operation of Congress or the sense of Congress.

Sometimes a bill begins in one chamber, is passed by that chamber, with or without amendments, and then moves to the other chamber. Sometimes the Senate and the House consider companion bills simultaneously to expedite the enactment process. As a general rule, in compiling a legislative history you will want to collect all available versions of the bill, from intro-duction to enactment, and track both the bill that passed and its companion, including proposed amendments (whether defeated or adopted).

The following describes the typical enactment process for a bill origi-nating in the House of Representatives, since most legislation originates in the House. Once the bill has been introduced and assigned its number, it is referred to the appropriate committee of the House and, as a general rule, from there to the appropriate subcommittee. At this point, the bill receives its most intensive consideration. Federal agencies interested in the bill submit reports. If the bill is sufficiently important or controversial, the subcommittee holds a public hearing on it. Witnesses before the subcommittee include members of Congress, other government officials, members of lobbying groups, and other interested private citizens.

It is difficult to predict how useful hearing records will be in revealing legislative intent. On the one hand, the testimony of well-informed and au-thoritative witnesses may provide considerable insight into the problem Con-gress sought to address. On the other hand, many witnesses speak to collateral issues or have little expertise. In some cases, the questions of subcommittee members point out their particular concerns.

After the hearing, the subcommittee deliberates and reports in writing on the bill to the full committee. The committee in turn considers the sub-committee report. It then votes to report the bill favorably to the full House, with or without amendments, or to table the bill. Since tabling a bill has the effect of preventing further action on it, adverse reports on bills are rare.

A bill reported favorably out of committee is accompanied by a com-mittee report—perhaps the single most important item of legislative history. A committee report may include a description of the bill's purpose and scope, a statement of the reasons it should be enacted, a section-by-section analysis, a report on changes the bill would make in existing law, committee amend-ments, communications from the executive branch (if any), minority reports (if any), and various other items.

The committee process also may generate a committee print. A com-mittee print may contain the views of one or more committee members on the bill or material prepared for the committee (by the staff, for example) as it considered the bill.

Once the bill clears the committee, it is placed on the appropriate House calendar and called up for consideration by the House through various con-voluted parliamentary devices. The House then debates the bill. Some bills are debated briefly; other debates take some time.

As an indicator of legislative intent, a record of floor debates generally is less helpful than a committee report, but more helpful than a hearing record. The usefulness of a record of floor debates varies greatly depending on how much serious discussion the bill received. Generally, you at least will discover what the bill's sponsor intended the bill to do. You also may find the views of several or many other members of Congress, some of whose views conflict.

Once the bill has passed the House, it becomes an "act" (although the popular term remains "bill"). It then is forwarded to the Senate.

The Senate's consideration of the act is similar in outline to that of the House, although procedural details differ. The act first is referred to the appropriate Senate committee and subcommittee, where it may receive the same detailed treatment as in the House. If the Senate committee reports favorably on the act, with or without amendment, the act is placed on the Senate's calendar and called up for debate and a vote.

If the act passes the Senate, it is sent back to the House along with any amendments that also passed the Senate. The House's response to the Senate's amendments depends on how substantial or controversial they are. If the amendments are relatively unimportant and unobjectionable, they may be agreed to by the House without conference committee deliberations.

If, however, the amendments are controversial, a conference committee is likely to be convened. The conference committee includes members of both the House and the Senate. The committee can consider only the discrepancies between the House and Senate versions, in essence deciding between the two versions. The conference committee must produce a report embodying its recommendations or conveying its inability to agree on a final version of the act. If the first conference committee cannot agree, another committee may be convened, generally with instructions from the House and the Senate. The conference committee report, like the House and Senate committees' reports, is a very important item of legislative history.

The Senate votes first on the conference committee report, choosing either to adopt it or to recommit the matter to the conference committee. When the conference report has passed the Senate, the House then debates and votes on it.

An act goes to the President only after identical versions have been passed by both the House and the Senate. Then an act passed by Congress becomes law if (1) the President signs it; (2) the President allows ten days to pass without signing or vetoing it (however, if the Congress adjourns before the ten days pass, the President's inaction amounts to a veto); or (3) the President vetoes it, but the House and the Senate override the veto by a two-thirds vote.

In addition to the documents described above, you may find it useful on occasion to read one of the many reports received by Congress. Congress receives presidential messages, reports from executive agencies, memoranda from private groups, and the like. These documents may pertain to pending or enacted legislation. They are called House or Senate documents.

According to the Congressional Information Service, which compiles and indexes federal legislative materials, Congress' committee working papers alone number 800,000 pages annually.

2. Your Research Situation Restated

Recall that one of the questions Ms. Selleck posed was whether the employees should or could be sanctioned, rather than or in addition to CSB Construction. The statute is ambiguous.

Section 654(b) creates a duty on the part of employees to comply with safety and health standards. 29 U.S.C. § 654(b) (1988). Furthermore, the statement of OSHA's purpose indicates that the Act provides "that employers and employees have separate but dependent responsibilities and rights." *Id.* § 651(b)(2).

On the other hand, the provisions pertaining to enforcement of the statute all refer to actions taken vis-à-vis "employers." *E.g., id.* §§ 658(a), 659(a). The statute provides for assessments of penalties only against employers. *Id.* § 666. The definitions define "employer" and "employee" separately, in terms reflecting ordinary usage of these terms. *Id.* § 652.

This ambiguity creates a classic occasion for research into legislative history.

3. Researching Federal Legislative History without CALR

a. Overview

As you no doubt have surmised, the federal legislative process and the documentation it produces can be lengthy and complicated. Thus, the process of researching legislative history tends to be lengthy and complicated. Keep in mind that you are researching a process, not a final result. It also is important to realize that the documents constituting a legislative history take various forms and are found in various sources.

You should see your research as involving two tasks:

(1) Figure out the steps the bill went through on its way to becoming law and the items of legislative history that were produced.
(2) Locate, read, and analyze the documents.

Your first step should be to determine whether there is a compiled source of legislative history on your statute. Because legislative history is so important and yet so difficult to research, persons particularly interested in specific statutes publish compiled histories of those statutes. Such a history may be a mere listing of events and documents, or it may be a volume of the key documents. As a general rule, this is done only for statutes of widespread importance. Of course, you can trim your research hours by using a compiled history.

To find out whether a compilation exists for your statute, consult Nancy P. Johnson, *Sources of Compiled Legislative Histories* (AALL Publication Series No. 14, 1988), a page of which is shown in Illustration 7-23 on page 285. As Illustration 7-23 shows, several publications containing OSHA's legislative history exist. They include law review articles, commercially published collections, and a Senate compilation. None is comprehensive, as the entries in the right-hand columns show. ("X" signifies that the cited source contains the full document; "E" signifies that the document is excerpted.)

For most statutes, no such compiled sources exist. Thus, you will need to compile the information and materials yourself. That process involves four sets of materials. The first is *United States Code Congressional and Administrative News,* a print legislative history source West has published for many years. The second set is the Congressional Information Service system, a more recent source, published primarily in microfiche. The third set consists of various government publications. As you will soon see, it is easier to research federal legislation through unofficial sources. Fourth, the use of CALR to research legislative history is covered in section 4 at page 303. Regardless of which legislative history material you use, your starting place is the statute itself.

Tables 7.1 and 7.2 on page 286 present an overview of federal legislative history. Table 7.1 is simply a list of the information you will need in order to locate the legislative history documents for your statute. Table 7.2 is a flowchart showing how you might work through some of the sources covered here.

b. The Statutory Codes

As a general rule, your research in legislative history will follow your reading of the statute in one of the federal statutory codes. You can get a good start on your legislative history research simply by reading the small print following the statutory sections. Please refer again to Illustrations 7-3,

ILLUSTRATION 7-23. Nancy P. Johnson, *Sources of Compiled Legislative Histories: A Bibliography of Government Documents, Periodical Articles, and Books, 1st Congress-99th Congress* [AALL Publication Series No. 14] B64 (1988).

285

PUBLIC LAW, BILL NUMBER	STATUTE	ACT. ENTRY	CONTENTS							
			ACTUAL DOCS.	CITES TO DOCS.						
			REPORTS	HEARINGS	DEBATES	INDEX	DISCUSSION	LISTS CITES		
91-581 S.368	84 Stat. 566	GEOTHERMAL STEAM ACT OF 1970								
		Bjorge, K.R. "Development of Geothermal Resources and the 1970 Geothermal Steam Act." 46 University of Colorado Law Review 1 (1974).						X	X	
91-596 S.2193	84 Stat. 1590	OCCUPATIONAL SAFETY AND HEALTH ACT OF 1970								
		Bureau of National Affairs. The Job Safety and Health Act of 1970: Text, Analysis, Legislative History. Wash., D.C.:Bureau of National Affairs, 1971. L.C.:KF3570.B8 $15	X	E	X		X	X		
		Gross, Marjorie E. "The Occupational Safety and Health Act: Much Ado About Something." 3 Loyola University of Chicago Law Journal 247 (1972).						X	X	
		Hogan, Roscoe B. and Hogan, R. Benjamin, III. Occupational Safety and Health Act. 2 vols. New York: Matthew Bender, 1977. $100	X		X					
		IHS Legislative Histories Microfiche Program. Indexed Guide, v. 1, pt. A, pg. 431.							X	
		Meeds, Lloyd. "Symposium: The Developing Law of Occupational Safety and Health: A Legislative History of OSHA." 9 Gonzaga Law Review 327 (1974).						X	X	
		Occupational Safety and Health Act of 1970. New York: Commerce Clearing House, 1971.	E		E		X			
		Perna, John B. Occupational Safety and Health Act, 1970: A Bibliography. Wash., D.C.: Library of Congress, Law Library, 1974.							X	
		U.S. Congress. Senate. Committee on Labor and Public Welfare. Subcommittee on Labor. Legislative History of the Occupational Safety and Health Act of 1970. Wash., D.C.:GPO, 1971 SuDoc: Y4.L11/2:Sa1/5 Microfiche: CIS, 71-S542-17	X		X	X				

TABLE 7.1. Information Needed to Research Legislative History.

public law number
date of approval
United States Statutes at Large citation
Congress and session numbers
bill numbers (for enacted bill and companion bills and related unenacted bills)
committees considering the bills (House, Senate, and conference)
committee report numbers
dates of consideration and passage in the House and Senate
Congressional Record citations for debates
date of approval by the President

TABLE 7.2. Flowchart of Legislative History Research.

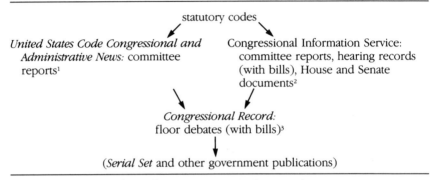

statutory codes

United States Code Congressional and Administrative News: committee reports[1]

Congressional Information Service: committee reports, hearing records (with bills), House and Senate documents[2]

Congressional Record: floor debates (with bills)[3]

(*Serial Set* and other government publications)

[1]also available on WESTLAW (LEXIS also contains recent committee reports)
[2]Index only also available on WESTLAW
[3]also available on WESTLAW and LEXIS (as of 1985)

7-11, and 7-13 (on pages 241, 252, and 259). The *United States Code, United States Code Annotated,* and *United States Code Service* all provide

(1) the statute's public law number,
(2) the date the statute was approved, and
(3) the *Statutes at Large* citation for the statute.

Remember that a statute's public law number is assigned when the bill becomes law; it reflects when the bill was enacted. Public Law 91-596, for example, was the 596th bill to be enacted during the 91st Congress. It was enacted December 29, 1970, and appears at 84 *United States Statutes at Large* 1593. *United States Statutes at Large* is the official session law service for federal legislation and is compiled in the order in which bills are enacted.

The three codes also provide a summary of the amendments made in the statute from its original enactment to date. Remember that you will want to research the history of all enactments—the original statute and amendments—relevant to your issue.

U.S.C.A. is the most helpful of the three codes because it provides an additional item of information—a citation to the statute's legislative history section in *United States Code Congressional and Administrative News.* Illustration 7-11 at page 253 refers you to "1970 U.S. Code Cong. and Adm. News, p. 5177."

c. **United States Code Congressional and Administrative News** (U.S.C.C.A.N.)

287

Statutes and
Constitutions:
Searching for
Primary Authority

United States Code Congressional and Administrative News (U.S.C.C.A.N.), West's publication in the area of federal legislative history, is one of the most accessible sources in this field. You will find it very useful in compiling a record of a statute's enactment process. As a repository of legislative documents, it is less useful because it is not comprehensive; but it still is worth consulting.

Each U.S.C.C.A.N. edition covers a particular session of Congress. U.S.C.C.A.N. contains two basic sections on each statute: (1) a reprint of the *Statutes at Large* version of the statute and (2) a legislative history section. Many editions span more than one volume, and these two sections generally are found in different volumes.

There are three ways to gain access to these two sections of U.S.C.C.A.N. First, if you know the *Statutes at Large* citation for your statute, as you would if you had read the statute in any code, you can look up the *Statutes at Large* reprint in U.S.C.C.A.N. directly because the organization of this part of U.S.C.C.A.N. mirrors that of *Statutes at Large*. From there, you can find the second section because the *Statutes at Large* reprint in U.S.C.C.A.N. refers to the legislative history section. Second, as has been noted above, U.S.C.A. also provides a direct reference to the legislative history section. Third, the subject index near the end of the final volume of each U.S.C.C.A.N. edition gives page references to both sections.

Consulting both the *Statutes at Large* reprint (Illustration 7-24 on page 288) and the legislative history section (Illustration 7-25 on page 289) should yield a wealth of useful information:

- the designation of the bill that was enacted, here S. 2193 (item 1 on Illustration 7-24);
- the designation of the bill that did not become law, here H.R. 16785 (item 2 on Illustration 7-25);
- the committees to which the bills were assigned, here Senate Labor and Public Welfare Committee and House Education and Labor Committee (items 3 and 4 on Illustration 7-25);
- the numbers and dates of the committee reports (again items 3 and 4);
- information about conference committee reports (item 5 on Illustration 7-25);
- dates of consideration and passage by both houses (item 6 on Illustration 7-25);
- the volume of the *Congressional Record* in which the debates appear (item 7 on Illustration 7-25); and
- the date the President approved the act (at the end of the *Statutes at Large* reprint, not reproduced here).

In some editions of U.S.C.C.A.N., you must consult both the *Statutes at Large* reprint and the legislative history section to obtain this material. In other editions, all of this information may appear in one section or the other.

In the second U.S.C.C.A.N. section—the legislative history section—you will also find whatever document(s) West deemed useful enough to print. As a general rule, West chooses whichever committee report best embodies the consideration given the bill during the legislative process; in some cases, two reports or extracts are published in U.S.C.C.A.N. In our example, West

P.L. 91–595   LAWS OF 91st CONG.—2nd SESS.   Dec. 28

FATHER'S DAY

PUBLIC LAW 91–595; 84 STAT. 1589

[S. J. Res. 187]

Joint Resolution to authorize the President to designate the third Sunday in June, 1971, as "Father's Day".

Resolved by the Senate and House of Representatives of the United States of America in Congress assembled, That:

The third Sunday in June of 1971 is hereby designated as "Father's Day". The President is authorized and requested to issue a proclamation calling on the appropriate Government officials to display the flag of the United States on all Government buildings on such day, inviting the governments of the States and communities and the people of the United States to observe such day with appropriate ceremonies, and urging our people to offer public and private expressions of such day to the abiding love and gratitude which they bear for their fathers.

Approved December 28, 1970.

OCCUPATIONAL SAFETY AND HEALTH ACT OF 1970

For Legislative History of Act, see p. 5177

PUBLIC LAW 91–596; 84 STAT. 1590

[S. 2193]

An Act to assure safe and healthful working conditions for working men and women; by authorizing enforcement of the standards developed under the Act; by assisting and encouraging the States in their efforts to assure safe and healthful working conditions; by providing for research, information, education, and training in the field of occupational safety and health; and for other purposes.

Be it enacted by the Senate and House of Representatives of the United States of America in Congress assembled, That:

This Act may be cited as the "Occupational Safety and Health Act of 1970".

CONGRESSIONAL FINDINGS AND PURPOSE

Sec. 2(a) The Congress finds that personal injuries and illnesses arising out of work situations impose a substantial burden upon, and are a hindrance to, interstate commerce in terms of lost production, wage loss, medical expenses, and disability compensation payments.

(b) The Congress declares it to be its purpose and policy, through the exercise of its powers to regulate commerce among the several States and with foreign nations and to provide for the general welfare, to assure so far as possible every working man and woman in the Nation safe and healthful working conditions and to preserve our human resources—

(1) by encouraging employers and employees in their efforts to reduce the number of occupational safety and health

1852

ILLUSTRATION 7-25. S. Rep. No. 91-1282, 91st Cong., 2d Sess. 1, *reprinted in*
1970 U.S.C.C.A.N. 5177.

289

OCCUPATIONAL SAFETY AND HEALTH
P.L. 91-596

OCCUPATIONAL SAFETY AND HEALTH ACT OF 1970

P.L. 91-596, see page 1852

③ ——Senate Report (Labor and Public Welfare Committee) No. 91-1282, Oct. 6, 1970 [To accompany S. 2193]

④ ——House Report (Education and Labor Committee) No. 91-1291, July 9, 1970 [To accompany H.R. 16785]—— ②

⑤ ——Conference Report No. 91-1765, Dec. 16, 1970 [To accompany S. 2193]

⑦ ——Cong. Record Vol. 116 (1970)

DATES OF CONSIDERATION AND PASSAGE

⑥ —— { Senate November 17, December 16, 1970
{ House November 24, December 17, 1970

The Senate bill was passed in lieu of the House bill. The Senate Report and the Conference Report are set out.

SENATE REPORT NO. 91-1282

𝕿HE Committee on Labor and Public Welfare, to which was referred the bill (S. 2193) to authorize the Secretary of Labor to set standards to assure safe and healthful working conditions for working men and women, to assist and encourage States to participate in efforts to assure such working conditions, to provide for research, information, education, and training in the field of occupational safety and health, and for other purposes, having considered the same, reports favorably thereon with an amendment (in the nature of a substitute) and recommends that the bill (as amended) do pass.

PURPOSE

The purpose of S. 2193 is to reduce the number and severity of work-related injuries and illnesses which, despite current efforts of employers and government, are resulting in ever-increasing human misery and economic loss.

The bill would achieve its purpose through programs of research, education and training, and through the development and administration, by the Secretary of Labor, of uniformly applied occupational safety and health standards. Such standards would be developed with the assistance of the Secretary of Health, Education and Welfare, and both their promulgation and their enforcement would be judicially reviewable. Encouragement is given to Federal-state cooperation, and financial assistance is authorized to enable states, under approved plans, to take over entirely and administer their own programs for achieving safe and healthful jobsites for the Nation's workers.

5177

Note: 2. Bill that did not become law
3. Senate committee report number and date
4. House committee report number and date
5. Conference committee report number and date
6. Dates of consideration and passage by both houses
7. Volume of the *Congressional Record* in which the debates appear

chose to publish the Senate and conference committee reports but not the House report. Obviously, this is not the end of your search for the documents created during your statute's enactment—but it is a good start.

One of the two reports printed in U.S.C.C.A.N. contains the passage in Illustration 7-26 (below). Note that the Senate wrote that "the fullest cooperation of affected employees" is necessary to achieve OSHA's purposes and that § 5(b) [29 U.S.C. § 654(b)] places on employees an "obligation to comply" with OSHA requirements. The next paragraph speaks not of sanctions, but rather of training and employee participation in developing safety programs. The final paragraph is most telling: Section 654(b) is not intended "to diminish in any way the employer's compliance responsibilities or his responsibility to assure compliance by his own employees. Final responsibility for compliance with the requirements of this act remains with the employer."

Check the spine of the U.S.C.C.A.N. volume you are using to find out which session of Congress passed the bill or created the legislative history you are reading, here the Second Session of the 91st Congress. (There are two one-year sessions per Congress.) You will need this information to cite certain sources.

> *Citation Note:* Rule 13 of *The Bluebook* governs citation to legislative materials, including several forms of committee reports. The core form is: S. Rep. No. 91-1282, 91st Cong., 2d Sess. 11 (1970). If the report is published in U.S.C.C.A.N., a U.S.C.C.A.N. citation should be added. For

ILLUSTRATION 7-26. S. Rep. No. 91-1282, 91st Cong., 2d Sess. 1, *reprinted in* 1970 U.S.C.C.A.N. 5187.

OCCUPATIONAL SAFETY AND HEALTH
P.L. 91–596

OBLIGATIONS OF EMPLOYEES

The committee recognizes that accomplishment of the purposes of this bill cannot be totally achieved without the fullest cooperation of affected employees. In this connection, Section 5(b) expressly places upon each employee the obligation to comply with standards and other applicable requirements under the act.

It should be noted, too, that studies of employee motivation are among the research efforts which the committee expects to be undertaken under section 18, and it is hoped that such studies, as well as the programs for employee and employer training authorized by section 18(f), will provide the basis for achieving the fullest possible commitment of individual workers to the health and safety efforts of their employers. It has been made clear to the committee that the most successful plant safety programs are those which emphasize employee participation in their formulation and administration; every effort should therefore be made to maximize such participation throughout industry.

The committee does not intend the employee-duty provided in section 5(b) to diminish in anyway the employer's compliance responsibilities or his responsibility to assure compliance by his own employees. Final responsibility for compliance with the requirements of this act remains with the employer.

example: S. Rep. No. 91-1282, 91st Cong., 2d Sess. 11 (1970), *reprinted in* 1970 U.S.C.C.A.N. 5177, 5187. You also may give the title of a report or document. Rule 13.4.

You should know that U.S.C.C.A.N. contains more material than that just described. For example, it prints presidential proclamations and executive orders. Its numerous cross-reference tables include provisions of U.S.C./U.S.C.A. that have been repealed or amended, as well as where public laws have been codified. For those of you who like your legislative history in table form, U.S.C.C.A.N. provides a table, Table 4, that synopsizes much of the information listed above at page 287.

d. Congressional Information Service

A second resource in the area of federal legislative history is the Congressional Information Service (C.I.S.) system. There are several components to the system. First, C.I.S. has created a microfiche collection with many of the sources you will need in order to conduct legislative history research. The core microfiche collection encompasses hearing records, committee reports, House and Senate documents, and special publications. C.I.S.'s Congressional Bills on Microfiche provides microfiche copies of bills, including amendments and revisions. C.I.S. also offers the *Congressional Record* on microfiche.

C.I.S.'s indexing and abstracting system enables you to locate and learn about pertinent microfiche documents before seeking them out in microfiche. The index/abstract system covers such critical documents as committee reports, hearing records, and special publications. It does not, however, cover the *Congressional Record.*

The C.I.S. system has evolved since its introduction in 1970. This text shows you how it works for OSHA, which was enacted in 1970, and the major difference between the 1970 system and the current system (begun in 1984). Be sure to consult the user's guide to the set you are using for more specific guidance. This text also shows you the print version of the C.I.S. index/abstract system; it is available as well on CD-ROM. Finally, this text shows you only the core C.I.S. system, used for statutes passed in 1970 or later; it does not cover the bulkier systems C.I.S. provides for older statutes.

For research into material predating 1984, such as OSHA, you would begin by locating the C.I.S. Abstracts volume compiled for the year of your statute. Consult first the Legislative Histories section. There C.I.S. presents a brief synopsis of every statute's legislative history, organized by PL (public law) number. This legislative history synopsis provides much the same information as U.S.C.C.A.N. does. For example, note the following information in Illustration 7-27 on page 292:

- the date of approval (item 1 on Illustration 7-27);
- the *Statutes at Large* citation (item 2);
- the numbers of the bill that passed and of related bills (items 3 and 4);
- the various report numbers (items 4 and 5);
- information about hearings on the bill (item 6);
- the dates of floor consideration and the outcome of the debates (item 7);
- the pertinent *Congressional Record* volume (item 8); and
- notations of presidential documents (there are none in Illustration 7-27).

ILLUSTRATION 7-27. Legislative History Synopsis of PL91-596: [Part One—Abstracts] *CIS/Annual 1970* at 794.

PL91-588

PL91-588 VETERANS PENSIONS, amendments.
Dec. 24, 1970. 91-2. •
●Item 575. 6 p.
84 STAT. 1580.

"To amend title 38 of the United States Code to increase the rates, income limitations, and aid and attendance allowances relating to payment of pension and parents' dependency and indemnity compensation; to exclude certain payments in determining annual income with respect to such pension and compensation; to make the Mexican border period a period of war for the purposes of such title; and for other purposes."
Legislative History (H.R. 15911 and related bills):
House Hearings: H761-2.
House Report: H763-9 (No. 91-1448).
Senate Report: S363-14 (No. 91-1439).
Congressional Record Vol. 116 (1970):
Sept. 21, considered and passed House.
Dec. 17, considered and passed Senate.

PL91-589 CONSTITUTION ANNOTATED, revised edition preparation and publication.
Dec. 24, 1970. 91-2. •
●Item 575. 2 p.
94 STAT. 1585.

"Authorizing the preparation and printing of a revised edition of the Constitution of the United States of America–Analysis and Interpretation, of decennial revised editions thereof, and of biennial cumulative supplements to such revised editions."
Legislative History (S.J. Res. 236):
House Report: H423-3 (No. 91-1598).
Senate Report: S683-10 (No. 91-1229).
Congressional Record Vol. 116 (1970):
Sept. 25, considered and passed Senate.
Dec. 15, considered and passed House.

PL91-590 INTERSTATE COMMERCE ACT, amendment.
Dec. 28, 1970. 91-2. •
●Item 575. 2 p.
84 STAT. 1587.

"To amend section 303(b) of the Interstate Commerce Act to moderni-

"To authorize the Secretary of Agriculture to receive gifts for the benefit of the National Agricultural Library."
Legislative History (H.R. 19402):
House Report: H163-23 (No. 91-1615).
Senate Report: [Agriculture and Forestry] (No. 91-1440).
Congressional Record Vol. 116 (1970):
Dec. 7, considered and passed House.
Dec. 17, considered and passed Senate.

PL91-592 NATIONAL MULTIPLE SCLEROSIS SOCIETY ANNUAL HOPE CHEST APPEAL WEEKS, proclamation.
Dec. 28, 1970. 91-2. •
●Item 575. 1 p.
84 STAT. 1588.

"To authorize the President to proclaim the period from May 9, 1971, Mother's Day, through June 20, 1971, Father's Day, as the 'National Multiple Sclerosis Society Annual Hope Chest Appeal Weeks.'"
Legislative History (S.J. Res. 226):
Senate Report: [Judiciary] (No. 91-1213).
Congressional Record Vol. 116 (1970):
Sept. 23, considered and passed Senate.
Dec. 10, considered and passed House, amended.
Dec. 15, Senate concurred in House amendment.

PL91-593 NATIONAL EMPLOY THE OLDER WORKER WEEK, proclamation.
Dec. 28, 1970. 91-2. •
●Item 575. 1 p.
84 STAT. 1589.

"To provide for the designation of the first full calendar week in May, 1971, as 'National Employ the Older Worker Week.'"
Legislative History (S.J. Res. 74):
Senate Report: [Judiciary] (No. 91-1207).
Congressional Record Vol. 116 (1970):
Sept. 23, considered and passed Senate.
Dec. 10, considered and passed House, amended.
Dec. 15, Senate concurred in House amendments.

PL91-595 FATHER'S DAY, proclamation.
Dec. 28, 1970. 91-2. •
●Item 575. 1 p.
84 STAT. 1589.

"To authorize the President to designate the third Sunday in June, 1971, as 'Father's Day.'"
Legislative History (S.J. Res. 187):
Senate Report: [Judiciary] (No. 91-1209).
Congressional Record Vol. 116 (1970):
Sept. 23, considered and passed Senate.
Dec. 10, considered and passed House, amended.
Dec. 15, Senate concurred in House amendments.

PL91-596 OCCUPATIONAL SAFETY AND HEALTH ACT OF 1970.
Dec. 29, 1970. 91-2. •
●Item 575. 31 p.
84 STAT. 1590.

"To assure safe and healthful working conditions for working men and women; by authorizing enforcement of the standards developed under the Act; by assisting and encouraging the States in their efforts to assure safe and healthful working conditions; by providing for research, information, education, and training in the field of occupational safety and health; and for other purposes."
Legislative History (S. 2193 and related bill):
Senate Hearings: S541-43; S541-44.
House Reports: H343-6 (No. 91-1291, accompanying H.R. 16785); H343-18 (No. 91-1765, Conference Report).
Senate Report: S543-37 (No. 91-1282).
Congressional Record Vol. 116 (1970):
Oct. 13, Nov. 16, 17, considered and passed Senate.
Nov. 23, 24, considered and passed House, amended, in lieu of H.R. 16785.
Dec. 16, Senate agreed to conference report.
Dec. 17, House agreed to conference report.

PL91-597 EGG PRODUCTS

Note: 1. Date of approval
2. *Statutes at Large* citation
3. Enacted bill
4. Bills that did not pass, as well as House and conference committee report numbers (including C.I.S. accession numbers)
5. Senate report number (including C.I.S. accession number)
6. Information about Senate hearings (including C.I.S. accession numbers)
7. Dates of consideration and passage by both houses
8. Volume of the *Congressional Record* in which the debates appear
9. Summary of the statute's purpose

Note also the summary of the statute's purpose (item 9). The C.I.S. legislative history synopsis provides more of this information than does U.S.C.C.A.N., because it refers you to documents and events pertaining to closely related legislation from previous sessions of Congress as far back as 1970. In addition, the C.I.S. legislative history synopsis refers you to the C.I.S. material you will consult next. Note the listings "S541-43" and "H343-6" in Illustration 7-27; these are called accession numbers.

You should always check the legislative histories in the Abstracts volume for the year following your statute's enactment as well. C.I.S. publishes an update when important documents are published after the year of a statute's enactment, which is not uncommon.

To gain further information about the material referred to in the C.I.S. legislative history synopsis, you may wish to read the abstracts, also found in the Abstracts volume and organized by accession numbers. An abstract provides both identifying information (for example, the title of the document and its report or hearing number) and a brief description of the document. The abstracts are organized first by the chamber and committee or body generating the document and then by the type of document—for example, committee report or hearing.

Abstract S541-43, for example, describes the record of hearings held by the Senate Labor and Public Welfare Committee. (See Illustration 7-28 on page 294.) As this excerpt shows, the Senate held hearings on various dates in 1969 and 1970 in various locations on two OSHA bills. Both government officials (Secretary of Labor Schultz and Assistant Secretary of HEW Egeberg) and private parties (the executive secretary of the American Industrial Hygiene Association) provided testimony.

Beginning with 1984 legislation, C.I.S. has replaced the legislative histories section in the Abstracts volume with a new volume, *Annual Legislative Histories of U.S. Public Laws.* In this volume, you will find a "standard legislative history" or a "special legislative history" on your act, depending on whether it qualifies as a major enactment. Both present the same information as the earlier legislative history and direct you to the abstracts in the accompanying Abstracts volume. You may find it unnecessary to read those abstracts, however, as the new legislative history statements provide much of the same information found in the abstracts. In particular, a special legislative history includes the full abstracts of the various documents on your statute as well as information on reports, hearings, documents, and debates related to the statute in the current and earlier Congresses. For an example of a standard legislative history from 1990, see Illustration 7-29 on page 295. (Note that the accession numbers are in parentheses and small print below the title of each document.)

An alternative means of gaining access to C.I.S. is through the Index volume. The main index covers subjects and names—for example, authors and witnesses. Illustration 7-30 on page 296 is from the 1990 Index volume. Note that the first item under "Occupational health and safety" refers you to PL 101-637—the legislative history of Public Law 101-637 shown in Illustration 7-29 on page 295, found in the Annual Legislative Histories volume. The second entry refers you to abstract S321-44.3, found in the Abstracts volume. The Index volume also has several specialized indexes including titles, bill numbers, report numbers, and document numbers.

The final step is to read the documents you have found. As noted at page 291, the C.I.S. system includes a microfiche library of the various documents abstracted and indexed as described above. The documents are filed by accession numbers. Using this library is clearly the most expeditious way to read the legislative history of your statute.

For example, if you pursued item S541-43, referred to in the legislative history of OSHA and abstracted in Illustration 7-28, you would find the transcript of hearings held before the Senate Subcommittee on Labor. Illustration 7-31 on page 297 is the first page of that document.

Citation Note: In citing a hearing transcript, give the subject matter title as it appears on the cover, the bill number, the names of the subcom-

S541–42.3

recommendations for action, including re-placement of paternalism by community ac-tion; possible role of guaranteed income in af-fecting power structure.

Insertions: Excerpt from the Colorado Mi-grant Council Annual Report, Mar. 1967 to Feb. 1968, describing migrant life-style (p. 916-920).

"M.A.Y.O. Del Campo," an article describ-ing the Mexican American Youth Organiza-tion and its goals (p. 921-922).

S541–42.4: July 16, 1969. p. 922-1072.

Witness: **KRUEGER, Edgar A. (Rev.),** Rio Grande Valley, Tex.

Statement and Discussion: Oversupply of labor on Texas border and its effect on wages, work-ing conditions, and employer-employee rela-tions; criticism of Texas Employment Com-mission; lack of migrant education and political power; alleged failure of Government programs, including the Farmers Home Ad-ministration, to reach people at the grass roots level; allegedly biased law enforcement; emer-gence, problems, and effect of indigenous groups (list, p. 943-944) including Colonias del Valle, Inc.; recommendations for legislative action.

Insertions: U.S. Commission on Civil Rights staff reports:

a. "Demographic, Economic and Social Cha-racteristics of the Spanish-Surname Popu-lation of Five Southwestern States": Arizona, California, Colorado, New Mex-ico, Texas (p. 945-951).

b. "The Mexican American Population of Texas" (p. 952-981).

c. "Farm Workers." Describes problems of farm labor force originating in Texas (p. 982-1011).

d. "Employment." Describes and presents statistics on the employment status of Mexican Americans in Texas (p. 1013-1024).

e. Excerpts from report on administration of justice concerning treatment of Mexican Americans (p. 1047-1057).

Information and statistics on the population of South Texas counties, including the role of the migrant in the Lower Rio Grande Valley economy, from an OEO Grant Application by Colonias Del Valle, Inc. (p. 1030-1035).

"La Huelga-In Starr County, Tex." by Irving J. Cohen, from Farm Labor Development, USDA. Describes efforts to organize field workers in the Lower Rio Grande Valley, Tex. (p. 1025-1028).

"Housing of Migrant Agricultural Workers" by Richard R. Brann, from the Texas Law Re-view, July 1968 (p. 1036-1047).

S541–42.5: July 17, 1969. p. 1073-1093.

Witness: **GODWIN, James L.,** executive di-rector, Coastal Progress, Inc., New Bern, N.C.

Statement and Discussion: Problems facing the rural poor in Jones, Pamlico, and Craven Counties, N.C., with particular emphasis on the lack of transportation; recommendations including funding of transportation for rural peoples and service to poor as alternative to military service; strike by Eastern Farm Work-ers Association blueberry pickers against Ja-son Morris Farms, Inc. and role of Coastal Progress, Inc.

S541–42.6: July 17, 1969. p. 1094-1099.

Witness: **MORRIS, Jason,** Jason Morris Farms, Inc., Bridgeton, N.C.

Statement and Discussion: Describes strike by blueberry pickers and wages and labor condi-tions on his farms.

S541–42.7: July 17, 1969. p. 1099-1109.

Witnesses: **KEYS, Emma Jean,** Trenton, N.C.
SMITH, Lena, cochairman, Eastern Farm Workers Association, New Bern, N.C.

Statements and Discussion: Participants' de-scription of North Carolina blueberry strike, including allegedly biased law enforcement during strike; working conditions in blueberry fields.

S541–42.8: July 17, 1969. p. 1109-1141.

Witnesses: **RICE, Ken,** law student, Duke University, appearing on behalf of:
WALLACE, Thomas B., deputy director, Coastal Progress, Inc.

Statement and Discussion: Alleged denial of justice to blacks in Craven County, N.C.; ar-rests during blueberry workers' strike.

Insertion: Selected newspaper articles and sup-plementary documentation dealing with the blueberry workers' strike and farmworker powerlessness (p. 1111-1141).

S541–42.9: July 17, 1969. p. 1141-1150.

Witness: **PARKER, T. W.,** deputy sheriff, Craven County, N.C.

Statement and Discussion: Alleged violations of law by blueberry workers and others during strike; alleged role of Coastal Progress, Inc. in strike.

S541–42.10: July 17, 1969. p. 1150-1157.

Witness: **GAVIN, James F.,** cochairman, Craven County Good Neighbor Council; ac-companied by **Burley, Delores,** and **Brown, Ernestine,** Trenton, N.C.

Statement and Discussion: Activities of Craven County Good Neighbor Council, N.C., alleged hostility between law enforcement offi-cials and black community in Craven County.

S541–43   OCCUPATIONAL SAFETY AND HEALTH ACT, 1970. Part 1.
Sept. 30, Nov. 4, 21, 24, 26, Dec. 9, 15, 16, 1969, Mar. 7, Apr. 10, 28, 1970. 91-1; 91-2.
† ●item 1043. xi + 1006 p.
Y4.L11/2:Sa1/3/970/pt.1.
11140(70).   71-608099.

Hearings before the *Subcommittee on Labor* on the following bills:

S. 2193 (text, p. 2-31), the Occupational Safety and Health Act of 1969, to authorize the Secretary of Labor to set standards to ensure safe and healthful working conditions, to as-sist and encourage States to participate in efforts to ensure such working conditions, and to provide for research, information, education, and training in occupational safety and health; and

S. 1788 (text, p. 32-73), the Administration's Occupational Safety and Health Act of 1969, to provide a program for safe and healthful working conditions by creating a National Occupational Safety and Health Board, appointed by the President, to set mandatory safety and health standards; by

authorizing enforcement; assisting State ef-forts; and by providing for research, infor-mation, education, and training.

Supplementary material includes submitted statements and correspondence (p. 872-878, 1004-1006).

Hearings held Mar. 7, 1970 in Jersey City, N.J.; Apr. 10, 1970 in Duquesne, Pa.; and Apr. 28, 1970 in Greenville, S.C.

(For summary of brief items of testimony, see S541-43.25.)

S541–43.1: Sept. 30, 1969. p. 76-95.

Witness: **SHULTZ, George P.,** Secretary of Labor; accompanied by **Hodgson, James D.,** Under Secretary; and **Silberman, Laurence H.,** Solicitor.

Statement: Support for S. 2788; need for com-prehensive safety legislation; analysis of exist-ing Federal, State, and private section safety and health activities. Analysis of S. 2788. (p. 76-87)

Discussion: Review of penalty provisions in S. 2788; reasons for extending coverage to large farms; operations of the proposed Board. (p. 87-95)

S541–43.2: Nov. 4, 1969. p. 98-163.

Witness: **EGEBERG, Roger O. (Dr.),** Assist-ant Secretary of HEW for Health and Scien-tific Affairs; accompanied by **Johnson, Charles C., Jr.,** Administrator, Consumer Protection and Environmental Health Service; **Key, Marcus M.,** Director, Bureau of Occu-pational Health and Safety; and **Meyer, Al-vin,** Special Assistant for Legislative Affairs.

Statement and Discussion: Support for S. 2788; extent of occupational health hazards; support for consensus method for determining stand-ards, and explanation of methodology in set-ting standards. Extent and nature of occupa-tional diseases from pesticides in agriculture, and byssinosis or "brown lung" in the textile industry. Anticipated funding and personnel requirements.

Insertions: Status of State and local govern-ment occupational health programs, Jan. 1969 (p. 103-109).

"A Review of State Occupational Health Legislation," by Andrew D. Hosey and Lorice Ede (p. 110-137).

S541–43.3: Nov. 21, 1969. p. 165-181.

Witnesses: **CLAYTON, George D.,** executive secretary, American Industrial Hygiene As-sociation.
ZAPP, John A., Jr., vice president and direc-tor, Haskell Laboratories, E. I. du Pont de Ne-mours & Co.

Statements and Discussion: Support for S. 2788 and consensus method for arriving at standards; changing social attitudes toward oc-cupational health hazards; need for emphasis on industrial hygiene.

S541–43.4: Nov. 21, 1969. p. 198-255.

Witness: **GORDON, Jerome B.,** president, Delphic Systems and Research Corp.

Statement and Discussion: Extent of air pollu-tion in industrial buildings; inadequacy of oc-cupational safety and health statistical report-ing systems, and of present Federal and State health and safety programs. Suggestions to re-organize executive responsibilities in occupa-tional safety and health by forming a Presi-dent's Occupational Safety and Health Advisory Committee.

ILLUSTRATION 7-29. Legislative History of Public Law 101-637: [Legislative Histories] *CIS/Annual 1990* at 747.

295

Public Law 101-637

104 Stat. 4589

Asbestos School Hazard Abatement Reauthorization Act of 1990

November 28, 1990

Public Law

1.1   Public Law 101-637, approved Nov. 28, 1990. (S. 1893)

(CIS90:PL101-637   10 p.)

"To reauthorize the Asbestos School Hazard Abatement Act of 1984."

Amends the Asbestos School Hazard Abatement Act of 1984 (ASHAA) to revise and authorize FY91-FY95 appropriations for the EPA program providing grants and loans to public school districts for school building asbestos hazards identification and abatement programs.

Amends the Asbestos Hazard Emergency Response Act of 1986 to require that the proceeds of any Government lawsuit against asbestos abatement contractors be deposited in the Asbestos Trust Fund.

Requires EPA to issue information or an advisory clarifying the circumstances under which in-place management or removal is the best method for asbestos abatement.

Makes technical corrections to ASHAA.

Amends the Toxic Substances Control Act to require asbestos abatement contractors working in public or commercial buildings to be accredited.

Authorizes EPA grants to nonprofit organizations to provide asbestos training programs.

P.L. 101-637 Reports

101st Congress

2.1   S. Rpt. 101-353 on S. 1893, "Asbestos School Hazard Abatement Reauthorization Act of 1989," June 28, 1990.

(CIS90:S323-9   8 p.)
(Y1.1/5:101-353.)

Recommends passage with amendments of S. 1893, the Asbestos School Hazard Abatement Reauthorization Act of 1989, to amend the Asbestos School Hazard Abatement Act of 1984 to authorize FY91-FY95 appropriations for EPA grants and loans to public school districts for school building asbestos hazards identification and abatement programs.

P.L. 101-637 Debate

136 Congressional Record
101st Congress, 2nd Session - 1990

4.1   Oct. 15, Senate consideration and passage of S. 1893.

4.2   Oct. 26, House consideration and passage of S. 1893.

101st Congress, 2nd Session

P.L. 101-637 Hearings

101st Congress

5.1   "Asbestos Issues," hearings before the Subcommittee on Toxic Substances, Environmental Oversight, Research and Development, Senate Environment and Public Works Committee, Apr. 26, 1990.

(CIS90:S321-44   iv+312 p.)
(Y4.P96/10:S.hrg.101-835.)

5.2   Hearings on H.R. 3677, the Asbestos School Hazard Abatement Reauthorization Act of 1989, before the Subcommittee on Transportation and Hazardous Materials, House Energy and Commerce Committee, June 19, 1990. (Not available at time of publication.)

ILLUSTRATION 7-31. *Occupational Safety and Health Act, 1970: Hearings on S. 2193 and S. 2788 before the Subcomm. on Labor and Public Welfare,* 91st Cong., 1st & 2d Sess. 76 (1970), *microformed on* CIS No. S541-43 (Congressional Info. Serv.).

297

OCCUPATIONAL SAFETY AND HEALTH ACT, 1970

HEARINGS

BEFORE THE

SUBCOMMITTEE ON LABOR

OF THE

COMMITTEE ON
LABOR AND PUBLIC WELFARE
UNITED STATES SENATE

NINETY-FIRST CONGRESS

FIRST AND SECOND SESSIONS

ON

S. 2193 and S. 2788

BILLS ON OCCUPATIONAL SAFETY AND HEALTH

SEPTEMBER 30, NOVEMBER 4, 21, 24, 26, DECEMBER 9, 15, 16, 1969;
MARCH 7, AND APRIL 10, 28, 1970

PART 1

Printed for the use of the Committee on Labor and Public Welfare

U.S. GOVERNMENT PRINTING OFFICE

42-537 O

WASHINGTON : 1970

mittee (if any) and the committee, the Congress and session, the page number, the year, and identifying information about the witness. For example: *Occupational Safety and Health Act, 1970: Hearings on S. 2193 and S. 2788 before the Subcomm. on Labor of the Comm. on Labor and Public Welfare*, 91st Cong., 1st & 2d Sess. 76 (1970) (statement of Secretary of Labor George P. Schultz). *See* Rule 13.3.

Although no witness may have testified to the question of employee sanctions, you would find a useful piece of information in this document: the bills under consideration by the Senate. Illustration 7-32 on page 299 is the first page of one of the bills being considered, S. 2788, which did not pass. That bill did not contain the language now found in § 654(b). Nor did S. 2193 (the bill that did pass), as of the hearing date.

Citation Note: Unenacted bills are cited as follows: S. 2788, 91st Cong., 2d Sess. § 1 (1970). If the unenacted bill can be found in published hearings, that information may be added. Enacted bills are cited as statutes unless they are used to document legislative history, in which case they are cited as unenacted bills. Rule 13.2.

For C.I.S. subscribers who lack the microfiche library, C.I.S. abstracts also provide information such as the Government Printing Office stock number that will enable you to locate the document through other methods.

e. The *Congressional Record* and Other Government Publications

(1) Congressional Record

Research beginning in U.S.C.C.A.N. and C.I.S. converges when it comes to floor debate on bills, and the point of convergence is the *Congressional Record*. The *Congressional Record* is published daily while Congress is in session; the daily editions periodically are compiled into hardcover or microform volumes. As noted above, C.I.S. publishes the *Record* in microfiche.

As a daily publication, the *Record* serves as a newspaper for Congress. More important for purposes of researching legislative history, the *Record* prints more or less verbatim transcripts of floor debates and proceedings. The transcripts include remarks by members of Congress (as revised by them), votes, proposed amendments, and on occasion the text of the bills under consideration. It also contains the text of messages from the President to Congress and some other House and Senate documents.

The daily edition of the *Record* differs from the compiled version in several respects. In the daily edition, House and Senate proceedings are paginated separately; the compiled version uses a continuous numbering system. Unlike the compiled version, the daily edition contains such information as notices of upcoming meetings.

There are several means of gaining access to the *Record*. Your research in U.S.C.C.A.N. or C.I.S. will yield the number of the volume you need. (In the case of recent major statutes, the C.I.S. legislative history may provide page numbers as well.) If you know the date when your bill was debated, you can simply page through the transcript for that date. However, this process frequently is very time-consuming.

It is much more efficient to use the index volume to the *Record*. For most compiled volumes of the *Record,* there is an index (a separate volume in print versions of the *Record*) with two parts: (1) a general index and (2) the History of Bills and Resolutions, with one section on House bills and resolutions and one section on Senate bills and resolutions. In addition to

ILLUSTRATION 7-32. S. 2788, 91st Cong., 2d Sess. (1970), *microformed on* CIS No. S541-43 (Congressional Info. Serv.).

299

91st CONGRESS
1st Session

S. 2788

IN THE SENATE OF THE UNITED STATES

August 6 (legislative day, August 5), 1969

Mr. Javits introduced the following bill; which was read twice and referred to the Committee on Labor and Public Welfare

A BILL

To provide a comprehensive program for assuring safe and healthful working conditions for working men and women by creating a National Occupational Safety and Health Board to be appointed by the President for the purpose of setting mandatory safety and health standards; by authorizing enforcement of the standards developed under the Act; by assisting and encouraging the States in their efforts to assure safe and healthful working conditions; by providing for research, information, education, and training in the field of occupational safety and health; and for other purposes.

1   *Be it enacted by the Senate and House of Representa-*

2 *tives of the United States of America in Congress assembled,*

3 That this Act may be cited as the "Occupational Safety and

4 Health Act of 1969."

    II—O

842   **CONGRESSIONAL RECORD INDEX**

O'BRIEN, LAWRENCE F.—Continued
Addresses
  Nixon Administration, Woman's National Democratic Club, 16633.
  Norman's National Democratic Club, 17378.
Articles and editorials
  Good Candidate, 9717.
  New Politics, 6245.
Letters
  Contribute funds to defeat Nixon and Agnew, 14417.
  Equal rights for women, 28018.
  Postal reform, 20474.
  Support for President Nixon, 24568.
Remarks in House
  Attack on Republicans: reply to, 24003.
  Campaign inconsistencies, 35262.
  Chairman, National Democratic Committee, 5827.
  Postal reform activities, 9851.
  Republicans attacked on drug problem, 35156.
  Vietnam war support: apology for, 26837.
Remarks in Senate
  Attacks on the administration, 17846, 17847.
  Contradictory statements, 16536.
  Nixon, Richard M.: accusations, 18130.
  Nixon-Agnew-Mitchell rhetoric, 16124.
  Tax returns: practice by executive branch of examining, 12217.
  TV speech: reply to, 23378.
Statements
  Administration's Failure To Meet Needs of Veterans, 19555.
  Campaign '70 Clearing House, 15979.
  Nixon Interim Cambodian Report, 18240.
O'BRIEN, TIM, article. Soldier Views Mylai, 2684.
O'BRIEN, W. E. remarks in Senate, commendation, 25620.
  Remarks in House, eulogy, 6867.
O'BRYAN, GERALD O., study, Federal Aid, 711.
OBSCENE MAIL MATTER. *See* DEPARTMENT OF THE POST OFFICE.
OBSCENE MATTER. *See* COURTS OF THE UNITED STATES; DEPARTMENT OF THE POST OFFICE.
OBSERVER (publication), article, Anti-Smith Exiles, 32270.
O'CALLAGHAN, DONAL N.
Bills and resolutions
  Relief (see bill S. 2755*).
  Pocket veto of bill (S. 2755), for relief of (no page).
OCARIZA, MRS. LEONARDA B., AND LUCILA, relief (see bill S. 3032*).
OCCHIPINTI, ROBERT B., decision in case of, 6412.
OCCUPATIONAL ACCIDENTS. *See* INDUSTRIAL.
OCCUPATIONAL HEALTH. *See also* PUBLIC HEALTH.
Articles and editorials
  Industrial Hazards (series), 108.
  Safety Standards, 2663.
OCCUPATIONAL SAFETY. *See* PUBLIC HEALTH.
OCCUPATIONAL SAFETY AND HEALTH ACT. *See also* PUBLIC HEALTH.
  Articles: Proposed (sundry), 30914–30916.
  Contract demands of oil, chemical, and Atomic Workers Union, 42235.
  Letter: Environmental Action Committee, 38054.
Remarks in House
  Bill (S. 2193) to set standards for, 41965, 42199–42210, 42235.
  Provisions of substitute bill (H.R. 19200) to enact, 31872–31889.
  Safety standards: bill (H.R. 16785) to improve, 33162.
OCDOL, AURORA P., relief (see bill S. 4600).
OCEANOGRAPHY, announcement, U.S. Oceans Policy, the President, 16883.
  Draft: U.N. Seabed Convention, 32034.

List: Federal marine science activities, 26154.
Press release: Youth programs, Department of Labor, 18515.
Review of book: Careers in Oceanography, Odom Fanning, 1280.
TV program: Ocean Dumping, Walter Cronkite, 43055.
Addresses
  Coastal States Organization, John E. Mock, 17932.
  Coastal Zone Management, Edward Wenk, Jr., 40036.
  Development of Ocean Resources, William B. Spong, Jr., 1278.
  Jurisdiction Over Ocean Floor, Robert H. Quinn, 6534.
  Marine Technology Society, George Murphy, 24151.
  National Oceanic and Atmospheric Administration, Rocco C. Siciliiano, 22515.
  ——— John G. Tower, 13681.
  National Oceanic Programs, Ernest F. Hollings, 19600.
  O. D. Waters, Jr., 15645.
  Ocean Resources and Foreign Aid, Claiborne Pell, 5370.
  Oceanic Education, Helen Delich Bentley, 5270.
  Oceanic Interests, William B. McLean, 38557.
  Offshore Technology Conference, Hollis Dole, 15087.
  ——— John G. Tower, 13689.
  Politics of the Oceans, Edward Wenk, Jr., 10853.
  U.S. Interest in the Oceans, George B Anderson, 4910.
  Using Our Pacific Treasure, Gov. John A. Burns, 5991.
Articles and editorials
  Cesspool of the Sea, 30978.
  Deep Sea Exploration Stalled, 37258.
  First Aquanaut Team Enters Undersea Laboratory, 11248.
  Food-From-the-Sea Myth, 26762.
  High Seas Treaty, 17480.
  Living by the Sea, 4276.
  LSU Professor Will Attend Seabed Meet, 20062.
  Ocean Dumping, 38257.
  Ocean Pollution, 4909, 35134.
  ——— (sundry), 28252, 28253.
  Oceans Are Dying (sundry), 35134.
  Pollution, 28393.
  Redefining the Law of the Sea, 8759.
  Seabed Riches, 20064.
  Sea's Resource Exceed Moon's, 18041.
  Tektite 2, 17448.
  Threat to Life in the Sea, 28893.
  Unified Research of Land and Sea, 24315.
  University of Miami's Laboratory, 29237.
  "Wet NASA": Will Nixon Take the Plunge? 12345.
Bills and resolutions
  International Conference on Ocean Dumping: convene (see S.J. Res. 247).
  Marine medicine: research (see bill H.R. 17211).
  Marine Resources and Engineering Development Act: amend (see bills H.R. 11766*, 18024).
  National Advisory Committee on the Oceans and Atmosphere: establish (see bill H.R. 19576*).
  National Marine Mineral Resources Trust: establish (see bill H.R. 18348).
  National resources: development of certain (see bill S. 3970).
  Quasi-public corporation for research and development: study feasibility of establishment (see bill H.R. 17590).
  Reorganization Plan No. 4: disapprove (see S. Res. 433*; H. Res. 1210*).
  Sea Grant College and Program Act: provide funds (see bill S. 2293*).
  Seabed: oppose vesting title to, in the United Nations (see H.J. Res. 1297, 1852).
  Sea Grant College and Program Act: provide funds (see bill S. 2293*).
  Tidal power: research (see S.J. Res. 185).

Messages
  By the President to prohibit ocean dumping (H. Doc. 91–399), 35364, 35523.
  From the President, Marine Science Affairs (H. Doc. 91–304), 11272, 11426.
  ——— Reorganization Plan No. 4, 23379, 23532.
Papers
  Hittle, James D., 7215.
  Lowe, George, 7214.
Remarks in House
  Create National Oceanic and Atmospheric Administration, 7176.
  International agency, 33201.
  Marine sanctuaries: provide, 37137.
  National Advisory Committee on the Ocean and Atmosphere: bill (H.R. 19576) to establish, 40209.
  National Oceanic and Atmospheric Administration, 24923.
  Ocean dumping: prohibit, 35899.
  Sea Grant College program: bill (H.R. 17902) to authorize funds for, 18160.
  Seaweed: natural fertilizer, 20535.
Remarks in Senate
  Continental Shelf: seaward limits, 11429.
  Federal organization for oceanic affairs: improve, 6086.
  Literature on sea and marine careers, 5646.
  Marine Environmental and Pollution Control Act: provisions of bill (S. 3484), 4088, 26152.
  National Marine Mineral Resources Trust: provisions of bill (S. 3631), 8820.
  National Marine Waters Pollution Control Act: provisions of bill (S. 3488), 4263.
  National Oceanic and Atmospheric Administration, 28480.
  ——— establish, 11253.
  ——— Hollings proposal, 6590.
  Pollution of the seas, 12673, 33389.
  President's message, 23465, 23480, 23768.
  President's program, 25741.
  Reorganization Plan No. 4, 28717, 29714.
  ——— National Oceanic and Atmospheric Administration, 28252.
  ——— resolution (S. Res. 433) disapproving, 34602.
  Seabed convention, 26289.
  Seabed resources: U.N. action, 42733.
  Seabed treaty, 26739, 27719.
  ——— President's policy, 24676.
  ——— provisions, 25740.
  Seabeds: President's message, 16883.
  Seaward limits, Continental Shelf, 12239–12242.
  Stratton Commission report, 25740.
  Texas Tektite program, 42486.
  Undersea resources agreement: U.S. giveaway, 21658.
  U.N. convention on international seabed Area, 32032.
  Urban wastes: disposal at sea, 5691.
Reports
  Management of Waste in Coastal Zone, 39142.
  Refuse Disposal at Sea? 4263.
  Research in Marine Sciences, University of Alaska, 11006.
Statements
  National Oceanic and Atmospheric Administration, Ernest F. Hollings, 26604.
  Resolution To Disapprove Reorganization Plan No. 4, Gaylord Nelson, 26150.
  Sea Grant Program, George Murphy, 11451.
  U.N. Seabed Committee, Claiborne Pell, 43037.
  ——— C. H. Phillips, 28298.
OCEANSIDE, LONG ISLAND, HIGH SCHOOL, article, Seniors Hold Own Graduation, 32658.
  Remarks in House, Lowenstein, Allard: refused permission to address graduating class, 20429, 20431, 20502–20507, 20511, 20540, 20556, 21028.
OCHOA, ROSARIO G., relief (see bill S. 5530).
O'CONNELL, BILL, statement, 32853.
O'CONNELL, DANIEL G., letter, Father's Day, 20526.

giving page references to the *Record,* the general index may refer you to the other two sections. Illustration 7-33 (above) is the general index entry for "Occupational Safety and Health Act" in the index to volume 116. Note the references to pages 41965, 42199-42210, and 42235 after "Bill (S. 2193) to set standards for."

You should consult both the House and the Senate History of Bills and Resolutions sections to catch all references to events pertaining to your statute.

These sections provide a synopsis of the bills' processes, insofar as they are reported in the volume to which the index pertains, and sometimes include lists of the sponsors of the bills. Thus, the *Record*'s synopses, like U.S.C.C.A.N. and the C.I.S. legislative history synopses, can be used to compile a legislative history. More important, the two bill sections list page references that direct you to the transcripts of the floor debates on your statute. Illustration 7-34 (below) is the Senate bills entry for S. 2193, the bill that became OSHA. Note that OSHA came before the Senate many times, in large part (it appears) because of disagreements between the House and Senate. Note the reference to page 41753, when the Conference report was presented and accepted.

If you read the material starting at page 41753, you would find first the entire text of the conference committee report and then three pages of commentary by the senators most closely involved in the bill. Note the statement at page 41763 of Senator Yarborough, chair of the Labor and Public Welfare Committee (see Illustration 7-35 on page 302) that one of the three key features of the bill is authorization of "sanctions to be used against those companies and employers who fail to meet [OSHA] standards." He did not speak of sanctions against employees. Of course, to conduct truly thorough research, you would read the rest of the congressional debates as well.

Citation Note: Congressional debates are cited to the *Congressional Record;* the compiled version is to be cited if available. For example: 116 Cong. Rec. 41,763 (1970). *See* Rule 13.5 of *The Bluebook.*

ILLUSTRATION 7-34. Senate Bills Entry for S. 2193, 116 Cong. Rec. 1268 (1970), *microformed on* Reel 561 (Princeton Microfilm Corp.).

2176-2362

SENATE BILLS

S. 2176—To implement the Convention on Offenses and Certain Other Acts Committed on Board Aircraft, and for other purposes.
From Committee on Commerce, 27879.—Reported (S. Rept. 91-1083), 27879.—Passed Senate, 28643.—Referred to House Committee on Interstate and Foreign Commerce, 28990.—Rules suspended. Passed House (in lieu of 14301), 34808.—Examined and signed, 35396, 35595.—Presented to the President, 35597.—Approved [Public Law 91-449], 37264.

S. 2193—To amend the title so as to read: "to assure safe and healthful working conditions for working men and women; by authorizing enforcement of the standards developed under the act; by assisting and encouraging the States in their efforts to assure safe and healthful working conditions; by providing for research, information, education, and training in the field of occupational safety and health; and for other purposes."
Cosponsor, 4266.—Cosponsors added, 14296, 37546.—Reported with amendment (S. Rept. 91-1282), 35087.—Debated, 35968, 36369, 36508, 36511, 36520, 36529, 36534, 37317, 37601, 37605, 37613, 37615.—Amended and passed Senate, 37632.—Amended and passed House (in lieu of H.R. 16785), 38724.—Title amended, 38733.—House insists on its amendments and asks for a conference, 38733.—Conferees appointed, 38733.—Senate disagrees to amendments of House and agrees to a conference, 39193.—Conferees appointed, 39193.—Conference report (H. Rept. 91-1765), submitted in Senate and agreed to 41753.—Conference report (H. Rept. 91-1765) submitted in House and agreed to, 41965, 42199.—Examined and signed, 42666, 43257.—Presented to the President, 43258.—Approved [Public Law 91-596], 44064.

S. 2208—To authorize the Secretary of the Interior to study the feasibility and desirability of a national lakeshore on Lake Tahoe in the States of Nevada and California, and for other purposes.
Cosponsor added, 12706.—From Committee on Interior ... ... 14918.—

vestment companies and their investment advisers and principal underwriters, and for other purposes.
Committee discharged, 33296.—Amended and passed House (in lieu of H.R. 17333), 33296.—House insists on its amendment and requests a conference, 33296.—Conferees appointed, 33296.—Senate disagrees to House amendment and agrees to conference, S. 17895, 36459.—Conferees appointed, 36459.—Conference report (H. Rept. 91-1631), submitted in House and agreed to, 38997, 39344.—Conference report submitted in Senate and agreed to, 39124.—Examined and signed, 39553, 39555.—Presented to the President, 39559.—Approved [Public Law 91-547], 41623.

S. 2229—For the relief of certain corporations, associations, and individuals.
From Committee on the Judiciary, 31998.—Reported (S. Rept. 91-1166), 31998.—Passed over, 32583.

S. 2236—To create a Federal Insurance Guaranty Corporation to protect the American public against certain insurance company insolvencies.
Reported with amendment (S. Rept. 1421), 40334.

S. 2253—To amend the act of August 7, 1961, providing for the establishment of Cape Cod National Seashore.
From Committee on Interior and Insular Affairs, 12702.—Reported (S. Rept. 91-779), 12702.—Passed over, 13100.—Indefinitely postponed, 13739.

S. 2264—To amend the Public Health Service Act to provide authorization for grants for communicable disease control.
Committee discharged, 31207.—Amended and passed House (in lieu of H.R. 11913), 31207.—Senate disagrees to House amendments and requests a conference, 32358.—Conferees appointed, 32358.—House insists on its amendments and agrees to conference, 32770.—Conferees appointed, 32770.—Conference report (H. Rept. 91-1462), submitted in House and agreed to, 33279, 33866, 33867, 33868.—Conference report, 34576.—Agreed to in Senate, 34579.—Examined and signed, 34880, 35431.—Presented to the President, ... [Public Law 91-

Co. and John A. Maxwell against the United States.
Reported (S. Rept. 91-1416), 40333.

S. 2306—To provide for the establishment of and international quarantine station and to permit the entry therein of animals from any country and the subsequent movement of such animals into other parts of the United States for purposes of improving livestock breeds, and for other purposes.
From Committee on Agriculture and Forestry, 1593.—Reported with amendment (S. Rept. 638), 1593.—Debated, 2019.—Amended and passed Senate, 2021.—Passed House, amended (in lieu of H.R. 11832), 5873.—Senate concurs in House Amendment with an amendment, 10360.—House concurs in Senate amendment, 12820.—Examined and signed, 13076, 13536.—Presented to the President, 13623.—Approved [Public Law 91-239], 14786.

S. 2308—To amend title 38 of the United States Code in order to provide for the payment of an additional amount of up to $100 for the acquisition of a burial plot for the burial of certain veterans.
Cosponsors added, 15536.

S. 2314—To amend section 4 of the Revised Organic Act of the Virgin Islands relating to voting age.
From Committee on Interior and Insular Affairs, 34241.—Reported (H. Rept. 91-1521), 34241.—Passed House, 34787.—Examined and signed, 35398, 35505.—Presented to the President, 35597.—Approved [Public Law 91-460], 37264.

S. 2315—To amend the Land and Water Conservation Fund Act of 1965, as amended, and for other purposes.
From Committee on House Administration, 11390.—Reported with amendment (H. Rept. 91-1000), 11390.—Made special order (H. Res. 953), 13325.—Debated, 20640.—Amended and passed House, 20654.—Title amended, 20654.—Senate concurs in House Amendment, 20993.—Examined and signed, 21206, 21308.—Presented to the President, 21374.—Approved [Public Law 91-308], 23379.

S. 2323—To authorize the Secretary of the Interior to consider a petition ...

the hearing procedure, for affected employers and employees to have a voice in the standards-making process.

As in the Senate bill, inspections would be made by the Labor Department, with authority to issue citations requiring the abatement of violations and to propose penalties, where appropriate. The conference agreement also contains the provision for an independent enforcement commission, which was adopted during Senate debate, on motion by Senator JAVITS. This provision was designed to separate the adjudication of violations from the other functions performed by the Secretary of Labor, in order to provide every assurance that fairness and due process would be fully served.

The conference agreement also contains the Senate bill's provisions which encourage State participation in the effort to bring safe and healthful conditions to the workplace, and which provide the workers and their representatives with an opportunity to participate in the standards-making and enforcement processes.

I might point out that the Senate bill contained a number of provisions that had no counterpart whatever in the House-passed bill. These include Senator JAVITS' proposals for a National Institute for Occupational Safety and Health to perform the all-important research functions which will be basic to this program's effectiveness, and a National Commission To Study the Problems of Workmen's Compensation, as well as Senator DOMINICK's proposal requiring the use of emergency locator beacons on certain small aircraft. All of these provisions remain in the bill agreed upon in conference.

Where the Senate conferees receded to the House, this was also done in accordance with views which had very substantial support in the Senate. I would cite in particular the bill's imminent danger provision. The Senate bill had provided that where an imminent danger was found to exist, the Secretary of Labor could not only go to court to obtain injunctive relief, but could, under certain circumstances, order the withdrawal of employees or closure of the plant for up to 72 hours. An amendment offered on the Senate floor by Senator SAXBE, which would permit all such imminent danger orders to be issued only by a court, failed by merely two votes. Under these circumstances, and in view of the insistence of the House Members on adhering to that portion of their bill which contained a provision similar to the Saxbe amendment, the Senate conferees felt warranted in receding to the House on this issue.

So I believe that in every respect we have been faithful to the wishes of the Senate, and in doing so, have brought back a bill which will be both strong and effective as well as fair and reasonable.

Mr. President, I am gratified that the administration announced its support yesterday of the bill agreed upon by the conference committee. I would also recall President Nixon's earlier remarks on this legislation in which he pointed out that "such a program ought to have been Federal law three generations ago. This

was not done, and three generations of American workers have suffered because of this."

Mr. President, the legislation is now before us, and I urge immediate approval of the conference report.

Mr. YARBOROUGH. Mr. President, today we are considering one of the truly great landmark pieces of social legislation in the history of this country. The occupational safety and health bill which has been agreed to by the House and Senate conferees provides the over 80 million American industrial workers with the protection that they so desperately need to insure that they have a safe and healthy place to work. I take special pride in this bill, not only because it was a product of long hours of hard work and investigation by the Senate Labor and Public Welfare Committee, of which I have had the honor to serve as chairman, but also because this is a measure I have worked on for many years. Actually this national industrial safety act is long overdue; for 30 years it has been advocated and urged. At long last this great remedial act is becoming law.

During the 90th Congress, I introduced in the Senate a comprehensive occupational safety and health bill and held extensive hearings on this measure. These hearings brought to the attention of the American people some startling facts about the conditions that exist in many of the industrial plants of this country. For example, in 1967 alone, there were over 7 million injuries in industrial employment, and of these, 2.2 million work-related injuries resulted in either temporary or permanent disabilities. Of these injuries, 6,900 resulted in death. Disregarding for the moment the human element of this pressing problem and looking only at the hard economic facts, industrial accidents and illnesses cost the American economy over $8 billion in 1967. Ten times more working days were lost as a result of industrial injuries than were lost because of strikes and lockouts. These figures stand as evidence to the truth that this law has been delayed much too long.

At the beginning of the 91st Congress, I joined with Senator HARRISON WILLIAMS in introducing again in Congress the occupational safety and health bill. Extensive hearings were held on this measure and the members of the Labor and Public Welfare Committee, both Democrats and Republicans, worked diligently to produce a bill that would protect the men and women of this country from the dangers that are present in the workplaces of America. In conference, the Senate conferees fought hard for those provisions which are so necessary if this bill is to be a truly effective means of curbing industrial injuries. The bill that came out of the conference stands as a tribute to the hard work of the conferees and particularly Senator WILLIAMS, chairman of the Senate Subcommittee on Labor with whom I worked in the conference.

I am extremely proud that I was able to take an active part in fashioning this bill and steering it through conference. If the 91st Congress is remembered for

nothing else than this bill, it will surely be recorded as one of the most productive legislative sessions in the history of this country. Contrary to the views expressed by the distinguished minority leader of the Senate, this occupational safety and health bill makes this session of Congress an unmitigated success.

The key features of this bill are:

First, it will authorize the establishment of health and safety standards;

Second, it provides the Secretary of Labor with the authority to enforce these standards; and

Third, it authorizes sanctions to be used against those companies and employers who fail to meet these standards.

This is not a passive measure but rather a strong and workable bill which deserves the support of all people who are concerned with industrial safety. Above all else, this bill stands as proof to the American people that Congress can respond in a constructive way to urgent needs. I am proud to have been a part of the fight for this measure and I urge the Senate to unanimously adopt the conference report.

Mr. PROUTY. Mr. President, I am one of the conferees appointed by the Senate to the joint conference on the occupational health and safety bill. Although I have misgivings over some of the provisions contained in the conference report, I have concluded that its overall effect will be beneficial and I shall vote for its adoption.

The original bills introduced in both bodies provided that the Secretary of Labor would promulgate all health and safety standards and would also be responsible for deciding appeals from employers who contested violations found or penalties assessed by inspectors employed by the Department of Labor.

The conference report, Mr. President, adopts provisions contained in both the House- and Senate-passed bills establishing an independent Commission to review all contested cases involving violations found or penalties assessed by the Secretary of Labor. The Commission's order in turn is subject to judicial review in an appropriate U.S. court of appeals.

The conference report also eliminates the authority granted to the Secretary of Labor by the Senate bill to partially or entirely arbitrarily shut down the operations of an employer on the grounds of imminent danger. Rather, it adopts the House provision requiring that the Secretary obtain an order from a U.S. district court if he concludes that a withdrawal order is warranted.

In addition, the conference report retains Senate language providing that where a withdrawal order is issued it must provide that sufficient numbers of employees may remain in the area in order to shut down the operation in an orderly and efficient manner. This provision is of primary importance to industries which utilize continuous flow operations.

While civil penalties are provided for willful violations, the conference report also eliminates criminal penalties for willful violations except where the vio-

---

(2) *The* Serial Set *and Related Materials*

The *Serial Set* is an official compilation of the committee reports and House and Senate documents produced during sessions of Congress. The *Serial Set* is compiled according to the order in which reports and documents are produced. As you can imagine, the *Serial Set* is a massive source. Few law school libraries own the entire *Serial Set,* although some libraries have it in microform. Some committee reports and other *Serial Set* materials also are available from the Government Printing Office (G.P.O.), federal depository libraries, and the Library of Congress. You also may wish to contact the clerk of the committee that issued the report or received the document.

Not all hearing records are published by the government. Those that are published generally include both the testimony taken and the exhibits submitted; some include the bill as it read at the time of the hearing. Some printed hearing records may be obtained from the committee that conducted the hearing, the G.P.O., federal depository libraries, and the Library of Congress.

You can determine whether a hearing record, committee report, or other document has been printed by the G.P.O. by consulting the *Monthly Catalog of U.S. Government Publications*. The *Monthly Catalog* is exactly what the name suggests—a catalog of the legislative, executive, and administrative documents published and sold by the federal government. One of its components resembles the *Index to Legal Periodicals:* a set of indexes that enables you to look up a document by author, title, subject, or series/report number, among other methods. The index entry provides a number that refers you to the *Catalog* text. The text, in turn, abstracts the document and tells you how to obtain it. Because the G.P.O. does not publish some documents until some time after the statute to which they pertain was enacted, you may need to consult the issues of the *Catalog* for the year of enactment and a year or two thereafter.

In addition, C.I.S. has published indexes to the *Serial Set* (committee reports and House and Senate documents) and to hearing records and committee prints created through 1969.

(3) Bills

Bills are available from various government sources. You may find the text of a bill in a hearing record or committee report or in the record of floor debates located in the *Congressional Record*. Libraries that have been designated federal depository libraries generally maintain a collection of bills, typically on microfiche. If none of these sources has the bill you seek, contact the Clerk of the House or Secretary of the Senate, the bill's sponsor, the committee that considered it, or the Law Library of the Library of Congress.

f. Other Legislative History Sources and Media

There are many other federal legislative history sources, both official and commercial, not discussed in detail here. For example, Commerce Clearing House (a private publisher) publishes a looseleaf service, *Congressional Index,* that is very useful in monitoring the progress of pending legislation. The *Congressional Record* recently has become available on CD-ROM from FD, Inc. Some of the sources described above, such as the *Congressional Record* and C.I.S., are available not only in print and microforms, but also online.

4. CALR in Legislative History

a. Introduction

Both WESTLAW and LEXIS offer databases useful in researching federal legislative history. This section demonstrates how several searches in the various databases work for the OSHA research situation and provides commentary on their usefulness. This section is not intended to exhaust the possibilities of legislative history research involving CALR, any more than the rest of this discussion exhausts the possibilities of print legislative history research.

b. WESTLAW

WESTLAW's LH database contains the collection of materials found in U.S.C.C.A.N. from 1948 to 1989 and a more extensive collection of committee reports as of 1990. LH also contains presidential signing statements beginning in 1986.

A simple way to begin a search in LH is to use a topic search, where the topic is the public law number of the statute. (Recall that you would know this number from researching the statute in the various codes.) The search [to(91-596)] in LH yielded two documents, the same Senate and conference committee reports published in U.S.C.C.A.N. (See Illustration 7-36 below.) If you wished to search for pertinent material within these documents, rather than browse through them, you could do a locate search. The search [lo compliance comply /s employee] in our example would bring you almost immediately to the most pertinent material in the Senate report. (See Illustration 7-37 on page 305.) Note that this search employs the terms used in the statute, as these are the terms Congress used; a search using terms you might have thought of without the aid of the statute, such as "sanctions" or "violation," would not have succeeded. Another possibility is to search for the pertinent section of the new law—not its designation in the code (which Congress would not have known). Here, the search [lo section +3 5(b)] yielded essentially the same results as the "compliance" search.

WESTLAW also offers the *Congressional Record* online in the CR database, but only as of 1985; the indexes and bill tables are not included. Because coverage began well after OSHA's enactment, the debates on OSHA itself are not available online. If you were interested in learning whether OSHA has

ILLUSTRATION 7-36. WESTLAW Citation List from the LH Database.

```
CITATIONS LIST (Page 1)                       Total Documents:  2
Database: LH

    1.    P.L. 91-596, OCCUPATIONAL SAFETY AND HEALTH ACT OF 1970
  CONFERENCE REPORT NO. 91-1765    DEC.16, 1970

    2.    P.L. 91-596, OCCUPATIONAL SAFETY AND HEALTH ACT OF 1970
  SENATE REPORT NO. 91-1282    OCT. 6, 1970
YOU ARE AT THE END OF THE CITATION LIST. PLEASE ENTER YOUR NEXT COMMAND.
```

ILLUSTRATION 7-37. WESTLAW Document Showing S. Rep. No. 91-1282, Available in the LH Database.

305

```
Citation                    Rank(R)        Page(P)        Database    Mode
S. REP. 91-1282             R 2 OF 2       P 1 OF 125     LH          P LOCATE
   S. Rep. No. 1282, 91ST Cong., 2ND Sess. 1970, 1970 USCC&AN 5177,
   1970 WL 5923 (Leg.Hist.)

            P.L. 91-596, OCCUPATIONAL SAFETY AND HEALTH ACT OF 1970
        SENATE REPORT (LABOR AND PUBLIC WELFARE COMMITTEE) NO. 91-1282,
                    OCT. 6, 1970 (TO ACCOMPANY S. 2193)
           HOUSE REPORT (EDUCATION AND LABOR COMMITTEE) NO. 91-1291,
                  JULY 9, 1970 (TO ACCOMPANY H.R. 16785)
                     CONFERENCE REPORT NO. 91-1765,
                  DEC.16, 1970 (TO ACCOMPANY S. 2193)
                      CONG. RECORD VOL. 116 (1970)
                   DATES OF CONSIDERATION AND PASSAGE
                 SENATE NOVEMBER 17, DECEMBER 16, 1970
                  HOUSE NOVEMBER 24, DECEMBER 17, 1970
     THE SENATE BILL WAS PASSED IN LIEU OF THE HOUSE BILL.  THE SENATE REPORT AND
                THE CONFERENCE REPORT ARE SET OUT.

  (CONSULT NOTE FOLLOWING TEXT FOR INFORMATION ABOUT OMITTED MATERIAL.  EACH
  COMMITTEE REPORT IS A SEPARATE DOCUMENT ON WESTLAW.)
```

```
S. REP. 91-1282             R 2 OF 2       P 23 OF 125    LH          T LOCATE

  UNSAFE.
     THE NEED FOR SUCH A CLAUSE WAS STRONGLY URGED BY GOVERNOR HOWARD PYLE,
  PRESIDENT OF THE NATIONAL SAFETY COUNCIL, IN TESTIMONY BEFORE THE SUBCOMMITTEE
  ON LABOR ON DECEMBER 9, 1969.  GOVERNOR PYLE STATED:
     IF NATIONAL POLICY FINALLY DECLARES THAT ALL EMPLOYEES ARE ENTITLED TO SAFE
  AND HEALTHFUL WORKING CONDITIONS, THEN ALL EMPLOYERS WOULD BE OBLIGATED TO
  PROVIDE A SAFE AND HEALTHFUL WORKPLACE RATHER THAN ONLY COMPLYING WITH A SET OF
  PROMULGATED STANDARDS.  THE ABSENCE OF SUCH A GENERAL OBLIGATION PROVISION
  WOULD MEAN THE ABSENCE OF AUTHORITY TO COPE WITH A HAZARDOUS CONDITION WHICH IS
  OBVIOUS AND ADMITTED BY ALL CONCERNED FOR WHICH NO STANDARD HAS BEEN
  PROMULGATED.

                      OBLIGATIONS OF EMPLOYEES

     THE COMMITTEE RECOGNIZES THAT ACCOMPLISHMENT OF THE PURPOSES OF THIS BILL
  CANNOT BE TOTALLY ACHIEVED WITHOUT THE FULLEST COOPERATION OF AFFECTED
  EMPLOYEES.  IN THIS CONNECTION, SECTION 5(B) EXPRESSLY PLACES UPON EACH
  EMPLOYEE THE OBLIGATION TO COMPLY WITH STANDARDS AND OTHER APPLICABLE
  REQUIREMENTS UNDER THE ACT.
     IT SHOULD BE NOTED, TOO, THAT STUDIES OF EMPLOYEE MOTIVATION ARE AMONG THE
  RESEARCH EFFORTS WHICH THE COMMITTEE EXPECTS TO BE UNDERTAKEN UNDER SECTION 18,
```

been discussed since 1985, perhaps in debates over proposed amendments, you might nonetheless search this database.

It is difficult to craft a useful search term, given the size of this database and its unstructured, expansive nature. The search ["occupational safety and health act" O.S.H.A.] yielded over 850 documents as of late 1991; adding [/p construction] reduced the number to 79. For an example of one of the documents, see Illustration 7-38 on page 306, extended remarks by a representative proposing an amendment to clarify OSHA's application to multi-employer worksites.

WESTLAW offers other services in the area of legislative history. For example, Billcast provides information on pending federal bills; CQ-ALERT provides the full text of these bills. Statenet provides information on pending

ILLUSTRATION 7-38. WESTLAW Document Showing 137 Cong. Rec. E2858-01,
Available in the CR Database.

```
Citation                    Rank(R)        Page(P)       Database    Mode
137 Cong.Rec. E2858-01      R 5 OF 79      P 1 OF 20     CR          T
1991 WL 145136 (Cong.Rec.)

              Congressional Record --- Extension of Remarks
        Proceedings and Debates of the 102nd Congress, First Session

    Material in Extension of Remarks was not spoken by a Member on the floor.

                     In the House of Representatives
                        Friday, August 2, 1991

        COMPREHENSIVE OCCUPATIONAL SAFETY AND HEALTH REFORM ACT

                  HON. WILLIAM D. FORD OF MICHIGAN

                     Thursday, August 1, 1991

    Mr. FORD of Michigan.
    Mr. Speaker, 20 years ago, the Congress enacted the Occupational Safety and
    Health Act, a milestone in the protection of American workers. Lives, limbs and
    the health of workers across the country have been protected by this law. But
    the job is far from over.
```

```
137 Cong.Rec. E2858-01     R 5 OF 79       P 18 OF 20     CR          P

                          3. General Duty Clause

    The general duty clause is also modified to clarify its application at
multiemployer worksites, where hazardous conditions or practices may affect not
only the employer's own employees, but also other employees working at the
site.
    The provision implements a recent recommendation of the John Gray Institute
that OSHA require plant management to assume responsibility for all workers on
site. Thus, a refinery owner would become responsible for the safety of all
workers at the site-even temporary contract workers. Likewise, a general
contractor at a CONSTRUCTION site would be ultimately responsible for the
safety of employees working for a subcontractor.

                          E. STATE PLANS

    The bill requires state plans to include provisions regarding employer
safety and health programs, joint safety and health committees, reporting,
nondiscrimination and access to information which are at least as effective as
those provided by federal law. In addition, the bill requires OSHA to
investigate complaints against State plans and modifies the procedures for
```

federal and state bills. Through DIALOG, WESTLAW also offers the Index to
the C.I.S. service online and *Congressional Record Abstracts,* covering the
Congressional Record from 1981 to date.

c. LEXIS

The LEXIS collection in legislative history is currently more limited than
that of WESTLAW. LEXIS does not offer U.S.C.C.A.N. or C.I.S., for example. It
does offer fairly recent volumes of the *Congressional Record* and committee
reports in full text.

The *Congressional Record* material appears in the LEGIS library, RECORD

```
                      Congressional Record -- House

                       Friday, November 22, 1991

                         102nd Cong. 1st Sess.

                        137 Cong Rec H 10856

REFERENCE: Vol. 137 No. 174

TITLE: DEPARTMENTS OF LABOR, HEALTH AND HUMAN SERVICES, AND EDUCATION, AND
RELATED AGENCIES APPROPRIATIONS ACT, 1992

SPEAKER: Mr. BLACKWELL; Mrs. BOXER; Mr. BURTON of Indiana; Mr. DANNEMEYER; Ms.
DeLAURO; Mr. DeLAY; Mr. DORNAN of California; Mr. DURBIN; Mr. EARLY; Mr.
EMERSON; Mr. FAZIO; Mr. FORD of Michigan; Mr. GOODLING; MR. GRADISON; MR. GREEN;
Mr. HEFNER; Mr. HOYER; Mr. HYDE; Mrs. KENNELLY; Mr. KOLBE; MR. LAGOMARSINO; MR.
LEVINE OF CALIFORNIA; Ms. LONG; Mrs. LOWEY of New York; Mr. MAVROULES; MR.
MCDADE; Mrs. MINK; Mr. MORAN; Mr. NATCHER; Ms. OAKAR; Mr. OBEY; Ms. PELOSI; Mr.
PORTER; MR. POSHARD; Mr. PURSELL; Mrs. SCHROEDER; MR. SERRANO; Mr. SHAW; Ms.
SLAUGHTER of New York; Mr. SMITH of Iowa; Mr. SMITH of New Jersey; MS. SNOWE;
Mr. STENHOLM; Mr. STOKES; Mrs. UNSOELD; Mr. VOLKMER; Mrs. VUCANOVICH; MR.
 Press ALT-H for Research Software Help; Press ESC for the Utilities Menu

                        137 Cong Rec H 10856, *

WEBER; MR. WEISS; Mr. WHITTEN; Mr. WOLPE; Mr. YOUNG of Florida


TEXT-1:

    ... [*H10883]   for administering the fund during the current fiscal year, as
authorized by section 9501(d)(5)(B) of that Act.

    Occupational Safety  and Health Administration

    SALARIES AND EXPENSES

    For necessary expenses for the  Occupational Safety  and Health
Administration, $304,157,000, including $66,344,000, which shall be the maximum
amount available for grants to States under section 23(g) of the  Occupational
 Safety  and Health Act, which grants shall be no less than fifty percent of the
costs of State  occupational safety  and health programs required to be incurred
under plans approved by the Secretary under section 18 of the  Occupational
 Safety  and Health Act of 1970: PROVIDED, That none of the funds appropriated
under this paragraph shall be obligated or expended to prescribe, issue,
administer, or enforce any standard, rule, regulation, or order under the
 Occupational Safety  and Health Act of 1970 which is applicable to any person
who is engaged in a farming operation which does not maintain a temporary
 Press Alt-H for Help or Alt-Q to Quit.

                        137 Cong Rec H 10856, *

WEBER; MR. WEISS; Mr. WHITTEN; Mr. WOLPE; Mr. YOUNG of Florida
```

file, which extended back to 1985 as of late 1991. If you entered a search comparable to that used above with WESTLAW—that is, ["occupational safety and health act" or OSHA or O.S.H.A. w/25 construction]—you would have obtained 77 documents. Illustration 7-39 (above) is the first to appear; it pertains to funding for OSHA activities for 1992.

Committee reports appear in the CMTRPT database, which extended to January 1990 as of early 1992. Again, the documents are provided in full text. The search set forth in the preceding paragraph yielded five documents, including Illustration 7-40 on page 308. That document pertains to a bill to establish an Office of Construction Safety, Health, and Education, perhaps in recognition of how common scenarios such as our research situation are.

In addition, LEXIS offers a broad array of files pertaining to current and fairly recent congressional operations. Several files, cumulated in the BILLS files, cover the text of current and recent session bills, bill tracking, and legislative forecasts. Other files cover such matters as member profiles, committee votes, and floor votes. In addition, LEXIS provides more extensive coverage of the legislative history of certain areas, such as tax and environmental law, in specialized files.

d.   Manual Research and CALR Compared

CALR in legislative history materials is, of course, feasible only for materials available online. Currently, less material is available online than in other formats.

The advantages and disadvantages of CALR searching over manual research methods vary by the documents searched. CALR is only moderately

ILLUSTRATION 7-40. LEXIS Document Showing S. Rep. 101-558, Available in the CMTRPT File.

```
                   LEVEL 1 - 17 OF 17 STORIES

                            Copyright
                             (c) 1990
                            Mead Data
                             Central,
                               Inc.

                            Committee
                             Reports


                        101st Congress

                    Senate Rept. 101-558


       TITLE CONSTRUCTION SAFETY, HEALTH, AND EDUCATION IMPROVEMENT
                               ACT

DATE:  October  27, 1990 (legislative day, October 2). Ordered to be printed

SPONSOR: Mr. Kennedy, from the Committee on Labor and Human Resources, submitted
the following

R E P O R T together with MINORITY VIEWS
(To accompany S. 930)

 TEXT:
   The Committee on Labor and Human Resources, to which was referred the bill
(S. 930) to amend the provisions of the Occupational Safety and Health Act of
1970 to establish an Office of Construction Safety, Health, and Education within
OSHA, to improve inspections, investigations, reporting, and recordkeeping in
the construction industry, to require certain construction contractors to
establish safety and health programs and onsite plans and appoint construction
safety specialists, and for other purposes, having considered the same, reports
favorably thereon with an amendment in the nature of a substitute and recommends
that the bill as amended do pass.

 CONTENTS
```

more efficient than print research in U.S.C.C.A.N. In both systems, it is easy to find the pertinent documents. CALR allows you to pinpoint the most pertinent material more quickly where there are distinctive terms in that material, although you should always at least browse an entire committee report for relevant comments in unlikely locations. For recent statutes, you may find CALR useful as a publication format for the *Congressional Record,* which can be difficult to use in microform, although the costs of reading or printing material online should be considered. If your research situation contains some very specific terms, it may be useful to use CALR to pinpoint key passages.

5. The Issue Resolved

The issue of employee sanctions has, in fact, been addressed by the Third Circuit Court of Appeals. In *Atlantic & Gulf Stevedores, Inc. v. OSAHRC,* 534 F.2d 541 (3d Cir. 1976), the court determined that OSHA does not permit sanctions against employees. ("OSAHRC" refers to the Occupational Safety and Health Review Commission.) The issue arose there in a somewhat different context, a challenge to the longshoring safety hat standard as infeasible on the grounds that employer discipline of employees would lead to a strike. Nonetheless, the court's holding resolves the issue. A portion of the decision appears as Illustration 7-41 on pages 310-311. (Discussion of this issue begins at headnote number 17.) Note in particular the court's reliance on the Senate report and a dialogue between two representatives at a hearing postdating the enactment of OSHA.

D. UNIFORM AND MODEL ACTS

1. What Are Uniform and Model Acts?

"Uniform acts" are proposed statutes drafted by public or private organizations for the purpose of attempting to standardize the statutory law of the many jurisdictions in the United States. "Model acts" often have the same purpose, but the term also is used to designate an act that does not have a reasonable possibility of passage in a substantial number of jurisdictions.

You are most likely to use a uniform or model act for one of two purposes: (1) to assist you in drafting new legislation or amendments to existing legislation or (2) to help you interpret an ambiguous statute that is based on a uniform or model act. In the latter setting, you could gain insight into the meaning of that statute by reading the drafter's comments on the uniform or model act and by reading cases and commentary interpreting similar statutes enacted in other jurisdictions. These sources would be highly persuasive authority.

Of course, the usefulness of these sources depends on the similarity between your ambiguous statute and the uniform or model act; they must be similar enough that the differences between them would not lead to different results under the facts in your research situation. This kind of "statutory analogy" must be carefully analyzed. The same kind of statutory analogy also can be drawn between the provision in your original statute and a similar provision in another state's enactment of the uniform or model act, if the similarities are great enough.

Like the Restatements, uniform and model acts are secondary authority.

ATLANTIC & GULF STEVEDORES v. OCCUPATIONAL SAFETY   **553**

Cite as 534 F.2d 541 (1976)

der § 5(b) would be "meaningless and a nullity" if the Commission and this court, in an enforcement proceeding, were powerless to sanction employee disregard of safety standards and commission orders.

In the proceedings before the Commission, the petitioners did not move to join their longshoremen as parties. Nevertheless, at least Commissioner Van Namee and possibly Chairman Moran relied upon the availability of such relief in rejecting the petitioners' challenge to the economic infeasibility of the hardhat standard. At oral argument counsel for the Secretary indicated in response to a question from the court that the Secretary might not oppose granting such relief in appropriate circumstances. After the argument, however, we were advised by letter that this is not the Secretary's position.[15] To the contrary—in two cases now pending before the Commission,[16] the Secretary has taken the position that he has no authority to issue citations, and that the Commission has no authority to issue cease and desist orders, against employees. Our authority under § 11(a) of the Act appears to be derivative of that of the Secretary and the Commission.

[17] With considerable misgivings, we conclude that Congress did not intend to confer on the Secretary or the Commission the power to sanction employees. Sections 2(b)(2) and 5(b) cannot be read apart from the detailed scheme of enforcement set out in §§ 9, 10 and 17 of the Act. It seems clear that this enforcement scheme is directed only against employers. Sections 9(a) and 10(a) provide for the issuance of citations and notifications of proposed penalties only to employers. 29 U.S.C. §§ 658(a), 659(a). Section 10(a) refers only

to an employer's opportunity to contest a citation and notification of proposed penalty. Only after an employer has filed a notice of contest does the Commission obtain general jurisdiction. Employees and their representatives may then elect to intervene under § 10(c). The only independent right granted employees by § 10(c) is to contest before the Commission the reasonableness of any time period fixed by the Secretary in a citation for the abatement of a violation. Section 17, 29 U.S.C. § 666, provides for the assessment of civil monetary penalties only against employers.[17] That the Act's use of the term "employer" is truly generic is made plain in § 3, the definitional section, where "employer" and "employee" are separately defined. See 29 U.S.C. § 652. We find no room for loose construction of the term of art.

We are likewise unable to find support in § 5(b) for the proposition that the Act's sanctions can be directed at employees. Although this provision's injunction to employees is essentially devoid of content if not enforceable, we reluctantly conclude that this result precisely coincides with the congressional intent. The House bill, H.R. 16785, did not even impose this nominal obligation on employees. The Senate version, § 5(b) of S. 2193, which was accepted in the Conference Committee, contained what is now § 5(b) of the Act. There was virtually no floor debate on the provision in the Senate, and none in the House following the action by the Conference Committee. In such circumstances it cannot be seriously contended that Congress intended to make the amenability of employees to coercive process co-extensive with employers. The Senate Report on the employee duty section, quoted in full, says:

15. In that letter the Secretary urged this court to disregard the issue until a case arises in which such a sanction is attempted. For the reasons explained in note 14 *supra,* we feel constrained to squarely address the issue in this case.

16. *See* Brief for the Secretary, *Dunlop v. Nacirema Operating Co.,* OSAHRC Docket Nos. 12099 & 13332, at 9–33.

17. Compare in this regard the Federal Coal Mine Health and Safety Act of 1969, 30 U.S.C. §§ 801–960. Section 109(a)(1)–(2) provides for civil penalties against miners as well as employers. 30 U.S.C. § 819(a)(1)–(2). In contrast to OSHA, § 109(a)(4) preserves the right to jury trial in the civil penalty enforcement proceeding. 30 U.S.C. § 819(a)(4). *See Frank Irey, Jr., Inc. v. OSHRC,* 519 F.2d 1200 (3d Cir. 1975) (en banc), *petition for cert. filed,* 44 U.S. L.W. 3363 (U.S. Nov. 21, 1975) (No. 75–748).

ILLUSTRATION 7-41. *(continued)* 311

The committee recognizes that accomplishment of the purposes of this bill cannot be totally achieved without the fullest cooperation of affected employees. In this connection, Section 5(b) expressly places upon each employee the obligation to comply with standards and other applicable requirements under the act.

It should be noted, too, that studies of employee motivation are among the research efforts which the committee expects to be undertaken under section 18, and it is hoped that such studies, as well as the programs for employee and employer training authorized by section 18(f), will provide the basis for achieving the fullest possible commitment of individual workers to the health and safety efforts of their employers. It has been made clear to the committee that the most successful plant safety programs are those which emphasize employee participation in their formulation and administration; every effort should therefore be made to maximize such participation throughout industry.

The committee does not intend the employee-duty provided in section 5(b) to diminish in anyway the employer's compliance responsibilities or his responsibility to assure compliance by his own employees. Final responsibility for compliance with the requirements of this act remains with the employer.

S.Rep. No. 91–1282, *supra*, at 10–11, U.S. Code Cong. & Admin.News 1970, p. 5187. We simply cannot accept the argument that a remedy for violations of § 5(b) can be implied from its terms. All the evidence points in the other direction.[18]

[18] Nor do we believe that the language in § 10(c) authorizing the Commission to issue orders "directing other appropriate relief" can be stretched to the point that it includes relief against employees. Rather, the generality of that language must be deemed limited by its context—relief in connection with the Secretary's citation. The Secretary appears not to have authority to issue a citation against an employee, and the Commission's powers cannot be any broader. "Other appropriate relief" refers to other appropriate relief against an employer.

[19, 20] This court's power under § 11(a) of the Act is framed in somewhat broader terms:

Upon [the filing of a petition for review], the court shall have jurisdiction of the

---

18. Our conclusion is fortified by reference to the following post-enactment colloquy between Representative Steiger, a co-sponsor of OSHA, and Representative Hungate:

MR. HUNGATE: Now, employer-employee. We have had a line of testimony about, tell this guy to wear a hardhat, or there are six guys on the job and five of them do and the other guy tosses it out, it is a hot day. And they come through and the employer gets fined and the employee does not. What can we do about that?

MR. STEIGER: Well, Mr. Chairman when this bill was being considered, that was a question on which we spent a considerable amount of time. I would have to say the business community, at the time the bill was under consideration, took a very hard line that they did not want the Federal government to be in the business of disciplining their employees . . . . But on balance, Mr. Chairman, I would not want to see us amend the law to impose Federal government discipline on employees. I think that is something left between management and labor.

MR. HUNGATE: No, there is not. The law says the employer is responsible . . . . but again I want to simply reiterate that I think it would be a mistake to interfere in labor-management relations in terms of who has discipline responsibility . . . . I think that is something where there are unions and managements negotiating that can be dealt with in the negotiation process.

MR. HUNGATE: Is fining the employer an act of discipline?

MR. STEIGER: Yes, I think it would be.

MR. HUNGATE: Then we are interfering in the field of discipline in labor-management relations.

MR. STEIGER: No, we are not.

MR. STEIGER: The employer is fined because, under the law, that is his responsibility. I would hope that the employer would be in the position to deal with his employee who put himself in the position of having his employer fined.

Hearings before the Subcomm. on Environmental Problems Affecting Small Business of the Select Comm. on Small Business, 92d Cong., 2d Sess. 490–91 (1972).

Only when their language is enacted by a state legislature does that language become primary authority in that state.

This final part of Chapter 7 will first examine the organizations that have drafted much of this legislation, then review some of the fruits of their labors, nd finally take a look at the research tools involved in this area.

a.   Drafting and Compiling Organizations

The National Conference of Commissioners on Uniform State Laws (NCCUSL) is by far the most prolific producer of uniform state legislation. It was established in 1892 in response to a resolution by the American Bar Association (ABA) in 1890 recommending that each state and the District of Columbia appoint several commissioners to figure out how to achieve more uniformity among the states in the laws on notaries, marriage and divorce, insolvency, wills, and deed acknowledgments. Walter P. Armstrong, Jr., *A Century of Service: A Centennial History of the National Conference of Commissioners on Uniform State Laws* 19 (1991). The mission of the NCCUSL is to "promote uniformity in state law on all subjects where uniformity is desirable and practicable." NCCUSL, *Handbook of the National Conference of Commissioners on Uniform State Laws* 459 (1990). The commissioners consist of attorneys, judges, legislators, and law professors appointed by the governor of each state. They participate in an annual meeting, serve on various ad hoc and standing committees, and work to persuade their states' legislatures to enact the statutes approved by the NCCUSL. Before the NCCUSL decides to draft a uniform or model act, a committee of the NCCUSL studies the feasibility of a uniform act in that subject area.

The American Law Institute (ALI) also engages in the drafting of model codes, in addition to its work on the Restatements and various studies and reports. The ALI also occasionally works in tandem with the NCCUSL on major acts.

Many other groups occasionally draft uniform and model acts to accomplish lobbying goals of the group. For instance, some creditor associations have offered uniform legislation on topics for which uniformity would be beneficial for the credit industry. Other groups draft such acts in order to inject their special expertise into the legislation process. For instance, the national organization of state motor vehicle commissioners drafted one of several uniform motor vehicle certificate-of-title acts.

The Council of State Governments has a Committee on Suggested State Legislation (CSSL), which collects, selects, and annually publishes pieces of legislation from various states. The issue involved must have national or regional significance and be sufficiently complex that a drafter would benefit from another state's legislation. The approach taken in the published legislation must be innovative, practical, and comprehensive. Finally, each bill must be logically consistent, clear, and unambiguous. 50 Council of State Governments, *Suggested State Legislation* xiv (1991). In addition, this annual publication also includes articles that survey areas of legislative focus, such as education reform.

Another source of state legislation is federal legislation, particularly in areas such as consumer protection, environmental protection, occupational health and safety, labor law, and antitrust law. Although the state laws adopted pursuant to federal authorization may not be "uniform," they often share common features, allowing you to do statutory interpretation by analogy. Once you recognize the federal source of the state legislation, you can research the resulting state act using the techniques in the earlier parts of this chapter.

313

Statutes and
Constitutions:
Searching for
Primary Authority

b. Some Effects of Uniform and Model Acts

The NCCUSL has approved more than 200 model and uniform acts, ranging from highly successful (the Uniform Partnership Act and the Uniform Controlled Substances Act) to less successful acts that have yet to be adopted by any state. Areas of coverage include child custody, arbitration, and anatomical gifts. (See Illustration 7-42 on page 314.) The effects of a uniform or model act can be far-ranging. For instance, the Uniform Commercial Code (UCC), a joint NCCUSL-ALI project, has standardized much of commercial practice in the areas of sales of goods, negotiable instruments, letters of credit, and secured transactions (to name a few) among the 50 states; it also serves as the federal common law. That is not to say that acts such as the UCC are enacted without changes. Most enacting states make at least some minor changes, despite vigorous lobbying by NCCUSL members. However, the act's effect, organization, and underlying policies generally remain unaltered, so that greater uniformity has been accomplished in nearly every instance.

The ALI also has drafted some very important model acts. Its Model Penal Code (MPC) really exemplifies a model act. Adopted to a substantial degree in only two jurisdictions, the MPC nonetheless has had considerable impact on criminal law jurisprudence because of the attention and debate it has attracted. It brought new definitions and rationales to the field as well. The ALI has drafted other model acts in the areas of evidence, land development, and pre-arraignment procedure.

2. How to Find Pertinent Uniform and Model Acts

a. Your Research Situation Restated

In the occupational safety and health dispute discussed throughout the preceding parts of this chapter, suppose that the location of the construction project was Rhode Island and that the occupational safety and health inspector was from the Rhode Island Division of Occupational Safety. You have found the state occupational safety and health statutes (found in R.I. Gen. Laws §§ 28-20-1 to 28-20-34 (1986 & Supp. 1991)) and want to research whether the state occupational safety and health regulations were validly adopted. Rhode Island's statute governing agency adoption of new rules appears in R.I. Gen. Laws §§ 42-35-2 to 42-35-3 (1988), as well as some other scattered provisions. These two sections present many issues, but the focus of this part of Chapter 7 is on whether the state agency complied with § 42-35-2 (see Illustration 7-43 on page 315), because subsection (b) prevents an agency rule from being effective until the rule has been made available for public inspection, as "herein required."

Because no decided cases interpreting that requirement are listed after the statute text or in the pocket part, you decide to look for a uniform or model act on which this statute was based, as well as similar statutes in other states based on the same uniform or model act.

b. *Uniform Laws Annotated*

The uniform and model acts of the NCCUSL that have been adopted by at least one state are published by West Publishing Company in *Uniform Laws*

314   ILLUSTRATION 7-42.   Directory of Uniform Acts, in NCCUSL, [Tables-Index] *U.L.A.*
Directory of Uniform Acts and Codes 1 (master ed. Supp.
1991).

DIRECTORY OF UNIFORM ACTS

List of Uniform Acts or Codes, in alphabetical order, showing where each may be found in Uniform Laws Annotated, Master Edition.

The designation "Pocket Part" under the page column indicates that the particular Act or Code is complete in the Pocket Part. The designation "Pamphlet" under the page column indicates that the particular Act is complete in a Supplementary or Special Pamphlet. The user should always, of course, consult the Pocket Part or Pamphlet for changes and subsequent material when an Act or Code appears in the main volume.

Title of Act	Uniform Laws Annotated Volume	Page
Abortion Act, Revised	9, Pt. I	1
Absence as Evidence of Death and Absentees' Property Act	8A	1
Acknowledgment Act	12	1
Notarial Acts, Uniform Law on	14	125
Administrative Procedure Act, State (1981) (Model)	15	1
Administrative Procedure Act, State (1961) (Model)	15	137
Adoption Act	9, Pt. I	11
Aircraft Financial Responsibility Act	12	21
Alcoholism and Intoxication Treatment Act	9	79
Anatomical Gift Act (1987 Act)	8A	Pocket Part
Anatomical Gift Act (1968 Act)	8A	15
Ancillary Administration of Estates Act	8A	69
Antitrust, State Antitrust Act	7B	711
Arbitration Act	7	1
Attendance of Witnesses From Without a State in Criminal Proceedings, Act to Secure	11	1
Audio-Visual Deposition Act [Rule]	12	Pocket Part
Brain Death Act	12	Pocket Part
Canada—U.S. Transboundary Pollution Reciprocal Access Act	9B	625
Certification of Questions of Law Act	12	49
Child Custody Jurisdiction Act	9, Pt. I	115
Children and minors,		
Abortion Act, Revised	9, Pt. I	1
Adoption Act	9, Pt. I	11
Child Custody Jurisdiction Act	9, Pt. I	115
Civil Liability for Support Act	9, Pt. I	333
Gifts to Minors Act (1966 Act)	8A	181
Gifts to Minors Act (1956 Act)	8A	225
Juvenile Court Act	9A	1
Parentage Act	9B	287
Paternity Act	9B	347
Putative and Unknown Fathers Act	9B	Pocket Part
Reciprocal Enforcement of Support Act (1968 Act)	9B	381
Reciprocal Enforcement of Support Act (1950 Act)	9B	553
Revised Abortion Act	9, Pt. I	1
Status of Children of Assisted Conception	9B	Pocket Part
Transfers to Minors Act	8A	Pocket Part

1

ILLUSTRATION 7-43. R.I. Gen. Laws § 42-35-2 (1988).   315

287   ADMINISTRATIVE PROCEDURES   42-35-3

ute, executive order or the constitution and which can effect the rights of private parties either through adjudication or rulemaking. In re Rhode Island Bar Ass'n, 118 R.I. 489, 374 A.2d 802 (1977).

The Rhode Island Bar Association is not an agency within the meaning of subsection (a).

In re Rhode Island Bar Ass'n, 118 R.I. 489, 374 A.2d 802 (1977).

A law enforcement agency hearing committee is not a state agency within the meaning of the Administrative Procedures Act (ch. 35 of title 42). Lynch v. King, 121 R.I. 868, 391 A.2d 117 (1978).

Collateral References. Construction and application of § 3(e)(5) of Privacy Act (5 U.S.C.S. § 552a(e)(5)), providing for proper maintenance of agency records used in determinations, 79 A.L.R. Fed. 585.

Construction and application of exemption

under 5 U.S.C.S. § 552b(c), to open meeting requirement of Sunshine Act, 82 A.L.R. Fed. 468.

Propriety of state or local government health officer's warrantless search — post-Camera cases, 53 A.L.R.4th 1168.

42-35-2. Public information — Adoption of rules — Availability of rules and orders. — (a) In addition to other rule making requirements imposed by law, each agency shall:

(1) Adopt as a rule a description of its organization, stating the general course and method of its operations and the methods whereby the public may obtain information or make submissions or requests;

(2) Adopt rules of practice, setting forth the nature and requirements of all formal and informal procedures available, and including a description of all forms and instructions used by the agency;

(3) Make available for public inspection all rules and all other written statements of policy or interpretations formulated, adopted, or used by the agency in the discharge of its functions;

(4) Make available for public inspection all final orders, decisions, and opinions.

(b) No agency rule, order, or decision is valid or effective against any person or party, nor may it be invoked by the agency for any purpose, until it has been made available for public inspection as herein required, except that this provision is not applicable in favor of any person or party who has actual knowledge thereof.

History of Section.
G.L. 1956, § 42-35-2; P.L. 1962, ch. 112, § 1.

42-35-3. Procedures for adoption of rules. — (a) Prior to the adoption, amendment, or repeal of any rule the agency shall:

(1) Give at least twenty (20) days' notice of its intended action. The notice shall include a statement of either the terms or substance of the intended action or a description of the subjects and issues involved, and of the time when, the place where, and the manner in which interested persons may present their views thereon. The notice shall be mailed to all persons who have made timely request of the agency for advance notice of its rule-making proceedings, and published in a newspaper or newspapers having aggregate general circulation throughout the state, provided, however, that if the ac-

Annotated (master ed. 1968-present) (U.L.A.). The acts are grouped by subject matter, as specified on the binding. Each act has its own index at the end of the act or at the end of the volume. These volumes are updated by annual pocket parts or supplements.

Although there is no overall table of contents, you can locate an act by consulting the *Directory of Uniform Acts and Codes: Tables-Index*, a pamphlet issued as part of the U.L.A. It contains the following research aids:

(1) Directory of Uniform Acts,
(2) Table of Jurisdictions Listing Uniform Acts Adopted, and
(3) Cross Reference Index to Acts.

The Directory of Uniform Acts, shown in Illustration 7-42 on page 314, is an alphabetical listing of all of the acts in the set, both by title and by subject, with volume and page references to their location in the U.L.A. It is, in effect, an abbreviated index for the U.L.A. Shown in Illustration 7-44 on page 317, the Table of Jurisdictions Listing Uniform Acts Adopted is an alphabetical listing, by state, of the uniform and model acts each state has enacted. Also in the Directory pamphlet is a more detailed index entitled Cross Reference Index to Acts, which appears in Illustration 7-45 on page 318. Unfortunately, it gives only U.L.A. volume numbers, not page numbers.

Using the Table of Jurisdictions shown in Illustration 7-44, you could surmise that the Rhode Island statute you are researching may be based on the 1961 Model State Administrative Procedure Act (MSAPA), which appears in volume 15 of the U.L.A. at page 137. If you knew that the Rhode Island statute you were researching was part of an "administrative procedure act," you could reach the same result by looking up that entry in the Directory of Uniform Acts, finding that there were both 1961 and 1981 versions of the act, and then consulting the adoption table on the first page of each act. (The adoption table for the 1961 version is shown in Illustration 7-46 at page 319.) This table notes which jurisdictions have adopted the act, the year of adoption, the public law or chapter number, the effective date, and the code citation. This same table appears at the beginning of the enacted version of the act in a state's annotated code, if the code is published by West Publishing Company (though many are, the Rhode Island code is not).

In U.L.A., the text of each act is preceded by this same table, an Historical Note, and a Prefatory Note. See Illustration 7-46 at pages 319 and 320. The Historical Note typically gives the date of adoption of an act and notes predecessor acts. The Prefatory Note may discuss the pressures that convinced the NCCUSL that a uniform or model act was needed in this area, the details of the act's approval by the NCCUSL, the content of the act, the major principles behind the act, and the variations in the act as adopted by the various states. Illustration 7-46 at page 321 contains the notes on Rhode Island's adoption and tells you that Rhode Island added sections to the act, but did not otherwise deviate much from it. In § 2 of the model act you will find a very close cousin of R.I. Gen. Laws § 42-35-2 (1988). See Illustration 7-47 on pages 322-323. The only differences between the model provision and the corresponding Rhode Island provision are a few differences in punctuation and phrasing, none of which is a substantive change. Thus, this section of the model act is an appropriate provision from which to draw a statutory analogy.

The individual sections of the model act (see Illustration 7-47) are followed by explanatory comments drafted by the NCCUSL, variations from the official text in the enacting jurisdictions, citations to legal periodicals (none here), references to West Key Numbers and C.J.S. sections, and a digest of

ILLUSTRATION 7-44. Table of Jurisdictions Listing Uniform Acts Adopted, in NCCUSL, [Tables-Index] *U.L.A. Directory of Uniform Acts and Codes* 53 (master ed. Supp. 1991).

317

JURISDICTIONS AND ACTS ADOPTED

RHODE ISLAND

Title of Act	Uniform Laws Annotated Volume	Page
Alcoholism and Intoxication Treatment Act	9, Pt. I	79
Anatomical Gift Act (1987 Act)	8A	Pocket Part
Attendance of Witnesses From Without a State in Criminal Proceedings, Act to Secure	11	1
Certification of Questions of Law Act	12	49
Child Custody Jurisdiction Act	9, Pt. I	115
Commercial Code[1]	1 to 3A	
Common Trust Fund Act	7	401
Condominium Act	7	421
Contribution Among Tortfeasors Act	12	57
Controlled Substances Act	9, Pt. II	1
Criminal Extradition Act	11	51
Custodial Trust Act	7A	Pocket Part
Declaratory Judgments Act	12	109
Determination of Death Act	12	Pocket Part
Divorce Recognition Act	9, Pt. I	355
Enforcement of Foreign Judgments Act (1964 Act)	13	149
Estate Tax Apportionment Act (1964 Act)	8A	287
Evidence, Rules of (1974)	13A	1
Facsimile Signatures of Public Officials Act	13	249
Fiduciaries Act	7A	391
Fraudulent Transfer Act	7A	639
Insurers Liquidation Act	13	321
Limited Partnership Act (1976 Act)	6	Pocket Part
Management of Institutional Funds Act	7A	705
Military Justice, Code of	11	335
Motor Vehicle Certificate of Title and Anti-Theft Act	11	421
Parentage Act	9B	287
Partnership Act	6	1
Paternity Act	9B	347
Post-Conviction Procedure Act (1966 Act)	11	477
Premarital Agreement Act	9B	369
Real Estate Time-Share Act (Model)	7B	351
Reciprocal Enforcement of Support Act (1968 Act)	9B	381
Rendition of Prisoners as Witnesses in Criminal Proceedings Act	11	547
Residential Landlord and Tenant Act	7B	427
Rules of Evidence (1974)	13A	1
Simplification of Fiduciary Security Transfers Act	7B	689
Simultaneous Death Act	8A	557
State Administrative Procedure Act (1961) (Model)	15	137
Trade Secrets Act	14	433
Transfers to Minors Act	8A	Pocket Part
Unclaimed Property Act (1981 Act)	8A	617
Veterans' Guardianship Act	8A	679

[1] Adopted 1977 Revision of Article 8, and 1972 Revision of Article 9.

CROSS REFERENCE INDEX TO ACTS

Citations are to U.L.A. Volumes

ABANDONED OR UNCLAIMED PROPERTY
Disposition of Unclaimed Property (1954 Act), Vol. 8A
Disposition of Unclaimed Property (1966 Act), Vol. 8A
Motor Vehicle Certificate of Title and Anti-Theft, Vol. 11
Probate Code, Art. III, Vol. 8
Unclaimed Property Act, Vol. 8A

ABANDONMENT
Disclaimer of Property Interests, Vol. 8A
Disclaimer of Transfers Under Nontestamentary Instruments, Vol. 8A

ABATEMENT
Probate Code, Art. III, Vol. 8

ABORTION
Penal Code, Part II, Vol. 10

ABORTION ACT
See Volume 9, Pt. I

ABSENCE AS EVIDENCE OF DEATH AND ABSENTEES PROPERTY ACT
See Volume 8A

ABSENCE WITHOUT LEAVE
Military Justice Code, Vol. 11

ABUSE OF OFFICE
Penal Code, Part II, Vol. 10

ACCEPTANCE
Commercial paper, Art. 3, Commercial Code, Vol. 2

ACCESS
Information Practices Code, Vol. 13

ACCIDENT AND HEALTH INSURANCE
Simultaneous Death, Vol. 8A

ACCIDENTS
Aircraft Financial Responsibility, Vol. 12
Brain Death, Vol. 12
Motor Vehicle Accident Reparations, Vol. 14
Periodic Payment of Judgment, Vol. 14

ACCOMMODATION PARTIES
Commercial paper, Art. 3, Commercial Code, Vol. 2

ACCOUNTS AND ACCOUNTING
Bank deposits and collections, Art. 4, Commercial Code, Vol. 2A
Commercial paper, Art. 3, Commercial Code, Vol. 2
Common Trust Funds, Vol. 7

ACCOUNTS AND ACCOUNTING—Cont'd
Consumer Credit Code (1968 Act), Vol. 7
Consumer Credit Code (1974 Act), Vol. 7A
Disposition of Unclaimed Property (1954 Act), Vol. 8A
Disposition of Unclaimed Property (1966 Act), Vol. 8A
Gifts to Minors (1956 Act), Vol. 8A
Gifts to Minors (1966 Act), Vol. 8A
Multiple-Person Accounts, Vol. 8A
Partnerships, Vol. 6
Preservation of Private Business Records, Vol. 14
Secured transactions, Art. 9, Commercial Code, Vols. 3, 3A
  Forms, Vol. 5
Transfers to Minors, Vol. 8A
Unclaimed Property, Vol. 8A
Veterans Guardianship, Vol. 8A

ACKNOWLEDGMENT ACT
See Volume 12

ACKNOWLEDGMENTS
Notarial Acts, Vol. 14
Recognition of Acknowledgments, Vol. 14

ACQUITTAL
Rules of Criminal Procedure, Art. V, Vol. 10

ADDICTS
Drug Dependence Treatment and Rehabilitation, Vol. 9, Pt. I

ADMINISTRATIVE PROCEDURE
State Administrative Procedure (1961 Act), Vol. 14
State Administrative Procedure (1981 Act), Vol. 14

ADMINISTRATORS
Executors and Administrators, generally, this index

ADMISSIBILITY OF EVIDENCE
Evidence Rules (1974), Vol. 13A

ADMISSION, PLEA OF
Rules of Criminal Procedure, Art. IV, Vol. 10

ADOPTION ACT
See Volume 9, Pt. I

ADVANCEMENTS
Intestate succession, Art. II, Probate Code, Vol. 8

ADVERSE OR PECUNIARY INTEREST
Trustees Powers, Vol. 7B

ADVERSE POSSESSION
Simplification of Land Transfers, Art. 3, Vol. 14

ADVERTISING
Consumer Credit Code (1968 Act), Vol. 7

ILLUSTRATION 7-46. Model State Admin. Proc. Act of 1961, Front Matter, 15 U.L.A. 137-38, 145 (1961) (superseded).

319

UNIFORM LAW COMMISSIONERS' MODEL STATE ADMINISTRATIVE PROCEDURE ACT (1961)

An Act Concerning Procedure of State Administrative Agencies and Review of Their Determinations

REVISED 1961 ACT

See, also, 1981 Model State Administrative Procedure Act, supra.

Table of Jurisdictions Wherein 1961 Act Has Been Adopted

Jurisdiction	Laws	Effective Date	Statutory Citation
Alabama	1981, No. 81–855, p. 1534	5–27–1981*	Code 1975, §§ 41–22–1 to 41–22–27.
Arizona [1]	1970, c. 101	1–1–1971	A.R.S. §§ 41–1001 to 41–1066.
Arkansas	1967 No. 434	3–17–1971	A.C.A § 25–15–201 to 25–15–214.
Connecticut	1971, P.A. 854	1–1–1972	C.G.S.A. §§ 4–166 to 4–189.
District of Columbia	1968, Pub.L. 90–614	10–21–1969	D.C.Code 1981, §§ 1–1501 to 1–1510.
Georgia	1964, p. 338	7–1–1965	O.C.G.A. §§ 50–13–1 to 50–13–22.
Hawaii	1961, c. 103		HRS §§ 91–1 to 91–18.
Idaho	1965, c. 273	1–1–1966	I.C. §§ 67–5201 to 67–5219.
Illinois	1975, P.A. 79–1083	9–22–1975	S.H.A. ch. 127, ¶¶ 1001 to 1021.
Iowa	1974, c. 1090	7–1–1975	I.C.A. §§ 17A.1 to 17A.23.
Louisiana	1966, No. 382	7–1–1967	LSA–R.S. 49:950 to 49:970.
Maine	1977, c. 551	7–1–1978	5 M.R.S.A. §§ 8001 to 11008.
Maryland	1957, c. 94	6–1–1957	Code, State Government, § 10–201 et seq.
Michigan	1969, No. 306	7–1–1970	M.C.L.A. §§ 24.201 to 24.315.
Mississippi	1976, c. 487	1–1–1977	Code 1972, §§ 25–43–1 to 25–43–19.
Missouri	1945, p. 1504		V.A.M.S. §§ 536.010 to 536.150.
Montana	1971, c. 2	12–31–1972	MCA 2–4–101 to 2–4–711.
Nebraska	1945, c. 255		R.R.S.1943, §§ 84–901 to 84–920.
Nevada	1965, c. 962		N.R.S. 233B.010 to 233B.150.
New York	1975, c. 167	9–1–1976	McKinney's State Administrative Procedure Act § 100 et seq.
Oklahoma	1963, c. 371		75 Okl.St.Ann. §§ 250.3 to 250.5, 302 to 323.
Oregon	1957, c. 717	6–13–1957*	ORS 183.310 et seq.
Rhode Island	1962, c. 112	1–1–1964	Gen.Laws 1956, §§ 42–35–1 to 42–35–18.
South Dakota	1966, c. 159		SDCL 1–26–1 to 1–26–41.
Tennessee	1974, c. 725	7–1–1975	T.C.A. §§ 4–5–101 et seq.
Vermont	1967, No. 360	7–1–1969	3 V.S.A. §§ 801 to 849.
West Virginia	1964, c. 1	7–1–1964	Code, 29A–1–1 to 29A–7–4.
Wisconsin	1955, c. 221		W.S.A. 227.01 to 227.60.
Wyoming	1965, c. 108	1–1–1966	W.S.1977, §§ 16–3–101 to 16–3–115.

* Date of approval.

[1] The Arizona act contains many of the major provisions of both the 1961 and 1981 Model State Administrative Procedure Acts. Accordingly, the citation of the Arizona act is set forth in the tables for both acts. For further details, see General Statutory Note, infra.

Historical Note

The Revised Model State Administrative Procedure Act was approved by the National Conference of Commissioners on Uniform State Laws in 1961. It superseded the orginal Model Act of the same name which was adopted in

STATE ADMINISTRATIVE PROCEDURE (1961)

1946. The 1961 Model Act was, in turn, superseded by the 1981 Model Act, set out supra.

PREFATORY NOTE

Administrative agencies have, during the last four decades become an essential and accepted part of state governmental organization, and the procedures by which such agencies adopt their rules and reach their decisions have attained paramount importance. Due very largely to the influence of the American Bar Association, the National Conference of Commissioners on Uniform State Laws and the state bar associations, substantial progress has been made in the direction of statutory codification of the procedures of state administrative agencies. Assurance has thereby been given of reasonable uniformity of practice and fair procedural methods for the benefit of all persons affected by state administrative action.

Preparation of the Model State Administrative Procedure Act

A brief resumé of the steps taken in the development of the Model State Administrative Procedure Act will reveal the careful attention it has received throughout the years. The act had its origin in the Section of Judicial Administration of the American Bar Association. In 1937, that Section created a Committee on Administrative Agencies and Tribunals. In 1938, at the American Bar Association meeting, the Committee presented a comprehensive report on the subject of Judicial Review of State Administrative Action in State Courts. The report was a scholarly and comprehensive document and drew much favorable comment. Again, in 1939, at the winter Section meeting, the same Committee reported,—this time setting forth a draft of a proposed act dealing with certain major phases of state administrative procedure. The act was prepared to serve as a model for state legislation on the subject.

In accordance with established practice, this draft act was referred by the Section to the National Conference of Commissioners on Uniform State Laws, and at the 1939 meeting of the Conference after discussion of the measure, a Conference Committee was appointed for the purpose of further study and development of the measure.

During the year 1939–1940, the Conference Committee met with the Committee of the Section on Judicial Administration, and numerous changes in the original draft were mutually agreed upon. A revised draft was presented at the 1940 session of the National Conference, and after careful revision it was adopted and forwarded to the House of Delegates of the American Bar Association for approval. However, in January of 1941, before action was taken by the House of Delegates, the United States Attorney General's Committee on Administrative Procedure filed its notable final report on the subject of federal administrative law, setting forth majority and minority drafts of bills for the regulation of federal administrative procedure. Thereafter, the Executive Committee of the National Conference decided that, in view of the Attorney General's Committee Report, it would be advisable to give still further consideration to the Conference measure, and accordingly it was recalled from the House of Delegates and recommitted to the Conference Committee.

Then in March of 1942, the so-called "Benjamin Report" was submitted to the Governor of New York. This report, entitled "Administrative Adjudication in the State of New York," was prepared by Robert M. Benjamin of the New York Bar as Commissioner appointed under Section 8 of the Executive Law of New York, for the purpose of studying the exercise of quasi-judicial functions of boards, commissions, and departments within the state. The report is a

138

ILLUSTRATION 7-46. *(continued)* 321

STATE ADMINISTRATIVE PROCEDURE (1961)

such manner that the various instances of substitution, omission, and additional matter cannot be clearly indicated by statutory notes.

Montana. While the Montana act is a substantial adoption of the major provisions of the Model Act, it departs from the official text in such manner that the various instances of substitution, omission, and additional matter cannot be clearly indicated by statutory notes.

Nebraska. While the Nebraska act is a substantial adoption of the major provisions of the Model Act, it departs from the official text in such manner that the various instances of substitution, omission, and additional matter cannot be clearly indicated by statutory notes.

Nevada. While the Nevada act is a substantial adoption of the major provisions of the Model Act, it departs from the official text in such manner that the various instances of substitution, omission, and additional matter cannot be clearly indicated by statutory notes.

New Hampshire. L. 1983, chs. 454 and 455, eff. Aug. 25, 1983, amended the New Hampshire act (formerly RSA 541-A:1 to 541-A:9), which previously had conformed substantially to the Model State Administrative Procedure Act of 1961, so that it consists of RSA 541-A:1 to RSA 541-A:21, and conforms substantially to the Model State Administrative Procedure Act of 1981. For further material relating to the New Hampshire act, see the Model State Administrative Procedure Act of 1981, supra.

New York. While the New York act is a substantial adoption of the major provisions of the Model Act, it departs from the official text in such manner that the various instances of substitution, omission, and additional matter cannot be clearly indicated by statutory notes.

North Carolina. The North Carolina act (G.S. §§ 150A-1 to 150A-64) was so amended by L.1985, c. 746, that it no longer constitutes a substantial adoption of the major provisions of the Uniform Act and, accordingly, has been deleted from the Table of Adopting Jurisdictions.

Oklahoma. While the Oklahoma act is a substantial adoption of the major provisions of the Model Act, it departs from the official text in such manner that the various instances of substitution, omission, and additional matter cannot be clearly indicated by statutory notes.

Oregon. While the Oregon act is a substantial adoption of the major provisions of the Model Act, it departs from the official text in such manner that the various instances of substitution, omission, and additional matter cannot be clearly indicated by statutory notes.

Rhode Island. Adds sections as follows:

"42-35-3.1. Form for filing—Failure to properly file. [Effective January 1, 1990.]— All administrative rules and regulations are to be filed in duplicate (one copy to be returned to the adopting agency, after proper stamping of date filed), pursuant to a form prepared by the secretary of state; all agencies must adhere to the form when submitting rules and regulations to the secretary of state pursuant to § 42-35-4.

"Should an agency fail to use the adopted format, the secretary of state shall reject the rule and/or regulation. The secretary of state shall reject the improper rule and/or regulation by returning the improperly drafted rule and/or regulation to the director of the agency which submitted the improper form within ten (10) days of receipt of said form."

"42-35-5.1. Regulatory agenda.—(a) On January 15 and June 15 of each year, each agency shall prepare and file with the governor, the secretary of state, the senate majority leader and the speaker of the house a regulatory agenda which shall contain:

"(1) a listing of all rules and orders promulgated since the preceding regulatory agenda, except orders of the human rights commission;

"(2) a brief description of the subject area of any rule which the agency expects to prepare or promulgate prior to the filing of the next regulatory agenda including the objectives and legal basis for such rules and approximate schedule for completing action on the rules;

"(3) the name and telephone number of an agency official knowledgeable concerning the items identified in subdivision (2).

"(b) The secretary of state shall compile the regulatory agendas and provide copies to the public upon request at a cost not to exceed the actual cost of publication.

"(c) Each agency shall endeavor to provide copies of its regulatory agenda to parties likely to be affected by proposed rules.

"(d) Nothing in this section precludes an agency from considering or acting upon any matter not included in the regulatory agenda nor does it require an agency to consider or act upon any matter listed in the agenda."

"42-35-15.1. Manner of taking appeals from administrative agencies.— (a) Appeals from decisions by administrative agencies of the state or officers thereof shall be taken to the superior court or to the district court as provided by the general laws in respect to each agency, provided, however, the time limits for the taking of steps necessary to perfect the appeal to the superior court or the district court shall be governed by the provisions of

§ 2. [Public Information; Adoption of Rules; Availability of Rules and Orders].

(a) In addition to other rule-making requirements imposed by law, each agency shall:

(1) adopt as a rule a description of its organization, stating the general course and method of its operations and the methods whereby the public may obtain information or make submissions or requests;

(2) adopt rules of practice setting forth the nature and requirements of all formal and informal procedures available, including a description of all forms and instructions used by the agency;

(3) make available for public inspection all rules and all other written statements of policy or interpretations formulated, adopted, or used by the agency in the discharge of its functions;

(4) make available for public inspection all final orders, decisions, and opinions.

(b) No agency rule, order, or decision is valid or effective against any person or party, nor may it be invoked by the agency for any purpose, until it has been made available for public inspection as herein required. This provision is not applicable in favor of any person or party who has actual knowledge thereof.

COMMENT

This section goes far beyond the provisions of Section 2 of the original Model State Administrative Procedure Act. Public information is substantially increased in scope. Subsection (a)(1) is made mandatory, whereas under the original act the obligation to promulgate descriptions of organization and the general course of operations was required only "so far as practicable." Also included are recommendations of the Hoover Commission Task Force to the effect that statements of policy and interpretive materials, as well as rules, orders, and opinions shall be made available for public inspection. Finally, the sanctions of Subsection (b) are included for the first time.

The corresponding provisions of the Federal Administrative Procedure Act are as follows:

"Sec. 3. Except to the extent that there is involved (1) any function of the United States requiring secrecy in the public interest or (2) any matter relating solely to the internal management of an agency—

"(a) *Rules.*—Every agency shall separately state and currently publish in the Federal Register (1) descriptions of its central and field organization including delegations by the agency of final authority and the established places at which, and methods whereby, the public may secure information or make submittals or requests; (2) statements of the general course and method by which its functions are channeled and determined, including the nature and requirements of all formal or informal procedures available as well as forms and instructions as to the scope and contents of all papers, reports, or examinations; and (3) substantive rules adopted as authorized by law and statements of general policy or interpretations formulated and adopted by the agency for the guidance of the public, but not rules addressed to and served upon named persons in accordance with law. No person shall in any manner be required to resort to organization or procedure not so published.

"(b) *Opinions and Orders.*—Every agency shall publish, or, in accordance with published rule, make available to public inspection all final opinions or orders in

ILLUSTRATION 7-47. *(continued)* 323

§ 2 STATE ADMINISTRATIVE PROCEDURE (1961)

the adjudication of cases (except those required for good cause to be held confidential and not cited as precedents) and all rules.

"(c) *Public Records.*—Save as otherwise required by statute, matters of official record shall in accordance with published rule be made available to persons properly and directly concerned except information held confidential for good cause found."

Action in Adopting Jurisdictions

Variations from Official Text:
Idaho. Omits subsec. (a)(1).

In subsec. (a)(2), omits clause beginning, "including a description".

Library References

American Digest System

Necessity of notice or publication of decision, see Administrative Law and Procedure ⊗504.

Necessity of notice or publication of rules after adoption, see Administrative Law and Procedure ⊗408.

Statutory basis of power to make rules, see Administrative Law and Procedure ⊗386.

Encyclopedias

Necessity of notice or publication of decision, see C.J.S. Public Administrative Law and Procedure § 152.

Necessity of notice or publication of rules after adoption, see C.J.S. Public Administrative Law and Procedure § 112.

Statutory basis of power to make rules, see C.J.S. Public Administrative Law and Procedure § 89.

WESTLAW Electronic Research

See WESTLAW Electronic Research Guide following the Explanation.

Notes of Decisions

Generally 1
Contracts 4
Exceptions to rule 5
Failure to promulgate rules 7
Internal procedure and management rules 3
Practice and procedure rules 2
Public inspection and disclosure 6

1. Generally

Under Michigan Administrative Procedures Act, where agency policy follows from its statutory authority, policy is considered exercise of permissible statutory authority and not rule requiring formal adoption. Matter of Park Nursing Center, Inc., Bkrtcy.Mich.1983, 28 B.R. 793.

Within constitutional limitations, statute may authorize administrative instrumentality to supply details of its operations by passing its own rules and regulations. Wilson v. Connect-icut Product Development Corp., 1974, 355 A.2d 72, 167 Conn. 111.

An administrative agency has the authority to promulgate guidelines constituting its attempt to construe provisions of statutory authority given to it by the legislature, subject to judicial review as to proper exercise of such authority. People ex rel. Petersen v. Turner Co., 1976, 346 N.E.2d 102, 37 Ill.App.3d 450.

Administrative agencies have broad authority to adopt regulations in furtherance of their legislative mandate, and the courts will not lightly interfere with promulgation or interpretation of such regulations. Fein v. Rent Stabilization Ass'n of New York City, Inc., 1979, 420 N.Y.S.2d 826, 101 Misc.2d 216.

2. Practice and procedure rules

Provision of the Administrative Procedure Act requiring that rules relating to practice and procedure be established and promulgated is cases from all jurisdictions construing this section. Additional information may appear in the pocket part or supplement.

In the occupational safety and health research situation, your next steps would be to look over the case digests, select those relevant to the research situation, and read those cases and the state statutes interpreted by those cases.

c.   Other Ways to Find Uniform and Model Acts

The organization sponsoring a new model or uniform act may first publish it in a legal periodical, sometimes accompanied by commentary.

Model and uniform acts also may be published separately. For instance, ALI model acts are entered in a library catalog under the author heading of "American Law Institute." NCCUSL uniform and model acts can be found under the subject heading of "Uniform State Laws," but individual acts are entered under the appropriate subject heading with the subdivision "United States—States."

The NCCUSL annually publishes *Handbook of the National Conference of Commissioners on Uniform State Laws.* This *Handbook* lists all of the NCCUSL uniform and model acts, not just those adopted by one or more states. It also discusses the progress of acts being considered for drafting and those currently being drafted. However, the text of a particular act only appears in the *Handbook* published in the year the act was approved.

The Council of State Government annually publishes *Suggested State Legislation,* which has a cumulative index at the back of each volume. You can locate this collection by doing an author or title search in your library catalog.

d.   ULA Database on WESTLAW

WESTLAW'S ULA database contains all uniform and model acts appearing in the hardbound U.L.A. You may retrieve a section of an act with the "find" command. To obtain the "find" abbreviations for a ULA act, use the scope command for the database: [sc ula]. Then to find a section of an act, for example, § 2 of the 1961 APA, use the "find" search [fi ula admin p 1961 s 2]. See Illustration 7-48 on page 325.

3. How to Find Sources Discussing Uniform and Model Acts

a.   Print Finding Tools

If you wish to learn where a section of a NCCUSL uniform or model act is discussed in Am. Jur. 2d, locate the Am. Jur. 2d volume entitled Table of Statutes, Rules, and Regulations Cited and use the table of contents on the inside front cover to find the table covering uniform and model acts.

Similarly, if you wish to learn where a section of a NCCUSL uniform or model act is discussed in A.L.R., locate the last A.L.R. *Index to Annotations* volume, which contains various tables. One of those tables is a table of statutes cited in A.L.R.3d, 4th, and 5th and A.L.R. Fed.; it only includes the NCCUSL model and uniform acts.

If you want to find cases from a particular jurisdiction that construe an adopted version of a NCCUSL uniform or model act, find the act in the annotated statutes for that jurisdiction. The U.L.A.'s table of jurisdictions adopt-

```
Citation                              Page(P)        Database   Mode
ULA ADMIN P 1961 s 2      FOUND DOCUMENT P 1 OF 16    ULA        P
 Model State Administrative Proc.Act 1961 s 2

                         UNIFORM LAWS ANNOTATED
 COPYRIGHT (c) 1991 By WEST PUBLISHING CO. Official Text and Comments Reproduced
  with Permission of the National Conference of Commissioners on Uniform State
                    Laws and the American Law Institute
   UNIFORM LAW COMMISSIONERS' MODEL STATE ADMINISTRATIVE PROCEDURE ACT (1961)
                          REVISED 1961 ACT

 s 2. [Public Information;  Adoption of Rules;  Availability of Rules and
   Orders].

  (a) In addition to other rule-making requirements imposed by law, each agency
 shall:
   (1) adopt as a rule a description of its organization, stating the general
 course and method of its operations and the methods whereby the public may
 obtain information or make submissions or requests;
   (2) adopt rules of practice setting forth the nature and requirements of all
 formal and informal procedures available, including a description of all forms
 and instructions used by the agency;
   (3) make available for public inspection all rules and all other written
```

ing that act may be a quick source of a cite to that state's version of the act. Also, if you are using a West annotated code to research a state statute based on a NCCUSL uniform or model act, you may turn to the beginning of the state act in the annotated code to find a table of jurisdictions that have adopted that particular uniform or model act, as well as cites to the adopting state's codes. This table allows you to skip using the U.L.A.

Another way to locate sources citing NCCUSL uniform acts is to use the specialized *Shepard's* sets, such as *Shepard's Uniform Commercial Code Citations* (covering the UCC) and *Shepard's Partnership Law Citations* (which covers the Uniform Partnership Act and both the original and the revised Uniform Limited Partnership Act). The advantages and limitations of *Shepard's* as compared with U.L.A. annotations are similar to those discussed earlier with regard to the Restatement appendix volumes. See Chapter 3, Part F, at pages 119 and 121.

b. Computer-Assisted Legal Research

At the beginning of each main U.L.A. volume or pocket part is a WESTLAW Electronic Guide, which suggests computer searches for locating cases that cite a section of a NCCUSL uniform or model act. The guide suggests the search [model +2 administrative /7 2] for locating cases citing § 2 of the Administrative Procedure Act. As of January 1992, this search brought up six cases in the ALLSTATES database. However, the courts of a state may not use the NCCUSL citation style, so you may need to search for a state-specific citation style.

Another strategy is to consult the NCCUSL uniform or model act to learn the West Topic and Key Number covering the section you are researching. Then perform a Key Number search to retrieve cases with that Key Number among their headnotes.

If you are researching a uniform or model act drafted by an organization other than the NCCUSL, WESTLAW and LEXIS will be equally capable of finding a mention of that act in various citing sources. Remember that the NCCUSL is not the only source of uniform and model laws.

Citation Note: Uniform and model acts that have been enacted as a statute are cited to the statute. Other acts are cited to U.L.A. as follows: Model State Admin. Proc. Act of 1961, § 2, 15 U.L.A. 137, 165 (1961) (superseded by 1981 act). Give the year in which the act was last amended, not the year of the U.L.A. volume. *See* Rules 12.8.4 and 12.8.5 of *The Bluebook.*

Administrative Materials: Searching for Primary Authority

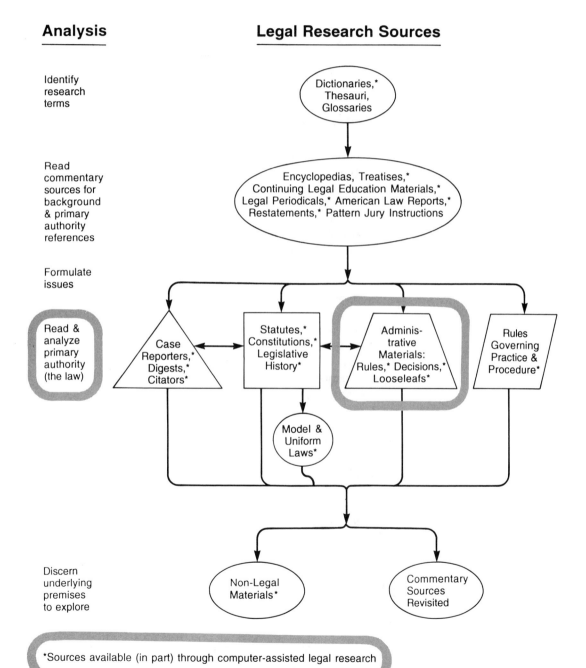

Analysis	Legal Research Sources

Analysis

Identify research terms

Read commentary sources for background & primary authority references

Formulate issues

Read & analyze primary authority (the law)

Discern underlying premises to explore

Legal Research Sources

Dictionaries,* Thesauri, Glossaries

Encyclopedias, Treatises,* Continuing Legal Education Materials,* Legal Periodicals,* American Law Reports,* Restatements,* Pattern Jury Instructions

Case Reporters,* Digests,* Citators*

Statutes,* Constitutions,* Legislative History*

Administrative Materials: Rules,* Decisions,* Looseleafs*

Rules Governing Practice & Procedure*

Model & Uniform Laws*

Non-Legal Materials*

Commentary Sources Revisited

*Sources available (in part) through computer-assisted legal research

A. INTRODUCTION

1. Preview

Thus far, you have learned how to use secondary authority tools to aid you in locating and understanding primary authority. You have learned to research two forms of primary authority: judicial decisions and statutory materials. In this chapter, you will learn to research an additional body of primary authority: the law made by administrative agencies.

Administrative agencies are involved in almost every field of American life and law from agriculture to zoning. For example, federal agencies regulate interstate trucking and aviation, allocate radio frequencies, monitor labor-management relations, license nuclear power plants, seek to reduce air and water pollution, and handle social security claims. State agencies handle worker's compensation claims, license drivers and barbers, review charges of employment and housing discrimination, and supervise charitable gambling. In some fields, there are overlapping federal and state agencies.

As you work through this chapter, be attentive to the similarities between cases and statutes on the one hand and the law made by administrative agencies on the other. Agencies promulgate regulations, which resemble statutes. Agencies also issue case adjudications, which resemble judicial decisions.

Also be attentive to the connections between cases and statutes on the one hand and the law made by administrative agencies on the other. As detailed below, statutes create agencies, which must operate within constitutional and statutory constraints. The judiciary monitors this compliance in its review of agency regulations and adjudications.

This chapter begins with an overview of how agencies come into being and operate. Part B then covers the official sources containing administrative agency law. Part C provides an introduction to administrative looseleaf services, which present a wide array of primary and secondary authority in various fields regulated by administrative agencies. Research in administrative agency law through online sources is then covered in Part D. The final part covers research into the law of state administrative agencies.

As you work through this chapter, you will learn more about the law pertinent to the CSB Construction problem introduced in Chapter 7. You may wish to refer to Table 8.1 below, which presents an overview of the sources in this area. As the flowchart in the table depicts, the process of research in

TABLE 8.1. Flowchart and Listing of Administrative Materials.

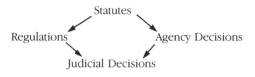

Each of the above materials is also analyzed in commentary sources.

Authority	Sources		
	Print	*CALR*	*Looseleafs*
Statutes:	U.S.C. U.S.C.A. U.S.C.S.	yes	yes
Regulations:	*Code of Federal Regulations* *Federal Register*	yes	yes
Agency Decisions:	official and unofficial reporters	yes	yes
Judicial Decisions:	official and unofficial reporters	yes	yes

administrative materials begins with a statute. The statute creates an agency, which promulgates regulations and issues decisions as permitted by the statute. The judiciary reviews the law made by the agency. Commentary, although not law itself, may be useful in understanding the law made by agencies.

2. Administrative Agencies

a. In General

As you no doubt know, the United States government has three branches: legislative, judicial, and executive. So pervasive is the administrative agency. that it has been called the fourth branch of government. Administrative agencies have existed for centuries, although many of them came about as a result of the regulatory reforms of the New Deal in the 1930s or the social reforms of the 1960s.

Agencies solve two general types of problems the other branches do not handle well alone. First, administrative agencies regulate an industry or a set of practices (such as employment relations or factory emissions) where the legislature perceives that the free market has failed to yield results consonant with social policy and the other branches cannot provide sufficiently close monitoring. An agency can provide close and constant supervision. For example, the Interstate Commerce Commission was created in 1887 to regulate railroads, which were perceived at the time to be operating contrary to the public interest.

Second, agencies administer systems that entail large volumes of claims or cases that would otherwise cripple the courts. For example, the predecessor of the Veterans Administration was created in 1789 to handle the large volume of claims by veterans for benefits under federal law.

Agencies are well equipped to handle these regulatory and bureaucratic tasks in part because of their expertise. Legislatures and judges are generalists; they address whatever problems constituents and litigants bring to them. An agency, by contrast, has a single subject on which it focuses. Its commissioners or members develop regulations or decide cases involving only that subject, its lawyers specialize in only that subject, and it generally can call upon a staff of technical experts.

Agencies also are well equipped for these tasks because they can use more than one form of law-making. Agencies engage in "an ongoing enterprise of regulation, of ordering and reordering." Louis L. Jaffe & Nathaniel L. Nathanson, *Administrative Law: Cases and Materials* 4 (1961). To the outside observer, the most obvious agency functions—the "occasional crystals of administrative energy," *id.*—are rulemaking and case adjudications.

When the agency promulgates rules or regulations (the terms are synonymous), it operates as a quasi-legislature. The agency typically solicits the views of persons likely to be affected by the regulation, conducts a hearing or prepares a written record, and then deliberates.

When the agency decides cases, it operates as a quasi-judiciary. That process generally entails a complaint and answer, a trial-type hearing, briefs and argument, deliberations, and a written order and decision explaining the outcome. In many situations, various agency employees serve as investigator, prosecutor, judge, jury, appeals court, and executioner.

The notion of separation of powers thus has little force in administrative agencies. Agencies merge legislative and judicial functions.

Agencies also operate in ways not typically employed by legislatures or courts. In enforcing quasi-criminal statutes, staff members of some agencies monitor an industry, identify wrongdoers, investigate instances involving violations of the law, cite the violators, and prosecute them in agency proceedings. Other agencies manage systems; an example is the Federal Reserve Board's activities in banking. Some agencies are charged with policy-making functions, typically carried out through studies of major problems that may yield new regulations or recommendations to Congress for legislation.

How do agencies acquire the authority to perform these tasks? Agencies are created by legislatures through enabling statutes. An enabling statute has two functions: to establish the agency and its powers and to set out the general substantive rules of law the agency is to carry out. Essentially the legislature sets out the general direction the law should take and delegates to the agency the power to settle the details.

A typical enabling statute specifies how members of an agency are to be selected and what those members may do—for example, make rules, decide cases, issue subpoenas, levy fines. An enabling statute also determines the forcefulness of the agency's actions. The legislature may provide that an agency decision in an individual case is enforceable by the agency, or it may provide that the courts must act to enforce the decision against an unwilling party. The legislature may provide that agency rules have authoritative weight comparable to that afforded a statute by providing a clear and specific delegation to the agency to make the rule and a penalty for violation of the rule (legislative or substantive rules). By contrast, when the legislature merely grants the agency the power to prosecute violators under general statutory language, the agency may issue an interpretive rule or guideline, expressing its understanding of what constitutes a violation.

The legislature's involvement with the agency continues well past the enactment of the enabling statute. The legislature appropriates funds for the agency; the amount of funding often determines how much real clout an agency will have. The legislature may reserve the right to review the executive's appointments of members of the agency. The legislature may conduct oversight hearings to determine whether the agency is properly pursuing its statutory mission and using its funds wisely. And the legislature may pass further legislation in response to actions the agency takes.

The legislature does not, however, oversee the agency alone. The courts also have a substantial responsibility for reviewing both agency regulations and case adjudications. Courts ask: Has the agency acted within its jurisdiction and according to the instructions set out in the enabling statute? Has the agency followed the procedures required by the statute and the Constitution? Is the agency's action adequately supported by the factual record? The subject of judicial review of agency actions is a rich and complex one, the details of which are beyond the scope of this text. In addition, the courts review the legislature's actions in creating the agency in order to be sure that the legislature has not unconstitutionally delegated its authority to the agency.

In thinking about the authoritative weight of administrative agency law, then, you should remember two principles. First, regulations and decisions issued by administrative agencies are primary authority because they issue from a government body empowered to make law. Second, the authoritative weight of a particular regulation or decision is ultimately determined by the legislature and the courts.

If you wish to explore how agencies operate in greater detail, you may wish to read the federal statutes governing administrative processes, 5 U.S.C. §§ 551-559, 601-612, 701-706 (1988).

b. Occupational Safety and Health as an Example

After passing several statutes protecting workers in specific industries during the late 1960s, Congress passed the Occupational Safety and Health Act (OSHA) in 1970. Pub. L. No. 91-596, 84 Stat. 1593. As you already know from Chapter 7, OSHA creates federal law regarding workplace safety and simultaneously permits equally stringent state laws. As you also know, OSHA imposes a general duty to provide a safe workplace and the specific duty to comply with regulations.

With OSHA, Congress chose a "standards enforcement model." Early on, the Secretary of Labor had the power to issue regulations, or standards, by adopting existing industry standards. Now the Secretary must follow rule-making procedures in adopting, modifying, or repealing new standards, although she may use an abbreviated process in emergency situations. Employers may seek variances from standards in limited situations.

The Occupational Safety and Health Administration of the Labor Department enforces the standards as well as the general duty clause through a system of inspections and citations. Compliance officers (COs) inspect workplaces on a scheduled basis, or as a follow-up to injuries, or when called in by employees. If the CO finds a violation of the law, the area director issues a citation that states the violation, penalty, and date by which the condition must be abated. Absent a contest by the employer, employees, or union, the citation takes effect.

Where there is a contest, OSHA provides for consideration by the Occupational Safety and Health Review Commission (OSAHRC), appointed by the President. The first stage involves a trial before an administrative law judge (ALJ), in which the Secretary must prove the violation. The Commission reviews the ALJ's recommended order at the request of a party or on its own initiative. Subsequent review is afforded by the federal courts of appeals.

OSHA also created the National Institute for Occupational Safety and Health (NIOSH), part of the Department of Health and Human Services. NIOSH conducts scientific research on occupational safety matters.

3. Your Research Situation

Reread the CSB Construction scenario first explored in Chapter 7 at pages 237-238.

The research detailed in Chapter 7 provided substantial information pertinent to this situation. You learned that there is a federal Occupational Safety and Health Act and that some states have "baby OSHAs" as permitted by the federal statute. You learned that the federal and probably state schemes do not afford direct sanctions against employees (although employers certainly are expected to discipline employees). You learned that employers have two duties: a general duty to provide a workplace free of recognized hazards and a duty to comply with specific agency regulations. This chapter explores the precise ramifications of the second duty.

For most of this chapter, we will assume that the facts arose in Georgia and are governed by the federal system.

B. RESEARCHING FEDERAL ADMINISTRATIVE MATERIALS WITHOUT LOOSELEAFS OR CALR

1. A Basic Strategy

As you may have deduced from Part A, thorough research in administrative materials entails locating and analyzing the pertinent enabling act and judicial opinions reviewing the agency's action as well as the law made by the agency itself. Again, agency law consists of regulations and case adjudications. The following materials describe a research sequence that begins with the statute, works through the agency's regulations and decisions, and concludes with judicial opinions. While there are other ways to proceed, the sequence presented here has two distinct advantages: It encompasses all forms of primary authority, and it tracks the evolution of the law, thus providing a depth of understanding that should prove helpful in figuring out a rule of law created jointly by the legislature, an agency, and the courts. You may wish to refer again to Table 8.1 on page 329 as you read through this part.

2. The Statutory Codes

Your point of departure for research in administrative materials should be the statute(s) pertaining to the agency. Although the statute is not law created by the agency, it is the law that creates the agency, providing guidance as to the substance of the law the agency may make and regulating the agency's procedures.

You should recall that there are various ways to locate a pertinent statute, including use of a reference provided in commentary sources and the statutory codes' indexes. Recall also that there are three federal statutory codes, the official *United States Code* (U.S.C.) and the two unofficial codes, *United States Code Annotated* (U.S.C.A.) and *United States Code Service* (U.S.C.S.). U.S.C.A. and U.S.C.S. are more helpful than U.S.C. because of the research leads provided by the annotations. Remember that it is crucial to update your research by consulting pocket parts, supplemental pamphlets, and legislative services.

Once you have located the pertinent statute, you should read it carefully to discern Congress' guidance on two questions: First, what has Congress said about your legal issue? Congress has provided fairly little guidance for our research situation. The statute requires employers to comply with OSHA standards. 29 U.S.C. § 654(a)(2) (1988). Congress also provided that standards must require practices "reasonably necessary or appropriate to provide safe or healthful employment," *id.* § 652(8), and imposed a feasibility requirement on standards pertaining to toxic substances, *id.* § 655(b)(5). As you can see, there is very little detail in the statute.

Second, in reading your statute, focus on what Congress has said about the operations of the agency and the role courts play. A thorough reading of OSHA would yield the information on the administrative scheme set forth in Part A on page 332.

Once you understand what the statute says, you should be ready to look in the annotations for references to agency regulations and decisions and judicial opinions. The U.S.C.S. annotations generally will be more helpful than those of U.S.C.A. because U.S.C.S. provides more references to agency decisions and regulations. In our research situation, U.S.C.S. is indeed more helpful. As Illustration 8-1 (on pages 335-336) shows, you would find a reference to "Administrative Rules" in the cross-references appearing below the legislative history section and citations to both federal court and OSAHRC decisions in the case annotations. In addition, references to several regulations, including 29 C.F.R. § 1926.28(a), appear in several of the paragraphs describing the key cases.

Before leaving the annotated codes, you also may wish to note any other useful references provided in the annotations, such as citations to legal encyclopedias or A.L.R. annotations.

3. Agency Regulations

Congress may do little more than provide a general standard and an instruction to the agency to issue appropriate regulations, as in our research situation. In form, agency regulations look very much like statutes. (See Illustration 8-2 on page 337.) In content, agency regulations generally are considerably more detailed and technical than the corresponding enabling statutes. This is not surprising, for regulations are promulgated after significant investigation by agencies with substantial technical expertise. Furthermore, the role of a regulation is to make Congress' vague intentions into explicit and precise rules of law.

There are close parallels between research into agency regulations and statutory research. The *Code of Federal Regulations* (C.F.R.) parallels U.S.C. A government publication containing almost all federal regulations, C.F.R. is organized by titles that basically parallel the titles of U.S.C. Happily, unlike U.S.C., portions of C.F.R. are revised and republished quarterly so that your volume should be no more than one year old. New regulations not yet published in C.F.R. appear in the *Federal Register,* the administrative agency equivalent of a session law service. There are, however, no commercial annotated publications for administrative regulations paralleling U.S.C.A. and U.S.C.S.

a. *Code of Federal Regulations*

As with the statutory codes, there are several means of locating a pertinent agency regulation. As noted above, U.S.C.S. and U.S.C.A. provide some citations to agency regulations. Commentary sources also are likely to provide these citations. You may also wish to determine whether your library carries a commercial index to C.F.R., such as Martindale-Hubbell's *Code of Federal Regulations Index* or Congressional Information Service's *CIS Index to the Code of Federal Regulations.* These indexes generally are more detailed than the official index.

C.F.R. itself provides several means of locating pertinent regulations, all found in the *CFR Index and Finding Aids* volume. First, the List of CFR Titles, Chapters, Subchapters, and Parts outlines the contents of C.F.R. C.F.R. compiles regulations into five units: titles, chapters, subchapters, parts, and sections, listed from largest to smallest. Because C.F.R. titles generally track those used in the statutory codes, you could determine the part where your regulation would appear by looking up the title paralleling your statutory title and skimming the contents. (See Illustration 8-3 on page 338.)

Second, the CFR Index, a subject matter index that uses rather general indexing terms, also directs you to the part of C.F.R. on point, although not

OCCUPATIONAL SAFETY AND HEALTH **29 USCS § 654**

§ 654. Duties of employers and employees

(a) Each employer—
(1) shall furnish to each of his employees employment and a place of employment which are free from recognized hazards that are causing or are likely to cause death or serious physical harm to his employees;
(2) shall comply with occupational safety and health standards promulgated under this Act.

(b) Each employee shall comply with occupational safety and health standards and all rules, regulations, and orders issued pursuant to this Act which are applicable to his own actions and conduct.
(Dec. 29, 1970, P. L. 91-596, § 5, 84 Stat. 1593.)

HISTORY; ANCILLARY LAWS AND DIRECTIVES

References in text:
"This Act", referred to in this section, is Act Dec. 29, 1970, P. L. 91-596, 84 Stat. 1590, popularly known as the Occupational Safety and Health Act of 1970, which appears generally as 29 USCS §§ 651 et seq. For full classification of this Act, consult USCS Tables volumes.

Effective date of section:
For the effective date of this section, see the Other provisions note to 29 USCS § 651.

CROSS REFERENCES

USCS Administrative Rules, OSHRC, 29 CFR Part 2200.
This section is referred to in 29 USCS §§ 658, 666.

RESEARCH GUIDE

Federal Procedure L Ed:
17 Fed Proc L Ed, Health, Education, and Welfare §§ 42:1085, 1260.

Am Jur:
2 Am Jur 2d, Administrative Law § 650.
61 Am Jur 2d, Plant and Job Safety—OSHA and State Laws §§ 1–3, 9, 21, 25, 26, 31, 34–38, 40, 43, 57, 58, 67, 78, 82, 88, 101, 102, 106, 112, 124.

Forms:
10A Fed Procedural Forms L Ed, Health, Education, and Welfare § 37:112.
16 Am Jur Pl & Pr Forms (Rev), Labor and Labor Relations, Forms 381, 382, 402–404.

American Law of Products Liability 3d:
4 Am Law Prod Liab 3d, Consumer Product Safety Laws § 62:7.

RIA Coordinators:
15 RIA Employment Coord, Employer Requirements ¶¶ WS-11,072; 13,802; 13,803.

37

to the specific section. In using this index, it is generally wise to start with the name of your agency. (See Illustration 8-4 on page 339.)

Finally, the Parallel Table of Authorities and Rules matches enabling statutes and regulations in C.F.R., generally by part. Note that this table lists the regulations not under 29 U.S.C. § 654 but rather under § 655, which establishes the agency's power to promulgate regulations. (See Illustration 8-5 on page 340.)

Once you have located your regulation, you should read it carefully and

LABOR

§§ 1910.23(a)(8), 1926.500(b)(8)) does not apply only to holes through which persons can fall. Bechtel Power Corp. (1979) OSHRC Docket No. 13832.

Employer was properly cited for willful violation of 29 CFR § 1910.22(c) in failing to provide guardrails around vats of molten zinc where employer had been previously cited under same standard for failure to have guardrails around galvanizing kettles and acid tanks and was thus aware of requirements of standard and employer's belief that guardrails would make certain operations impossible or create greater hazard, however "sincere," could not be considered "good-faith" belief since employer failed to exercise reasonable diligence to find alternative protection for employees. Acme Fence & Iron Co. (1980) OSHRC Docket No. 78-0982.

129. —Safety lines and belts

Terms "lifeline" and "lanyard" have distinct meanings under OSHA regulations; construction company violated standard requiring use of lifeline (29 CFR § 1926.451(1)(4)) even though employee used lanyard. Fluor Constructors, Inc. v Occupational Safety & Health Review Com. (1988, CA6) 861 F2d 936, 13 BNA OSHC 1956, 1988 CCH OSHD ¶ 28350.

Construction industry personal protective equipment standard (29 CFR § 1926.28(a)) properly can be read to require use of tied-off safety belts where employee is exposed to falling hazard. PPG Industries, Inc. (1977) OSHRC Docket No. 15426.

Prima facie violation of 29 CFR § 1926.105(a) is established if employees are subject to falls of more than 25 feet and none of devices listed in standard are used; complete failure to use safety belts is not excused simply because they cannot be tied off in ideal manner. Sierra Constr. Corp. (1978) OSHRC Docket No. 13638.

Requirement of standard (29 CFR § 1926.556(b)(2)(v)) that tied off body belt be worn when "working" from aerial lift includes act of being transported in aerial lift to or from work level. Salah & Pecci Constr. Co. (1978) OSHRC Docket No. 15769.

Employer can be found in violation of 29 CFR § 1926.28(a) for failing to require wearing of tied-off safety belts even if belts cannot be tied off in ideal manner; employer is not excused from compliance with § 1926.28(a) merely because it is not possible to secure lifelines as required by 29 CFR § 1926.104(b) or to limit length of lanyards as required by 29 CFR § 1926.104(d). Valley Roofing Corp. (1978) OSHRC Docket No. 15800.

Standard at 29 CFR § 1926.451(u)(3) is directed at separate fall hazard associated with

118

OCCUPATIONAL SAFETY AND HEALTH

working anywhere on sloped roof due to its pitch rather than working proximate to its edge and does not preempt general standard at 29 CFR 1926.28(a). John's Roofing & Sheet Metal Co. (1978) OSHRC Docket No. 76-114.

Impossibility of compliance with requirement of 29 CFR § 1926.104(b) that lifelines be secured above point of operation is not defense to alleged violation of 29 CFR § 1926.28(a) based on non-use of safety belts. S & H Riggers & Erectors, Inc. (1980) OSHRC Docket Nos. 76-1104, 76-1739.

Language of 29 CFR § 1910.252(e)(1)(i), requiring fall protection for workers on platforms, scaffolds or runways, imposes specific duty on employers in that it assumes existence of fall hazard and lists alternative ways in which employer may fulfill duty to provide effective protection against falling such as use of railings, safety belts, or lifelines, and Secretary need not, therefore, prove feasibility of remedial measures in order to make out prima facie violation of standard. Marion Power Shovel Co., Inc. (1980) OSHRC Docket No. 76-4114.

Argument that employee's failure to tie off his safety belt is unpreventable employee misconduct does not establish defense to citation where violation alleged is lack of standard guardrail around open-sided floor. Secretary of Labor v Capform, Inc. (1986, OSHRC ALJ) 13 BNA OSHC 1011.

For purposes of standards such as 29 CFR § 1926.104, regulating use of lifelines, safety belts, and lanyards, terms "lifeline" and "lanyard" have distinct meanings and are not interchangeable. Fluor Constructors, Inc. (1987) OSHRC Docket No. 86-1393.

130. — —Particular cases

Employer is in violation of 29 USCS § 651 where inspection by Occupational Safety and Health Act compliance officers reveals lifelines not installed on any of 4 scaffolds in place and none of workers on scaffolds wearing safety belts. Western Waterproofing Co. v Marshall (1978, CA8) 576 F2d 139, cert den 439 US 965, 58 L Ed 2d 423, 99 S Ct 452.

Where employer took all feasible steps to insure compliance with safety standards, it is not liable for employee's failure to use safety belt and resulting fall to death from temporary catwalk. Daniel International Corp. v Occupational Safety & Health Review Com. (1982, CA11) 683 F2d 361 (disagreed with by Brock v L.E. Myers Co., High Voltage Div. (CA6) 818 F2d 1270, 13 BNA OSHC 1289, 1987 CCH OSHD ¶ 27919, cert den 484 US 989, 98 L Ed 2d 509, 108 S Ct 479, 13 BNA OSHC 1531, 1988 CCH OSHD ¶ 28131).

119

discern its impact on your problem. Note that the key regulation here, § 1926.28 (see Illustration 8-2 on page 337), simply makes the employer "responsible for requiring the wearing of appropriate personal protective equipment" where there are hazards or other rules so require. You would, of course, consult other rules for further detail, much as it is imperative to consult related statutory sections. If you did so, you would not in this case find

ILLUSTRATION 8-2. 29 C.F.R. §§ 1926.20-.28 (1991).   337

in., Labor   § 1926.20

assumes all obligations prescribed as employer obligations under the standards contained in this part, whether or not he subcontracts any part of the work.

(c) To the extent that a subcontractor of any tier agrees to perform any part of the contract, he also assumes responsibility for complying with the standards in this part with respect to that part. Thus, the prime contractor assumes the entire responsibility under the contract and the subcontractor assumes responsibility with respect to his portion of the work. With respect to subcontracted work, the prime contractor and any subcontractor or subcontractors shall be deemed to have joint responsibility.

(d) Where joint responsibility exists, both the prime contractor and his subcontractor or subcontractors, regardless of tier, shall be considered subject to the enforcement provisions of the Act.

Subpart C—General Safety and Health Provisions

AUTHORITY: Sec. 107, Contract Work Hours and Safety Standards Act (Construction Safety Act) (40 U.S.C. 333); secs. 4, 6, 8, Occupational Safety and Health Act of 1970 (29 U.S.C. 653, 655, 657); Secretary of Labor's Order No. 12-71 (36 FR 8754), 8-76 (41 FR 25059), or 9-83 (48 FR 35736), as applicable.

§ 1926.20 General safety and health provisions.

(a) *Contractor requirements.* (1) Section 107 of the Act requires that it shall be a condition of each contract which is entered into under legislation subject to Reorganization Plan Number 14 of 1950 (64 Stat. 1267), as defined in § 1926.12, and is for construction, alteration, and/or repair, including painting and decorating, that no contractor or subcontractor for any part of the contract work shall require any laborer or mechanic employed in the performance of the contract to work in surroundings or under working conditions which are unsanitary, hazardous, or dangerous to his health or safety.

(b) *Accident prevention responsibilities.* (1) It shall be the responsibility

19

Occupational Safety and Health Admin., l

§ 1926.25 Housekeeping.

(a) During the course of construction, alteration, or repairs, form and scrap lumber with protruding nails, and all other debris, shall be kept cleared from work areas, passageways, and stairs, in and around buildings or other structures.

(b) Combustible scrap and debris shall be removed at regular intervals during the course of construction. Safe means shall be provided to facilitate such removal.

(c) Containers shall be provided for the collection and separation of waste, trash, oily and used rags, and other refuse. Containers used for garbage and other oily, flammable, or hazardous wastes, such as caustics, acids, harmful dusts, etc. shall be equipped with covers. Garbage and other waste shall be disposed of at frequent and regular intervals.

§ 1926.26 Illumination.

Construction areas, aisles, stairs, ramps, runways, corridors, offices, shops, and storage areas where work is in progress shall be lighted with either natural or artificial illumination. The minimum illumination requirements for work areas are contained in Subpart D of this part.

§ 1926.27 Sanitation.

Health and sanitation requirements for drinking water are contained in Subpart D of this part.

§ 1926.28 Personal protective equipment.

(a) The employer is responsible for requiring the wearing of appropriate personal protective equipment in all operations where there is an exposure to hazardous conditions or where this part indicates the need for using such equipment to reduce the hazards to the employees.

(b) Regulations governing the use, selection, and maintenance of personal protective and lifesaving equipment are described under Subpart E of this part.

§ 1926.29 Acceptable certifications.

(a) *Pressure vessels.* Current and valid certification by an insurance company or regulatory authority shall

21

additional information about how an employer is to "require" the use of protective equipment.

While the regulation has made the rule of law somewhat more specific, questions remain. Is the regulation valid? What does "requiring the wearing" of protective equipment entail?

List of CFR Titles, Chapters, Subchapters, and Parts

TITLE 29—LABOR—Continued

1470	Uniform administrative requirements for grants and cooperative agreements to State and local governments.
1471	Governmentwide debarment and suspension (nonprocurement) and government-wide requirements for drug-free workplace (grants).

Chapter XIV—Equal Employment Opportunity Commission (Parts 1600–1699)

1600	Employee responsibilities and conduct.
1601	Procedural regulations.
1602	Records and reports.
1604	Guidelines on discrimination because of sex.
1605	Guidelines on discrimination because of religion.
1606	Guidelines on discrimination because of national origin.
1607	Uniform guidelines on employee selection procedures (1978).
1608	Affirmative action appropriate under Title VII of the Civil Rights Act of 1964, as amended.
1610	Availability of records.
1611	Privacy Act regulations.
1612	Government in the Sunshine Act regulations.
1613	Equal employment opportunity in the Federal Government.
1615	Enforcement of nondiscrimination on the basis of handicap in programs or activities conducted by the Equal Employment Opportunity Commission.
1620	The Equal Pay Act.
1621	Procedures—The Equal Pay Act.
1625	Age Discrimination in Employment Act.
1626	Procedures—Age Discrimination in Employment Act.
1627	Records to be made or kept relating to age; notices to be posted: administrative exemptions.
1690	Procedures on interagency coordination of equal employment opportunity issuances.
1691	Procedures for complaints of employment discrimination filed against recipients of Federal financial assistance.

Chapter XVII—Occupational Safety and Health Administration, Department of Labor (Parts 1900—1999)

1901	Procedures for State agreements.
1902	State plans for the development and enforcement of State standards.
1903	Inspections, citations and proposed penalties.
1904	Recording and reporting occupational injuries and illnesses.
1905	Rules of practice for variances, limitations, variations, tolerances, and exemptions under the Williams-Steiger Occupational Safety and Health Act of 1970.
1906	Administration witnesses and documents in private litigation. (Reserved)
1908	Consultation agreements.
1910	Occupational safety and health standards.
1911	Rules of procedure for promulgating, modifying, or revoking occupational safety or health standards.
1912	Advisory committees on standards.
1912a	National Advisory Committee on Occupational Safety and Health.
1913	Rules of agency practice and procedure concerning OSHA access to employee medical records.
1915	Occupational safety and health standards for shipyard employment.
1917	Marine terminals.
1918	Safety and health regulations for longshoring.
1919	Gear certification.
1920	Procedure for variations from safety and health regulations under the Longshoremen's and Harbor Workers' Compensation Act.
1921	Rules of practice in enforcement proceedings under Section 41 of the Longshoremen's and Harbor Workers' Compensation Act.
1922	Investigational hearings under Section 41 of the Longshoremen's and Harbor Workers' Compensation Act.
1924	Safety standards applicable to workshops and rehabilitation facilities assisted by grants.
1925	Safety and health standards for Federal service contracts.
1926	Safety and health regulations for construction.
1928	Occupational safety and health standards for agriculture.

ILLUSTRATION 8-4. CFR Index, in *CFR Index and Finding Aids* 528 (1991).

339

Table I—Authorities

29 U.S.C.—Continued	CFR
621	29 Part 1625
626	29 Part 1627
628	29 Part 1626
631	29 Parts 1625, 1627
633a	29 Part 1613
651 et seq	29 Part 42
651—653	29 Part 1975
651	34 Part 75
653	29 Parts 1910-1912, 1915, 1917-1919, 1926, 1975, 1990
655—657	29 Part 1912
655	29 Parts 1905, 1910, 1911, 1915, 1917-1920, 1926, 1928, 1990
	40 Part 311
655 note	29 Part 1910
656—657	29 Part 1912a
656	29 Part 1908
657—658	29 Part 1903
657	29 Parts 1901-1905, 1909-1913, 1915, 1917-1919, 1926, 1928, 1975, 1977, 1978, 1990
	30 Part 11
	42 Parts 85-87
660	29 Parts 1977, 1978
661	29 Parts 2200-2203
665	29 Part 1905
667	29 Parts 1901, 1902, 1952-1956
668	29 Part 1960
670	29 Parts 1908, 1949
	42 Part 86
672	29 Parts 1950, 1951
673	29 Parts 1904, 1960
705—706	34 Part 361
706	10 Part 4
	28 Part 42
	29 Part 32
	32 Part 56
	34 Parts 350, 363, 366, 367, 369, 385
	38 Part 18
	41 Parts 60-1, 60-741
710—711	34 Part 361
711—711a	34 Part 376
711	34 Parts 365-367, 369, 371-375, 378-380, 385-390
711—712	34 Part 363
717	34 Part 350
721—723	34 Part 361
721—722	34 Part 371
721	34 Parts 350, 365, 367, 369, 372, 385
723	34 Parts 365, 369, 385
730—731	34 Part 361
732	34 Parts 369, 370
740—741	34 Part 361
744	34 Parts 385, 386, 387, 388, 396
750—759	34 Part 351
750	34 Parts 361, 371
759g	34 Part 379
760—762	34 Parts 350-357, 360
761—761a	34 Part 359
761a	34 Part 358
762	34 Part 358

29 U.S.C.—Continued	CFR
762a	34 Part 350
766	34 Part 350
771	34 Part 374
774	34 Parts 385-390, 396
775—777a	34 Part 369
775—776	34 Part 372
776	29 Parts 1, 5
	34 Part 385
777—777a	34 Part 373, 376
777	34 Part 378
777a	34 Parts 359, 373-375, 380
777b	34 Part 375
777f—777g	34 Part 369
777f	34 Part 378
780	34 Part 362
791	5 Part 720
	29 Part 1613
	39 Part 255
792	36 Parts 1150, 1151, 1153, 1155, 1190
793	31 Part 202
	41 Parts 60-1, 60-30, 60-250, 60-741
794	1 Parts 326, 457, 500
	3 Part 102
	5 Parts 723, 900, 1207, 1411, 1720, 1850, 2416
	7 Parts 15, 15b
	10 Parts 4, 1041, 1535
	11 Part 6
	12 Parts 410, 606, 794
	13 Parts 113, 136
	14 Part 1251
	15 Parts 8b, 8c
	16 Parts 6, 1034
	17 Parts 149, 200
	18 Parts 1307, 1313
	19 Part 201
	20 Part 365
	21 Part 1615
	22 Parts 142, 144, 217, 219, 530, 607, 711, 794, 1005, 1103, 1304, 1510, 1600
	24 Part 8
	25 Part 720
	28 Parts 39, 41, 42
	29 Parts 32, 33, 100, 2205, 2608, 2706
	32 Parts 56, 1699
	34 Parts 104, 222, 300
	35 Part 257
	36 Parts 406, 812, 906, 909, 1154, 1208
	38 Parts 15, 18, 21
	39 Part 255
	40 Parts 7, 12
	41 Part 51-9
	43 Part 17
	44 Part 16
	45 Parts 84, 85, 605, 606, 707, 1151, 1153, 1170, 1175, 1180, 1181, 1232, 1706, 1803, 2104
	46 Part 507
	47 Part 1

regulations. The general citation form for a final rule consists of the title
number in C.F.R., the section number, and the year. For example: 29
C.F.R. § 1926.28 (1991). The name should also be provided when it is
commonly known.

While looking at C.F.R., you also may wish to take note of the "administrative history" reference in small print at the start of the part or after your section. That reference tells you when the rule was published in final form and where in the *Federal Register* to find that publication. (There is no example in Illustration 8-2 because the reference appears at the start of part 1926.)

b. *Federal Register* and *LSA—List of CFR Sections Affected*

Each volume of C.F.R. is out-of-date almost as soon as it is published, for agency regulations are revised, repealed, and promulgated virtually daily. New and amended regulations are published on a daily basis in the *Federal Register,* as are proposed regulations and notices of repealed regulations.

Attorneys who specialize in highly regulated areas scan the *Federal Register* daily, watching not only for new final rules but also for proposed rules that may affect their clients. Agencies provide notice of proposed rules so that affected persons and organizations may comment on them before they become law. As you would expect, it frequently is worth the effort to make comments on a proposed rule and perhaps prompt a change in the troublesome language before it takes effect, rather than wait and be forced to challenge the final rule. Indeed, some lawyers specialize in drafting rules, not just providing comments, for agency consideration.

The contents of each edition of the *Federal Register* are organized alphabetically by issuing agency. Nonetheless, it generally would be unwieldy and time-consuming to flip through each issue of the *Federal Register* published after the volume of C.F.R. you are using. It is far more efficient to check for most of the changes in a regulation published in C.F.R. by using the monthly companion to C.F.R., *LSA—List of CFR Sections Affected* [hereinafter L.S.A.].

First, consult the beginning of your C.F.R. volume to determine when its coverage ends. Next, find the most recent L.S.A. pamphlet(s) needed to update your specific title of C.F.R. In our research situation, for example, as of late 1991 (the time this text was written) the most current C.F.R. volume available covered developments as of July 1, 1991. The October 1991 L.S.A. extended coverage to October 31, 1991.

Next, look up your regulation by title and section number. If it is not listed, there have been no changes made during the period covered. If there has been a change, you will see a one- or two-word explanation and a page number. (See Illustration 8-6 on page 342.) Illustration 8-6 reveals no changes in § 1926.28 itself, although the agency made several revisions in other standards regulating the construction industry, in particular §§ 1926.1052 and 1926.1053, reported at page 41794.

The page number indicates where in the *Federal Register* the change appears. Some L.S.A. issues cover two years; boldface numbers refer to pages in the current year, while standard-type numbers refer to actions taken the previous year. To locate the page you need, you first will want to know the date of the issue containing that page. Consult the Table of Federal Register Issue Pages and Dates at the end of your L.S.A. pamphlet.

There almost always will be a gap between the period covered in the

112　　　**LSA—LIST OF CFR SECTIONS AFFECTED**

CHANGES JULY 1, 1991 THROUGH OCTOBER 31, 1991

TITLE 29
Chapter XIV—Equal Employment Opportunity Commission (Parts 1600—1699)

Page

1600　Technical correction............ 30502
1600.735-501—1600.735-519
　(Subpart E) Technical correction..................................... 30502
1602　Heading and authority citation revised............................ 35755
1602.1—1602.6　(Subpart A)
　Heading revised........................ 35755
1602.1　Revised; transferred to
　Subpart A................................. 35755
1602.2　Removed............................ 35755
1602.3　Removed............................ 35755
1602.4　Removed............................ 35755
1602.5　Removed............................ 35755
1602.6　Removed............................ 35755
1602.7　Amended............................ 35755
1602.10　Revised............................ 35755
1602.11　Amended........................... 35755
1602.12　Amended; OMB numbers.................................... 35755
1602.14　(a) amended; (a) designation and (b) removed;
　OMB numbers........................ 35755
1602.19　Amended.......................... 35755
1602.21　(b) amended..................... 35755
1602.26　Amended.......................... 35755
1602.28　(a)　amended;　OMB
　numbers................................. 35755
1602.31　(a) designation and (b)
　removed;　amended;　OMB
　numbers................................. 35755
1602.37　Amended.......................... 35756
1602.40　(a) designation and (b)
　removed;　amended;　OMB
　numbers................................. 35756
1602.45　Amended.......................... 35756
1602.49　(b) removed; (c) redesignated as (b); (a) amended;
　OMB numbers........................ 35756
1602.54　Amended.......................... 35756
1602.56 (Subpart R)　Added......... 35756
1627.3　(b)(3) removed;　(b)(4)
　redesignated as (b)(3) and
　amended................................. 35756
1627.4　(a)(2)　removed;　(a)(3)
　redesignated as (a)(2) and
　amended................................. 35756
1627.5　(c) amended...................... 35756
1630　Added; eff. 7-26-92.............. 35734

NOTE: **Boldface entries indicate October changes.**

Chapter XVII—Occupational Safety and Health Administration, Department of Labor (Parts 1900—1999)

Page

1910.1001　Note revised................ 43700
1910.1048　(m)(1)(i)　through
　(4)(ii) stayed to 11-6-91........... 37651
1910.1101　Note revised................ 43700
1926.58　Note revised................... 43700
1926.1052　(c)(1) revised............... 41794　◄
1926.1053　(a)(3) revised............... 41794
1952　Enforcement....................... 55192

Chapter XXV—Pension and Welfare Benefit Administration, Department of Labor (Parts 2500—2599)

2570.62　(a) amended................... 54708

Chapter XXVI—Pension Benefit Guaranty Corporation (Parts 2600—2699)

2603　Authority　citation　revised.................................... 55818
2603.2　(d) and (e) added; interim.................................... 55818
2603.18　(f) added; interim.......... 55818
2603.37　(b)　redesignated　as
　(b)(1); (a) and new (b)(1)
　amended; (b)(2) added; interim.................................... 55818
2603.41　(a)　amended;　(a) and
　(c) redesignated in part as
　(a)(1) and (c)(1); (a)(2) and
　(c)(2) added; interim.............. 55819
2610　Authority　citation　revised.................................... 52193
2610.11　(b)(2) amended............. 52193
2610.21　Amended....................... 52193
2610.22　(a)(1)　revised;　(a)(2)
　and　(3)　introductory　text
　amended................................. 52193
2610　Appendixes　A　and　B
　amended................................. 32089
Appendixes A and B amended.................................... 51820
2619　Appendix B amended......... 46526
2622　Appendix A amended......... 32089
Appendix A amended................ 51821
2644　Appendix A amended......... 32090
Appendix A amended................ 51822

most recent L.S.A. pamphlet and the date you are conducting your research. To close that gap, find the most recent *Federal Register* issue published and the last *Federal Register* issue for each month not covered by L.S.A. For example, if you were researching this chapter's research situation in December 1991, you would consult the last *Federal Register* issue for November of 1991 and the most recent December 1991 issue. In each, look for the CFR Parts Affected Table at the end of the Reader Aids section. (See Illustration 8-7 on page 344.) This table functions just like L.S.A. does, although it provides less detail. Note that Illustration 8-7 shows a proposed rule for part 1926, appearing at page 57036. Again, to find the issue containing any pages you need to read, use the *Federal Register* pages and dates chart adjacent to the CFR Parts Affected Table.

You now should be ready to locate any *Federal Register* issue you need and the pertinent pages within it. If you pursued the revisions to construction regulations §§ 1926.1052 and 1926.1053 that you found a reference to in Illustration 8-6, you would find Illustration 8-8 (see page 345). When a new or amended regulation is published in the *Federal Register,* there is more information than just the rule itself. As Illustration 8-8 shows, you also will find a summary of the regulation, key dates, background information, and a person at the agency to contact for more information. While this information is not law, as the regulation is, these sections do provide valuable insight into the new or amended regulation.

In our research situation, you also should consult the proposed new rule at 57036. Although it may not become law and in any event would not apply to the recent inspection of CSB, it may signal the agency's current thinking. You would find that OSHA is proposing exposure limits for a toxic substance—not your concern here.

> *Citation Note:* Regulations not yet appearing in C.F.R. should be cited to the *Federal Register,* with the expected C.F.R. citation provided as well. For example: 56 Fed. Reg. 41,794 (1991) (to be codified at 29 C.F.R. § 1926.1052). Proposed regulations also are cited to the *Federal Register.* *See* Rule 14.2 in *The Bluebook.*

c.   *Shepard's Code of Federal Regulations Citations*

The research steps set forth above should yield the agency's current regulation. As noted in Part A, courts pass on the validity of regulations, determining whether they are constitutional, conform to the statutory mandate, and were promulgated according to proper procedures. They also interpret regulations in light of specific facts. The courts' role here roughly parallels their role in implementing statutes.

As you might expect, the methods of locating judicial opinions dealing with a regulation to some extent parallel the methods of locating opinions construing a statute. You probably will come across references to these opinions in commentary sources. Your research into the annotated statutory codes would yield citations to cases interpreting regulations. There is, however, no comprehensive annotated code of regulations. Finally, you should consult *Shepard's Code of Federal Regulations Citations.*

The *Shepard's* covering C.F.R. functions just like the *Shepard's* volumes covering statutes. The citation lists are organized by title and then by C.F.R. section. The citing sources include federal and state court decisions and selected law reviews. The list of citing sources includes a special feature that acknowledges the frequent republication of C.F.R.: The date of the C.F.R. edition cited or the date of the citing reference is noted after each citation.

229.............................57237
230.............................56294
239.................56294, 57237
240.............................57237
270.................56154, 56294
274.............................56294
Proposed Rules:
30...............................58527
180.............................56482
240.................57605, 58194
249.............................57605

18 CFR
2.............56544, 57255, 58844
11.............................58497
154........56544, 57255, 58844
157........56544, 57255, 58844
271.............................56466
284........56544, 57255, 58844
375........56544, 57255, 58844
380........56544, 57255, 58844
381.............................58498

19 CFR
101.............................57487
Proposed Rules:
101.............................56179
141.............................56608
142.............................56608

20 CFR
404........57928, 58845, 60059
416.............................57928
655.............................56860
Proposed Rules:
416.............................58198

21 CFR
3...............................58754
5...............................58758
101.............................60880
520.............................59331
Proposed Rules:
5.....................60421, 60856
20...................60537, 60856
100........60528–60534, 60856
101........60366–60394, 60421,
 60478–60507, 60523, 60557,
 60566–60825, 60856, 60877
102.............................60877
105...................60421, 60856
130........60512, 60856, 60877
131.............................60877
133.............................60877
135.............................60877
136.............................60877
137.............................60877
139.............................60877
145.............................60877
146.............................60877
150.............................60877
152.............................60877
155.............................60877
156.............................60877
158.............................60877
160.............................60877
161.............................60877
163.............................60877
164.............................60877
166.............................60877
168.............................60877
169.............................60877
803.............................60024
807.............................60024

22 CFR
Proposed Rules:
514...................59822, 59837

23 CFR
140.............................56576
1327.................57255, 57373
Proposed Rules:
1212.............................56692

24 CFR
86.............................57488
Ch. I...........................56544
570.............................56902
813.............................57489
888.............................59996
913.............................57489
Proposed Rules:
10...............................57869
17...............................56336
81...............................58653
203.............................58762
207.............................59150
213.................58762, 59150
214.............................58158
215.............................59150
220.............................59150
221.............................59150
231.............................59150
232.............................59150
234.................58762, 59150
236.............................59150
242.............................59150
880.............................59150
881.............................59150
882.............................59150
883.............................59150
884.............................59150
885.............................59150
886.............................59150
887.............................59150
961.............................57871
965.............................59150

25 CFR
Ch. III.........................57373
Proposed Rules:
83...............................59843
211.............................58734
212.............................58734
225.............................58734
502........56278, 56282, 57373

26 CFR
1...............................58003
52.............................56303
602.............................56303
Proposed Rules:
1...............56545, 56609, 57374,
 57605, 58003, 60077
301.................56545, 58199

27 CFR
9.....................59213, 60920
Proposed Rules:
4...............................58199

28 CFR
0...............................56578
16...............................58304
542.............................58634

29 CFR
508.............................56860
516.............................61100

570.............................58026
778.............................61100
1910.............................57593
2615.............................57977
2617.............................57980
2676.............................57983
Proposed Rules:
1910.............................57036
1915.............................57036
1926.............................57036
2617.............................58014

30 CFR
202.............................57256
206.............................57256
210.............................57256
212.............................57256
800.............................59992
914.............................60060
915.............................56578
944.............................58846
948.............................58306
Proposed Rules:
48...............................59235
75...............................59235
77...............................59235
795.............................57376
816.................59904, 60012
817.............................60012
870.............................57376
872.............................57376
873.............................57376
874.............................57376
875.............................57376
876.............................57376
886.............................57376
916.............................58018
925.............................60077

31 CFR
211.............................56931
800.............................58774

32 CFR
Ch. I...............58179, 60062
199.................59870, 59873
247.............................58179
275.............................57984
285.............................58179
286.................58179, 59217
287.............................58501
290.............................56932
292a...............56595, 57799
292.............................58501
293.............................59217
294.............................57984
295.............................58179
297.............................58179
298.............................58180
298b.............................58180
299.............................58501
310.............................57800
311.............................57801
313.............................57801
314.............................57801
315.............................57801
317.............................57802
318.............................57802
319.............................56595
321.............................57802
322.............................57802
323.............................57803
701.............................59217
719.............................57803
806b.............................60923
1286.............................57803

Proposed Rules:
199.............................57498
251.............................59236

33 CFR
100.............................60062
117........57287, 57490, 59880
 60063
330.............................59110
Proposed Rules:
26...............................58292
95...............................56180
100.............................56180
117.................56609, 56610
155.................58202, 60949
157.............................56284
173.............................56180
174.............................56180
175.............................56180
177.............................56180
179.............................56180
181.............................56180
183.............................56180
207.............................59913

34 CFR
318.............................57198
328.............................56456
690.............................56911
Proposed Rules:
363.............................57778
772.............................59158

35 CFR
60...............................59881

36 CFR
228.............................56155
1254.............................58311
Proposed Rules:
62...............................58790

37 CFR
201.............................59884
202.................59884, 60064
203.............................59884
204.............................59884
211.............................59884
304.............................60924
307.............................56157

38 CFR
1...............................59217
3...............................57985
4...............................57985
8...............................57492
Proposed Rules:
21...............................60078

39 CFR
111.................57724, 58858
265........56933, 57805, 57984
602.............................58858
Proposed Rules:
3001.............................56955

40 CFR
51...............................57288
52.............56158, 56159, 56467,
 57492, 58501, 60924
60...............................59886
62...............................56320
80...............................57986
81...............................56694
122.............................56548

ILLUSTRATION 8-8. 56 Fed. Reg. 41,794 (1991).   345

(36 cm) apart, as measured along the ladder's side rails.

(ii) Rungs, cleats, and steps of step stools shall not be not less than 8 inches (20 cm) apart, nor more than 12 inches (31 cm) apart, as measured between center lines of the rungs, cleats, and steps.

(iii) Rungs, cleats, and steps of the base section of extension trestle ladders shall not be less than 8 inches (20 cm) nor more than 18 inches (46 cm) apart, as measured between center lines of the rungs, cleats, and steps. The rung spacing on the extension section of the extension trestle ladder shall be not less than 6 inches (15 cm) nor more than 12 inches (31 cm).

OSHA has determined that paragraph (a)(3)(i) does not accurately reflect the requirements that the Agency both proposed and intended to promulgate for "individual-rung/step ladders" (as defined in § 1926.1050 of the final rule). In particular, the final rule was intended to require that the spacing for all fixed ladders, including individual-rung/step ladders, be measured in the same way (along the side rails), even though individual-rung/step ladders do not have side rails. The Agency notes that proposed paragraph (a)(3)(ii) took this circumstance into account appropriately, by requiring that the spacing be measured between the center lines of the rungs, cleats, and steps.

To correct the error, OSHA is revising paragraph (a)(3)(i) of the final rule to require that the spacing for all fixed ladders be measured between the center lines of the rungs, cleats, and steps. In this way, the Agency will provide proper guidance to employers who use individual-rung/step ladders, without substantively changing the requirements for other fixed ladders. In addition, OSHA is adding language to paragraph (a)(3)(i) of the final rule to indicate clearly that individual-rung/step ladders are covered by that provision.

As set out above, paragraph (a)(3)(iii) of the final rule indicates how the spacing of rungs, cleats, and steps of the base section of extension trestle ladders is to be measured, but does not indicate how the spacing of the extension section is to be measured. OSHA had intended that the required spacing in the extension section, like that in the base section, be measured between the center lines of the rungs, cleats, and steps. To correct this oversight, the Agency is adding language to paragraph (a)(3)(iii) of the final rule that requires spacing to be measured accordingly.

List of Subjects in 29 CFR Part 1926

Construction safety; Construction industry; Ladders and scaffolds; Occupational safety and health; Protective equipment; Safety.

Authority: This document was prepared under the direction of Gerard F. Scannell, Assistant Secretary of Labor for Occupational Safety and Health, U.S. Department of Labor, 200 Constitution Avenue, NW., Washington, DC 20210.

Accordingly, pursuant to sections 4, 6, and 8 of the Occupational Safety and Health Act of 1970 (29 U.S.C. 653, 655, and 657), section 107 of the Contract Work Hours and Safety Standards Act (40 U.S.C. 333), Secretary of Labor's Order No. 1–90 (55 FR 9033), and 29 CFR part 1911, subpart X of 29 CFR part 1026 is amended as set forth below.

Signed at Washington, DC, this 17th day of July, 1991.

Gerard F. Scannell,
Assistant Secretary of Labor.

PART 1926—[AMENDED]

1. The authority citation for subpart X of part 1926 continues to read as follows:

Authority: Sec. 107, Contract Work Hours and Safety Standards Act (Construction Safety Act) (40 U.S.C. 333); Secs. 4, 6, and 8, Occupational Safety and Health Act of 1970 (29 U.S.C. 653, 655, and 657); Secretary of Labor's Order No. 1–90 (55 FR 9033); and 29 CFR part 1911.

2. Subpart X is amended as follows:

§ 1926.1052 [AMENDED]

The text of paragraph (c)(1) of § 1926.1052 is revised to read as follows:

*   *   *   *   *

(c)(1) Stairways having four or more risers or rising more than 30 inches (76 cm), whichever is less, shall be equipped with:

(i) At least one handrail; and

(ii) One stairrail system along each unprotected side or edge.

Note: When the top edge of a stairrail system also serves as a handrail, paragraph (c)(7) of this section applies.

*   *   *   *   *

§ 1926.1053 [AMENDED]

The text of paragraph (a)(3) of § 1926.1053 is revised to read as follows:

(a) * * *

(3)(i) Rungs, cleats, and steps of portable ladders (except as provided below) and fixed ladders (including individual-rung/step ladders) shall be spaced not less than 10 inches (25 cm) apart, nor more than 14 inches (36 cm) apart, as measured between center lines of the rungs, cleats, and steps.

(ii) Rungs, cleats, and steps of step stools shall be not less than 8 inches (20 cm) apart, nor more than 12 inches (31 cm) apart, as measured between center lines of the rungs, cleats, and steps.

(iii) Rungs, cleats, and steps of the base section of extension trestle ladders

shall not be less than 8 inches (20 cm) nor more than 18 inches (46 cm) apart, as measured between center lines of the rungs, cleats, and steps. The rung spacing on the extension section of the extension trestle ladder shall be not less than 6 inches (15 cm) nor more than 12 inches (31 cm), as measured between center lines of the rungs, cleats, and steps.

*   *   *   *   *

[FR Doc. 91–17460 Filed 8–22–91; 8:45 am]
BILLING CODE 4510-26-M

DEPARTMENT OF THE INTERIOR

30 CFR Part 901

Alabama Regulatory Program; Regulatory Reform; Correction

AGENCY: Office of Surface Mining Reclamation and Enforcement (OSM), Interior.

ACTION: Final rule; correction.

SUMMARY: OSM is correcting two errors in the final rule notice approving Alabama Program Amendment Number AL–005B published on Wednesday, July 3, 1991 (56 FR 30502). Alabama's proposed revision at section 880–X–9C–.03(7) of the Alabama Surface Mining Commission Rules (ASMCR) is approved. The required amendment to include certain definitions relating to terms and conditions of bonds is removed as these definitions are addressed at section 880–X–2A–.06 of the ASMCR. Alabama's proposed revision at section 880–X–10D–.17 of the ASMCR is approved. The required amendment to address the treatment of point-source discharge of water is removed as this provision is addressed at section 880–X–10D–.13(1)(a) of the ASMCR.

FOR FURTHER INFORMATION CONTACT: Jesse Jackson, Jr., Director, Birmingham Field Office, 135 Gemini Circle, suite 215, Birmingham, Alabama 35209; Telephone: (205) 290–7282.

SUPPLEMENTARY INFORMATION: On page 30507, second column, § 901.16, paragraphs (l) and (m) are removed.

Dated: August 15, 1991.

Jeffrey Jarrett,
Acting Assistant Director; Eastern Support Center.

[FR Doc. 91–20231 Filed 8–22–91; 8:45 am]
BILLING CODE 4310-05-M

You should watch for citations preceded by the following abbreviations: C (constitutional), U (unconstitutional), Up (unconstitutional in part), V (void or invalid), Va (valid), Vp (void or invalid in part). You should read those opinions carefully, for they bear on the validity of your regulation. (See Illustration 8-9 on page 347.)

Illustration 8-9 indicates that § 1926.28 has been cited in over 30 federal cases and in a handful of state cases as well. Of particular concern are the citations preceded by "U" and "C"; these would be required reading. Finally, note that the regulation is cited in several A.L.R. annotations.

4. Administrative Agency Decisions

a. Reporters of Agency Decisions

Thus far you have studied rules of law created through agency regulations. Many agencies also make law by adjudicating cases, much as courts do. In some situations, the agency decision reflects the application of the agency's regulation. In other situations, the agency decision does not involve a regulation, but merely the application of the agency's enabling statute.

The Administrative Procedure Act, 5 U.S.C. § 552(a)(2)(A) (1988), requires agencies to make final opinions in adjudicated cases available to the public. While there is no single, comprehensive reporter of agency decisions (as there is in the West Reporter System for opinions of the federal courts), some agencies do publish their own reporters. A list of these reporters and their publication dates appears in Table T.1 of *The Bluebook*.

While the details vary from reporter to reporter, there are some consistent features. As with reporters of judicial opinions, agency decisions are compiled in chronological, rather than topical, order. Thus, critical features of these reporters are the index or digest systems used to locate relevant decisions. Some of these systems are rather awkward, so it may be more helpful to locate citations to agency decisions through annotated codes or commentary sources.

In the early 1970s, the United States government published *OSAHRC Reports*, containing decisions of the Occupational Safety and Health Review Commission. It has since ceased publication, although decisions are available on microfiche. The *Index-Digest to OSAHRC Reports* operates as a finding tool for the reporter.

In any research involving agency reporters, your first step is to find the appropriate topic in the reporter's finding tool. In the case of the OSAHRC *Index-Digest,* you could do so by consulting the listing of major topic headings (Illustration 8-10 on page 348) or the so-called cross-reference table (Illustration 8-11 on page 349). The first is equivalent to a table of contents; the second suggests an index. In our research situation, both would point you to topic "8.000 Hazards, by Standard." A scope note in the *Index-Digest* volume explains that § 8.000 digests cases involving violations of specific regulations and is organized by regulation number.

Your second task is to read the digest paragraphs or listings under the appropriate topic (much as you read Key Number paragraphs in West's Digest System). Among the cases you would find a reference to is *Miller & Long Co.,* case #320, decided August 3, 1972, and reported at 1 O.S.A.H.R.C. 626 (Illustration 8-12 on page 350).

The third step is to locate and read the decision. Illustration 8-13 (on page 351) is an excerpt from the decision in *Miller & Long Co.* (The *Miller & Long Co.* decision in Illustration 8-13 is actually the decision of the ad-

ILLUSTRATION 8-9. *Shepard's Code of Federal Regulations Citations* 817 (1986).

347

CODE OF FEDERAL REGULATIONS			TITLE 29
§1926.10 609F2d1122 △1980	**§1926.21** 727F2d427 △1984	**§1926.28(a)** U546F2d282 *1972 573F2d821 △1978	**§1926.32(h)** 491F2d1344 △1974
§1926.11 et seq. 423FS805 △1976	**§1926.21(a)** La 383So2d474 △1980	574F2d223 △1978 581F2d1056 △1978 C583F2d1366 △1978 590F2d1364 △1979	**§1926.32(i)** 548F2d249 △1977
§1926.16 516F2d1087 △1975 591F2d321 △1979 423FS807 △1976 592FS721 △1983	**§1926.21(b)(1)** La 383So2d474 △1980	597F2d247 △1979 598F2d913 △1979 601F2d719 △1979 608F2d581 △1979 612F2d942 △1980	**§1926.32(j)** 548F2d249 △1977 **§1926.32(p)** 535F2d374 △1976
§1926.16(b) Del 415A2d504 △1980	**§1926.21(b)(2)** C583F2d1050 *1977 604F2d887 *1978 640F2d267 △1981	C625F2d728 △1980 625F2d1076 *1979 645F2d825 △1981 C647F2d1065 *1979	**§1926.50** et seq. 526F2d57 △1975
§1926.16(c) 592FS722 △1983 124Az219 *1974 Ariz 603P2d111 *1974 Del 415A2d504 △1980	652F2d978 △1981 Va656F2d927 △1981 698F2d424 △1983 Ala 462So2d927 △1985 La 383So2d474 △1980	649F2d460 △1981 649F2d1165 △1981 659F2d1275 △1981 659F2d1287 △1981 659F2d1292 △1981 672F2d430 △1982 673F2d112 △1982	**§1926.51(a)(1)** 519F2d1207 △1975 **§1926.51(c)** 519F2d1207 △1975 **§1926.52** 538FS288 *1975 43ARF164n △1979
§1926.20 et seq. 526F2d57 △1975	**§1926.21(b)(3)** 592FS721 △1983	674F2d1187 *1980 683F2d362 △1982 685F2d668 △1982 685F2d880 △1982	**§1926.55** 647F2d1310 *1979
§§1926.20 to 1926.32 685F2d667 *1981	**§1926.25** 609F2d1122 △1980 429FS907 △1977	693F2d120 △1982 698F2d509 *1981 718F2d1343 △1983 744F2d179 *1983	**§1926.56** 609F2d1122 △1980 429FS907 △1977
§1926.20(a)(1) Ala 462So2d926 △1985 La 383So2d474 △1980	**§1926.25(a)** 507F2d1043 △1974 519F2d1259 △1975 647F2d1065 △1981 655F2d42 △1981 718F2d1343 △1983	763F2d482 △1985 766F2d806 △1985 298Md672 △1984 73NCA427 △1985 La 383So2d474 △1980	**§1926.56(a)** 507F2d1043 △1974 **§1926.57** 647F2d1310 *1979
§1926.20(b)(1) 516F2d1091 *1974 Ala 462So2d927 △1985 La 383So2d474 △1980	124Az219 *1974 Ariz 603P2d111 *1974 DC 441A2d946 *1980 **§1926.25(b)** 507F2d1043 △1974	Md 472A2d66 △1984 NC 326SE340 △1985 39ARF141s △1978 45ARF807n △1979 47ARF350n △1980	**§§1926.100 to 1926.107** 685F2d667 *1981 39ARF144n △1978 **§1926.100** 528F2d647 △1976
§1926.20(b)(2) La 383So2d474 △1980	**§1926.25(c)** 507F2d1043 △1974	**§1926.28(a)(2)** Ala 462So2d927 △1985	**§1926.100(a)** 766F2d805 △1985
§1926.20(b)(3) La 383So2d474 △1980	**§1926.26** 609F2d1122 △1980 124Az219 *1974 Ariz 603P2d111 *1974	**§1926.28(b)** La 383So2d475 △1980	**§1926.102** 723F2d412 △1984 Ind 457NE185 △1983
§1926.20(b)(4) La 383So2d474 △1980	**§1926.28** 683F2d365 △1982	**§1926.32(a)** 548F2d249 △1977 **§1926.32(d)** 491F2d1344 △1974	**§1926.102(a)** 723F2d412 △1984 **§1926.102(a)(1)** C723F2d411 △1984 Ala 462So2d927 △1985

* followed by a year refers to the CFR edition, if cited. If not cited,
△ followed by a year indicates the date of the citing reference

817

MAJOR TOPIC HEADINGS

v

ministrative law judge, not an opinion of OSAHRC.) If you were to read the entire decision, you would observe that it follows a fairly standard format: introductory material, findings of fact, conclusions of law, and order. You would also observe that Miller & Long was inspected following a fatal accident, that the employer's net worth at the time was $750,000, that the judge found a violation of § 1926.28, and that the penalty was $600. The employer had a safety program involving incentives, training for supervisors, and rules requiring protective equipment, but no orientation of new employees even though most were inexperienced. (A technical note: The decision refers to § 1518.28—the prior C.F.R. codification of the current § 1926.28.)

ILLUSTRATION 8-11. Cross-Reference Table, [Apr. 28, 1971-Mar. 9, 1975] *Index-Digest to OSAHRC Reports* lxxx.

349

➤ PROTECTIVE EQUIPMENT (INCLUDING PERSONAL) - See 6.210 (Employers, Duties, Knowledge); 6.275 (Employers, Duties, Payment for Protection Equipment); 8.000-1910.132(a), 1926.28, 1926.102, 1926.103, 1926.104, 1926.106, 1926.353(e)(2), 1926.650(e); 12.100 (Penalties, Assessment Factors); 14.320 (Proof, Defenses, Disobedience); 14.350 (Proof, Defenses, No Knowledge); 14.470 (Proof, Evidence, Community Practice); 18.110 (Standards, General); 18.120-1910.132(a), 1926.28(a); 18.130 (Standards, Ambiguous).

PROTECTIVE FOOTWEAR - See Safety Shoes.

PROTECTIVE GOGGLES - See 8.000-1910.132(a), 1910.133(a)(1). rt: Eye/Face Protection.

PROTECTIVE GLOVES - See Hand Protection.

PROTECTIVE HAT, HELMET, ETC. - See Hard Hat.

"PROVIDING" (PROTECTIVE EQUIPMENT) - See 6.275 (Employers, Duties, Payment For Protective Equipment).

PROXIMATE CAUSE - See 14.410 (Proof, Evidence, Sufficiency).

"PRUDENT MAN TEST" - See 2.300 (Act, Constitutionality of); 15.110 (RC, Re Standards).

PUBLIC DISCLOSURE (TRADE SECRETS) - See Disclosure; "Privilege," Statutory (Employers).

PUBLIC LAW 91-596 - See Act.

PUBLIC WORKSITE - See 9.250 (Inspections, Presentation of Credentials).

PUBLISHING OF STANDARDS - See 16.220 (Secretary, Responsibilities, Dissemination of Standards). rt: Federal Register.

PUERTO RICO, APPLICATION OF ACT TO - See 2.120 (Act, Specific Sections); 10.200 (Jurisdiction, Personal).

PULLEYS, GUARDS - See 8.000-1910.219(d)(1).

PULPWOOD LOGGING - See 8.000-1910.266.

PULP, PAPER AND PAPERBOARD MILLS - See 8.000-1910.261.

PUNCH PRESS, GUARDING - See 8.000-1910.212(a)(1), 1910.217(c).

PURPOSE OF ACT - See 2.110 (Act, General).

QUALIFICATIONS OF INSPECTOR - See 9.280 (Inspections, Miscellaneous).

lxxx

Citation Note: Rule 14.3 of *The Bluebook* governs citation of agency decisions. The rule requires citation to an official reporter if the decision appears there. *See* Table T.1. The citation consists of the full name of the first private party or subject name (as modified by Rule 10), volume, abbreviation of the reporter name, page number, and year. For example: *Miller & Long Co.,* 1 O.S.A.H.R.C. 626 (1972) (administrative law judge decision).

```
                        8.000


    [#3948; 7/22/74; --.]
    TREADWELL CORP.                        11 OSAHRC 353
    [#3936; 9/3/74; --.]
    CHICAGO BRIDGE AND IRON CO.            11 OSAHRC  933
    [#6902; 9/26/74; --.]
    AMERICAN BRIDGE,DIV.of U.S. STEEL CORP12 OSAHRC   22
    [#2249; 10/2/74; RC, C/d.]
    LODEN and COMPANY,INC.                 13 OSAHRC  420
    [#6163; 11/21/74; --.]
    JULIUS NASSO CONCRETE CORP.            14 OSAHRC. 863
    [#2150 & 2212; 1/10/75; --.]


    1926.28(a)  --     (Personal   protective   equipment).
    Non-serious violation;  no penalty.
    UNITED STATES TESTING COMPANY, INC.    11 OSAHRC  311
    [#5220; 8/29/74; --.]
    MARTIN MASONRY CO.                     13 OSAHRC    1
    [#1735; 11/1/74; RC, M, C/c.]
```

```
    1926.28(a)and(b) --    Failure to require  the  use  of
    appropriate   protective  or  lifesaving  equipment  by
    employees engaged in operations  where  there  was  an
```

303

```
                        8.000


    exposure  to  hazardous  conditions,  namely falling from
    points along the outside edge of the   4th  floor  of  a
    building  where they were working at a height more than
    25 ft above the surface of the ground warranted a  $600
    penalty.
    MILLER & LONG CO., INC.                1 OSAHRC  626
    [#320; 8/3/72; --.]
```

b. *Shepard's* Covering Agency Decisions

The process of updating a published agency decision parallels the process used to update a judicial opinion: consult *Shepard's*. The decisions of some agencies are covered by *Shepard's United States Administrative Citations*. Decisions of the OSAHRC are covered by a special *Shepard's, Shepard's Federal Occupational Safety and Health Citations*. (The same is true of other areas such as energy, immigration and naturalization, labor, patents, tax, and trademarks.)

The citing sources include opinions of the federal and state courts, administrative agency decisions, and selected law reviews. *Shepard's United States Administrative Citations* uses an extensive set of abbreviations to signify the subsequent history and treatment of an agency decision. Watch for V

SECRETARY v. MILLER AND LONG CO., INC.

OSAHRC Docket No. 320   August 3, 1972

BATES, JUDGE, OSAHRC: This is a proceeding under section 10(c) of the Occupational Safety and Health Act of 1970, 29 U.S.C. 651, *et seq.* (hereinafter referred to as the Act), to review citations issued by the Secretary of Labor pursuant to section 9(a) and proposed assessments of penalties thereon issued pursuant to section 10(c) of the Act.

By citations issued on December 20, 1971, and by complaint filed on January 10, 1972, it is alleged that Miller & Long Co., Inc., the employer (hereinafter respondent), on or about November 1, 1971, at a workplace under its ownership, operation or control, violated an occupational safety and health standard promulgated pursuant to section 6 of the Act (29 C.F.R. 1518.28), and that on November 10, 1971, respondent also violated the standard at 29 C.F.R. 1518. 500(d)(1). The standards at 29 C.F.R. 1518 were adopted as occupational safety and health standards by 29 C.F.R. 1910.12. Notification of proposed penalties issued to respondent on December 20, 1971, proposed to assess a total of $615.00 penalties, as referred to more fully below.

As noted above, the complainant charged the respondent with failure to comply with the standard at 29 C.F.R. 1518.28 and thereby violating section 5(a)(2) of the Act, in that respondent failed to require the use of appropriate protective or lifesaving equipment by its employees engaged in operations where there was an exposure to hazardous conditions, namely falling from

626

(void), Va (valid), and Vp (void in part), in addition to the designations you learned to watch for when studying case law research. You can find a table of these abbreviations and their meanings near the beginning of most volumes.

As with a *Shepard's* covering judicial opinions, you first look up the volume of the reporter and then the page number. The first citations are parallel citations, including references to commercial publications, described in Part C at pages 372-373. Citations to other OSAHRC decisions, judicial opinions, law review articles, and A.L.R. annotations citing your case follow. It is possible to Shepardize OSAHRC decisions by various official and unofficial reporter citations. *Shepard's Federal Occupational Safety and Health Citations* also covers federal cases and OSHA regulations as cited sources.

As Illustration 8-14 (below) shows, *Miller & Long Co.* has not been cited often.

The *OSAHRC Reports* system offers a partial alternative to *Shepard's* for cases covered by that system. The *Index-Digest* contains a table of subsequent citations of cases. That table allows you to find citations to OSAHRC decisions in later OSAHRC decisions and uses abbreviations to signify the significance of a citation, much as *Shepard's* does.

5. Judicial Opinions

The federal courts bear the responsibility of reviewing agency regulations for compliance with constitutional and statutory requirements. The courts also review agency decisions to be sure, for example, that the agency has not exceeded its statutory authority and has substantial evidence to support its fact findings. Thus, it is critical to locate and read any pertinent judicial opinions.

The major methods of locating these opinions have been covered already: the annotations in the statutory codes, *Shepard's,* and commentary. In some cases, the agency's index or digest will cover court decisions. You should read these cases for two purposes: to discern the ultimate rule of law in the

ILLUSTRATION 8-14. *Shepard's Federal Occupational Safety and Health Citations* 261 (1984).

OSAHRC REPORTS								Vol. 1
(OSHD	OSHD	OSHD	– 680 –	78/63/B2	11OSHR819	73/32/C3	75/77/E4	
¶15138)	[¶18338	[¶20603	(72/8/D2)	2OSHC3274	12OSHR155	73/35/G3	75/78/A2	
78/86/C4	OSHD	(OSHD	6OSHC1896	12OSHR400	73/39/A2	75/78/E6	
OSHD	[¶18536	– 657 –	¶15170)	OSHD	12OSHR468	73/39/B5	75/80/E7	
[¶23117	OSHD	(72/8/B7)		[¶19139	12OSHR600	73/40/A2	75/82/E3	
	[¶19154	(OSHD	– 683 –	OSHD	12OSHR650	73/41/C10	d75/82/E12	
– 609 –	OSHD	¶16308)	(72/8/D5)	[¶22936	12OSHR752	73/48/F9	75/86/D7	
(72/7/E8)	[¶19161	(OSHD	(1OSHC		13OSHR7	73/53/C1	76/3/A11	
(1OSHC	OSHD	¶16309)	1070)	– 731 –	13OSHR183	d73/54/A2	76/12/C4	
3106)	[¶19399		(OSHD	(72/9/A2)	13OSHR204	73/61/A2	76/53/A2	
(OSHD	OSHD	– 660 –	¶15289)	(1OSHC	13OSHR221	73/61/B1	76/54/A2	
¶15139)	[¶20238	(72/8/B10)	4OSHR583	1049)	13OSHR234	74/1/E12	76/108/A2	
2OSHR1438	OSHD	(1OSHC	14OSHR882	(OSHD	14OSHR109	74/3/D8	76/132/A6	
3OSHR239	[¶21061	1047)	73/38/D6	¶15028)	14OSHR306	74/4/C8	77/35/E8	
3OSHR769	OSHD	(OSHD	75/27/F2	(OSHD	15OSHR33	74/6/E5	77/195/C11	
3OSHR984	[¶23358	¶15159)	1OSHC1318	¶15188)	15OSHR439	74/6/F3	77/199/A2	
4OSHR496			OSHD	1OSHR574	15OSHR635	74/13/A2	77/216/B10	
9OSHR209	– 626 –	– 662 –	[¶16361	1OSHR921	15OSHR710	74/21/B6	77/218/B3	
11OSHR196	(72/7/F11)	(72/8/B12)	OSHD	1OSHR933	15OSHR795	74/21/E2	78/10/C6	
11OSHR227	(1OSHC	(OSHD	[¶16506	1OSHR1136	15OSHR862	74/21/F11	78/19/C8	
11OSHR725	3088)	¶15162)		2OSHR105	15OSHR874	74/27/A2	78/42/E2	
14OSHR352	(OSHD		– 686 –	2OSHR307	d16OSHR108	74/30/A2	78/51/A2	
14OSHR402	¶15152)	– 666 –	(72/8/D8)	2OSHR384	16OSHR179	74/42/F14	79/5/B8	
20OSHR159	17OSHR202	(72/8/C2)	(OSHD	2OSHR488	16OSHR222	74/48/E11	79/9/E13	
73/16/B11	75/51/E5	(1OSHC	¶16143)	2OSHR543	16OSHR345	74/49/B10	79/18/E4	
73/20/E3	3OSHC1117	3005)	(OSHD	2OSHR868	16OSHR434	74/51/C6	79/35/G1	
73/26/D10	OSHD	(OSHD	¶16144)	2OSHR924	16OSHR713	74/56/D11	79/41/A2	
73/29/A2	[¶17908	¶15178)		2OSHR951	17OSHR324	74/60/C3	79/68/C5	
73/37/D11	OSHD		– 690 –	2OSHR1005	17OSHR456	74/60/F4	79/81/D2	
74/38/C13	[¶19549	4OSHR779	(72/8/D12)	2OSHR1168	17OSHR550	d74/61/E2	79/83/C10	
74/61/B13		7OSHR119	(OSHD	2OSHR1455	17OSHR663	74/65/A2	79/100/C7	
74/61/E2	– 638 –	8OSHR949	¶16147)	3OSHR19	17OSHR672	74/66/D12	80/11/F6	
74/67/A2	(72/8/A2)	11OSHR108	(OSHD	3OSHR137	17OSHR711	74/67/E14	80/17/C9	
74/91/F10	(74/3/A2)	17OSHR149	¶16148)	3OSHR163	17OSHR852	74/68/A7	80/20/B1	
74/92/D1	(1OSHC	73/40/F9		3OSHR302	18OSHR53	74/72/E5	80/36/B6	
75/21/A2	1505)	74/11/C8	– 693 –	3OSHR393	18OSHR144	74/75/C9	80/43/A2	
75/82/E12	(OSHD	74/35/E5	(72/8/E1)	3OSHR414	18OSHR708	74/76/A9	80/46/D4	
79/7/A2		74/60/B10		3OSHR493	19OSHR7	74/77/D10	80/49/D	

case and to assess how well the agency's action has fared. As with all case law research, be sure to Shepardize your cases.

In our research situation, one obvious set of cases to consult would be those labeled "U" or "C" in *Shepard's*. If you read these cases, you will learn that some courts consider the standard unconstitutionally vague in that the employer's duty arises where there is exposure to hazardous conditions, even though no other rule requires protective equipment. The more recent cases have rejected this argument. *See, e.g., Austin Bldg. Co. v. OSAHRC,* 647 F.2d 1063 (10th Cir. 1981); *Ray Evers Welding Co. v. OSAHRC,* 625 F.2d 726 (6th Cir. 1980). Obviously, you should study this line of cases carefully.

You would also find *Daniel Int'l Corp. v. OSAHRC,* 683 F.2d 361 (11th Cir. 1982), important. (Both U.S.C.S. and *Shepard's* provide citations to this case.) As you can see from the excerpt in Illustration 8-15 (on page 354), the facts and employer's argument closely resemble those of your case. And the decision, as an Eleventh Circuit decision, is binding precedent.

C. RESEARCHING FEDERAL ADMINISTRATIVE MATERIALS IN LOOSELEAF SERVICES

1. The Role and Advantages of Looseleafs

It would be handy if a legal researcher could have access to a "mini-library" containing all relevant primary and secondary authority needed to research an area of administrative agency law. This mini-library would contain the full text of primary sources such as statutes, cases, administrative regulations, agency decisions, and executive orders. It also would include current awareness information detailing pending legislation, proposed regulations, and docketed cases. Both federal and state law would be covered. The mini-library would include commentary by experts; practice aids and finding tools, such as practice forms and citators; and, where pertinent, uniform and model laws.

Looseleaf services, to some extent, are just such mini-libraries. A looseleaf service provides access to current, comprehensive information in a discrete, specialized area of the law.

The first looseleaf services came into existence in the early 1900s, but they did not begin to proliferate until the New Deal era of the 1930s. This proliferation occurred because the law—and hence legal research—became more complex due to a sharp increase in legislative activity and the related creation and expansion of administrative agencies. As lawyers soon learned, finding administrative decisions and regulations is often not an easy task; most administrative materials are poorly organized and indexed. Furthermore, many are not published in a timely fashion. Looseleafs were created to make research in administrative agencies easier.

Looseleaf services have become an important part of an attorney's library. Today, there are more than 3,400 looseleaf services and treatises covering more than 100 legal topics. Each looseleaf service covers a specialized, discrete area of the law. Looseleafs are especially useful in heavily regulated areas such as tax, labor, energy, insurance, environment, pensions, securities, banking, trade, employment, transportation, antitrust, and estate planning. Other looseleafs cover recent court decisions or congressional activities covering many areas of law or court rules.

815 (5th Cir. 1981); *Accu-Namics, Inc. v. OSHRC,* 515 F.2d 828, 834 35 (5th Cir. 1975), *cert. denied,* 425 U.S. 903, 96 S.Ct. 1492, 47 L.Ed.2d 752 (1976). Nevertheless, the effectiveness of Daniel's safety program, as evidenced by the record, negates any conclusion that the company violated 29 C.F.R. § 1926.28(a).

Daniel maintains that the accident on October 16, 1975 was the product of isolated and negligent misconduct on the part of four employees who simply wanted to get their paycheck and go home early. To prevail on this affirmative defense, Daniel must demonstrate that it took all feasible steps to prevent the accident, and that the actions of its employees were a departure from a uniformly and effectively communicated and enforced work rule of which departure Daniel had neither actual nor constructive knowledge. *H. B. Zachry Co. v. OSHRC,* 638 F.2d 812, 818 (5th Cir. 1981); *see General Dynamics Corp. v. OSHRC,* 599 F.2d 453 (1st Cir. 1979); *Horne Plumbing & Heating Co. v. OSHRC,* 528 F.2d 564 (5th Cir. 1976). Daniel points to several crucial findings in the record which indicate that the company effectively supports and enforces a strong safety program.

When Daniel employees are hired, they are given full instructions on all of Daniel safety rules. They also receive a published pamphlet outlining each of the rules and describing in detail compliance standards. As a follow up to this preliminary training program, employees attend safety meetings every Monday for half an hour. At these meetings, the need to tie off safety belts whenever an employee is over ten feet off the floor always is emphasized. The company also provides all necessary safety equipment. Thus, we have little doubt that Daniel has a work rule requiring employees to tie off and which is communicated effectively to all of its employees.

[2] The only real question on appeal is whether Daniel took all feasible steps to prevent employee misconduct. The Commission concludes that, because all four men involved in the accident had failed to tie off, tie off violations by Daniel employees were frequent. The Commission acknowledges that Daniel discharged employees for violating tie off rules, but argues that Daniel failed to communicate these discharges to other employees. Finally, the Commission maintains that Daniel enforcement practices are not uniform.

The evidence, however, overwhelmingly points to the conclusion that Daniel is a company which takes its safety program seriously and indeed took all steps to enforce its safety rules effectively. Initially, Daniel employs a full time safety engineer at construction sites whose primary duty is to enforce the company's safety rules. Any employee who violates the tie off rule is reprimanded immediately, and prior to this accident, seven Daniel employees had been terminated for failing to comply with the rule.[6] Although the Commission notes that two of the ironworkers involved in the accident were unaware of the specific employee discharges, both employees were aware of the safety rule, and that a failure to tie off was grounds for termination. In addition, the company's foreman, George Woolsey, each morning had his crewmembers check their safety equipment, and during the course of the day Woolsey would check his workers seven to ten times to be certain they were tied off. Daniel also points to the fact that just two days prior to the accident, an OSHA compliance officer inspected the construction site and evaluated Daniel's safety program. The compliance officer found all the employees tied off and concluded that Daniel's enforcement of its safety rules was "effective."

Finally, the Commission attempts to prove that Daniel was aware of a lax atti-

---

6. The Commission argues that because some employees were reprimanded and others terminated, Daniel's safety rules were not uniformly enforced. This view fails to account for differing circumstances under which a violation may occur. Those employees who were reprimand-

ed may represent less serious or first time offenders. This type of graduated enforcement does not weaken the overall effectiveness of the program; it merely recognizes mitigating circumstances.

Looseleaf services are so named because of their format: The individual pages are loose for easy removal and replacement. They are typically comprised of multi-ringed binders containing individually filed pages and are updated frequently by removing pages from the binders and adding new pages. Most looseleaf services contain several binders, each binder serving a specific function or covering a particular topic or jurisdiction.

Looseleaf services have two important characteristics: (1) they offer comprehensive coverage of a discrete, specialized area of the law, and (2) the research materials are current.

a. Comprehensiveness

Looseleafs exist to ease the difficulties inherent in collecting all the relevant authorities for a particular area of the law. Comprehensive in scope, looseleafs often contain the following:

Primary Authority
Federal and state statutes
Federal and state administrative regulations
Federal and state case law
Federal and state agency decisions
Executive orders
Municipal ordinances
Legislative histories
Rules of court

Secondary Authority
Commentary of experts and editors
Model acts
Uniform laws

Finding Aids and Practice Aids
Indexes
Citators
Annotations and references to other sources
Practice forms

Let's focus first on some of the specific primary source documents you may find in a looseleaf service, and then we will examine secondary materials and finding aids.

To research the law governing health and safety issues raised by the CSB Construction situation, you need to consider many primary source documents. As you have already discovered, you will need to consider federal statutes and regulations as well as agency and court decisions. Additionally, the commentary by experts (secondary authority) may provide valuable analysis of each of the materials previously shown in the Table 8.1 flowchart:

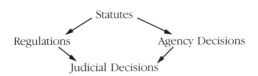

A useful looseleaf service, such as the *Employment Safety and Health Guide* published by Commerce Clearing House, Inc. (CCH), contains the text of these documents. This looseleaf service contains applicable passages of federal safety legislation, such as the Occupational Safety and Health Act of 1970, its amendments, and the related health and safety regulations. Often, legislative history, such as House or Senate Reports that are helpful for determining the intent of Congress, are reproduced or cited in a looseleaf service as well.

A major portion of virtually all looseleaf services is devoted to recent court and agency decisions. For example, the *Occupational Safety and Health Decisions* series, which is part of the complete looseleaf service published by CCH, contains the full text of federal and state court decisions and OSAHRC (i.e., agency) decisions. Many looseleaf services contain decisions that are not yet published in a reporter system; hence, looseleafs may be the best source for finding recent decisions. Additionally, you may recall from the discussion in Chapter 5 on case reporters that not all decisions of the lower federal and state courts are published. Looseleaf publishers seek to be comprehensive; they make no judgment about the value of decisions written by the federal courts and thus publish many decisions that are not published elsewhere.

Looseleafs contain a great deal of secondary authority materials as well. In the *Employment Safety and Health Guide* service, for example, commentary about the law fills a large portion of the looseleaf binders. Written by experts in the field or by the commercial publisher's editorial staff, the commentary explains the law. The footnotes and annotations refer the researcher to other valuable sources.

Additionally, most looseleaf services contain a digest section, arranged by topic, which uses headnotes to list and summarize court and agency decisions. Some looseleaf services also contain citators that indicate the status and treatment of the cases, statutes, and regulations; citators also provide citations to additional sources, which makes them helpful research aids.

Many looseleaf services contain practice forms. Although there are no practice forms in the *Employment Safety and Health Guide* service, looseleaf services covering other administrative agencies, such as environmental law or taxation, contain the forms needed to make reports to the federal or state agencies.

b. Currentness

Because the law is always evolving, attorneys must be aware of the current law and upcoming developments. Looseleaf services, because of their format, excel in providing current awareness information.

Looseleaf services are updated frequently. Many are updated weekly, some biweekly, others annually or semiannually; some include daily alert bulletins. Some looseleafs are updated primarily by interfiling pages; other looseleaf services are updated by use of successive additions in the form of a pamphlet.

(1) Interfiling Looseleafs

Most of the larger looseleaf services are updated by interfiling new pages. Pages that contain outdated information or errors are removed and discarded, and new pages that supersede the outdated pages are inserted. CCH, Callaghan

& Co. (Callaghan), Bureau of National Affairs (BNA), Thomson Professional Publishing, and Research Institute of America (RIA) are examples of publishing companies that use this method for updating.

357

Administrative
Materials: Searching
for Primary
Authority

The process of filing the new pages is a painstaking task and creates the potential for errors in filing. Hence, you should be certain that the pages you are using have been placed in the right order and are truly the current pages. One means of ascertaining whether the information is current is to note the dates printed in small type on each page of the looseleaf service. Another good checkpoint is the "release" or "supplementation" information, usually filed in the first volume of the looseleaf service, in the index volume, or in the back of the last volume of the looseleaf service. This information indicates the date the new information was released for insertion into the service. As already noted, for legal research to be accurate, it is critical that the information be current.

(2) Supplemental Pamphlets

Some looseleaf services are updated using supplemental pamphlets known as cumulative releases. Typically, one- or two-volume looseleaf services use small pamphlets containing recent cases or legislation. Because the pamphlets contain additional information that does not supersede earlier texts, no pages of text are removed. The additional pamphlets are filed in successive, chronological order.

(3) New Releases and Report Letters

A new release or supplementation typically contains new case decisions, new legislation, new regulations, and additional commentary on the law. Thus, the release presents an excellent means of staying abreast of new changes in the law and may be routed to interested attorneys before filing.

Most looseleaf publishers also include a brief "report letter" that summarizes and highlights the information contained in the release. This report letter permits persons to scan just a few pages that, in turn, will index specific paragraphs, sections, or pages of the release.

On occasion, the report letter will contain the full text of a major act or the text of a congressional report. Many libraries retain these letters and shelve them near the looseleaf service.

c. Looseleaf Treatises

Not all books that are published in a looseleaf format are true looseleaf services. Some treatises use a looseleaf format rather than pocket parts as a means of updating the text. These treatises are not true looseleaf services because the text is largely secondary authority in the form of commentary. The updating information is usually issued as supplemental pages or pamphlets and is predominantly additional annotations, commentary, or appendices to the text.

The distinction is important because looseleafs and treatises fulfill different needs. Looseleaf services are valuable research tools because they compile all available information, including primary source documents. Treatises are useful because they provide explanatory commentary. You also should understand this distinction between looseleafs and treatises to ensure that you can find materials in your library: Some libraries shelve looseleaf services in a separate area.

2. Organization of Looseleaf Services

Looseleaf services are published by many different publishing companies and government agencies. They are marketed in a variety of shapes and sizes and employ varied methods of organization and indexing. Thus, there is no one method for approaching all looseleaf services. Some general points can be made, however.

a. Binders

Looseleaf services usually are made up of several binders or volumes. Each binder typically contains a specific segment of the looseleaf's material (commentary, for example) or covers a specific subtopic or jurisdiction.

Most of the larger looseleaf services have a master index binder that contains topical listings directing the user to the appropriate looseleaf binders. The master index binder may include a digest for recent cases and agency decisions.

b. Topical or Jurisdictional Tabs

Each binder is organized by type of material, subtopic, or jurisdiction, as indicated by divider tabs that separate material into these categories. The divider tabs make it easier to find materials in the binder. For instance, federal statutes may be compiled under one tab, state statutes under another tab, and case law and agency decisions each under individual tabs. Hence, research on our OSHA topic will require you to examine materials filed under many different tabs.

c. Paragraphs or Sections

When updating materials, such as amendments to a statute or regulation, are lengthier than the original statute or regulation to be amended, many pages may be inserted to replace a single, dated page. A sequential numbering of pages is therefore not practical because supplements would confuse the numbering sequence. Consequently, looseleaf services use paragraphs (par. or ¶) or sections (sec. or §) rather than pages. The indexes refer you to the relevant material by paragraph or section.

Do not be dismayed if you find gaps in the sequence of paragraphs or sections. Publishers often reserve numbers for new paragraphs or sections to be developed later. There will be a notation describing the gap in such a situation.

Some looseleafs include page numbers as well, usually in smaller print. Often the pages will employ decimals and subsections—for example, page 230.56-e. This makes it possible to handle the ever-expanding numbering scheme and is helpful in finding gaps caused by errors in filing.

d. Reporters and Transfer Binders

Agency decisions and court decisions constitute an important part of the looseleaf service. When agency decisions and court decisions are first decided, the decisions are filed within the binders, usually under the heading of "Current Decisions." In the *Employment Safety and Health Guide,* OSAHRC decisions and court decisions are collected in the fourth binder under a tab entitled "OSHA, MSHA Court Decisions." ("MSHA" refers to the decisions of the Federal Mine Safety and Health Review Commission, which are part of the looseleaf service but are irrelevant to our research problem.)

When the binders become too full to hold additional decisions, which occurs annually or semiannually depending on the service, the materials under the "Current Decisions" tab are pulled from the binder and are collected into separate bound or softcover volumes. Some looseleaf publishers then bind the decisions in permanent, hardbound volumes that are separately issued as reporters. For example, the agency decisions are first filed in binder 4 of the *Employment Safety and Health Guide* as soon as they are rendered; later, CCH collects the decisions and separately publishes a hardbound reporter series entitled *Occupational Safety and Health Decisions*. The looseleaf pages in the binders that contain "Current Decisions" are removed and discarded when the hardbound reporter volume is received by the library.

Some looseleaf publishers do not issue new hardbound reporters. Instead, these publishing companies provide "transfer binders" to hold the dated decisions. Transfer binders are paper or cardboard folders with metal posts that hold in place the individual looseleaf pages removed from the looseleaf binders.

Access to the transfer binders or hardbound reporters is often assisted by bound digests and indexes. Some publishing companies cumulate the headnotes and indexes that were initially filed in the master index binder and produce a separate volume in book format. The headnotes or indexing terms used in the master index binder can be used in these cumulative digest and index volumes, which facilitates research of older cases.

Many looseleaf services do not publish their own reporters. However, most provide footnotes or annotations to other reporters, which contain the primary source documents.

3. How to Use Looseleaf Services

If you have little understanding of a particular area of the law, you may need to consult an encyclopedia, treatise, or legal periodical before beginning research in a looseleaf service, so that you know you are consulting an appropriate looseleaf service and using appropriate search terms. *Legal Looseleafs in Print,* compiled by Arlene L. Eis, is helpful for finding a looseleaf service by topic. Once you have located an appropriate looseleaf service, you should consider the following steps:

(1) Consult the "How to Use" materials and finding lists.
(2) Find pertinent information using the indexes.
(3) Read pertinent commentary.
(4) Locate and read pertinent statutes and regulations.
(5) Locate and read pertinent agency and court decisions.

a. "How to Use" Information and Finding Lists

If you are unfamiliar with a particular looseleaf service, you should start with the "how to use this service" section, which is typically filed in the front of the first binder or in the master index binder. The "how to use" section generally explains the arrangement of the particular looseleaf service, provides helpful research tips, and lists the abbreviations used throughout the looseleaf. Most important, it tells what the service covers. For instance, the "How to Use This Guide" section of the *Employment Safety and Health Guide* (CCH) indicates that the service contains the full text of all decisions of the Occupational Safety and Health Review Commission, but that the substantive decisions of the administrative law judges are only digested.

Of particular value are the various finding lists contained in looseleaf services, particularly if you are already familiar with major statutes or regulations. For example, as Illustration 8-16 (on pages 361-362) shows, this CCH service has tables that direct the user to well-known laws, regulations, cases, or agency directives. Often, there is also a table of cases covering both court and agency decisions. As you can see from the illustration, the "Finding Lists—Laws by Title" has a handy cross-reference table that refers you to paragraphs in the looseleaf service where OSHA is given in full text accompanied by commentary and annotations. Of course, this is not a good place to start your research unless you are already familiar with at least the statute.

The abbreviations you encounter may not make sense unless you are familiar with the listing of abbreviations found in the front of the master index binder. The "Abbreviations and References" table found in ¶ 225 in the *Employment Safety and Health Guide,* which is reproduced in Illustration 8-17 on page 363, tells you that OSHRC is the Occupational Safety and Health Review Commission.

b. Indexes

If you are unfamiliar with your research topic, the best strategy is to first gain a general background or overview of the law. In a looseleaf service, that means the best starting strategy is to use a topical approach using the several available indexes. When using the indexes, you need to be aware that some are general in scope and others are more specific. This further explains why it is important to read the "how to use this guide" section of the looseleaf service, which does a good job of describing the coverage of each index.

At first, the indexes seem cumbersome to use because they are located in different binders. For instance, the *Employment Safety and Health Guide* comprises four large looseleaf binders; the "Topical Index" is located in the first. The topical index is the most general of the indexes and directs the user to commentary material. This is often a good starting point because the commentary section provides an overview of the topic; contains references to specific statutory or regulatory provisions; and sets out annotations with citations to cases, agency decisions, statutes, regulations, and other materials.

Most looseleafs also have updates to their indexes that direct the user to specific parts of the looseleaf service. For example, in the third binder of the *Employment Safety and Health Guide,* you will find the section entitled "Cumulative Index—Current Topical Index." Although filed behind one tab in this binder, these are really two separate indexes that cover more recent information. The Current Topical Index updates your research by subject and directs you to more recent commentary, which may include new annotations and references to proposed statutes or proposed regulations. The Cumulative Index directs you to new material, including recent court and agency decisions, keyed to paragraph numbers in the compilation.

The Current Topical Index is updated frequently by a separate index entitled "Latest Additions to Current Topical Index," and the Cumulative Index is updated frequently by a separate index entitled "Latest Additions to Cumulative Index." Hence, to be completely current, you also must check listings under these supplementary indexes.

There also are more specific indexes in the other binders that index specific legal information and are filed in the binders containing that material. For instance, the "Index to Standards" in the second binder is a detailed index covering the OSHA standards contained within that binder.

ILLUSTRATION 8-16. Finding Lists, 1 Employ. Safety & Health Guide (CCH) 201, 205, 211 (Mar. 27, 1990).

361

985   3-27-90

201

FINDING LISTS
CASE TABLE

TABLE OF CONTENTS

[The next page is 205.]

1048   5-28-91

205

FINDING LISTS

¶ 100

Laws by Title

CONTRACT WORK HOURS AND SAFETY STANDARDS ACT

Law Sec.	Par.	Law Sec.	Par.	Law Sec.	Par.
1	6326	103(b)	6331	107(c)	6336
2	6327	105	6332	107(d)	6337
101	6328	106	6333	107(e)	6338
102(b)	6329	107(a)	6334	107(f)	6339
103(a)	6330	107(b)	6335		

FEDERAL MINE SAFETY AND HEALTH ACT OF 1977

Law Sec.	Par.	Law Sec.	Par.	Law Sec.	Par.
1	7900.1	115	7900.20	313	7900.39
2	7900.2	201	7900.21	314	7900.40
3	7900.3	202	7900.22	315	7900.41
4	7900.4	203	7900.23	316	7900.42
5	7900.5	204	7900.24	317	7900.43
101	7900.6	205	7900.25	318	7900.44
102	7900.7	206	7900.26	501	7900.45
103	7900.8	301	7900.27	502	7900.46
104	7900.9	302	7900.28	503	7900.47
105	7900.10	303	7900.29	504	7900.48
106	7900.11	304	7900.30	505	7900.49
107	7900.12	305	7900.31	506	7900.50
108	7900.13	306	7900.32	507	7900.51
109	7900.14	307	7900.33	508	7900.52
110	7900.15	308	7900.34	509	7900.53
111	7900.16	309	7900.35	510	7900.54
112	7900.17	310	7900.36	511	7900.55
113	7900.18	311	7900.37	512	7900.56
114	7900.19	312	7900.38	513	7900.57

OCCUPATIONAL SAFETY AND HEALTH ACT OF 1970

Law Sec.	29 USC Sec.	Par.	Law Sec.	29 USC Sec.	Par.
1	651 (note)	6101	4(b)(1)	653(b)(1)	6106
2(a)	651	6102	4(b)(2)	653(b)(2)	6107
2(b)	651	6103	4(b)(3)	653(b)(3)	6108
3	652	6104	4(b)(4)	653(b)(4)	6109
4(a)	653(a)	6105	5(a)	654(a)	6110

Employment Safety and Health Guide

¶ 100

¶ 101

Regulations by Law Title

CONTRACT WORK HOURS AND SAFETY STANDARDS ACT

Code of Federal Regulations, Title 29, Chapter XVII, Part 1926

Reg. Sec.	Par.	Reg. Sec.	Par.
1926.1—1926.4	7701.1—7701.4	1926.500—1926.502	7731.1—7731.8
1926.10—1926.16	7701.5—7702.3	1926.550—1926.556	7732.1—7734.6
1926.20—1926.32	7702.4—7703.9	1926.600—1926.606	7735.6—7738.1
1926.50—1926.59	7704.2—7706.951	1926.650—1926.652	7738.7—7740.7
1926.100—1926.107	7707.1—7708.8	1926.700—1926.706	7741.1—7741.16
1926.150—1926.155	7709.1—7712.8	1926.750—1926.752	7742.1—7742.5
1926.200—1926.203	7713.1—7714.1	1926.800—1926.804	7743.1—7746.4
1926.250—1926.252	7714.5—7717.4	1926.850—1926.860	7747.1—7748.2
1926.300—1926.305	7717.7—7719.4	1926.900—1926.914	7748.7—7750.6
1926.350—1926.354	7720.1—7722.2	1926.950—1926.960	7751.1—7755.2
1926.400—1926.449	7722.3—7723.70	1926.1000—1926.1003	7755.7—7758.5
1926.450—1926.452	7724.8—7730.5	1926.1050—1926.1060	7759.3—7759.9

LONGSHOREMEN'S AND HARBOR WORKERS' COMPENSATION ACT

Code of Federal Regulations, Title 29, Chapter XVII, Parts 1919 and 1920

Reg. Sec.	Par.	Reg. Sec.	Par.
1919.1—1919.2	7873.3—7873.4	1919.50—1919.51	7874.13—7874.14
1919.3—1919.9	7873.5—7873.11	1919.60	7874.15
1919.10—1919.12	7873.12—7873.14	1919.70—1919.90	7874.16—7874.28
1919.13—1919.25	7873.15—7873.27	1920.1	7875.1
1919.26—1919.37	7874.1—7874.12	1920.2	7875.2

OCCUPATIONAL SAFETY AND HEALTH ACT OF 1970

Code of Federal Regulations, Title 29, Part 2

Reg. Sec.	Par.	Reg. Sec.	Par.
2.20	6529.2	2.23	6529.5
2.21	6529.3		
2.22	6529.4	2.24	6529.6

Code of Federal Regulations, Title 29, Part 11

Reg. Sec.	Par.	Reg. Sec.	Par.
11.1—11.3	6562.1—6562.3	11.10—11.14	6562.4—6562.8

Code of Federal Regulations, Title 29, Chapter XVII, Part 1901

Reg. Sec.	Par.	Reg. Sec.	Par.
1901.1	6501.1	1901.5	6501.5
1901.2	6501.2	1901.6	6502.1
1901.3	6501.3		
1901.4	6501.4	1901.7	6502.2

Code of Federal Regulations, Title 29, Chapter XVII, Part 1902

Reg. Sec.	Par.	Reg. Sec.	Par.
1902.1—1902.2	6502.4—6503.3	1902.10—1902.23	6508.2—6510.4
1902.3—1902.6	6504.1—6508.1	1902.30—1902.53	6510.5—6510.73

Code of Federal Regulations, Title 29, Chapter XVII, Part 1903

Reg. Sec.	Par.	Reg. Sec.	Par.
1903.1	6511.2	1903.4	6512.1
1903.2	6511.3	1903.5	6512.2
1903.3	6511.5	1903.6	6512.3

ILLUSTRATION 8-17. Abbreviations and References Table, 1 Employ. Safety & Health Guide (CCH) ¶ 225, at 271 (Feb. 14, 1989).

363

927   2-14-89   **271**

ABBREVIATIONS AND REFERENCES
¶ 225

ACGIH—American Conference of Governmental Industrial Hygienists
ANPR—Advance Notice of Proposed Rulemaking
ANSI—American National Standards Institute
ASTM—American Society for Testing and Materials
ASSE—American Society of Safety Engineers
BLS—Bureau of Labor Statistics
BMOA—Board of Mine Operations Appeals
BOM—Bureau of Mines
CAS—Chemical Abstracts Service
CDC—Centers for Disease Control
CFR—Code of Federal Regulations
CPSC—Consumer Product Safety Commission
CSHO—Compliance Safety and Health Officer
DHHS—Department of Health and Human Services
DOD—Department of Defense
DOL—Department of Labor
DOT—Department of Transportation
EAJA—Equal Access to Justice Act
EPA—Environmental Protection Agency
ETS—emergency temporary standard
FAA—Federal Aviation Administration
FACOSH—Federal Advisory Council on Occupational Safety and Health
FDA—Food and Drug Administration
FIFRA—Federal Insecticide, Fungicide and Rodenticide Act
FMSHRC—Federal Mine Safety and Health Review Commission
FOM—Field Operations Manual
F.R.—Federal Register
FRA—Federal Railroad Administration
FRCP—Federal Rules of Civil Procedure
GAO—General Accounting Office
GFCI—ground fault circuit interrupter

GPO—Government Printing Office
HCS—hazard communication standard
HHS—Department of Health and Human Services (same as DHHS above)
IARC—International Agency for Research on Cancer
IHTM—Industrial Hygiene Technical Manual
mg/m^3—milligrams per cubic meter
MSDS—Material Safety Data Sheet
MSHA—Mine Safety and Health Administration
NACOSH—National Advisory Committee on Occupational Safety and Health
NCI—National Cancer Institute
NFPA—National Fire Protection Association
NIOSH—National Institute for Occupational Safety and Health
NLRB—National Labor Relations Board
NRTL—Nationally Recognized Testing Laboratory
NSC—National Safety Council
NTP—National Toxicology Program
OMB—Office of Management and Budget
OSHA—Occupational Safety and Health Administration
OSHD—Occupational Safety and Health Decisions
OSHRC—Occupational Safety and Health Review Commission
PEL—permissible exposure limit
ppb—parts per billion
ppm—parts per million
SBA—Small Business Administration
SIC—standard industrial classification
STAA—Surface Transportation Assistance Act
TLV—threshold limit value
TWA—time weighted average
$\mu g/m^3$—micrograms per cubic meter

In summary, it is likely that you will use multiple indexes to find the relevant material. It probably is best to begin with the general topical index for access to general information and explanatory commentary. Then use the current topical and cumulative indexes to update your research. Remember that these indexes are further updated by supplementary indexes.

In our research situation, you will find the subject headings "Safety belts, life lines, and lanyards" and "Personal protective equipment" in the Topical Index of the *Employment Safety and Health Guide*. In Illustration 8-18 on page 364, you will note that there are multiple subtopics under the heading "Personal protective equipment" and that the subtopic of "construction standards" appears to pertain most directly to construction projects. We will focus on the first entry, ¶ 2106.

The material is identified by paragraphs, not pages. This is important to remember because these paragraphs may, in fact, span several pages of text,

1062 8-27-91   **Topical Index**   **133**
See also Current Topical Index at page 5851 and Index to Standards at page 3201.
References are to paragraph (¶) numbers.

and you will end up at the wrong place in the looseleaf service if you try to search by page number.

c. Commentary

One logical approach is to read commentary first, both for its explanation of the law and for references to material. For instance, ¶ 2106 begins with about five pages of explanatory commentary. Illustration 8-19 on pages 366-369 contains the first two pages of that commentary as well as examples of two later pages.

While scanning this text, note that there are frequent references to § 1926.28(a); we know that these are references to a regulation. As mentioned before, because most looseleafs function as "mini-libraries," it is likely that the full text of primary materials, such as statutes and agency regulations, are contained in the looseleaf service. However, before finding that statute and any related regulations, first explore the other material in this commentary section.

As a part of the commentary, you would find about 15 pages of annotations, which is too much to scan quickly. Note that at page 902 of Illustration 8-19 (on page 368) there is a brief directory or index of these annotations. Of the entries found in this short directory, it appears that the following may be the most likely to provide relevant information:

Employee misconduct 30
Employer knowledge 32
Employer's safety program 33

The decimals refer to subtopics within ¶ 2106. Note that subtopic .31 does not exist; this decimal has been intentionally reserved by the editors of the looseleaf service so that later legal developments can then be inserted without renumbering the entire service.

After examining each of these subtopics, you would probably conclude that ¶ 2106.33 is the most relevant for our research problem. These annotations begin on page 909 of the looseleaf service. Look at page 909 of Illustration 8-19 (on page 369) and note the several cases and agency decisions that deal with the issue before us. Indeed, one of the agency decisions you are already familiar with, *Miller & Long Co., Inc.* Additionally, there is a headnote of another familiar case, *Daniel International Corp. v. OSHRC.*

You also will notice that subtopic ¶ 2106.33 is expanded further by subparagraphs ¶ 2106.331 and ¶ 2106.332, both of which may be relevant. (The decimal designations make it easier to add new annotations without renumbering the entire sections.)

Having found these references, the next step is to check the updating indexes. These indexes are located behind the Cumulative Index-Current Topical Index tab in the same looseleaf binder. Examine Illustration 8-20 on page 370, which shows part of the relevant page of the Cumulative Index. Note that ¶ 2106 has been updated by several new development paragraphs. All of the new development references that appear relevant, such as the entry to ¶ 29,333, should be examined fully.

It is necessary to also check the Latest Additions to Cumulative Index (Illustration 8-21 on page 371). There is only one entry for ¶ 2106, and the reference to ¶ 29,439 pertains specifically to painting bridges, which is probably not relevant to our research project.

ILLUSTRATION 8-19. Commentary Excerpts: 1 Employ. Safety & Health Guide (CCH) ¶ 2106, at 898-99, 902, 909 (Sept. 17, 1991).

---

with ladders, boxes, clothing, lumber, and various pieces of metal created a tripping hazard. *Bechtel Power Corp.,* Rev. Com. Judge 1976, 79 OSAHRC 34/A2, 1975-1976 OSHD ¶ 20,592; affirmed Rev. Com. 1979, 1979 OSHD ¶ 23,575.

.35 Fire equipment [24]. Failure to provide fire equipment at the worksite was affirmed as a § 1926.24 violation. This violation was considered minimal because the building was concrete. *Underhill Construction Corp.,* Rev. Com. Judge 1974, 76 OSAHRC 89/A2, 1973-1974 OSHD ¶ 17,881; affirmed without comment on this issue, Rev. Com. 1976, 1976-1977 OSHD ¶ 20,918.

.36 First aid [23]. There was sufficient evidence to find that the employer failed to provide first aid kits as required by § 1926.23; the nearest hospital was more than 11 miles away. *Tilo Company, Inc.,* Rev. Com. Judge 1972, 73 OSAHRC 15/F5, 1971-1973 OSHD ¶ 15,150; affirmed without comment on this issue Rev. Com. 1973, 1971-1973 OSHD ¶ 15,678.

.81 Subcontractor's responsibility [25(a)]. A subcontractor installing elevators was held in violation of § 1926.25(a), even though it had cleaned up its work areas two days before the inspection and the remaining debris had been left by one or more of five other subcontractors using the area. The subcontractor had the expertise to recognize and eliminate the housekeeping hazard; at a minimum it should have requested the responsible subcontractor or general contractor to correct the condition. *Otis Elevator Co.,* Rev. Com. 1976, 76 OSAHRC 57/E5, 1975-1976 OSHD ¶ 20,693.

Accord:

Jack Parker Construction Corp., Rev. Com. Judge 1973, 73 OSAHRC 55/C3, 1973-1974 OSHD ¶ 16,841.

Metro-Mechanical, Inc., Rev. Com. Judge 1974, 75 OSAHRC 72/A2, 1973-1974 OSHD ¶ 17,181; other issues considered Rev. Com. 1975, 1974-1975 OSHD ¶ 19,795.

Bob McCaslin Steel Erection Co., Rev. Com. Judge 1974, 75 OSAHRC 69/C10, 1973-1974 OSHD ¶ 17,314; affirmed one-to-one Rev. Com. 1975, 1974-1975 OSHD ¶ 19,755.

Hancock Heating and Air Conditioning Co., Rev. Com. Judge 1974, 74 OSAHRC 14/C6, 1973-1974 OSHD ¶ 17,350.

Star Circle Wall Systems, Inc., Rev. Com. Judge 1974, 76 OSAHRC 38/C9, 1973-1974 OSHD ¶ 17,390; review declined Rev. Com. 1976, 1975-1976 OSHD ¶ 20,502.

Las Vegas Painting & Drywall, Inc., Rev. Com. Judge 1975, 76 OSAHRC 82/D8, 1975-1976 OSHD ¶ 20,371.

John S. Parnon Construction Corp., Rev. Com. Judge 1975, 76 OSAHRC 8/D5, 1975-1976 OSHD ¶ 20,374.

Badaracco Bros. & Co., Rev. Com. Judge 1977, 77 OSAHRC 146/F14, 1977-1978 OSHD ¶ 22,062.

Emile M. Babst Co., Inc., Rev. Com. Judge 1978, 78 OSAHRC 71/D12, 1978 OSHD ¶ 23,008.

New Jersey Bell Telephone Co., Rev. Com. Judge 1980, 80 OSAHRC 53/A2, 1980 OSHD ¶ 24,513.

Lassel and Karst Co., Rev. Com. Judge 1984, 84 OSAHRC 47/B5, 1984-1985 OSHD ¶ 27,082.

Reliable Electric Co., Inc., Rev. Com. Judge 1989, 89 OSAHRC 50/A3, 1987-1990 OSHD ¶ 28,669.

BFW Construction Co., Inc., Rev. Com. Judge 1987, 87 OSAHRC 7/B9, 1986-1987 OSHD ¶ 27,823.

.811 Although a plumbing subcontractor did not create or control violative § 1926.25(a) housekeeping conditions at the worksite, its employees were exposed to the hazards, and the Judge erred in vacating the citation. The duration of exposure was brief, however, since the employees were exposed only while passing through the areas where the conditions existed in order to reach their actual work stations. *Robert E. Lee Plumbers, Inc.,* Rev. Com. 1975, 75 OSAHRC 56/C2, 1974-1975 OSHD ¶ 19,594.

.812 A § 1926.25(a) charge was vacated because the employer, a subcontractor working on a multi-employer jobsite, was not required to remove debris created by other subcontractors from all areas through which its employees had to pass. The employer made reasonable efforts to compel the general contractor to carry out its obligations and went beyond its own contractual obligation by participating in general cleanup. *Truland Corp.,* Rev. Com. Judge 1976, 77 OSAHRC 23/A2, 1976-1977 OSHD ¶ 20,974.

.813 Allowing employees digging a trench for a gas supply line to work in and around an area where debris (consisting of plywood, gas cylinders and plastic pipe) constituted tripping and falling hazards constituted a nonserious § 1926.25(a) violation. The subcontractor argued that it neither created nor controlled the condition, but it failed to show that it had taken the required realistic measures to protect employees; supervisory personnel were well aware that the materials were strewn about the working area. *Laclede Gas Co.,* Rev. Com. Judge 1983, 83 OSAHRC 32/A2, 1983-1984 OSHD ¶ 26,553.

.91 Waste containers [25(c)]. A nonserious § 1926.25(c) waste disposal charge was reduced to de minimis. Although garbage was removed daily, it still overflowed the garbage pails near a break area. However, because the overflow conditions did not exist long enough each day to create a significant fire hazard, the violation did not pose a direct danger. *D. Fortunato, Inc.,* Rev. Com. 1979, 79 OSAHRC 69/B12, 1979 OSHD ¶ 23,781.

 ¶ 2106 PERSONAL PROTECTIVE EQUIPMENT (§ 1926.28)

Section 1926.28(a) states that employers are responsible for requiring the wearing of personal protective equipment by employees in all operations where there is an exposure to hazardous conditions *or* where Part 1926 (i.e., the construction standards) indicates a need for using such equipment to reduce the hazard to employees. In 1986,

¶ 2106

ILLUSTRATION 8-19. *(continued)* 367

the Review Commission in *L.E. Myers Co.* reversed its own precedent, ruling that the standard as written was invalid and that the earlier version of the standard is in effect. According to the Commissioners, establishment of a violation under the earlier version of the standard requires a showing by the Secretary that employees are exposed to a hazard requiring the use of personal protective equipment *and* that Part 1926 indicates a need for using such equipment to reduce the hazard to employees (.92).

In a recent application of the *Myers* test, the Commissioners ruled that the Secretary established a steel erection employer's violation of § 1926.28(a) by demonstrating that welders working without protection at a 30-foot height were exposed to a hazardous condition that warranted the use of safety belts, that another section of the construction standards (i.e., § 1926.105(a)) indicated a need for belts, and that the employer failed to require the use of the equipment (.34).

In another case, the Commissioners vacated a § 1926.28(a) charge of failing to require safety belt use by employees installing insulation and decking to form the roof of a one-story metal building because the Secretary did not meet his burden of proof under *Myers.* The roof in question had a slope of 1 to 12 and varied in height from 16 to 21 feet. No other construction standards indicated a need for fall protection under the conditions existing at the worksite. Section 1926.105(a), safety nets, applies only to fall distances greater than 25 feet, the Commissioners noted. Section 1926.500(g) mentions the use of safety belts on low-pitched roofs, but applies only to "built-up roofing work," which by definition excludes the construction of roof decks. Other construction standards provide for protection from falls of less than the 16 to 21 feet involved in the instant case, but by means of guardrails, catch platforms, nets, or other protective devices that are not "personal" equipment as called for in § 1926.28(a) (.341).

A subcontractor applying fireproofing material to a high-rise building under construction was held in violation of § 1926.28(a) for allowing an employee to work without a safety belt on a steel beam 40 feet above ground level and one or two feet beyond the cable guarding the open side of the building. The Secretary had amended the citation by adding the § 1926.28(a) charge as an alternative to a § 1926.105(a) safety net charge. The employer's argument that the Secretary's position was patently inconsistent because the standard appearing in the citation indicated that a safety net should have been used, while the evidence presented at the hearing focused entirely on safety belts, was rejected. The Judge pointed out that the Commission noted in *Myers* that § 1926.105(a) indicates the need for belts where the workplace is more than 25 feet above the ground. Sections 1926.105(a) and 1926.28(a) are therefore inextricably linked in instances in which an employee working more than 25 feet above the ground is exposed to a fall hazard (.343).

Scope. The standard has most often been used to cite employers for failure to require employees working at elevations to wear safety belts and lifelines. The standard has also been used on occasion to cite employers for not requiring workers to wear face, foot, and head protection.

As noted in § 1926.28(b), regulations governing the use, selection, and maintenance of personal protective equipment appear in § 1926.104 (see ¶ 2111). In addition, requirements covering the selection and use of safety belts, safety nets, and protective equipment for work over water are covered at ¶ 2113 through 2117.

Validity of standard. Section 1926.28(a), as initially adopted in 1971, stated that the "employer is responsible for requiring the wearing of personal protective equipment in all operations where there is an exposure to hazardous conditions and where this part indicates the need for using such equipment to reduce the hazard to the employees." The standard was amended the following year to substitute the word "or" for the word "and." The Review Commission, in its 1979 *S&H Riggers* decision, ruled that the 1972 amendment was not a substantive change in the standard requiring formal rulemaking procedures (.921), but later reversed itself and ruled the amendment invalid (.92).

902   **Construction Standards**   1058   7-31-91

erection standards applied to the hazard in question (.83). In a similar decision, the Commissioners held that a reasonable person familiar with the circumstances would not have recognized that workers engaged in structural steel bolting operations at a height of ten feet were exposed to a hazard requiring protective equipment (.831).

In a recent decision, the Commissioners ruled that the steel erection standard at § 1926.750(b)(2)(i) addresses only falls to the interior of a building and was not specifically applicable to the exterior fall hazard at issue (.832).

Work on roofs. The Commissioners upheld a § 1926.28(a) charge of not providing fall protection to employees working near the edge of a roof sloped two inches in 12 inches, rejecting the employer's argument that application of the standard was precluded by a scaffolding standard requirement that catch platforms be provided for roofs having a slope greater than four in 12. The latter standard, the Commissioners stated, addresses the fall hazard associated with working anywhere upon a sloped roof because of its pitch rather than the hazard of working near its edge. Accordingly, the more general requirements of the personal protective equipment standard applied (.75).

In rejecting an employer's contention that its employee had no suitable place to tie off while leaning over the edge of a structure, the Commissioners ruled that impossibility of compliance with § 1926.104(b)—which requires that lifelines be secured to an anchorage or structural member capable of supporting 5,400 pounds— was no defense to a § 1926.28(a) charge (.19).

Fall distances. A Judge's ruling that a construction firm violated § 1926.28 by allowing employees to work beneath a bridge at a height of less than 25 feet without tying off was upheld over the employer's argument that the standard was too generalized to support a citation and that § 1926.105(a), though specific, did not apply to a height of less than 25 feet. Previous Commission decisions holding § 1926.28(a) applicable to fall distances less than the 25 feet specified in § 1926.105(a) were controlling (.38).

Current OSHA guidelines state that, in general, construction fall hazards of 10 through 25 feet are governed by § 1926.28(a), while those of more than 25 feet are addressed by § 1926.105(a). According to the guidelines, OSHA interprets § 1926.28(a) as not generally requiring the use of safety belts for heights of less than 10 feet due to the need for maneuverability and the common use of belts with a six-foot lanyard. In addition, § 1926.28(a) will be cited in situations in which employees engaged in structural steel construction of tiered buildings are exposed to fall hazards of 10 to 25 feet to the interior of buildings (.382).

Annotations by Topic

¶ **2106**

ILLUSTRATION 8-19. (*continued*)

nary measures intended to implement the program were not imposed. The deterrent effect of the rules was undermined by emphasizing construction deadlines over safety requirements. *Henry J. Kaiser Co.*, Rev. Com. Judge 1984, 84 OSAHRC 44/A2, 1984-1985 OSHD ¶ 27,066.

.324 Because the Secretary failed to prove that an employer knew or could have known that an employee whose duties as a union steward included safety responsibilities was not wearing a safety belt, a § 1926.28(a) charge was vacated. The employee's knowledge was not imputable to an employer, since the steward was not a foreman and had no safety authority delegated by the employer. The employer could anticipate that a union safety representative would comply with regulations, and the alternative would be constant supervision, which the work did not require. *Atlas Electric Construction, Inc.*, Rev. Com. Judge 1978, 78 OSAHRC 23/F8, 1978 OSHD ¶ 22,621.

.33 Employer's safety program. The Commissioners erred in rejecting the employer's employee misconduct defense to a § 1926.28(a) charge on the ground that the company's safety program was inadequately enforced. The employer took all feasible steps to ensure compliance with workrules requiring workers to wear tied-off safety belts during elevated work; the violative actions of its employees were an unforeseeable departure from these effectively communicated and enforced rules. Safety training was given upon hiring, and weekly meetings emphasized the need to tie off belts during work over ten feet above ground. A full-time safety manager was employed at construction sites, employees violating the safety rules were reprimanded, and seven workers had been terminated for such violations. Each morning the foreman had the crew check safety equipment, and checked workers ten times a day to be certain they were tied off. He could not have been expected to remain to watch the crew's every move. *Daniel International Corp. v. OSHRC and Secretary of Labor*, CA-11 1982, 683 F2d 361, 1982 OSHD ¶ 26,185.

See also:

Miller and Long Co., Inc., Rev. Com. Judge 1972, 72 OSAHRC 7/F11, 1971-1973 OSHD ¶ 15,152.

Charles Vrana & Son Construction Co., Rev. Com. Judge 1976, 77 OSAHRC 4/E10, 1975-1976 OSHD ¶ 20,603.

Irvin H. Whitehouse and Sons Co., Inc., Rev. Com. Judge 1978, 78 OSAHRC 73/B12, 1978 OSHD ¶ 22,995; appeal (CA-6, No. 78-3543) dismissed 11/15/79.

Rodgers Construction, Inc., Rev. Com. Judge 1982, 82 OSAHRC 61/B6, 1982 OSHD ¶ 26,308.

Henry J. Kaiser Co., Rev. Com. Judge 1984, 84 OSAHRC 44/A2, 1984-1985 OSHD ¶ 27,066.

Pressure Concrete Construction Co., Inc., Rev. Com. Judge 1985, 85 OSAHRC 35/A3, 1984-1985 OSHD ¶ 27,357.

Regina Construction Corp., Rev. Com. Judge 1987, 87 OSAHRC 19/A6, 1986-1987 OSHD ¶ 27,911; affirmed (CA DofC, No. 87-1159) 1988.

Walters & Wolf Glass Co., Rev. Com. Judge 1989, 89 OSAHRC 16/B14, 1987-1990 OSHD ¶ 28,500 (employer's safety program was not effectively enforced).

.331 In reversing the Judge's affirmance of a § 1926.28(a) charge of failure to require employees working over power lines to use safety belts, the Review Commission misallocated the burden of proving the adequacy of the company safety program. The Commissioners failed to justify their rejection of the Judge's factual findings that the foreman's conduct raised an inference of lax enforcement and communication of the program. One employee was electrocuted and a second injured in the accident that gave rise to the citation, and the injured worker testified that the supervisor specifically stated that no safety belts would be needed on the job. The employer argued unsuccessfully that once it alleged the existence of a comprehensive safety program, the burden shifted to the Secretary to prove that the program was inadequate to make the supervisor's noncompliance with safety belt rules unforeseeable. A claim of unforeseeable employee misconduct is most appropriately regarded as an affirmative defense to be proved by the employer after the Secretary had shown a *prima facie* OSH Act violation. A *prima facie* case was established in the instant case by evidence that safety belts were not provided as required by § 1926.105(a) for work more than 25 feet above the ground. The employer is obligated to prevent hazardous noncomplying conduct by supervisory employees. The Commissioners erred in accepting the employer's evidence on the adequacy of the safety program as written while selectively ignoring evidence credited by the Judge showing that the program was actively disregarded in practice. The employer could produce no records of safety booklets distributed to the workers or manuals to the supervisor or of any tailgate meeting conducted by the supervisor. The injured worker could not remember when a safety meeting had last been held, and a company secretary testified that the supervisor had not filed any safety reports prior to the accident. *Brock, Secretary of Labor v. The L.E. Myers Co., High Voltage Div. and OSHRC*, CA-6 1987, 818 F2d 1270, 1986-1987 OSHD ¶ 27,919; cert denied, SCt 1987, 1987-1990 OSHD ¶ 28,131.

.332 The Judge properly found the employer in violation of § 1926.28(a) for permitting employees to work on a 50-foot-high bridge girder without safety belts. The employer's imperfectly enforced workrule requiring safety belt use under the cited conditions indicated its recognition of the hazard. That a supervisor himself breached the company safety policy showed that implementation of the policy was lax. *Jensen Construction Co.*, Rev. Com. 1979, 79 OSAHRC 49/D3, 1979 OSHD ¶ 23,664.

.34 Establishing a violation under the *Myers* test. The Secretary established a steel erection employer's violation of § 1926.28(a) personal protective equipment requirements by demonstrating that welders working without protection at a 30-foot height were exposed to a hazardous condition that warranted the use of safety belts, that some other section of the construction standards (i.e., § 1926.105(a)) indicated a need for belts, and that the employer failed to require the use of the equipment. *Bratton Corp.*, Rev. Com. 1990, 1987-1990 OSHD ¶ 29,152.

See also:

Employment Safety and Health Guide

¶ 2106

1061 8-20-91	**Cumulative Index**	**5829-19**

See also Latest Additions to Cumulative Index at page 5805.

From Compilation Paragraph No.		**To New Development Paragraph No.**

2106	§ 1926.28(a); employees working without fall protection (RC)	25,491
	§ 1926.28(a); full-face respirators, full-length gloves; need for protection	29,232
	§ 1926.28(a); safety belt use on scaffold; employee misconduct (RC)	29,333
	§ 1926.28(a); safety belt while working on roof edge	28,503
	§ 1926.28(a); safety belt, work near unguarded elevator shaft; review ordered	29,019
	§ 1926.28(a); safety belt, work near unguarded elevator shaft; settlement (RC)	29,360
	§ 1926.28(a); safety belts for bridges painting; review ordered	28,149
	§ 1926.28(b); safety belt use for outrigger scaffold; review ordered	27,898
	Unguarded elevated bridges; review ordered	27,315
2108	§ 1926.52(a); duration of employee exposure to excessive noise (RC)	27,868
	§§ 1926.55(a), (b); lead exposure, engineering controls; review ordered	28,928
	§ 1926.50(f); failure to post medical telephone numbers at site	29,319
	§ 1926.51(f); washing facilities; coke oven emissions; review ordered.	29,216
	Lead hazards in construction; OSHA/NIOSH publication	10,907
	Posting telephone numbers of physicians, hospitals, ambulances; OMB review	10,402
2109	§§ 1926.58(e)(6)(i), (j)(2)(i); "regulated area," small-scale, short-duration exemption; review ordered	28,704
	§§ 1926.58(e)(6)(i), (j)(2)(i); citations withdrawn (RC)	29,102
	§ 1926.58(e)(1); regulated area, asbestos encapsulation project	29,107
	§ 1926.58(e)(6)(i); negative pressure enclosure; fiber levels below PEL	29,182
	asbestos encapulation project	29,107

The next step is to check the Current Topical Index for additional commentary and news items about relevant statutory or regulatory activities. In Illustration 8-22 on page 372 you can observe that there are several entries related to safety belts and lines under the topic "Personal protective equipment," which is the same subject heading used previously in the Topical Index. This index is further updated by the Latest Additions to Current Topical Index, reproduced in Illustration 8-23 on page 373. The paragraph references are to more recent cases, regulations, proposed regulations, legislative changes, or additional analysis and commentary that is found within the looseleaf binder filed behind the "New Developments" tab.

In total, the researcher has checked five indexes: the general Topical Index, the Cumulative Index, the Latest Additions to Cumulative Index, the Current Topical Index, and the Latest Additions to Current Topical Index. Looseleafs published by companies other than CCH may use different labels; for example, the Bureau of National Affairs uses a "Master Index" updated by supplemental "Cumulative Digests and Indexes." Nonetheless, the methodology employed to complete the research is very similar.

The commentary section of a looseleaf service is frequently and regularly updated through the issuance of new "releases" that are interfiled in the looseleaf binders or through separate supplementation. In addition, new material will be found in a new or current developments section, which will contain news items, such as news about major appointments of persons to the agency, or editorial comments about proposed regulations, or comments about observed trends in agency activities regarding enforcement.

d. Statutory Authority and Administrative Regulations

The commentary in our example includes analysis of the pertinent statute and agency regulations. Most looseleafs, as mini-libraries, contain the full text

ILLUSTRATION 8-21. Updating Indexes: Latest Additions to Cumulative Index, 3 Employ. Safety & Health Guide (CCH) 5806 (Oct. 8, 1991).

371

5806 Cumulative Index—Current Topical Index 1068 10-8-91
See also Cumulative Index at page 5825.

From Compilation Paragraph No.		To New Development Paragraph No.
1149	§ 1910.145(f)(8); biological hazard labels on nursing home waste;review ordered	29,460
1159	§ 1910.178(n)(4); "obstructed forward view" defined; review ordered	29,428
1177	§ 1910.252(e)(1)(ii) [now 1910.252(b)(1)(ii)]; keeping passageways clear of welding cable; review ordered	29,423
	§ 1910.252(e)(2)(i)(a); two-man welding operation, "proper" eye protection (RC)	29,442
	§ 1910.252(e)(4)(iv) [now 1910.252(b)(4)(iv)]; attendant required outside confined space; review ordered	29,423
	§ 1910.252(e)(4)(iv) [now 1910.252(b)(4)(iv)]; quick removal of welders from confined spaces; review ordered	29,423
	§ 1910.252(e)(4)(i) [now 1910.252(b)(4)(i)]; submarine compartment was a "confined space"; review ordered	29,423
1186	§ 1910.304(f)(1)(iv); missing ground prong; citation withdrawn (RC)	29,436
1190	Indoor air pollutants; request for information	11,055
1193	Nonasbestiform minerals; extension of administrative stay	11,040
1199	§ 1910.1029(g)(3); Secretary's interpretation of requirements (CA-10)	29,431
1204	§ 1910.1048(m)(1)(i)—(m)(4)(ii); stay extended	11,020
	Formaldehyde standard; comments on proposed revision	11,045
1301	§ 1910.1200(e)(1)(i); non-existent chemical on required list; citation withdrawn	29,445
	Exemption for pesticides; removal by California	11,016

Construction Standards

2102	§ 1926.20(b); inspection by "competent persons" (CA-11)	29,432
2106	§ 1926.28(a); safety belts for bridge painting; wilful (RC)	29,439
2109	Nonasbestiform minerals; extension of administrative stay	11,040
2110	§ 1926.59(e)(4); failure to make program available to Secretary	29,437
2111	§ 1926.100(a); head protection for steel erection employees; review ordered	29,456
2115	§ 1926.105(a); failure to prove fall existed	29,437
	§ 1926.105(a); proof of practicality of safety belts; review ordered	29,426
2117	§ 1926.106(a); life jackets for work beneath bridge; provision vs. use (RC)	29,454
	§ 1926.106(c); ring buoy (RC)	29,454
2128	§ 1926.399(b)(2); inadequate guarding of rotating blades on a muller mixer; repeat violation	29,447
	§ 1926.601(b)(4); lift truck did not have obstructed rear view	29,447
2139	§ 1926.451(a)(13); access ladder for buggy scaffold; not wilful (RC)	29,439
	... bracing, securing	29,438

of statutes and agency regulations. There are several related methods for finding the full text of the statute and the regulations.

An efficient approach is to pursue the references found in the commentary section. Another approach is to use the title of the act as a search term in the topical index and in the other updating indexes. Because the index is exhaustive, this approach is more valuable if you are also looking for commentary on a specific provision of a statute or regulation. An alternative to the index for finding the full text of a statute or a regulation is to use one of the finding aids included in the looseleaf service. In the *Employment Safety and Health Guide,* filed behind a separate tab covering "Laws and Executive Orders," there are tables listing the primary documents contained in this looseleaf service. As demonstrated in Illustration 8-24 on page 374, the full text of the Occupational Safety and Health Act of 1970 begins at ¶ 6100.

Looseleaf services also typically contain finding aids that assist the user in finding federal administrative regulations by section. In the *Employment Safety and Health Guide,* filed behind the tab "Finding Lists—Case Table" (see Illustration 8-16) is a listing of regulations sections arranged by section number. In the commentary material in Illustration 8-19, we noticed several references to regulation § 1926.28(a). Now examine Illustration 8-25 on pages

5889-50   **Cumulative Index—Current Topical Index**   1046   5-14-91

See also Topical Index at page 91 and Index to Standards at page 3201.
References are to paragraph (¶) numbers.

Personal protective equipment—continued
. fall hazard—continued
. . work at flat roof edge . . . 26,477
. fall protection, proposed amendments
. . CCH Publication, Part 2 . . . 10,443
. . comments . . . 10,601; 10,642
. . hearing scheduled . . . 10,576
. firefighters
. . effective date of clothing requirement . . .
   27,317
. . validity of standard . . . 27,317
. flame retardant clothing
. . arm sleeves near plastic molds . . . 27,397
. . long sleeved shirts . . . 26,840
. . metal pouring workers . . . 27,268; 27,568; 28,844
. flat roof work
. . hazard recognition . . . 25,510
. flotation devices . . . 27,975
. foundry molten metal operations
. . protection above vs. below the waist . . .
   25,059
. general industry, revised standard proposal
. . comment request . . . 10,189
. . comments . . . 10,599
. . hearing schedule, comment period
   reopening . . . 10,355
. gloves
. . barrier cream or glove feasibility . . . 25,326
. . chemical hazards . . . 29,177; 29,192; 29,206
. . fiberglass industry safety program . . .
   25,744
. . flame resistant, coke oven workers . . .
   28,873
. . sharpening slicer blades . . . 29,088
. hard hats . . . 27,798; 27,991; 28,183; 28,227
. . automobile test driving . . . 27,593
. . disciplinary action . . . 28,543; 28,559
. . falling objects protection . . . 28,045; 28,320;
   28,543; 28,581; 28,816
. . high voltage wire contact . . . 27,857
. . ironworkers . . . 28,921
. . provi . . .   28,930

Personal protective equipment—continued
. protective clothing—continued
. . provision for rescue work . . . 25,995
. . welding work . . . 26,331
. reasonable man test
. . hard hats . . . 25,347; 27,964
. . safety belts in bridge construction . . .
   27,222
. . safety shoes . . . 26,961; 28,907
. reflective clothing
. . jurisdiction, FAA vs. OSHA . . . 29,051
. rubber gloves
. . grounding electrical wires . . . 26,165
. . incontinent patients . . . 27,499
. safety belts and lines
. . applicability to steel erection . . . 26,395;
   26,593; 28,246
. . chimney demolition . . . 26,437
. . employee misconduct . . . 26,114; 26,308
. . exposure to hazardous conditions . . .
   25,991
. . feasibility, ironworkers . . . 26,501
. . feasibility, welding workers . . . 26,395
. . greater hazards . . . 26,030; 26,114
. . hazard showing for yarn blending bin
   workers . . . 26,263
. . notice of applicability . . . 25,982
. . oil derrick servicing rigs . . . 26,401
. . safety program, adequacy . . . 28,489
. . scaffold platform . . . 28,188
. . supplier of workers vs. building owner . . .
   26,767
. . use decision left to employees . . . 26,231
. . work on mobile home roofs . . . 26,390
. safety glasses—see eye and face protection,
   this entry
. safety nets
. . provision in lieu of safety belts . . . 26,178
. safety shoes
. . airline freight handlers and luggage ramp
   workers . . . 25,339
. . auto parts handling . . . 26,239
. . auto parts warehouse . . . 27,309

376-377, which is the table of agency regulations arranged by section number. This table indicates that the text of § 1926.28 begins at ¶ 7703.5 of the service.

Often there is commentary accompanying the full text of the regulation, which may include information about the enabling statutory authority. Note that is the situation here; the introductory material of ¶ 7701, reproduced in Illustration 8-25 on page 376, includes a brief description of the authority OSHA was granted under the Occupational Safety and Health Act authorizing the creation of the safety and health regulations, which are pertinent to our research problem.

e.   Reporters

In addition, the commentary section directs you to court and agency decisions. The citations found in the annotations are to the reporters accompanying the *Employment Safety and Health Guide*. In Illustration 8-19 at page 369, note the citation in *Miller & Long Co., Inc.* to 1971-1973 OSHD ¶ 15,152. This citation is to the *Occupational Safety and Health Decisions* reporter. At ¶ 15,152 of the reporter covering years 1971 to 1973, you will find the digest of the decision rendered by the administrative law judge. That digest entry is reproduced in Illustration 8-26 on page 378.

ILLUSTRATION 8-23. Updating Indexes: Latest Additions to Current Topical Index, 3 Employ. Safety & Health Guide (CCH) 5836 (Oct. 1, 1991).

373

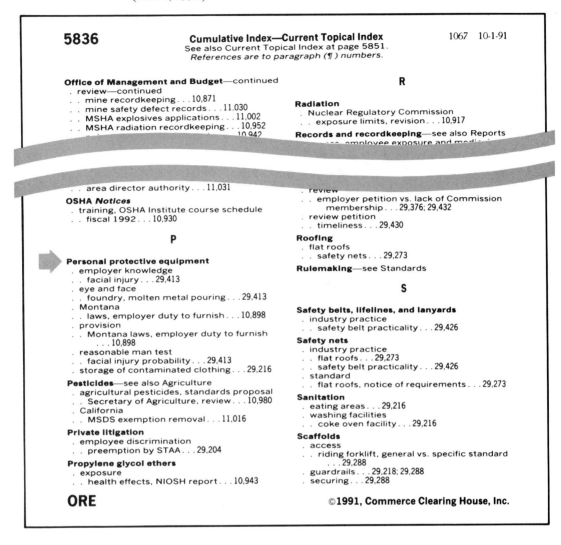

5836   **Cumulative Index—Current Topical Index**   1067   10-1-91
See also Current Topical Index at page 5851.
References are to paragraph (¶) numbers.

Office of Management and Budget—continued
. review—continued
. . mine recordkeeping. . .10,871
. . mine safety defect records. . . 11,030
. . MSHA explosives applications. . . 11,002
. . MSHA radiation recordkeeping. . .10,952
                                    10,942

. . area director authority. . .11,031
OSHA *Notices*
. training, OSHA Institute course schedule
. . fiscal 1992. . .10,930

P

Personal protective equipment
. employer knowledge
. . facial injury. . .29,413
. eye and face
. . foundry, molten metal pouring. . .29,413
. Montana
. . laws, employer duty to furnish. . .10,898
. provision
. . Montana laws, employer duty to furnish
. . . 10,898
. reasonable man test
. . facial injury probability. . .29,413
. storage of contaminated clothing. . . .29,216

Pesticides—see also Agriculture
. agricultural pesticides, standards proposal
. . Secretary of Agriculture, review. . .10,980
. California
. . MSDS exemption removal. . .11,016

Private litigation
. employee discrimination
. . preemption by STAA. . .29,204

Propylene glycol ethers
. exposure
. . health effects, NIOSH report. . .10,943

ORE

R

Radiation
. Nuclear Regulatory Commission
. . exposure limits, revision. . .10,917
Records and recordkeeping—see also Reports
. . . employee exposure and medical

. review
. . employer petition vs. lack of Commission
. . . membership. . .29,376; 29,432
. review petition
. . timeliness. . .29,430

Roofing
. flat roofs
. . safety nets. . .29,273
Rulemaking—see Standards

S

Safety belts, lifelines, and lanyards
. industry practice
. . safety belt practicality. . .29,426
Safety nets
. industry practice
. . flat roofs. . .29,273
. . safety belt practicality. . .29,426
. standard
. . flat roofs, notice of requirements. . .29,273
Sanitation
. eating areas. . .29,216
. washing facilities
. . coke oven facility. . .29,216
Scaffolds
. access
. . riding forklift, general vs. specific standard
. . . 29,288
. guardrails. . .29,218; 29,288
. securing. . .29,288

©**1991, Commerce Clearing House, Inc.**

Similarly, the annotations in ¶ 2106 have a brief headnote for the Eleventh Circuit Court of Appeals decision for *Daniel International Corp.,* which can be found at 1982 O.S.H.D. (CCH) ¶ 26,185; that decision is not reproduced here. Again, the looseleaf service, together with the accompanying reporters, have provided the user with a mini-library on OSHA decisions.

Citation Note: If the decision is published in a reporter, you should cite to the reporter, as dictated by Rule 10.3.1(b) and Table T.1 of *The Blue-book.* If you are citing an unreported decision or to a digest of a decision that is not available in a reporter, cite to the looseleaf service, using Rule 18. The citation to a service includes the name of the publisher and the exact date. For example: *Miller & Long Co.,* 1971-73 O.S.H.D. (CCH) ¶ 15,152 (July 3, 1972). Table T.16 provides the abbreviations of the most common looseleaf services and their publishers. Citations may be to paragraphs (¶) or sections (§) instead of pages.

Because *Daniel International Corp.* is a reported case, it should be cited to *West's Federal Reporter* and not to a service.

1048   5-28-91   **2585**

LAWS
EXECUTIVE ORDERS

TABLE OF CONTENTS

ILLUSTRATION 8-24. *(continued)* 375

[The next page is 2589.]

f.   Summary

Following this research process, you have found the following: commentary on the pertinent primary authority, the text of the governing federal regulation, the text of the enabling legislation, court decisions, agency decisions, and any important updating information. As noted in Part E at page 389, you could also find state statutes, state regulations, and state agency decisions.

The looseleaf services provide you with a mini-library of materials needed to complete legal research. They are comprehensive and current, but sometimes they are complex and bulky. In many ways, research using looseleafs is a synthesis of research you would use if you had the entire law library within easy reach.

CONTRACT WORK HOURS AND SAFETY STANDARDS ACT

REGULATIONS 29 CFR PART 1926

SAFETY AND HEALTH REGULATIONS FOR CONSTRUCTION

[¶ 7701]

These regulations were first adopted under the Construction Safety Act [1] on April 13, 1971, applicable only to government contracts. They were adopted by reference under the Occupational Safety and Health Act on May 29, 1971, effective August 27, 1971, by § 1910.12 (¶ 6625.4). Subparts A and B are not incorporated by reference under OSHA. The regulations were reissued with amendments on December 16, 1972, and are now codified as 29 CFR, Chapter XVII, Part 1926, §§ 1926.1 through 1926.1052.[2] Section 1926.58 covering asbestos, tremolite, anthophyllite, and actinolite, was added to Subpart D—Occupational Health and Environmental Controls—June 20, 1986, effective July 21, 1986. Subpart K, Electrical, was amended July 11, 1986 (51 F.R. 25318), effective October 9, 1986. Section 1926.59, covering hazard communication, was added on August 24, 1987. Section 1926.700 was completely revised June 16, 1988 (53 F.R. 22643) to cover concrete and masonry construction. Section 1926.800 was completely revised June 2, 1989 (54 F.R. 23850) to cover underground construction. Subpart P, beginning with § 1926.650, was completely revised to cover excavations on October 31, 1989 (F.R. 45959). The effective date was delayed from January 2, 1990, to March 5, 1990, by a December 27, 1989, notice (54 F.R. 43055).

[[1] Issued under the authority contained in Sec. 1, 83 Stat. 96, 97, adding Sec. 107 to Public Law 87-581, 76 Stat. 357; 40 U.S.C. 333.]

[[2] Originally 29 CFR, Chapter XII, Part 1518, Sections 1518.1 through 1518.1051. Redesignated at 36 F.R. 25232, Dec. 30, 1971.]

[Authority: Secs. 6 and 8, Occupational Safety and Health Act (29 U.S.C. 655, 657); Sec. 107, Contract Work Hours and Safety Standards Act (40 U.S.C. 333); Secretary of Labor's Order No. 9-83 (48 FR 35736); 29 CFR Part 1911.]

TABLE OF CONTENTS

ILLUSTRATION 8-25. *(continued)* 377

Let's review the steps you took in researching the CSB Construction problem. You started with the index, which led you to commentary that provided general information about the topic and also provided you with references to other sources.

The commentary section cited governing legislation and federal administrative regulations. These were found by using finding aids, and the statutes and the regulations were reproduced in full text within the looseleaf binder. The annotations also contained digests and citations to relevant court and agency decisions. These decisions were reproduced in the accompanying reporters.

As a final step, although the process was not reviewed within this chapter, you would, of course, have Shepardized the cases, statutes, regulations, and agency decisions you found. Many looseleafs contain a citator as part of the service, but many do not—the *Employment Safety and Health Guide* does

Decisions   **20,225**

exercise sufficient supervision to insure that a portable ladder used on the construction project at a private residence was properly secured to avoid sideways slippage (§ 1926.450). There was sufficient evidence to find that the employer failed to provide first aid kits, although the nearest hospital was more than 11 miles distant (§ 1926.23). The Secretary failed to prove, however, that the employer had a duty to provide a portable toilet since the employees had access to the owner's toilet while the owner was present. Section 1926.51(c)(1) can be construed to not require the constant availability of toilet facilities, providing that periods of privation are not long. The Judge vacated that portion of a proposed penalty relating to the catch platform since the existence of a less stringent standard at § 1910.28(s)(3) was possibly confusing. A penalty of $67 was assessed.

[¶ 15,151] Canrad Precision Industries, Inc.

Digest of Judge's Decision dated July 21, 1972. OSHRC Docket No. 89. David G. Oringer, Judge. **For further action, if any, see Case Table at page 5901.**

General Duty Clause—Electrical Hazards—Employer Responsibility—Employee Negligence. Although an employee engaged in electrical research was responsible for creating hazardous electrical conditions that caused his electrocution, the employer's failure to exercise adequate supervision justified a Citation for serious violation of the General Duty Clause. The employee's supervisor had not inspected the laboratory to examine the equipment being used for a "considerable period of time." The employer had the primary duty to furnish a safe place of employment, and it must guard even those employees who carelessly disregard their own safety, if reasonably and prudently possible with the exercise of reasonable diligence. In this instance, the employer could have determined through the exercise of reasonable diligence, that the employee's place of work contained unguarded electrical sources of 2200 volts, no protection against abrasion of all conductors entering service boxes, and pull boxes open during servicing. The Citation and a proposed penalty of $800 were sustained.

[¶ 15,152] Miller and Long Company, Inc.

Digest of Judge's Decision dated July 3, 1972. OSHRC Docket No. 320. Herbert E. Bates, Judge. **For further action, if any, see Case Table at page 5901.**

Construction—Personal Protective Equipment—Safety Nets—Fatality. An employer was held to have seriously violated § 1926.28 by failing to provide personal protective equipment or safety nets for employees working more than 25 feet above the ground. The employer was cited after an investigation into the death of an employee who stepped onto a platform designed to prevent falling objects from falling onto employees. The platform was not capable of supporting the weight of a human. The employee had little experience with construction work and had not been given any general safety training, although he had been warned not to step on the platforms. The employer should have been aware that failure to provide adequate safety measures for employees working on the job site would cause death or serious physical injuries, and a proposed penalty of $600 was sustained.

Guard Rails—Construction. An employer who failed to provide guardrails around spaces near a trash container on the fifth floor of a building under construction was properly cited for violating § 1926.500(d)(1). A proposed penalty of $15 was vacated on the ground that the violation resulted from an oversight, a relatively small area was unprotected, and the employer immediately abated the violation.

[¶ 15,153] Cable Car Advertisers, Inc.

Digest of Judge's Decision dated July 11, 1972. OSHRC Docket No. 354 and 480. Robert N. Burchmore, Judge. This report will become the final order of the OSHRC if no Commissioner directs review within thirty days. **For further action, if any, see Case Table at page 5901.**

Posting—Employee Rights Poster—Citations. An employer was properly cited for failure to comply with § 1903.2(a) and § 1903.16. A Compliance Officer had given an not. Regardless of whether you use the looseleaf's citator or one of the *Shepard's* citators, you need to consider and thoroughly research the status and treatment of the law you have found.

379

Administrative
Materials: Searching
for Primary
Authority

Although there is not one method that works for every looseleaf service, it is appropriate to anticipate that every looseleaf service functions as a mini-library. Access to the library begins with the indexes or digests, which lead you to the primary and secondary authorities you need to solve your research situation.

D. CALR IN FEDERAL ADMINISTRATIVE MATERIALS

1. Introduction

You can research administrative regulations and agency decisions online, through WESTLAW and LEXIS, just as you can research federal statutes and judicial decisions online. This section demonstrates some possible searches in the key databases and comments on their usefulness compared to print research. It assumes that you already have located and read the pertinent statute, but have not found references to agency regulations or decisions.

2. WESTLAW

WESTLAW offers current regulations in the CFR database, which encompasses the *Code of Federal Regulations,* and the FR database, which encompasses the *Federal Register.*

A useful first step in searching in the CFR database is to take advantage of C.F.R.'s close parallel to U.S.C. and confine your search to the appropriate title. For example, entering [pr("title 29")] would limit your search to the regulations in title 29. Unfortunately, title 29 contains over 7,000 documents; adding [& o.s.h.a. "occupational safety"] to limit the scope to OSHA regulations reduced the number only to 1,625.

Thus, you would need to further narrow your search by adding terms pertinent to your factual situation. If you emphasized the equipment the employees were failing to use, you might add [& harness scaffold (safety /5 belt line)]. This search yielded 64 documents. If you scanned the list (see Illustration 8-27 on page 380), you would be able to exclude many of them as unlikely to be relevant. The most relevant regulation listed is § 1926.104, which does indeed cover safety lines on construction sites. However, it does not pertain to the employer's obligation to compel employees to wear the safety lines. (See Illustration 8-28 on page 381.) You could obtain the pertinent regulation, § 1926.28, along with nearly 50 others, by adding instead a search such as [& personal employee /5 protective safety /5 equip!]. Note that you will obtain historical information about your regulation online. (See Illustration 8-29 on page 382.)

Next, you would simply enter [update] to essentially switch from the CFR database (which covered developments as of June 1991 when this was written in December 1991) into the FR database (which was current to mid-December 1991). You would then obtain information on any changes in your regulation; in our example, there were none. (See Illustration 8-30 on page 383.)

WESTLAW presents agency decisions in databases specialized by subject matter. The decisions of the Occupational Safety and Health Review Com-

```
CITATIONS LIST (Page 5)                    Total Documents:  64
Database: CFR

   34.    29 C.F.R. s 1917.49
 s 1917.49 Spouts, chutes, hoppers, bins, and associated equipment.

   35.    29 C.F.R. s 1917.73
 s 1917.73 Terminal facilities handling menhaden and similar species of fish.

   36.    29 C.F.R. s 1917.118    s 1917.118 Fixed ladders.

   37.    29 C.F.R. s 1917.119    s 1917.119 Portable ladders.

   38.    29 C.F.R. s 1918.98    s 1918.98 Grain fitting.

   39.    29 C.F.R. s 1926.104
 s 1926.104 Safety belts, lifelines, and lanyards.

   40.    29 C.F.R. s 1926.105    s 1926.105 Safety nets.

   41.    29 C.F.R. s 1926.107
 s 1926.107 Definitions applicable to this subpart.

-->
```

mission, for example, appear in the FLB-OSRC database (one of the collection of databases in the area of federal labor law). That database contains decisions from 1971, when the OSAHRC was first created, to the present. There are comparable databases for many other areas governed by administrative agencies.

One way to locate decisions interpreting a regulation if you already have a citation to the relevant regulation is to search for references to the regulation. Of course, this search will work best when the regulation is cited rarely. In our example, the search [29 +5 1926.28] yielded 774 documents; obviously, the protective equipment regulation is an often cited standard. To narrow such a search, add words referring to key aspects of your situation. In our example, quite a few terms were needed to reduce the number of documents to a reasonable number. Ultimately, the search [29 +5 1926.28 /s (safety /5 line belt) /p fire* disciplin! suspen! terminat! discharge*] worked very well. It yielded seven very relevant documents; the first five appear at Illustration 8-31 on page 383.

Unfortunately, it is not always as easy to update agency decisions online as it is to update judicial decisions. WESTLAW did not carry *Shepard's Federal Occupational Safety and Health Citations* as of the time this book was written. You could, however, enter the name of the decision (with or without an accompanying citation) in the relevant database with a date restrictor in order to find later cases citing your decision. In this research example, you would conduct this search in the ALLFEDS database to locate any federal court review of your decision, as well as in the FLB-OSRC database.

3. LEXIS

LEXIS' coverage of official agency materials quite closely parallels that of WESTLAW. One difference is that LEXIS divides the federal regulations into specialized databases that are joined with agency decisions and other materials to form subject matter libraries. (WESTLAW clumps agency decisions and judicial decisions this way.)

To search for the regulation pertinent to our research situation in LEXIS,

ILLUSTRATION 8-28. WESTLAW Document Showing 29 C.F.R. § 1926.104, Available in the CFR Database.

381

```
Citation                    Rank(R)         Page(P)         Database    Mode
29 CFR s 1926.104           R 39 OF 64      P 1 OF 3        CFR         P
29 C.F.R. s 1926.104

                     CODE OF FEDERAL REGULATIONS
                          Title 29--Labor
              Subtitle B--Regulations Relating to Labor
    Chapter XVII--Occupational Safety and Health Administration, Department of
                                Labor
         PART 1926--SAFETY AND HEALTH REGULATIONS FOR CONSTRUCTION
         SUBPART E--PERSONAL PROTECTIVE AND LIFE SAVING EQUIPMENT

  s 1926.104 Safety belts, lifelines, and lanyards.

    (a) Lifelines, safety belts, and lanyards shall be used only for employee
  safeguarding. Any lifeline, safety belt, or lanyard actually subjected to in-
  service loading, as distinguished from static load testing, shall be
  immediately removed from service and shall not be used again for employee
  safeguarding.
    (b) Lifelines shall be secured above the point of operation to an anchorage or
  structural member capable of supporting a minimum dead weight of 5,400 pounds.
    (c) Lifelines used on rock-scaling operations, or in areas where the lifeline
  may be subjected to cutting or abrasion, shall be a minimum of 7/8 -inch wire
  -->

  29 CFR s 1926.104           R 39 OF 64      P 2 OF 3        CFR         P
    TEXT

  core manila rope. For all other lifeline applications, a minimum of 3/4 -inch
  manila or equivalent, with a minimum breaking strength of 5,400 pounds, shall
  be used.
    (d) Safety belt lanyard shall be a minimum of 1/2 -inch nylon, or equivalent,
  with a maximum length to provide for a fall of no greater than 6 feet. The
  rope shall have a nominal breaking strength of 5,400 pounds.
    (e) All safety belt and lanyard hardware shall be drop forged or pressed
  steel, cadmium plated in accordance with type 1, Class B plating specified in
  Federal Specification QQ-P-416. Surface shall be smooth and free of sharp
  edges.
    (f) All safety belt and lanyard hardware, except rivets, shall be capable of
  withstanding a tensile loading of 4,000 pounds without cracking, breaking, or
  taking a permanent deformation.

         PART 1926--SAFETY AND HEALTH REGULATIONS FOR CONSTRUCTION

    Source:  44 FR 8577, Feb. 9, 1979;  44 FR 20940, Apr. 6, 1979;  51 FR 24526,
  24528, July 7, 1986, unless otherwise noted.

    Editorial Note:  At 44 FR 8577, Feb. 9, 1979, OSHA reprinted without change
  -->
```

you thus would start in the LABOR library and then proceed to the CFR database. That database contains eight titles of C.F.R.; to narrow your search to title 29, you would conduct a [title (29)] segment search. If you proceeded as described above in the WESTLAW section, you would obtain much the same results. The successful search would be [title (29) and o.s.h.a. or osha or occupational safety and personal or employee w/5 protective or safety w/5 equip!]. That search would yield the pertinent regulation, along with many others. See Illustration 8-32 (on page 384) for a partial citation list and Illustration 8-33 (on page 384) for the regulation itself.

To update your search, you would then shift to the FEDREG file, which encompasses the *Federal Register* from 1980 to date, and conduct a focused search for material pertinent to the regulation—that is, [29 pre/3 1926.28]. This search would yield four documents, none affecting the currency of your regulation. Illustration 8-34 on page 385 is one of the four; it pertains to

```
Citation                Rank(R)        Page(P)       Database   Mode
29 CFR s 1926.28        R 30 OF 50     P 1 OF 2      CFR        T
  29 C.F.R. s 1926.28

                    CODE OF FEDERAL REGULATIONS
                           Title 29--Labor
                Subtitle B--Regulations Relating to Labor
      Chapter XVII--Occupational Safety and Health Administration, Department of
                                  Labor
           PART 1926--SAFETY AND HEALTH REGULATIONS FOR CONSTRUCTION
              SUBPART C--GENERAL SAFETY AND HEALTH PROVISIONS

 s 1926.28 Personal protective equipment.

  (a) The employer is responsible for requiring the wearing of appropriate
personal protective equipment in all operations where there is an exposure to
hazardous conditions or where this part indicates the need for using such
equipment to reduce the hazards to the employees.
  (b) Regulations governing the use, selection, and maintenance of personal
protective and lifesaving equipment are described under Subpart E of this part.

       PART 1926--SAFETY AND HEALTH REGULATIONS FOR CONSTRUCTION

--> p

29 CFR s 1926.28          R 30 OF 50        P 2 OF 2        CFR          P
   TEXT

  Source:  44 FR 8577, Feb. 9, 1979;  44 FR 20940, Apr. 6, 1979;  51 FR 24526,
24528, July 7, 1986, unless otherwise noted.

  Editorial Note:  At 44 FR 8577, Feb. 9, 1979, OSHA reprinted without change
the entire text of 29 CFR Part 1926 together with certain General Industry
Occupational Safety and Health Standards contained in 29 CFR Part 1910, which
have been identified as also applicable to construction work.  This developed a
single set of OSHA regulations for both labor and management forces within the
construction industry at 44 FR 20940, Apr. 6, 1979, Part 1926 was corrected.

         SUBPART C--GENERAL SAFETY AND HEALTH PROVISIONS

  Authority: Sec. 107, Contract Work Hours and Safety Standards Act
(Construction Safety Act) (40 U.S.C. 333);  Secs. 4, 6, 8, Occupational Safety
and Health Act of 1970 (29 U.S.C. 653, 655, 657);  Secretary of Labor's Order
No. 12-71 (36 FR 8754), 8-76 (41 FR 25059), or 9-83 (48 FR 35736), as
applicable.

  29 C. F. R. s 1926.28
  29 CFR s 1926.28
-----------------------------------------------------------------------
```

approval of California's state standards paralleling the federal regulations. By adding a date restrictor, you could confine your search to recent material.

LEXIS offers the decisions of the OSAHRC dating back to 1971 in the OSAHRC file in the LABOR library. A search for cases there citing § 1926.28 also retrieved 774 cases as in WESTLAW. A more focused search, [29 pre/3 1926.28 w/30 (safety w/5 line or belt) w/30 fire* or disciplin! or suspen! or terminat! or discharge*], yielded 12 documents, including the seven listed on WESTLAW. (The numbers vary slightly because of the differences in grammatical searches available on WESTLAW and numerically based searches used with LEXIS.) Illustration 8-35 on page 385 shows a portion of the most recent, very pertinent case, *Atlas Industrial Painters*.

ILLUSTRATION 8-30. WESTLAW Document Showing 29 C.F.R. § 1926.28
Updated, Available in the CFR Database.

383

```
 update
Citation                                 Page(P)       Database   Mode
29 CFR s 1926.28          FOUND DOCUMENT  P 1 OF 2      CFR        P
29 C.F.R. s 1926.28

                         CODE OF FEDERAL REGULATIONS
                              Title 29--Labor
                     Subtitle B--Regulations Relating to Labor
         Chapter XVII--Occupational Safety and Health Administration, Department of
                                     Labor
              PART 1926--SAFETY AND HEALTH REGULATIONS FOR CONSTRUCTION
                  SUBPART C--GENERAL SAFETY AND HEALTH PROVISIONS

 s 1926.28 Personal protective equipment.

  (a) The employer is responsible for requiring the wearing of appropriate
 personal protective equipment in all operations where there is an exposure to
 hazardous conditions or where this part indicates the need for using such
 equipment to reduce the hazards to the employees.
  (b) Regulations governing the use, selection, and maintenance of personal
 protective and lifesaving equipment are described under Subpart E of this part.

            PART 1926--SAFETY AND HEALTH REGULATIONS FOR CONSTRUCTION

 --> update

 There are currently no UPDATE documents for 29 CFR s 1926.28.

 More complete information on UPDATE and other Related Material services is
 available in SCOPE for the statutes, and legislative service databases.
```

ILLUSTRATION 8-31. WESTLAW Citation List from the FLB-OSRC Database.

```
 --> L

 CITATIONS LIST (Page 1)                          Total Documents:  7
 Database: FLB-OSRC

     1.   SECRETARY OF LABOR, Complainant    v.
 ATLAS INDUSTRIAL PAINTERS, Respondent    OSHRC Docket No. 87-619
 August 9, 1991.   Slip Copy, 1991 WL 165881 (O.S.H.R.C.)

     2.   SECRETARY OF LABOR v. F.A. GRAY, INC.   OSHRC DOCKET NO. 83-517
 April 26, 1985   OSHRC DOCKET NO. 83-517, 1985 WL 44840 (O.S.H.R.C.)

     3.   SECRETARY OF LABOR, v. ELECTRICAL CORPORATION OF AMERICA, INC.
 OSHRC DOCKET NO. 81-1012   April 14, 1982
 OSHRC DOCKET NO. 81-1012, 1982 WL 22383 (O.S.H.R.C.)

     4.   SECRETARY OF LABOR, v. MIDWEST TANK COMPANY, INC.
 OSHRC DOCKET NO. 80-4305   October 22, 1981
 OSHRC DOCKET 80-4305, 1981 WL 19544 (O.S.H.R.C.)

     5.   SECRETARY OF LABOR, v. MEL JARVIS CONSTRUCTION COMPANY, INC.
 OSHRC DOCKET NOS. 77-207 and 77-671 (Consolidated)   June 10, 1980
 OSHRC DOCKET NO. 77-207, 1980 WL 10257 (O.S.H.R.C.)

 -->
```

```
                        FOCUS - 49 SECTIONS

Subpart X--Effective Dates, @ 1926.Subject Index to Part 1926 -- Safety and
Health Regulations for Construction, 29 CFR 1926.Subject Index to Part 1926 --
Safety and Health Regulations for Construction

29. Title 29--Labor; Revised as of July 1, 1991 Subtitle B--Regulations Relating
to Labor, CHAPTER XVII--OCCUPATIONAL SAFETY AND HEALTH ADMINISTRATION,
DEPARTMENT OF LABOR, PART 1926--SAFETY AND HEALTH REGULATIONS FOR CONSTRUCTION
Subpart C--General Safety and Health Provisions, @ 1926.28 Personal protective
equipment., 29 CFR 1926.28

30. Title 29--Labor; Revised as of July 1, 1991 Subtitle B--Regulations Relating
to Labor, CHAPTER XVII--OCCUPATIONAL SAFETY AND HEALTH ADMINISTRATION,
DEPARTMENT OF LABOR, PART 1926--SAFETY AND HEALTH REGULATIONS FOR CONSTRUCTION
Subpart D--Occupational Health and Environmental Controls, @ 1926.52
Occupational noise exposure., 29 CFR 1926.52

31. Title 29--Labor; Revised as of July 1, 1991 Subtitle B--Regulations Relating
to Labor, CHAPTER XVII--OCCUPATIONAL SAFETY AND HEALTH ADMINISTRATION,
DEPARTMENT OF LABOR, PART 1926--SAFETY AND HEALTH REGULATIONS FOR CONSTRUCTION
Subpart D--Occupational Health and Environmental Controls, @ 1926.58 Asbestos,
tremolite, anthophyllite, and actinolite., 29 CFR 1926.58

Press Alt-H for Help or Alt-Q to Quit.
```

ILLUSTRATION 8-33. LEXIS Document Showing 29 C.F.R. § 1926.28, Available in the LABOR-CFR File.

```
                        29 CFR 1926.28
                                                              FOCUS
          PART 1926--SAFETY AND HEALTH REGULATIONS FOR   CONSTRUCTION
              Subpart C--General Safety and Health Provisions

              @ 1926.28 Personal protective equipment.

                        29 CFR 1926.28

   (a) The employer is responsible for requiring the wearing of appropriate
personal protective equipment in all operations where there is an exposure to
hazardous conditions or where this part indicates the need for using such
equipment to reduce the hazards to the employees.

   (b) Regulations governing the use, selection, and maintenance of personal
protective and lifesaving equipment are described under Subpart E of this part.

   SOURCE: 44 FR 8577, Feb. 9, 1979; 44 FR 20940, Apr. 6, 1979

   AUTHORITY: Sec. 107, Contract Work Hours and Safety Standards Act
( Construction  Safety Act) (40 U.S.C. 333); secs. 4, 6, 8, Occupational Safety
and Health Act of 1970 (29 U.S.C. 653, 655, 657); Secretary of Labor's Order No.
12-71 (36 FR 8754), 8-76 (41 FR 25059), or 9-83 (48 FR 35736), as applicable.

Press Alt-H for Help or Alt-Q to Quit.
```

ILLUSTRATION 8-34. LEXIS Document, Available in the FEDREG File.   385

```
                        LEVEL 1 - 4 OF 4 DOCUMENTS

                           DEPARTMENT OF LABOR
                Occupational Safety and Health Administration

                              46 FR 11383

                            February 6, 1981


California State Standards; Approval

TEXT:

    ... 23), 1910.264, 1910.265, 1910.266 and 1910.268; National Electrical Code
29 CFR 1910.309; Toxic and Hazardous Substances 29 CFR 1910.1000(e) and
1910.1001 (c) and (h); General Safety and Health Provisions  29  CFR  1926.28;
Occupational Health and Environmental Controls 29 CFR 1926.50(c) and 1926.55 (a)
through (c); Tools -- Hand and Power 29 CFR 1926.304(f); Electrical 29 CFR
1926.400; Cranes, Derricks, and ...




Press Alt-H for Help or Alt-Q to Quit.
```

ILLUSTRATION 8-35. LEXIS Document Showing *Atlas Industrial Painters,*
                  Available in the LABOR-OSAHRC File.

```
                        LEVEL 2 - 1 OF 12 CASES

                        ATLAS INDUSTRIAL PAINTERS

                        OSHRC Docket No. 87-619

              Occupational Safety and Health Review Commission

                          1991 OSAHRC LEXIS 105

                            August 9, 1991

 OPINION:
   ... [*9]    BNA OSHC at 1019, 1986-87 CCH OSHD at p. 36,341.  We therefore
affirm the violation as willful.

- - - - - - - - - - - - - - - - - -Footnotes- - - - - - - - - - - - - - - - - -

   n5 In Constructora Maza, the employer was issued a citation for a willful
violation of  29  C.F.R. @  1926.28 (a), in which it was alleged that the
company's employees failed to wear  safety belts  while exposed to a fall of 138
feet.  In affirming the allegation that the violation was willful, the
Commission noted that, although the employer had a company rule requiring the
employees' use of safety belts, no  disciplinary  action was taken against the
 Press Alt-H for Help or Alt-Q to Quit.

                        1991 OSAHRC LEXIS 105, *9

employees, despite their repeated failure to wear safety belts.

- - - - - - - - - - - - - - - -End Footnotes- - - - - - - - - - - - - - - - - -
[*10]

   II.  Citation Item 1b

   Atlas was additionally cited for violating 29 C.F.R. @ 1926.451( ...
```

LEXIS does not carry *Shepard's* for OSAHRC decisions. However, LEXIS offers a service not available on WESTLAW: Auto-Cite covers OSAHRC decisions. Illustration 8-36 (see below) is the Auto-Cite print-out for *Atlas Industrial Painters.*

4. CALR for Looseleafs

Both LEXIS and WESTLAW have included online a few administrative looseleaf services and a few administrative law reporters. Most of the titles carried online cover heavily regulated areas such as tax and labor. You can check the print database directories or scan the online directories to determine which looseleaf services are carried online.

The *Employment Safety and Health Guide,* for instance, is not carried online. However, under related topics such as labor, employment, or health, you will find that the *BNA Occupational Safety & Health Daily* is on LEXIS and WESTLAW. This publication is not a traditional looseleaf service; it is a daily service (available only online) that contains highlights of recent information relating to OSHA. In effect, it updates the *Occupational Safety & Health Reporter* (BNA).

The *BNA Occupational Safety & Health Daily* is found in many LEXIS libraries, including the BNA library. Before using the update, a useful step is to use the related reporter. In LEXIS, the directory's file screen displays information about the dates covered by individual files, as seen for the OSHR example in Illustration 8-37 on page 387.

WESTLAW contains the *BNA Occupational Safety & Health Daily* in the BNA-OSHD database. Entering [sc bna-oshd] provides information about the dates covered by that database.

Access to the *BNA Occupational Safety & Health Daily* on WESTLAW or LEXIS can be gained in two ways—by scanning the daily highlights and by performing a search, much as you have already done. Gaining access to the

ILLUSTRATION 8-36. LEXIS Auto-Cite Display for *Atlas Industrial Painters.*

```
Auto-Cite (R) Citation Service, (c) 1991 Lawyers Cooperative Publishing

1991 OSAHRC LEXIS 105:                            Screen 1 of 1

CITATION YOU ENTERED:

Atlas Industrial Painters, 1991 OSAHRC LEXIS 105, 1991 CCH OSHD P 29439 (OSHRC
1991)

PRIOR HISTORY:

Atlas Industrial Painters, Inc., 1988 OSAHRC LEXIS 142 (OSHRC ALJ 1988),

    affd, in part (BY CITATION YOU ENTERED)



-------------------------------------------------------------------------
To check another citation, type it and press the TRANSMIT key.
Alternate presentation formats are available.
For further explanation, press the H key (for HELP) and then the TRANSMIT key.
To return to LEXIS, press the EXIT SERV key.
 Press Alt-H for Help or Alt-Q to Quit.
```

highlights is quick and easy: The highlights for the current day are displayed automatically when you enter the database or file.

To obtain the daily highlights on the WESTLAW BNA-OSHD database, merely enter [bna-oshd]. As seen in Illustration 8-38 on page 388, there are several one-line highlights describing the information added to the system on that date. Over the course of several days, you may find recent information about agency or judicial decisions, proposed regulations or legislation, or simply news items about the agency. If you scan the one-line descriptions in Illustration 8-38, you will see examples. This information is very current since the highlights are added to the system daily. To see the text of the material referred to by the one-line descriptions, you may "page through" the document.

You may also search this database. Earlier in this chapter, a search was used to obtain regulations regarding the CSB Construction issue, and a good search for this database can be structured using those same terms. Because you are already in a database that deals with OSHA information, the search [personal or employee w/5 protective or safety w/5 equip!] is appropriate without the further limiters of C.F.R. title 29. If you were to enter this search, you would retrieve over 100 updating documents. These documents are displayed in reverse chronological order, the most current displayed first.

This same approach can be used in the BNA OHD file of LEXIS. After you ascertain the scope of that file, you can scan for daily entries or perform a key word search for documents pertinent to your research situation.

To search the traditional looseleafs online, use a key word search. You may likely find the text of statutes and regulations, as well as case or agency decisions. It is probably more efficient and less costly to scan the actual documents in print format rather than online.

5. CALR and Print Research Compared

The usefulness of CALR research in C.F.R. is determined in large part by the uniqueness of the terms used in your regulation. It is possible to focus your attention on the relevant title and even chapter fairly easily, as is also true of print research. But you are unlikely to be able to locate a specific regulation without unique terms or substantial information about the precise

ILLUSTRATION 8-37. LEXIS Screen Showing Scope of the OSHR File.

```
    Please TRANSMIT the NAME (only one) of the file you want to search.  You may
    TRANSMIT the NAME of any file, not only those listed below.  To see other
    descriptions, press the NEXT PAGE or PREV PAGE key.  To see the menu page
    containing the first file described below, press the TRANSMIT key.
                        DESCRIPTIONS -- PAGE 5 of 14
    NAME    FILE                        NAME    FILE

    BNALAB Combined DLABRT, PENSN, GOVEMP,  BENDAY Benefits Today
            BENDAY & OSHR                          from 1/01/88

                                        OSHR    Occupational Safety
                                                & Health Reporter-
                                                Current Report
                                                from 1/06/88

    For further explanation, press the H key (for HELP) and then the TRANSMIT key.
```

```
BNA Occupational Safety & Health Daily
Dec. 13, 1991
BNA OCCUPATIONAL SAFETY & HEALTH DAILY Dec. 13, 1991 (copr. BNA, Inc.)

IN TODAY'S ISSUE:

JOB SAFETY: OSHA Agrees To Drop Contempt Order After Home Allows Inspection
LITIGATION: Employee Not Criminally Liable For Employer's OSHA Violation
FINES: OSHA Fine Collection Improved During Recent Years, Data Show
NTP: Studies Show Adverse Effects For Diethanolamine, Dimethylformamide
ACRYLAMIDE: EPA Sets Hearing On Proposed Ban; Comment Period Extended To Jan.
ERGONOMICS: Food Industry Plans March '92 Release Of Guidelines For Warehouses
CALIFORNIA: CAL/OSHA Budget Cuts Could Lead To Closing Of Offices, Others
GENERAL POLICY: OSHA Injury Reporting Requirement Proposal Clears OMB
ENFORCEMENT: OSHA Cites NY Contractor Following Employee Death From Roof Fall
OCCUPATIONAL SAFETY & HEALTH CASES: Two Cases Summarized

BNA OCCUPATIONAL SAFETY & HEALTH DAILY Dec. 13, 1991

Safety
```

wording of the regulation. On the other hand, CALR is very useful in facilitating rapid updating of any regulations you may find.

CALR offers some distinct advantages over print research in the area of agency decision research. Certainly, where the agency does not publish its opinions in a reporter with an index or digest, CALR makes access to the opinions more efficient. Where the official indexing system is hard to use and full-text search methods are suitable (recall the discussion in Chapter 6 at pages 219-221), CALR also can improve your efficiency. There is likely to be an advantage in the area of updating as well.

Some online services are not available in print format; the *BNA Occupational Safety & Health Daily,* for example, is not. Some online services are very current in that they provide daily awareness information; in fact, the *BNA Tax Updates* is updated more than once each day. It should be noted, however, that many of these services are indeed available in print format and their currentness is affected only by the few days it takes for the mail to reach a practitioner's desk.

Although it can be time-consuming to use the several indexes that are a necessary part of looseleaf services, those indexes are usually very comprehensive and detailed, so that it is possible to narrow your search. For those looseleaf services that are available online, it is possible to avoid the multiple indexes by using a key word search; however, as with any key word search, it is also difficult to frame a search to a specific, narrow issue.

Hence, as with any research tool, these tools must be used prudently. LEXIS and WESTLAW are excellent finding tools; as you become more familiar with them, you will better understand when they can genuinely facilitate your research project. For example, as you have already learned, you should select the narrowest useful databases or libraries to expedite your research. Thus, if you are searching for the full text of statutes or administrative regulations, it makes more sense to use the databases and libraries that are limited specifically to those materials rather than to search through the looseleaf databases. Similarly, it does not make sense to use the online systems to scan or read the actual text of the commentary or reporters using the online looseleaf services; it is much easier, faster, and much less expensive to use the looseleafs or reporters in their traditional print format for that purpose.

E. RESEARCHING STATE ADMINISTRATIVE MATERIALS

As noted in Part A, there are many state administrative agencies. They create law much as federal agencies do.

In terms of official sources, most states publish agency regulations in both regulatory codes parallel to C.F.R. and registers parallel to the *Federal Register*. In general, it is much more difficult to research state agency decisions because they rarely are compiled and indexed as thoroughly as federal agency decisions are. It may well be useful to call the agency whose decisions you wish to read to determine whether there is a compilation and index available at the agency's offices.

Illustration 8-39 on page 390 is the first page of the occupational safety and health rules in Minnesota. (Minnesota has its own federally approved occupational safety and health system.) Note that Minnesota Rule 5205.0010 chose to incorporate the federal rules by reference. This incorporation encompasses the rules found in part 1926 of C.F.R. Minnesota also has promulgated some of its own rules, as listed in the table of contents. You would be able to locate these rules from a cross-reference in *Minnesota Statutes Annotated* or through the finding tools in the *Minnesota Rules* series itself.

On the other hand, looseleafs are often a good place to begin research on state administrative rules. There are two methods, for example, for finding state administrative material in the *Employment Safety and Health Guide*. One approach is to use the Topical Index and the related updating indexes. Using the name of the state as a search term would direct you to appropriate references, if any.

A second approach is to use the material filed behind the tab "State Activity—Plans, Standards, Cooperation." This section contains information about state plans adopted and authorized by the Secretary of Labor for the 20 or so states that have prepared plans that have been approved. The best approach is to scan the table of contents to find a reference to the appropriate state. (See Illustration 8-40 on pages 391-392.) This approach leads the user to ¶ 5410 for Georgia, the state where our research situation arose. That paragraph indicates that Georgia has opted to rely on the federal system. (See Illustration 8-41 on page 392.)

By contrast, we would find that Minnesota has adopted a detailed occupational safety and health plan. The *Employment Safety and Health Guide* looseleaf service contains the text of that plan; commentary about the plan, including annotations to specific administrative rules; and citations to cases that have been decided regarding the plan and rules. This material is often useful in stating which is the appropriate state administrative agency, explaining the jurisdiction of that agency, and describing enforcement methods. (See Illustration 8-42 on page 393.) You will note (see Illustration 8-43 on page 394) that the looseleaf contains a reference table to applicable Minnesota state administrative rules (here 5207.0100) regarding personal protective equipment as required by state construction standards. The text of the Minnesota state rules is not contained in the looseleaf, so you would need to contact the state agency or consult the appropriate volume of state administrative rules, if published.

CHAPTER 5205
DEPARTMENT OF LABOR AND INDUSTRY
SAFETY AND HEALTH STANDARDS

5205.0010 ADOPTION OF FEDERAL OCCUPATIONAL SAFETY AND HEALTH STANDARDS BY REFERENCE.

Subpart 1. **Title 29.** The Minnesota Department of Labor and Industry Occupational Safety and Health Codes and rules are amended by incorporating and adopting by reference, and thereby making a part thereof, Title 29 of the Code of Federal Regulations as listed in subparts 2 to 7.

ILLUSTRATION 8-40. State Administrative Activity Plans—Table of Contents, 1 Employ. Safety & Health Guide (CCH) 2001, 2002 (Apr. 3, 1990).

391

986   4-3-90   **2001**

STATE ACTIVITY PLANS • STANDARDS COOPERATION

TABLE OF CONTENTS

2002	State Activity	986 4-3-90

	Par.
Connecticut Public Employee Plan	5370
Delaware	5380
District of Columbia...............................	5390
Florida	5400
Georgia	5410
Guam	5415
Hawaii State Plan	5420
Idaho	5430
Illinois	5440
Indiana State Plan	5450
Iowa State Plan	5460
Kansas	5470
Kentucky State Plan	5480
Louisiana	5490
Maine...	5500
Maryland State Plan	5510
Massachusetts	5520
Michigan State Plan	5530
Minnesota State Plan	5540
Mississippi.......................................	5550
Missouri..	5560

ILLUSTRATION 8-41. Commentary Covering Georgia's State Activity Plan: 1
Employ. Safety & Health Guide (CCH) ¶ 5410, at 2191
(May 8, 1990).

991   5-8-90   **2191**

¶ 5410

GEORGIA

There is no state plan in effect in Georgia. A developmental plan was submitted to OSHA in February 1973 (.01), but was withdrawn by the governor in April 1973 (.02). Consequently, OSHA retains jurisdiction over private sector job safety and health in Georgia and enforces federal requirements.

.01 38 *Federal Register* 3556, February 7, 1973.   .02 40 *F.R.* 15468, April 7, 1975.

[The next page is 2193.]

ILLUSTRATION 8-42. Commentary Covering Minnesota's State Activity Plan: 1
Employ. Safety & Health Guide (CCH) ¶ 5540, at 2307
(Oct. 1, 1991).

393

¶ 5540

MINNESOTA STATE PLAN

COVERAGE OF PLAN

¶ 5540.01   Submission and Approval of Plan

The Minnesota plan was submitted to federal OSHA in 1972 and received initial approval in August 1973 (.011). OSHA certified completion of all developmental steps in September 1976 (.012) and suspended its concurrent enforcement in June 1982 (.013). The plan received final approval in July 1985 (.014).

The steps of OSHA approval of the Minnesota plan are described in the federal regulations at § § 1952.200 *et seq.*, reproduced in Volume 2 of the GUIDE beginning at ¶ 6594.7.

.011 38 *Federal Register* 15076, June 8, 1973.
Plan supplements were approved 40 *F.R.* 13211,
March 25, 1975; 40 *F.R.* 18995, May 1, 1975; 41
F.R. 36650, August 31, 1976;

.012 41 *F.R.* 42659, September 28, 1976.

.013 47 *F.R.* 25323, June 11, 1982.

.014 50 *F.R.* 30821, July 30, 1985.

¶ 5540.02   Enabling Legislation

The Minnesota Occupational Safety and Health Act of 1973 (MOSHA) is found at Chapter 182 of the Minnesota Statutes (Minn. Stats.). The Employee Right to Know Act of 1983 is codified as part of MOSHA. Implementing regulations adopted by the Commissioner of Labor and Industry are found at Minnesota Rules (Minn. Rules) Chapters 5206 and 5210.

¶ 5540.03   Scope of Plan

The Minnesota plan covers all activities and areas covered by the federal OSH Act except for offshore maritime employment in the private sector, federal employment, and employment at the Twin Cities Army Ammunition Plant, which remain under federal OSHA jurisdiction. Minnesota's jurisdiction over working conditions in the maintenance shop of an interstate railroad was not preempted by the Federal Railroad Administration, the state supreme court ruled in 1976, because FRA regulations did not cover the general aspects of occupational safety or health (.031). The supreme court's reasoning was followed in 1987 to permit the application of state standards to railroad employees inspecting track at a highway crossing (.032).

As under the federal OSH Act, employers have a general duty to furnish employees with a place of employment free from recognized hazards likely to cause death or serious injury. Both employers and employees have a duty to comply with all specific standards and regulations (Minn. Stats. § § 182.653 and 182.654). An employer must not request or require an employee to waive any rights under the Act or standards (Minn. Stats. § 182.6575).

Private Litigation. There is no private right of action to enforce MOSHA regulations, but an employee may bring a private suit under the discrimination provisions of the Act claiming that he was discharged in retaliation for exercising his right to make a safety complaint (.033). Department of Labor personnel are not subject to subpoena for testimony on matters relating to an occupational safety and health inspection except in enforcement proceedings under the Act. Written reports and documents prepared or gathered by the Department are public information once the inspection file is closed (Minn. Stats. § 182.659, Subd. 8).

.031 *State of Minnesota v. Burlington Northern, Inc.,* Minn SCt 1976, 247 NW2d 54, 1976-1977 OSHD ¶ 21,278.

.032 *State of Minnesota v. Duluth, Winnipeg & Pacific Railway Co.,* Minn Ct App 1987, 408 NW2d 671, 1987-1990 OSHD ¶ 27,981.

2311-2	State Activity	1067 10-1-91

Minn. Rules

Confined Spaces

Scope	5205.1000
Definitions	5205.1010
Operating Procedures and Worker Training	5205.1020
Pre-Entry Procedures	5205.1030
Entry Into and Work Within Confined Spaces	5205.1040

Cranes and Hoists

Cranes and Hoists	5205.1200
Hoist Hook Safety Devices	5205.1210
Warning Signal	5205.1220

Personnel Platforms Suspended from Cranes and Derricks

Scope and Application	5205.1230
Definitions	5205.1240
General Requirements	5205.1250
Operational Criteria	5205.1260
Personnel Platform	5205.1270
Inspection and Testing	5205.1280
Safe Work Practices	5205.1290
Prelift Meeting	5205.1300

Hoppers

Inspection of Hoppers	5205.1400

Construction Standards

General

Anchor Bolts	5207.0010
Bar, Floor, and Roof Joists	5207.0020
Demolition Operations	5207.0030
Demolition, Restoration, Remodeling Asbestos Survey	5207.0035
Spray Painting of Building Interiors	5207.0040
Wire Rope Clips	5207.0050
Flammable Liquid Tank Supports	5207.0060

Personal Protective Equipment

High Visibility Personal Protective Equipment	5207.0100 ⬅

Walking, Working Surfaces

Ships Ladders	5207.0200
Ships Ladders, Special Requirements	5207.0210
Walking, Working Surfaces	5207.0250
Suspension Scaffolds	5207.0260
Confined Spaces	5207.0300
Carbon Monoxide Monitoring	5207.0310

Environmental Controls

Gas Fired Machines and Appliances	5207.0320

Cranes, Hoists, and Derricks

Cranes, Hoists, and Derricks	5207.0400
Personnel Platforms Suspended from Cranes and Derricks	5207.0410
Enclosures at Construction or Engineering Projects	5207.0500
Wells, Pits, Shafts, and Other Similar Spaces	5207.0510
Warning Signs at Construction or Engineering Projects	5207.0520
Sidewalk Sheds	5207.0530
Lights at Sidewalk Sheds	5207.0540

Machine Guarding

Lockout Devices	5207.0600
Motor Start Button	5207.0610
Machine Controls and Equipment	5207.0620
Foot Actuated Machines	5207.0630

Maintenance and Repair of Equipment

Compressed Gas Containers	5207.0700
Pressure Hoses	5207.0710
Alteration of Tools and Equipment	5207.0720

¶ 5540.30

Rules Governing Practice and Procedure: Searching for Primary Authority

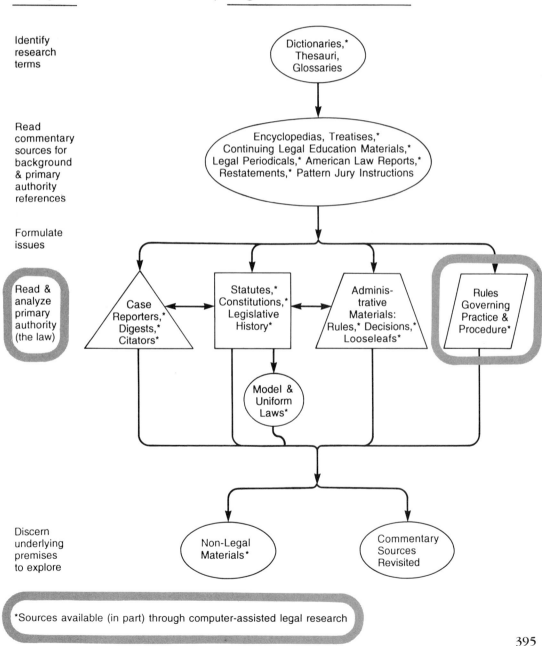

Analysis

Identify research terms

Read commentary sources for background & primary authority references

Formulate issues

Read & analyze primary authority (the law)

Discern underlying premises to explore

Legal Research Sources

Dictionaries,* Thesauri, Glossaries

Encyclopedias, Treatises,* Continuing Legal Education Materials,* Legal Periodicals,* American Law Reports,* Restatements,* Pattern Jury Instructions

Case Reporters,* Digests,* Citators*

Statutes,* Constitutions,* Legislative History*

Administrative Materials: Rules,* Decisions,* Looseleafs*

Rules Governing Practice & Procedure*

Model & Uniform Laws*

Non-Legal Materials*

Commentary Sources Revisited

*Sources available (in part) through computer-assisted legal research

396

**Rules Governing
Practice and
Procedure:
Searching for
Primary Authority**

A. INTRODUCTION

397
Rules Governing
Practice and
Procedure:
Searching for
Primary Authority

This chapter explores approaches to researching rules that govern the operation of the courts and the litigation process, evidentiary issues at trial, and proper professional conduct for attorneys. Because procedural and evidentiary questions are generated in every lawsuit, a lawyer specializing in litigation is apt to research these topics more frequently than other areas of law. The rules of ethics, of course, are vital to the practice of every lawyer. The specific topics discussed in this chapter often are the subject of separate courses in the law school curriculum (for example, civil procedure, criminal procedure, trial advocacy, evidence, and professional responsibility). The scope of each topic is outlined briefly below.

Litigation procedure usually is governed by state and federal rules of civil, criminal, and appellate procedure. The initiation of lawsuits, the forms of pleadings, pre-trial discovery, motion practice, trial and post-trial procedures, and appellate procedure are often governed by a jurisdiction's formal rules. Case law and statutes also may have an impact on litigation procedure.

In addition, local rules of court adopted by each court for its own operations describe details of practice not governed by more general rules of procedure. These local rules cover such topics as dress codes for attorneys, the form of pleadings, the color and size of the paper upon which pleadings may be submitted, and similar matters.

Evidentiary issues are governed by the Federal Rules of Evidence in all federal courts and by state rules of evidence in state courts, or by case law where formal rules have not been adopted. The rules or the case law prescribe presentation and admissibility of various types of testimony, documents, and other evidence offered by a party to prove its case.

The standards for ethical conduct by lawyers have not been (and cannot be) completely codified. However, the American Bar Association has drafted several sets of model rules for professional ethics during this century. These ABA codifications have served as models for the majority of state ethics codes. Violations of ethical standards may result in professional sanctions and civil or criminal liability. In addition, professional malpractice standards may be found in case law in each jurisdiction.

B. RESEARCHING RULES GOVERNING THE LITIGATION PROCESS

1. Overview

a. Federal Procedural Rules and Rules of Court

At the federal level, commentators agree that Congress has the right to prescribe rules of procedure for the federal courts, while the individual courts are free to issue local rules on items not covered by the rules of procedure. *See generally* 4 Charles Alan Wright & Arthur R. Miller, *Federal Practice and Procedure* § 1001 (2d ed. 1987). The Constitution is silent on the matter, and the United States Supreme Court has never addressed the issue. As a practical matter, Congress delegates any rulemaking authority to the Supreme Court.

The enactment of the Federal Rules of Civil Procedure (FRCP) is an example of such a delegation. By the Rules Enabling Act of 1934, ch. 651, 48

398

Rules Governing
Practice and
Procedure:
Searching for
Primary Authority

Stat. 1064, Congress gave, or purported to give, the Supreme Court power to prescribe rules of procedure for the federal district courts and the District of Columbia. In 1935, the Supreme Court appointed an advisory committee to prepare a draft of the rules. After making some changes in the advisory committee's draft, the Supreme Court adopted the rules in 1937. The Attorney General reported the rules to Congress in January 1938. The rules met opposition in both houses of Congress, particularly in the Senate Judiciary Committee, which never approved the rules. However, the opposition was apparently meaningless because the Rules Enabling Act allowed the rules to become effective on September 6, 1938, even though when Congress adjourned in the early summer of 1938, only the House Judiciary Committee had voiced approval of the rules. The FRCP have since been amended by the Supreme Court periodically during their decades of application.

A separate set of rules, the Federal Rules of Criminal Procedure, govern criminal pre-trial procedures and trials. A third set of rules, the Federal Rules of Appellate Procedure, govern criminal and civil appeals. In addition, there are separate rules governing litigation before the Supreme Court and the specialized subsidiary courts such as the Court of Claims and the Court of International Trade. These rules were enacted in a manner similar to the FRCP and are amended from time to time by the courts to which these rules apply.

There has been a proliferation of local rules that are not incorporated in the published rules. Recently these local rules have become the source of increasing controversy. In some instances, local rules have been applied to modify or contravene the formal procedural rules. In many cases, the local rules are not formally published and are available only from the bench or from the office of the clerk of the court in question. The potential impact of these local rules requires an attorney to carefully research both the formally published rules and the local rules, which usually may be secured from the bench or from the office of the clerk of the court in question.

b. State Rules of Procedure

The success of the Federal Rules of Civil Procedure perhaps is best indicated by the subsequent adoption of similar rules in many states that are modeled after the FRCP. State rules may be promulgated by the state legislature, by the state courts, or through an interaction between both branches of government. In any case, the interpretation of the FRCP may prove helpful in interpreting state procedural rules.

c. Interpretation of Procedural Rules

Irrespective of the original source of procedural rules, courts must interpret and apply the rules. As in other legal issues, mandatory or persuasive precedent may be used to argue the meaning or proper application of procedural rules. In addition, commentary sources and articles may be helpful in interpreting procedural rules.

Only a small percentage of state procedural decisions are ever published because disputes involving rules of procedure are often resolved in trial court opinions, which rarely are published. Conversely, the case law in the federal system is rather well developed because many federal trial court opinions are published and because the federal procedural system has wide application. Thus, while recognizing the differences between the state and federal procedural rules, state courts accord great weight to federal case law construing those federal rules that correspond to the state rules.

399

Rules Governing
Practice and
Procedure:
Searching for
Primary Authority

Keep in mind that a court in State A is not bound by case law from State B or by a federal court that construes a rule with wording similar, or even identical, to the rule in State A. Similarly, a court may or may not be bound by its own decisions construing an earlier version of the rule, if the language or policy of the rule has been changed.

Advisory comments accompany most procedural rules. These comments reflect the history of each rule and the reasoning process of the drafters. They are not binding authority because they usually are not part of the officially adopted rules, but they are highly persuasive and should be utilized in much the way you would utilize legislative history sources. Furthermore, if you are researching a state rule that was patterned after a federal rule, you should refer to the advisory comments to both the state rule and the federal rule.

2. The Research Situation

This chapter concentrates on the rules governing civil litigation in federal district courts. Again, in the federal system, there are separate sets of rules that govern civil litigation, criminal litigation, and appellate practice. You will use similar skills and strategies to research all three sets of federal procedural rules.

Because your client may have a choice between state and federal court, this chapter will introduce you to both state and federal research materials by tracing the initiation of a lawsuit in federal court with references to sources for state court procedure. This comparison will enable you to examine some of the similarities and important differences between state and federal procedural rules. In real life, awareness of these differences will help you choose between state and federal court.

Recall the scenario involving the "Mega-Mall" that you have already explored in Chapters 7 and 8.

In spite of the best efforts of CSB Construction, an employee was injured near the worksite. The injury occurred when a vehicle, driven by a visitor to the construction site, collided with the vehicle of a worker who had just pulled out of the employee parking lot. The worker was seriously injured, and Carlotta Selleck has asked your firm to represent her employee in a personal injury action against the driver of the car that caused the accident.

Your client, the injured employee, lives in a neighboring state but the negligent acts occurred in your state. The defendant resides in your state. Even though negligence issues are governed by state law, your client has a choice between federal and state courts because federal courts have jurisdiction over cases involving residents of different states, if potential damages exceed $50,000 (28 U.S.C. § 1332 (1988)).

Assume that you have drafted a complaint and filed it with the clerk in a federal district court. (Form complaints are in an appendix to the Federal Rules of Civil Procedure and are discussed later in this chapter. See the form complaint for negligence in Illustration 9-10 on page 415.)

A few days later, you learn that the complaint and summons were not delivered directly to the defendant, but instead were delivered to a ten-year-old child at the defendant's home. Not feeling completely comfortable with that method of delivery, or "service of process," you decide to research whether the service of process was effective. If it was not, you will need to have the defendant served properly in order to initiate the lawsuit. Thus, your initial research issue is whether the service of process at the defendant's home was performed according to the applicable rules of civil procedure.

400

Rules Governing
Practice and
Procedure:
Searching for
Primary Authority

3. Sources Containing the Federal Rules of Civil Procedure

Rules of procedure are published in unannotated and annotated codes. At the federal level, *United States Code* (U.S.C.) contains the Federal Rules of Civil Procedure. *United States Code Annotated* (U.S.C.A.) contains the FRCP and related annotations in several volumes filed under title 28. *United States Code Service* (U.S.C.S.) has separate "Court Rules" volumes (following title 50) containing the FRCP and related annotations. These sources also contain the Federal Rules of Criminal Procedure, the Federal Rules of Appellate Procedure, the Supreme Court Rules, and the rules of the subsidiary federal courts.

Rules of procedure are published in their most compact form in "deskbooks." Deskbooks generally contain a particular jurisdiction's rules of procedure, evidence, and ethics. One deskbook, *Federal Civil Judicial Procedure and Rules,* published by West, contains the FRCP, the Federal Rules of Evidence, the Federal Rules of Appellate Procedure, and selected federal statutes affecting issues of jurisdiction and procedure. Most deskbooks are republished annually and are a convenient source of up-to-date rules that are easier to browse than a full code.

Because the problem we have chosen is a civil case, our research will focus on the Federal Rules of Civil Procedure. Your first step is to locate the rule that applies to the situation you are researching. A useful first step would be to use the index or the table of contents of a deskbook or another source that contains the FRCP. Illustration 9-1 on page 401 shows part of the table of contents for the FRCP in the West deskbook. Reading the Roman numeral headings in this table would acquaint you with the scope and organization of the Rules.

Rules 3, 4, and 5 discuss the commencement of an action and service of process. Your next step would be to read these rules and look at the accompanying Advisory Committee Notes. The Notes summarize the intent of the drafters and list previous rules that have been superseded and proposed amendments that were rejected. Remember that the Notes are only commentary, not authority.

After reading Rules 3, 4, and 5, you would have narrowed the scope of your research to Rule 4(d). This subsection discusses service of the complaint and summons "[u]pon an individual other than an infant or an incompetent person." Fed. R. Civ. P. 4(d)(1). (See Illustration 9-2 on page 402, showing the rule as presented in U.S.C.)

Leaving the documents at the defendant's home instead of his office was certainly an acceptable practice. However, the defendant's ten-year-old child may not have been an acceptable person with whom to leave the summons and complaint. Thus, you have narrowed your research issue to whether the defendant's ten-year-old child is a "person of suitable age and discretion" according to Rule 4(d)(1). The rule and its Advisory Committee Note do not answer this question.

Citation Note: Rule 12.8.3 of *The Bluebook* dictates the following form for citation to one of the Federal Rules of Civil Procedure: Fed. R. Civ. P. 4(d)(1). However, when discussing one of the Federal Rules of Civil Procedure in text, you should use the following form: "Rule 4 of the Federal Rules of Civil Procedure" or simply "Rule 4" (if it is clear that you are discussing Rule 4 of the Federal Rules of Civil Procedure). For example: "A complaint need only state a 'short and plain statement of

ILLUSTRATION 9-1. Table of Rules, in *Federal Civil Judicial Procedure and Rules* 1 (West rev. ed. 1991).

401

FEDERAL
RULES OF CIVIL PROCEDURE

FOR THE

UNITED STATES DISTRICT COURTS

As Amended to July 1, 1991

TABLE OF RULES

the court's jurisdiction and the plaintiff's claim.' Fed. R. Civ. P. 8(a). In addition, Rule 8(a)(3) requires the inclusion of 'a demand for judgment.'" *See* Practitioners' Note P.4(b) and Rule 12.9 of *The Bluebook*.

4. Sources Containing State Procedural Rules

State rules of civil procedure govern most, but not all, civil proceedings in each state. These rules may be numbered similarly but not identically to the federal rules. In some states, narrow statutory provisions preempt or supplement related provisions of the state rules of civil procedure.

The annotated code in your state may contain your state's rules of civil procedure, criminal procedure, appellate procedure, and related annotations. As with the federal rules, you generally would use a state deskbook to locate the state rules of procedure.

Rule 4   TITLE 28, APPENDIX—RULES OF CIVIL PROCEDURE   Page 556

4. This rule provides that the first step in an action is the filing of the complaint. Under Rule 4(a) this is to be followed forthwith by issuance of a summons and its delivery to an officer for service. Other rules provi...

(iii) pursuant to an order issued by the court stating that a United States marshal or deputy United States marshal, or a person specially appointed for that purpo...

Filing with the court defined, see rule 5.

Rule 4. Process

(a) SUMMONS: ISSUANCE. Upon the filing of the complaint the clerk shall forthwith issue a summons and deliver the summons to the plaintiff or the plaintiff's attorney, who shall be responsible for prompt service of the summons and a copy of the complaint. Upon request of the plaintiff separate or additional summons shall issue against any defendants.

(b) SAME: FORM. The summons shall be signed by the clerk, be under the seal of the court, contain the name of the court and the names of the parties, be directed to the defendant, state the name and address of the plaintiff's attorney, if any, otherwise the plaintiff's address, and the time within which these rules require the defendant to appear and defend, and shall notify the defendant that in case of the defendant's failure to do so judgment by default will be rendered against the defendant for the relief demanded in the complaint. When, under Rule 4(e), service is made pursuant to a statute or rule of court of a state, the summons, or notice, or order in lieu of summons shall correspond as nearly as may be to that required by the statute or rule.

(c) SERVICE.

(1) Process, other than a subpoena or a summons and complaint, shall be served by a United States marshal or deputy United States marshal, or by a person specially appointed for that purpose.

(2)(A) A summons and complaint shall, except as provided in subparagraphs (B) and (C) of this paragraph, be served by any person who is not a party and is not less than 18 years of age.

(B) A summons and complaint shall, at the request of the party seeking service or such party's attorney, be served by a United States marshal or deputy United States marshal, or by a person specially appointed by the court for that purpose, only—

(i) on behalf of a party authorized to proceed in forma pauperis pursuant to Title 28, U.S.C. § 1915, or of a seaman authorized to proceed under Title 28, U.S.C. § 1916,

(ii) on behalf of the United States or an officer or agency of the United States, or

age prepaid) to the person to be served, together with two copies of a notice and acknowledgment conforming substantially to form 18-A and a return envelope, postage prepaid, addressed to the sender. If no acknowledgment of service under this subdivision of this rule is received by the sender within 20 days after the date of mailing, service of such summons and complaint shall be made under subparagraph (A) or (B) of this paragraph in the manner prescribed by subdivision (d)(1) or (d)(3).

(D) Unless good cause is shown for not doing so the court shall order the payment of the costs of personal service by the person served if such person does not complete and return within 20 days after mailing, the notice and acknowledgment of receipt of summons.

(E) The notice and acknowledgment of receipt of summons and complaint shall be executed under oath or affirmation.

(3) The court shall freely make special appointments to serve summonses and complaints under paragraph (2)(B) of this subdivision of this rule and all other process under paragraph (1) of this subdivision of this rule.

(d) SUMMONS AND COMPLAINT: PERSON TO BE SERVED. The summons and complaint shall be served together. The plaintiff shall furnish the person making service with such copies as are n...

(1) Upon an individual other than an infant or an incompetent person, by delivering a copy of the summons and of the complaint to the individual personally or by leaving copies thereof at the individual's dwelling house or usual place of abode with some person of suitable age and discretion then residing therein or by delivering a copy of the summons and of the complaint to an agent authorized by appointment or by law to receive service of process.

person, by serving the summons and complaint in the manner prescribed by the law of the state in which the service is made for the service of summons or other like process upon any such defendant in an action brought in

Citation Note: State rules of procedure are cited as statutes (Rule 12 of *The Bluebook*), if they are numbered as part of the statutory codification. On the other hand, if the rules are not codified statutes (even though they may appear in the annotated statute volumes), they are cited in much the same manner as the federal rules under Rule 12.8.3, but you should use an abbreviation that reflects the official name of the state rules. For example: Ariz. R. Civ. P. 26.

5. Researching Cases Interpreting the Federal Rules of Civil Procedure

403

Rules Governing
Practice and
Procedure:
Searching for
Primary Authority

a. *West's Federal Rules Decisions*

Federal cases decided at the appellate level in which procedural issues appear along with other issues are reported in *West's Federal Reporter* (F. and F.2d) and in the various Supreme Court reporters. Procedural issues also may be decided in district court opinions that are reported in *West's Federal Supplement* (F. Supp.). An entire set of case reporters, *West's Federal Rules Decisions* (F.R.D.), is devoted to cases involving only the Federal Rules of Civil Procedure and the Federal Rules of Criminal Procedure, as well as to articles on federal judicial issues. Opinions appearing in F.R.D. do not appear in any other West case reporters. See the case citations to F.R.D. in Illustrations 9-3 and 9-4 on pages 404-405.

Note: At the state level, the only reported cases are likely to be those decided by the state high court and intermediate appellate court. A few states also have separate reporters for rules decisions or published trial court decisions.

b. Annotated Codes

As you may recall from Chapter 7 (see page 263), U.S.C.A. annotations contain cross-references to the West Key Numbers and the encyclopedia *Corpus Juris Secundum;* U.S.C.S. annotations contain cross-references to A.L.R. annotations and law review articles. Both codes contain Advisory Committee Notes and annotations to cases that interpret the FRCP.

If you used the annotations to Rule 4 of the FRCP in either code to locate one or more case annotations encompassing your service of process issue, you should find *De George v. Mandata Poultry Co.,* 196 F. Supp. 192 (E.D. Pa. 1961). *De George* is listed in the U.S.C.A. case annotations to Rule 4 under the heading "Persons residing therein." (See Illustration 9-3 on page 404.) *De George* is also contained in the U.S.C.S. case annotations to Rule 4 under the heading "Person of suitable age and discretion then residing therein." (See Illustration 9-4 on page 405.) In *De George* the court held that delivery of the complaint to the defendant's 16-year-old daughter was sufficient to comply with the rule. As with statutory research, always update your research by consulting pocket parts and other updating materials.

Note: Similar annotations to the state rules of civil procedure appear in your state's annotated code.

c. West's Key Number Digests

Digests are fertile sources of citations interpreting procedural rules. Because the digests are not arranged by rule number, they are most useful after you have obtained the appropriate Key Number, perhaps by means of a U.S.C.A. annotation. In addition, having a relevant case citation will allow you to locate an appropriate Key Number. (See pages 163-172 in Chapter 5 on using digests.)

You may use *West's Federal Practice Digest, 4th, West's Federal Practice Digest, 3d, West's Federal Practice Digest, 2d,* and the *Modern Federal Practice Digest* to research the FRCP, because these digests encompass the case law after the enactment of the FRCP. Note that you first would use the most recent digest. The procedural topics are dispersed alphabetically among other digest

RULES OF CIVIL PROCEDURE

house or usual place of abode should be liberally construed so as to effectuate service at that location. Capitol Life Ins. Co. v. Rosen, D.C.Pa.1975, 69 F.R.D. 83.

189. —— Persons residing therein

Service of process upon defendant's cook at defendant's residence was sufficient under rule requiring service made at person's usual place of abode to be upon individual residing there, absent showing that cook did not reside at defendant's home. Home–Stake Production Co. v. Talon Petroleum, C.A., C.A.10 (Okl.) 1990, 907 F.2d 1012.

Substituted service of process on defendant made by serving apartment complex manager who resided in different building than defendant was effective under this rule permitting service at defendant's dwelling house or usual place of abode. Nowell v. Nowell, C.A.Tex.1967, 384 F.2d 951, certiorari denied 88 S.Ct. 1053, 390 U.S. 956, 19 L.Ed.2d 1150.

Where suit papers in a civil action were served upon defendant by a marshal by handing them to defendant's named landlady at an address where defendant resided, jurisdiction over defendant was acquired in accordance with this rule dealing with service of process, notwithstanding the fact that defendant was not personally served with such process or did not personally at any time receive such process. Smith v. Kincaid, C.A.Ohio 1957, 249 F.2d 243.

Service of process at defendant's place of abode "with Dawn Doe, a person over the age of 18 believed to be residing there," failed to comply with provisions of federal civil rule; thus, default judgment against that defendant based on that defective service would be set aside. Hasenfus v. Corporate Air Services, D.D.C.1988, 700 F.Supp. 58.

Delivery of summons and complaint to one guarantor's 18–year-old son at guarantor's residence complied with rule which permitted service by delivery at dwelling house or usual place of abode with some person of suitable age or discretion residing there. Azuma N.V. v. Sinks, S.D.N.Y.1986, 646 F.Supp. 122.

Service on defendant's adult daughter at defendant's residence satisfied provision of this rule permitting service on person residing at place of abode, although daughter was visiting home from

260

PROCESS

college. M. Lowenstein & Sons, Inc. v. Austin, D.C.N.Y.1977, 430 F.Supp. 844.

Service upon defendant's wife at defendant's residence, in New York, was valid under this rule, regardless of whether it complied with requirements of New York rule. U.S. v. Scheiner,

Sixteen-year-old daughter of defendant was proper person to receive summons and complaint under this rule, authorizing service on individual by delivering copy of summons and complaint at his dwelling house with some person of suitable age and discretion residing therein. De George v. Mandata Poultry Co., D.C.Pa.1961, 196 F.Supp. 192.

dant's home during day but who did not live there was not a person "then residing therein" for purposes of subd. (d)(1) of this rule and McKinney's N.Y. Business Corporation Law § 307; thus, service of process on defendant's nonlive-in housekeeper during her working hours was insufficient, and district court had no personal jurisdiction over defendant in a trademark infringement action. Polo Fashions Inc. v. B. Bowman & Co., D.C.N.Y.1984, 102 F.R.D. 905.

Leaving of service of process with a person described as defendant's housekeeper at a house owned by nonresident defendant but which was not used as his usual and normal residence was insufficient. Shore v. Cornell–Dubilier Elec. Corp., D.C.Mass.1963, 33 F.R.D. 5.

Where return of deputy marshal stated that summons and complaint were left with an elderly Negro who answered door and said that he was janitor of house, but janitor spent only a part of day at defendant's rooming house doing janitor work, the janitor was not "residing therein" within subdivision (d)(1) of this rule and service was defective. Zuckerman v. McCulley, D.C.Mo.1948, 7 F.R.D. 739, appeal dismissed 170 F.2d 1015.

190. —— Suitable age and discretion

Service was sufficient in forfeiture proceeding, where officers of the court served complaint and warrant of arrest in rem on daughter-in-law of owners who was on the property and signed for the complaint and warrant of arrest, and notice of action was published in newspaper of general circulation. U.S. v. One

261

ILLUSTRATION 9-4. Annotations to Fed. R. Civ. P. 4, in [Court Rules] U.S.C.S. [Fed. R. Civ. P.] 88 n.41 (1984).

405

Rule 4, n 39

RULES OF CIVIL PROCEDURE

or place of abode method of service. Gipson v Bass River (1979, DC NJ) 82 FRD 122, 27 FR Serv 2d 397

or place of abode method. Lamont v Haig (1982, DC SD) 539 F Supp 552, 34 FR Serv 2d 1192.

Service of summons and complaint upon defendant's place of work or business does not satisfy requirements of Rule 4(d)(1) which governs personal service upon individual by delivery of copy of summons and complaint to him personally. Thompson v Kerr (1982, SD Ohio) 555 F Supp 1090.

Individual defendant is not properly served where summons and complaint are served on his supervisor at his place of employment while he is vacationing in another state and where plaintiffs make no showing that his supervisor is authorized by appointment or law to accept service; similarly, defendant is not properly served where plaintiffs serve his secretary at his place of employment and where there is no indication that his secretary is agent authorized to receive service of process. Betlyon v Shy (1983, DC Del) 573 F Supp 1402, 83-2 USTC ¶ 9707, 38 FR Serv 2d 275.

40. —Other places

Hotel apartment rented and occupied by defendant's wife and woman friend after defendant had returned to England was not defendant's usual place of abode so as to render effective service on defendant by service of summons and complaint on his wife. Leigh v Lynton (1949, DC NY) 9 FRD 28.

In action by injured seaman against owner and captain of

Rule 4 that process be at defendant's "dwelling house or usual place of abode." Hysell v Murray (1961, SD Iowa) 28 FRD 584, 5 FR Serv 2d

41. "Person of suitable age and discretion then residing therein"

Delivery of papers to resident manager of apartment complex was valid service on defendant, notwithstanding that manager resided in one of two buildings and defendant resided alone in other. Nowell v Nowell (1967, CA5 Tex) 384 F2d 951, 11 FR Serv 2d 20, 32 ALR3d 107, cert den 390 US 956, 19 L Ed 2d 1150, 88 S Ct 1053.

Leaving summons and complaint with resident manager of apartment hotel where defendant resided did not comply with Rule 4. Judson v Judson (1943, DC Dist Col) 8 FRD 336.

Service was not effective when left at premises owned by defendant with janitor who answered door, where janitor spent only part of day at roominghouse, having his residence elsewhere. Zuckerman v McCulley (1947, DC Mo) 7 FRD

Sixteen-year-old daughter of defendant, upon whom summons and complaint were served at defendant's residence, was a "person of suitable age and discretion then residing therein." De George v Mandata Poultry Co. (1961, ED Pa) 196 F Supp 192, 4 FR Serv 2d 32.

individual may be made by leaving copy of summons at his dwelling house with person of suitable age and discretion "then residing" therein is broad enough to include student returning home from college to stay at least over-

topics; they also are grouped under the topic heading "Federal Civil Procedure." The case we already have located is at Key Number 420, "Usual place of abode," under the "Federal Civil Procedure" topic heading. (See Illustration 9-5 at page 406.)

Note: It is likely that the digest or digests in your state are not organized according to the rules of civil procedure, but rather discuss procedural and substantive topics in alphabetical order. For this reason, research using the annotated rules may be easier, especially if your research is concentrating on only one or two rules.

d. *Federal Rules Service* and *Federal Rules Digest*

Federal Rules Service, currently in its third edition, is published by Lawyers Cooperative Publishing (which succeeded Callaghan & Co. in 1991) in bound volumes and looseleaf binders. It indexes and reports decisions con-

---

33A F P D 2d—289   **FEDERAL CIVIL PROCEDURE**   ⚷**420**

For references to other topics, see Descriptive-Word Index

Inasmuch as plaintiff at least by January 11, 1963, properly served process after defendant filed motion on December 11, 1962, to dismi~~

~~a person specified~~ that process must be served by United States marshal, by a deputy, or by some person specially appointed by the court for that purpose. Fed.Rules Civ.Proc. rule 4(c, e), 28 U.S.C.A.; 16 A.R.S. Rules of Civil Procedure, rule 4(e)(2); West's Ann.Cal.Code Civ.Proc. § 414.10.

> Veeck v. Commodity Enterprises, Inc., 487 F.2d 423.

see United States Code Annotated

D.C.Cal. 1960. Responsibility for service of process is upon plaintiff.

> Huffmaster v. U. S., 186 F.Supp. 120.

for that purpose. Fed.Rules Civ.Proc. rule 4(c, e), 28 U.S.C.A.

> Veeck v. Commodity Enterprises, Inc., 487 F.2d 423.

⚷**420. Usual place of abode.**

Library references

> C.J.S. Federal Civil Procedure § 197.

33A F P D 2d—291   **FEDERAL CIVIL PROCEDURE**   ⚷**421**

For references to other topics, see Descriptive-Word Index

D.C.Mass. 1963. If a defendant is not served personally or through an agent authorized by appointment or by operation of law to receive process, the service is valid only if left at his dwelling house or usual place of abode or his last and usual place of abode. Fed.Rules Civ.Proc. rule 4(d) (1, 7), 28 U.S.C.A.

> Shore v. Cornell-Dubilier Elec. Corp., 33 F.R.D. 5.

D.C.N.J. 1979. Leaving process at the defendants' place of employment did not qualify under the dwelling house or place of abode method for service or process. Fed.Rules Civ.Proc. rule 4(d)(1), 28 U.S.C.A.

> Gipson v. Bass River Tp., 82 F.R.D. 122.

D.C.N.Y. 1977. Service on defendant's adult daughter at defendant's residence satisfied rule permitting service on person residing at place of abode, although daughter was visiting home from college. Fed.Rules Civ.Proc. rule 4(d)(1), 28 U.S.C.A.

> M. Lowenstein & Sons, Inc. v. Austin, 430 F.Supp. 844.

D.C.Pa. 1975. Whether a particular location is a person's dwelling house or usual place of abode for purposes of federal rule pe~~

Compliance with rule relating to service of process at a person's dwelling house or usual place of abode is sufficient to give personal jurisdiction regardless of unsubstantiated assertions that the defendant never received or had notice of the complaint and summons. Fed.Rules Civ.Proc. rule 4(d)(1), 28 U.S.C.A.

> Capitol Life Ins. Co. v. Rosen, 69 F.R.D. 83.

D.C.Pa. 1961. Sixteen-year-old daughter of defendant was proper person to receive summons and complaint under Federal Rule of Civil Procedure authorizing service on individual by delivering copy of summons and complaint at his dwelling house with some person of suitable age and discretion residing therein. Fed.Rules Civ.Proc. rule 4(d)(1), 28 U.S.C.A.

> De George v. Mandata Poultry Co., 196 F.Supp. 192.

⚷**421. Agent of party, service on.**

Library references

> C.J.S. Federal Civil Procedure § 198.

C.A.Nev. 1977. Service on in-state "general agent" is effective at that time against the principal. Fed.Rules Civ.Proc. rule 4(d)~~

---

struing the FRCP and the Federal Rules of Appellate Procedure. The *Service* is augmented by *Federal Rules Digest,* which is organized by rules and contains abstracts of the cases reported in the *Service.*

The *Digest* and the *Service* have an index, the Findex, which is organized according to the FRCP. The *De George* case appears in the *Digest* at Findex Number 4d.123. (See Illustration 9-6 on page 407.) The "Finding Aids" volume contains the Findex, as well as a descriptive word index for use when you are not certain which federal rule applies. Complete instructions on how to use this publication are located at the beginning of the Finding Aids volume.

ILLUSTRATION 9-6. [Rules 1-9] Fed. R. Dig. 3d 215-16 (1987). 407

PROCESS   **4d.123**

notice of the suit, (2) paid the apartment rent, (3) made no effort to leave a forwarding address or disconnect telephone service until after the date of service, and (4) left all the furniture and both family automobiles in Phoenix. Blackhawk Heating & Plumbing Co., Inc. v. Turner, 14 FR Serv2d 433; 50 FRD 144 (DCD Ariz, 1970).

Although there was no question that defendant's wife was a "person of suitable age and discretion" and that defendant had actually received notice of

at defendant's last known address w~

v. Marshall, 38 Fed Rules Serv 2d 1107, 100 FRD 480 (WD Pa, 1984).

4d.123 "Person of suitable age and discretion"

COURTS OF APPEALS

Service on apartment manager residing in a different building from the defendant but in the same apartment complex was valid where defendant received notice of the suit. Where defendant has received notice, Rule 4(d)(1) should be broadly construed. Nowell v. Nowell, 11 FR Serv2d 20, 384 F2d 951 (CA 5th, 1967).

215

4d.13   FEDERAL RULES DIGEST

DISTRICT COURTS

Defendant's sixteen-year-old daughter is a "person of suitable age and discretion" within the meaning of Rule 4(d). De George v. Mandata Poultry Co., 4 FR Serv2d 32, 196 F Supp 192 (DCED Pa, 1961).

summons and complaint with defendant's 20-year-old daughter at an apartment until recently occupied by defendant and his family will be upheld notwithstanding defendant's contention that he had recently established a permanent residence in California, where it appeared that defendant (1) received actual notice of the suit, (2) paid the apartment rent, (3) made no effort to leave a forwarding address or disconnect telephone service until after the date of service, and (4) left all the furniture and both family automobiles in Phoenix. Blackhawk Heating & Plumbing Co., Inc. v. Turner, 14 FR Serv2d 433; 50 FRD 144 (DCD Ariz, 1970).

Service upon defendant's wife at defendant's residence was valid under Rule 4(d)(1); its validity was not affected by the fact that it did not also comply with the requirements of state law. United States v. Scheiner, 14 FR Serv2d 896; 308 F Supp 1315 (DCSDNY, 1970).

When a person is imprisoned, his family residence remains his usual place of abode. Service of process upon the wife of an incarcerated defendant at defendant's family residence was in compliance with Rule 4(d) and effective to give the district court jurisdiction over the person of defendant. United States v. Davis, 17 FR Serv2d 1493, 60 FRD 187 (DCD Neb, 1973).

In an action brought against a corporate officer and his corporation, service of the summons and complaint on the maid at the officer's home was sufficient to give the court personal jurisdiction over the officer, but not over the

408

Rules Governing
Practice and
Procedure:
Searching for
Primary Authority

The "Current Volume" of *Federal Rules Service* contains recent cases. These cases are indexed by Findex numbers in the Federal Findex Case Table. They also are indexed alphabetically in the current Table of Cases.

Some cases cited in *Federal Rules Service* carry a parallel citation blank (for example, __ F.2d __). If the editors do not include a parallel citation blank, they do not anticipate this case will be published elsewhere. Nevertheless, you should use the table of cases in the appropriate West digest to determine whether the case subsequently has been published in a preferred case reporter.

Familiarity with *Federal Rules Service* may give you a competitive advantage in a trial practice because (1) decisions usually appear here sooner than in other publications and (2) some opinions appearing in *Federal Rules Service* are not published in West's case reporters and thus are not accessible through other research tools.

Note: There is no equivalent of this service in most states.

> **Citation Note:** If a case in *Federal Rules Service* also has been published in an official or a West case reporter, the official or West citation is preferred, to the exclusion of the *Federal Rules Service* citation. *See* Table T.1 in *The Bluebook*. The correct citation form for cases reported only in *Federal Rules Service* is governed by Rule 18.1 on services (looseleaf and bound). This rule requires any citation to a bound volume of a service to contain the case name; the volume number; the name of the service (abbreviated per Table T.16); the abbreviated name of the publisher, placed within parentheses; the page number where the case begins; and a final parenthetical containing the name of the court and the year. For example, a case in a bound volume of *Federal Rules Service* is cited as follows: *Wilson v. Kenny,* 20 Fed. R. Serv. 3d (Law. Coop.) 940 (4th Cir. 1991).

6. Sources Containing Commentary on the Federal Rules of Civil Procedure

A handful of influential treatises interpret the rules of civil procedure and practice in the federal courts. The texts of these treatises contain analysis of the rules and accompanying case law, as well as discussion of historical and drafting considerations. Furthermore, the citations in these treatises will lead you to a variety of additional sources. (Refer to Chapter 3 on treatises if you need more information on how to use or cite treatises.)

The following are some of the treatises that discuss the Federal Rules of Civil Procedure:

> Fleming James, Jr. & Geoffrey C. Hazard, Jr., *Civil Procedure* (3d ed. 1985) (a single-volume treatise).
>
> James Wm. Moore et al., *Moore's Federal Practice* (2d ed. 1982-present) (this looseleaf 32-volume treatise is brought up-to-date by new insert pages and covers civil, criminal, and appellate rules).
>
> James Wm. Moore et al., *Moore's Manual: Federal Practice and Procedure* (1991) (3 volumes).
>
> Charles Alan Wright, *The Law of Federal Courts* (4th ed. 1983) (a single-volume treatise).
>
> Charles Alan Wright et al., *Federal Practice and Procedure* (1969-present) (this 40-volume treatise covers civil and criminal rules).

Note that some treatises are organized by rule, while others are organized by topic. You would use either the index or table of contents approach to locate the sections of the treatise that discuss the "suitable age and discretion" language mentioned in Rule 4(d)(1). Some of the treatises refer to *De George v. Mandata Poultry Co.* (See Illustrations 9-7 and 9-8 on pages 409-410 and 412-413.)

> *Citation Note:* Most multi-volume treatises are updated annually, and outdated volumes occasionally are replaced by new volumes. This practice may result in changes in names of authors, dates of publication, and even edition numbers. Thus, when citing to a particular volume of a treatise, you must check the title page of that volume to ascertain the

409

Rules Governing
Practice and
Procedure:
Searching for
Primary Authority

ILLUSTRATION 9-7. 2 James Wm. Moore et al., *Moore's Federal Practice* ¶ 4.11[3] (2d ed. 1991).

4–135 **SOME PERSON RESIDING THEREIN** ¶ 4.11[3]

cess at a house which the career serviceman is purchasing and to which he expects someday to retire, is also invalid.[19]

usual place of abode.[23]

[3]—"Some Person of Suitable Age and Discretion Then Residing Therein."

Rule 4(d)(1) provides for leaving a copy of the summons and complaint at the defendant's dwelling house or usual place of abode "with some person of suitable age and discretion then residing therein." The quoted requirement is not always found in state stat-

---

visited it only occasionally. The court added: "The fact that he is a career servicemen shows me that his sojourn with the Armed Forces is neither involuntary or temporary as in the case of a draftee. Cf. Shore v. McFadden . . ."); Eckman v. Grear (1936) 14 NJ Misc 807, 187 Atl 556.

[19] Hysell v. Murray (SD Iowa 1961) 30 FRD 56 (where defendant was a career serviceman living in South Carolina, service on lessee of house defendant was purchasing in Iowa, in which he had lived and to which he planned someday to return, was invalid).

[20] Di Leo v. Shin Shu (SD NY 1961) 30 FRD 56 (service on daughter of defendant who resided in same building as defendant, but in a separate apartment in another part of the building, was invalid). See also Cugno v. Kaelin (1951) 138 Conn 341, 343, 84 A2d 576.

[21] Clover v. Urban (1928) 108 Conn 13, 142 A 389.

[22] Nowell v. Nowell (CA5th, 1967) 384 F2d 951, citing **Treatise**, cert denied (1968) 390 US 956, 88 S Ct 1053, 19 L ed2d 1150.

[23] See United States v. N. Tully Semel, Inc. (D Conn 1949) 88 F Supp 732.

(Rel.70–6/86 Pub.410)

R 4 **PROCESS** 4–136

utes and rules of court.[1] Therefore, under Rule 4(c)(2)(C)(i), permitting service in accordance with the law of the state in which the district court is held, a substituted service may be valid that does not meet the requirements of Rule 4(d)(1).[2] Conversely, if service complies with Rule 4(d)(1), the fact that state law provides a different method which could have been followed does not affect the validity of the service in a federal court action.[3]

In providing for delivery of the summons and complaint to "some person of suitable age and discretion then residing" in the party's dwelling house or usual place of abode, Rule 4(d)(1) made some changes in federal law. Under former Equity Rule 13, delivery was to be made to "some adult person who is a member of or resident in the family." Rule 4(d)(1), however, permits service upon a person who is not an adult, but is "of suitable age and discretion,"[4] while it forbids service upon an adult who has not "suitable discretion."[5] The person with whom the copies of the summons and complaint are left must reside in the defendant's dwelling house or usual place of abode.[6] This would seem to exclude a person, such as a servant who

---

[1] For example, the Connecticut statute provides:

"Except as otherwise provided, process in any civil action shall be served by leaving a true and attested copy of it, including the declaration or complaint, with the defendant, or at his usual place of abode, in this state. . . ." Conn General Statutes Annotated (1973) § 52–57.

[2] ¶ 4.19, *infra.*

[3] United States v. Scheiner (SD NY 1970) 308 F Supp 1315.

See also the discussion of Hanna v. Plumer (1965) 380 US 460, 85 S Ct 1136, 14 L ed2d 8, in subhead [1], *supra* and in ¶ 0.306[1], *supra.*

[4] De George v. Mandata Poultry Co. (ED Pa 1961) 196 F Supp 192, citing **Treatise** (service on sixteen-year-old daughter of defendant held proper).

[5] Joyce v. Bauman (1933) 11 NJ Misc 237, 165 Atl 425 (service on illiterate maid not valid).

[6] See United States v. Scheiner, n 3, *supra* (service on defendant's wife with whom he resided would be valid if indeed she was actually notified); First National City Bank v. Gonzalez & Co. Sucr. Corp. (D PR 1970) 308 F Supp 596 (service of process on defendant's daughter with whom the defendant was residing at the daughter's home was valid despite allegation that defendant was a judicially undeclared incompetent at the time of service; see also ¶ 4.21, *infra*); De Fazio v. Wright (D NJ 1964) 229 F Supp 111 (delivery of process to husband not valid service upon his wife and daughter who were not residing with him at time of service); John Hancock Mutual Life Ins. Co. v. Gooley (1938) 196 Wash 357, 83 P2d 221, 118 ALR 1484 (woman visiting mother-in-law, who was ill in a hotel room, was not "permanent resident in the house of the usual abode" of her parents-in-law

authors and the publication date of that volume. Rules 3.2 and 15 of *The Bluebook* provide further explanation.

In addition to treatises, you also can look to other sources for commentary on civil procedure. The general-scope encyclopedias, *American Jurisprudence 2d* and *Corpus Juris Secundum,* contain topics relating to civil procedure. There are also more specialized sources such as the *Cyclopedia of Federal Procedure* (published by Callaghan & Co.). Legal periodicals frequently provide scholarly analysis and research on narrow procedural topics. A.L.R. annotations provide a similar narrow coverage of procedural topics, especially in the A.L.R. Federal series.

Note that, at the state level, the collection of research sources available may include treatises, encyclopedias, legal periodicals, and continuing legal education publications. You could use a state treatise to locate a case arising out of a court in your state that has considered the issue of whether a person is of "suitable age and discretion" or has applied an equivalent standard.

Make sure that the case arose under the current version of the state's rule (or an earlier version of the rule with very similar language). If the earlier version would give rise to a different result under your facts, the earlier cases no longer will be binding precedent on the issue you are researching. If your state's courts have not yet published an opinion on the current version, your research would have to rely on cases arising in jurisdictions with similarly worded rules.

7. *Shepard's Citations*

As with cases, statutes, and administrative materials, procedural rules should be Shepardized to be certain that each rule is current, as well as to find additional sources that cite or construe a particular rule.

Shepard's United States Citations includes federal court rules in the Statute Edition volume, which also covers *Statutes at Large* and treaties. The number of the rule, the "cited source," is printed in boldface at the top of a list of "citing sources." Citing sources include selected official and unofficial federal reporters, A.L.R. annotations, and the *American Bar Association Journal.* Each list is further divided to correspond to the rule's subdivisions.

In addition, *Shepard's Federal Rules Citations* covers, in a similar format, all federal court rules and state rules similar to the federal rules. Citing sources include state and federal reporters, numerous law reviews, and A.L.R. annotations.

Note: State court rules also can be Shepardized in the Statute Edition of *Shepard's Citations* for each state.

To Shepardize Rule 4(d), you first would locate the boldface heading for Rule 4 and continue to scan the list until you locate "Subd. d." One-letter abbreviations precede the citations to some citing sources. This abbreviation may refer to legislative action—for example, amended (A) or renumbered (Rn)—or to judicial action—for example, void (V) or unconstitutional (U). Pay particular attention to these citations because they may indicate the validity of the rule you are researching.

In Illustration 9-9 on page 414, you will see a *Shepard's Federal Rules Citations* entry for Arizona Rule of Civil Procedure 4, subdivision d, which parallels the federal rule.

The remainder of your research on the sample research project would consist of finding, reading, and Shepardizing the cases you located. While reading these cases, you would be looking for the standard or the test em-

412

Rules Governing
Practice and
Procedure:
Searching for
Primary Authority

ployed by the courts involved. The important point is why the court ruled as it did, not just at what age a child is "of suitable age and discretion."

8. Other Print Sources

a. Sources Containing Form Pleadings

In each jurisdiction, many practitioners often rely on form books, which publish sample forms and pleadings that can serve as a basis for pleadings drafted by an attorney. These sample forms have great utility, but they must be used with care. Major difficulties can result from selection of the wrong form, an outdated form, or a standard form that does not precisely fit the needs of a particular case.

Some sample forms are published in an appendix to the Federal Rules of Civil Procedure in West's deskbook, *Federal Civil Judicial Procedure and Rules*. Note that the appendix contains model forms for typical pleadings. A model complaint for negligence, the cause of action for this chapter's research example, is presented in Illustration 9-10 on page 415.

Other sources of forms for use in federal cases are *Bender's Federal Practice Forms, West's Federal Forms,* and *Federal Procedural Forms, Lawyers Edition.* State forms are available in local publications. General purpose forms appear in *American Jurisprudence Pleading and Practice Forms Annotated* and other sources.

b. Sources Containing Rules of Court or Local Rules

Rules of court (or local rules) governing practice before a particular court do not correspond in numbering to the federal or state rules of civil procedure. Some of these rules are mundane and cover such issues as filing fees and procedure, paper size, and the color of brief covers. Other rules set up crucial procedures such as mandatory pre-trial conferences or the division

ILLUSTRATION 9-8. 4A Charles Alan Wright & Arthur R. Miller, *Federal Practice and Procedure* § 1096 (2d ed. 1987).

---

§ 1095   **PROCESS**   **Ch. 3**
Rule 4

defendant does not take the papers into possession. Since this procedure satisfies the objective of giving notice to the party to be served, it seems to be entirely sufficient to satisfy Rule 4(d)(1).

§ 1096. —— **Service on Person Residing in Defendant's Dwelling House or Usual Place of Abode**

As an alternative to personal delivery, Rule 4(d)(1) permits service of process to be made upon an individual by leaving a copy of the summons and complaint at the individual's "dwelling house or usual place of abode with some person of suitable age and discretion then residing therein."[1] Contrary to the practice in some states, this method of service is entirely optional, and plaintiff need not show an inability to obtain service by personal

When service is made at defen-

ILLUSTRATION 9-8. *(continued)* 413

Rule 4(d)(1) not only requires that a copy of the summons and complaint be left at defendant's "dwelling house or usual place of abode," but it also must be left "with some person of suitable age and discretion then residing therein." The person to whom it is given need not necessarily be an adult, however. In De George v. Mandata Poultry Company,[26] the court upheld service under Rule 4(d)(1) when delivery was made to defendant's 16 year old daughter. The court pointed out that Rule 4(d)(1) had omitted the

24. Unrealistic

Van Buren v. Glasco, 1975, 217 S.E.2d 579, 582, 27 N.C.App. 1, **quoting Wright & Miller,** overruled on another point Love v. Moore, 1982, 291 S.E.2d 141, 305 N.C. 575.

25. Spirit of rules

See § 1029.

Alternative theory

"[C]onsider the totality of the circumstances surrounding the substituted service to determine whether in all probability the procedure used would inform the defendant of the proceedings against him." Note, 1968, 17 U.Kan.L.Rev. 125, cited with approval in Blackhawk Heating & Plumbing Co. v. Turner, D.C.Ariz.1970, 50 F.R.D. 144, **citing Wright & Miller,** noted 1971, 19 Kan.L.Rev. 519.

But see

Despite actual notice, service attempted on defendant at her "dwelling house or usual place of abode" was not proper when there was no compliance at all with the required procedure. Chilcote v. Shertzer, D.C.Wis.1974, 372 F.Supp. 86.

Service was made upon defendant's wife at his place of business and thus did

not comply with Rule 4(d)(1). Accordingly, despite the receipt of notice, the court relying on the Cohen case, below, held service patently insufficient. Tart v. Hudgins, D.C.N.C.1972, 58 F.R.D. 116.

The federal courts, however, have not lost sight of the fact that Rule 4(d)(1) requires that service be made at the usual place of abode. Thus in Cohen v. City of Miami, D.C.Fla.1972, 54 F.R.D. 274, the court held that service under Rule 4(d)(1) by delivering process to a secretary in a doctor's office (the doctor living elsewhere) patently was inadequate regardless of whether notice was received.

26. De George case

D.C.Pa.1961, 196 F.Supp. 192.

See also

Azuma N.V. v. Sinks, D.C.N.Y.1986, 646 F.Supp. 122 (delivery of summons and complaint to 18-year-old son at residence sufficient)]

Blue Cross & Blue Shield of Michigan v. Chang, D.C.Mich.1986, 109 F.R.D. 669 (service on defendant's seventeen-year-old son at defendant's residence held sufficient)]

80

of responsibilities between judges and magistrates. Too often, local rules are ignored by unprepared attorneys; such rules are not ignored, however, by the judges enforcing the rules.

The local rules of federal courts appear in *Federal Rules Service* and in *Federal Local Court Rules for Civil and Admiralty Proceedings.* Rules applicable to individual federal courts of appeals also are located in U.S.C.A. and U.S.C.S. The local rules of state courts may appear in a deskbook or in an annotated code containing state procedural rules, or they may be available only from the office of the clerk of court. You should have ready access to the local rules of every court in which you practice.

FEDERAL RULES OF CIVIL PROCEDURE — Art. 2 / Rule 4

498P2d169	400P2d125	297P2d344	468FS521	524P2d1323	136Az336	**Rule 4(i)**	688SW2d744
601P2d289	406P2d845	480P2d30	505FS31	529P2d234	144Az300	136Az308	33AkL13
11AzL416	409P2d292	493P2d944	609FS206	533P2d714	146Az442	1AzA117	¶ 2
	486P2d786	650P2d1239	Cir. 10	537P2d994	149Az19	8AzA441	33AkL13
Rule 4(c)	496P2d144	**Subd. 8**	445FS687	542P2d24	1AzA258	400P2d125	¶ 3
A135Az	514P2d1042	133Az257	Va93Az361	542P2d1131	3AzA295	446P2d950	33AkL15
lix	527P2d294	14AzA7	94Az365	543P2d454	3AzA320	666P2d53	¶ 4
84Az9	608P2d68	16AzA398	100Az251	555P2d1121	5AzA136	82Az669n	275Ark453
90Az324	609P2d596	480P2d30	104Az308	557P2d522	6AzA506		631SW2d286
135Az365	653P2d693	493P2d944	107Az286	563P2d307	11AzA348		33AkL16
137Az245	669P2d1022	650P2d1239	112Az365	564P2d916	13AzA100		¶ 5
138Az386	674P2d1384		113Az485	565P2d864	15AzA560		15AkA177
17AzA357	680P2d198	**Rule 4(e)**	115Az52	573P2d91	16AzA45		16AkA251
322P2d891	684P2d167	(1)	115Az227	585P2d1235	22AzA293		690SW2d746
367P2d668	703P2d561	102Az326	115Az358	586P2d971	25AzA333	**Arkansas**	701SW2d384
498P2d169	706P2d1209	107Az286	117Az400	591P2d1005	27AzA771	**Rules of**	33AkL13
661P2d215	**Subd. 2**	113Az485	120Az323	596P2d698	380P2d1016	**Civil**	¶ 6
669P2d1022	83Az207	127Az283	120Az410	604P2d670	382P2d686	**Procedure**	33AkL13
674P2d1384	90Az341	136Az306	121Az517	619P2d742	401P2d743	**1979**	¶ 7
	99Az372	136Az335	122Az560	622P2d472	413P2d732		33AkL13
Rule 4(d)	125Az138	144Az299	124Az408	634P2d987	413P2d861		¶ 8
Cir. 9	132Az408	146Az443	127Az233	639P2d1059	414P2d169	**Rule 4**	712SW2d296
513F2d140	140Az595	3AzA295	127Az525	661P2d232	424P2d178	Cir. 9	**Subd. e**
90Az324	318P2d676	4AzA460	130Az175	666P2d51	429P2d438	96FRD39	279Ark83
93Az361	367P2d950	5AzA136	131Az234	666P2d80	433P2d998	269Ark10	282Ark28
94Az365	409P2d292	10AzA474	135Az382	674P2d902	452P2d101	276Ark174	3AkA28
99Az372	608P2d68	13AzA100	136Az306	683P2d305	464P2d668	279Ark29	621SW2d501
110Az522	646P2d293	13AzA343	136Az335	693P2d906	474P2d459	279Ark81	648SW2d484
114Az257	684P2d167	14AzA569	138Az348	710P2d473	489P2d1262	A279Ark471	665SW2d288
115Az227	**Subd. 3**	15AzA560	140Az506	711P2d634	490P2d1173	282Ark286	33AkL11
120Az323	99Az372	16AzA184	143Az251	724P2d40	509P2d615	282Ark519	¶ 1
120Az410	140Az595	19AzA453	147Az363	20AzL869	526P2d1248	286Ark420	279Ark81
123Az84	409P2d292	22AzA293	147Az495	1976AzS263	543P2d454	3AkA27	648SW2d483
140Az595	684P2d167	25AzA333	1AzA258	19A348n	558P2d966	598SW2d83	¶ 2
2AzA127	**Subd. 4**	413P2d861	2AzA267	19A3175n	569P2d1353	621SW2d500	279Ark81
14AzA290	99Az372	421P2d542	3AzA295	27A3553n	666P2d81	633SW2d39	648SW2d483
16AzA125	125Az138	424P2d178	4AzA460	**Subd. a**	697P2d693	648SW2d465	Cir. 8
16AzA398	409P2d292	429P2d438	6AzA338	Cir. 9	706P2d1209	648SW2d483	613FS884
20AzA206	608P2d68	459P2d753	11AzA348	513F2d140	716P2d80	A651SW2d63	275Ark226
367P2d668	**Subd. 5**	474P2d459	14AzA569	121Az232	**Rule 4(e)**	668SW2d30	279Ark81
380P2d1016	99Az372	476P2d864	17AzA354	136Az306	(4)	669SW2d468	628SW2d323
385P2d234	409P2d292	485P2d292	18AzA94	136Az335	Cir. 9	692SW2d246	648SW2d483
406P2d845	**Subd. 6**	486P2d184	18AzA491	6AzA506	513F2d140	33AkL9	A712SW2d...
409P2d292			...28	17AzA240		**Subd. a**	

9. Computer-Assisted Legal Research in Procedural Rules

a. Introduction

The Federal Rules of Civil Procedure and state procedural rules are available online through both WESTLAW and LEXIS. The CALR research techniques for the FRCP and state rules that have been codified as statutes are exactly the same as those you have already employed in Chapter 7 when researching other types of statutes.

b. WESTLAW

The Federal Rules of Civil Procedure are in three of the WESTLAW databases: (1) United States Code (USC), (2) United States Code Annotated (USCA), and (3) Federal Rules (US-RULES). An index for the FRCP can be found in the United States Code Annotated Index (USCA-IDX) database. The US-RULES database draws on the USCA database but is smaller and probably will be

ILLUSTRATION 9-10. Form 9, Complaint for Negligence, in *Federal Civil Judicial Procedure and Rules* 205 (West rev. ed. 1991).

415

Form 12

Form 8.

COMPLAINT FOR MONEY HAD AND RECEIVED

1. Allegation of jurisdiction.
2. Defendant owes plaintiff _____ dollars for money had and received from one G. H. on June 1, 1936, to be paid by defendant to plaintiff.

Wherefore (etc. as in Form 3).

(As amended Jan. 21, 1963, eff. July 1, 1963.)

NOTES OF ADVISORY COMMITTEE ON RULES
1963 AMENDMENT

This form was amended in 1963 by deleting the stated dollar amount and substituting a blank, to be properly filled in by the pleader. See Note of Advisory Committee under Form 3.

Form 9.

COMPLAINT FOR NEGLIGENCE

1. Allegation of jurisdiction.
2. On June 1, 1936, in a public highway called Boylston Street in Boston, Massachusetts, defendant negligently drove a motor vehicle against plaintiff who was then crossing said highway.
3. As a result plaintiff was thrown down and had his leg broken and was otherwise injured, was prevented from transacting his business, suffered great pain of body and mind, and incurred expenses for medical attention and hospitalization in the sum of one thousand dollars.

Wherefore plaintiff demands judgment against defendant in the sum of _____ dollars and costs.

(As amended Jan. 21, 1963, eff. July 1, 1963.)

NOTES OF ADVISORY COMMITTEE ON RULES
1937 ADOPTION

Since contributory negligence is an affirmative defense, the complaint need contain no allegation of due care of plaintiff.

1963 AMENDMENT

This form was amended in 1963 by deleting the stated dollar amount and substituting a blank, to be properly filled in by the pleader. See Note of Advisory Committee under Form 3.

Form 10.

COMPLAINT FOR NEGLIGENCE WHERE PLAINTIFF IS UNABLE TO DETERMINE DEFINITELY WHETHER THE PERSON RESPONSIBLE IS C. D. OR E. F. OR WHETHER BOTH ARE RESPONSIBLE AND WHERE HIS EVIDENCE MAY JUSTIFY A FINDING OF WILFULNESS OR OF RECKLESSNESS OR OF NEGLIGENCE

A. B., Plaintiff

    v.   *Complaint*

C. D. and E. F., Defendants

1. Allegation of jurisdiction.
2. On June 1, 1936, in a public highway called Boylston Street in Boston, Massachusetts, defendant C. D. or defendant E. F., or both defendants C. D. and E. F. wilfully or recklessly or negligently drove or caused to be driven a motor vehicle against plaintiff who was then crossing said highway.
3. As a result plaintiff was thrown down and had his leg broken and was otherwise injured, was prevented from transacting his business, suffered great pain of body and mind, and incurred expenses for medical attention and hospitalization in the sum of one thousand dollars.

Wherefore plaintiff demands judgment against C. D. or against E. F. or against both in the sum of _____ dollars and costs.

(As amended Jan. 21, 1963, eff. July 1, 1963.)

NOTES OF ADVISORY COMMITTEE ON RULES
1963 AMENDMENT

This form was amended in 1963 by deleting the stated dollar amount and substituting a blank, to be properly filled in by the pleader. See Note of Advisory Committee under Form 3.

Form 11.

COMPLAINT FOR CONVERSION

1. Allegation of jurisdiction.
2. On or about December 1, 1936, defendant converted to his own use ten bonds of the _____ Company (here insert brief identification as by number and issue) of the value of _____ dollars, the property of plaintiff.

Wherefore plaintiff demands judgment against defendant in the sum of _____ dollars, interest, and costs.

(As amended Jan. 21, 1963, eff. July 1, 1963.)

NOTES OF ADVISORY COMMITTEE ON RULES
1963 AMENDMENT

This form was amended in 1963 by deleting the stated dollar amount and substituting a blank, to be properly filled in by the pleader. See Note of Advisory Committee under Form 3.

Form 12.

COMPLAINT FOR SPECIFIC PERFORMANCE OF CONTRACT TO CONVEY LAND

1. Allegation of jurisdiction.
2. On or about December 1, 1936, plaintiff and defendant entered into an agreement in writing a copy of which is hereto annexed as Exhibit A.
3. In accord with the provisions of said agreement plaintiff tendered to defendant the purchase price and requested a conveyance of the land, but defendant re-

Complete Annotation Materials, see Title 28 U.S.C.A.

416

Rules Governing
Practice and
Procedure:
Searching for
Primary Authority

the most efficient for locating either a rule or material interpreting the rule. The US-ORDERS database picks up very recent changes in the FRCP.

Thus, a search in the US-RULES database might begin with several key words such as [pr("rules of civil procedure") & "service of process" /s age]. This search would reveal that Rule 4 of the Rules of Civil Procedure provides for service of process and that there are over 1,000 pages of annotations associated with the document. (See Illustration 9-11 below.)

Your search results could be further narrowed by using the locate function to find the most relevant text and annotations. For example, the search [lo "suitable age" /s discretion] will yield the text of the rule and annotations that discuss "suitable age and discretion" in such cases as *De George v. Mandata Poultry.* (See Illustration 9-12 on page 417.)

c. LEXIS

To access the text of the Federal Rules of Civil Procedure, you would begin by entering the GENFED library. You would find a RULES File (see Illustration 9-13 on page 418). If you transmit the number that corresponds to the file, you would obtain a description of the file. You also would note that there are separate files for various federal rules (see Illustration 9-14 on page 418). Once you have accessed a file, you may use a LEXIS search to find

ILLUSTRATION 9-11. WESTLAW Document 1 of Fed. R. Civ. P. 4, 28 U.S.C.A.,
Available in US-RULES Database.

```
Citation                    Rank(R)         Page(P)        Database   Mode
FRCP Rule 4                 R 1 OF 3        P 1 OF 1131    US-RULES   T
Fed.Rules Civ.Proc. Rule 4 , 28 U.S.C.A.

           COPR. (c) WEST 1991  No Claim to Orig. Govt. Works
                   UNITED STATES CODE ANNOTATED
        RULES OF CIVIL PROCEDURE FOR THE UNITED STATES DISTRICT COURTS
II. COMMENCEMENT OF ACTION;  SERVICE OF PROCESS, PLEADINGS, MOTIONS, AND ORDERS

Rule 4. Process

 (a) Summons:  Issuance. Upon the filing of the complaint the clerk shall
forthwith issue a summons and deliver the summons to the plaintiff or the
plaintiff's attorney, who shall be responsible for prompt service of the
summons
```

```
                  notice and acknowledg
be executed under oath or affirmation.
 (3) The court shall freely make special appointments to serve summonses and
complaints under paragraph (2)(B) of this subdivision of this rule and all

 (d) Summons and Complaint:  Person to be Served.  The summons and complaint
shall be served together.  The plaintiff shall furnish the person making
service with such copies as are necessary.  Service shall be made as follows:
 (1) Upon an individual other than an infant or an incompetent person, by
delivering a copy of the summons and of the complaint to the individual
personally or by leaving copies thereof at the individual's dwelling house or
usual place of abode with some person of suitable age and discretion then
residing therein or by delivering a copy of the summons and of the complaint to
an agent authorized by appointment or by law to receive service of process.
 (2) upon an infant or an incompetent person, by serving the summons and
complaint in the manner prescribed by the law of the state in which the
service is made for the service of summons or other like process upon any such
defendant in an action brought in the courts of general jurisdiction of that
state.
 (3) Upon a domestic or foreign corporation or upon a partnership or other
```

the particular rule or language that is the object of your search. If you know the number of the rule you seek, you may use a rule segment search to retrieve the rule—for example, [rule (4)].

417

Rules Governing
Practice and
Procedure:
Searching for
Primary Authority

Some sources necessary for researching procedural rules are not in computer databases. State and federal rules are available, as are published cases interpreting the rules. However, all local rules are not yet included in the databases, nor are all treatises or form books. Consult the WESTLAW or LEXIS database directories for an up-to-date listing of sources that are available for your jurisdiction.

Shepard's Citations, Statutes Editions, are not yet available online on either WESTLAW or LEXIS.

Locating a procedural rule in a print volume, such as a deskbook, is probably the most efficient method to locate the language of a particular rule. Computer-assisted research is most useful for locating cases that interpret the rule and some commentary sources. Print sources are necessary for the text of most commentary material, other than commentary of the advisory committee appended to the rule itself.

C. RESEARCHING EVIDENTIARY ISSUES

1. Introduction

Unlike civil procedure, for which formal rules exist in every jurisdiction, the law of evidence in some jurisdictions is governed exclusively by case law. On the other hand, many jurisdictions rely on codified rules of evidence as interpreted by case law, a scheme very similar to the Federal Rules of Civil Procedure that we have just examined.

ILLUSTRATION 9-12. WESTLAW Document 1 of Annotations for Fed. R. Civ. P. 4, Available in US-RULES Database.

```
FRCP Rule 4                  R 1 OF 3        P 343 OF 1131   US-RULES    T
   ANNOTATIONS     (Notes of Decisions Index - enter p157 )

D.D.C.1988, 700 F.Supp. 58.

   Delivery of summons and complaint to one guarantor's 18-year-old son at
guarantor's residence complied with rule which permitted service by delivery at
dwelling house or usual place of abode with some person of suitable age or
discretion residing there.  Azuma N.V. v. Sinks, S.D.N.Y.1986, 646 F.Supp. 122.

   Service on defendant's adult daughter at defendant's residence satisfied
provision of this rule permitting service on person residing at place of abode,
although daughter was visiting home from college.  M. Lowenstein & Sons, Inc.
v. Austin, D.C.N.Y.1977, 430 F.Supp. 844.

   Where actual delivery of copies of summons and complaint was made to defendant
three times personally at his most recent address in Virginia discovered
subsequent to substituted service made by registered mail, even though that was
not required by North Carolina long-arm statute, G.S. s 1-105, and s 1-105.1,
defendant received sufficient notice of action against him and his employer.
Denton v. Ellis, D.C.N.C.1966, 258 F.Supp. 223.

   Sixteen-year-old daughter of defendant was proper person to receive summons
and complaint under this rule, authorizing service on individual by delivering
copy of summons and complaint at his dwelling house with some person of
suitable age and discretion residing therein.  De George v. Mandata Poultry
Co., D.C.Pa.1961, 196 F.Supp. 192.
```

```
Please TRANSMIT, separated by commas, the NAMES of the files you want to search.
You may select as many files as you want, including files that do not appear
below, but you must transmit them all at one time.  To see a description of a
file, TRANSMIT its page (PG) number.
         FILES - PAGE 1 of 8 (NEXT PAGE for additional files)

NAME    PG DESCRIP         NAME    PG DESCRIP         NAME    PG DESCRIP

 ---COURT GROUP FILES--    ----ADMINISTRATIVE-----     ---LEGAL DEVELOPMENTS--
COURTS   1 Fed Cases & ALR  ALLREG 16 FEDREG & CFR     USLIST 11 Sup.Ct Summaries
CURRNT   1 Cases aft 1990   FEDREG 16 Fed. Register    APPSUM 13 Ct App Summaries
NEWER    3 Cases aft 1944   CFR    16 Code of Fed.Reg  USLW   12 US Law Week
SUPCIR   1 US,USAPP & CAFC  COMGEN 14 Comp.Gen.Decs.   USLWD  12 US Law Wk Daily
 ---U.S. COURT FILES---     --SUPREME COURT BRIEFS-    PUBS   37 Legal Pubs
US       1 US Supreme Ct    BRIEFS 11 Argued aft 9/79  ------LEGISLATIVE------
USAPP    1 Cts of Appeal                               RECORD 26 CongRec aft 1984
DIST     1 District Courts  RULES  31 Federal Rules    USCODE 15 USCS & PUBLAW
CLCT     2 Claims Court     CIRCUI 33 Circuit Ct Rules BLREC  26 CongRec & BLTEXT
                                                       BILLS  27 All Bills Files
To search by Circuits press NEXT PAGE.  NOTE:  Only court files can be combined.
Press Alt-H for Help or Alt-Q to Quit.
```

ILLUSTRATION 9-14. LEXIS Description of the FRCP File.

```
Please TRANSMIT, separated by commas, the NAMES of the files you want to search.
You may select as many files as you want, including files that do not appear
below, but you must transmit them all at one time.  To see the menu page
containing the first file described below, press the TRANSMIT key.
    DESCRIPTIONS - PAGE 31 of 39 (NEXT PAGE or PREV PAGE for additional files)

NAME    FILE                          NAME    FILE

------------------- FEDERAL COURT RULES (page 1 of 4) ------------------------

RULES  -Combined Federal Rules        FRE     -Federal Rules of Evidence,
                                               as amended to 12/91
FRCP   -Federal Rules of Civil
        Procedure, as amended to 12/91 FRAP   -Federal Rules of Appellate
                                               Procedure, as amended to 12/91
FRCRP  -Federal Rules of Criminal
        Procedure, as amended to 12/91 SUPRUL -U.S. Supreme Ct. Rules,
                                               effective 1/1/90
Press Alt-H for Help or Alt-Q to Quit.
```

2. Evidentiary Rules and Advisory Comments

At the federal level, the Federal Rules of Evidence (FRE) govern many evidentiary issues before the federal courts. Drafted by an advisory committee appointed by the United States Supreme Court, the FRE were revised and then jointly adopted by the Court and the Congress. They took effect in 1975. (See Illustration 9-15 on page 419, which shows the FRE table of contents.) The FRE have served as a model for state evidentiary rules in about half of the states.

Like the Federal Rules of Civil Procedure, advisory committee comments accompany the FRE and many of the state rules. These comments detail the

ILLUSTRATION 9-15. Federal Rules of Evidence, *Federal Civil Judicial Procedure and Rules* 289 (West rev. ed. 1991).

419

FEDERAL RULES OF EVIDENCE

FOR

UNITED STATES COURTS

AND

MAGISTRATES

Pub.L. 93–595, § 1, January 2, 1975, 88 Stat. 1926

As amended to July 1, 1991
EFFECTIVE DATE AND APPLICABILITY

Section 1 of Pub.L. 93–595 provided in part: "That the following rules shall take effect on the one hundred and eightieth day beginning after the date of the enactment of this Act [January 2, 1975]. These rules apply to actions, cases, and proceedings brought after the rules take effect. These rules also apply to further procedure in actions, cases, and proceedings then pending, except to the extent that application of the rules would not be feasible, or would work injustice, in which event former evidentiary principles apply."

For legislative history and purpose of Pub.L. 93–595, see 1974 U.S. Code Congressional and Administrative News, p. 7051.

Article I. General Provisions

Rule
101. Scope.
102. Purpose and Construction.
103. Rulings on Evidence:
    (a) Effect of erroneous ruling:
        (1) Objection.
        (2) Offer of proof.
    (b) Record of offer and ruling.
    (c) Hearing of jury.
    (d) Plain error.
104. Preliminary Questions:
    (a) Questions of admissibility generally.
    (b) Relevancy conditioned on fact.
    (c) Hearing of jury.
    (d) Testimony by accused.
    (e) Weight and credibility.
105. Limited Admissibility.
106. Remainder of or Related Writings or Recorded Statements.

Article II. Judicial Notice

201. Judicial Notice of Adjudicative Facts:
    (a) Scope of rule.
    (b) Kinds of facts.
    (c) When discretionary.

Rule
201. Judicial Notice of Adjudicative Facts:—Cont'd
    (d) When mandatory.
    (e) Opportunity to be heard.
    (f) Time of taking notice.
    (g) Instructing jury.

Article III. Presumptions in Civil Actions and Proceedings

301. Presumptions in General in Civil Actions and Proceedings.
302. Applicability of State Law in Civil Actions and Proceedings.

Article IV. Relevancy and Its Limits

401. Definition of "Relevant Evidence".
402. Relevant Evidence Generally Admissible; Irrelevant Evidence Inadmissible.
403. Exclusion of Relevant Evidence on Grounds of Prejudice, Confusion, or Waste of Time.
404. Character Evidence Not Admissible to Prove Conduct; Exceptions; Other Crimes:
    (a) Character evidence generally:
        (1) Character of accused.
        (2) Character of victim.
        (3) Character of witness.
    (b) Other crimes, wrongs, or acts.

Complete Annotation Materials, see Title 28 U.S.C.A.

289

reasoning underlying many of the drafting choices made by the advisory committee, as well as the history and the evolution of the rules.

The current version of FRE and the advisory committee comments appear in the *Federal Civil Judicial Procedure and Rules* deskbook, U.S.C., U.S.C.S., and U.S.C.A. Similarly, state rules of evidence may appear in a state deskbook or a state code, unless the state lacks codified rules of evidence and relies exclusively on the common law.

420

**Rules Governing
Practice and
Procedure:
Searching for
Primary Authority**

3. Cases and the Role of Common Law Evidentiary Rulings

Compared to civil procedure, the law of evidence relies heavily on the common law. The federal and state rules of evidence do not presume to cover every evidentiary issue; they presuppose the existence of a well-developed body of evidentiary case law. Thus, your research should start with legislatively adopted rules of evidence, then proceed to the cases dealing with evidentiary issues. Some cases supplement and apply the standards set out in the rules. Other cases set out common law rules of evidence not covered by the legislatively adopted rules of evidence. If a common law rule directly conflicts with a rule enacted by the legislature, the latter rule governs, unless the courts have declared the legislative enactment unconstitutional or otherwise invalid.

If you are researching an evidentiary question in a jurisdiction having no codified rules of evidence, your research should focus on cases, finding tools related to cases, and commentary sources on the law of evidence. If you are researching in a jurisdiction with codified rules of evidence, you should use research techniques similar to the research techniques for civil procedure questions, because your task then involves the application and interpretation of particular codified rules.

4. Commentary Sources on Evidence

Commentary sources are a great help in sorting out the common law rules and the legislatively adopted rules. The following is a list of some treatises on the FRE and the law of evidence in general:

> David W. Louisell & Christopher B. Mueller, *Federal Evidence* (1977-present) (a multi-volume treatise).
> *McCormick on Evidence* (Edward W. Cleary ed., 3d ed. 1984 & Supp. 1987) (a single-volume treatise).
> James Wm. Moore et al., *Moore's Federal Practice* (2d ed. 1982-present) (more than 30 volumes).
> James Wm. Moore et al., *Moore's Manual: Federal Practice and Procedure* (1991) (3 volumes).
> Jack B. Weinstein & Margaret A. Berger, *Weinstein's Evidence: Commentary on Rules of Evidence for the United States Courts and Magistrates* (1975-present) (a multi-volume treatise).
> John Henry Wigmore, *Evidence in Trials at Common Law* (rev. ed. Peter Tillers 1983-present) (a multi-volume treatise).
> Charles Alan Wright et al., *Federal Practice and Procedure* (1969-present) (40 volumes).

These treatises contain references to federal decisions construing the FRE as well as to state decisions construing state adaptations of the FRE. There also are treatises encompassing evidentiary law in individual states.

Treatises are not the only source of commentary on evidence. The general-scope encyclopedias, *American Jurisprudence 2d* and *Corpus Juris Secundum,* contain evidentiary topics covering the FRE and the common law at the state and federal levels. Encyclopedias at the state level are another research possibility. Legal periodicals contain articles on narrow subjects in evidence; these articles are excellent sources of current scholarly criticism and analysis. Some A.L.R. annotations also pertain to narrow evidentiary subjects; A.L.R. Federal is especially useful on federal evidentiary issues.

United States Code Annotated and *United States Code Service* contain case annotations to the FRE in volumes filed under title 28. Both give references to law reviews and other commentary sources such as encyclopedias.

West's Key Number Digests contain topics devoted to evidentiary subjects. These topics are a fruitful source of case citations. Because the FRE did not take effect until 1975, you should use *West's Federal Practice Digest, 3d* or *West's Federal Practice Digest, 4th* for research at the federal level.

Another source of cases construing the FRE is the *Federal Rules of Evidence Service,* formerly published by Callaghan & Co. and now published by Lawyers Cooperative Publishing. Like the *Federal Rules Service* discussed earlier, the *Federal Rules of Evidence Service* is published in bound volumes and looseleaf binders. It is devoted exclusively to indexing and reporting decisions construing the FRE and is augmented by a digest. The instructions on how to use this publication are located in the "Finding Aids" volume.

Shepard's Federal Rules Citations and the Statute Edition of *Shepard's United States Citations* cover *Statutes at Large* and treaties, and contain citations to cases and other sources construing the FRE. Shepardizing the FRE is similar to the process of Shepardizing procedural rules. Recent decisions construing the FRE also appear in the *Federal Rules of Evidence News.*

6. Computer-Assisted Research

The Federal Rules of Evidence and state rules of evidence are available online in both WESTLAW and LEXIS. Computerized research techniques for evidentiary codes are similar to those applicable to procedural codes, which are discussed in more detail at pages 414-417. Jurisdictions lacking an evidentiary code require research techniques used with other common law questions.

a. WESTLAW

The Federal Rules of Evidence are compiled in the same databases as the Rules of Civil Procedure: USC, USCA, USCA-IDX, and US-RULES. (See Illustration 9-16 on page 422.) The US-RULES database includes all the procedural and evidentiary rules for the federal courts. By doing the field search [pr(evidence /s rules)], you will find the 73 documents that encompass the Federal Rules of Evidence. (See Illustration 9-17 on page 422.) You should update your research in the US-ORDERS database, which picks up any very recent changes in rules. Merely enter [update] when viewing a rule.

b. LEXIS

The Federal Rules of Evidence are in the GENFED library of LEXIS. The GENFED library has a directory of files for the various federal rules. (See Illustration 9-18 on page 423.) The FRE file contains the Federal Rules of Evidence. (See Illustration 9-19 on page 423.) You could then use one of the LEXIS segment names to form a search request. For example, [name (evidence)] (see Illustration 9-20 on page 424) would put the first page of the Federal Rules of Evidence on your screen (see Illustration 9-21 on page 424).

```
_____WESTLAW DIRECTORY WELCOME SCREEN_____P1_____
_____GENERAL FEDERAL DATABASES                                       P4_____

        STATUTES & REGULATIONS                    STATUTES & REGULATIONS
  BC        Billcast                       LH        Legislative History
  US-BILLTRK Federal Bill Tracking         CR        Congressional Record
  BILLTRK   State & Fed. Bill Tracking     US-RULES  Federal Rules
  USCA      U.S. Code Annotated            US-ORDERS Federal Orders
  USCA-IDX  U.S. Code Anno. - Gen. Idx     US-FSG    Sentencing Guidelines
  USC       U.S. Code                      CFR       Code Fed. Regulations
  US-PL     U.S. Public Laws               FR        Federal Register
  US-PL90   U.S. Public Laws - 1990        US-REGTRK Fed. Regulation Tracking
  US-PL89   U.S. Public Laws - 1989        REGTRK    State & Fed. Reg. Tracking


                                         Note: For local federal district and
                                               bankruptcy court rules,
                                               enter P15.


  If you wish to:
     Select a database, type its identifier, e.g., USC and press ENTER
     View information about a database, type SCOPE followed by its identifier
        and press ENTER
```

ILLUSTRATION 9-17. WESTLAW Document 1 of Fed. R. Evid. Prec. R. 101,
Available in US-RULES Database.

```
Citation              Rank(R)        Page(P)         Database   Mode
FRE Prec. R. 101, Refs    R 1 OF 73      P 1 OF 1        US-RULES   T
  Fed.Rules Evid. Prec. R. 101, Refs & Annos , 28 U.S.C.A.

              COPR. (c) WEST 1992  No Claim to Orig. Govt. Works
                        UNITED STATES CODE ANNOTATED
            RULES OF EVIDENCE FOR UNITED STATES COURTS AND MAGISTRATES

                           HISTORICAL NOTE

  Effective Date and Application of Rules

   Section 1 of Pub.L. 93-595 provided in part:  "That the following rules shall
  take effect on the one hundred and eightieth day beginning after the date of
  the enactment of this Act [Jan. 2, 1975].  These rules apply to actions, cases,
  and proceedings brought after the rules take effect.  These rules also apply to
  further procedure in actions, cases, and proceedings then pending, except to
  the extent that application of the rules would not be feasible, or would work
  injustice, in which event former evidentiary principles apply."

  Fed. Rules Evid. Prec. R. 101, Refs & Annos , 28 U.S.C.A.
  FRE Prec. R. 101, Refs & Annos
  END OF DOCUMENT
```

D. RESEARCHING ETHICAL ISSUES

1. Introduction

Given the unique role of the legal profession in our society, it is hardly surprising that the practice of law has been viewed as much with skepticism and suspicion as it has been admired and valued. The suggestion found in

```
Please TRANSMIT, separated by commas, the NAMES of the files you want to search.
You may select as many files as you want, including files that do not appear
below, but you must transmit them all at one time.  To see a description of a
file, TRANSMIT its page (PG) number.
            FILES - PAGE 1 of 8 (NEXT PAGE for additional files)

 NAME   PG DESCRIP          NAME   PG DESCRIP          NAME   PG DESCRIP

  ---COURT GROUP FILES--    ----ADMINISTRATIVE-----     ---LEGAL DEVELOPMENTS--
 COURTS  1 Fed Cases & ALR ALLREG 16 FEDREG & CFR      USLIST 11 Sup.Ct Summaries
 CURRNT  1 Cases aft 1990  FEDREG 16 Fed. Register     APPSUM 13 Ct App Summaries
 NEWER   3 Cases aft 1944  CFR    16 Code of Fed.Reg   USLW   12 US Law Week
 SUPCIR  1 US,USAPP & CAFC COMGEN 14 Comp.Gen.Decs.    USLWD  12 US Law Wk Daily
  ---U.S. COURT FILES---    --SUPREME COURT BRIEFS-    PUBS   37 Legal Pubs
 US      1 US Supreme Ct   BRIEFS 11 Argued aft 9/79   ------LEGISLATIVE------
 USAPP   1 Cts of Appeal   ---------RULES---------    RECORD 26 CongRec aft 1984
 DIST    1 District Courts RULES  31 Federal Rules    USCODE 15 USCS & PUBLAW
 CLCT    2 Claims Court    CIRRUL 33 Circuit Ct Rules BLREC  26 CongRec & BLTEXT
                                                      BILLS  27 All Bills Files
 To search by Circuits press NEXT PAGE.  NOTE:  Only court files can be combined.
 Press Alt-H for Help or Alt-Q to Quit.
```

ILLUSTRATION 9-19. LEXIS Description of the FRE File.

```
Please TRANSMIT, separated by commas, the NAMES of the files you want to search.
You may select as many files as you want, including files that do not appear
below, but you must transmit them all at one time.  To see the menu page
containing the first file described below, press the TRANSMIT key.
     DESCRIPTIONS - PAGE 31 of 39 (NEXT PAGE or PREV PAGE for additional files)

 NAME    FILE                        NAME    FILE

 ------------------- FEDERAL COURT RULES (page 1 of 4) -------------------

 RULES  -Combined Federal Rules      FRE    -Federal Rules of Evidence,
                                             as amended to 12/91
 FRCP   -Federal Rules of Civil
         Procedure, as amended to 12/91  FRAP   -Federal Rules of Appellate
                                             Procedure, as amended to 12/91
 FRCRP  -Federal Rules of Criminal
         Procedure, as amended to 12/91  SUPRUL -U.S. Supreme Ct. Rules,
                                             effective 1/1/90
 Press Alt-H for Help or Alt-Q to Quit.
```

Shakespeare, "The first thing we do, let's kill all the lawyers," is echoed in recent surveys that place the legal profession well down the list of vocations that inspire confidence and trust.

Perhaps this perception is a natural consequence of the adversarial process that can cast attorneys in the role of "hired guns," or is a reaction to the monopoly over the practice of law granted to lawyers in each state, or stems from the personal characteristics of individuals who are drawn to the practice of law, or is caused by other factors too numerous to catalog. Nevertheless, the legal profession has an enormous responsibility to regulate the practice of law in a fashion that not only inspires public confidence, but also reflects an appreciation for the enormous power that the legal profession exercises over the affairs of our society.

```
name (Evidence)




The following names may be used as a segment name in your search request:

NAME            CITE            DATE            PART
RULE            FORM            TEXT            HISTORY
COMMENTS

The following name may be used with the arithmetic operators:

DATE


Please type your search request then press the TRANSMIT key.
What you transmit will be Search Level 1.

For further explanation, press the H key (for HELP) and then the TRANSMIT key.
 Press Alt-H for Help or Alt-Q to Quit.
```

ILLUSTRATION 9-21. LEXIS Screen of the Federal Rules of Evidence.

```
                    LEVEL 1 - 1 OF 63 RULES

                 FEDERAL RULES OF  EVIDENCE

                  FED. R. EVID. 101; FRE 101

                 November 1, 1988 Effective

               ARTICLE I. GENERAL PROVISIONS

                     Rule 101. Scope

    These rules govern proceedings in the courts of the United States and before
United States bankruptcy judges and United States magistrates, to the extent and
with the exceptions stated in rule 1101.

(As amended Mar. 2, 1987, eff. Oct. 1, 1987; Apr. 25, 1988, eff. Nov. 1, 1988.)

COMMENTS:
 EFFECTIVE DATE AND APPLICATION OF RULES

   Pub. L. 93-595, @ 1, Jan. 2, 1975, 88 Stat. 1926, provided: "That the
following rules shall take effect on the one hundred and eightieth day beginning
after the date of the enactment of this Act [Jan. 2, 1975].  These rules apply
 Press Alt-H for Help or Alt-Q to Quit.
```

In the main, the response of the legal profession has been to establish codes of ethics and professional responsibility. Over time, pure self-regulation has given way to a modified form of self-regulation under which a branch of government, either a court or legislature, enfranchises a single organization as the licensing and oversight agency in each state. The state-recognized organization or agency establishes an enforcement mechanism that usually involves a disciplinary committee or similar body that hears complaints re-

425

Rules Governing
Practice and
Procedure:
Searching for
Primary Authority

garding professional conduct. Sanctions for violations of ethical or professional standards include such penalties as public or private censure, suspension of one's license to practice law, or disbarment. In addition to the state-authorized disciplinary agency, local bar associations also may have ethics committees that hear complaints about attorney misconduct, but which lack enforcement power.

Violations of ethical or professional standards can have additional legal implications. Serious violations can expose an attorney to civil liability for malpractice. In some cases professional misconduct also can result in criminal penalties. Frequently, courts will look to the ethical and professional standards enforced by the state regulatory body in determining the seriousness of the misconduct and establishing legal liability. In short, failure to meet professional standards can have grave consequences.

2. The ABA Model Code and Model Rules

The American Bar Association has been a major source for the development of ethical standards and rules of professional responsibility. The most recent expressions of the ABA concern for these issues are the Model Code of Professional Responsibility, published in 1969, and the Model Rules of Professional Conduct, adopted in 1983. These professional and ethical standards have served as models for many of the ethics codes adopted by the states. Because the ABA is a voluntary association to which only a portion of all lawyers belong, the standards set by the ABA are not binding on any attorney.

The older Model Code of Professional Responsibility contains nine general "Canons" of ethics. Each Canon is accompanied by Ethical Considerations (EC) and Disciplinary Rules (DR). (See Illustration 9-22 on page 426.) The purpose and significance of the Ethical Considerations and Disciplinary Rules are set forth in the short Preamble and Preliminary Statement of the Code. The Model Rules of Professional Conduct consist of numbered black letter rules followed by Comments, which explain the application of the rules. (See Illustration 9-23 on page 427.) Your state rules may follow the format of the Model Code or the Model Rules or may have another organizing scheme.

Both the older Model Code and the current Model Rules are available in pamphlet form from the ABA. Additional sources for copies of the ABA models are the American Bar Foundation's *Annotated Code of Professional Responsibility* (published prior to the adoption of the Model Rules) and the ABA's *Annotated Model Rules of Professional Conduct.* These sources also include commentary and case decisions concerning the meaning and application of the Model Code or Model Rules. The ABA has published the *Legislative History of the Model Rules of Professional Conduct: Their Development in the ABA House of Delegates,* which provides additional insight into the meaning of the rules. Other sources for the Model Code and the Model Rules are the *ABA/BNA Lawyers' Manual on Professional Conduct* and the *National Reporter on Legal Ethics and Professional Responsibility.*

3. Advisory Opinions and Disciplinary Decisions

The ABA's Standing Committee on Ethics and Professional Responsibility issues formal and informal opinions interpreting the Model Rules and, in the past, the Model Code. The ABA formal opinions are on subjects of general interest to the bar. Informal opinions are responses to specific questions regarding particular factual situations. Although these opinions neither have the force of law nor carry enforceable professional sanctions, they often are

LIMITING LIABILITY TO CLIENT

EC 6-6   **A lawyer should not seek, by contract or other means, to limit his individual liability to his client for his malpractice.** A lawyer who handles the affairs of his client properly has no need to attempt to limit his liability for his professional activities and one who does not handle the affairs of his client properly should not be permitted to do so. A lawyer who is a stockholder in or is associated with a professional legal corporation may, however, limit his liability for malpractice of his associates in the corporation, but only to the extent permitted by law.[5]

DR 6-102   **Limiting Liability to Client.**

(A)   **A lawyer shall not attempt to exonerate himself from or limit his liability to his client for his personal malpractice.**

TEXTUAL AND HISTORICAL NOTES

In the tentative draft of October 1968, provisions relating to limitations on the lawyer's liability for malpractice were found under EC IV-6 and DR IV-1(5) (DR 4-101(A)(5) in the preliminary draft of January 1969). In the final draft of July 1969, the Disciplinary Rule was renumbered DR 6-102(A).

In the tentative draft, EC IV-6 (EC 4-6 in the preliminary draft; now EC 6-6) read as follows:

> **A lawyer should not seek to limit his liability to his client for malpractice, whether by contract, limitation of corporate liability, or otherwise. Thus the liability of lawyers who are stockholders in a professional legal corporation should be the same as it would be if they were practicing as partners.**

Minor changes were made in this text in the preliminary draft; the current wording was adopted in the final draft.

The current text of DR 6-102(A) was adopted in the final draft; the corresponding provision in the preliminary draft (DR 4-101(A)(5)) stated that a lawyer shall not **"[e]xonerate himself from liability for malpractice or limit his liability for malpractice by contract with his client or by use of a corporate structure."**

RELATED PROVISIONS

EC 6-6, DR 6-102(A):

None

---

5. *See ABA Opinion* 303 (1961); *cf.* CODE OF PROFESSIONAL RESPONSIBILITY, EC 2-11.

ILLUSTRATION 9-23. *Model Rules of Professional Conduct and Code of Judicial Conduct* 62 (1989).

427

Rule 3.1   **ABA MODEL RULES**

recognized in the legal profession. Such a procedure is set forth in the American Bar Association Statement of Policy Regarding Lawyers' Responses to Auditors' Requests for Information, adopted in 1975.

Model Code Comparison

There was no counterpart to this Rule in the Model Code.

ADVOCATE

RULE 3.1   MERITORIOUS CLAIMS AND CONTENTIONS

A lawyer shall not bring or defend a proceeding, or assert or controvert an issue therein, unless there is a basis for doing so that is not frivolous, which includes a good faith argument for an extension, modification or reversal of existing law. A lawyer for the defendant in a criminal proceeding, or the respondent in a proceeding that could result in incarceration, may nevertheless so defend the proceeding as to require that every element of the case be established.

Comment

The advocate has a duty to use legal procedure for the fullest benefit of the client's cause, but also a duty not to abuse legal procedure. The law, both procedural and substantive, establishes the limits within which an advocate may proceed. However, the law is not always clear and never is static. Accordingly, in determining the proper scope of advocacy, account must be taken of the law's ambiguities and potential for change.

The filing of an action or defense or similar action taken for a client is not frivolous merely because the facts have not first been fully substantiated or because the lawyer expects to develop vital evidence only by discovery. Such action is not frivolous even though the lawyer believes that the client's position ultimately will not prevail. The action is frivolous, however, if the client desires to have the action taken primarily for the purpose of harassing or maliciously injuring a person, or, if the lawyer is unable either to make a good faith argument on the merits of the action taken or to support the action taken by a good faith argument for an extension, modification or reversal of existing law.

Model Code Comparison

DR 7-102(A)(1) provided that a lawyer may not "[f]ile a suit, assert a position, conduct a defense, delay a trial, or take other action on behalf of his client when he knows or when it is obvious that such action would serve

428

**Rules Governing
Practice and
Procedure:
Searching for
Primary Authority**

used by state regulatory bodies and even by courts as persuasive authority in resolving questions involving attorney conduct.

These ABA ethics opinions are reported in *Recent Ethics Opinions,* which is published by the ABA Standing Committee on Ethics and Professional Responsibility. ABA ethics opinions also are published in the *ABA/BNA Lawyers' Manual on Professional Conduct.* This source also includes commentary on various ethical problems and related historical developments, digests of relevant court opinions, and digests of ethics opinions of state and local bar association committees and disciplinary agencies.

4. State Rules and Codes of Professional Responsibility

There are no nationally recognized and enforceable standards of professional ethics or conduct for attorneys. Rather, each state undertakes to establish ethical and professional standards that are specific to that state and that are enforced by regulatory procedures particular to that state. Often these standards are patterned after either the ABA Model Code or Model Rules. Although the Model Rules replaced the Model Code in 1983, state regulatory bodies may continue to refer to the Model Code when interpreting state standards that are based on the earlier code.

State ethics rules generally are published by the state bar association, in publications of the state supreme court, in the state's annotated code, or in another form unique to the state. A single source for all the state rules and codes is the *National Reporter on Legal Ethics and Professional Responsibility.* This source includes cases construing state rules.

The state regulatory bodies governing ethics and professional conduct also issue advisory opinions on questions arising under the state rules on ethics and professional conduct. These state advisory opinions are published in the *National Reporter on Legal Ethics and Professional Responsibility.* In addition, each state has its own reporting system that publishes advisory opinions. For example, the New York State Bar Association publishes *Opinions of the Committees on Professional Ethics of the Association of the Bar of the City of New York and the New York County Lawyers' Association,* which collects New York's advisory opinions construing the New York code. Your librarian or the state regulatory body will be able to help you locate the publication in your state that reports advisory opinions on ethics and professional conduct.

In addition to advisory opinions that merely comment on ethical questions and are often issued by bar organizations that lack enforcement power, state regulatory bodies issue binding disciplinary decisions that may involve imposition of professional penalties. Ethics opinions issued by these bodies are published in varying publications in each state. Generally, the state bar association publishes disciplinary opinions, but methods vary from state to state. In some jurisdictions certain decisions may be held confidential unless they are appealed by the attorney. Usually, opinions of the disciplinary agencies may be appealed to the state courts.

5. Cases Interpreting Ethical Rules

Cases construing the enacted version of the Model Rules or Model Code may involve disciplinary actions against attorneys, legal malpractice issues in civil actions, criminal prosecutions against attorneys, or even constitutional questions at the federal or state level.

a. Disciplinary Actions

The propriety of a particular disciplinary action is directly at issue in court when the decision of the state's governing body has been appealed by the attorney who has been found subject to discipline. Disciplinary cases that arise directly from interpretations of the Model Code or Model Rules may be located by referring to the annotations to the state ethics code accompanying your state's annotated statutes.

Similarly, as noted earlier, case annotations and commentary involving the ABA Model Rules are published in the ABA's *Annotated Model Rules of Professional Conduct*. The American Bar Foundation published an *Annotated Code of Professional Responsibility* prior to the adoption of the Model Rules. The *National Reporter on Legal Ethics and Professional Responsibility* also publishes the full text of state supreme court and appellate court opinions involving the review of disciplinary decisions.

b. Malpractice Opinions

Another source of interpretations of ethics rules is civil claims brought against lawyers based on claims of legal malpractice. Ethical rules or rules of conduct are often implicated in, or relevant to, the questions of the professional standards that may have been violated. Like other forms of civil liability, malpractice can be researched using conventional and computerized research tools discussed in earlier chapters, including West's Key Number digests (usually under the heading "attorney and client"). Treatises, encyclopedias, and law review articles also cover malpractice cases that cite state codes and rules.

c. Criminal Prosecutions

When professional misconduct involves questions of misappropriation of assets or other gross violations of a client's interests, attorneys may suffer criminal liability in addition to any civil or professional sanctions that might apply. Research into criminal violations can be accomplished using conventional methods of statutory research in the statutes of the jurisdiction in question.

d. Constitutional Issues and Other Litigation

Because enforceable ethics rules are state rules, the case law interpreting ethical or conduct rules is generally state case law. Occasionally, however, federal courts will be called on to interpret issues arising under state disciplinary or ethical rules. Some state malpractice claims, for example, may arise in cases that are properly in federal court, and the federal court may be called on to interpret the state rules in the way a state court would in the same situation. In some cases the application of particular professional rules may raise questions regarding the extent to which the legal profession may govern itself consistent with the Constitution.

For example, professional rules that improperly interfere with rights of free speech may furnish the basis for litigation either in state or federal court. Allegations that professional rules have a monopolizing impact that improperly restrains trade or prevents competition also may be the subject of a constitutional or federal statutory challenge. Professional rules may improperly interfere with the rights of clients as well. Conventional research approaches are useful in this type of research, as are specialized sources such

429

Rules Governing
Practice and
Procedure:
Searching for
Primary Authority

430

Rules Governing
Practice and
Procedure:
Searching for
Primary Authority

as the *National Reporter on Legal Ethics and Professional Responsibility* and the *ABA/BNA Lawyers' Manual on Professional Conduct*. These sources include cases at the federal and state level that involve issues of professional ethics and conduct.

6. Treatises and Commentary Sources

As in other substantive areas, professional ethics and conduct issues are discussed in a variety of secondary sources. Charles W. Wolfram's *Modern Legal Ethics* (1986) is a comprehensive treatise in the area of legal ethics and professional conduct. The *ABA/BNA Lawyers' Manual on Professional Conduct* provides references to articles and other commentary sources. Local bar publications also may be a source for commentary on issues arising under the ethics code or rules of a particular state.

ILLUSTRATION 9-24. 12 *Shepard's Professional and Judicial Conduct Citations* [No. 2] 217 (Supp. Feb. 1992).

CODE OF PROFESSIONAL RESPONSIBILITY			CANON 7
30SCR244	336So2d356	W Va	**DR 6-102(A)(6)**
36SCR373	370So2d1146	367SE773	105NJ247
41SR1175	385So2d96	67ABA1625	NJ
7SwR626	390So2d1192	26AzL340	520A2d1
61TxL235	477So2d561	29AzL583	
90UTLR281	489So2d728	31Buf375	**DR 6-102(B)**
26VR1185	Ill	81BYU70	29AzL580
43W&L127	522NE1234	26DR90	
79WLR1027	Ind	15FSU307	**DR 6-102(J)(9)**
35WnL212	366NE166	48GW734	746F2d288
	426NE684	27HUL129	
DR 6-102(A)	444NE852	771BJ192	**DR 6-103(A)(2)**
	452NE935	21InLR321	Minn
796F2d983	482NE726	23InLR475	381NW431
667FS1422	516NE36	49JBK10	
275Ark160	526NE973	74KLJ179	**DR 6-103(A)(3)**
111Az102	Iowa	75KLJ795	Fla
163Az552	463NW35	46Law189	486So2d591
195Col179	Kan	20LoyC585	La
8DC3d400	709P2d988	40LR8	512So2d414
12DC3d493	La	67MBJ878	Minn
13DC3d529	491So2d1330	55NDL498	381NW431
14DC3d389	504So2d829	9ONU4	
C16DC3d227	545So2d990	61TLQ1192	**DR 6-106**
20DC3d226	Md	11Tol227	144Wis2d382
20DC3d453	470A2d343	61TxL237	
22DC3d491	475A2d468	13UCD427	
25DC3d213	Minn	90UTLR281	**CANON 7**
49DC3d374	368NW926	23VaL61	
122Il2d165	374NW721	42VLR53	
266Ind626	402NW548	32W&L627	
211Kan285	439NW11	83WLR661	510F2d270
238Kan452	Miss		511F2d960
298Md377	480So2d1085	**DR 6-102(A)(2)**	515F2d436
299Md736	NC	Minn	526F2d42
62NCA176	302SE651	395NW82	537F2d815
81NJ33	NJ		541F2d835
98NJ401	404A2d1138	**DR 6-102(A)(3)**	558F2d1297
99NJ479	486A2d1251	138Il2d330	563F2d652
99NJ491	493A2d1231	105NJ247	564F2d371
100NJ539	493A2d1238	Fla	576F2d733
		474So2d1198	579F2d402

431

Rules Governing
Practice and
Procedure:
Searching for
Primary Authority

7. *Shepard's Professional and Judicial Conduct Citations*

Shepard's Professional and Judicial Conduct Citations is a particularly useful finding tool in this area of research. This volume lists a wide variety of sources that cite to the ABA Model Code and the ABA Model Rules. If the ABA models are applicable to your research, you will be able to find federal cases, state cases, many law reviews, and A.L.R. annotations in which the ABA models are cited. Sources that cite the ABA Model Code or Model Rules are listed under the boldface listing of the ABA model provision being cited. (See Illustration 9-24 on page 430 and Illustration 9-25 below.)

ILLUSTRATION 9-25. 12 *Shepard's Professional and Judicial Conduct Citations* [No. 2] 28 (Supp. Feb. 1992).

Rule 1.16	MODEL RULES OF PROFESSIONAL CONDUCT		
813P2d1016 37CLA1153 19Hof354 791BJ275	589A2d1143 W Va 408SE69 Wyo	**Rule 3.3(a)** 486US441 108SC1903 Ind 577NE993	**Rule 3.3(a)(4)** 131BRW519 Minn 469NW94
587A2d282 20Cap377 37CLA874 79Geo37 19Hof312 30Wsb255	Minn 467NW621 474NW167 Mo 808SW357 Okla 807P2d267		1ExER244 79CaL352 79Geo34
	808P2d670 809P2d67	**Rule 3.3(a)(2)** 131BRW519 53C3d655 323Md91	**Rule 3.3(e)** 323Md91 Md 591A2d494
Rule 2.3 79CaL316 19Hof312	20CoL1082 50MdL970 100YLJ1263	Calif 280CaR710 Fla 581So2d909	**Rule 3.4** 33MJ604
Rules 3.1 **to 3.9** 67NDR389	**Rule 3.3** 931F2d1161 764FS344	La 582So2d197 585So2d519 Md	Ala 579So2d1388 Del 593A2d549
Rules 3.1 **to 3.4** 52OhLJ576	32MJ535 245Mt53 Ill 578NE1137	591A2d494 42Mer775 60MLJ524 60MLJ575	Fla 583So2d733 Ill 578NE1137
Rule 3.1	1ExER244 1991BYU967	52OhLJ568 64SCL966	Mo 808SW358
938F2d966 7DC4d131 Ariz 813P2d725	79CaL316 20Cap374 79Geo34 104HLR481	**Rule 3.3(a)(3)** La 583So2d1166	79CaL352 79Geo34 104HLR472 50MdL951
Md 596A2d1056 Minn 468NW543	19Hof332 42Mer774 60MLJ524 52OhLJ574	NM 808P2d44 Pa 597A2d170	60MLJ533 60MLJ576 52OhLJ574 1990WLR1036
Mo 807SW74 Okla 807P2d267 809P2d67 Pa	64SCL966 1990WLR1017 37WnL1028 100YLJ1263	42FLR615 104HLR517 60MLJ575 73MqL430 52OhLJ601 64SCL966	100YLJ1263
			Continued

28

432
Rules Governing
Practice and
Procedure:
Searching for
Primary Authority

8. Computer-Assisted Research

The ABA Model Rules and the Model Code are available through computer research. However, not all state rules or codes are in the database. Cases interpreting ABA rules and specific legal or ethical issues may be obtained using standard search query methods.

a. WESTLAW

The WESTLAW directory lists ABA material (see Illustration 9-26 below). This includes several "Professional Conduct" databases, among them LS-ABAEO (ABA Ethics Opinions) and LS-MRPC (Rules of Professional Conduct) (see

ILLUSTRATION 9-26. WESTLAW Directory Screen Highlighting American Bar Association (ABA) Material.

```
_____ WELCOME to the WESTLAW DIRECTORY _____ P1_____

GENERAL MATERIAL     TEXT & PERIODICAL       CITATORS        SPECIALIZED MAT'L
Federal       P2     Law Reviews,  P337   Insta-Cite,  P374  ABA            P376
State         P6       Texts & CLEs        Shepard's,        DNA
DIALOG       P159    Restatements          Shepard's PreView C. Board. Cal. P382
News & Info. P198      & Unif. Laws P373   & QuickCite       Dictionary     P384
------------------   TOPICAL MATERIAL -------------------    Directories    P385
Antitrust    P207    Family Law    P248   Legal Ser.   P295  Gateways (D&B, P389
Bankruptcy   P210    Financial Ser P251   Maritime Law P299    Dow Jones, etc.)
Business     P213    First Amend.  P256   Military Law P301  Historical     P390
Civil Rights P219    Gov't Benefit P258   Product Liab P303  Other Pub's    P407
Commun. Law  P222    Gov't Cont.   P261   Real Prop.   P306  TaxSource      P418
Corporations P224    Health Ser.   P267   Sci. & Tech. P309  WESTLAW        P419
Crim. Just.  P229    Immigration   P273   Securities   P312   Highlights
Education    P233    Insurance     P275   Soc. Science P320  Other Serv.    P421
Energy       P236    Intell. Prop. P279   Taxation     P324   (NEW, FIND, etc.)
Environment  P241    International P283   Transport.   P332  EZ ACCESS      P422
                     Labor         P288   Worker Comp. P334  Customer Info  P423
If you wish to:
   View another Directory page, type P followed by its number and press ENTER
   Select a known database, type its identifier and press ENTER
   Obtain further information, type HELP and press ENTER
```

ILLUSTRATION 9-27. WESTLAW Directory Screen of ABA Databases Highlighting Professional Conduct Databases.

```
____WESTLAW DIRECTORY WELCOME SCREEN_____ P1_____
____AMERICAN BAR ASSOCIATION DATABASES                              P376_____

   The following databases are provided through an agreement between West
Publishing Company and the American Bar Association (ABA).

     INDEX TO ABA DATABASES                PROFESSIONAL CONDUCT DATABASES
AMBAR .................. This Page    LS-ABAEO    ABA Ethics Opinions
Prof. Conduct Databases . This Page   CJ-SCJ      ABA Standards for
Specialized Databases ... This Page               Criminal Justice
Texts & Periodicals ..... Next Page   LS-CJC      Code of Judicial Conduct
                                      LS-MRPC     Rules of Professional
             AMBAR                                 Conduct
AMBAR      ABA Summaries                       SPECIALIZED DATABASES
AMBAR-LE   ABA Legal Education        SCT-PREVIEW Preview of U.S. Supreme
AMBAR-TP   ABA Journals                           Court Cases


If you wish to:
   Select a database, type its identifier, e.g., AMBAR and press ENTER
   View information about a database, type SCOPE followed by its identifier
     and press ENTER
```

433

Rules Governing
Practice and
Procedure:
Searching for
Primary Authority

Illustration 9-27 on page 432). All LS databases in WESTLAW contain documents that relate to the regulation of the practice of law. The LS-ABAEO database includes formal and informal ethics opinions issued by the American Bar Association's Standing Committee on Ethics and Professional Responsibility. The older Model Code of Professional Responsibility is not online, although opinions interpreting the Code are in the LS-ABAEO database.

State ethics opinions and codes are online for most states and are compiled in the "Specialized" database for a state. (See Illustration 9-28 below.) For example, Minnesota ethics opinions are included in the MNLS-EO database. (See Illustration 9-29 below.) Minnesota's Rules on Lawyers Professional

ILLUSTRATION 9-28. WESTLAW Directory Screen of Sample State (Minnesota) Database.

```
_____WESTLAW DIRECTORY WELCOME SCREEN_____P1_____
_____GENERAL STATE DATABASES:  MINNESOTA                     P83_____

              GENERAL CASE LAW
MN-CS     Minnesota Courts            MN-ST-ANN   Annotated Statutes
MNTX-TCT  Tax Court                   MN-ST       Unannotated Statutes
                                      MN-ST-IDX   General Index
         GENERAL ADMINISTRATIVE       MN-LEGIS    Legislative Service
MN-AG     Attorney General Opinions
MN-REGTRK Regulation Tracking               HISTORICAL STATUTES
                                      Annotated Statutes 1990
TOPICAL/SPECIALIZED DATABASES INDEX   e.g., MN-STANN90
Topical Case Law ....... Next Page    Legislative Service 1988-1991
                                      e.g., MN-LEGIS88
Specialized Databases ... Enter P85
                                               COURT RULES
                                      MN-RULES   Court Rules
                                      MN-ORDERS  Court Orders

If you wish to:
    Select a database, type its identifier, e.g., MN-CS and press ENTER
    View information about a database, type SCOPE followed by its identifier
      and press ENTER
    View the Index to State Databases, type P6 and press ENTER
```

ILLUSTRATION 9-29. WESTLAW Directory Screen of Sample State (Minnesota) Specialized Databases Highlighting MNLS-EO Database.

```
_____WESTLAW DIRECTORY WELCOME SCREEN_____P1_____
_____GENERAL STATE DATABASES:  MINNESOTA                     P85_____

       SPECIALIZED DATABASES
MN-REGTRK  Minnesota Bill Tracking
MNLS-EO    Minnesota Ethics Opinions
MN-INDEX   Minnesota Index
MN-PUR     Minnesota PUR
MNPRI-WLD  West Legal Directory -
             Private Practice
       DIALOG DATABASES
SP-PPD     St. Paul Pioneer Press




If you wish to:
    Select a database, type its identifier, e.g., MN-INSUR and press ENTER
    View information about a database, type SCOPE followed by its identifier
      and press ENTER
    View the Index to State Databases, type P6 and press ENTER
```

```
Citation                  Rank(R)        Page(P)         Database   Mode
MN R LAWYERS PROF RESP     R 1 OF 29     P 1 OF 2        MN-ST      T
52 M.S.A., Lawyers Prof.Resp., Rule 1

            RULES ON LAWYERS PROFESSIONAL RESPONSIBILITY
            COPR. (c) WEST 1992 No Claim to Orig. Govt. Works

RULE 1. DEFINITIONS

   As used in these Rules:
   (1) "Board" means the Lawyers Professional Responsibility Board.
   (2) "Chair" means the Chair of the Board.
   (3) "Executive Committee" means the committee appointed by the Chair under
Rule 4(d).
   (4) "Director" means the Director of the Office of Lawyers Professional
Responsibility.
   (5) "District Bar Association" includes the Range Bar Association.
   (6) "District Chair" means the Chair of a District Bar Association's Ethics
Committee.
   (7) "District Committee" means a District Bar Association's Ethics Committee.
   (8) "Notify" means to give personal notice or to mail to the person at the
person's last known address or the address maintained on this Court's attorney
registration records, or to the person's attorney if the person is represented
```

ILLUSTRATION 9-31. LEXIS Screen Highlighting ETHICS and ABA Libraries.

```
                       LIBRARIES -- PAGE 1 of 2
Please TRANSMIT the NAME (only one) of the library you want to search.
- For more information about a library, TRANSMIT its page (PG) number.
- To see a list of additional libraries, press the NEXT PAGE key.
NAME   PG NAME   PG NAME   PG NAME   PG NAME   PG NAME    PG NAME     PG

- - - - - L E X I S - U S - - - - - - - - - - PUBLIC      FINANCIAL  --NEXIS--
GENFED  1 CODES  1 LEGIS   1 STATES  1 CITES   6 RECORDS  COMPNY 15 NEXIS   13
                                               ASSETS   6 MERGER 15 BACKGR  13
ADMRTY  2 FEDCOM 3 MILTRY  4 CORP    2 LAWREV  6 DOCKET   6 NAARS  15 BANKS   14
BANKNG  2 FEDSEC 3 PATENT  4 EMPLOY  2 MARHUB  6 INCORP   6          CMPCOM  13
BKRTCY  2 FEDTAX 3 PENBEN  4 HEALTH  3 _____    LIENS    6 --INT'L-- CONSUM  13
COPYRT  2 IMMIG  3 PUBCON  4 INSRLW  3 ABA     6          WORLD  16 ENRGY   14
ENERGY  2 INTLAW 3 PUBHW   4 MEDMAL  3 ___      --MEDIS-- ASIAPC 16 ENTERT  13
ENVIRN  2 ITRADE 3 REALTY  4 PRLIAB  4 TAXRIA  6 GENMED  12 EUROPE 16 INSURE  13
_____  2 LABOR  3 TRADE   5 STENV   4 TAXANA  6 MEDEX   12 MDEAFR 16 LEGNEW  14
ETHICS  2 LEXPAT 3 TRDMRK  5 STSEC   4 ALR     6 MEDLNE  12 NSAMER 16 MARKET  14
_____    M&A    4 TRANS   5 STTAX   4 -ASSISTS-                    PEOPLE  14
FEDSEN  3 MSTORT 5            UCC     5 PRACT   12 POLITICAL          SPORTS  13
                             UTILTY  5 GUIDE   12 CMPGN   14         TRAN    14
                                                 EXEC    14
   AC for AUTO-CITE   LXE (LEXSEE) to retrieve a case/document by cite
   SHEP for SHEPARD'S LXT (LEXSTAT) to retrieve a statute by cite
Press Alt-H for Help or Alt-Q to Quit.
```

Responsibility are included in the MN-ST-ANN and the MN-ST databases, and
a search such as [pr(rules & lawyers & professional)] will locate the Rules
within the databases. (See Illustration 9-30 above.)

b.   LEXIS

There are two points of entry for researching ethics materials on LEXIS.
(See Illustration 9-31 above.) The ABA library contains separate files for formal

ILLUSTRATION 9-32. LEXIS Description of ETHICS Library.   435

```
Please TRANSMIT the NAME (only one) of the library you want to use.  You may
TRANSMIT the NAME of any library, not only those listed below.  To see other
descriptions, press the NEXT PAGE or PREV PAGE key.  To see the menu page
containing the first library described below, press the TRANSMIT key.
                    DESCRIPTIONS -- PAGE 2 of 16
    NAME    LIBRARY                        NAME    LIBRARY

    ADMRTY  Federal Admiralty Cases and    EMPLOY  State Private & Public Sector
              Arbitrators Awards                     Employment Cases, Codes, plus
            UK Admiralty Cases, statutes            Related Topical Materials
              and statutory instruments    ENERGY  Federal Energy Cases & Admin.
    BANKNG  Federal Banking Cases, Agency           Decisions & Orders
              Material and Publications    ENVIRN  Federal Environmental Cases
    BKRTCY  Federal Bankruptcy Cases,      ESTATE  Federal and State Estate, Gift
              Bankruptcy Court Decisions &           & Trust cases and publications
              Title 11                     ETHICS  State Ethics Cases, Codes
    COPYRT  Federal Copyright Cases,                 and Related Publications
              Regulations, Statutes & Treaties FAMILY State Family Law cases and
    CORP    State Corporate Cases and              Statutory Materials
              Corporate information from the
              Secretary of State Offices

For further explanation, press the H key (for HELP) and then the TRANSMIT key.
Press Alt-H for Help or Alt-Q to Quit.
```

ILLUSTRATION 9-33. LEXIS Screen of Files in ETHICS Library.

```
Please type, separated by commas, the NAMES of the files you want to search and
then press the TRANSMIT key.  To see the description of a particular file, type
its page number and then press the TRANSMIT key.
                         FILES -- PAGE 1 of 1
NAME    PG NAME  PG NAME  PG NAME  PG NAME  PG NAME  PG DESCRIP

------------     STATE ETHICS CASE LAW  ----------  ------  ABA MATERIALS  -----
OMNI   12 HAW     3 MINN   5 OHIO    7 WASH   10 FOPIN  11 Formal Opinions
ALA     1 IDA     3 MISS   5 OKLA    7 WVA    10 INFOP  11 Informal Opinions
ALAS    1 ILL     3 MO     5 ORE     7 WISC   10 CODES  11 Professional and
ARIZ    1 IND     3 MONT   5 PA      8 WYO    10                Judicial Conduct
ARK     1 IOWA    3 NEB    5 RI      8                          Codes and Rules
CAL     1 KAN     4 NEV    5 SC      8 AGENCIES
COLO    1 KY      4 NH     6 SD      8 CABAR   13  ----- COMBINED FILES -----
CONN    2 LA      4 NJ     6 TENN    8 NYBAR   13 OMNI   12 Comb. State Cases
DEL     2 ME      4 NM     6 TEX     9 NYCBAR  13 ALLCDE 12 Comb. State Codes
DC      2 MD      4 NY     6 UTAH    9            ETHICS 12 Comb. FOPIN, INFOP
FLA     2 MASS    4 NC     6 VT      9                      and CODES Files
GA      3 MICH    5 ND     7 VA      9
*Use the OMNI File to search all State Case Law Files with one Search.
*Use the Custom File Selection to combine State Ethics Case Law Files.

Press Alt-H for Help or Alt-Q to Quit.
```

ethics opinions (FOPIN), informal opinions (INFOP), and the Codes of Professional Responsibility and Judicial Conduct (CODES). The "Ethics" file in that library combines both the formal and informal opinions and the current Codes.

The ETHICS library (see Illustration 9-32 above) includes state files that contain ethics cases, the Codes of Professional and Judicial Conduct, formal and informal ABA opinions, and opinions of the California, New York, and New York City Bar Associations (see Illustration 9-33 above). At the time this was written, there were ethics cases, ethical codes, and formal and informal opinions from 39 states online in LEXIS.

Researching Non-Legal Materials | Chapter 10

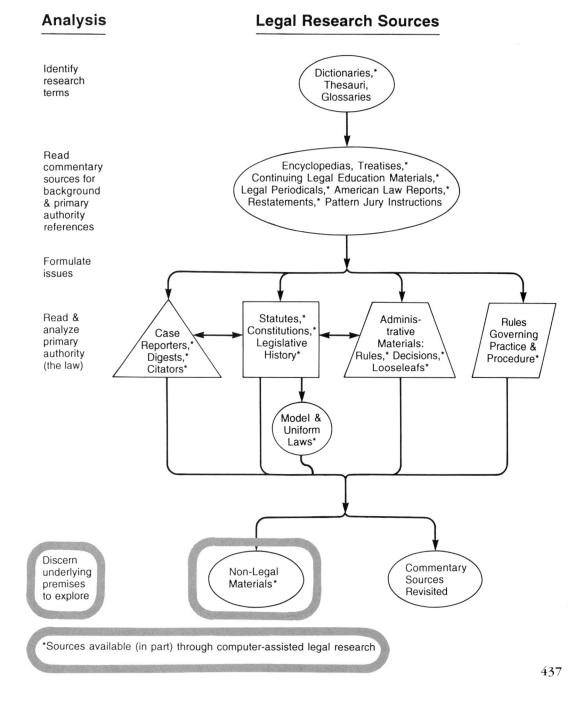

Analysis

Identify research terms

Read commentary sources for background & primary authority references

Formulate issues

Read & analyze primary authority (the law)

Legal Research Sources

Dictionaries,* Thesauri, Glossaries

Encyclopedias, Treatises,* Continuing Legal Education Materials,* Legal Periodicals,* American Law Reports,* Restatements,* Pattern Jury Instructions

Case Reporters,* Digests,* Citators*

Statutes,* Constitutions,* Legislative History*

Adminis-trative Materials: Rules,* Decisions,* Looseleafs*

Rules Governing Practice & Procedure*

Model & Uniform Laws*

Discern underlying premises to explore

Non-Legal Materials*

Commentary Sources Revisited

*Sources available (in part) through computer-assisted legal research

437

A. INTRODUCTION

The law exists to regulate interactions among people or between people and their environments and to resolve disputes arising from these interactions. Interactions that prompt the development and applications of legal rules are also of interest to other disciplines. For example, biologists and chemists are as concerned with environmental protection as the law is. Economists are as concerned with securities regulation as the law is. Physicians and human resource managers are as concerned with occupational safety and health as the law is. Sociologists, psychologists, and historians are as concerned with racist behavior as the law is.

This chapter provides a *basic* introduction to locating and reading information from other disciplines. This chapter focuses on social sciences information pertinent to the Perkins problem set out in Chapter 2 on pages 15-16, although much of what is said here would apply to the physical sciences as well. Furthermore, this chapter emphasizes the sources available in many law libraries. Our goals are to demonstrate the availability and importance of law-related information, not to provide a definitive method for this area of research.

B. WAYS OF KNOWING: LAW vs. SOCIAL SCIENCE

Lawyers and social scientists know what they know in fundamentally different ways. Lawyers rely on authority; scientists (whether social scientists or physical scientists) rely on the scientific method or observation.

1. Law as a System of Authority

Law is a system of "revealed truth." That is, judges, legislators, and members of administrative agencies pronounce the law. Lawyers know they have discovered authoritative law when they have found judicial or agency decisions, statutes, or rules that are both relevant and mandatory. Scholars of the law critique these pronouncements, and lawyers apply them to the situations of clients (or argue for new rules of law).

Pronouncements of law entail proscriptions and prescriptions of future conduct and declarations of the legal consequences of various courses of action. In prescribing how people are to behave, lawmakers thus act primarily normatively. The law of intentional infliction of emotional distress, for example, proscribes racist actions against a person in a position of powerlessness vis-à-vis the tortfeasor.

Lawmakers implicitly rely on assumptions regarding human behavior. These assumptions are unstated in many contexts and only rarely tested through the legal system. For example, in applying the law of intentional infliction of emotional distress, courts assume that the use of racist epithets by persons in a position of power inflicts harm on the target. The courts base this assumption in part on the facts of the case at hand, but also in part on their understanding of human nature and the power of words.

2. Social Scientists and the Scientific Method

Social scientists do test assumptions (or hypotheses) about human behavior, and they do so in large part through the "scientific method." The scientific method is aimed at describing what occurs, explaining why it occurs, and predicting future events. The scientist (1) begins with an observation about the real world; (2) formulates an explanation of it through inductive thinking; (3) predicts what will occur in the future based on that explanation, through deductive thinking; and (4) then verifies the prediction, as well as the explanation, through controlled observation or experimentation. If the prediction plays out repeatedly, the scientist knows the fact under investigation.

For example, social psychologists have been curious for some time about how racism spreads—a topic of some significance to the Perkins problem. According to one theory, the use of a racial epithet has consequences not only for the speaker and the target, but also for those who overhear the epithet. When a third party overhears the epithet, negative stereotypes about the target's racial group are evoked. The third party, as well as the speaker, may then engage in negative behavior toward the target.

Various experiments to test this theory have been run in recent years. In a 1987 study at the University of Arizona and the University of North Carolina (Chapel Hill), the researchers had small groups of white undergraduate students read materials about a trial. The materials included a transcript and a picture of the defense attorney. In some instances, the defense attorney was African-American; in others, he was white. During the discussion of the trial, a confederate of the researchers, posing as a student, either said nothing, simply criticized the defense attorney, or criticized the defense attorney by use of an epithet. For the African-American attorney, the epithet was "nigger" (described by the researchers as a "derogatory ethnic label"). The students provided verdicts, ratings of the two attorneys, and an impression of the defendant.

Illustration 10-1 on page 440 shows a page from the study, Shari L. Kirkland, Jeff Greenberg & Tom Pyszczynski, *Further Evidence of the Deleterious Effects of Overheard Derogatory Ethnic Labels: Derogation beyond the Target,* 13 Pers. & Soc. Psych. Bull. 216, 224 (1987). If you were to read the entire article, you would see that it follows the standard format for such studies: discussion of prior research, description of the experiment (who the "subjects" were and what they did) and the results, and a discussion of the study's implications. Illustration 10-1 presents some of the conclusions of this study in numbers and words.

The facts obtained through the scientific method often come in numerical or statistical form. While the fine points of statistics are rarely compre-

ILLUSTRATION 10-1. Shari L. Kirkland et al., *Further Evidence of the Deleterious Effects of Overheard Derogatory Ethnic Labels: Derogation beyond the Target,* 13 Pers. & Soc. Psych. Bull. 216, 224 (1987).

TABLE 2   Means and F Values for the Comment Variable Main Effect in the Black Defense Attorney Condition

Ratings	DEL	Nonethnic Label	No Comment	Main Effect
Defense attorney	25.46	27.96	32.92	$F(2, 73) = 3.40$, p < .05
Prosecuting attorney	43.18	40.69	40.28	$F(2, 73) = 1.74$, ns
Defendant	10.29	13.92	13.50	$F(2, 74) = 5.98$, p < .004
Verdict measure	14.15	10.38	11.17	$F(2, 72) = 4.67$, p < .02

Note: Attorney ratings could range from 6 = most unfavorable to 54 = most favorable. Defendant ratings could range from 3 = most unfavorable to 27 = most favorable. The means for the verdict measures are collapsed across the intermediate and final measures and could range from 1 = not guilty with maximum certainty to 18 = guilty with maximum certainty.

showed that subjects were more certain that the defendant was guilty in the DEL condition than in the other conditions, t (76) = 2.15, p<.05. As with the defendant ratings, there was no hint of a nonethnic label versus no comment difference (t<1).

In the white defense attorney condition, the 2 × 2 analyses of variance revealed no significant effects. There was, however, a marginal main effect of the competence variable on ratings of the prosecuting attorney's opening statement, F (1, 48) = 3.58, p<.07. The prosecuting attorney's opening statement was rated slightly more favorably when the defense attorney's opening statement was incompetent than when it was competent, means of 13.2 and 12.00, respectively; again, only a slight hint of an effect of the competence manipulation.

DISCUSSION

The present results demonstrated a deleterious effect of overheard derogatory ethnic labels generally similar to the effect found previously by Greenberg and Pyszczynski (1985). Thus the effect appears to generalize to (a) situations in which the target is remote, (b) situations in which there is a substantial time delay and further exposure to information about the target between the slur and evaluation of the target, and (c) situations in which the target is of high occupational status. Because the competence manipulation was weak and the defense attorney was rated lower than the prosecutor, it is still unclear whether the effect occurs when the target does not perform poorly.

Most interestingly, the present results indicate that the effects of the derogatory ethnic label can extend to evaluations of an individual associated · with the target who is not a member of the slurred group (i.e., the white defendant). To explain the effects of the DEL on derogation of the target, we suggest that the DEL accesses negative attitudes and beliefs regarding members hensible without training in statistics, some basics are easily understood. In Table 2, for example, the African-American defense attorney's favorability rating was 25.46 where the epithet was used, 27.96 when there was a non-racial critical comment, and 32.92 when there was no comment. The higher the score, the more favorably the students viewed the attorney. A similar pattern occurs in the students' impressions of the defendant, who was white in all trials. Note also that the guilty verdict was most likely when the racial epithet occurred.

The numbers in the "Main Effect" column are the least comprehensible without training in statistics—and, of course, the most important. Scientific researchers use statistical tests to determine whether their results are likely due to mere chance or due to the phenomenon they have predicted. Here, "$p < .05$" signifies that the difference between the favorability ratings of the defense attorneys has less than a 5 percent (1 out of 20) likelihood of being due to mere chance. This result and the results regarding assessments of the defendant and the verdict are considered statistically significant.

The Kirkland, Greenberg, and Pyszczynski study confirms the results of an earlier study (as detailed in the Discussion in Illustration 10-1). Thus, the researchers assert, although not without reservation, that racial epithets "have reliable, detrimental effects on evaluations of targeted individuals and others associated with them as well." *Id.* at 225.

3. Social Sciences and Observation

Social scientists use other methods of knowing as well. Historians, anthropologists, sociologists, and others rely on careful observation of events, whether current or in the past. This observation may be firsthand or secondhand, through the recorded observations of others.

For example, Illustration 10-2 on page 442 is the first page of an article on racial slurs written by an anthropologist, S. Allen Counter, *Racial Slurs,* The Crisis, May 1985, at 37. The article presents his conclusions about the historical use of the term "nigger," based on a review of documents, and current usage of the term, based on his observation of current culture.

Similarly, Illustrations 10-3 and 10-4 on pages 443 and 444 present the results of recent polls of American citizens. Opinion polls are a means of obtaining and synopsizing the observations or judgments of many persons at one time. Illustration 10-3 presents the responses of over 1,500 Americans surveyed in May 1991 by telephone. When asked to state what they perceived to be the most important issues facing the country, 2 percent of the respondents mentioned racism. Illustration 10-4 is a report on the results of a psychological well-being survey of African-Americans conducted in the late 1980s. According to the survey, the African-Americans participating in the survey score low on such measures of life satisfaction, regardless of social class.

C. WAYS OF INFORMING: USE OF SOCIAL SCIENCES INFORMATION IN LAW

Accomplished lawyers understand not only the law of a problem but also the perspectives of other pertinent disciplines such as the social sciences. They use these perspectives as they apply existing law to fact situations, advise

DR. S. ALLEN COUNTER DIRECTOR OF THE HARVARD FOUNDATION ON THE ISSUE OF

A CRISIS COMMENTARY

Sticks and stones may break my bones, but racial epithets go straight to the heart. We have all heard some of them, whether from acquaintances, friends or enemies; sometimes in jokes, sometimes in general conversation and occasionally in angry confrontations. There is even a hierarchy of racial and cultural epithets for most groups. Some epithets are mere crass expressions that describe generalized characteristics of an identifiable group. Others may relate to a people's origin or intelligence or failure to live up to another group's expectations. The most menacing can provoke violent reaction. Some feel that in a pluralistic society such as ours with so many different races and cultures living together, often in apparent competition, it is natural for one group to have uncharitable names for non-group members. I disagree. Biases are learned, not innate, and derogatory ethnic names for nongroup members represent prejudices that are passed on from generation to generation. In a pluralistic society, racial epithets are an impediment to racial harmony. All racial epithets,

however "mild," are ultimately pernicious and have no place in civilized society.

Recently the issue of racial epithets and ethnic slurs has received a great deal of media coverage. To the chagrin of many, this issue has become divisive and has served only to distract the national discourse from more substantive topics. While the recent accusations and counter-accusations in the press are clearly part of the election year rhetoric, with its attendant political overtones, some feel it unfortunate that this issue arose in the first place and would simply like for us to get beyond it. Others, however, feel that open discussion of this subject is long overdue.

Although the current widespread media attention to the subject might make it appear that racial epithets are something new in our society, certain Americans have for over a century been the victims of the most vulgar racial defamation. While there are numerous racial epithets used against specific ethnic groups and nationalities both here and around the world (most of which

originated outside of this country), I would like to focus on the most American, the most vulgar and historically the most violent: "nigger."

What is the origin of the word? Some feel that it derives from the Latin word *niger* which means black, or from the name of the Niger River area from which many of the later-enslaved Africans were abducted. Others feel that the term is simply an American invention. Historical documents suggest that this term entered America at about the same time the first chained blacks were pushed upon these shores from the holds of Dutch slaveships at Jamestown, Virginia in 1619. In fact, the word most likely comes from the Dutch language, where the official word *Neger* (pronounced "nayger") simply means "black person." This fact confronted me frequently while conducting ethnographic research in Holland and Suriname (formerly Dutch Guiana). I was often jolted when my Dutch-speaking hosts and well-educated officials referred to blacks as "Naygers."

When first introduced to this

37

clients, advocate for their clients, and work toward legal reform through litigation or lobbying.

In advising Perkins, the information in Illustrations 10-1 through 10-4 would be helpful. For example, her distress triggered by the trash dumping and use of racial epithets makes sense when you know the historical and current connotations of "nigger."

In advocating for Perkins before a court or an administrative agency deciding her case, you might find this information useful as well. For example, a court might give greater credence to the argument that Perkins' distress is severe if the effects of a racial epithet on Perkins and bystanders were under-

[Survey organization: Hart and Teeter Research Companies.
Research sponsor: NBC News/*Wall Street Journal.* Data provided
by the Roper Center for Public Opinion Research at the University
of Connecticut.]

```
                    (COPR. ROPER CNTR/U. CONNECTICUT)
           Rank(R)                Page(P)         Database      Mode
           R 5 OF 33              P 1 OF 4        POLL          T

006   What  would  you  say  are  the two or three most important issues or
problems  facing the nation today that you personally would like to see the
federal government in Washington do something about? (Open-ended)

Bank failures                                    2%
Economy generally                                21
Farm problems, agriculture, drought              1
Inflation, prices                                2
Interest rates                                   1
Jobs, unemployment                               19
New industry needed                              1
Recession                                        4
Savings and Loan industry                        1
Trade, imports                                   3
Wages, better jobs                               1
Defense spending--cut defense budget             1
Defense--strengthen                              1
Foreign aid--reduce                              3
Foreign policy                                   4

                    (COPR. ROPER CNTR/U. CONNECTICUT)
           R 5 OF 33              P 3 OF 4        POLL          T

Environment, pollution, toxic wastes             7
Government corruption                            1
Gun control--against                             1
Gun control--for                                1
Morality/Values                                 1
Racism                                          2
Other                                           5
None/Not sure                                   4

QUESTION NOTES: Adds to more than 100% due to multiple responses

ORGANIZATION CONDUCTING SURVEY: HART AND TEETER RESEARCH COMPANIES (NBCWSJ)
SPONSOR:                        NBC News/Wall Street Journal
SOURCE:                         NBC NEWS/WALL STREET JOURNAL

SURVEY BEGINNING DATE: 05/10/91
SURVEY ENDING DATE:    05/14/91
SURVEY RELEASE DATE:   05/24/91

INTERVIEW METHOD:      Telephone
NO. OF RESPONDENTS:    1508
                    (COPR. ROPER CNTR/U. CONNECTICUT)
           R 5 OF 33              P 4 OF 4        POLL          P

SURVEY POPULATION:     National registered voters

DESCRIPTORS:           PROBLEMS; GOVERNMENT

(c) Roper Center for Public Opinion Research, U. of Connecticut
END OF DOCUMENT
```

ILLUSTRATION 10-4. LEXIS Document Showing an Article, *Blacks Gain, but Far from Satisfied,* in the PSYTDY File of the NEXIS Library.

17TH STORY of Level 1 printed in FULL format.

Psychology Today Copyright (c) 1988 Information Access Company;
Copyright (c) American Psychological Assn. 1986

July, 1986

SECTION: Vol. 20; Pg. 72

LENGTH: 711 words

HEADLINE: Blacks gain, but far from satisfied

BYLINE: Kroehler, Carolyn J.

BODY:
   Blacks gain, but far from satisfied Despite significant improvements in the social status of blacks during the past 25 years, whites continue to report better psychological well-being and quality of life than do blacks.

   Sociologists Melvin Thomas and Michael Hughes examined national survey data showing that race, not social class, is the major factor linked to blacks' low scores on questions related to life satisfaction, marital happiness, trust in people, general happiness and even physical health.

   "Being black in and of itself is the problem," says Thomas, who explains that the effects of racism and discrimination are felt by blacks in all social classes. The researchers accounted for differences in education, income, employment, age and marital status among those surveyed and found that, regardless of social class, whites still report significantly greater life satisfaction and psychological well-being than do blacks.

   What's more, things have not changed much since the early 1970s. The data examined by Thomas and Hughes, from the National Opinion Research Center's General Social Survey, included 11 national samples collected between 1972 and 1984. Although they found slight variations from year to year, the basic pattern--in which blacks report a lower quality of life than do whites--did not change with time.

   The researchers suggest that the social and economic improvements blacks have experienced in the past 25 years may have driven up their expectations unrealistically, leaving them dissatisfied with their actual progress. But for the most part, their feelings reflect reality: "The United States is still stratified by race with whites on top and blacks and other minorities on the bottom," Thomas says. "Being black in a white-dominated society is still detrimental to life satisfaction and psychological well-being."

   SUBJECT:
Afro-Americans, social conditions

04292217

LOAD-DATE-MDC: March 30, 1988

stood. This information could reach the court or agency in various ways. You could present the testimony of an expert witness who would describe the research and present observations regarding Perkins' case. Or you could cite the study by Kirkland and her colleagues, as you would cite legal commentary. Many legal rules have evolved from "Brandeis briefs," which cite not only legal authorities but also economic and social studies. The Brandeis brief is named after Louis Brandeis, associate justice of the United States Supreme Court, who pioneered its use while practicing law.

   Lawyers also advocate for clients and promote the development of the law through lobbying legislative bodies. The information in Illustrations

10-1 through 10-4 could be useful in discussions about the necessity of a statute to regulate racist conduct. For example, according to the study described in Illustration 10-4, discrimination has a powerful negative effect on the psychological well-being of African-Americans; there is a problem to be remedied. One could make various arguments based on the low percentage of respondents in the opinion poll who cited racism as a concern (Illustration 10-3). Perhaps there should not be a statute on a subject of such little apparent interest. Or perhaps a statute is needed to address racist conduct that is occurring but is little noticed or rarely perceived as troublesome due to pervasive bias in our society. As this example demonstrates, empirical information does not always yield clear or consistent implications, any more than legal authorities do.

D. RESEARCHING SOCIAL SCIENCES INFORMATION

Of course, extensive research in social science literature or other fields requires use of a university or specialized library. Nonetheless, you may find helpful information in your law library.

1. Guides to Research Sources

Just as this text describes the research methods and sources used in law, so other texts describe the research methods and sources used in other fields. Your library may contain one or more of these texts. The *Guide to Reference Books,* for example, is a publication of the American Library Association that provides general guidance about research in a wide variety of fields. It covers such divergent topics as fine arts, sports, genealogy, religion, and education, as well as the social sciences.

If you consulted this text for guidance on researching the psychological dimensions of racism, for example, you would discover over ten pages listing texts in psychology. The texts are categorized by information format, such as guides, bibliographies, periodicals, manuscripts, abstracts to journals and indexes, book reviews, dictionaries and encyclopedias, handbooks, biographies, style manuals, and tests and measurements. Upon reading the list, you would have references to several guides to psychological research, the major texts on various subjects, and the index services used in psychology. (See Illustration 10-5 on page 446.) You would learn, for example, that *Psychological Abstracts* provides synopses of books, articles, and reports. If you then consulted *Psychological Abstracts* for 1987, you would find a reference to the article by Kirkland and her colleagues.

2. Print Sources Available in a Law Library

Many law libraries carry some social science materials that are related to law, mainly in the form of books and periodical articles. The methods of locating treatises described in Chapter 3 should yield any pertinent books (see page 60). Similarly, you may find references to articles in one of the indexes described in Chapter 3, such as the *Index to Periodical Articles Related to Law*, on pages 82-89.

In addition, your library may have one or more social sciences indexes. For example, the *Social Sciences Index* covers about 350 English-language periodicals in the various social sciences. It dates to 1974. The Kirkland article betically by title; a special section includes periodicals published by international organizations. A short analysis of each periodical provides editorial information, and a concise description of one issue notes average number and length of articles, number and average length of research notes, regular features, etc. Indexes by title, by institution, and by subject. Z7203.P974

Markle, Allen and **Rinn, Roger C.**, eds. Author's guide to journals in psychology, psychiatry and social work. N.Y., Haworth Pr., [1977]. 256p. **CD62**

A guide to help authors locate the professional journals in which acceptance of their articles is most probable. *Psychological abstracts* and the 1976 edition of *Ulrich's International guide to periodicals* were used as the guides for choosing the English-language journals for inclusion. The types of information given for the journals include: address, major content areas, type of articles usually accepted and inappropriate manuscripts, topics preferred, publication lag time, acceptance rate, style requirement, location of indexing and abstracting, and circulation. BF76.8.M37

Osier, Donald V. and **Wozniak, Robert H.** A century of serial publications in psychology, 1850–1950: an international bibliography. Millwood, N.Y., Kraus Internat. Pubns., [1984]. 805p. (Bibliographies in the history of psychology and psychiatry [2]) **CD63**

Some 1,107 serials are fully described in a chronological main-entry listing, with an appendix of 739 serials "not primarily psychological but which contain material relevant to psychology or written by psychologists" (*p.641*) grouped in 11 subject categories. Focus is historical and there is no data past 1950 on continuing publications; however, a number of pre-1850 publications have been included. Title and name indexes. Z7203.O8

Tompkins, Margaret and **Shirley, Norma.** Serials in psychology and allied fields. 2d ed. Troy, N.Y., Whitston, 1976. 472p. **CD64**

1st ed. (1969) had title: *A checklist of serials in psychology and allied fields.*

More than 800 current serials listed, with annotations. A title and subject index and a listing of serials by subject are added to this edition. Z7203.T65

Manuscripts

Sokal, Michael M. and **Rafail, Patrice A.** A guide to manuscript collections in the history of psychology and related areas. Millwood, N.Y., Kraus Internat., [1982]. 212p. **CD65**

In two main sections: the first describes more than 500 individual manuscript collections in the United States relating to psychology, psychiatry, psychoanalysis, child development, parapsychology, phrenology, neurology, and mental health; the second describes the most important archival repositories in the United States, Canada, and Western Europe. Indexed. BF81.S58

Abstract journals and indexes

L'année psychologique. v.1, 1894– . Paris, Presses Universitaires de France, 1895– . **CD66**

Includes signed abstracts of periodical articles and critical book reviews, with exact references to sources. International coverage. Periodical article abstracts were discontinued after v.65 (1965). Author and subject indexes to v.1–25 are contained in v.26. BF2.A6

Bibliographic guide to psychology. 1975– . Boston, G. K. Hall, [1976]. Annual. **CD67**

Continues the same publisher's *Psychology book guide* (1974) which covered Library of Congress materials only.

A comprehensive annual subject bibliography which brings together "publications cataloged by The Research Libraries of the New York Public Library and the Library of Congress."—*Pref.* Arranged alphabetically by main entry and subject. Z7203.N47a

Developmental disabilities abstracts. v.12–13, Jan. 1977– Oct. 1978. [Wash], Developmental Disabilities Office, [1977–78]. Quarterly. **CD68**

Represents a continuation of two earlier publications, whose numbering it assumes: *Mental retardation abstracts,* v.1–10, 1964–73, and *Mental retardation & developmental disabilities abstracts,* v.11, 1974–76.

Prep. under a grant to the American Assoc. on Mental Deficiency, with support services provided by Herner and Co., Wash., D.C.

In 1978, abstracted about 3,600 scientific and professional articles dealing with the medical, developmental, training, programmatic, family, and personnel aspects of developmental disabilities. Author and subject indexes. RC570.M4

Psychological abstracts, 1927– . Lancaster, Pa., Amer. Psychological Assoc., 1927– . v.1– . Monthly. **CD69**

An important bibliography listing new books, journal articles, technical reports, and other scientific documents, with a signed abstract of each item. Abstracts are now arranged in 16 major classification categories, some with subsections. Author index, and, beginning with 1963, brief subject index to each number; cumulated author and subject indexes issued quarterly and annually. BF1.P65●

—— Cumulative subject index to Psychological abstracts, 1927/60– . Boston, G. K. Hall, 1966– .

Title, publisher and frequency vary: 1927/60 (publ. in 2v.), Suppl.1 (1961/65) and Suppl.2 (1966/68 in 2v.) publ. by G. K. Hall, 1966–71; Suppls. for 1969/71– publ. triennially by American Psychological Assoc.

A cumulation of the subject indexes for the period indicated, with some revision and consolidation of headings. References are to year and abstract number only. BF1.P652

Columbia University. Libraries. Psychology Library. Author index to Psychological index, 1894 to 1935, and Psychological abstracts, 1927 to 1958. Boston, G. K. Hall, 1960. 5v. **CD70**

Reproduced photographically directly from the cards without further editing; consists of a cumulation of the author entries appearing in these two sets, combined with an earlier card file which preceded the *Psychological index.* These volumes, reproducing card files made by cutting out the actual entries, pasting them on cards, and filing them alphabetically, provide an author index to psychological books and articles in many languages from 1890 to 1958. Z7203.P975

—— Cumulative author index to Psychological abstracts. Supplement. 1st– . Boston, G. K. Hall, 1965– .

Publisher and frequency vary: Suppls. 1–2 (1959/63, 1964/68) publ. by G. K. Hall, 1965–69; Suppls. for 1969/71– publ. triennially by American Psychological Assoc. The 1981/83 cumulative author and subject indexes are to be the final volumes of the series.

Psychological index, 1894–1935, an annual bibliography of the literature of psychology and cognate subjects. Princeton, N.J., Psychological Review Co., 1895–1936. 42v. **CD71**

Lists original publications in all languages, both books and periodical articles, together with translations and new editions in English, French, German, and Italian. A classified subject list, with an alphabetical author index but no subject index. Lists about 5,000 titles each year, and indexes about 350 periodicals. The list of the principal periodicals indexed, with abbreviations used, is given in v.30. Very useful for advanced work.

Continued by *Psychological abstracts* (CD69). Z7203.P97

—— Abstract references. . . . Columbus, Ohio, Amer. Psychological Assoc., 1940–41. 2v. (v.1, 1941) **CD71a**

Contents: v.1, v.1–25, 1894–1918; v.2, v.26–35, 1919–28.

Editor, H. L. Ansbacher. Prepared by the American Psychological Association in cooperation with the Work Projects Administration of the City of New York.

relevant to the Perkins problem is indexed in the April 1987/March 1988 *Social Sciences Index.* (See Illustration 10-6 on page 448.) Observe that the terms used in this index are not legal terms; the Kirkland article appears under "Race prejudice."

3. Online and CD-ROM Materials

Thanks to computer technology, you can gain access to a tremendous amount of non-legal information in a law library. The two major online services are DIALOG (available through WESTLAW) and NEXIS (related to LEXIS). This short discussion does not cover all of the data available through these services, and new databases are added periodically. Nor does it cover all research methods. Finally, this information is current to September 1991. Thus, you should familiarize yourself with the current user's manual before beginning your research.

a. DIALOG

DIALOG provides access to information on a wide variety of subjects, including the following:

biosciences and biotechnology	engineering
business information	industry analysis
chemistry	intellectual property
company information	medicine and drug information
computers and electronics	news and current affairs
defense and aerospace	science and technology
directories and reference	social science and humanities
energy and environment	

There are over 250 separate databases pertaining to these subjects available to law schools and even more available to full-service customers. Some DIALOG databases contain the full text of sources. Most are reference databases, such as indexes and abstracts.

For example, Illustration 10-3 on page 443 is a print-out of material available in full-text form in the POLL database. POLL is Public Opinion Online, which contains the full text of public opinion surveys on a wide variety of topics conducted by the Roper Center for Public Opinion.

Illustration 10-7 on page 449 presents listings from the NEWSINDEX database that might be useful in presenting Perkins' case. NEWSINDEX is the National Newspaper Index online; the National Newspaper Index lists articles from such leading newspapers as the *Wall Street Journal* and *New York Times.* Note that research in an online index does not yield the indexed article itself, any more than a search in a print index does; you still need to locate the periodical in which the article is published.

Research in DIALOG on WESTLAW entails two basic steps: selecting your database and entering your search.

Begin by selecting the page number for the DIALOG directory from the WESTLAW menu. You will then be presented with an index to the DIALOG databases. You may wish to page through this index to identify potentially useful databases. Alternatively, you could consult a print DIALOG catalog. To ascertain the scope of a database, type [scope database name]. Once you have selected a database, simply enter its identifier.

The second step is to enter your search. As with computer-assisted research in legal sources, the purpose of a search is to identify terms likely to

Race identity—*cont.*
Benton revised visual retention test performance of black adolescents according to age, sex, and ethnic identity. E. P. Knuckle and C. A. Asbury. bibl *Percept Mot Skills* 63:319-27 Ag '86
Identity and marginality: issues in the treatment of biracial adolescents. J. T. Gibbs. bibl *Am J Orthopsychiatry* 57:265-78 Ap '87

Race identity in literature
Race, politics, and literary techniques in recent books on Brazilian literature [review article] E. de S. Rego. *Lat Am Res Rev* 21 no3:249-56 '86

Race prejudice
See also
  Race attitudes
Anthropology, ethnology and ethnic and racial prejudice. Y. V. Bromley. il *Int Soc Sci J* 39:31-43 F '87
Further evidence of the deleterious effects of overheard derogatory ethnic labels: derogation beyond the target. S. L. Kirkland and others. bibl *Pers Soc Psychol Bull* 13:216-27 Je '87
A prejudice against prejudice. M. S. Kimmel. *Psychol Today* 20:46-8+ D '86
Race prejudice and economic beliefs. P. C. L. Heaven and A. Furnham. bibl *J Soc Psychol* 127:483-9 O '87
Racial and ethnic stereotypes in professional wrestling. B. Maguire and J. F. Wozniak. bibl *Soc Sci J* 24 no3:261-73 '87
Racial prejudice in a capitalist state: what has happened to the American creed? R. T. Schaefer. *Phylon* 47:192-8 S '86
Religious orientation and prejudice: a comparison of racial and sexual attitudes. G. M. Herek. bibl *Pers Soc Psychol Bull* 13:34-44 Mr '87
The rhetoric of miscegenation: Thomas Jefferson, Sally Hemings, and their historians. B. R. Burg. *Phylon* 47:128-38 Je '86
Shaping the organizational context for black American inclusion. T. F. Pettigrew and J. Martin. bibl *J Soc Issues* 43:41-78 Spr '87; Discussion. 43:79-156 Spr '87
Sixth amendment—right to inquire into jurors' racial prejudices. M. Wyckoff. *J Crim Law Criminol* 77:713-42 Fall '86

Race relations
See also
  Asians and blacks
  Ethnic relations
  Genocide
  Immigration and emigration
  Interracial adoption
  Interracial marriage
  Jewish question
  Jews and blacks
  Minorities
  Native races
  Race discrimination
  Racism
Ethnicity beyond compare; review article. S. Fenton. *Br J Sociol* 38:277-82 Je '87

International aspects
See also
  International Convention on the Elimination of All Forms of Racial Discrimination
  United Nations. Committee on the Elimination of Racial Discrimination
Assembly appeals for intensified activities to combat racism, condemns increased use of mercenaries. *UN Chron* 24:126 F '87
Race, votes and power: the numbers game. *Economist* 305:63-6 D 26 '87

Australia
Blackfellas and Whitefellas: the concepts of domain and social closure in the analysis of race-relations. D. S. Trigger. bibl il *Mankind (Aust)* 16:99-117 Ag '86

Canada
See also
  Canada—Minorities
History
The idea of Chinatown: the power of place and institutional practice in the making of a racial category. K. J. Anderson. bibl map *Ann Assoc Am Geogr* 77:580-98 D '87

Great Britain
See also
  Great Britain—Minorities
The anti-anti-racists. J. Jenkins. *New Statesman* 112:13 N 28 '86
'Arab pigs' and the Attorney-General. G. Bindman. *New Statesman* 113:17 Ja 9 '87

Coloured and coded; census questions on race. *Economist* 304:52 Ag 1 '87
Mediating race relations: British Community Relations Councils revisited. A. M. Messina. *Ethn Racial Stud* 10:186-202 Ap '87
Race prejudice and economic beliefs. P. C. L. Heaven and A. Furnham. bibl *J Soc Psychol* 127:483-9 O '87
Recent Marxist theories of nationalism and the issue of racism. R. Miles. *Br J Sociol* 38:24-43 Mr '87
This isn't the way to deal with racism. J. Jenkins. *New Statesman* 112:10-11 O 31 '86

Israel
See also
  Israel—Minorities

Malaysia
Of races and tongues. S. Aznam. *Far East Econ Rev* 137:9-10 Jl 30 '87

South Africa
See also
  South African question
United Nations. Special Committee against Apartheid
Apartheid at home and sabotage abroad. Guang Hexin. *Beijing Rev* 30:12-13 Ja 12 '87
Apartheid—an outstanding issue in world politics. Ge Ji. *Beijing Rev* 30:14-17 Mr 9 '87
Apartheid's slow road. *Economist* 303:47 My 16 '87
Battle for conscience in Washington. J. Harding. *Africa (Lond Engl)* no183:42-4+ N '86
Chief Buthelezi's poisoned chalice. *Economist* 304:50-1 S 19 '87
Comparing the comparers: white supremacy in the United States and South Africa: review essay. G. R. Andrews. *J Soc Hist* 20:585-99 Spr '87
Conversation with Luke J. Mwananshiku Minister of Foreign Affairs, Zambia. *Afr Rep* 31:30-1 S/O '86
Doors do open. *Economist* 305:48-9 N 14 '87
Economic sanctions against South Africa. C. M. Becker. *World Polit* 39:147-73 Ja '87
Frantz Fanon and black consciousness in Azania (South Africa). T. K. Ranuga. *Phylon* 47:182-91 S '86
Important step to ending apartheid. Xu Dewen. *Beijing Rev* 30:13 Jl 27 '87
Laager quarrels. *Economist* 302:42+ F 7 '87
Making foreign policy: the Congress and apartheid. R. G. Lugar. *Afr Rep* 31:33-6 S/O '86
The nature of the agrarian land question in the Republic of South Africa. R. Daniels. *Am J Econ Sociol* 46:1-16 Ja '87
The OAU: a new militancy. M. A. Fitzgerald. *Afr Rep* 31:66-9 S/O '86
Olusegun Obasanjo and Malcolm Fraser: Co-Chairmen, the Commonwealth Eminent Persons Group [interview] *Afr Rep* 31:4-11 S/O '86
Perceptions of race groups by South African white women. D. J. A. Edwards. *J Soc Psychol* 127:539-41 O '87
Pretoria remains on treacherous road. Wang Nengbiao. *Beijing Rev* 30:34-5 D 21 '87
Sanctions and beyond. map *Africa (Lond Engl)* no181:8-11+ S '86
Singing out in protest. M. Shaw. *Africa (Lond Engl)* no182:78-9 O '86
South Africa and the American South. G. Sorin. *Dissent* 34:28-9 Wint '87
South Africa embattled. J. De St. Jorre. *Foreign Aff* 65 no3:538-63 '87
South Africa: violence, myths, and democratic reform [review article] D. D. Laitin. *World Polit* 39:258-79 Ja '87
The state of psychiatry in South Africa today. J. Dommisse. *Soc Sci Med* 24 no9:749-57 '87; Discussion. 24 no9:758-61 '87
The structure of the South African labor market, 1970-83. R. Daniels. *Rev Black Polit Econ* 15:63-78 Spr '87
Surplus people and expendable children: the structure of apartheid and the mortality crisis in South Africa. T. R. De Gregori and W. A. Darity. *Rev Black Polit Econ* 15:47-62 Spr '87
Toward a new South Africa. G. P. Shultz. *Afr Rep* 31:16-19 S/O '86
Under Thatcher's coattails. D. Herbstein. *Afr Rep* 31:20-3 S/O '86
History
Apartheid planning in South Africa: the case of Port Elizabeth. A. J. Christopher. bibl maps *Geogr J* 153:195-204 Jl '87
Public opinion
An editor's report on attitudes in South Africa. K. H. Keene. *Public Opin* 9:55 S/O '86

ILLUSTRATION 10-7. WESTLAW Citation List from the NEWSINDEX Database in
DIALOG.

449

```
                                                              PAGE    1

           Rank(R)                  Page(P)        Database      Mode
           R 101 OF 202             P 1 OF 1       NEWSINDEX     P

The subtler shades of RACISM; private emotions lag behind public discourse.
Gladwell, Malcolm
Washington Post  v114 col 1 pA3 July 15, 1991
SOURCE FILE: NNI File 111
EDITION: Mon  22 col in
NAMED PEOPLE: Gaertner, Samuel--Research
DESCRIPTORS:   RACISM--PSYCHOLOGICAL   aspects;   Psychologists--Research;
    Avoidance (Psychology)--Social aspects

                                                  (COPR. 1991 IAC)

           Rank(R)                  Page(P)        Database      Mode
           R 109 OF 202             P 1 OF 1       NEWSINDEX     P

New  way  to  battle  bias:  fight  acts,  not  feelings. (the psychology of
    prejudice;  research  done  by  Fletcher  Blanchard  at  Smith College;
    includes related article) (Living Arts Pages)
Goleman, Daniel
New York Times  v140 col 4 pB1(N) pC1(L) July 16, 1991
SOURCE FILE: NNI File 111
EDITION: Tue  39 col in
CODEN: NYTIA
illustration; portrait
CAPTIONS: Fletcher Blanchard. (portrait)
NAMED PEOPLE: Blanchard, Fletcher--Research
DESCRIPTORS:  Prejudices--Psychological  aspects;  RACISM--RESEARCH; Smith
    College--Research

                                                  (COPR. 1991 IAC)


           Rank(R)                  Page(P)        Database      Mode
           R 197 OF 202             P 1 OF 1       NEWSINDEX     P

Whites'  racial  stereotypes  persist;  most  retain negative beliefs about
    minorities, survey finds. (National Opinion Research Center report)
Duke, Lynne
Washington Post  v114 col 1 pA1 Jan 9, 1991
SOURCE FILE: NNI File 111
EDITION: Wed  28 col in
DESCRIPTORS: Whites--Attitudes; RACISM--SURVEYS; Stereotype (Psychology)--
    Surveys; National Opinion Research Center--Reports; Minorities--Public
    opinion

                                                  (COPR. 1991 IAC)
```

appear in documents pertinent to your problem. Unlike WESTLAW databases, which are all produced by West, DIALOG databases are produced by various companies. Consequently, the database structure varies from database to database, and so does the search process. Each database has a default search procedure, which you can ascertain from the scope screens or by pressing "f" and "enter" once you are in the database. The default procedure sets the fields to be searched absent contrary directions. For example, company and product names, descriptors (subject headings), captions, named persons, and titles are automatically searched in the NEWSINDEX database. You may specify additional fields to search as well.

There are several differences in search procedures between WESTLAW itself and DIALOG on WESTLAW. You can learn of these differences by entering [scope dialog]. Fortunately, using DIALOG on WESTLAW allows you to use the familiar WESTLAW commands or connectors because the WESTLAW system translates these commands as the search request is passed on to DIALOG. For example, DIALOG does not accept grammatical connectors; it converts each to a numerical connector. Thus, [/s] becomes [/10].

The search [pd(>1990) & racism] in NEWSINDEX asked for articles on racism published since 1990. It yielded 202 article listings in the fall of 1991, some of which are found in Illustration 10-7. The search in POLL that yielded Illustration 10-3 was [pd(>1990) & racis!]. In both searches, [pd(>1990)] was used to obtain only documents published since 1990.

DIALOG also is available separately from WESTLAW. If you gain access to DIALOG other than through WESTLAW, be aware that there are differences in search strategies.

b. NEXIS

Similarly, accompanying LEXIS is NEXIS, an online presentation of material found in a wide collection of newspapers, magazines, wire services, and newsletters. As of fall 1991, there were over 600 files available to law school users. NEXIS includes material on general and business topics.

Again, the first step is to select your database. NEXIS has grouped its databases in various ways. Thus, NEXIS permits you to focus your search on the most useful files by designating one of the subjects listed below or by selecting dates and format choice, type of publication, and region of the country. For example, the CURRNT file includes articles from the past two or three years in all publications in NEXIS. The PAPERS file includes all newspapers in NEXIS.

Format and date choices

full text
currnt	for recent articles (past 2-3 years)
archiv	for older articles
omni	for both

abstract
curabs	for recent abstracts
arcabs	for older abstracts
allabs	both

Types of publications

majpap	major newspapers
papers	all newspapers
mags	magazines
nwltrs	newsletters
wires	wire services
script	transcripts

Regions

mwest
neast
seast
west

      business
      finance
      international
      legal news
      news
      people
      trade and technology

In the alternative, you may identify a specific file or publication to search. You might, for example, wish to search in the *Psychology Today* file, PSYTDY, if you were researching the Perkins problem.

As with DIALOG, the second step is to enter your search. Again, the purpose of the search is to locate documents containing key terms. NEXIS uses the same commands and connectors as LEXIS. If you were searching the PSYTDY database for material pertinent to the Perkins problem, you might use [racis!] as a query. [Racis!] would be a very broad search term, undoubtedly too broad to be effective, if you were searching more files. This search in PSYTDY yielded 18 articles in late 1991. One of them appears as Illustration 10-4 on page 444. Note that NEXIS provides the full text of this article.

c. Materials on CD-ROM

As with legal periodicals, some social science and other non-legal material is available on CD-ROM disks, and more is likely to be available in this format each year. For example, WILSONDISC (referred to in Chapter 3 on pages 88-89 because it includes the *Index to Legal Periodicals*) contains nearly 20 indexes, including the *Applied Science and Technology Index, Business Periodicals Index, Education Index, Religion Indexes,* and *Social Sciences Index.*

E. CONCLUDING OBSERVATIONS

Most of this text focuses on legal authorities and the skills needed to research legal authorities. It is important to remember that, for any particular problem, law provides only one perspective. Other disciplines provide valuable perspectives and information as well. Hence it is important to draw on non-legal information in resolving "legal" problems.

Happily, the skills you have developed by reading and working through this text should prove useful as you conduct research in other disciplines. No matter which discipline you are researching, you must identify the question you need to answer based on careful analysis of your situation, develop terms to use as research terms, discern the sources that might contain useful information and locate those sources, use your research terms to locate pertinent material, and update your results.

Developing an Integrated Research Strategy

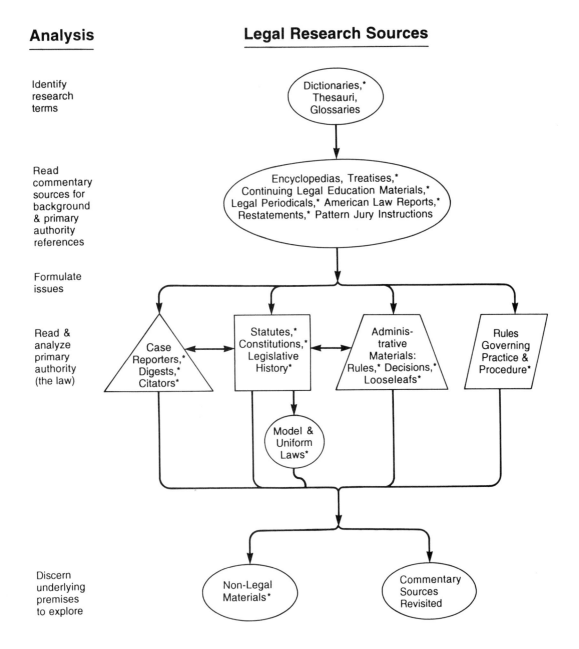

Analysis

Identify research terms

Read commentary sources for background & primary authority references

Formulate issues

Read & analyze primary authority (the law)

Discern underlying premises to explore

Legal Research Sources

Dictionaries,* Thesauri, Glossaries

Encyclopedias, Treatises,* Continuing Legal Education Materials,* Legal Periodicals,* American Law Reports,* Restatements,* Pattern Jury Instructions

Case Reporters,* Digests,* Citators*

Statutes,* Constitutions,* Legislative History*

Administrative Materials: Rules,* Decisions,* Looseleafs*

Rules Governing Practice & Procedure*

Model & Uniform Laws*

Non-Legal Materials*

Commentary Sources Revisited

*Sources available (in part) through computer-assisted legal research

A. INTRODUCTION

In Chapter 2, we began to explore the research process. Now that you have at least a passing familiarity with a range of legal research sources, we want to leave you with the message that research strategies vary from person to person, depending on familiarity with the general subject matter and specific topic, acquired biases regarding certain research sources, the contents of the library at hand, and overall research expertise. Nonetheless, there are certain constants in legal research.

To prove our point, one of us, Deborah Schmedemann, drafted a research situation for her four co-authors to research. The remainder of the chapter includes four research scenarios, followed by Deborah's commentary on them.

First, a caveat: This chapter is derived from a research exercise conducted jointly by the authors in the fall of 1988. You might test your updating skills by researching more recent developments in this fast-moving area.

Second, another caveat: The following descriptions of the research process are not complete. Ann Bateson exhaustively researched this problem (reflecting her experience as a reference librarian well versed in employment law tools—and the amount of time she put in). As for the others, each writer chose to stop when he or she determined that there were some legal theories to pursue on behalf of the client. This decision is sensible given the very preliminary posture of the dispute. Perhaps a simple letter to the client's employer setting out the most straightforward claims the client has will suffice. At this point, the lawyer can provide competent advice to the client for a reasonable price. Should the dispute persist and the stakes increase, all the writers would engage in further research.

Third, an observation: You may be surprised that the writers pursued somewhat different theories and have somewhat different perceptions of the helpfulness of the authorities they found. An experienced lawyer would not be surprised at this. In many situations, there are several, indeed sometimes many, ways "to skin the cat." And legal texts are not self-explanatory; they require interpretation by lawyers viewing concrete facts. It is up to the lawyer to ascertain the legal possibilities, develop them, and choose those best suited to the facts of the situation and the goals of the client. It takes creativity, intelligence, judgment—and highly developed research skills—to accomplish this task.

B. RESEARCH SITUATION

Your client is Anna Hale. She works as an assistant artisan in a studio that makes custom stained-glass windows in Cherry Hill, New Jersey. As you might expect, there are not many stained-glass studios in the country. Hale feels very fortunate to have her job and to be able to practice her chosen craft. She enjoys the people she works with, and the pay, benefits, and hours are good.

Hale, however, has a complaint: Over the past few months, she has suffered from a series of respiratory ailments. Several times, she has been forced to stay home from work; other times, she simply has felt rather worn-out and tired. On the recommendation of a colleague, she finally went to see a doctor. After running a battery of tests and taking an exhaustive medical history, the doctor determined that Hale has an allergy to cigarette smoke. Hale, a nonsmoker, has always had a significant aversion to smoke. She avoids smoky places as much as she can. However, she is exposed to smoke on a daily basis at work—three of the seven artisans who share the studio with her are heavy smokers.

The studio is fairly large, with several workstations positioned throughout. Each worker also has an individual space with a desk and set of personal supplies. Part of each worker's day is spent at his or her desk, but most of the day is spent at the various workstations. There is a separate employee lounge, where all of the workers take breaks and frequently eat lunch. The building is rather old and not very well ventilated.

The current rules regarding smoking are sketchy at best. The practice is that employees smoke while on break in the lounge and fairly regularly while working at their desks. One or two of the artisans also smoke periodically at the workstations. Thus, although Hale's desk is as far removed as possible from the desks of her smoking colleagues, she nonetheless is exposed to smoke both in the studio and the lounge.

Hale has had a brief conversation with the owner of the studio. He indicated that he would ask her colleagues not to smoke at the workstations, but he did not feel that it was necessary to forbid smoking at the personal desks or in the lounge. He expressed concern that a no-smoking rule would prompt one or more of the smokers, who are among the senior artisans, to quit. Hale feels that her employer is not particularly sympathetic to her situation, as he is a smoker himself.

Hale wants to prompt her employer to impose a no-smoking rule and, if possible, to keep her job. If that is not possible, she feels compelled to quit and would like remuneration. Your task at this point is to evaluate whether she has any legal theories to support her goals.

C. FOUR RESEARCH PROCEDURES

Ann L. Bateson

When I read the research situation, I immediately categorized the major issue as a labor and employment law issue. Although I suspected that the issue would be governed by state law, I thought federal law also might apply. I also believed that many types of primary authority (statutes, regulations, and cases) might be relevant. Thus, I decided to begin my research in a looseleaf service. Because I was already familiar with BNA's *Labor Relations Reporter,* I began there.

I started with the Master Index in the *Individual Employment Rights Manual.* I skimmed the entries under "Smoking" and "New Jersey," copying the references that seemed relevant. All of these references fell within two sections: 511, covering smoking in the workplace, and 571, covering New Jersey laws. There also was a reference to § 220.09 in the Outline of Classifications; that is the number assigned to cases on workplace safety and smoking.

I turned first to the New Jersey statutes in the state laws section of the *Manual.* Anna Hale's situation did not seem to be covered by the New Jersey statutes governing smoking in the workplace, because one of them defines a place of employment as one "at which 50 or more individuals perform any type of service or labor. . . ." N.J. Stat. § 26:3D-24.

Next I turned to the *Manual's* commentary section on smoking in the workplace. The introduction told me that local ordinances are sometimes applicable. I made a note to check with the Cherry Hill City Hall or library.

The commentary contained a discussion of the theories under which suits relating to smoking in the workplace have been brought and the relevant cases. The first theory discussed was that of a constitutional right to a smoke-free environment under the first, fifth, ninth, and fourteenth amendments. The commentary noted these challenges have been unsuccessful. Although I assumed that the cases and commentary were still good law, I Shepardized the cited cases and also used WESTLAW to update *Shepard's.* I concluded that the commentary was accurate.

The second theory was that the employer has a common law duty to provide a safe and healthful workplace. The discussion cited two New Jersey cases. In the first, *Shimp v. New Jersey Bell Tel. Co.,* 145 N.J. Super. Ct. 516, 368 A.2d 408 (1976), the court found a common law right to a safe work environment and ordered the employer to restrict employee smoking to non-work areas. Of course, I read *Shimp.* On the basis of *Shimp,* it seemed unlikely Anna could get a court to agree to impose a total ban on smoking in the workplace, but she could probably get some relief.

In the second New Jersey case, *Smith v. Blue Cross & Blue Shield,* No. C-3617-81E (N.J. Super. Ct. 1983), the court denied an employee's request to force his employer to adopt broad smoking restrictions and criticized the *Shimp* case as "too sweeping" and going "well beyond what is necessary to ensure a safe working place." I tried to find the text of *Smith,* but the case was not available in this looseleaf or on LEXIS or WESTLAW. Before I gave Anna Hale advice, I would want to obtain this case and compare it with *Shimp.* I could request it from the clerk of the court.

I Shepardized *Shimp* and used the computer as a citator to track references to *Shimp* and *Smith.* That process did not yield any other significant New Jersey decisions, but I did note the citations to relevant cases from other jurisdictions.

Because the applicability of the *Shimp* and *Smith* decisions to Anna's case seemed unclear, I decided to look for commentary on the *Shimp* case. I turned to the Table of Cases in the *Legal Resource Index.* It produced one reference, Tammy Turner Walsh & Phillip David Wool, Recent Development, *Nonsmokers' Rights,* 26 Wash. U. J. Urb. & Contemp. L. 211 (1984), which in turn referred to two additional commentaries on *Shimp.* Unfortunately, none of the commentaries was particularly useful.

I returned to the *Manual's* discussion of the employer's common law duty to provide a safe workplace and noted two non-New Jersey cases that might help me compare and contrast the two New Jersey cases. I found and read both *Smith v. Western Elec. Co.,* 643 S.W.2d 10 (Mo. Ct. App. 1982), and *Gordon v. Raven Sys. & Research, Inc.,* 462 A.2d 10 (D.C. 1983). These cases reach conflicting results on the employer's duty to accommodate nonsmokers. Shepardizing *Smith* and *Gordon* and running the case names through the computer did not turn up any new significant cases. The cumulative lesson from these cases seems to be that to recover on a common law theory a plaintiff must prove that smoke in the workplace really causes harm both to herself and to nonsmokers in general.

A third theory discussed in the *Manual* was breach of an implied contract to provide the employee with a smoke-free work environment, but this theory has been rejected in at least one case, and there was no indication in the facts that Anna Hale might have such a claim. A fourth theory was intentional or negligent infliction of emotional distress; this theory too has been rejected by at least one court.

A fifth theory is that an employee who is hypersensitive to smoke might be regarded as handicapped under the federal Rehabilitation Act of 1973 or a similar state or local law prohibiting discrimination against the handicapped. The employee would then be able to obtain some relief from the employer. I decided first to find the federal law to see if it might be applicable in our case. I used the Popular Name Table for U.S.C.A. to retrieve the citation, 29 U.S.C.A. §§ 701 et seq. I skimmed through the list of sections at the beginning of the chapter and picked out the sections that define persons protected by the statute and employers governed by the statute. Section 701 defines "individual with handicaps" broadly. That section was followed by cross-references to related sections in the *Code of Federal Regulations*. The Notes of Decisions indicated a split of authority about whether a person harmed by tobacco smoke is a "handicapped person" for purposes of the act. *See GASP v. Mecklenburg County,* 42 N.C. App. 225, 256 S.E.2d 477 (1979); 63 Op. Comp. Gen. 115 (1983); *Vickers v. Veterans Admin.,* 549 F. Supp. 85 (W.D. Wash. 1982). The split would become relevant if the federal act applied or if New Jersey had a similar act and used the federal definition to help interpret its own (as North Carolina did).

However, the federal statute has a limited scope: private employers who obtain government contracts and programs receiving federal financial assistance. Nothing in the facts indicates Anna Hale's employer was covered by the act. If he were, it would be necessary to read the related regulations.

I thus went to the index to *New Jersey Statutes Annotated* to see if New Jersey had a statute that prohibited discrimination against the handicapped. Under the heading "Handicapped Persons," I found a reference to §§ 10:5-1 et seq. I looked for the current text of the sections in the main volume and pocket part. The statute does forbid employment discrimination on the basis of being handicapped and defines "handicapped" in rather broad, general terms. I read the annotations to the pertinent sections. They did not clearly indicate whether Anna Hale would be "handicapped" under the statute or whether refusal to accommodate her needs would fall within the prohibited acts. One case does establish that the statute is not restricted to severe disabilities. It is possible Anna Hale would qualify for protection.

To confirm this reseach, I checked the Descriptive Word Index to *West's New Jersey Digest, 2d* under "Handicapped." I found a reference to Civil Rights 9.16, but the digests there did not provide any additional useful information. I also looked for recent decisions interpreting the relevant statutory sections by using WESTLAW. I did not find any new relevant material.

Next, the *Manual* noted that if an employee demonstrates that workplace smoke has impaired his or her ability to work, the employee may be entitled to disability pay, worker's compensation, or unemployment benefits, even if the employer has made a reasonable attempt to accommodate the employee. The discussion cited one case, *Parodi v. Merit Sys. Protection Bd.,* 690 F.2d 731 (9th Cir. 1982), where the court decided that, under the disability statute governing federal employees, a worker with an allergy to tobacco smoke was entitled to disability payments if her employer could not provide her with "suitable employment in a safe environment." Here, "safe" meant smoke-free. I read and Shepardized the case and used the computer as a citator to retrieve additional cases.

I then turned to the main volume and the pocket part of the index to New Jersey statutes to see if state statutes regulated disability pay. I found the section on "compensable disability" and concluded the law was probably not applicable, because it covered accidents and sickness *not* arising out of or in the course of an individual's employment or, if so, not compensable under worker's compensation law.

The entries in the index to New Jersey statutes for "Worker's Compensation" led me to § 34:15-1, the heart of the law. It provided for coverage "[w]hen personal injury is caused to an employee by accident arising out of and in the course of his employment . . . ." I wondered if the word "accident" could rule out a claim in Anna Hale's situation, so I read the annotations to this section and concluded that I would have to analyze the cited cases carefully. Section 34:15-8 also was especially important because it provided that acceptance of worker's compensation coverage constitutes waiver of other forms of compensation. *Shimp* had, however, indicated that this statute did not preclude an injunction. Section 34:15-31 provided an additional theory for worker's compensation coverage: occupational disease.

The statutes provided that decisions governing worker's compensation are made first in the Division of Workers' Compensation in the Department of Labor and Industries. Thus, the decisions of that agency would be useful. I knew we did not have state agency decisions from other states in our library, unless those decisions were included in a looseleaf. I decided to try to find one. Using *Legal Looseleafs in Print,* a subject guide to looseleafs, I found a reference to CCH's *Workers' Compensation Law Reporter.* I went to the reporter and learned from the "How to Use This Reporter" section that the reporter did not include agency decisions. I glanced quickly at the index to see if it included entries under "smoking." It did not. I concluded that the subject headings seemed to be based in great part on terminology that would only be familiar to those who already knew worker's compensation law. I decided not to spend time with this looseleaf.

I did, however, check the *New Jersey Digest, 2d* annotations for Workers' Compensation, where I did pick up some useful citations that I had not found in the annotated statutes.

I returned to the New Jersey statutes. The index entries for "Unemployment Compensation" led to §§ 43:21-1 et seq. I noted references to the New Jersey Administrative Code. I skimmed the statute and annotations. It seemed Anna might qualify for benefits if she quit but made herself available for work as the concept is defined by state case law and administrative regulation.

I returned to the *Manual.* The commentary had a section on how the smoking issue might be resolved in a union environment, but because the facts did not indicate such an environment, I decided to ignore the section.

I completed my work in the *Labor Relations Reporter* by searching for entries under § 220.09 in the Cumulative Digest and Indexes covering individual employee rights and by skimming the cases published in releases subsequent to the index. There were no additional New Jersey cases.

The *Labor Relations Reporter* had shown me that many legal theories might be applicable to our smoking-in-the-workplace issue. These theories could show up in a New Jersey case digest under a multitude of different

Key Numbers, and the Key Numbers could have changed over time. To be sure I had found all likely New Jersey cases on the subject of smoking in the workplace, I decided to do a very broad WESTLAW search using the term "smoking." The only useful case I retrieved was *Shimp*. The search, of course, would not have retrieved analogous cases that did not involve smoking. That is one of the drawbacks of a fact-specific computer search.

The *Labor Relations Reporter* had been very useful, but it had not told me everything I wanted to know. It had not, for example, cited many decisions relating to disability benefits, worker's compensation, or unemployment compensation issues; it had also not discussed the applicability of the Occupational Safety and Health Act (OSHA). I decided to check additional secondary sources.

I went next to a second looseleaf, RIA's *Employment Coordinator,* because I spotted it when I returned the first looseleaf to the shelf. While this set did not contain as many citations, it provided a few additional (but non-New Jersey) citations to cases in which employees won worker's compensation and unemployment compensation benefits when they left work to avoid severe health risks imposed by tobacco smoke. It provided one additional twist on the injunction issue. In *Lee v. Massachusetts,* No. 15385 (Sup. Ct. Bristol Cty. 1982), a court lifted a ban on smoking when a smoker, claiming addiction to nicotine, asserted she could not work in a smoke-free environment. RIA observed, "[i]t may be alleged that a smoker is addicted to smoking and is therefore handicapped and entitled to accommodation for the handicap from an employer under the laws restricting bias against the handicapped." RIA noted one additional theory on which a smoking in the workplace case had been brought—assault and battery. *See McCracken v. Sloan,* 40 N.C. App. 214, 252 S.E.2d 250 (1979).

In addition, the looseleaf made a reference to OSHA. I recalled that one of the articles I had retrieved when looking for discussion of *Shimp* discussed the applicability of OSHA. I had ignored it at the time because of its age, but I went back to Larry Bracken, Note, 9 Tex. Tech. L. Rev. 353 (1977-78). The article stated that the "general duty" clause of OSHA, 29 U.S.C. § 654(a)(1), might be used to obtain relief. In situations not covered by specific standards established under the act, employers must furnish to each employee a place of employment that is "free from recognized hazards that are causing or are likely to cause death or serious physical harm to his employees." I retrieved OSHA and verified that Anna Hale's employer came within the statutory definition of employer and that the statutory requirement was still valid. The article also noted that smoking could lead to problems under specific OSHA standards on workplace toxins that also are generated by cigarette smoke. I noted that if the employee wants relief, the employee must request that OSHA investigate; the statute does not provide for a private cause of action. To be sure that OSHA statutes and regulations had not changed, I searched on WESTLAW and found no changes.

Next I decided to check whether New Jersey has a state occupational safety and health act. I found an index reference to the New Jersey Worker Health and Safety Act, Chapter 34:6A, under the subject heading "Safety." I turned to the act and skimmed all of its sections, because I know that sections are frequently interrelated. I skimmed the Notes of Decisions, which did not provide any useful citations. Under the section giving the commissioner the power to promulgate rules, I noticed an Administrative Code reference indicating that New Jersey had decided to rely on federal standards rather than promulgating its own. I ran the current and previous statutory section numbers through the New Jersey case database in WESTLAW. The search produced two new cases, which only indirectly mattered because they deal with fired employees.

Next, I went to *Legal Resource Index* to locate periodical articles on smoking in the workplace. I skimmed the entries under "Smoking—Law and Legislation" and under the cross-reference "Passive Smoking." I picked out the most recent articles in major law reviews. I read the newest available article, Elizabeth M. Crocker, *Controlling Smoking in the Workplace,* 38 Lab. L.J. 739 (1987), first. It cited the Surgeon General's 1986 report, *The Health Consequences of Involuntary Smoking,* as presenting data supporting the adverse effects of a tobacco smoke environment on the nonsmoker. In addition, the article cited some additional (non-New Jersey) cases to support the argument that a particularly sensitive nonsmoker may be entitled to worker's compensation benefits or unemployment benefits.

I chose the next article, Raymond L. Paolella, *The Legal Rights of Non-smokers in the Workplace,* 10 U. Puget Sound L. Rev. 591 (1987), because it had been cited in some of the cases I had already read. That article was valuable because it described and cited numerous studies about the bad effects of environmental tobacco smoke. The article suggested one additional tort theory nonsmokers might use: nuisance. However, it acknowledged that nonsmokers have not yet had much success arguing outrage, battery, or nuisance theories.

I decided to go next to the *Index to Annotations* for the A.L.R.s because I knew the A.L.R.s have comprehensive coverage of any topic they cover. I checked the subject heading "Smoking," which referred me to "Tobacco and Tobacco Products." I checked both the main volume and pocket parts and picked five annotations. I checked the pocket part update for each annotation, and I called the toll-free number for the most up-to-date citations. The annotations did not yield any New Jersey cases.

In checking the card catalog under the subject heading "Smoking—Law and Legislation—United States," I found the title *Where There's Smoke: Problems & Policies Concerning Smoking in the Workplace* (2d ed. 1987). That source provided many citations to studies on the effects of workplace smoke on nonsmokers, and it introduced an additional (but untried) theory on which nonsmokers might bring suit: negligent hiring or retention. Under this theory an employer might be liable if a smoking employee injured a nonsmoking employee by an action the employer could have anticipated and prevented. This source also noted two theories on which smoking employees might try to protect their interests: reverse handicap claims or racial discrimination claims.

By the time I skimmed the last source, the theories, statutes, and leading cases were becoming very familiar. It seemed I had done enough secondary research to be reasonably certain I had found the major theories to support Anna Hale's interests. I also had done enough research in New Jersey statutes and cases to have found the significant primary sources. What remained was to analyze the materials I had and to update any cases I had not yet Shepardized and tracked using the computer as a citator.

Matthew P. Downs

I did not have much specific knowledge about smoking in the workplace, but knew from news articles that smoking had become a controversial topic resulting in legislative activity and court action. Thus, I decided to start with secondary sources. I expected that the right secondary sources would provide background commentary and references to other sources and assist me in determining some of the issues raised by the research situation.

I started with the periodical indexes. I was not sure which search terms would be most useful: "smoking," "employment," "employees," or "labor." I was successful on the first try by using "smoking" as a search term. Many law journal articles listed in the *Legal Resource Index* directly addressed smoking in the workplace. I ignored the references to legal newspapers because I wanted articles that were heavily footnoted.

Two of the stronger law review articles were Elizabeth M. Crocker, *Controlling Smoking in the Workplace,* 38 Lab. L.J. 739 (1987), and Douglas Messengill & Donald J. Petersen, *Smokers vs. Nonsmokers in the Workplace: Clearing the Air,* 10 Emp. Rel. L.J. 505 (1984-85). I have a somewhat peculiar way of reading law reviews—I read footnotes and skim the text. Using this method, I was able to learn quickly some of the current legal theories, and the footnotes provided citations to relevant primary authority. I paid particular attention to any references about New Jersey law, primarily because Anna Hale was employed in Cherry Hill, New Jersey.

I found that many states, including New Jersey, have clean indoor air acts directed at smoking in workplaces (among others). I also found that Occupational Safety and Health Act standards and guidelines are applicable in some situations and that, in some cases, recovery has been sought through worker's compensation.

Furthermore, the law review footnotes provided me with references to two New Jersey cases. *Shimp v. New Jersey Bell* was one of the early, landmark cases on smoking in the workplace and affords injunctive relief to nonsmokers adversely affected by co-employee smoking. But *Shimp* is questioned in a more recent unreported case, *Smith v. Blue Cross & Blue Shield.*

After I skimmed four or five of the law review articles, I checked the A.L.R.s. Because the A.L.R. index had no entries under "smoking," I found it important to search under other terms, including "occupational safety and health," "workers' compensation," "tobacco and tobacco products," and "labor and employees." Three or four annotations seemed relevant. Two that I found of particular value were *Right of Employee to Injunction Preventing Employer from Exposing Employee to Tobacco Smoke in Workplace* and *Employer's Liability to Employee for Failure to Provide Work Environment Free from Tobacco Smoke.* While both were relatively short, they did provide some additional background.

Because I had determined that most state legislatures had enacted legislation addressing smoking in the workplace, I started my search for primary authority with New Jersey statutes. The index to West's *New Jersey Statutes Annotated* contained a reference to "smoking" with a sub-reference to "places of employment." I was surprised and pleased to find that the New Jersey legislature had enacted §§ 26:3D-23 et seq., which became effective March 1, 1986. I was surprised because this legislation was enacted after the articles I read had been published, and after *Shimp* had been decided, so I had not seen thus far any discussion of the legislation. I looked for cases in the annotations to the statutes, but found none. I would have next attempted to examine some of the legislative history to determine what prompted the legislative enactments, but I did not have ready access to New Jersey legislative history.

By now, I had developed significant reservations about the status of *Shimp* and wondered if it still remained authoritative. I thus used *Shepard's New Jersey Citations* to check the status of *Shimp.* There were only two federal cases that had cited *Shimp. Shepard's* did cite several additional New Jersey cases; the case has not received any adverse judicial consideration.

Because the law review articles referred to the unreported case, I went in search of that case; at the same time I looked for other New Jersey cases that might have discussed smoking in the workplace. There were three options available to me: computer-assisted research tools (WESTLAW and LEXIS), *West's New Jersey Digest,* and looseleaf services.

Based on experience, I have found WESTLAW and LEXIS to be much easier to use than looseleaf services, so I started there. Although they often contain unreported cases, neither WESTLAW nor LEXIS had *Smith;* nor did they have any other relevant New Jersey cases.

I then tried the digests. I used the headnotes for *Shimp* in *West's Atlantic Reporter,* second series, to find topics and Key Numbers to use in *West's New Jersey Digest.* There were several relevant headnotes in *Shimp* (Workmen's Compensation 2088, Master and Servant 101(1) and 203(1), and Labor Relations 7 and 791), but none led to additional relevant cases.

My final search strategy was to use a looseleaf service. I had some difficulty in finding the appropriate looseleaf service. The looseleaf services on fair employment practices and on occupational safety and health that I first attempted to use did not cover smoking. However, BNA's *Individual Employment Rights Manual* was a gold mine. That looseleaf contained the text of the New Jersey legislation, general federal legislation, and a chapter of commentary on smoking. I used the Master Index and the table of cases to find a reference to *Smith.* Unfortunately, the looseleaf did not carry the full text of *Smith,* but it had sufficient discussion of *Smith* to cast doubt on *Shimp.* I would want to get a copy of *Smith* from the clerk of the court.

Because there were no cases interpreting the New Jersey statute, I looked in the looseleaf for cases decided by courts in other states, concentrating on states with similar legislation restricting smoking in the workplace (such as Minnesota, Missouri, Kansas, Washington, and New York). I did find cases to use in arguing by analogy. The looseleaf provided a quick means of doing this comparative research.

Thus, my strategy was to first gain background information about the research situation, while gleaning some important references to primary authority through the use of secondary authority. I concentrated my search for primary authority on the jurisdiction in question, New Jersey, and expanded my research only after I found scant questionable authority there. I would perhaps continue by exploring federal legislation and federal case law, as well as worker's compensation law at the state level.

C. Peter Erlinder

Because I am not very familiar with employment, environmental, or health issues, I began by reviewing the fragmentary information I could recall from my general understanding of workplace regulation. I remembered that both state and federal law govern employment situations, but I had little specific knowledge about particular statutory or common law principles that might apply to this situation. I made a short list of the principles I could remember:

(1) Federal OSHA (Occupational Safety and Health Administration) regulations govern health and safety issues in some way.

(2) Some state regulations of workplace conditions also exist, but the extent of the coverage of state regulations was not clear to me.

(3) Some common law causes of action can arise in the employment context, such as breach of contract, interference with contract, and tort claims.

(4) Many tort claims from workplace injury are covered by state worker's compensation statutes.

(5) There is no constitutional right to employment, and I did not think that there is a constitutional right to clean air.

(6) The Surgeon General has been providing warnings against smoking for years and had recently stated that nicotine was addictive.

I decided to begin by focusing on the federal level because I knew of OSHA, a federal workplace safety regulation that would be relatively easy to locate. I also thought that once I found commentaries or case law that discussed federal limitations on smoking in the workplace, it would be relatively easy to locate similar issues in New Jersey statutes or case law.

I decided to begin with secondary sources to increase my understanding of the area of law I had identified as a starting place. The first source I actually opened was the most recent update of the *Index to Legal Periodicals*. I reasoned that limitations on smoking would be found in fairly recent commentary sources. I also knew that OSHA was not very old. In addition, I was interested in the most recent authority I could find. I decided to work my way back from the most recent update.

I began by looking for headings with several possible alternatives in mind. I looked under "smoking" and found no heading, but I did find a reference to "smoke prevention," which referred me to "air pollution," under which I found references to several articles that seemed as though they might be useful. I made note of Gladys W. Gruenberg, *Smoking in the Workplace: The Issues Heat Up,* Arb. J., Sept. 1988, at 8; E. Patrick McGuire, *Hazards in the Workplace,* Trial, June 1988, at 24; and Arthur J. Marinelli, Jr., *Worker Protection and the Law of the Occupational Safety and Health Act,* 21 Suffolk U. L. Rev. 1053 (1987).

I also noted some articles under "air pollution" that mentioned the Environmental Protection Agency (EPA). This reminded me that I had forgotten another major federal regulatory body and another possible source of legal limitation on smoking. I then remembered that Minnesota has a Clean Indoor Air Act and that other states also might have similar environmental regulations that might affect my research. I made note of these ideas.

I then began reading the articles I had already found. The articles in *Arbitration Journal* and *Trial* proved not to be very helpful. (The first was limited to employer/employee rights under union contracts, and the *Trial* article was too general.) The third article, however, was quite useful. The article described enough about how OSHA works to allow me to conclude that it was possible that the cancer-causing effects of passive smoking might be analogized to other health risks. I made note to check on possible regulations on smoking.

I went back to the *Index to Legal Periodicals* to try to find more relevant articles, continuing to look under "air pollution" and "OSHA." I found even more articles, and I began collecting the periodical volumes to continue my reading.

On top of the pile was Les Nelkin, Note, *No Butts About It: Smokers Must Pay,* 12 Colum. J. Envtl. L. 317 (1987). I read it first. That article mentioned that New Jersey had enacted an anti-smoking law. I made note of the reference and congratulated myself for having found the first reference to a primary source in the jurisdiction that concerned me. I decided to continue reading the articles because they were already in front of me and I still needed a better understanding of all potential legal theories.

Another article referred to the Surgeon General's report I had vaguely recalled earlier. I also noticed a reference to a New Jersey case that established a common law cause of action to work in a safe environment. Now I had both the cite to a New Jersey statute and a New Jersey case that seemed to have a direct bearing on my assignment. I decided that the discussion of the law stemming from the case and statute in New Jersey would give me what I needed to get started. I abandoned my commentary search.

The case I located, *Shimp,* clearly established that my client had a common law right to a smoke-free environment under New Jersey law; furthermore, she could bring an injunction to force the employer to limit smoking to non-work areas. I Shepardized *Shimp* to see whether it had been overturned or modified. I found that it had been cited favorably in more recent cases. In *Lepore v. National Tool & Mfg. Co.,* 224 N.J. Super. 463, 540 A.2d 1296 (App. Div. 1988), the court indicated that a statute, the New Jersey Worker Health and Safety Act, had essentially codified *Shimp.* Moreover, *Lepore* made clear that an employee has a cause of action in tort for lost wages, reinstatement, punitive damages, and counsel fees for retaliatory firing arising from reporting possible safety violations. I then read the provisions of the statutes in question in the *New Jersey Statutes Annotated.*

At this point I concluded that we could compel the employer to provide a smoke-free working environment under New Jersey law. Furthermore, if Anna Hale were fired as a result of this action we probably would be able to get her reinstated and obtain back pay, punitive damages, and attorney's fees.

Then I talked to a colleague about the problem. She asked me what would happen if, in spite of the potential remedies, the client no longer wished to work for the employer. Because I had not considered that possibility, I had to do more research.

I knew that state statutes governed the ability of a worker to claim benefits for constructive termination. This knowledge came from personal experience and news sources. I went to *West's New Jersey Digest* to locate the law on constructive termination. I read the digests of several cases and concluded that New Jersey recognizes health risks as a legitimate basis for quitting work under the state unemployment compensation system. Even if she decided to quit, my client would be able to receive unemployment benefits.

Christina L. Kunz

My first step was to read the last paragraph of the problem to find out the scope of the problem and the issues to be researched. I then read the problem twice—the first time to get a general sense of the facts and the second time to start analyzing which facts were significant to the problem. Meanwhile, I began to mentally "spin" through possible solutions. When I was through reading, I made a jot list of ideas and solutions. I then sorted this jot list into a list of research directions, separated by issue, starting with the "quickest fix" and ending with the least likely solution. Here's what I came up with:

> instigate no-smoking rule at work?
> > ck card catalog for smoking literature (seems more likely to be helpful than law revs.)

ck my state Clean Indoor Air Acts for cross-refs to other statutes,
    encyclopedia topics, law revs., etc.
ck NJ statutes for same
ck NJ state encyc. on smoking
    if nothing there, then try NJ digest
    if nothing there, then try Am Jur or CJS
ck fed statutes and regs (doubtful)
    OSHA standards
    EPA indoor air regs
    National Labor Relations Act bargaining topic?
    what procedure?
any state NJ equiv of NLRA, etc.?
quit work & seek remuneration
    unemploymt comp
        should she quit?
        what grounds?
        what procedure?
        how much $? how long?
    worker's comp
        allowable injury?
        what procedure?
tort claim? unlikely

I then went to the library. I looked in the card catalog under "smoking" and found two sources: (1) the 1983 Surgeon General's report on smoking's health consequences and (2) a BNA pamphlet, *Where There's Smoke: Problems and Policies Concerning Smoking in the Workplace* (1986 and 1987 versions). My initial research direction paid off well. I know that BNA is a respected publisher of labor and employment law looseleaf services and reporters.

Why did I favor the card catalog as my first research direction? I knew that my research in this unfamiliar area would be made much easier by a good commentary source; otherwise I would be forced to research each substantive area of law separately and from scratch. Coverage in a treatise was unlikely because a treatise tends to cover a single broad substantive area, rather than tie together the many diverse areas my jot list showed. Encyclopedias might pay off, if one of their major topics was "smoking," but I was concerned that the coverage might focus on fairly conventional (and perhaps dated) means of legal recourse, rather than emerging theories on the cutting edge. I wanted a source that could pinpoint trends as well as established lines of analysis. Legal periodicals showed more promise because they do pick up on emerging legal theories fairly quickly. However, if I didn't luck out with an index topic on smoking, research in legal periodicals could be very difficult. I also briefly considered A.L.R., but decided against using it because it focuses on case law and usually does not examine the breadth of statutory and regulatory solutions that I was contemplating. So I resolved to try the card catalog first. If that didn't work, I was prepared to try legal periodicals.

When I skimmed the table of contents of the BNA pamphlet, I decided that none of the appendices was useful to me but that most of the text was well worth reading. I focused on 42 pages of relevant text. After reading these pages, I gained new indexing vocabulary (second-hand smoke, sidestream smoke, environmental tobacco smoke (ETS), involuntary smoking, passive smoking). I read synopses of the major studies showing adverse health effects on passive smokers, which told me that my client's allergy and health complaints are far from uncommon. I learned that desktop smoke filters and central heating/cooling filters are not effective enough; other alternatives include designated no-smoking areas, designated smoking areas, and separation of smoking and nonsmoking employees by area.

In the discussion of legal developments, the pamphlet noted that an employer has a common law duty to provide a safe workplace. The court in *Shimp*, a 1976 New Jersey case, used that duty to compel an employer to protect an employee with smoke allergies by restricting smoking and providing smoke-free work and break locations. The pamphlet speculated that a similar case today could be even easier to win with the recent passive smoking health studies, but only if you could show more than one smoke-sensitive employee. I realized that I now had a New Jersey case that I could use to obtain digest Key Numbers and that I could Shepardize. In addition, New Jersey and eight other states had statutes on smoking by May 1986. There also are numerous local ordinances.

The pamphlet said that there were no federal OSHA regulations on point by the end of 1986, so I made a note to update that information. On the other hand, the federal Rehabilitation Act of 1973 (something I had not thought of) and similar state and local statutes allow an employee to raise a handicap discrimination claim if the employee can demonstrate bona fide illness due to tobacco smoke.

The pamphlet also noted legal developments in the areas of worker's compensation, unemployment compensation, and negligence, but by this time I had decided to narrow the focus of my research to concentrate on the option of helping my client obtain a smoke-free workplace. If *Shimp*, the New Jersey smoking statute, and the handicap statutes did not work out, then I might return to the option of my client quitting and obtaining remuneration.

I reshelved the BNA pamphlet and went to Shepardize *Shimp*. Aside from the parallel cite, there was nothing notable—no criticisms, overruling, etc. I copied down the New Jersey and federal cases, just in case I needed them later. There was also a cite to an A.L.R. annotation.

I decided to look for the New Jersey smoking statute first, before investigating *Shimp* further, because a new statute might well preempt the preexisting case law. I located the collection of New Jersey materials in the library. The collection included *New Jersey Statutes Annotated* (NJSA) and the accompanying *Session Law Service,* as well as two sequential digest series. The collection contained no regulations or ordinances, so I made a mental note that those materials might be available online if I needed them.

I found "smoking" in the NJSA index; the main volume included only the subtopic of "public places," but the pocket part contained references to "place of employment," all of them within §§ 26:3D-23 to 26:3D-31.

I pulled out that statute volume, intending to return to my table to read the act, but first I did two more things while I was up. (I try not to do much of this, because I tend to lose my research direction when I take a stack of books back to the table, but I was really curious about two things.) First, I looked up "smoking" in the index to *West's New Jersey Digest, 2d.* I found nothing, even in the pocket part. As it turns out, this subject appears under "health and environment" in the West system.

Second, I couldn't return to my table without finding and reading *Shimp*. As I read it, I knew right away that it was a very useful case. I jotted down the relevant West Key Numbers and topics (labor relations, workers' compensation, evidence, injunction, and—the most important one—master and servant). I should have guessed—a lot of employment law concepts are under "master and servant."

Unfortunately, the New Jersey statute turned out to be probably inapplicable, even when I updated it through the current month. The statute applies only to structurally enclosed locations where 50 or more individuals perform service or labor for consideration under any kind of employment relation. My client works with seven artisans. I need to find out from her how many employees work in that building; if it is fewer than 50, this statute is of limited help. I also need to check with her to make sure this is not an area generally accessible to the public; if so, then another similar statute may apply, NJSA §§ 26:3D-38 to 26-3D-45. At any rate, the place-of-employment statute does have an introductory section that makes legislative findings about smoking as a substantial health hazard and a nuisance (I had not thought about nuisance as a cause of action before). Another section states that an employer who has adopted a nonsmoking policy in compliance with the statute shall not be subject to a personal injury action by anyone for secondhand tobacco smoke; the legislature must have thought that such an action might otherwise be feasible. The same section makes an exception for employee actions brought under title 34, which I decided to look at next.

I turned to the table of contents to title 34 and scanned its contents. The most relevant provisions seemed to be New Jersey's equivalent of OSHA and the worker's compensation provisions. The mini-OSHA encompasses my client's place of employment and her employer. Several sections deal with the employer's duty to furnish a safe and healthful work environment and the building owner's duty to furnish adequate ventilation. The act provides for inspection and enforcement by the Commissioner of the Department of Labor and Industry. It also requires the promulgation of regulations that must meet the standards of the federal OSHA. Now I knew I could skip researching the federal OSHA. By this point, I was speculating that the stained-glass studio probably had a lot more in the air than just cigarette smoke. Most likely a mini-OSHA inspection would find something wrong with the workplace air that would require greater ventilation, and the smoking also might be a concern.

Next I turned to the table of contents for the worker's compensation act and scanned for definitional and operative sections. I'm not a worker's compensation expert at all, but the language of the act seemed potentially applicable, and *Shimp* had discussed the applicability of worker's compensation to that fact situation.

By this point, I had enough legal alternatives to convince the employer that this smoking problem could get very expensive and aggravating if it wasn't solved. Because my client's first goal was to stay in this job if at all possible (and because out-of-work employees have a hard time paying legal bills), I decided to finish up my case law research surrounding *Shimp* and to put off for now what options would be available if she quit.

I selected several Key Numbers to pursue the case law a bit further. Using the second series of *West's New Jersey Digest,* I found that Master and Servant 101 and 134 had been moved to a new topic, Employers' Liability. I located that topic and used the conversion table on the first page of the topic to find relevant sections 30 to 36 and 70. There was nothing worthwhile there besides *Shimp,* even in the pocket part. I gave up on the digest and went on to skim the cases I had jotted down from Shepardizing *Shimp.* They did not add anything to what I had.

The only other source I wish I had access to was the New Jersey regulations. They might be available online or in some looseleaf service. Regardless, though, I think my case is solid enough right now without them.

D. COMMENTARY

At first glance, it may seem that my colleagues' research approaches are more different than similar. While there are many differences among the four research scenarios set forth above, the differences are matters of detail. The fundamental similarities in the four approaches are much more important. Each writer worked through essentially the same steps. Furthermore, each writer had a clear sense of the tasks he or she needed to accomplish at each step and chose research tools to accomplish those tasks. In other words, each writer's research process was driven by tasks, not by tools.

Each writer began by figuring out what he or she already knew about the law; no one saw the task as beginning from scratch. Peter, for example, listed general legal principles he had picked up along the way that might bear on the problem. Chris began by focusing on the assignment and the options she thought the law might offer Hale. Ann considered her knowledge of the research tools in employment law. Even after a brief time in law school, you will acquire useful information about legal issues and authorities. Furthermore, your general knowledge of public issues will come in handy in many instances.

Next, each writer chose words to express the factual and legal issues he or she perceived in the problem. The law operates through language; your research must be conducted through words. In this situation, there was an obvious indexing term—smoking—deriving from the facts of the case. Even so, a good researcher thinks of alternative terms. Compare, for example, the different indexing terms used by Matt and Peter in approaching the two major indexes to legal periodicals. Note also what Chris discovered about the West digesting system; the basic term for employment law had changed from master/servant to employer's liability. Words are one of the chief tools you use in legal research; be aware of how you choose your terms, and be deliberate in your choices.

Each writer also took note of the jurisdiction of the problem before beginning to research. Events occurring in Cherry Hill, New Jersey, could be covered by federal, New Jersey, and Cherry Hill law. The writers focused on federal and state law, understandably so, for local law tends to be less important in most situations. Note, however, that Ann observed that there may be local ordinances on point that should be reviewed if possible. Furthermore, while all writers focused on this mandatory law, they remained open to the possibility of broadening their research—that is, using law from sister jurisdictions to aid in interpreting the mandatory authorities. This sense of jurisdictional priorities makes it possible to perform efficient yet properly expansive research.

Although each writer knew that he or she was looking for primary authority (federal, state, or local statutes; cases; or administrative law), each writer started with secondary authority. Why? As the very organization of this book is meant to convey, secondary authority is typically the first place to look. As the writers explain and their research scenarios demonstrate, secondary authority provides an overview of an area of law, insight into the pertinent legal theories, and citations to primary authority. Furthermore, in areas such as this where knowledge of scientific facts and public policy trends can further one's legal analysis, commentary can provide some useful "extra-legal" information. Each writer thus perceived that his or her first research task was to obtain the information provided through commentary.

At the same time, note that the writers chose different secondary authorities: articles and A.L.R. annotations (Matt), articles only (Peter), a monograph (Chris), and the commentary section of a looseleaf service (Ann). It is predictable that each writer chose a source that is generally quite up-to-date and specialized, since smoking in the workplace is a relatively new and narrow legal problem. In making his or her specific choice, each writer implicitly or explicitly assessed the strengths and weaknesses of the possibilities, as well as his or her general preferences.

Commentary can play other roles as well. While all of the writers relied on commentary mostly in the initial stages of research, you should observe that commentary can be useful at later stages as well. Observe, for example, that Ann consulted periodicals toward the end of her process to verify her primary research. Furthermore, the relationship between primary and secondary authorities is a two-way street. While one generally uses secondary authority to locate primary authority, the reverse can also be done. For example, Ann used *Shimp* in the table of cases in a periodical index to find periodical articles.

One final point about the search for primary authority: Services related to primary sources can, of course, be used to obtain citations to primary sources. Consider, for example, Chris' use of *Shepard's* to obtain additional case citations and the use by all writers of statutory annotations.

The ultimate focus of the research process for all writers was, of course, mandatory primary authority. While an exhaustive analysis of the problem would entail the use of federal as well as state law, and perhaps even local law, it would be sensible to focus attention at this preliminary stage on the *Shimp* case and the New Jersey statutes on occupational health and safety in general and workplace smoking in particular. All writers found these authorities—as indeed they must to accomplish this project successfully. Unlike secondary authority, primary authority is not optional. Having found one case, you may not stop until you know that you have found all of the pertinent cases. Nor may you stop after finding a pertinent statute, without determining whether there is pertinent case law. Many legal issues, like this one, involve the interaction of case and statutory law. Indeed, it could well be useful here to look also at administrative regulations (which the writers did not do, partly because of concerns about their availability, partly because the cases and statutes provided the crucial legal rules).

Although finding and reading primary authority are necessary steps, you will have some discretion at this stage in selecting the sources you will use. Note, for example, that the same statutes and cases could be found in the West publications and the BNA looseleaf service. Indeed, some authorities were also available online. Again, the task to be accomplished is fixed; the writers used their judgment in choosing the tools to accomplish the task.

Finally, note that all writers updated their research results regularly. Some updated near the end of the process; others updated each source as it was discovered. The classic means of updating cases is through *Shepard's;* the use of electronic citators is newer and perhaps more expedient. The classic means of updating statutes is through pocket parts and update pamphlets. Note, however, that other means exist as well. Both Ann and Matt used looseleaf services to find the latest information readily available to them. And Ann used the telephone—to call the publisher of the A.L.R. annotations. Again, the task must be accomplished, and there are various ways to do it.

As you might expect, the writers talked periodically while working on this problem. At one point, Chris indicated that she "lucked out" in finding the BNA monograph that proved very useful in her research. At times, you too may feel that your research turns out well only because you "lucked out." Of course, luck does play a part in research. But you also can enhance your chances of "lucking out," just as Chris did, by making a calculated guess. We hope that working through this book has provided you with information about and insights into legal research, so that your luck will be "smart luck." We hope that you have some sense of the tasks you will need to accomplish as you research and knowledge of the tools that will enable you to accomplish those tasks. If so, as Deborah's husband likes to say, you will be able to "make your own luck."

Problem Sets

There are five Problem Sets for Chapter 3. They cover the following areas of research:

Problem Set 1   Encyclopedias
Problem Set 2   Treatises
Problem Set 3   Legal Periodicals
Problem Set 4   A.L.R. Annotations
Problem Set 5   Restatements

With the exception of Problem Set 5, you will be selecting one of the following Research Situations in each of these Problem Sets. We suggest that you leave pages 473-475 in your book (or at least do not turn them in to your professor), so you will have ready access to the texts of the Research Situations as you work through Problem Sets 1 through 4.

Note: These Research Situations will appear again in the Chapter 10 Problem Set on non-legal materials.

Research Situation A:

Your client, Ms. Cambridge, sought the help of a marriage counselor, Dr. Braxton. Ms. Cambridge often met with Dr. Braxton in his home without her husband. Occasionally, Dr. Braxton would encourage Ms. Cambridge to engage in sexual relations with him during her sessions as a way to open up, relieve tension, and compensate her for the love she never got as a child. She did so at his urging. Ms. Cambridge changed counselors two months ago and now would like to know whether she can sue Dr. Braxton for malpractice.

Research Situation B:

Your client, Mr. Piper, has no permanent address or residence. The local police recently discovered Mr. Piper wandering the streets of the warehouse district. When they approached him, he became hostile and violent. When asked for identification, he screamed that he was invisible. The officers took Mr. Piper to the county hospital for a psychiatric evaluation, where he was diagnosed as a paranoid schizophrenic. He again became hostile, punching a nurse while demanding to be released. The psychiatrist who examined Mr. Piper recommends that he remain in the hospital for further testing and to ensure his and others' safety from his violent behavior. Mr. Piper refuses to remain hospitalized, insisting that he is competent to care for himself. He would like to know whether the hospital has the right to commit him against his will.

Research Situation C:

Your client, Mr. Carsberg, was a mechanic at Quality Transmission Company. He was an "at-will" employee, meaning that he could be fired for any or no reason. His job was to work on transmissions after the manager diagnosed the problem. One day Mr. Carsberg observed the manager placing metal filings in the transmission fluid of a car before it was tested. As Mr. Carsberg predicted, the test then indicated that the transmission would need a complete overhaul, a long and expensive undertaking. Mr. Carsberg asked a former employee about this practice, who confirmed that this was common. Mr. Carsberg was outraged and reported the practice to the Better Business Bureau. Mr. Carsberg was fired the next day. He would like to take action against his former employer for wrongful discharge.

Research Situation D:

Your client, Ms. Hunter, lives in an apartment owned by Prism Management Company. Her building is in a high-crime neighborhood of Central City. While coming home late one night, Ms. Hunter observed a man lingering around the entrance to her building. He appeared to be looking for directions, but as Ms. Hunter approached the entrance he took a gun from his overcoat. He forced Ms. Hunter into some overgrown bushes on the side of the dimly lit building, where he severely beat and robbed her. Other tenants in the building previously had made calls to the management company about the lack of safe conditions around the building, but no action was taken to make it safer. Ms. Hunter would like to take action against Prism Management for its failure to protect her from this criminal act.

Research Situation E:

Your clients, a tenants' group from Central City, live in a five-story apartment building owned and managed by Cost-Mor Company. Cost-Mor's maintenance staff, protesting their low wages, went on strike one month ago. The garbage hauler has refused to cross their picket line to empty the building's garbage receptacle. As a result, the garbage has accumulated to a height equal to that of the first-floor windows. Central City has declared a health emergency because of the harmful refuse odors and because of the rodents and cockroaches that have since infested the building. The tenants would like to know if they must continue to live in these uninhabitable conditions.

Research Situation F:

Your client, Ms. Ling, owns a house next door to a family with children of ages three, four, and seven. The children often play in their backyard. Ms. Ling has a toolshed in her backyard that usually is locked, but once every week or two she leaves the shed unlocked so that a teenager down the block can mow her lawn with the riding mower. She leaves the key in the mower on those days. One morning before the teenager came over to mow the lawn, the seven-year-old from next door got into the unlocked shed, started the mower with the key, fell off, and injured himself severely. The boy's parents assert that, even though their son was trespassing, Ms. Ling should pay for the injuries because she created a nuisance that attracted children.

Research Situation G:

Your client, Pizza Works, is a local pizza restaurant and delivery service. Although there is no state law requiring that food-service employees be clean-shaven, Pizza Works strictly enforces its own dress code, which requires all customer-service employees to be clean-shaven. Mr. Borm applied for a customer-service position and was qualified for the job, but he refused to shave his beard. Mr. Borm's religion requires him to wear a beard. Pizza Works then offered him an alternative position on the late-night cleanup crew. Mr. Borm wants to know whether he has a discrimination claim against Pizza Works for refusing to accommodate his religious practices.

Research Situation H:

Your client, Ms. Orns, is a drill-press operator for Plastiform, Inc. Plastiform bought the drill press from Precision Machine Co., at which time Precision's sales representative knew that Plastiform was ordering the drill press in order to drill holes in plastic. Ms. Orns drills holes in plastic parts and uses the drill press at its highest speed to keep the drill bit from "binding." In the trade, plastic generally is known to bind at lower drill speeds. One day, a plastic part that Ms. Orns was drilling "bound," flew off the drill press, and severely injured Ms. Orns. Although Ms. Orns is receiving worker's compensation payments, she also wants to sue Precision because it had a duty to recommend that Plastiform buy the "optional bind-indicator with emergency-stop device" for the drill press, as well as a duty to warn Plastiform of the dangers of not purchasing the device.

Research Situation I:

For about a year, the police have suspected your client, Mr. Wallace, of being a drug dealer. The police, after obtaining a valid search warrant, recently searched Mr. Wallace's house, but found no evidence of illegal substances or drug money. Three days later Mr. Wallace suffered severe abdominal pains and subsequently lost consciousness. A neighbor rushed him to the nearby hospital. The medical staff suspected an appendicitis attack, but surgery revealed that Mr. Wallace's stomach contained 21 balloons of crack cocaine, as well as over $1,700 in paper currency. The surgeon removed these items, then immediately notified the police. Mr. Wallace was arrested for possession of illegal drugs. You want to know whether the physician-patient privilege was breached when the doctor notified police.

Research Situation J:

Your clients, Mr. and Mrs. Walker, lost their daughter in an auto accident. Julia, 16 years old, sustained severe head injuries after a car entered an interstate freeway from the exit ramp, colliding with the car in which Julia was a passenger. The driver of the car was legally intoxicated. Paramedics administered first aid to Julia and rushed her to the county hospital where she died later that day. The Walkers already have initiated a wrongful death action in Julia's name. They now want to know whether they can recover from the driver for their own loss of their daughter's companionship, society, and services during the remainder of their lives.

PROBLEM SET 1: ENCYCLOPEDIAS

Name _____   Professor _____

Circle the letter of the Research Situation you selected from those set out on pages 473-475:

A   B   C   D   E   F   G   H   I   J

Questions 1 through 5 build heavily on the material in Chapter 2. You should read Chapter 2 before completing this Problem Set.

You may skip Questions 1 through 4 if you already have worked on the same Research Situation in Problem Set 2 (treatises), 3 (legal encyclopedias), or 4 (A.L.R. annotations). You should copy your previous answer to Question 5 onto this Problem Set to provide a starting point for your research here. If you have not yet completed all of the above Problem Sets, you should keep a copy of this Problem Set when you hand it in, so that you will not have to redo Questions 1 through 5 in each Problem Set.

1. Perform a factual and preliminary legal analysis on your Research Situation, using the six categories from Chapter 2. See page 17.

Persons or Parties: _____

_____

_____

Item or Subject Matter: _____

_____

_____

Timing and Location: _____

_____

_____

Relief Sought: _____

_____

_____

Legal Theories: _____

_____

_____

Procedure: _____

_____

_____

2. Locate the legal terms from Question 1 that you need defined. Using law dictionaries and glossaries (but not thesauri), locate the relevant definitions. Then record them here, restating the definitions in your own words as much as possible.

_____

_____

_____

_____

_____

_____

_____

_____

_____

_____

_____

_____

_____

3. Construct a "ladder of abstraction" for each category or sub-category in Question 1. Push yourself to expand these ladders vertically, adding as many rungs as possible. Then expand these ladders horizontally, adding as many synonyms as possible. Consult dictionaries, glossaries, and thesauri as needed. See pages 18-30 in Chapter 2 if you need to refresh your memory on this process.

_____

_____

_____

_____

_____

_____

_____

_____

_____

_____

_____

_____

_____

_____

_____

_____

_____

_____

_____

_____

_____

_____

_____

_____

_____

_____

_____

_____

_____

_____

_____

_____

_____

_____

_____

_____

_____

_____

_____

_____

_____

4. Where did you find your answers to Questions 1 through 3? Use correct citation form to record the sources and their exact pages. You need not cite more than three sources.

_____

_____

_____

_____

_____

_____

_____

_____

_____

_____

5. Create a flowchart or outline (see pages 33-35) of the legal categories (relief sought, legal theories, and procedure). If you run into difficulties, go back and expand your answers to Questions 1 through 3. You now have completed the first segment of this Problem Set and can return the books you used thus far to the appropriate place.

The Topic Outline Approach

6. Locate the two national encyclopedias, C.J.S. and Am. Jur. 2d. Choose one. If your research doesn't go well in one encyclopedia, change to the other encyclopedia. (Do not use a state encyclopedia.) Which major topics in the List of Titles (C.J.S.) or the Table of

Abbreviations (Am. Jur. 2d) seem to pertain to your Research Situation? Be sure to look for topics related to your ladders of abstraction and your outline or flowchart.

_____

_____

_____

_____

_____

7. Using the encyclopedia's topic outlines, not the index, find the section(s) of those topics that pertain specifically to your Research Situation. Read all relevant material, including material in any supplement. Don't hesitate to reassess or expand your answer to Question 6. What guidance does the material provide on your Research Situation? (If you were doing actual research, you would, of course, read the sources cited to determine whether they are applicable.)

_____

_____

_____

_____

_____

_____

_____

_____

_____

_____

_____

_____

_____

_____

_____

_____

_____

8. Give the correct citation to the encyclopedia sections that you used. (See page 42. See also Rule 3.4 in _The Bluebook_ on how to cite multiple sections and subsections.)

_____

_____

_____

_____

9. Does the material you read in this encyclopedia alter or expand your outline or flowchart in Question 5? If so, record the revised outline or flowchart here. Return all encyclopedia volumes to the appropriate place.

The Index Approach

10. Switch to the other encyclopedia. Use the index to find encyclopedia topic(s) and section(s) that seem to pertain to your Research Situation. Be sure to look for items related to your ladders of abstraction and your outline or flowchart. Read all relevant material, including material in any supplement. What guidance does the material provide on your Research Situation? (If you were doing actual research, you would, of course, read the sources cited to determine whether they are applicable.)

_____

_____

_____

_____

_____

_____

_____

_____

11. Give the correct citation to the encyclopedia sections that you used. (See page 42. See also Rule 3.4 in *The Bluebook* on how to cite multiple sections and subsections.)

_____

_____

_____

_____

12. Does the material you read in this encyclopedia alter or expand your outline or flowchart in Question 5? If so, record the revised outline or flowchart here. Return all encyclopedia volumes to the appropriate place.

PROBLEM SET 2: TREATISES

Name _____ Professor _____

Circle the letter of the Research Situation you selected from those set out on pages 473-475:

A   B   C   D   E   F   G   H   I   J

Questions 1 through 5 build heavily on the material in Chapter 2. You should read Chapter 2 before completing this Problem Set.

You may skip Questions 1 through 4 if you already have worked on the same Research Situation in Problem Set 1 (encyclopedias), 3 (legal periodicals), or 4 (A.L.R. annotations). You should copy your previous answer to Question 5 onto this Problem Set to provide a starting point for your research here. If you have not yet completed all of the above Problem Sets, you should keep a copy of this Problem Set when you hand it in, so that you will not have to redo Questions 1 through 5 in each Problem Set.

1. Perform a factual and preliminary legal analysis on your Research Situation, using the six categories from Chapter 2. See page 17.

Persons or Parties: _____

_____

_____

Item or Subject Matter: _____

_____

_____

Timing and Location: _____

_____

_____

Relief Sought: _____

_____

_____

Legal Theories: _____

_____

_____

Procedure: _____

_____

_____

2. Locate the legal terms from Question 1 that you need defined. Using law dictionaries and glossaries (but not thesauri), locate the relevant definitions. Then record them here, restating the definitions in your own words as much as possible.

_____

_____

_____

_____

_____

_____

_____

_____

_____

_____

_____

3. Construct a "ladder of abstraction" for each category or sub-category in Question 1. Push yourself to expand these ladders vertically, adding as many rungs as possible. Then expand these ladders horizontally, adding as many synonyms as possible. Consult dictionaries, glossaries, and thesauri as needed. See pages 18-30 in Chapter 2 if you need to refresh your memory on this process.

_____

_____

_____

_____

_____

_____

_____

_____

_____

_____

_____

_____

_____

_____

_____

_____

4. Where did you find your answers to Questions 1 through 3? Use correct citation form to record the sources and their exact pages. You need not cite more than three sources.

_____

5. Create a flowchart or outline (see pages 33-35) of the legal categories (relief sought, legal theories, and procedure). If you run into difficulties, go back and expand your answers to Questions 1 through 3. You now have completed the first segment of this Problem Set and can return the books you used thus far to the appropriate place.

6. Circle the area(s) of the law involved in your Research Situation:

Property   Torts   Contracts   Constitutional Law
Civil Procedure   Criminal Law

7. Using any of the methods for finding treatises (see page 60), locate at least two treatises on the area of law in your Research Situation. Explain how you found the treatises and give their titles and lead authors (not their full cites).

_____

_____

_____

_____

_____

_____

8. Using the criteria for selecting the best treatise (see pages 68-69), select the treatise best suited to your needs. Explain how the treatises compared to each other and how you made your choice.

_____

_____

_____

_____

_____

_____

_____

9. Using the index or table of contents of the treatise selected in Question 8, locate a discussion that seems to pertain to your Research Situation. Be sure to look for entries or topics related to your ladders of abstraction and your outline or flowchart. Which entries seemed most to the point?

_____

_____

_____

10. Read all relevant material. (Feel free to reevaluate your choice in Question 8.) What guidance does the material provide on your Research Situation? (If you were doing actual research, you would, of course, read the sources cited to determine whether they are applicable.)

_____

_____

_____

_____

_____

_____

_____

11. How is this treatise updated or supplemented, if at all? If there is a supplement, does this supplement or update change your answer to Question 10 in any way? Explain.

_____

_____

_____

_____

12. Give the correct citation to the relevant portions of the treatise. (See page 60. See also Rule 3.4 in *The Bluebook* on how to cite multiple sections and subsections.)

_____

_____

_____

_____

13. Does the material you read in this treatise alter or expand your outline or flowchart in Question 5? If so, record the revised outline or flowchart here. Return all treatises to the appropriate place.

PROBLEM SET 3: LEGAL PERIODICALS

Name _____   Professor _____

Circle the letter of the Research Situation you selected from those set out on pages 473-475:

A   B   C   D   E   F   G   H   I   J

Questions 1 through 5 build heavily on the material in Chapter 2. You should read Chapter 2 before completing this Problem Set.

You may skip Questions 1 through 4 if you already have worked on the same Research Situation in Problem Set 1 (encyclopedias), 2 (treatises), or 4 (A.L.R. annotations). You should copy your previous answer to Question 5 onto this Problem Set to provide a starting point for your research here. If you have not yet completed all of the above Problem Sets, you should keep a copy of this Problem Set when you hand it in, so that you will not have to redo Questions 1 through 5 in each Problem Set.

1. Perform a factual and preliminary legal analysis on your Research Situation, using the six categories from Chapter 2. See page 17.

Persons or Parties: _____

_____

_____

Item or Subject Matter: _____

_____

_____

Timing and Location: _____

_____

_____

Relief Sought: _____

_____

_____

Legal Theories: _____

_____

_____

Procedure: _____

_____

_____

2. Locate the legal terms from Question 1 that you need defined. Using law dictionaries and glossaries (but not thesauri), locate the relevant definitions. Then record them here, restating the definitions in your own words as much as possible.

_____

_____

_____

_____

_____

_____

_____

_____

_____

_____

_____

_____

3. Construct a "ladder of abstraction" for each category or sub-category in Question 1. Push yourself to expand these ladders vertically, adding as many rungs as possible. Then expand these ladders horizontally, adding as many synonyms as possible. Consult dictionaries, glossaries, and thesauri as needed. See pages 18-30 in Chapter 2 if you need to refresh your memory on this process.

_____

_____

_____

_____

_____

_____

_____

_____

_____

_____

_____

_____

_____

_____

_____

_____

_____

_____

_____

_____

_____

_____

_____

_____

_____

_____

_____

_____

_____

_____

_____

_____

_____

_____

_____

_____

_____

_____

4. Where did you find your answers to Questions 1 through 3? Use correct citation form to record the sources and their exact pages. You need not cite more than three sources.

_____

_____

_____

_____

_____

_____

_____

_____

_____

_____

5. Create a flowchart or outline (see pages 33-35) of the legal categories (relief sought, legal theories, and procedure). If you run into difficulties, go back and expand your answers to Questions 1 through 3. You now have completed the first segment of this Problem Set and can return the books you used thus far to the appropriate place.

6. Assume that the major articles on your Research Situation were indexed in the year listed below:

Research Situation A: 1990
Research Situation B: 1989
Research Situation C: 1990
Research Situation D: 1986
Research Situation E: 1987
Research Situation F: 1987
Research Situation G: 1988
Research Situation H: 1990
Research Situation I: 1987
Research Situation J: 1989

Find the appropriate volume of *Index to Legal Periodicals* (I.L.P.) or *Current Law Index* (C.L.I.). Circle your choice of index.

I.L.P.   C.L.I.

Look in your index for entries related to your ladders of abstraction and your outline or flowchart. List two or three subject headings used in your index that appear to be good possibilities.

_____

_____

_____

7. Assume that the most useful subject heading for your Research Situation is the one listed below:

Research Situation A:	I.L.P.—Psychiatric malpractice
	C.L.I.—Psychotherapist and patient
Research Situation B:	I.L.P.—Civil commitment
	C.L.I.—Mentally ill
Research Situation C:	I.L.P.—Employment at will
	C.L.I.—Employees, dismissal of
Research Situation D:	I.L.P.—Landlord and tenant
	C.L.I.—Landlord and tenant
Research Situation E:	I.L.P.—Landlord and tenant
	C.L.I.—Landlord and tenant
Research Situation F:	I.L.P.—Attractive nuisance
	C.L.I.—Attractive nuisance
Research Situation G:	I.L.P.—Freedom of religion
	C.L.I.—Freedom of religion
Research Situation H:	I.L.P.—Products liability
	C.L.I.—Products liability
Research Situation I:	I.L.P.—Privileged communications
	C.L.I.—Confidential communications
Research Situation J:	I.L.P.—Wrongful death
	C.L.I.—Loss of consortium

Scan the listings under this heading. (Ordinarily, you would scan the listings under cross-referenced subject headings as well to ensure thoroughness.) Set out the entries for two articles that seem pertinent. (You need not use proper citation form.)

_____

_____

_____

_____

_____

8. To compare print and CD-ROM indexes, locate either *LegalTrac* or WILSONDISC. Acquaint yourself with the operation of the reader and printer. Enter the subject heading listed in Question 7 or one of the terms you listed in your answer to Question 6. Scan the headings and subheadings until you find a promising place to look for articles.

(a) List the heading and subheading you searched.

_____

_____

(b) How many articles appear there?

_____

(c) Provide the title of the most recent article listed.

_____

_____

9. Move to the legal periodicals collection, and locate one of the volumes listed below for your Research Situation. (Do not be alarmed if it did not appear on your list of references. I.L.P. and C.L.I. do not follow identical schedules in indexing articles.) Circle your choice.

Research Situation A:	19 Golden Gate University Law Review or
	14 Law and Psychology Review
Research Situation B:	19 Columbia Human Rights Law Review or
	2 Journal of Law and Health
Research Situation C:	15 Employee Relations Law Journal or
	58 University of Cincinnati Law Review
Research Situation D:	29 Howard Law Journal or
	38 Vanderbilt Law Review
Research Situation E:	55 Mississippi Law Journal or
	35 University of Kansas Law Review
Research Situation F:	20 Georgia State Bar Journal or
	22 Wake Forest Law Review
Research Situation G:	1987 Detroit College Law Review or
	39 Labor Law Journal
Research Situation H:	27 Duquesne Law Review or
	65 New York University Law Review
Research Situation I:	33 Medical Trial Techniques Quarterly or
	63 University of Detroit Law Review
Research Situation J:	22 John Marshall Law Review or
	13 Southern Illinois University Law Journal

In this volume, locate an article (lead article, student piece, or other form) pertaining to your Research Situation.

(a) Which type of article is it?

_____

(b) Give its proper citation. See page 79 in Chapter 3.

_____

_____

_____

10. Read the introduction and conclusion of your article; if you wish, skim the body as well. What guidance does the article give you regarding your Research Situation?

_____

_____

_____

_____

_____

11. Now look at the footnotes. List two or three sources found in the first three footnotes that you might pursue if you researched this topic further.

_____

12. Based on your quick review of the article, would you cite this article if you were writing a brief to a court about your Research Situation, should litigation arise? Why, or why not?

_____

13. OPTIONAL QUESTION: Locate the first volume of *Shepard's Law Review Citations* to cover your article. (Recall that you ordinarily would check all *Shepard's* volumes to date.) Look up your article by journal name, then volume, then page number. Remember that *Shepard's* does not cover all periodicals. Record the first two entries listed (if any). Use the table of abbreviations at the front of the volume to decipher the entry or entries, and provide the explanation.

_____

_____

_____

_____

_____

_____

14. Does the legal periodical material you read alter or expand your outline or flow-chart in Question 5? If so, record the revised outline or flowchart here. Return all materials to the appropriate place.

PROBLEM SET 4: A.L.R. ANNOTATIONS

Name _____   Professor _____

Circle the letter of the Research Situation you selected from those set out on pages 473-475:

A   B   C   D   E   F   G   H   I   J

Questions 1 through 5 build heavily on the material in Chapter 2. You should read Chapter 2 before completing this Problem Set.

You may skip Questions 1 through 4 if you already have worked on the same Research Situation in Problem Set 1 (encyclopedias), 2 (treatises), or 3 (legal periodicals). You should copy your previous answer to Question 5 onto this Problem Set to provide a starting point for your research here. If you have not yet completed all of the above Problem Sets, you should keep a copy of this Problem Set when you hand it in, so that you will not have to redo Questions 1 through 5 in each Problem Set.

1. Perform a factual and preliminary legal analysis on your Research Situation, using the six categories from Chapter 2. See page 17.

Persons or Parties: _____

_____

_____

Item or Subject Matter: _____

_____

_____

Timing and Location: _____

_____

_____

Relief Sought: _____

_____

_____

Legal Theories: _____

_____

_____

Procedure: _____

_____

_____

2. Locate the legal terms from Question 1 that you need defined. Using law dictionaries and glossaries (but not thesauri), locate the relevant definitions. Then record them here, restating the definitions in your own words as much as possible.

_____

_____

_____

_____

_____

_____

_____

_____

_____

_____

_____

3. Construct a "ladder of abstraction" for each category or sub-category in Question 1. Push yourself to expand these ladders vertically, adding as many rungs as possible. Then expand these ladders horizontally, adding as many synonyms as possible. Consult dictionaries, glossaries, and thesauri as needed. See pages 18-30 in Chapter 2 if you need to refresh your memory on this process.

_____

_____

_____

_____

_____

_____

_____

_____

_____

_____

_____

_____

_____

_____

_____

_____

_____

_____

_____

_____

_____

_____

_____

_____

_____

_____

_____

_____

_____

_____

_____

_____

_____

_____

_____

_____

_____

_____

4. Where did you find your answers to Questions 1 through 3? Use correct citation form to record the sources and their exact pages. You need not cite more than three sources.

_____

_____

_____

_____

_____

_____

_____

_____

_____

_____

5. Create a flowchart or outline (see pages 33-35) of the legal categories (relief sought, legal theories, and procedure). If you run into difficulties, go back and expand your answers to Questions 1 through 3. You now have completed the first segment of this Problem Set and can return the books you used thus far to the appropriate place.

6. Locate A.L.R. Use the *Index to Annotations,* not the digest, to find annotations in the third, fourth, fifth, or federal series that seem to pertain to your Research Situation. Be sure to look for entries related to your ladders of abstraction and your outline or flowchart. What index entries seemed to be most on point?

_____

_____

_____

_____

_____

7. Read the scope notes in each of the annotations you have located. Select the annotation best suited to your needs. Explain how the annotations under consideration compared to each other and how you made your choice.

_____

_____

_____

_____

_____

_____

_____

_____

_____

_____

_____

8. Locate a discussion that seems to pertain to your Research Situation in the annotation you selected in Question 7. Use the annotation's index or table of contents. Be sure to look for entries or topics related to your ladders of abstraction and your outline or flowchart. Read all relevant material, including material in any supplement. (Feel free to reevaluate your choice in Question 7.) What guidance does the material provide on your Research Situation? (If you were doing actual research, you would, of course, read the sources cited to determine whether they are applicable.)

_____

_____

_____

_____

_____

_____

_____

_____

9. Give the correct citation to the annotation, including the specific portions that pertain to your Research Situation. (See page 96. See also Rule 3.4 in _The Bluebook_ on how to cite multiple sections and subsections.)

_____

_____

_____

_____

10. Does the material you read in this annotation alter or expand your outline or flowchart in Question 5? If so, record the revised outline or flowchart here. Return all A.L.R. volumes to the appropriate place.

PROBLEM SET 5: RESTATEMENTS

Name _____   Professor _____

Research Situation A:

Your client, Ms. Holmes, is a landowner with a large front yard. Mr. Nate, her neighbor, wanted to run a buried cable through her yard. Ms. Holmes consented to the cable, but with the restriction that Mr. Nate would only bury the cable in a specified area of the yard; Mr. Nate agreed to those restrictions. However, when Mr. Nate buried the cable, he went outside the designated area, which resulted in damage to Ms. Holmes' oak trees. Examine the Restatement of Torts, focusing on Ms. Holmes' consent to allow Mr. Nate to enter her yard: Has Mr. Nate trespassed on Ms. Holmes' land by exceeding the area restriction given by Ms. Holmes in the consent to enter her land?

Research Situation B:

Your client's child, Lynn, was physically abused by an employee at the Child Care Co-op. (C.C.C.). Although C.C.C. screened potential employees by checking police records, C.C.C. had not checked all of the prior job references. At trial, the court awarded Lynn and her parents compensatory and punitive damages. C.C.C. asserts that it had not negligently hired the employee in question and has appealed the punitive damages award. Examine the Restatement of Torts, focusing on sections that address circumstances when punitive damages are appropriately assessed against an employer.

Research Situation C:

Mr. Holden is a member of the community who does volunteer work with a community organization dealing with illiteracy. The "Book at Lunch" campaign was his idea and has been very successful. Recently, a local newspaper wrote an article on Mr. Holden, falsely accusing him of having an affair with his assistant. Mr. Holden is married and has asserted that the allegations of immorality are libelous. Examine the Restatement of Torts. Determine whether the newspaper is liable for the defamatory article under a claim of libel, even if Mr. Holden is unable to show any special harm. (Mr. Holden is not a "public figure.")

Research Situation D:

Your client, Mr. Renchie, wishes to convey property as a gift to his nephew, Julian, with the restriction that Julian first must convert to the Islamic faith. According to the Restatement of Property, is the provision contained within this donative transfer a valid restraint?

Research Situation E:

Mr. Virgil hired Mr. Roy as his agent to sell his home. During negotiations with the buyer, Mr. Roy misrepresented the age and condition of the roof. The buyer has now learned that the roof is defective and has asked to rescind the purchase contract. Mr. Virgil, the principal, had not authorized his agent to make the misrepresentations and has refused to rescind the contract. Under the Restatement of Agency, can the buyer, who is an innocent third party in this case, obtain rescission of the contract because of the fraudulent or misrepresentational statements made by the agent?

Research Situation F:

Source Insurance is the professional liability insurer for Mr. Scott, a licensed psychologist. Allegedly, Mr. Scott engaged in improper conduct with one of his clients. The client filed a complaint with Mr. Scott's professional board and threatened to file a civil suit as well. Mr. Scott brought a declaratory judgment action against Source when the insurer refused coverage. The court held that the policy covered the claims filed by Mr. Scott's client. Then the client filed the civil suit against Mr. Scott, who brought the insurance company into the lawsuit as a third-party defendant. Find the Restatement of Judgments section that discusses whether the declaratory judgment is res judicata in the civil suit.

Research Situation G:

Ms. Barnet is a research chemist who was employed for several years by ChemLab to develop a fabric treatment for sportswear. Under the terms of her contract, Ms. Barnet promised that she would refrain from ever working for a competitor if she were to leave ChemLab. Shortly after Ms. Barnet developed the fabric treatment, she accepted a position with ChemLab's competitor. ChemLab sued Ms. Barnet for breach of contract. According to the Restatement of Contracts, is ChemLab's restraint-of-trade clause valid?

Research Situation H:

Ms. Manbeck began cohabitating with Mr. Hemlish in 1945, but they never married. They bought property together, raised their two children, and generally held themselves out to be married. Until two years ago, Manbeck and Hemlish lived in a state that recognized "common law marriages," but at that time they moved to a state that does not. Mr. Hemlish died earlier this year; whether Ms. Manbeck will inherit his property depends on whether she is treated as his wife. According to the Restatement of Conflicts of Law, which state law is applied to determine whether the time the couple lived together creates a common law marriage?

Research Situation I:

Mr. Han contracted with Wilkerson Builders to renovate a commercial building that he had already leased to a French bakery. Wilkerson was unable to complete the renovations by the agreed-upon date. Wilkerson finished several weeks after the beginning of the lease, and the French bakery was forced to find another building to rent. Under the Restatement of Contracts, can Mr. Han seek lost profits because of the lost rent as part of the damages he plans to seek from Wilkerson?

Research Situation J:

Mr. Enteng drafted his will in 1935. Under the applicable clause, the will devised all of his property to his nieces and nephews. This type of donative transfer in a will is known as a "class gift." At the time of his death, Mr. Enteng's only heirs were his three nieces, one of whom was adopted. According to the Restatement of Property, does this class gift include the adopted niece?

Circle the letter of the Research Situation you selected:

A   B   C   D   E   F   G   H   I   J

Questions 1 through 5 build heavily on the material in Chapter 2. You should read Chapter 2 before completing this Problem Set.

1. Perform a factual and preliminary legal analysis on your Research Situation, using the six categories from Chapter 2. See page 17.

Persons or Parties: _____

_____

_____

Item or Subject Matter: _____

_____

_____

Timing and Location: _____

_____

_____

Relief Sought: _____

_____

_____

Legal Theories: _____

_____

_____

Procedure: _____

_____

_____

2. Locate the legal terms from Question 1 that you need defined. Using law dictionaries and glossaries (but not thesauri), locate the relevant definitions. Then record them here, restating the definitions in your own words as much as possible.

_____

_____

_____

_____

_____

_____

_____

_____

_____

_____

_____

_____

3. Construct a "ladder of abstraction" for each category or sub-category in Question 1. Push yourself to expand these ladders vertically, adding as many rungs as possible. Then expand these ladders horizontally, adding as many synonyms as possible. Consult dictionaries, glossaries, and thesauri as needed. See pages 18-30 in Chapter 2 if you need to refresh your memory on this process.

_____

_____

_____

_____

_____

_____

_____

_____

_____

_____

_____

_____

_____

_____

_____

_____

_____

_____

_____

_____

_____

_____

_____

_____

_____

4. Where did you find your answers to Questions 1 through 3? Use correct citation form to record the sources and their exact pages. You need not cite more than three sources.

_____

_____

_____

_____

_____

_____

_____

_____

_____

_____

_____

5. Create a flowchart or outline (see pages 33-35) of the legal categories (relief sought, legal theories, and procedure). If you run into difficulties, go back and expand your answers to Questions 1 through 3. You now have completed the first segment of this Problem Set and can return the books you used thus far to the appropriate place.

The First Series

6. Using the first-series Restatement index(es) for the subject indicated, locate index entries that seem to pertain to your Research Situation. Be sure to look for entries related to your ladders of abstraction and your outline or flowchart. Which entries seem helpful?

_____

_____

_____

7. Read all relevant first-series sections, including their comments and illustrations. What guidance does the material provide on your Research Situation? (If you were doing actual research, you would, of course, determine whether that Restatement section had been adopted by the courts of that jurisdiction.)

_____

_____

_____

_____

_____

_____

_____

_____

_____

_____

_____

_____

_____

_____

_____

_____

_____

_____

_____

_____

_____

_____

_____

_____

_____

8. Give the correct citation to the first-series Restatement material you used, including specific subsections, comments, and illustrations, if applicable. (See pages 109 and 112. See also Rule 3.4 in _The Bluebook_ on how to cite multiple sections.)

_____

_____

_____

_____

9. Does the material you read in the first-series Restatement alter or expand your outline or flowchart in Question 5? If so, record the revised outline or flowchart here. Return all Restatement volumes to the appropriate place.

The Second Series

10. Convert your first-series section numbers to second-series section numbers, using the methods mentioned on page 115. Also consult the second-series Restatement index(es) on the subject indicated to find pertinent sections, including those not present in the first series. Which additional entries seemed helpful?

_____

_____

_____

11. Read all relevant second-series sections, including their comments, illustrations, Reporter's Notes, and Statutory Notes (if any). What guidance does the material provide on your Research Situation? (If you were doing actual research, you would, of course, determine whether that Restatement section had been adopted by the courts of that jurisdiction.)

_____

_____

_____

_____

_____

_____

_____

_____

_____

_____

_____

_____

_____

_____

_____

12. Give the correct citation to the second-series Restatement material you used, including specific subsections, comments, and illustrations, if applicable. (See pages 109 and 112. See also Rule 3.4 in _The Bluebook_ on how to cite multiple sections.)

_____

_____

_____

13. List a case that cites a Restatement section you cited in Question 12.

_____

_____

14. What other types of sources are contained in the annotations to the second-series sections you cited in Question 12?

_____

_____

_____

_____

15. With regard to your Research Situation, how does the material you read in the second-series Restatement differ from what you read in the first-series Restatement? Return all Restatement volumes to the appropriate place.

_____

_____

_____

_____

_____

_____

Case Law

Name _____   Professor _____

Research Situation:

Lucille B. Brandow was recently dismissed from her position at American National First Bank, City Office. Ms. Brandow held the position of manager of the commercial loan division for several years. When Ms. Brandow received her dismissal notice, the vice president of personnel at the main office told her by phone that "the national office had reviewed her file and considered all of the relevant circumstances and recommended her dismissal." When asked for specifics, the vice president indicated that "specifics were not important; the decision had already been made."

Ms. Brandow is upset because she was given no specific reasons for her dismissal and had no opportunity to meet with her supervisors to hear their concerns and to respond. Before this period, Ms. Brandow's work record had been very good and she had routinely received high evaluations.

Ms. Brandow has shown you an employee policy manual that she said was given to her when she first started work. The policy manual, entitled "Employee Policies and Procedures for Loan Officers and Managers: American National First Bank," describes procedures for dismissal of loan officers and managers. It specifically outlines that an employee would only be dismissed "for cause." "In such circumstances," the policy manual reads, "an officer or manager with a less than satisfactory work record will first receive a written statement of reasons as to why performance has been considered to be unsatisfactory, and a probationary period of at least one quarter (three months) will be imposed before a permanent dismissal will take place."

You have been asked to conduct case law research, focusing on any contract rights Ms. Brandow may have.

Assume that Ms. Brandow may bring suit in the state jurisdictions listed. Select one of the jurisdictions to perform your case law research. You will know that you are on the right track for this Problem Set if you find a case with the following characteristics:

Jurisdiction	Characteristics
A. Illinois	1985 Illinois Appellate Court decision
B. Nebraska	1987 Nebraska Supreme Court decision
C. Massachusetts	1988 Massachusetts Supreme Judicial Court decision
D. North Carolina	1985 North Carolina Court of Appeals decision
E. Washington	1988 Washington Supreme Court decision
F. Tennessee	1988 Tennessee Court of Appeals decision
G. Wyoming	1986 Wyoming Supreme Court decision
H. South Dakota	1989 South Dakota Supreme Court decision
I. Michigan	1986 Michigan Supreme Court decision
J. Texas	1987 Texas Court of Appeals decision

Circle the letter of the jurisdiction you selected:

A   B   C   D   E   F   G   H   I   J

1. Facts obtained through a client interview often raise more than one issue. For this Problem Set, focus on the question of the employee policy manual (or handbook). Precisely state the issue that the Research Situation poses.

_____

_____

_____

2. Remember that the most important consideration in case law research is the persuasiveness of the authority found. Thus, one goal is to find binding precedent—mandatory primary authority—which in this instance is case law from your jurisdiction. Keep in mind the jurisdiction of the Research Situation that you selected.

(a) Give the titles for two or three digest sets you could use to find binding state case law precedent on this issue.

_____

_____

_____

(b) Which digest would you prefer to use and why?

_____

_____

_____

3. Before you open the Descriptive Word Index for the digest you have chosen, list as many potential research terms as you can think of. (You may need to use a legal dictionary or thesaurus to find appropriate legal terms. Remember to use legal vocabulary—for example, "employee" rather than "worker.")

_____

_____

_____

_____

4. Using a West digest, locate the Descriptive Word Index volumes that are part of the digest series. Use the research terms you think most appropriate to find two or more potential topics and Key Numbers in the Descriptive Word Index that pertain to your issue. State the topics and the Key Numbers.

_____

_____

_____

5. Using these topics and Key Numbers, now find the digests of cases that may provide primary mandatory authority for your Research Situation. Recall that the West digests are organized alphabetically by topic and then by Key Number. Remember to check the pocket part or pamphlet supplement for current digests. For your own research notes, it is prudent to jot down the names and citations of the cases that appear relevant for future reference lest you need to retrace your steps.

For this exercise, you should find and focus on the case that matches the characteristics given for the jurisdiction you have selected for this Research Situation. Use the topic "Master and Servant," Key Number 3(2) to complete the following questions:

(a) Give the name of the case and the citation as it appears in the digest; the citation may not be in correct *Bluebook* format. This is the cited case.

_____

_____

(b) Keep in mind that a digest is an editor's analysis of an issue in a case. To ensure accurate research, do not rely on the digest; you must read the entire case. Find your case in the appropriate reporter and read it quickly. If the cited case addresses the issue posed by your Research Situation, briefly describe the facts of the case and give the court's holding.

_____

_____

_____

_____

_____

_____

_____

_____

(c) If there is a dissenting opinion, separately note the reasoning in the dissenting opinion.

_____

_____

_____

_____

6. The next step is to analyze the current status of the case you found and its applicability to your Research Situation. A valuable research tool for accomplishing these tasks is a citator. Focus on the governing jurisdiction for your Research Situation.

(a) Which *Shepard's Citations* could you use to "Shepardize" the case you found in Question 5?

_____

_____

(b) Which *Shepard's Citations* would you most prefer to use and why?

_____

_____

_____

_____

_____

(c) Indicate which *Shepard's Citations* you selected to use to complete these questions.

_____

_____

7. Collect all of the *Shepard's* volumes and paper pamphlets that cover the case you found in Question 5; the *Shepard's Citations* will list cases that have cited this case. To ensure thorough research whenever you use *Shepard's Citations,* begin with the most recent paper supplement. Check the cover for the listing of "What Your Library Should Contain" and then Shepardize your case using the volumes listed; you will note that the dates or reporter volumes covered in each citator are indicated on the spine of the bound volumes and on the front cover of the paper pamphlets. It is best to work backward from the most recent supplementary pamphlet to the first volume containing the cited case. This task will likely require you to use more than one bound volume and more than one paper pamphlet.

For these exercises use the regional reporter citation of the cited case. You can use this citation in either the regional *Shepard's* citator or the state *Shepard's* citator. Because you are most interested in mandatory primary authority, for this Problem Set cite only cases from your jurisdiction from the list of cases in *Shepard's*.

(a) Shepardize the cited case: Examine the table entitled "Abbreviations—Analysis" that appears in the front of the *Shepard's* volumes. Note abbreviations for "History of Case." Now, scan the citations listed in the *Shepard's Citations* and note all historical abbreviations. Pay special attention to citations that affirm ("a"), modify ("m"), or reverse ("r") your case, or citations that are listed as being "s," the same case.

Give the citations to the cases listed in *Shepard's* that may affect the history of the cited case—for example, r 234 Cal. App. 1023.

_____

_____

_____

_____

(b) Now consider the treatment of the cited case. Review the meaning of "treatment" by looking again at the "Abbreviations—Analysis" table. Look especially for cases that criticize ("c"), overrule ("o"), or question ("q") your case. Identify one state court case from your jurisdiction that has a *Shepard's* treatment code, if any, and indicate the treatment given the cited case—for example, o 123 N.Y.S. 567. If there is no treatment, list the first citing case in *Shepard's*.

_____

_____

_____

_____

(c) Based on the information gathered in *Shepard's,* do you think that the cited case still carries mandatory authority? Why or why not? (It is always necessary, of course, to read the actual text of cases to make a fully informed decision.)

_____

_____

_____

_____

8. *Shepard's* can be used to find parallel citations. The parallel citation is contained only in the earliest volume of *Shepard's* for which it is available; it will be contained within parentheses. Table T.1 in *The Bluebook* will assist you in determining which states have parallel citations.

Find the parallel citation, if any, for the cited case. If there is no parallel citation, explain why there is not.

_____

_____

_____

9. Give the complete, proper citation to the case as it would appear in documents submitted to a court in that jurisdiction. Be sure to include parallel cites (if any) and the history of the case (if any). You can best accomplish this by incorporating the information obtained from *Shepard's* as given in your answers to Questions 7 and 8. You may need to review the section on prior and subsequent history in Rule 10.7 of *The Bluebook.*

_____

_____

_____

10. Assume that your Research Situation involves a federal law question.

(a) What digest titles would you most likely use to find federal cases decided since 1990?

_____

_____

(b) For the region in which your school is located, which federal district court carries mandatory authority?

_____

(c) For the region in which your school is located, which federal court of appeals carries mandatory authority? Illustration 5-1 on page 141 provides a map depicting the federal judicial circuits.

_____

11. If you were to limit your search to United States Supreme Court cases only, what digests would you use? Give the titles to two digest systems.

_____

_____

12. On some occasions, you may already know the name of an important case. If that is the situation, one quick means of finding the citation and the topic and Key Number is to make use of the Table of Cases volume(s) of the relevant digest. Continue to use the same jurisdiction selected above.

Locate the Table of Cases volume(s) of an appropriate West digest and find the case listed below:

A. Illinois: *Pundt v. Millikin University*
B. Nebraska: *Stratton v. Chevrolet Motor Division, General Motors Corporation*
C. Massachusetts: *Garrity v. Valley View Nursing Home, Inc.*
D. North Carolina: *Rucker v. First Union National Bank*
E. Washington: *Hibbert v. Centennial Villas*
F. Tennessee: *Hamby v. Geneseo, Inc.*
G. Wyoming: *McDonald v. Mobil Coal Producing, Inc.*
H. South Dakota: *Larson v. Kreiser's, Inc.*
I. Michigan: *Kari v. General Motors Corporation*
J. Texas: *Hicks v. Baylor University Medical Center*

Give the complete and correct citation for the case as it would appear in court documents to be submitted to a court in that jurisdiction. Be sure that you have the accurate title of the case, applicable parallel citations, and the date. Remember that you should also check *Shepard's* for any relevant subsequent or prior history.

_____

_____

_____

_____

Chapter 6

Introduction to Computer-Assisted Legal Research

Name _____   Professor _____

PROBLEM SET 1: ELECTRONIC CITATORS—LEXIS

Complete both Problem Sets 1 and 2 unless your professor tells you otherwise.

> Note: For this Problem Set any characters you are asked to type are enclosed in brackets. Do not include the brackets when you type your search. The names of the function keys are printed in capital letters.

Sign on to LEXIS. If you are using a LEXIS 2000 workstation, follow these directions. Otherwise, ask your librarian for assistance.

  (1) Turn on the printer. (Switch is on left front.)
  (2) Turn on the monitor. (Switch is on right side.)
  (3) Turn on the computer. (Switch is on right front.)
  (4) Wait for the "Star Wars" screen. Press the spacebar.
  (5) If necessary, use the arrow keys to move the yellow highlighting bar so that "LEXIS(R) 2000 Research Software for MS-DOS(R)" is highlighted. Press ENTER (a green key).
  (6) Wait while the computer connects to the system. When it displays the "Welcome to LEXIS and NEXIS" screen, type your personal ID (password) and press ENTER.
  (7) On the next screen, type your client ID—that is, your last name, your professor's last name, and the course name—and press ENTER. For example: [Jones,Smith,legal writing].

Once you are signed on, you will be looking at the first screen of the Libraries Menu. From this screen, or any LEXIS screen, it is easy to Shepardize a case. Just type the *Shepard's* command, followed by your case citation, and press ENTER. The *Shepard's* command is [sh]. Your case citation must include a volume number, reporter abbreviation, and page number, in that order, with spaces between them, and you must use the proper *Shepard's* abbreviation for the name of the reporter.

> Note: The *Shepard's* abbreviation for a reporter may be different from the abbreviation in *The Bluebook*. You may find the abbreviation for the name of a reporter in the *Reference Manual for the LEXIS/NEXIS Services,* or you may find it online. To find it online (do not do this now), you would type [sh] and press ENTER to enter the *Shepard's* service. Then you would type [h] for "help" and press ENTER. You would be directed to a list of tutorials from which you could select the list of *Shepard's* reporter abbreviations. Although you may use periods and spaces within the name of the reporter, you need not do so. Omitting periods and spaces saves time and thus makes your research more economical.

Now Shepardize the case of *Walker v. Westinghouse Electric Corp.,* 335 S.E.2d 79 (N.C. App. 1985). Type [sh 335 se2d 79] and press ENTER.

Note: On a LEXIS terminal, you may type the citation and press the SHEP key. If you are viewing a case and want to Shepardize it, you only have to press SHEP or type [sh] and press ENTER.

1. The top of the screen that you have reached tells you how many documents you have retrieved. How many documents did this citation retrieve?

---

2. Next the screen verifies the citation you Shepardized in the "CITATIONS TO" line, and then it identifies the print series and the division within that series to which the online display corresponds.

(a) Look at the "SERIES" line. To which print *Shepard's* title does the online *Shepard's* display correspond?

(b) Look at the "DIVISION" line. To which division within the print title does the online *Shepard's* display correspond?

---

3. Look at the "COVERAGE" line.

(a) With what volume of the print *Shepard's* does the online display for the case begin?

(b) What is the most recent supplement to *Shepard's Southeastern Reporter Citations* included in the display?

---

4. You may have noticed that the LEXIS *Shepard's* does not automatically tell you how many pages there are in the *Shepard's* document you are viewing. To find out, type [p] and press ENTER. How many online pages of full text are there in the document you are viewing?

To return to the page you had been viewing, press ENTER.

5. Now look at the first page of the *Shepard's* display. If it gives a parallel citation for the case you Shepardized, identify the parallel citation.

---

6. You can page through a *Shepard's* display on LEXIS by pressing the NEXT PAGE key. Page through the first document. Circle yes or no to indicate which of the categories of citing documents appear in the *Shepard's* display for the case in the regional reporter *Shepard's*.

Citations for decisions from other state courts	Yes	No
Citations from A.L.R. or L. Ed. 2d annotations	Yes	No
Citations from law reviews other than the *ABA Journal*	Yes	No

The last citations in this display are to treatises published by Shepard's/McGraw-Hill.

7. You can return to the first page of a *Shepard's* display by pressing the FIRST PAGE key. Do that. Then page forward in the *Shepard's* display until you find a citation to the

first case in which *Walker* was cited in a dissenting opinion. What is the citation for that case?

---

8. You can retrieve a citing case that is of interest to you by typing the number in the "NUMBER" column that corresponds to that case. Retrieve the case you found in Question 7.

(a) What number did you ENTER?

You will come to a display of the citing case and you may see the first reference it contains to the cited case. (If the citation to your case does not appear on the first screen, press NEXT PAGE.) You are in KWIC mode. In KWIC, you see your search request (in this case a citation to *Walker*) highlighted, and you are shown 25 searchable words on either side of your search request. If you want to read more of a citing case than you see in the KWIC format, press the FULL key. Do that now. Page through the case until you find *Walker* cited in the dissenting opinion.

(b) Why does the *dissent* say the cited case is not controlling?

---

9. Return to the *Shepard's* display. Type [res] (meaning "resume") and press ENTER. [Res] takes you back to the last service or library you were searching, in this case *Shepard's*. The online version of *Shepard's* allows you to limit the *Shepard's* display to any paragraph number or editorial code of your choice. ("PARA" is the heading on the screen under which LEXIS puts headnote numbers. LEXIS calls headnotes "paragraphs" because most official reporters refer to them that way. WESTLAW calls the equivalent column "headnotes" because that is what they are called in the West reporters.) This limiting feature is especially useful when a *Shepard's* display is very long and you are only interested in parts of it. To limit the display, you must press the SEGMTS (segments) key. Do that now. To limit the display to cases that list headnote 2 in the "PARA" column, type [2] and press ENTER. How many citations does *Shepard's* display with this restriction?

---

10. To retrieve the full display again, press the FULL key. Do that now. Next retrieve the second *Shepard's* document for your case. Press the NEXT DOC key. What is the *Shepard's* series of the second document?

---

11. Page through the document you have retrieved. Circle yes or no to indicate which of the categories of citing documents appear in the *Shepard's* for citations to a case by its regional reporter citation in the state *Shepard's* volumes.

Citations for decisions from other state courts	Yes	No
Citations from A.L.R. or L. Ed. 2d annotations	Yes	No
Citations from law reviews other than the *ABA Journal*	Yes	No

Return to the first page of the document. Press the FIRST PAGE key.

12. Now Shepardize the case using its official state reporter citation. What do you ENTER?

_____

13. Page through the documents by pressing the NEXT PAGE key. Circle yes or no to indicate which of the categories of citing documents appear in the *Shepard's* for citations to the case by its official state reporter citation.

Citations for decisions from other state courts	Yes	No
Citations from A.L.R. or L. Ed. 2d annotations	Yes	No
Citations from law reviews other than the *ABA Journal*	Yes	No

14. To view the Auto-Cite display for the same case, type [ac] and press ENTER.

Note: To see the Auto-Cite display for a case you are not viewing, type [ac] followed by the case citation. Use the volume number, reporter abbreviation, and page number of the case with spaces between them. To find the proper Auto-Cite abbreviation for a reporter, use either the *Reference Manual for the LEXIS/NEXIS Services* or first go into Auto-Cite by typing [ac] and pressing ENTER. Then type [h] for help and press ENTER. You would be directed to a list of tutorials from which you could select the Auto-Cite reporter abbreviations.

(a) Cite the appellate history of the case, if any.

_____

_____

(b) Cite the prior history of the case, if any.

_____

_____

(c) Cite the first subsequent treatment case, if any.

_____

_____

15. Auto-Cite lists A.L.R. and L. Ed. 2d annotations that cite any case listed on an Auto-Cite screen. It identifies cases that have annotations by an asterisk and a reference number indicating the number to check for annotations related to the case.

(a) How many annotations are there for the citation you entered? (You may need to "turn the page" of the display to answer this question.)

_____

(b) Cite the annotation discussing the relationship between an employer's promulgated policies and the employer's right to discharge an employee.

_____

You may retrieve a document listed on an Auto-Cite display by typing [lxe] followed by its citation. You need not do that now.

Since you were viewing the *Shepard's* display for this case immediately before you came to the Auto-Cite display, you can return to the *Shepard's* display by typing [res] and pressing ENTER. If you had gone to Auto-Cite first and then had wanted to reach the *Shepard's* display for the case, all you would have to do is type [sh] and press ENTER.

Now sign off LEXIS. Press the SIGN OFF key and follow the directions on the screen.

PROBLEM SET 2: ELECTRONIC CITATORS—WESTLAW

Name _____   Professor _____

Complete both Problem Sets 1 and 2 unless your professor tells you otherwise.

Note: For this Problem Set any characters you are asked to type are enclosed in brackets. Do not include the brackets when you type your search. The names of the function keys are printed in capital letters.

Sign on to WESTLAW. If you are using a WALT terminal, follow these directions. Otherwise, ask your librarian for assistance.

(1) Turn on the printer. (Switch is on left front.)
(2) Turn on the computer. (Blue button on right front.)
(3) The monitor should already be on. (If it is not, the switch is on right side.)
(4) The WESTLAW icon should be highlighted pink. (If not, use the arrow keys.) Press ENTER.
(5) Wait for the screen that says WESTLAW in asterisks.
(6) Type your password and press ENTER.
(7) The next screen will say "Welcome to WESTLAW." Type your client ID—that is, your last name, your professor's last name, and the course name—and press ENTER. For example: [Jones,Smith,legal writing].

Once you are signed on, you will be looking at the first page of the WESTLAW Directory. From this screen, or any WESTLAW screen, it is easy to Shepardize a case. Just type the *Shepard's* command, followed by your case citation, and press ENTER. The *Shepard's* command is [sh]. Your case citation must include a volume number, reporter abbreviation, and page number, in that order, and you must use the proper *Shepard's* abbreviation for the name of the reporter.

Note: The *Shepard's* abbreviation for a reporter may be different from the abbreviation in *The Bluebook.* You may find the abbreviation for the name of a reporter in the *WESTLAW Reference Manual,* or you may find it online. To find it online (do not do this now), you would type [sh] and press ENTER to enter the *Shepard's* service. Then you would type [pubs] for "publications" and press ENTER. (If you were already in *Shepard's,* you would just type [pubs] and press ENTER.) Although you may use periods and spaces within the name of the reporter, you need not do so. Omitting periods and spaces saves time and thus makes your research more economical. On WESTLAW, unlike LEXIS, you do not need a space after the volume number and before the page number.

Now Shepardize the case of *Walker v. Westinghouse Electric Corp.,* 335 S.E.2d 79 (N.C. App. 1985). Type [sh 335 se2d 79] and press ENTER.

Note: You also may type the citation and press the SHEPARDIZE key. If you are viewing a case and want to Shepardize it, you only have to type [sh] and press ENTER or press the SHEPARDIZE key.

1. The top of the screen that you have reached tells you how many documents you have retrieved and which ranked document you are viewing. How many documents did this citation retrieve?

_____

2. Next the screen verifies the citation you Shepardized in the "CITATIONS TO" line, and then it identifies the citator series and the division within that citator to which the online display corresponds.

(a) Look at the "CITATOR" line. To which print *Shepard's* title does the online *Shepard's* display correspond?

_____

(b) Look at the "DIVISION" line. To which division within the print title does the online *Shepard's* display correspond?

_____

3. Look at the "COVERAGE" line.

(a) With what volume of the print *Shepard's* does the online display for the case begin?

_____

(b) What is the most recent supplement to *Shepard's Southeastern Reporter Citations* included in the display?

_____

4. How many online full-text pages are there in the document you are viewing?

_____

5. Now look at the first page of the *Shepard's* display. If it gives a parallel citation for the case you Shepardized, identify the parallel citation.

_____

6. You can page through a *Shepard's* display on WESTLAW by pressing the ENTER key. Page through the first document. Circle yes or no to indicate which of the categories of citing documents appear in the *Shepard's* display for the case in the regional reporter *Shepard's*.

Citations for decisions from other state courts	Yes	No
Citations from A.L.R. or L. Ed. 2d annotations	Yes	No
Citations from law reviews other than the *ABA Journal*	Yes	No

The unrecognizable citations at the end of this display, if any, are to treatises published by Shepard's/McGraw-Hill.

7. You can return to the first page of a *Shepard's* display by typing [p1] and pressing ENTER. Do that. Then page forward in the *Shepard's* display until you find the citation to the first case in which *Walker* is cited in a dissenting opinion. What is the citation for that case?

_____

8. You can retrieve a citing case that is of interest to you by typing the number in the "Retrieval No." column that corresponds to that case. Retrieve the case you found in Question 7.

(a) What number did you ENTER?

You will come to a display of the citing case, and the words "CITING CASE" will be highlighted. You will be in term mode. In term mode, every time you press ENTER, you come to the next page of the case that contains your search terms. In this case, your search is for a citation. If the citation to your case does not appear on the first screen, press ENTER, and you will come to the first page on which the citation appears. The citation will be highlighted. The first page on which the citation occurs is not part of the dissenting opinion. To verify that, note the number of the page you are viewing by checking the highlighted cite line at the top of the page. Compare that number with the page number in Question 7. Page through the case. To do so, press ENTER. You may switch at any time from term mode to page mode, which allows you to see each page in the document. Just type [p] or [t] as appropriate and press ENTER to switch between term and page mode.

(b) Why does the *dissent* say the cited case is not controlling?

---

9. Return to the *Shepard's* display. Type [gb] (meaning "go back") and press ENTER or press the GO BACK key. [Gb] takes you back to the last service or database you were searching. The online version of *Shepard's* allows you to limit the *Shepard's* display to any headnote number or editorial code of your choice. This limiting feature is especially useful when a *Shepard's* display is very long and you are only interested in parts of it. To limit the display, type [lo] (meaning "locate"), followed by the editorial code or headnote number you wish to find. To locate all cases that discuss the issue in headnote 2, type [lo2] and press ENTER. How many citations does *Shepard's* display with this restriction? You may need to page through the display.

---

10. To retrieve the full display again, type [xl] (meaning "cancel locate") and press ENTER. Do that now. Next, retrieve the second *Shepard's* document for your case. Type [r] (meaning "rank") and press ENTER, or press the NEXT DOC key.

(a) From which citator is the second document taken?

(b) From which division of the citator is the document taken?

---

11. Page through the document you have retrieved. Circle yes or no to indicate which of the categories of citing documents appear in the *Shepard's* for citations to a case by its regional reporter citation in the state *Shepard's* volumes.

Citations for decisions from other state courts	Yes	No
Citations from A.L.R. or L. Ed. 2d annotations	Yes	No
Citations from law reviews other than the *ABA Journal*	Yes	No

Return to the first page of the document. Type [p1] and press ENTER.

12. Now Shepardize the case using its official state reporter citation. What do you ENTER?

_____

13. Page through the document by pressing the NEXT PAGE key. Circle yes or no to indicate which of the categories of citing documents appear in the *Shepard's* for citations to the case by its official state reporter citation.

Citations for decisions from other state courts	Yes	No
Citations from A.L.R. or L. Ed. 2d annotations	Yes	No
Citations from law reviews other than the *ABA Journal*	Yes	No

14. WESTLAW gives you a "sneak preview" of new citations from the National Reporter System advance sheets in its service, *Shepard's Preview.* To obtain the citations to the case you Shepardized, type [sp] (meaning *"Shepard's Preview"*) and press ENTER. What is the first citation on the list?

_____

15. QuickCite, another WESTLAW service, can retrieve citing cases that are so new they do not yet even appear in *Shepard's Preview.* QuickCite does so by searching case law databases for citations to your case. To search QuickCite, type [qc] and press ENTER. Do that now. Read the screen display to see your QuickCite options. Then press ENTER. Notice that WESTLAW displays on the screen the search it is running.

(a) How many citations did your QuickCite search retrieve? (Hint: Look under the "Rank" column.)

_____

(b) List the first citation you retrieved. (Since these are likely to be very new cases, they may only have "WL" citations.)

_____

16. To view the Insta-Cite display for *Walker,* type [ic 335 se2d 79] and press ENTER. (You may also type the citation and press the INSTA-CITE key.)

Note: To find the proper Insta-Cite abbreviation for a reporter, use either the *WESTLAW Reference Manual* or first go into Insta-Cite by typing [ic] and pressing ENTER, then type [pubs] and press ENTER.

(a) Cite the appellate history of the case, if any. Include the language that indicates the relationship between the two cases.

_____

(b) Cite the prior history of the case, if any.

(c) Cite the first indirect history case, if any.

You may retrieve a document listed on an Insta-Cite display by typing its number. You need not do that now.

Now sign off WESTLAW. Type [off] and press ENTER.

PROBLEM SET 3: FULL-TEXT SEARCHING—LEXIS

Name _____ Professor _____

Complete both Problem Sets 3 and 4 unless your professor tells you otherwise.

Note: For this Problem Set any characters you are asked to type are enclosed in brackets. Do not include the brackets when you type your search. The names of the function keys are printed in capital letters.

Research Situation:

You are an attorney practicing in Minnesota. Your client became gravely ill with aplastic anemia after being treated for an infection with the antibiotic chloromycetin. The doctor never advised your client of the possibility of side effects from the drug.

This Problem Set will focus on two of the possible approaches to writing a computer search from this hypothetical. The first approach focuses on the facts; the second focuses on the legal issue raised by those facts. A search based only on fact words will find cases involving those words (i.e., chloromycetin) regardless of the legal issue involved (e.g., a product tampering case instead of a medical malpractice case). A search based only on the legal issue will find cases involving that issue regardless of whether the facts are the same (e.g., complications of surgery rather than the side effects of drug therapy). In the following questions, you will write searches taking each approach.

Fact Approach

1. Look again at the hypothetical. Two terms associated with the facts are quite specific: aplastic anemia and chloromycetin. Write a search to find cases that have *both* these terms in them.

_____

2. Using those same two terms, write a search to find cases containing *either* one *or* the other (or both) terms.

_____

Issue Approach

3. What legal issue is raised by the Research Situation? State the issue in the form of a question. (Hint: Do not use words that describe the specific facts—that is, aplastic anemia, antibiotic, or chloromycetin. The issue is not simply "medical malpractice." Think about what it was that the doctor should or should not have done.)

_____

_____

_____

_____

_____

4. List the key terms as they appear in your answer to Question 3.

_____

_____

_____

5. Pick the three or four most important key terms from your answer to Question 4. Write them down again, and list the alternative words for each term below it. If applicable, show the use of the * or ! root expansion symbols on your terms.

_____

_____

_____

_____

_____

_____

_____

6. Use the terms from Question 5 to write a search that will retrieve cases on your legal issue without limiting your results to the specific facts. Remember to use the alternatives for key terms and to add the appropriate connectors.

_____

_____

_____

Running the Search

7. Sign on to LEXIS. If you are using a LEXIS 2000 workstation, follow these directions. Otherwise, ask your librarian for assistance.

(1) Turn on the printer. (Switch is on left front.)
(2) Turn on the monitor. (Switch is on right side.)
(3) Turn on the computer. (Switch is on right front.)
(4) Wait for the "Star Wars" screen. Press the spacebar.
(5) If necessary, use the arrow keys to move the yellow highlighting bar so that "LEXIS(R) 2000 Research Software for MS-DOS(R)" is highlighted. Press ENTER (a green key).
(6) Wait while the computer connects to the system. You will reach the "WELCOME TO LEXIS AND NEXIS" screen. Type your personal ID (password) and press ENTER.
(7) On the next screen, type your client ID—that is, your last name, your professor's last name, and the course name—and press ENTER. For example: [Jones,Smith,legal writing].

You will be on the first page of the LEXIS Libraries directory. To see the next page, press the NEXT PAGE key. Then return to the first page by pressing PREV PAGE. Select the STATES library. Type [states] and press ENTER. You will come to a list of files. Which file should you select if you wish to find only mandatory primary case authority for the Research

Situation? (Hint: To obtain a description of a file, type the number to the right of the file name.)

8. On what date does LEXIS coverage begin for the state supreme court cases in the file? (See the "Hint" parenthetical for Question 7.)

Note: LEXIS has online a GUIDE library and some GUIDE files that contain more detailed information than you will find by entering the page number for the file in the directory. When this was written, LEXIS did not have a GUIDE file for the MINN (Minnesota) file.

9. Select the MINN file. ENTER [minn]. Then run the search you wrote for Question 1. How many cases did you retrieve?

Press the KWIC key. Skim through the cases in KWIC mode by pressing the NEXT PAGE key.

Making a Record of Your Search Results

10. When you have completed a search, you may want to "make notes" of both your search and your search results. Press FIRST DOC to return to the first page of your search results.

(a) Then to display your search on LEXIS, type [r] and press ENTER. Use the PRINT SCREEN key to print this screen. Attach the print-out to this Problem Set.

(b) To display the list of citations retrieved by your search, press CITE, then PRINT SCREEN. Attach the print-out to this Problem Set. (Remember that it is expensive to read cases online or to print entire cases.)

Editing Your Search

11. You may sometimes wish to edit a search. ENTER [1m] to edit your last search. (The number 1 refers to the level you are editing. Think of "m" as a "modify" command.) Edit the search to match the search you wrote in Question 2. Move the cursor to the end of the line (or drop it a line) to make sure the cursor is at the end of the text you want to enter. Then ENTER your edited search.

(a) How many cases did you retrieve?

(b) Skim through the cases in KWIC. Cite the first additional relevant case you retrieved (if any).

Running a New Search

12. Press NEW SEARCH to clear the screen so you can run a new search. Then run the search you wrote for Question 6. How many cases did you retrieve?

Even though your issue search does not use the term chloromycetin, you should be able to retrieve the relevant cases retrieved by your search in Question 9, because they are on the same issue.

13.   (a) Write a second level to narrow the search results to cases that contain the word chloromycetin. (Hint: Each new level must start with a connector.)

_____

_____

_____

_____

(b) Type [m] and press ENTER to tell LEXIS you want to add a level to your search. Then ENTER the level 2 search you wrote in Question 13(a). How many cases did you retrieve on level 2? Press CITE to see the list. Write their citations below.

_____

_____

_____

_____

_____

Note: On LEXIS you also have the focus feature that allows you to focus your browsing on particular terms, whether those terms were in your search or not. Focus could be used to find the cases mentioning chloromycetin without adding a level to this search. It can also speed up browsing. For searches that have one or more terms that appear frequently in retrieved documents, use focus to limit browsing to the less common terms. Why did we use levels instead of focus? Level searching is useful because it allows you to separately browse and print separate lists of citations for each level of specificity of your search. You can move between levels by typing a level number and pressing the DISPLAY DIF LEVEL key. It also allows you to do some editing of your search without incurring a new search charge. When you edit any level of your search, you are charged for a new search, but you can add levels indefinitely for no charge.

14.   If the results of your issue search did not include the cases involving chloromycetin, rewrite your search.

(a) What is your new search?

_____

_____

(b) Press the NEW SEARCH key and ENTER the search (or type [1m] and edit your old search). Which of the cases involving chloromycetin did you retrieve?

_____

_____

Changing Libraries and Files

15.   You may sometimes wish to run a search in more than one library and file. For example, since federal courts sometimes apply state law, you may wish to extend your

search to federal court cases decided in Minnesota. (Since Minnesota is in the 8th Circuit, for this example we will search a file containing both 8th Circuit Court of Appeals cases and district court cases from that circuit.) Press the CHG LIB key. Type [genfed;8th] and press ENTER. (Using the semicolon between the library name—GENFED—and the file name—8th—saves time by skipping over the display of files. Notice that the last search you used is displayed on the screen so you would not have to type it in to use it again. You will not use this search now, but it is not necessary to delete it.) Type the search you wrote for Question 2 at the top of the screen. Make sure your cursor is at the end of what you typed and before the beginning of the last search. Press ENTER. How many documents did you retrieve?

Segment Searching

16. If you know the name of a case but not its citation, you can find it on LEXIS with a name segment search. (Hint: See Chapter 6.) Write a search to find the case of *Reinhardt v. Colton.*

---

17. Return to the STATES library's MINN file and run the search you wrote for Question 16. What is the citation of that case?

Using the System as a Citator

18. Because LEXIS contains the full text of documents, you can search for citations contained within those documents. For example, cases are always cited by the parties' names followed by the volume, reporter, and page. If you know the citation of a case, you can use the words and numbers from that citation and their proximity to each other to write a search for other documents containing that citation. This is a very useful technique to find cases that are more recent than those listed in *Shepard's.* Write a search to find documents that contain citations to *Reinhardt v. Colton* and are dated after 1990.

---

19. Press the NEW SEARCH key, then run the search you wrote for Question 18. How many cases did you retrieve?

Press the SIGN OFF key and follow the directions on the screen to sign off LEXIS.

PROBLEM SET 4: FULL-TEXT SEARCHING—WESTLAW

Name _____   Professor _____

Complete both Problem Sets 3 and 4 unless your professor tells you otherwise.

Note: For this Problem Set any characters you are asked to type are enclosed in brackets. Do not include the brackets when you type your search. The names of the function keys are printed in capital letters.

Research Situation:

You are an attorney practicing in Minnesota. Your client became gravely ill with aplastic anemia after being treated for an infection with the antibiotic chloromycetin. The doctor never advised your client of the possibility of side effects from the drug.

This Problem Set will focus on two of the possible approaches to writing a computer search from this hypothetical. The first approach focuses on the facts; the second focuses on the legal issue raised by those facts. A search based only on fact words will find cases involving those words (i.e., chloromycetin) regardless of the legal issue involved (e.g., a product tampering case instead of a medical malpractice case). A search based only on the legal issue will find cases involving that issue regardless of whether the facts are the same (e.g., complications of surgery rather than the side effects of drug therapy). In the following questions, you will write searches taking each approach.

Fact Approach

1. Look again at the hypothetical. Two terms associated with the facts are quite specific: aplastic anemia and chloromycetin. Write a search to find cases that have *both* these terms in them.

_____

2. Using those same two terms, write a search to find cases containing *either* one *or* the other (or both) terms.

_____

Issue Approach

3. What legal issue is raised by the Research Situation? State the issue in the form of a question. (Hint: Do not use words that describe the specific facts—that is, aplastic anemia, antibiotic, or chloromycetin. The issue is not simply "medical malpractice." Think about what it was that the doctor should or should not have done.)

_____

_____

_____

_____

4. List the key terms as they appear in your answer to Question 3.

_____

_____

_____

5. Pick the three or four most important key terms from your answer to Question 4. Write them down again, and list the alternative words for each term below it. If applicable, show the use of the * or ! root expansion symbols on your terms.

_____

_____

_____

_____

_____

_____

_____

6. Use the terms from Question 5 to write a search that will retrieve cases on your legal issue without limiting your results to the specific facts. Remember to use the alternatives for key terms and to add the appropriate connectors.

_____

_____

_____

Running the Search

7. Sign on to WESTLAW. If you are using a WALT terminal, follow these directions. Otherwise, ask your librarian for assistance.

(1) Turn on the printer. (Switch is on left front.)
(2) Turn on the computer. (Blue button on right front.)
(3) The monitor should already be on. (If it is not, the switch is on the right side.)
(4) The WESTLAW icon should be highlighted pink. (If not, use the arrow keys.) Press ENTER.
(5) Wait for the screen that says WESTLAW in asterisks.
(6) Type your password and press ENTER.
(7) The next screen will say, "Welcome to WESTLAW." Type your client ID—that is, your last name, your professor's last name, and the course name—and press ENTER. For example: [Jones,Smith,legal writing].

In what database should you run your search? (Hint: You want a general, rather than a topical, database.)

_____

8. On what date does coverage begin for Minnesota Supreme Court cases in this database? Type [scope] followed by the database identifier, then press ENTER.

_____

9. Select the Minnesota case database, and run the search you wrote for Question 1. How many cases did you retrieve? (The number appears in the "Rank" column.)

Skim through the cases in term mode.

Making a Record of Your Search Results

10. When you have completed a search, you may want to "make notes" of the search and your search results.

(a) To display your search, type [g] and press ENTER. Use the PRINT SCREEN key to print this screen. Attach the print-out to this Problem Set.

(b) To display the list of citations, type [l] (for "list"), then press ENTER, then press PRINT SCREEN. Attach the print-out to this Problem Set. (Remember that it is expensive to read cases online or to print entire cases.)

Editing Your Search

11. Type [q] and press ENTER to retrieve your search for editing. Edit the search to match the search you wrote in Question 2 and run it.

(a) How many cases did you retrieve?

(b) Browse through the cases in term mode. Cite the first additional relevant case you retrieved, if any.

Running a New Search

12. Clear your last search so you can run a new search. Type [s] and press ENTER. Now run the search you wrote for Question 6. How many cases did you retrieve?

Even though your issue search does not use the term chloromycetin, you should be able to retrieve the relevant cases retrieved by your search in Question 9, because they are on the same issue.

13.   (a) Use the locate command to find if any of the cases retrieved by your search contains the term chloromycetin. (Hint: Make sure you are on the first page of the first ranked document before you start locate, because locate will run forward through the documents starting with the screen you are on. To get to the first page of the first document, type [r1] or [p1] as appropriate, and press ENTER.) Type [lo chloromycetin] and press ENTER.

(b) How many documents contained the term? Write their citations below.

_____

_____

_____

_____

14. If the results of your issue search did not include the cases involving chloromycetin, rewrite your search.

(a) What is your new search?

_____

_____

(b) Type [s] (for new search) and press ENTER. Then type and ENTER your new search. Which of the cases involving chloromycetin did you retrieve?

_____

_____

Changing Databases

15. You may sometimes wish to run a search in more than one database. For example, since federal courts sometimes apply state law, you may wish to extend your search to federal court cases decided in Minnesota. Since Minnesota is in the 8th Circuit, for this example we will search the database of 8th Circuit Court of Appeals cases. There are several ways to change databases on WESTLAW. (Do not type anything yet.) The command [db] will take you back to the directory. If you already know the name of the database, you can add that to your command and go directly to that database. For example, [dbcta8] would skip the directory screen and take you directly to the database of 8th Circuit Court of Appeals cases. If you want to take the search you just ran with you to the new database, you can add [q] (for editing) or [s] (for running the same search) to the [db] command to skip the step of having to type the search in again. For our example, we want to run the same search in the cta8 database. Type [sdbcta8] and press ENTER. How many documents did you retrieve?

_____

Field Searching

16. If you know the name of a case but not its citation, you can find it on WESTLAW with a title field search. (Hint: See Chapter 6.) Write a search to find the case of _Reinhardt v. Colton._

_____

17. Return to the MN-CS (Minnesota cases) database and run the search you wrote for Question 16. What is the citation of that case?

_____

Using the System as a Citator

18. Because WESTLAW contains the full text of documents, you can search for citations contained within those documents. For example, cases are always cited by the parties' names followed by the volume, reporter, and page. If you know the citation of a case, you can use the words and numbers from that citation and their proximity to each other to write a search for other documents containing that citation. The QuickCite function on WESTLAW will do this for you when you are looking for cases that are more recent than those listed in *Shepard's*. If you understand how to do so yourself, you can create your own citator for any type of material, not just cases. Write a search to find documents that contain citations to *Reinhardt v. Colton* and are dated after 1990.

---

19. Type [s] and press ENTER, then run the search you wrote for Question 18. How many cases did you retrieve?

Type [off] and press ENTER and then follow the directions on the screen to sign off WESTLAW.

Statutes and Constitutions

There are four Problem Sets for Chapter 7. They cover the following areas of research:

Problem Set 1	Researching Federal Statutes in Print Sources
Problem Set 2	Researching Federal Statutes on CALR
Problem Set 3	Researching Federal Legislative History without CALR
Problem Set 4	Researching Federal Legislative History with CALR

You will be selecting one of the following Research Situations in each of these Problem Sets. We suggest that you leave pages 545-547 in your book (or at least do not turn them in to your professor), so you will have ready access to the texts of the Research Situations as you work through each Problem Set.

Research Situation A:

Your client is the owner of a small business that has always provided generous medical benefits for its employees and their dependents. The premiums for these benefits have increased significantly in the last two years, and your client must cut costs by reducing benefits. He prefers to do so by maintaining the current level of benefits for his employees but reducing the level of benefits for their dependents. He asks if a policy that offers greater pregnancy benefits to female employees than to spouses of male employees would violate federal law prohibiting discrimination on the basis of sex.

Research Situation B:

Your client is the owner of a Tennessee Walking Horse. Tennessee Walking Horses have a high-stepping gait achieved through selective breeding and training. The gait also can be created in less talented horses by making the horses' forelimbs sore. Your client was charged with showing a "sore" horse, an action prohibited by federal law. Is intent to cause the horse harm an element of a violation of the federal law?

Research Situation C:

Your client, a lifelong environmentalist, has successfully petitioned to place a small fish known as the "snail darter" on the federal endangered species list. With that battle behind her, she seeks to halt the completion of a dam that would destroy the snail darter's only habitable territory. The dam, begun seven years ago by a federal agency, is a few weeks from completion. To abandon the project now would result in the waste of millions of taxpayer dollars, but would save a species from extinction. Is your client likely to succeed?

Research Situation D:

Your client manufactures the Spinner, an amusement park ride that consists of a boom that rotates in a 360-degree arc when the machine is operating. Attached to the boom at equidistant points are 12 cars that move along the boom and also rotate through the 360-degree arc. Each car has two latching systems. The Consumer Product Safety Commission alleges that at least four Spinner riders have died in falls that occurred when doors of Spinner cars opened in mid-air. It has filed suit against your client, asking the court to declare the Spinner an imminently hazardous consumer product and to enjoin its operation until corrective action is taken. Is the Spinner a product subject to regulation by the Commission?

Research Situation E:

Your client attempted to demonstrate the inadequacy of security measures on a federal computer network by introducing a virus into the network. He was charged with violating a federal computer fraud and abuse law that punishes anyone who intentionally accesses a federal interest computer without authorization and damages or prevents authorized use, causing a loss of $1,000 or more. May he be convicted if he did not intend the damage? [Note: As of April 1992 U.S.C.A. contained an error in the "Legislative History" section cross-reference to *United States Code Congressional and Administrative News.* Use the index to U.S.C.C.A.N. to find the correct location for the committee report.]

Research Situation F:

You recently petitioned successfully for United States citizenship for your client. The Immigration and Naturalization Service had contested your client's naturalization in federal court and, as a result, the process was lengthy and complex. You now seek the award of attorney's fees for your work in representing your client in his suit against the United States. Are you entitled to them?

Research Situation G:

Your client is a part-time law student who works for the Department of Justice as a program analyst. She recently took a leave of absence to study for and take the bar exam. Her supervisor, who was suspicious about whether your client was using her time as she claimed, contacted the state board of bar examiners to confirm her attendance at the bar exam. When your client learned of this, she became furious and filed suit against the Department, claiming it violated her statutory right to privacy because it failed to obtain the information directly from her to the extent practicable before seeking the information from a third party. Is your client likely to prevail?

Research Situation H:

Your client's application for a federally insured home loan was initially denied on the basis of a mortgage report prepared by a credit reporting agency for the mortgage company. Although the credit reporting agency accurately reported the information it received from creditors, some of that information was inaccurate. Your client would like to know if a credit reporting agency has a duty to do more than correctly report information supplied to it by creditors.

Research Situation I:

Hi-Wire Corporation sells telecommunication services. Your client, a Fortune 500 corporation, subscribes to Hi-Wire's cellular telephone service for some of its executives. Recently, your client discovered that the company's major competitor had intercepted one of its marketing director's cellular telephone calls and as a result learned of the company's new marketing strategy. Your client is outraged by this interception and disclosure of the contents of its communications and wants to know if it may obtain damages from a provider of cellular telephone services who fails to scramble its transmissions or to prevent interceptions by some other means.

Research Situation J:

You represent a wholesaler of "plush" infant toys. Your client purchased a large order of plush kittens and discovered that the eyes on the kittens were not securely enough attached to comply with United States consumer product safety standards. Most of the merchandise was either unsalable or required repair before sale. As a result, your client suffered economic harm and would like to sue the manufacturer and supplier. Can your client recover damages from the manufacturer and supplier?

PROBLEM SET 1: RESEARCHING FEDERAL STATUTES IN PRINT SOURCES

Name _____   Professor _____

Circle the letter of the Research Situation you selected from those set out on pages 545-547:

A   B   C   D   E   F   G   H   I   J

1. Locate in U.S.C.A. or U.S.C.S. the statute that pertains to your Research Situation. If you use the index to U.S.C.S. to help you, remember that you may need to use the looseleaf update to the index as well as the main index. Statutes are often very difficult to locate. If you have difficulty locating the relevant statute in the index to one of the sets, switch to the index for the other set.

(a) Which index did you use? _____ U.S.C.A. _____ U.S.C.S.

(b) Under which main heading and subheading did you locate a reference to the applicable statute?

_____

_____

(c) Write the proper *Bluebook* citation for the relevant statute as found in the source you used. Remember to check both the main volume and the pocket part or annual supplement to it.

_____

_____

2. Has the code section you found been amended since it was originally enacted? Use the main volume and pocket part or supplementary pamphlet to answer this question.

(a) _____ Yes   _____ No

(b) If it has been amended, write the *United States Statutes at Large* citation for the most recent amendment.

_____

_____

3. Read the text of the statute you located. What guidance does it offer for your Research Situation?

_____

_____

_____

_____

_____

4. Using the same annotated code, write the *United States Statutes at Large* citation for the public law that originally created the statutory section.

5. Using the case annotations for the section you identified in Question 1, find and cite in *Bluebook* form a case that appears to address the Research Situation you selected. For purposes of this exercise, you should find and cite the case identified below, which will be directly on point. You should remember, however, that your research often will not lead to a case directly on point. It may, however, lead you to a number of cases that may be relevant to your Research Situation.

Research Situation A: a 1983 United States Supreme Court case
Research Situation B: a 1984 Ninth Circuit case
Research Situation C: a 1977 Sixth Circuit case for which the United States Supreme Court issued a 1978 opinion
Research Situation D: a 1977 District of Columbia district court case
Research Situation E: a 1991 Second Circuit case
Research Situation F: a 1989 Ninth Circuit case
Research Situation G: a 1989 D.C. Circuit case
Research Situation H: a 1982 Sixth Circuit case
Research Situation I: a 1990 Third Circuit case
Research Situation J: a 1989 federal district court case

6. What answer to the Research Situation is provided by the case annotation? (If you were doing actual research, you would, of course, read the entire case to determine if the case annotation is applicable and correct, and you would use a citator to determine the current weight of authority of the case. You would not rely on the annotation.)

7. Now look at the editorial material following the text of the statute you identified in Question 1. Indicate which of the following types of information the source you are using provides for the section by placing a check mark in front of each type of information you found. Be sure to check both the main volume and the pocket part or supplementary pamphlet.

_____ A cross-reference to a related statute
_____ A citation to a law review article
_____ A citation to a legal encyclopedia
_____ A citation to the *Code of Federal Regulations*
_____ A citation to a West topic and Key Number
_____ A citation to an A.L.R. or L. Ed. 2d annotation
_____ A citation to a treatise
_____ A citation to forms

8. Determine if the statute that pertains to your Research Situation has been amended since the annual pocket part or supplementary pamphlet was issued. Use the update services for the same source you used in Question 1. Review pages 252-263 if you need help answering this question.

(a) Identify each title and issue you checked.

_____

_____

_____

(b) If you found an amendment to the statutory section you cited in Question 1, identify the amendment by public law and section number.

_____

9. Now turn to the same section you identified in Question 1 in the annotated code you did not use in Question 1. Identify which of the following information that code provides for the statutory section by placing a check mark in front of each type of information you find. Remember to check both the main volume and pocket part or supplementary pamphlet.

_____ A cross-reference to a related statute
_____ A citation to a law review article
_____ A citation to a legal encyclopedia
_____ A citation to the *Code of Federal Regulations*
_____ A citation to a West topic and Key Number
_____ A citation to an A.L.R. or L. Ed. 2d annotation
_____ A citation to a treatise
_____ A citation to forms

10. Since *Bluebook* rules require that you cite statutes currently in force to the official code if they are available there, give the proper official citation for the section you identified in Question 1. If you do not provide an official citation for the section, explain why you did not.

_____

_____

_____

_____

_____

11. Using the tables for one of the three versions of the code, determine if Pub. L. No. 101-239, § 7714 was codified (added to the code). If it was, give the title and section

number where you would find it. If it was not, find the section in *United States Statutes at Large* and then explain why the section was not codified.

_____

_____

_____

_____

_____

PROBLEM SET 2: RESEARCHING FEDERAL STATUTES ON CALR

Name _____ Professor _____

Circle the letter of the Research Situation you selected from those set out on pages 545-547. (We recommend that you use the same Research Situation that you used in Problem Set 1, unless your professor instructs you otherwise.)

A   B   C   D   E   F   G   H   I   J

1. Circle the online service you have chosen.

LEXIS   WESTLAW

2. Set out your search exactly as you will enter it.

_____

_____

_____

3. Identify the WESTLAW database or LEXIS library and file in which you will do your full-text search. If the system you chose has both an annotated and an unannotated code database, select the unannotated database.

_____

4. Sign on to the system you have chosen, select your database or library and file, and enter your search.

Note: LEXIS automatically searches the full text of the statutes and the annotations unless you limit your search to the text segment. Therefore, for your first LEXIS search, do a text segment search. Add the word "text" to the search you wrote in Question 2 and enclose your search terms in parentheses. Follow this format: text (your search terms).

(a) How many documents did your search retrieve? _____

(b) Did your search retrieve the relevant code section for your Research Situation? _____ If so, identify the section.

_____

(c) If your search did not retrieve the relevant code section, rewrite your search. What is your new search?

_____

_____

(d) Did your new search retrieve the relevant code section? _____ If so, identify the section.

_____

(e) Now run your search in the annotations as well as the text. On LEXIS just edit your search. Enter [1m]; then delete the word "text" and the parentheses. On WESTLAW transfer your search to the USCA database by entering [sdb usca]. How many documents did your search retrieve? _____ Page through the documents in term or kwic mode. Did you retrieve the relevant section?

_____

(f) Skip this question if you are using LEXIS. If you are using WESTLAW and have retrieved the relevant statutory section, update your search results while viewing that section by entering [update]. If your statutory section has been updated, note the public law number of the act that has amended it.

_____

5. To update your research further, enter the PUBLAW file on LEXIS (if you have not already searched a combined file, which includes public law information) or the US-PL database on WESTLAW. To enter the PUBLAW file on LEXIS, enter [.cf] for "change file"; then enter [publaw] and follow the directions on the screen. To enter the US-PL file on WESTLAW, enter [sdb us-pl] if you wish to run the same search or [db us-pl] if you wish to run a different search.

(a) What is your search?

_____

(b) Has your statutory section been amended? If so, cite the public law number of the act that has amended it.

_____

_____

Now sign off the system you are using. Use [.so] on LEXIS and [off] on WESTLAW.

6. Was your print research or your online research more effective for your Research Situation? Explain your answer.

_____

_____

_____

_____

_____

_____

_____

_____

PROBLEM SET 3: RESEARCHING FEDERAL LEGISLATIVE HISTORY WITHOUT CALR

Name _____   Professor _____

Circle the letter of the Research Situation you selected from those set out on pages 545-547. (We recommend that you use the same Research Situation that you used in Problem Set 1, unless your professor instructs you otherwise.)

A   B   C   D   E   F   G   H   I   J

1. If you have not already done so in Problem Set 1, locate your statute in one of the three federal codes (U.S.C., U.S.C.A., or U.S.C.S.). Read the section pertinent to the problem and the legislative history material, generally located immediately below the statute. Research the public law enacted in the following year:

Research Situation A: 1978 act listed first
Research Situation B: 1976
Research Situation C: 1973
Research Situation D: 1972
Research Situation E: 1986
Research Situation F: 1985
Research Situation G: 1974
Research Situation H: 1970
Research Situation I: 1986
Research Situation J: 1972

Record the following legislative history information:

(a) Public law number _____

(b) *Statutes at Large* citation _____

(c) Date of approval _____

(d) Anything else? _____

2. Find and scan the legislative history section of the *United States Code Congressional and Administrative News* (U.S.C.C.A.N.) pertinent to your statute. Record the following information, as found there:

(a) House bill number, committee, report number, and date (if any):

_____

_____

(b) Senate bill number, committee, report number, and date (if any):

_____

_____

(c) Conference committee report number and date (if any):

_____

(d) Which bill passed:

_____

(e) Date(s) of consideration by the House:

_____

_____

(f) Date(s) of consideration by the Senate:

_____

_____

(g) Volume(s) of the *Congressional Record* that record these events:

_____

(h) Session of Congress that passed your bill (check the spine):

_____

_____

3. Unless your Research Situation is listed below, read the pertinent portions of the first document of legislative history in U.S.C.C.A.N.

Research Situation H: Read the second document.
Research Situation J: Read the second document.

Does the document provide any guidance on your Research Situation? If so, note what you have learned:

_____

_____

_____

_____

4. Provide the proper citation to the first page of the document you just read:

_____

_____

_____

5. Find the pertinent Abstract volume (if your statute predates 1984) or Legislative Histories volume (if your statute dates to 1984 or later) of the *CIS/Annual*. Read the legislative history on your statute. Compare the information there to your answers to Questions 1 and 2. Does the volume provide any new information? If so, record it (or part of it, if there is a lot of new information) here.

_____

_____

_____

6. Record the "accession numbers" for up to five House and up to five Senate documents pertaining to your statute.

_____

_____

7. Locate and read the following abstract in the Abstract volume pertinent to your statute, or read the information pertinent to the following document in the Legislative Histories volume:

Research Situation A:	H341-48 from 1977
Research Situation B:	H501-16
Research Situation C:	H561-10 from 1973
Research Situation D:	S261-3
Research Situation E:	S521-78
Research Situation F:	H521-25 from 1983
Research Situation G:	H401-40
Research Situation H:	S241-19
Research Situation I:	H521-41
Research Situation J:	S261-4

What type of document does the abstract describe?

_____

_____

8. Obtain the C.I.S. microfiche card(s) containing the document listed above. Scan the following pages:

Research Situation A:	3-5
Research Situation B:	54-58
Research Situation C:	201-206
Research Situation D:	141-145
Research Situation E:	34-40
Research Situation F:	33-37
Research Situation G:	118-128
Research Situation H:	56-59
Research Situation I:	19-21
Research Situation J:	401-405

Does this document provide any guidance on your Research Situation? If so, note what you have learned.

_____

_____

_____

_____

9. Provide the proper citation to the first page of the document you just read.

_____

_____

_____

10. Now locate the volume of the *Congressional Record* you listed in your answer to Question 2(g); use the more recent if two volumes are listed. Locate the two entries for your statute in the House and Senate bills and resolutions sections of the index. On what pages are the presentation of the bill to the President and approval of the bill reported?

_____

11. Find the pages where the following floor debate is reported, again by use of the House and Senate bills and resolutions sections of the index.

Research Situation A: Conference report considered and agreed to in House.
Research Situation B: Senate concurred in House amendments.
Research Situation C: Conference report submitted in Senate and agreed to.
Research Situation D: Conference report submitted in House and agreed to (second page referred to).
Research Situation E: House concurs in Senate amendment.
Research Situation F: Passed Senate.
Research Situation G: House concurs in Senate amendment with amendments.
Research Situation H: Conference report submitted in Senate and agreed to.
Research Situation I: House concurs in Senate amendments.
Research Situation J: Conference report submitted in Senate and agreed to.

Read the first statement by the first legislator to speak during this debate (not the report or bill). Does the debate provide any guidance on your Research Situation? If so, note what you have learned.

_____
_____
_____
_____
_____

12. Provide the proper citation to the first page of the material you just read.

_____
_____
_____

13. If all of the documents you just read provided guidance on your Research Situation, which would you rely on? Why?

_____
_____
_____
_____
_____

PROBLEM SET 4: RESEARCHING FEDERAL LEGISLATIVE HISTORY WITH CALR

Name _____   Professor _____

Circle the letter of the Research Situation you selected from those set out on pages 545-547. (We recommend that you use the same Research Situation that you used in Problem Set 1, unless your professor instructs you otherwise.)

A   B   C   D   E   F   G   H   I   J

Note: This Problem Set asks you to look for recent consideration by Congress of the general area covered by your statute; you will not be researching the history of your statute.

1. Circle the online service you will be using.

LEXIS   WESTLAW

2. Which database will you research for:

(a) recent committee reports?

_____

(b) recent debates in the *Congressional Record?*

_____

3. Set out here the search you will enter in the database containing committee reports, exactly as you intend to enter it.

_____

_____

4. Run your search. Edit your search if necessary until you are satisfied you have written a good search. Copy down your final search and explain why you edited it as you did.

_____

_____

_____

5. Provide citation information for the most pertinent document you located through this search.

_____

_____

_____

_____

6. Set out here the search you will enter in the database containing the *Congressional Record,* exactly as you intend to enter it.

_____

_____

7. Run your search. Edit your search if necessary until you are satisfied you have written a good search. Copy down your final search and explain why you edited it as you did.

_____

_____

_____

8. Provide citation information for the most pertinent document you located through this search.

_____

_____

_____

9. Was your print research or your online research more effective for your Research Situation? Explain your answer.

_____

_____

_____

_____

_____

_____

_____

_____

There are three Problem Sets for Chapter 8. They cover the following areas of research:

Problem Set 1	Researching Administrative Materials without Looseleafs or CALR
Problem Set 2	Researching Administrative Materials in Looseleafs
Problem Set 3	CALR in Federal Administrative Materials

You will be selecting one of the following Research Situations in each of these Problem Sets. We suggest that you leave pages 561-563 in your book (or at least do not turn them in to your professor), so you will have ready access to the texts of the Research Situations as you work through each Problem Set.

Research Situation A:

Your client, Lucille Songco, has developed a line of beauty products called "CoCo," which she has used in her beauty salons located throughout the city. Because the "CoCo" line has become popular, Ms. Songco has decided to set up franchises of beauty salons in other cities. Ms. Songco has contacted you to draft a franchise agreement. What are the disclosure requirements and prohibitions concerning franchising? Should the franchise information also suggest the income likely to be earned?

Looseleaf Service:	*Business Franchise Guide,* Commerce Clearing House, Inc. (CCH).
Statute:	Federal Trade Commission Act, Franchise Disclosure Rule, 15 U.S.C. §§ 45-46.

Research Situation B:

Brenda Tshe, president of Fabulous Gowns, Inc., a controlled corporation, has operated a fashion apparel business for the past ten years. Fabulous Gowns included a successful line of jewelry, but the corporate officers now wish to market a moderately priced line of jewelry in order to expand their share of the national market. For valid business reasons, Fabulous Gowns, Inc. wishes to transfer the entire jewelry business to a new corporation, Quality Bobbles, Inc. Analyze the income tax consequences for the shareholders: What effect will the corporate reorganization have on the shareholders if the securities (shares) are distributed or divided as part of a "Type D" corporate reorganization by spin-off, split-off, or other similar plan?

Looseleaf Service:	*Business Transactions: Tax Analysis,* Research Institute of America (RIA).
Statute:	Type D Reorganizations—Internal Revenue Code, 26 U.S.C. § 355(a).

Research Situation C:

Ted Therrien employs a neighbor, Jeff Luther, to assist him with work on the family horse farm. Mr. Therrien is concerned that he should be withholding unemployment compensation taxes, known as FICA (Federal Insurance Contributions Act) taxes, from Jeff's wages. Analyze the income tax consequences: Should Mr. Therrien be withholding and collecting unemployment taxes?

> Looseleaf Service: *Unemployment Insurance Reports,* Commerce Clearing House, Inc. (CCH).
>
> Statute: Federal Insurance Contributions Act, 26 U.S.C. § 3121(g).

Research Situation D:

Because of corporate growth, Dobins & Lopez, Ltd. (D & L) has found it necessary to relocate several of its executives to offices in other states. This has occurred so frequently that the CEO, Maria Dobins, has drafted an employee relocation policy. Under the policy, D & L will provide loans that are below the market mortgage rate to assist relocated employees with the purchase of a home in the new location. Analyze the income tax consequences of this employee benefit: Are these "below-market-rate loans" taxable as income to the employees?

> Looseleaf Service: *Benefits Coordinator,* Warren, Gorham, Lamont (WGL).
>
> Statute: Tax Reform Act of 1986, 26 U.S.C. § 7872.

Research Situation E:

Your client, Kao Jaixin, is a Chinese national who entered the United States in 1983 to evade the national draft due to political and moral convictions. The Immigration and Naturalization Service has initiated deportation proceedings against Mr. Kao. You wish to present a case in support of your client for political asylum. You are unsure how to develop the "well-founded fear of persecution" standard to meet your client's requisite burden of proof in his asylum request. Must your client show that he has individually been threatened previously by the authorities of his native country?

> Looseleaf Service: *Federal Immigration Law Reporter,* Washington Service Bureau, Inc. (WSB).
>
> Statute: Immigration and Naturalization Act, 8 U.S.C. § 1101(a)(42)(A).

Research Situation F:

Your client, Alexia Floyd, age 70, was admitted to the United States under a temporary visa. The visa has now expired but Ms. Floyd has not been deported because of her serious illness. She has sought treatment at a hospital located in your state, but has been denied Medicare coverage because she is neither a citizen nor a permanent resident. Ms. Floyd has no other social security benefits. Regarding her entitlement under Medicare: Is Ms. Floyd ineligible for hospital insurance under Medicare because of her lack of citizenship?

> Looseleaf Service: *Medicare and Medicaid Guide,* Commerce Clearing House, Inc. (CCH).
>
> Statute: Social Security Act—Medicare; Health Insurance for the Aged and Disabled, 42 U.S.C. § 1395o.

Research Situation G:

Your client, Virginia D. DuLuc, is planning to open a sandwich and cheese deli in a local suburban mall. She plans to employ teenagers to work in the deli. These teenagers would be trained to wait on customers, run the cash register, prepare the various sandwiches, and market the various cheeses. Among their other duties, the teenagers will be trained to operate a large slicing machine, used to slice cheese and meat, and a meat grinder. Because Ms. DuLuc plans to hire teenagers who will operate the slicer and grinder, you have concerns about the hazardous occupation provisions of the child labor law.

Looseleaf Service: *Labor Relations Reporter,* Bureau of National Affairs, Inc. (BNA).
Statute: Fair Labor Standards Act—Child Labor Provisions, 29 U.S.C.
                                § 212(c).

Research Situation H:

Vince Hoch seeks to manufacture and market "all natural products" ski gloves. The linings of the gloves are a combination of wool and other man-made products. What information must be disclosed on the labels of the gloves if he wishes to advertise them as a wool product?

Looseleaf Service: *Federal Trade Regulation Reporter,* Commerce Clearing
                                House, Inc. (CCH).
Statute: Wool Products Labeling Act of 1939, 15 U.S.C. § 68b.

Research Situation I:

Joan Jackson, owner of World-Wide Books Distributors, wants to establish an account in Libya in order to more easily buy and sell books within that country. Ms. Jackson specializes in official documents and books published by foreign governments. The Libyan government is requiring a substantial advance for its documents. Is Ms. Jackson precluded from establishing an account in Libya and transferring funds from the United States to a foreign account located in Libya?

Looseleaf Service: *Federal Banking Law Reporter,* Commerce Clearing
                                House, Inc. (CCH).
Statute: Trading with the Enemy Act of 1917, 50 App. U.S.C. § 5.

Research Situation J:

Your client, Luke Grant, applied for a VistaExcess credit card with Bank Corp. The brief credit application form did not contain detailed information about any charges or fees connected with the card. The application was approved and Mr. Grant received a credit card by mail; that mailing did not include any additional information. Mr. Grant used the card at the local department store for several purchases. Later, when the billing statement arrived, Mr. Grant was very upset to discover that a transaction charge had been included for each credit card purchase. Mr. Grant seeks your advice. Is there any recourse under truth-in-lending law because VistaExcess did not disclose sufficient credit information regarding the transaction fees?

Looseleaf Service: *Consumer Credit Guide,* Commerce Clearing House, Inc. (CCH).
Statute: Consumer Credit Protection Act, 15 U.S.C. § 1637.

PROBLEM SET 1: RESEARCHING ADMINISTRATIVE MATERIALS WITHOUT LOOSELEAFS OR CALR

Name _____   Professor _____

Circle the letter of the Research Situation you selected from those set out on pages 561-563.

A   B   C   D   E   F   G   H   I   J

1. In U.S.C.A. or U.S.C.S., locate the statute referred to in your Research Situation. Read the section setting out the substantive rule governing your situation.

(a) Summarize the rule and the probable effect of this statute on your client.

_____

_____

_____

_____

(b) Provide the proper citation to that section of the statute.

_____

2. Now read the section(s) setting out the powers of your agency. State the name of the enforcing agency and list some of its powers or duties.

_____

_____

_____

_____

3. Scan the annotations. Look for references to pertinent judicial decisions, agency regulations, and agency decisions. Note: Your annotations may not contain references to all of these sources. List the references from the annotations that look the most promising.

(a) Judicial decisions: _____

_____

_____

(b) Agency regulations: _____

_____

(c) Agency decisions: _____

_____

4. Even if the code annotations had a reference to C.F.R., it may not be on point precisely. Locate the most current *CFR Index and Finding Aids* volume. Look for a pertinent regulation in the CFR Titles, Chapters, Subchapters, and Parts; subject matter index; or Parallel Table of Authorities and Rules. Remember that you can use your agency's name or statute's title as an indexing term. Record those parts of C.F.R. that may be applicable.

_____

_____

5. Scan the parts of C.F.R. you located through Questions 3(b) and 4. Locate and read the C.F.R. section pertinent to your situation.

(a) What guidance does it provide?

_____

_____

_____

_____

(b) Give its proper citation.

_____

6. Collect the first L.S.A. pamphlet necessary to update your research. (In practice, of course, you would consult all appropriate L.S.A. pamphlets.)

(a) Look up the regulation cited in Question 5. Record here information about your regulation that appears in L.S.A., if any.

_____

(b) Check the table to determine the date of the *Federal Register* in which this information, if any, appears, and record it here as well.

_____

7. Although your next step in practice will be to check the Reader Aids chart in the very recent *Federal Register* issues that have not been covered by the most recent L.S.A. pamphlets, move directly to the issue of the *Federal Register* referred to in your answer to Question 6(b), if any, and read the material noted.

(a) If it bears on your situation, summarize its impact. If it does not bear on your situation, describe the agency's action.

_____

_____

_____

(b) Provide the proper citation to this material.

_____

8. Shepardize the regulation you have been working with. Provide the *Shepard's* citations to any decisions declaring your regulation constitutional or unconstitutional, valid or invalid. If there are no such citations, list the first three citations to your regulation, if any.

---

9. OPTIONAL: State the title of the official reporter containing your agency's decisions, if any. Then locate the reporter. Use citations found previously or use the index, digest, or outline system of the reporter to locate a relevant decision. Read that decision.

(a) Explain the impact of the decision on your situation.

(b) Provide the proper citation.

---

10. OPTIONAL: Shepardize the decision cited in your answer to Question 9. Update your citation, if necessary, to reflect subsequent judicial or administrative action.

---

11. Based on your research thus far, are there any judicial decisions you would read to complete your research? Which ones, and why?

PROBLEM SET 2: RESEARCHING
ADMINISTRATIVE MATERIALS IN LOOSELEAFS

Name _____   Professor _____

Circle the letter of the Research Situation you selected from those set out on pages 561-563. (We recommend that you use the same Research Situation that you used in Problem Set 1, unless your professor instructs you otherwise.)

A   B   C   D   E   F   G   H   I   J

1. Using the recommended looseleaf service, locate the general, topical, or master index as well as all updating indexes and current supplements. It is likely that you will need to consult more than one index located in more than one binder to find all of the necessary material. First, locate the commentary in the looseleaf service.

(a) What guidance does it provide?

_____

_____

_____

_____

_____

(b) Provide the proper citation to this commentary.

_____

_____

_____

2. Locate the section of the looseleaf service where the applicable federal legislation is included.

(a) What guidance does it provide? (If you have previously worked with the same Research Situation, you may refer to a previous answer.)

_____

_____

_____

_____

_____

(b) Provide the proper citation to this legislation.

_____

_____

3. Locate the section of the looseleaf service where the applicable federal regulation is included.

(a) What guidance does it provide? (If you have previously worked with the same Research Situation, you may refer to a previous answer.)

_____

_____

_____

_____

_____

(b) Provide the proper citation to this regulation.

_____

_____

4. Use the case or agency digests, or scan the textual annotations, to find citations to court and agency decisions. Be sure to use the updating materials as well.

(a) Record references to at least one court and one agency decision, if any. These decisions may be found in the looseleaf or in companion reporters, official reporters, or transfer binders.

Court decision(s): _____

_____

_____

Agency decision(s): _____

_____

_____

(b) Based on the annotations or digest material, what guidance do these decisions provide? (If you have previously worked with the same Research Situation and the same decisions, you may refer to a previous answer.)

_____

_____

_____

_____

5. OPTIONAL: Now search for information about state regulations, state agency decisions, or state statutes found in the looseleaf service that are relevant to your Research Situation, if any.

(a) What state material is contained in the looseleaf, if any, and what guidance does this material provide?

_____

_____

(b) Provide the proper citation to the portion of the looseleaf where you found this information.

PROBLEM SET 3: CALR IN FEDERAL ADMINISTRATIVE MATERIALS

Name _____ Professor _____

Circle the letter of the Research Situation you selected from those set out on pages 561-563. (We recommend that you use the same Research Situation that you used in Problem Set 1, unless your professor instructs you otherwise.)

A   B   C   D   E   F   G   H   I   J

1. Circle the online service you will be using.

LEXIS   WESTLAW

2. Which non-looseleaf database(s) will you research for:

(a) regulations promulgated by your agency?

_____

_____

(b) decisions (if any) of your agency?

_____

_____

3. Begin by searching for a pertinent regulation. Set out your search here, exactly as you intend to enter it.

_____

_____

_____

4. Run your search. Edit your search if necessary until you are satisfied you have written a good search. Copy down your final search, and explain why you edited it as you did.

_____

_____

_____

_____

_____

_____

_____

_____

5. Provide citation information for the most pertinent document you located through this search. What guidance does it provide for your Research Situation? (If you have previously worked with the same Research Situation, you may refer to a previous answer.)

_____

_____

_____

_____

6. Update your research. Is there any change in your regulation? If so, describe it here and its impact on your Research Situation.

_____

_____

_____

_____

7. If your agency issues decisions as well, set out the search you would use to locate pertinent decisions, exactly as you intend to enter it. (You may need to change databases to perform this search.)

_____

_____

_____

8. Run your search. Edit your search if necessary until you are satisfied you have written a good search. Copy down your final search, and explain why you edited it as you did.

_____

_____

_____

_____

_____

_____

_____

_____

9. Provide citation information for the most pertinent document you located through this search. What guidance does it provide for your Research Situation? (If you have previously worked with the same Research Situation, you may refer to a previous answer.)

_____

_____

_____

_____

10. Update your research. Is the decision still good law? Why, or why not?

_____

_____

_____

11. Focusing on those looseleaf services carried online, find recent information in the form of commentary, proposed legislation or regulations, or new decisions.

(a) What database(s) did you use? _____

_____

(b) What is the scope or coverage of this database? _____

_____

_____

(c) Set out your search here.

_____

_____

_____

(d) What information did you find?

_____

_____

_____

_____

12. Now that you have used print materials, looseleaf services, and online databases, what have you found to be the relative strengths and weaknesses of these research tools?

_____

_____

_____

_____

_____

_____

_____

_____

_____

_____

_____

_____

Rules Governing Practice
and Procedure

There are three Problem Sets for Chapter 9. They cover the following areas of research:

Problem Set 1	Researching Federal Rules of Civil Procedure without CALR
Problem Set 2	Researching Federal Rules of Civil Procedure on CALR
Problem Set 3	State Rules of Civil Procedure

You will be selecting one of the following Research Situations in Problem Sets 1 and 2. We suggest that you leave pages 577-578 in your book (or at least do not turn them in to your professor), so you will have ready access to the texts of the Research Situations as you work through Problem Sets 1 and 2.

Research Situation A:

Your firm recently won a motion for summary judgment in the federal district court in Alaska. The opposing side is appealing that decision on the grounds that it established a genuine issue of material fact through a legal memorandum and oral statements by counsel; the opposing side did not submit affidavits or other material. Research the federal rule that governs summary judgment to determine if the opposing side has a strong basis for an appeal.

Research Situation B:

Your client has brought a wage discrimination claim against her former employer in federal district court in Michigan. During discovery you served the employer with a request for admissions regarding discriminatory employment practices. The employer responded well after the deadline passed, and you want to know whether you can bring a motion for summary judgment based upon the employer's failure to respond properly to the request for admissions. Research the federal rule governing the effect of a late response to a request for admissions.

Research Situation C:

Your client is an automobile manufacturer who is suing a foreign parts supplier for breach of contract in Puerto Rico. In preparing the case during discovery, you have requested copies of all pertinent documents. The supplier has complied with this request, but sent the documents in the supplier's native language. Who must pay for the translation of the documents? Research the federal rule governing production of documents.

Research Situation D:

A month after obtaining a favorable judgment in federal court in New York, you noticed that the order for judgment omits the pre-judgment interest to which your client is clearly entitled. You view the omission as a simple clerical error. Research the federal rule governing motions to amend the judgment for reasons of clerical mistakes.

Research Situation E:

Your client, a New York dessert manufacturer, alleges that a T-shirt manufacturer is improperly spoofing its desserts. The T-shirts carry pictures with parodies of your client's logo and product names. You have identified trademark infringement and unfair competition as potential causes of action. Because your client fears a drop in sales due to the rather effective parody, you are considering obtaining a preliminary injunction against the sale of the T-shirts. Research the federal rule pertaining to preliminary injunctions.

Research Situation F:

You are representing an Indian tribe in federal district court in Nevada in a dispute over "riparian rights," arising from the use of water in a river adjoining their reservation. Your analysis of the claim indicates that the rights of each member are essentially the same even though they reside in different locations in the river's watershed; at the least, their rights are not adverse to each other's. Your clients want to know whether a single class action against the 13,000-member irrigation district is appropriate, or whether each member must be sued individually. Research the federal rule governing class actions.

Research Situation G:

Your client is a lessee whose property was destroyed by a fire that took place after a riot in Washington, D.C. He wants to depose members of the municipality where the riot occurred. However, he is currently unable to develop a set of facts to support a cause of action against the municipality. Research the federal rule governing depositions before complaints are filed.

Research Situation H:

During trial of an employment dispute in Virginia, your client, the defendant company, would like to use statements made by the employee plaintiff during her pre-trial deposition. You would like to use the statements for purposes of impeaching her testimony during your cross-examination of her during the trial. For that matter, some of the statements are favorable enough that you would like to use them as direct proof of the matters discussed. Research the federal rule governing use of deposition testimony during trial.

Research Situation I:

You represent a large manufacturer, which is a defendant in a contracts case in federal district court in Massachusetts. The plaintiff has served a set of interrogatories, seeking information that is covered in documents in your headquarters in Texas. You would like to simply refer the plaintiff to those documents and permit the plaintiff to locate them in the files and review them on-site. Research the federal rule governing responding to interrogatories.

Research Situation J:

You represent, on appeal, a plaintiff who lost before the jury on a negligence case brought in federal district court in Maryland. Trial counsel did not object to a jury instruction that you deem both harmful to the plaintiff and clearly contrary to settled law in that it stated the wrong standard of care. You view the plaintiff's case as so compelling that the jury would have found for her had it been properly instructed. Research the federal rule governing objections to jury instructions.

PROBLEM SET 1: RESEARCHING FEDERAL RULES OF CIVIL PROCEDURE WITHOUT CALR

Name _____ Professor _____

Circle the letter of the Research Situation you selected from those set out on pages 577-578.

A   B   C   D   E   F   G   H   I   J

1. In a deskbook, locate the Federal Rule of Civil Procedure that governs the Research Situation you selected. Record the proper citation to that rule.

_____

2. What guidance does the rule provide for your Research Situation?

_____

_____

_____

_____

3. Now read the Advisory Committee Notes. Do they provide any further guidance? If so, note it here.

_____

_____

_____

_____

4. Locate the section(s) or paragraph(s) in either *Moore's Federal Practice* or Wright et al.'s *Federal Practice and Procedure* relating to your issue. What does the treatise discussion tell you about your Research Situation?

_____

_____

_____

_____

5. Record the proper citation to the treatise material you just read.

_____

_____

6. Using the U.S.C.A. or U.S.C.S. case annotations, locate a case that pertains to your Research Situation and conforms to the guidelines listed below. Read the case, and note any guidance it provides for your Research Situation.

Research Situation A:	1974 Ninth Circuit decision
Research Situation B:	1981 Eastern District of Michigan decision
Research Situation C:	1982 First Circuit decision
Research Situation D:	1968 District of New York decision
Research Situation E:	1983 Eastern District of New York decision
Research Situation F:	1975 District of Nevada decision
Research Situation G:	1978 district court decision from District of Columbia
Research Situation H:	1963 Fourth Circuit decision
Research Situation I:	1988 District of Massachusetts decision
Research Situation J:	1980 Fourth Circuit decision

_____

_____

_____

_____

_____

7. Record the proper citation to the case you just read. (You need not provide any subsequent history that is not apparent in the case annotation or the case report.)

_____

_____

PROBLEM SET 2: RESEARCHING FEDERAL RULES OF CIVIL PROCEDURE ON CALR

Name _____ Professor _____

Circle the letter of the Research Situation you selected from those set out on pages 577-578. (We recommend that you use the same Research Situation that you used in Problem Set 1, unless your professor instructs you otherwise.)

A   B   C   D   E   F   G   H   I   J

1. Circle the online service you have chosen.

LEXIS   WESTLAW

2. Which database(s) will you research for:

(a) Federal Rules of Civil Procedure?

_____

(b) Cases interpreting or applying the rule?

_____

3. Begin by searching for a pertinent rule. Set out your search as you intend to enter it.

_____

_____

4. Run your search. Edit your search if necessary until you are satisfied you have written a good search. Copy down your final search, and explain why you edited it as you did.

_____

_____

5. (a) Provide citation information for the most pertinent rule located through your search.

_____

(b) What guidance does the most pertinent rule provide?

_____

_____

_____

_____

(c) When was the rule most recently updated?

_____

_____

6. Set out the search you would use to locate pertinent cases interpreting your rule. (You may need to change databases to perform this search.)

_____

_____

7. Run your search. Edit your search if necessary until you are satisfied you have written a good search. Copy down your final search, and explain why you edited it as you did.

_____

_____

8. Provide citation information for the most pertinent case your search revealed.

_____

_____

9. Update your research on that case. Is the case still good law? Why or why not?

_____

_____

PROBLEM SET 3: STATE RULES OF CIVIL PROCEDURE

Name _____   Professor _____

Research Situation:

Your client recently purchased a hair coloring enhancer. After one application, her hair began to fall out. In preparing your case against the manufacturer in state court, you have requested disclosure of the lotion's formula. The manufacturer has refused this request, asserting that the formula is a trade secret and therefore is protected from discovery. Locate the state rule of civil procedure governing discovery practice and determine whether trade secrets are subject to a protective order that might prevent you from obtaining the formula.

Complete the Research Situation in one of the following states (circle one):

Arizona   California   Hawaii   Idaho   Kansas
Kentucky   Minnesota   Montana   Pennsylvania   South Dakota

1. Locate the state rule of civil procedure that governs the Research Situation. Record the proper citation to the rule.

_____

_____

_____

2. Does the language of the rule resolve the Research Situation? If so, how?

_____

_____

_____

3. Using annotations to the state rules, can you find a case annotation that pertains to the Research Situation? Remember to check the pocket parts. If so, read the case itself, record the case citation, and write down the answer to the Research Situation. If you can find no relevant cases, simply say so.

_____

_____

_____

_____

_____

_____

Name _____   Professor _____

Select one of the following Research Situations, preferably one you worked in Problem Sets 1 through 4 in Chapter 3.

Research Situation A:

Your client, Ms. Cambridge, sought the help of a marriage counselor, Dr. Braxton. Ms. Cambridge often met with Dr. Braxton in his home without her husband. Occasionally, Dr. Braxton would encourage Ms. Cambridge to engage in sexual relations with him during her sessions as a way to open up, relieve tension, and compensate her for the love she never got as a child. She did so at his urging. Ms. Cambridge changed counselors two months ago and now would like to know whether she can sue Dr. Braxton for malpractice.

Research Situation B:

Your client, Mr. Piper, has no permanent address or residence. The local police recently discovered Mr. Piper wandering the streets of the warehouse district. When they approached him, he became hostile and violent. When asked for identification, he screamed that he was invisible. The officers took Mr. Piper to the county hospital for a psychiatric evaluation, where he was diagnosed as a paranoid schizophrenic. He again became hostile, punching a nurse while demanding to be released. The psychiatrist who examined Mr. Piper recommends that he remain in the hospital for further testing and to ensure his and others' safety from his violent behavior. Mr. Piper refuses to remain hospitalized, insisting that he is competent to care for himself. He would like to know whether the hospital has the right to commit him against his will.

Research Situation C:

Your client, Mr. Carsberg, was a mechanic at Quality Transmission Company. He was an "at-will" employee, meaning that he could be fired for any or no reason. His job was to work on transmissions after the manager diagnosed the problem. One day Mr. Carsberg observed the manager placing metal filings in the transmission fluid of a car before it was tested. As Mr. Carsberg predicted, the test then indicated that the transmission would need a complete overhaul, a long and expensive undertaking. Mr. Carsberg asked a former employee about this practice, who confirmed that this was common. Mr. Carsberg was outraged and reported the practice to the Better Business Bureau. Mr. Carsberg was fired the next day. He would like to take action against his former employer for wrongful discharge.

Research Situation D:

Your client, Ms. Hunter, lives in an apartment owned by Prism Management Company. Her building is in a high-crime neighborhood of Central City. While coming home late one night, Ms. Hunter observed a man lingering around the entrance to her building. He appeared to be looking for directions, but as Ms. Hunter approached the entrance he took a gun from his overcoat. He forced Ms. Hunter into some overgrown bushes on the side of the dimly lit building, where he severely beat and robbed her. Other tenants in the building previously had made calls to the management company about the lack of safe conditions around the building, but no action was taken to make it safer. Ms. Hunter would like to take action against Prism Management for its failure to protect her from this criminal act.

Research Situation E:

Your clients, a tenants' group from Central City, live in a five-story apartment building owned and managed by Cost-Mor Company. Cost-Mor's maintenance staff, protesting their low wages, went on strike one month ago. The garbage hauler has refused to cross their picket line to empty the building's garbage receptacle. As a result, the garbage has accumulated to a height equal to that of the first-floor windows. Central City has declared a health emergency because of the harmful refuse odors and because of the rodents and cockroaches that have since infested the building. The tenants would like to know if they must continue to live in these uninhabitable conditions.

Research Situation F:

Your client, Ms. Ling, owns a house next door to a family with children of ages three, four, and seven. The children often play in their backyard. Ms. Ling has a toolshed in her backyard that usually is locked, but once every week or two she leaves the shed unlocked so that a teenager down the block can mow her lawn with the riding mower. She leaves the key in the mower on those days. One morning before the teenager came over to mow the lawn, the seven-year-old from next door got into the unlocked shed, started the mower with the key, fell off, and injured himself severely. The boy's parents assert that, even though their son was trespassing, Ms. Ling should pay for the injuries because she created a nuisance that attracted children.

Research Situation G:

Your client, Pizza Works, is a local pizza restaurant and delivery service. Although there is no state law requiring that food-service employees be clean-shaven, Pizza Works strictly enforces its own dress code, which requires all customer-service employees to be clean-shaven. Mr. Borm applied for a customer-service position and was qualified for the job, but he refused to shave his beard. Mr. Borm's religion requires him to wear a beard. Pizza Works then offered him an alternative position on the late-night cleanup crew. Mr. Borm wants to know whether he has a discrimination claim against Pizza Works for refusing to accommodate his religious practices.

Research Situation H:

Your client, Ms. Orns, is a drill-press operator for Plastiform, Inc. Plastiform bought the drill press from Precision Machine Co., at which time Precision's sales representative knew that Plastiform was ordering the drill press in order to drill holes in plastic. Ms. Orns drills holes in plastic parts and uses the drill press at its highest speed to keep the drill bit from "binding." In the trade, plastic generally is known to bind at lower drill speeds. One day, a plastic part that Ms. Orns was drilling "bound," flew off the drill press, and severely injured Ms. Orns. Although Ms. Orns is receiving worker's compensation payments, she also wants to sue Precision because it had a duty to recommend that Plastiform buy the "optional bind-indicator with emergency-stop device" for the drill press, as well as a duty to warn Plastiform of the dangers of not purchasing the device.

Research Situation I:

For about a year, the police have suspected your client, Mr. Wallace, of being a drug dealer. The police, after obtaining a valid search warrant, recently searched Mr. Wallace's house, but found no evidence of illegal substances or drug money. Three days later Mr. Wallace suffered severe abdominal pains and subsequently lost consciousness. A neighbor rushed him to the nearby hospital. The medical staff suspected an appendicitis attack, but surgery revealed that Mr. Wallace's stomach contained 21 balloons of crack cocaine, as well as over $1,700 in paper currency. The surgeon removed these items, then immediately notified the police. Mr. Wallace was arrested for possession of illegal drugs. You want to know whether the physician-patient privilege was breached when the doctor notified police.

Research Situation J:

Your clients, Mr. and Mrs. Walker, lost their daughter in an auto accident. Julia, 16 years old, sustained severe head injuries after a car entered an interstate freeway from the exit ramp, colliding with the car in which Julia was a passenger. The driver of the car was legally intoxicated. Paramedics administered first aid to Julia and rushed her to the county hospital where she died later that day. The Walkers already have initiated a wrongful death action in Julia's name. They now want to know whether they can recover from the driver for their own loss of their daughter's companionship, society, and services during the remainder of their lives.

Circle the letter of the Research Situation you selected:

A   B   C   D   E   F   G   H   I   J

1. Refer back to the terms, outline, and legal principles you developed in your answers to Problem Sets 1 through 4 for Chapter 3, or simply think through your Research Situation carefully. What non-legal facts of a general nature would you like to know? List several areas to research.

_____

_____

_____

2. List research terms you would use in consulting social sciences literature on your Research Situation. Remember that your terms should not be legal terms.

_____

_____

_____

3. Select DIALOG or NEXIS for your research. Scan the online directory, or consult a current print manual or list to acquaint yourself with the current databases. Which computer service did you select? Circle one.

DIALOG   NEXIS

4. Identify the database you expect to contain useful information. State your database choice.

_____

5. List the research terms you expect to find in pertinent documents. Then state your search as you intend to enter it.

(a) research terms _____

_____

(b) search _____

_____

6. Run your search. Edit your search if necessary until you are satisfied you have written a good search. Copy down your final search, and explain why you edited it as you did.

_____

_____

_____

_____

7. How many documents did your final search yield? _____ Scan the documents until you find a useful one. Print the first screen of that document to hand in with this Problem Set.

8. How does your document advance your analysis of your Research Situation? Stated another way, what insight does it provide on the legal rule(s) applicable to your Research Situation?

_____

_____

_____

_____

_____

9. OPTIONAL QUESTION: Locate a print index to periodicals that covers articles that would be useful to your research, such as the *Social Sciences Index*. Select the most recent volume available, and look for promising articles.

(a) What is the most pertinent subject heading?

_____

_____

(b) Give the entry for the most pertinent article listed under that subject heading.

_____

_____

Developing an Integrated Research
Strategy

Name _____   Professor _____

Generally, the fact situations you research in practice are amalgams of facts drawn from various sources. For this, the final Problem Set of the book, we thus present statements by various persons with various perspectives on a single event. Assume that Genevieve Finlay has brought a claim against the federal government as a result of this event.

Your professor will give you instructions for this Problem Set.

Claim No. 91-123456
Claimant: Genevieve Finlay
Date: October 15, 1991
Location of Occurrence: Yosemite National Park

Statement of Otis Finlay

I am a resident of El Cerrito, California and have been for seven years. I build and repair boats for a living. I am the son of Genevieve Finlay, the claimant. She was injured at my wedding in Yosemite National Park on April 9, 1991.

My wife, Nanci Su Selleck, and I met nearly five years ago through mutual friends in Berkeley, California. After years of dating, in December of 1990 we decided to get married. We decided on a small wedding: just twenty members of our family and close friends. We wanted to be married in a unique location featuring the natural beauty of California. We thought about a boat on the San Francisco Bay, but they are very expensive. Nanci suggested Yosemite. She knew it from camping there as a child with her parents. After talking over this idea with our families, we decided to go with it.

Of course, we needed someone to officiate at the ceremony. Nanci's brother Bert has a high school classmate, Mike Best, who started out as a minister in the United Church of Christ, then switched to a career as a park ranger. Mike, as it turned out, works in Yosemite. We contacted him to see if he would officiate at a nonsectarian ceremony. He agreed to do so. He also sent us a short pamphlet with photos of several spots in the park, a map, and information about the services available there.

Spring came to Yosemite several days before the wedding, as we had hoped it would. Most of the snow in the valley melted, and the air warmed up. Apparently, however, there was a sharp freeze the night before the wedding, and certain spots froze over.

We all drove into the park through one of the main entrances at about 9:00 a.m. (We all stayed in a bed-and-breakfast in a small town a few miles outside the park the nights before and after the wedding.) We met Mike at his home in the park. I paid him $100 for his services. He directed us to the spot he had chosen, a meadow with a nice view of Half-Dome. It was gorgeous. He conducted the ceremony there; it took about twenty minutes.

When the ceremony was over, we decided to take pictures on a nearby bridge extending over a stream about fifty yards away. We walked over and lined up on the bridge as Bert (our family photographer) told us to. After he took a few pictures of the whole group, he asked Nanci, our parents, and me to stay on the bridge. Somehow in the shuffling of people, as my mother stepped aside, she slipped on a very icy spot that was virtually undetectable. As she slipped, she fell against one of the side posts on the bridge and sustained a serious head injury.

We have consulted a lawyer, who in turn consulted an expert on bridge surfaces. According to the expert, the bridge is an accident waiting to happen. The bridge was recently resurfaced with a compound that is not appropriate for rough wood bridges. (The surface now holds ice longer than it should, and the ice is very difficult to see.) According to the expert, the bridge should carry warnings or restrictions on use during the winter.

It has been months since my mother was injured. Although her life was never in danger, she is not the same person as she was before, and the doctors expect little additional improvement. She has significant problems with memory and speech. Her balance is impaired. She suffers from blinding headaches. She can no longer work.

Claim No. 91-123456
Claimant: Genevieve Finlay
Date: December 15, 1991
Location of Occurrence: Yosemite National Park

Statement of Genevieve Finlay

I am 63 years old, a physician, and a resident of Montecito, California. I am the mother of Otis Finlay and the mother-in-law of Nanci Su Selleck.

I was injured at their wedding. Due to the nature of the injury, I do not remember much about the accident itself. I remember going into Yosemite Park for Otis and Nanci's wedding, watching and participating in the ceremony, and then going to a little bridge over a creek for pictures. After that, I have no recollection. To be frank, I can't even describe the area very much, as my attention was focused on the wedding and keeping warm.

Since the injury, I have been in either the hospital or a rehabilitation center. As I understand it, I suffered a traumatic brain injury. It has caused some continuing problems for me. Although I have some long-term memory, I have difficulty remembering events that have just occurred. My speech is slurred, although I can write. My balance is impaired. Most significant are the headaches, which occur nearly every day. As a result of these effects as well as my need to work on my rehabilitation, I have resigned my position as a pediatrician at the Cottage View Hospital in Santa Barbara.

I have, of course, wondered on and off why Nanci and Otis chose to be married in such an unusual location. I have never been very outdoorsy and think that weddings are better conducted in a church. I vaguely recall talking with Nanci and Otis about possible outdoor locations in northern California and believe that I urged them at least to avoid the mountains unless they chose to be married in the summer. Of course, the decision was theirs to make. They did send all of us a copy of the park brochure along with the invitation to the wedding. I remember thinking that it looked like a nice place for a park; I had never been there myself.

Claim No. 91-123456
Claimant: Genevieve Finlay
Date: October 20, 1991
Location of Occurrence: Yosemite National Park

Statement of Mike Best

I am a federal park ranger, stationed in Yosemite National Park. As a resident ranger, I live in a cabin in the park. Before I became a park ranger in 1987, I was a United Church of Christ minister assigned to a congregation in Sacramento. I have maintained my standing as an ordained U.C.C. minister, which permits me to conduct weddings in California.

I have known Bert Selleck since the mid-1970s, when we were in college in Santa Barbara. We kept in touch on and off thereafter. Sometime in the winter of 1991, Bert's sister Nanci called me to ask if I would officiate at her wedding to Otis Finlay in April. After talking with her and then Otis about the ceremony, I agreed. They wanted an informal ceremony in one of the valleys against the backdrop of Half-Dome with just a few friends and relatives, so that's what we planned. We set April 9 as the date, in part because I had that morning off.

Otis, Nanci, their relatives, and friends met me at my cabin about 9:30 that morning. Otis gave me a check for $50. We drove to a valley just off the main road. There is a nice clearing there, sheltered by a grove of aspen, where spring flowers bloom early and you can see Half-Dome. Since spring came early this year, I knew it would look wonderful—and it did.

After a few minutes of orientation, we went through the simple ceremony. It took about twenty minutes.

Then Bert suggested taking pictures on a bridge that's about eighty yards from the clearing. Everyone went over to the bridge, and Bert had everyone line up on the bridge. After a few pictures he indicated that he wanted to take some smaller group shots. I walked off the bridge and turned around to watch the rest of the picture-taking. Meanwhile, other people were walking off the bridge or moving around. In a flash, Mrs. Finlay was flat on her back on the bridge; she was not moving. We got her into my car as soon as we could and to the nearest hospital.

I don't know for sure what caused Mrs. Finlay to fall. I assume she slipped, since no one recalls bumping her. I do know there were some very slippery spots on that bridge that morning for some reason—I assume from the overnight freeze. I've slipped once or twice on that bridge myself, though I've never fallen. The bridge was resurfaced in the fall of 1990.

I understand Mrs. Finlay still has some disability as a consequence of the accident. That's too bad—she seemed to be a lovely person.

Claim No. 91-123456
Claimant: Genevieve Finlay
Date: October 20, 1991
Location of Occurrence: Yosemite National Park

Statement of Jerome Shaw

I am Chief Ranger and Park Manager, Yosemite National Park. I have been in my current position nearly ten years and was a ranger in Yosemite for nearly twenty years before that.

I was not present when Mrs. Finlay was injured, so I have no firsthand information about the incident. I can comment, however, on several background matters.

Yosemite is widely regarded as one of the jewels of the National Park System. Its chief allure is its sheer beauty, not any developed recreational facilities. There are hiking trails, a few pedestrian bridges, a simple system of two-lane roads leading into and through the park, and a number of campsites (rated primitive to basic—some pit toilets, no bathing facilities). The only real development is the Awahnee Inn, a classic lodge built early in this century.

Yosemite is, simply put, one of the benefits the federal government affords citizens and visitors. There are no entrance or user fees, although persons staying in the Awahnee, of course, pay room rental to the Park System concessionaire that runs the Inn.

In all of my years here, Yosemite has never advertised. People come to know of it by word-of-mouth or, I suppose, by reading Park Service directories or materials travel agents or tourist bureaus circulate about the area. We do have a two-page pamphlet we hand out at the main entrances to the park. The pamphlet consists of a simple map and description of the topography, wildlife, flora, and fauna of the park. I suppose some people may be drawn in by the signs at the park entrances, although they are simply $4' \times 4'$ signs stating "Welcome to Yosemite."

The area where the incident occurred is several miles into the park, down the road from Mike Best's cabin. It is one of many lovely small valleys in the park adjacent to a mountain stream. The bridge over the stream is about twenty years old and was resurfaced in the fall of 1990. The resurfacing was done to increase the bridge's long-term durability. From what I understand, the bridge received virtually no traffic between the time of its resurfacing and the April 9 incident. That area of the park is not used much during the winter because it is closest to an entrance that is closed during the winter. And the traffic in Yosemite typically does not pick up until late April. According to my records, the bridge involved in this incident was the only one resurfaced last fall. I believe, although I am not positive, that the Service used a different resurfacing compound in prior years.

Weddings are not a common occurrence in the park, but they do occur from time to time. I understand from Mike Best that he has conducted three other weddings here since he has been a ranger. So long as they occur when he is off-duty, I am fine with his "moonlighting." It is more common to see a minister come in from outside the park.

Claim No. 91-123456
Claimant: Genevieve Finlay
Date: October 30, 1991
Location of Occurrence: Yosemite National Park

Statement of Elizabeth Bower

I am the Director of Facilities Maintenance for the national parks located on the West Coast, Yosemite included. In this role, I am responsible for determining which man-made structures in the parks receive major repairs each season, selecting materials, and arranging for the work to be done. I have been in my post for seven years.

One man-made structure found in many parks is the pedestrian bridge. The Park Service constructs such bridges rarely. We do so where they are necessary to enable visitors to reach locations that are otherwise inaccessible, yet should be open to visitors. In all bridge construction and maintenance, we seek to serve not only the goal of access, but also to disturb the natural environment as little as possible, to ensure the highest level of visitor safety possible, and to do so cost effectively. These goals conflict somewhat. It is my duty to resolve the conflicts.

An issue of particular concern recently has been the durability of the pedestrian bridges. Left untreated, the natural wood we use deteriorates fairly rapidly; thus, we treat it with a sealant. In the past we have used various sealants, each chosen for specific combinations of wood and climate. We have hoped recently to change this situation, since it precludes bulk purchasing and standardized application procedures. Of course, any such sealant must produce a safe, durable, natural-appearing bridge.

In the fall of 1990, seven natural bridges were resurfaced with a single, new compound in seven different parks in my region. (As I understand it, Mrs. Finlay slipped on the resurfaced bridge in Yosemite.) The bridges are in parks with fairly varied climates. This resurfacing project is basically an experiment, aimed at establishing how useful the new compound is. Its manufacturer has asserted that it is usable across climates and wood types. The studies we received from the manufacturer support this claim.

Since Mrs. Finlay's injury, I have received a report on the new compound's performance at the seven test sites. The compound has scored well compared to our prior compounds on the dimensions of cost effectiveness, natural appearance, and durability. Its major flaw has been that experienced, apparently, by Mrs. Finlay: slipperiness in freeze conditions. Ranger Best has indicated that the Yosemite bridge was slippery this past spring, since the snow melted and re-froze. I have received similar reports regarding the bridges in the other winter climates. We had hoped, of course, that the slipperiness would be minimal. This information will be combined with information we receive over the next year to determine whether to use the compound more widely.

Note to Students: The information about Yosemite National Park in this Problem Set is part truth, part fiction. It is a beautiful park with scenic valleys and an inn named the Awahnee. However, it is much more developed than the individual statements suggest. The facts about the Park, as well as the facts about the wedding and the injury, are drafted to create an interesting story under the applicable legal rules.

Index